I'M AWAKE!

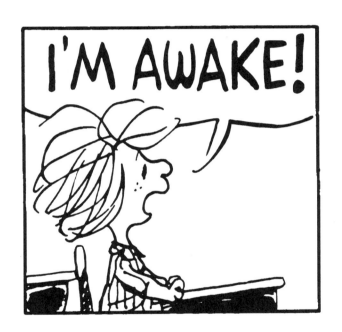

THE COMPLETE PEANUTS
by Charles M. Schulz

Fantagraphics Books, Inc.

Editor: Gary Groth

Designer: Kayla E.

Production, assembly, and restoration: Paul Baresh

Archival and production assistance: Marcie Lee,
Kristen Bisson, Tom Graham, and Ben Horak

Associate Publisher: Eric Reynolds

Publisher: Gary Groth

Special thanks to Jean Schulz, without whom
this project would not have come to fruition.

Thanks to Timothy Chow, and to Charles M. Schulz Creative
Associates, especially Paige Braddock and Kim Towner.

**Fantagraphics Books, Inc.,
7563 Lake City Way NE,
Seattle, WA 98115, USA**

www.peanuts.com

www.fantagraphics.com

ISBN: 978-1-68396-903-7

Library of Congress Control Number: 2023931265

First softcover printing: 2023

Printed in China

PEANUTS

The COMPLETE PEANUTS by CHARLES M. SCHULZ 1987–1988

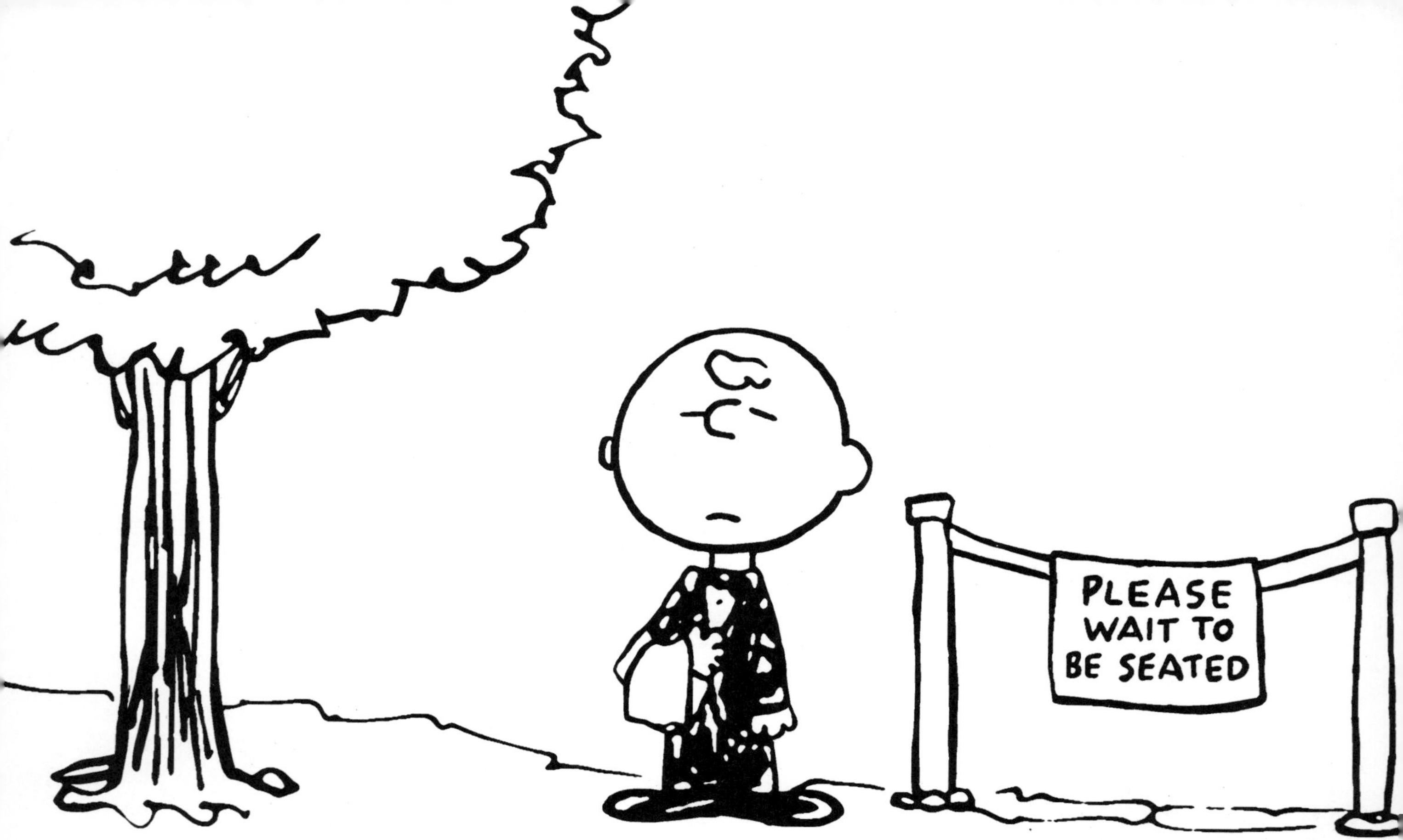
PLEASE
WAIT TO
BE SEATED

Introduction by
GARRY TRUDEAU

IT WAS AN HOUR BEFORE GEORGE W. BUSH WAS TO make his forensics debut at a New Hampshire television station. At a nearby Holiday Inn, two well-known columnists and a visiting cartoonist were sharing pre-debate gossip over a meal of barbecue chicken. As they were finishing up, the conversation turned unexpectedly reflective.

"You know," said the first scribe, "I wrote scores of columns condemning the Vietnam War, and it didn't make the slightest bit of difference. With one small exception, nothing I have ever written has remotely affected an outcome." The other columnist nodded solemnly. He too had no sense of ever having had any meaningful effect on the course of events. Sighing deeply, the cartoonist reached for his slice of the same humble pie. He had made a lot of noise in his life, he admitted, but he had no pretensions about leaving the world a better place than he had found it. In fact, he knew

of only two people in his profession who could make such a claim — Bill Mauldin and Charles Schulz.

Schulz, of course, would have narrowed that list down to one — Mauldin. Such was Mauldin's stature in his eyes that Schulz paid him the extraordinary compliment of regularly referencing him in *Peanuts* (although because he was a grown-up, Mauldin could only appear off-panel). Schulz included him in full knowledge that most of his readers would have to ask their elders who Bill Mauldin was, but that was the point: If they didn't know, they should. Mauldin had chronicled the grubby, dangerous lives of World War II soldiers, and millions of ordinary grunts like Pvt. "Sparky" Schulz had loved him for providing the balm of laughter when they needed it most. Mauldin, Schulz knew firsthand, had made a difference.

So has Schulz, profoundly, but you wouldn't know it by him. It's not that Schulz had been unmoved by the remarkable adulation that had come his way — he just never seemed to trust it much. For his colleagues, this has been perplexing, for they were among the first to appreciate how truly transformative his stripped-down little creation was. *Peanuts* was the first (and still the best) postmodern comic strip. Everything about it was different. The drawing was graphically austere but beautifully nuanced. It was populated with complicated, neurotic characters speaking smart, haiku-perfect dialogue. The stories were interwoven with allusions from religion, classical music, psychiatry and philosophy. And such was Schulz's quiet faith in the power of observational truth, he often passed up punch lines in favor of aphorisms and little throwaway codas — literary devices rarely seen in a gag-oriented medium.

On the surface, Schulz's message was filled with a uniquely American sense of optimism — "Li'l Folks" with big dreams, never giving up, always trudging out to the mound one more time. But the pain of sustaining that hope showed everywhere. Schulz subjected his clueless anti-hero Charlie Brown to the full range of childhood cruelties (it's worth noting that the very first *Peanuts* punch line was, "I hate Charlie Brown"). His strip vibrated with '50s alienation, making it, I always thought, the first Beat strip. Although Schulz would have said the very notion is preposterous and grandiose, he completely revolutionized the art form, deepening it, filling it with possibility, giving permission to all who followed to write from the heart and intellect.

I sometimes teased Sparky that my career was all his fault, but I'm far from alone. Study *B.C.* or *Feiffer* or *Calvin and Hobbes* or *Bloom County* carefully, and you'll see his influence everywhere — stylistically, narratively, rhythmically. While the public at large regards *Peanuts* as a cherished part of our shared popular culture, cartoonists also see it as an irreplaceable source of purpose and pride, our gold standard for work that is both illuminating and aesthetically sublime. More than a decade after his death, Schulz remains sorely missed by the many colleagues to whom his work was as good as it gets.

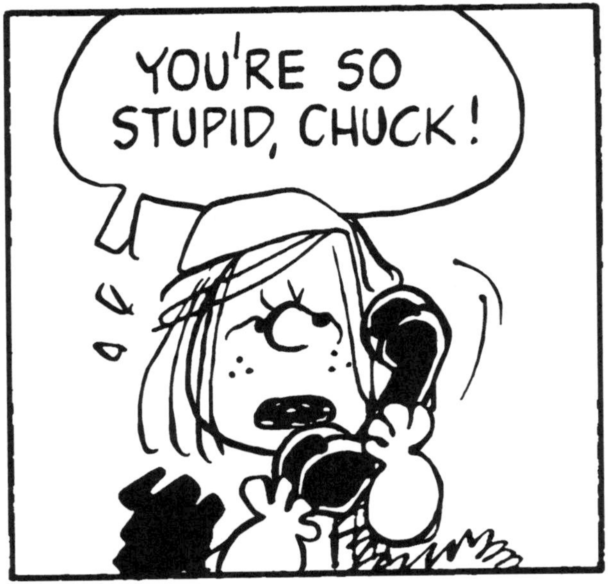
YOU'RE SO STUPID, CHUCK!

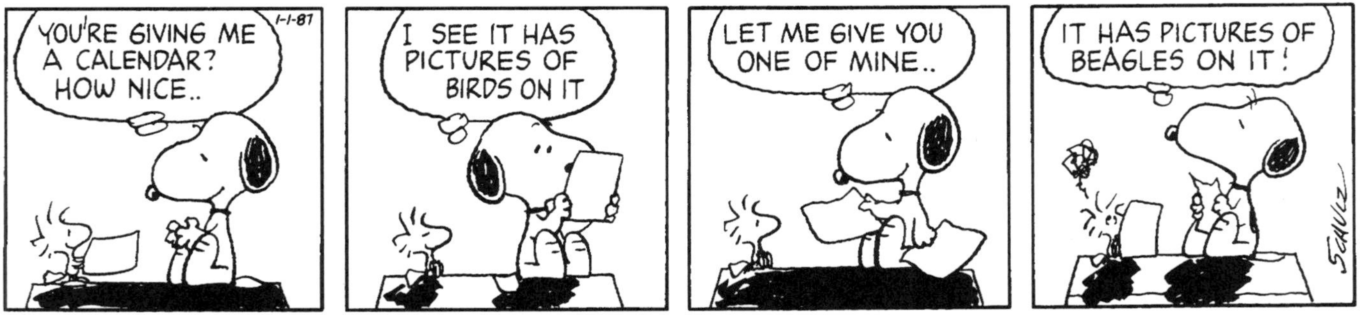
1-1-87
YOU'RE GIVING ME A CALENDAR? HOW NICE..
I SEE IT HAS PICTURES OF BIRDS ON IT
LET ME GIVE YOU ONE OF MINE..
IT HAS PICTURES OF BEAGLES ON IT!
SCHULZ

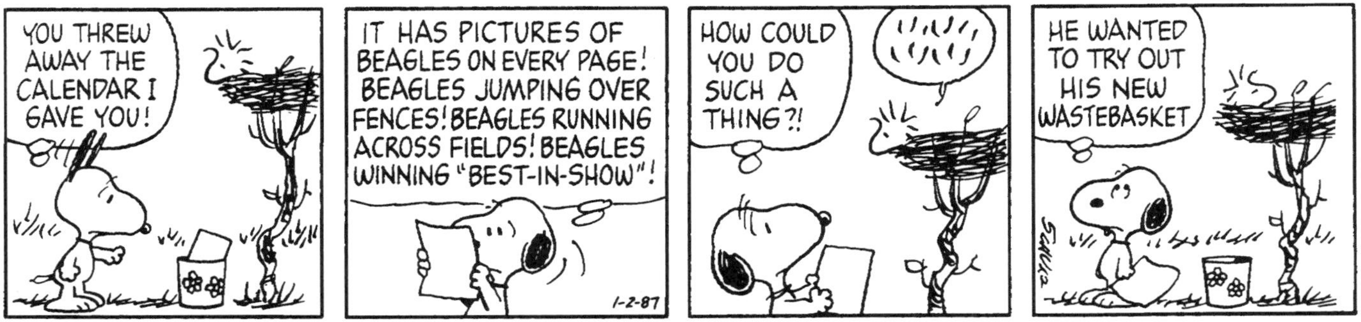
YOU THREW AWAY THE CALENDAR I GAVE YOU!
IT HAS PICTURES OF BEAGLES ON EVERY PAGE! BEAGLES JUMPING OVER FENCES! BEAGLES RUNNING ACROSS FIELDS! BEAGLES WINNING "BEST-IN-SHOW"!
1-2-87
HOW COULD YOU DO SUCH A THING?!
HE WANTED TO TRY OUT HIS NEW WASTEBASKET
SCHULZ

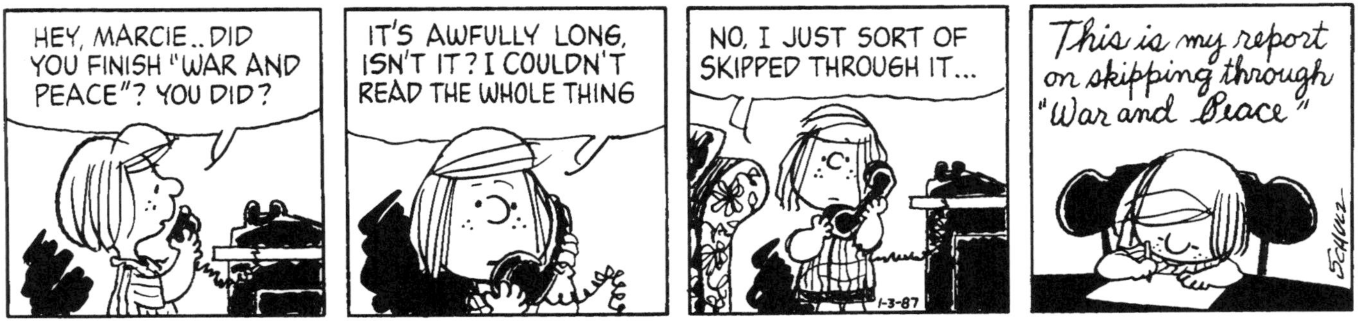
HEY, MARCIE..DID YOU FINISH "WAR AND PEACE"? YOU DID?
IT'S AWFULLY LONG, ISN'T IT? I COULDN'T READ THE WHOLE THING
NO, I JUST SORT OF SKIPPED THROUGH IT...
1-3-87
This is my report on skipping through "War and Peace"
SCHULZ

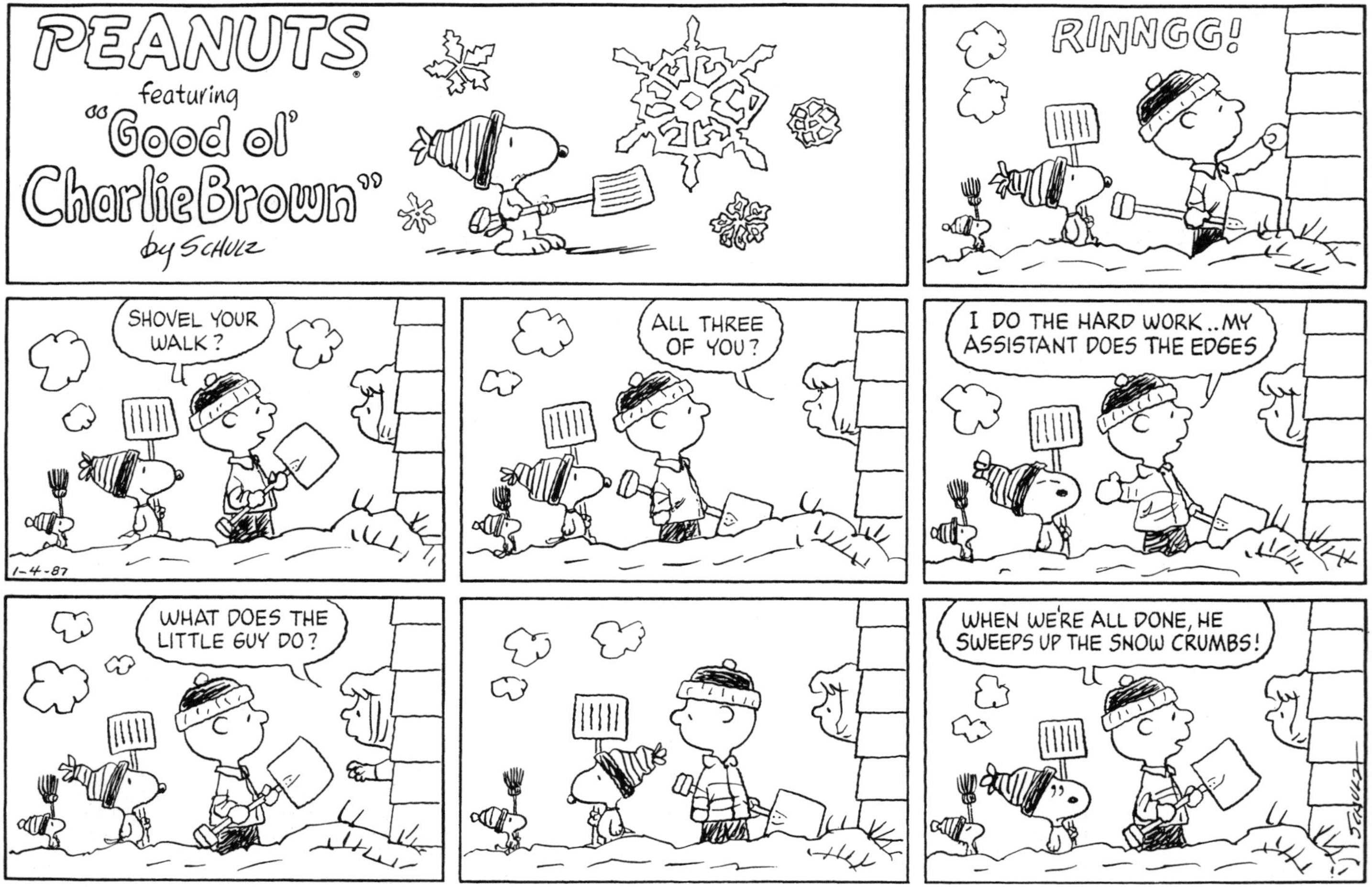
PEANUTS
featuring
"Good ol' Charlie Brown"
by SCHULZ
RINNGG!
SHOVEL YOUR WALK?
1-4-87
ALL THREE OF YOU?
I DO THE HARD WORK.. MY ASSISTANT DOES THE EDGES
WHAT DOES THE LITTLE GUY DO?
WHEN WE'RE ALL DONE, HE SWEEPS UP THE SNOW CRUMBS!
SCHULZ

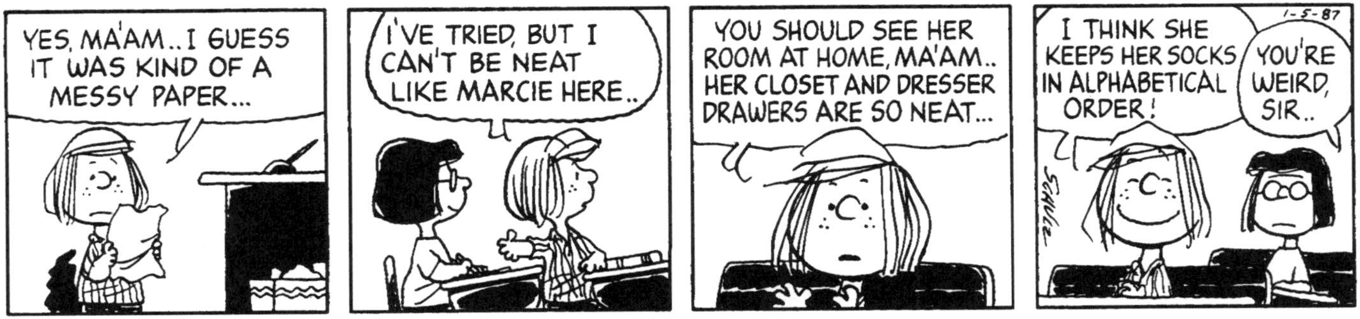
YES, MA'AM.. I GUESS IT WAS KIND OF A MESSY PAPER...
I'VE TRIED, BUT I CAN'T BE NEAT LIKE MARCIE HERE..
YOU SHOULD SEE HER ROOM AT HOME, MA'AM.. HER CLOSET AND DRESSER DRAWERS ARE SO NEAT...
I THINK SHE KEEPS HER SOCKS IN ALPHABETICAL ORDER!
YOU'RE WEIRD, SIR..
1-5-87

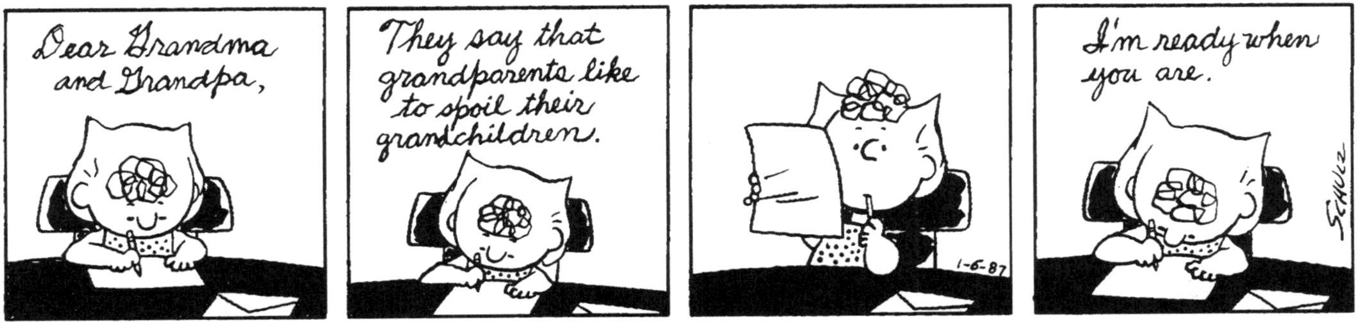
Dear Grandma and Grandpa,
They say that grandparents like to spoil their grandchildren.
1-6-87
I'm ready when you are.

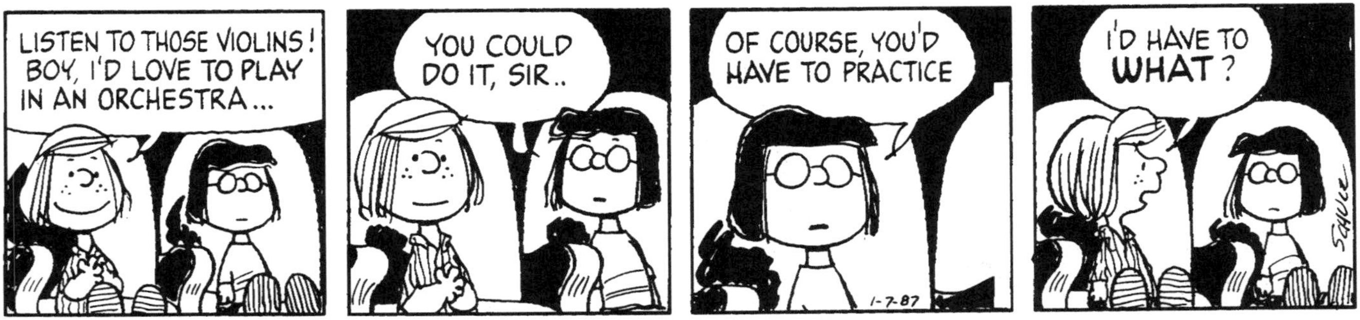
LISTEN TO THOSE VIOLINS! BOY, I'D LOVE TO PLAY IN AN ORCHESTRA...
YOU COULD DO IT, SIR..
OF COURSE, YOU'D HAVE TO PRACTICE
1-7-87
I'D HAVE TO **WHAT**?

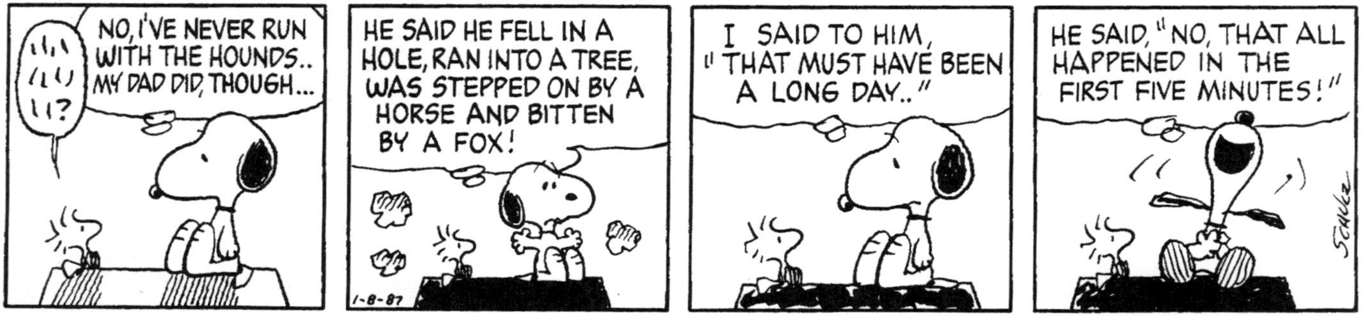
NO, I'VE NEVER RUN WITH THE HOUNDS.. MY DAD DID, THOUGH...
HE SAID HE FELL IN A HOLE, RAN INTO A TREE, WAS STEPPED ON BY A HORSE AND BITTEN BY A FOX!
1-8-87
I SAID TO HIM, "THAT MUST HAVE BEEN A LONG DAY.."
HE SAID, "NO, THAT ALL HAPPENED IN THE FIRST FIVE MINUTES!"
SCHULZ

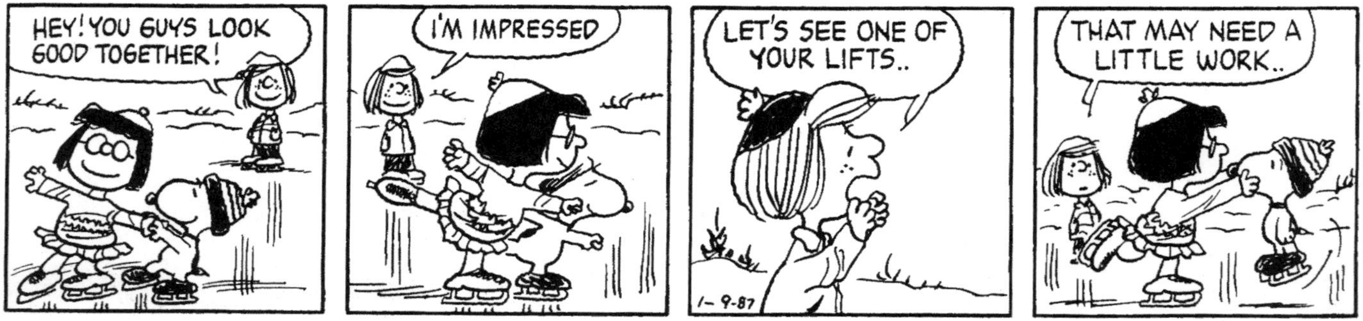
HEY! YOU GUYS LOOK GOOD TOGETHER!
I'M IMPRESSED
LET'S SEE ONE OF YOUR LIFTS..
1-9-87
THAT MAY NEED A LITTLE WORK..

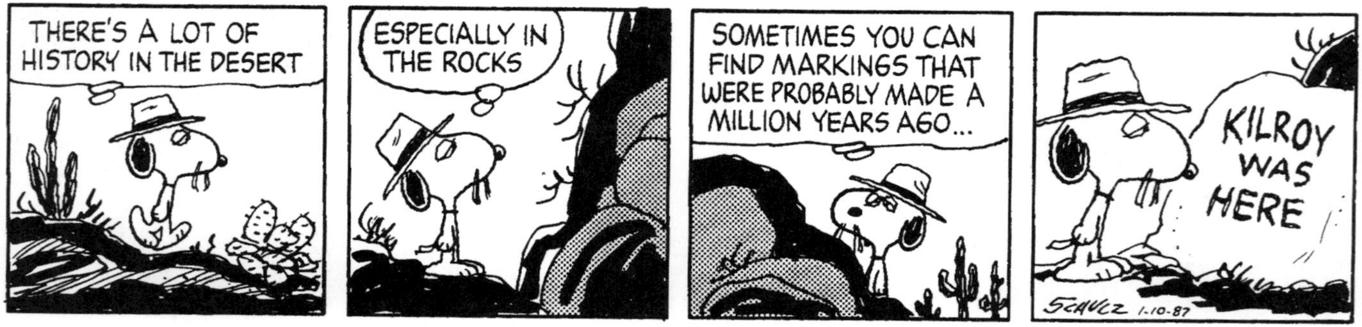
THERE'S A LOT OF HISTORY IN THE DESERT
ESPECIALLY IN THE ROCKS
SOMETIMES YOU CAN FIND MARKINGS THAT WERE PROBABLY MADE A MILLION YEARS AGO...
KILROY WAS HERE
SCHULZ 1-10-87

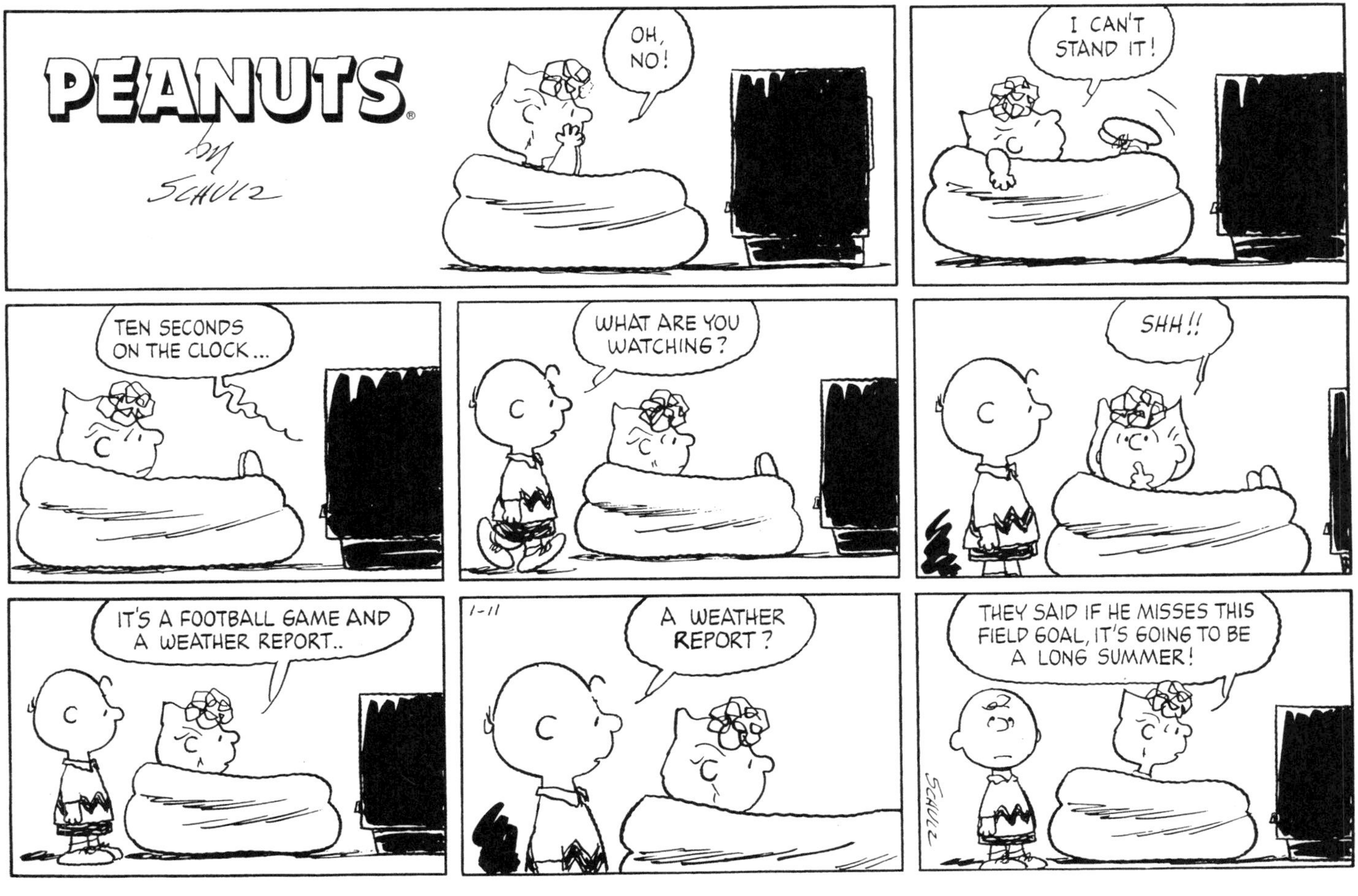
PEANUTS
by SCHULZ
OH, NO!
I CAN'T STAND IT!
TEN SECONDS ON THE CLOCK...
WHAT ARE YOU WATCHING?
SHH!!
IT'S A FOOTBALL GAME AND A WEATHER REPORT..
1-11
A WEATHER REPORT?
THEY SAID IF HE MISSES THIS FIELD GOAL, IT'S GOING TO BE A LONG SUMMER!
SCHULZ

I THINK I'LL ASK THAT LITTLE RED HAIRED GIRL IF I CAN WALK HOME FROM SCHOOL WITH HER..

I THINK I'LL MAKE A REMARK ABOUT HOW COLD IT IS..

1-12

I THINK I'LL SUGGEST THAT MAYBE I SHOULD HOLD HER HAND...

I THINK I'LL WALK VERY SLOW IN CASE I BUMP INTO A TREE..

IF I WINK AT THAT LITTLE RED HAIRED GIRL, MAYBE SHE'LL NOTICE ME

1-13

I'M NOT GETTING ANY DISTANCE..

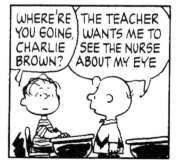

WHERE'RE YOU GOING, CHARLIE BROWN?

THE TEACHER WANTS ME TO SEE THE NURSE ABOUT MY EYE

SHE SAW ME WINKING AT THE LITTLE RED HAIRED GIRL.. SHE THINKS SOMETHING'S WRONG WITH MY EYE...

WHAT AM I GOING TO TELL THE NURSE?

1-14

I NEVER KNEW LOVE COULD BE SO MUCH TROUBLE..

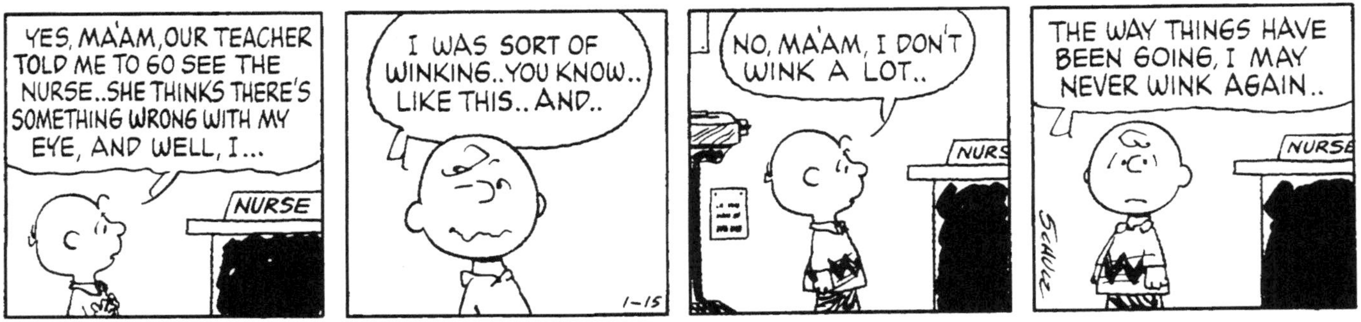
YES, MA'AM, OUR TEACHER TOLD ME TO GO SEE THE NURSE..SHE THINKS THERE'S SOMETHING WRONG WITH MY EYE, AND WELL, I...
NURSE
I WAS SORT OF WINKING..YOU KNOW.. LIKE THIS.. AND..
1-15
NO, MA'AM, I DON'T WINK A LOT..
NURS
THE WAY THINGS HAVE BEEN GOING, I MAY NEVER WINK AGAIN..
NURSE
SCHULZ

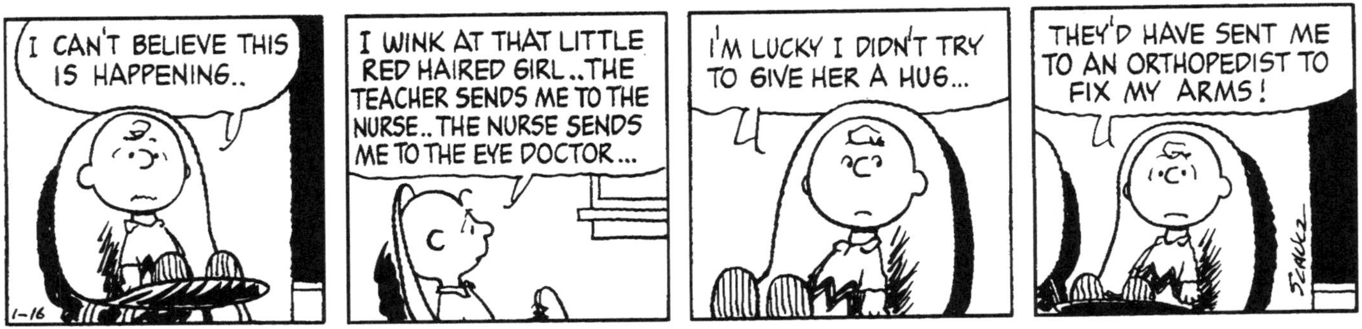
I CAN'T BELIEVE THIS IS HAPPENING..
1-16
I WINK AT THAT LITTLE RED HAIRED GIRL..THE TEACHER SENDS ME TO THE NURSE..THE NURSE SENDS ME TO THE EYE DOCTOR...
I'M LUCKY I DIDN'T TRY TO GIVE HER A HUG...
THEY'D HAVE SENT ME TO AN ORTHOPEDIST TO FIX MY ARMS!
SCHULZ

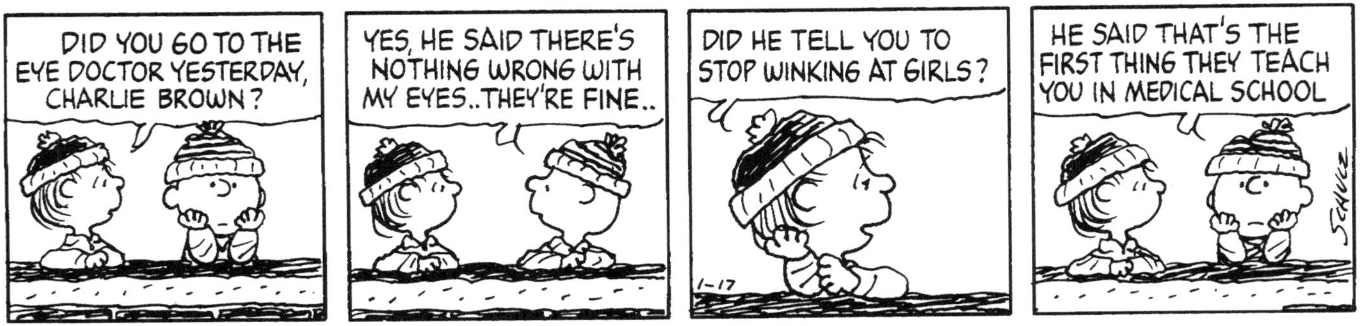
DID YOU GO TO THE EYE DOCTOR YESTERDAY, CHARLIE BROWN?
YES, HE SAID THERE'S NOTHING WRONG WITH MY EYES..THEY'RE FINE..
DID HE TELL YOU TO STOP WINKING AT GIRLS?
1-17
HE SAID THAT'S THE FIRST THING THEY TEACH YOU IN MEDICAL SCHOOL
SCHULZ

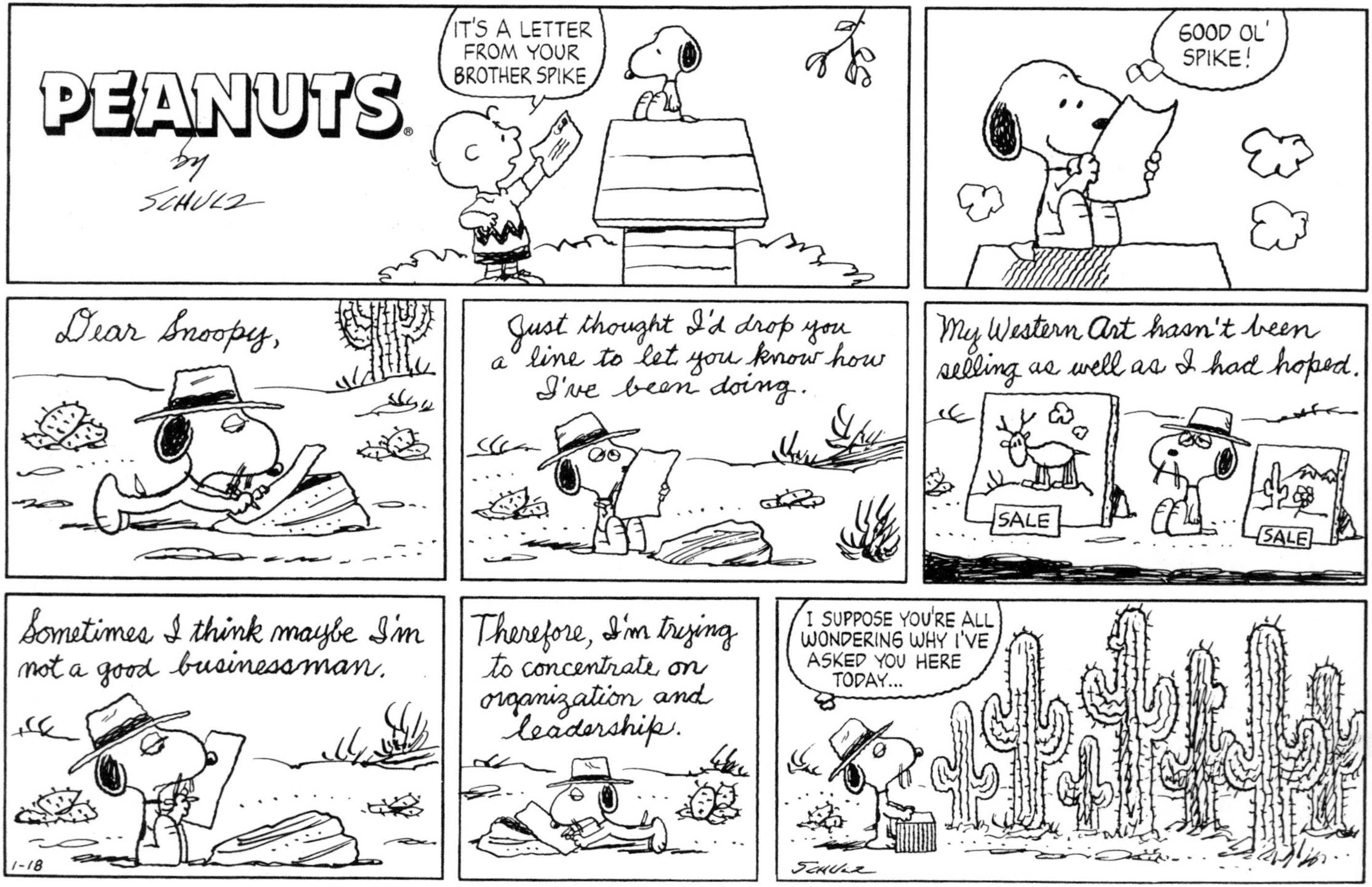
PEANUTS
by SCHULZ
IT'S A LETTER FROM YOUR BROTHER SPIKE
GOOD OL' SPIKE!
Dear Snoopy,
Just thought I'd drop you a line to let you know how I've been doing.
My Western Art hasn't been selling as well as I had hoped.
SALE
SALE
Sometimes I think maybe I'm not a good businessman.
1-18
Therefore, I'm trying to concentrate on organization and leadership.
I SUPPOSE YOU'RE ALL WONDERING WHY I'VE ASKED YOU HERE TODAY...
SCHULZ

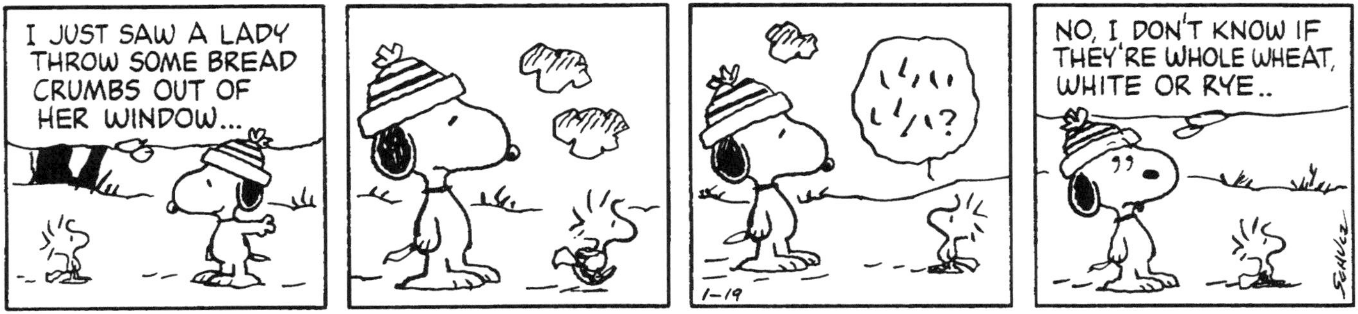
I JUST SAW A LADY THROW SOME BREAD CRUMBS OUT OF HER WINDOW...
1-19
NO, I DON'T KNOW IF THEY'RE WHOLE WHEAT, WHITE OR RYE..

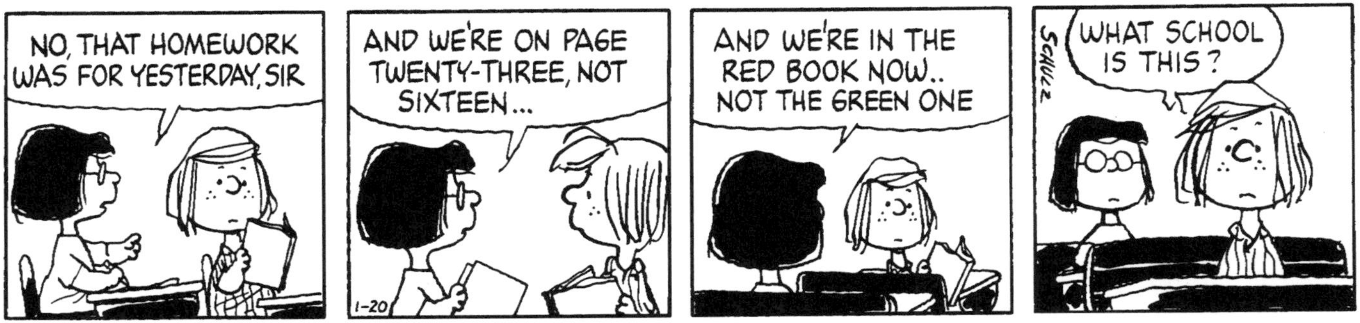
NO, THAT HOMEWORK WAS FOR YESTERDAY, SIR
AND WE'RE ON PAGE TWENTY-THREE, NOT SIXTEEN...
1-20
AND WE'RE IN THE RED BOOK NOW.. NOT THE GREEN ONE
WHAT SCHOOL IS THIS?

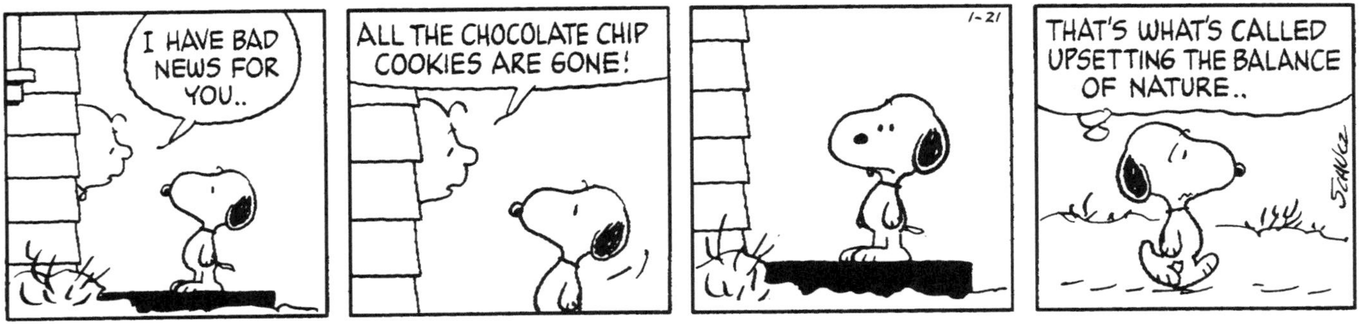
I HAVE BAD NEWS FOR YOU..
ALL THE CHOCOLATE CHIP COOKIES ARE GONE!
1-21
THAT'S WHAT'S CALLED UPSETTING THE BALANCE OF NATURE..

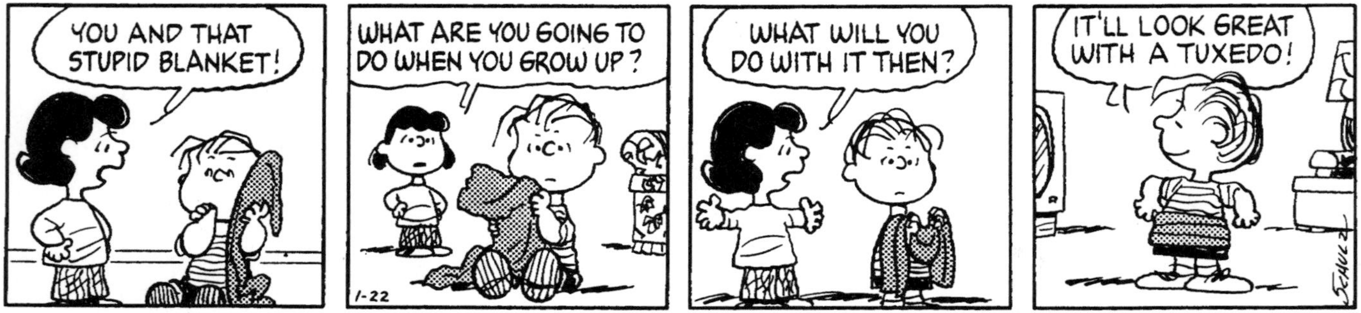
YOU AND THAT STUPID BLANKET!
WHAT ARE YOU GOING TO DO WHEN YOU GROW UP?
1-22
WHAT WILL YOU DO WITH IT THEN?
IT'LL LOOK GREAT WITH A TUXEDO!
SCHULZ

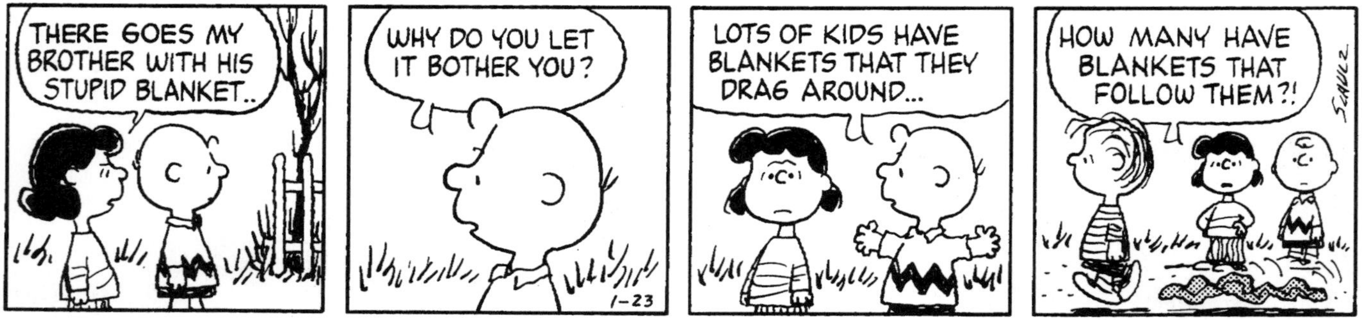
THERE GOES MY BROTHER WITH HIS STUPID BLANKET..
WHY DO YOU LET IT BOTHER YOU?
1-23
LOTS OF KIDS HAVE BLANKETS THAT THEY DRAG AROUND...
HOW MANY HAVE BLANKETS THAT FOLLOW THEM?!
SCHULZ

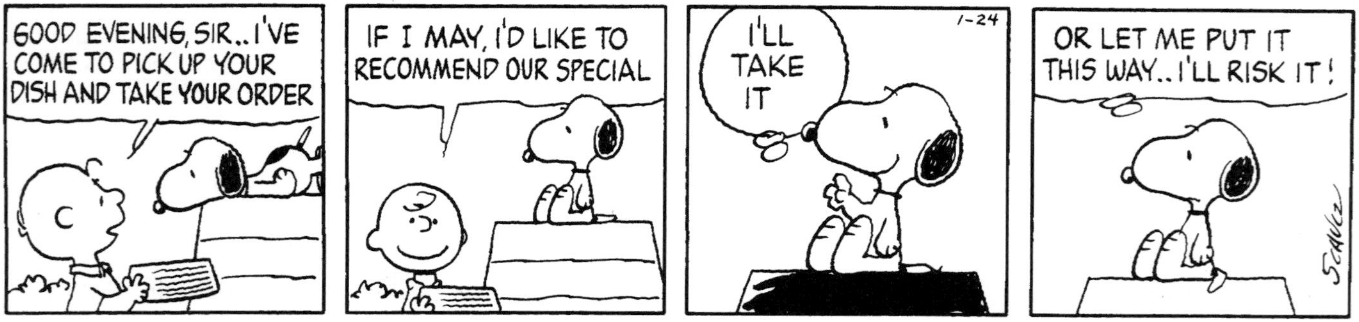
GOOD EVENING, SIR.. I'VE COME TO PICK UP YOUR DISH AND TAKE YOUR ORDER
IF I MAY, I'D LIKE TO RECOMMEND OUR SPECIAL
1-24
I'LL TAKE IT
OR LET ME PUT IT THIS WAY.. I'LL RISK IT!
SCHULZ

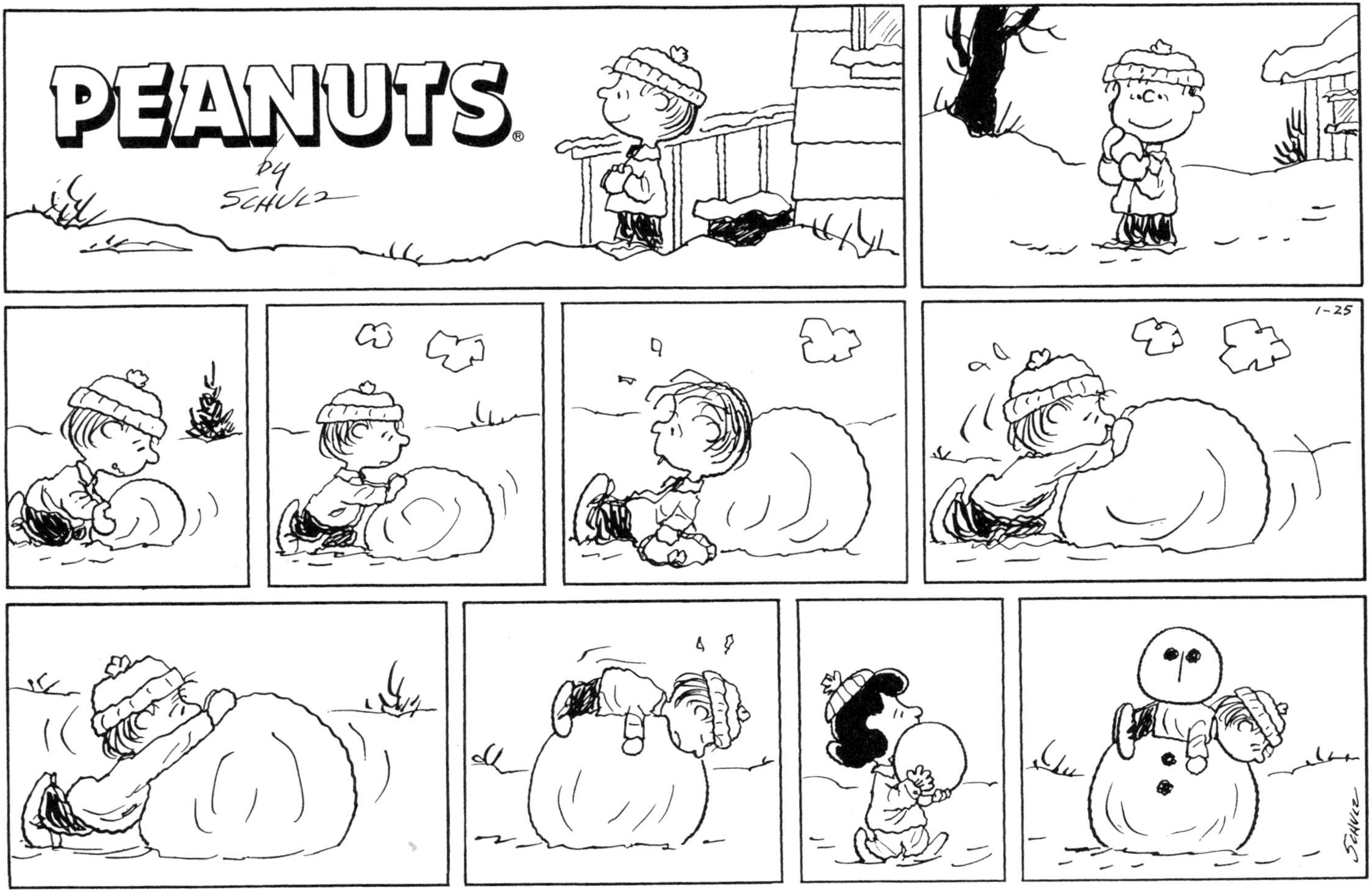
PEANUTS®
by SCHULZ
1-25
SCHULZ

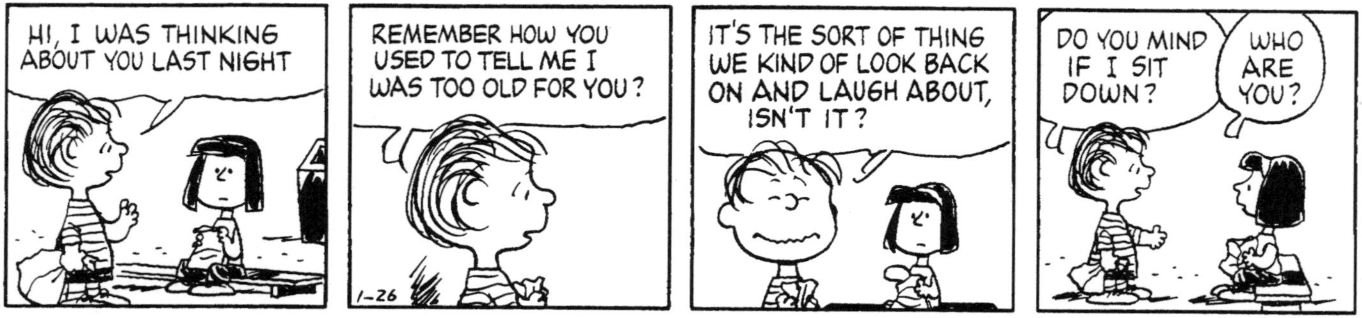
HI, I WAS THINKING ABOUT YOU LAST NIGHT
REMEMBER HOW YOU USED TO TELL ME I WAS TOO OLD FOR YOU?
1-26
IT'S THE SORT OF THING WE KIND OF LOOK BACK ON AND LAUGH ABOUT, ISN'T IT?
DO YOU MIND IF I SIT DOWN?
WHO ARE YOU?

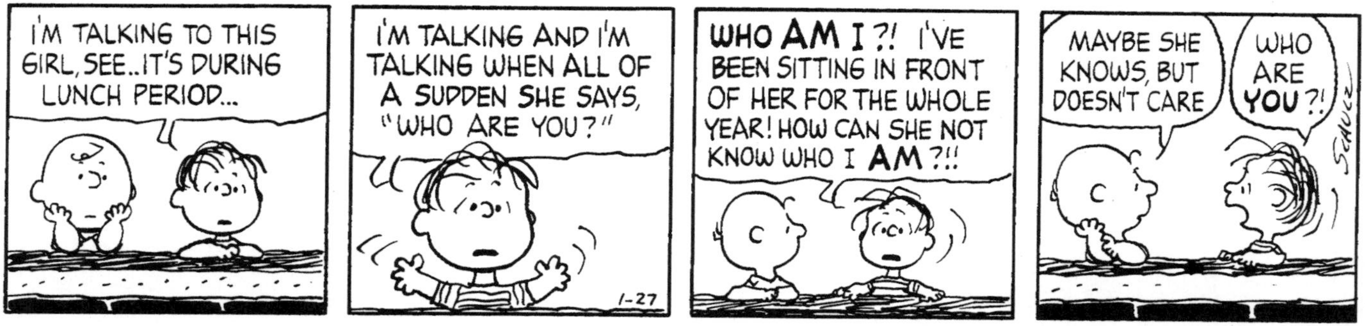
I'M TALKING TO THIS GIRL, SEE..IT'S DURING LUNCH PERIOD...
I'M TALKING AND I'M TALKING WHEN ALL OF A SUDDEN SHE SAYS, "WHO ARE YOU?"
1-27
WHO AM I?! I'VE BEEN SITTING IN FRONT OF HER FOR THE WHOLE YEAR! HOW CAN SHE NOT KNOW WHO I AM?!!
MAYBE SHE KNOWS, BUT DOESN'T CARE
WHO ARE YOU?!
SCHULZ

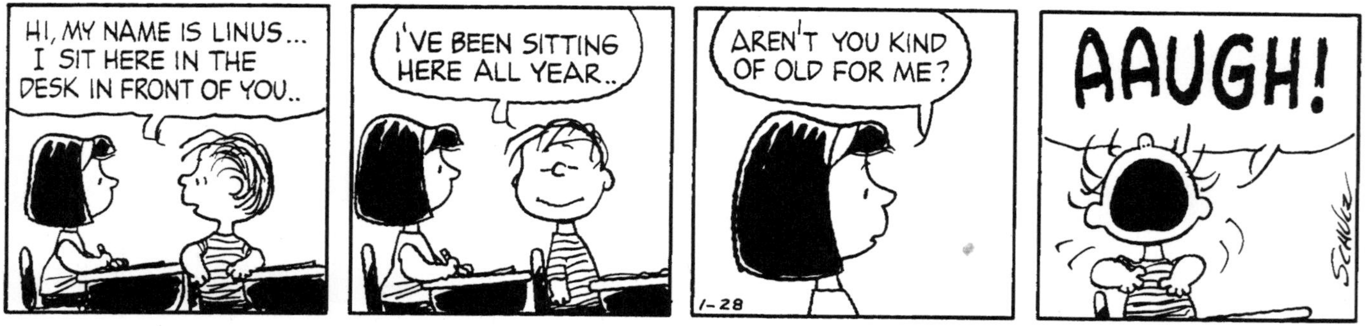
HI, MY NAME IS LINUS... I SIT HERE IN THE DESK IN FRONT OF YOU..
I'VE BEEN SITTING HERE ALL YEAR..
AREN'T YOU KIND OF OLD FOR ME?
1-28
AAUGH!
SCHULZ

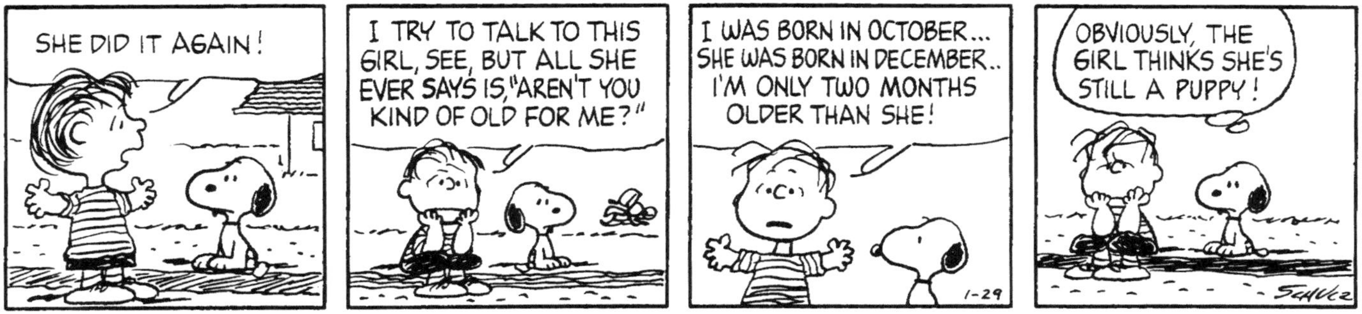
SHE DID IT AGAIN!
I TRY TO TALK TO THIS GIRL, SEE, BUT ALL SHE EVER SAYS IS, "AREN'T YOU KIND OF OLD FOR ME?"
I WAS BORN IN OCTOBER... SHE WAS BORN IN DECEMBER.. I'M ONLY TWO MONTHS OLDER THAN SHE!
1-29
OBVIOUSLY, THE GIRL THINKS SHE'S STILL A PUPPY!
SCHULZ

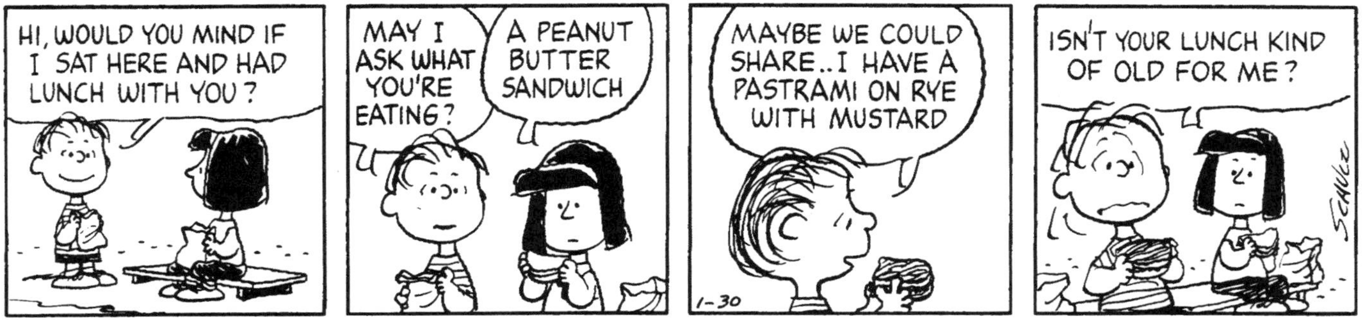
HI, WOULD YOU MIND IF I SAT HERE AND HAD LUNCH WITH YOU?
MAY I ASK WHAT YOU'RE EATING?
A PEANUT BUTTER SANDWICH
MAYBE WE COULD SHARE..I HAVE A PASTRAMI ON RYE WITH MUSTARD
1-30
ISN'T YOUR LUNCH KIND OF OLD FOR ME?
SCHULZ

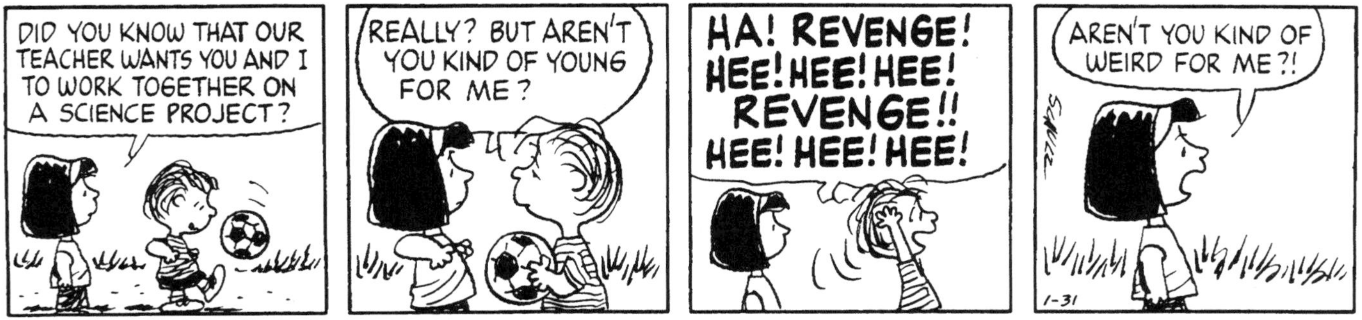
DID YOU KNOW THAT OUR TEACHER WANTS YOU AND I TO WORK TOGETHER ON A SCIENCE PROJECT?
REALLY? BUT AREN'T YOU KIND OF YOUNG FOR ME?
HA! REVENGE! HEE! HEE! HEE! REVENGE!! HEE! HEE! HEE!
SCHULZ
AREN'T YOU KIND OF WEIRD FOR ME?!
1-31

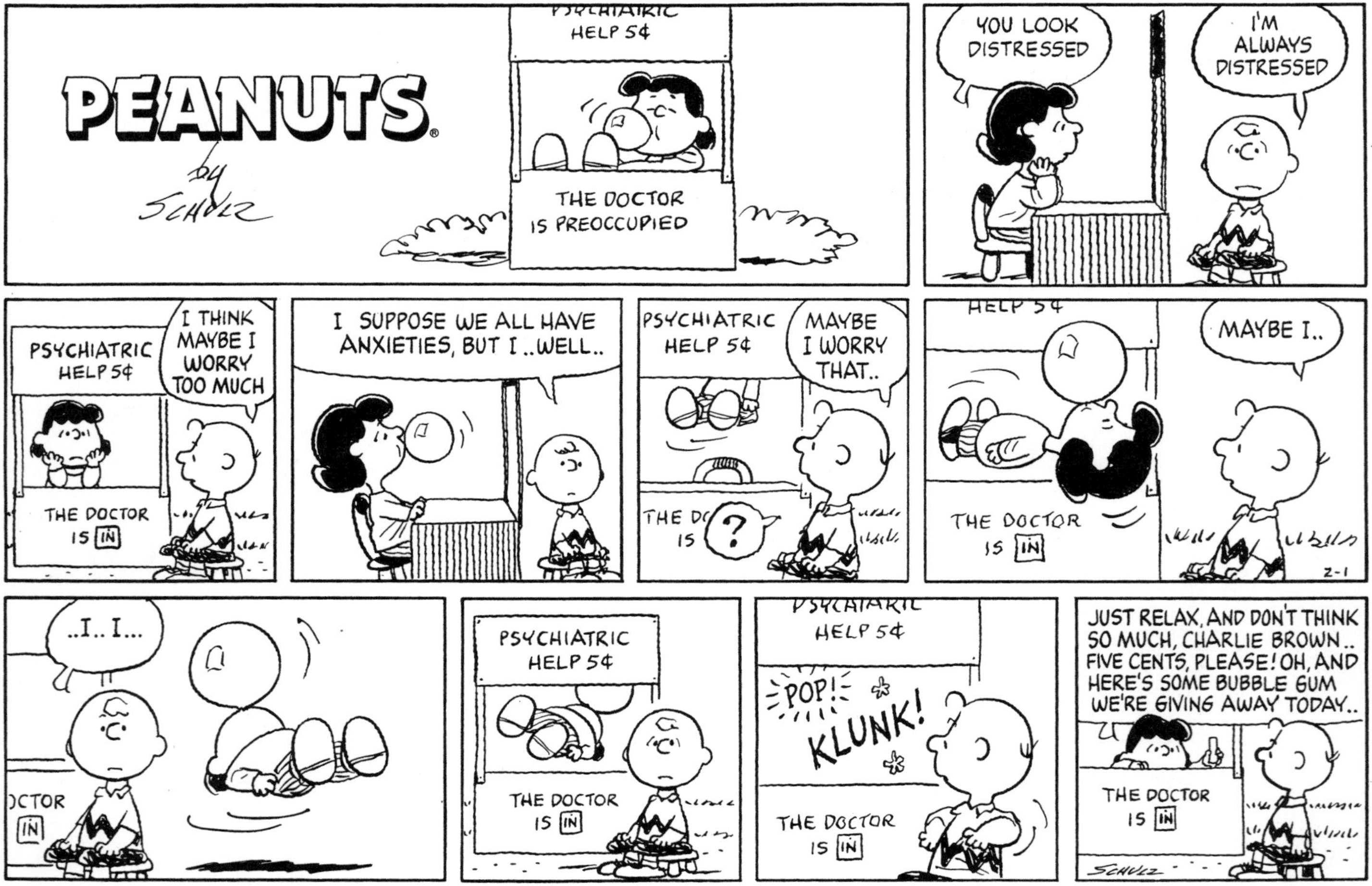
PEANUTS
by SCHULZ
PSYCHIATRIC HELP 5¢
THE DOCTOR IS PREOCCUPIED
YOU LOOK DISTRESSED
I'M ALWAYS DISTRESSED
PSYCHIATRIC HELP 5¢
THE DOCTOR IS IN
I THINK MAYBE I WORRY TOO MUCH
I SUPPOSE WE ALL HAVE ANXIETIES, BUT I ..WELL..
PSYCHIATRIC HELP 5¢
MAYBE I WORRY THAT..
?
HELP 5¢
THE DOCTOR IS IN
MAYBE I..
2-1
..I.. I...
IN
PSYCHIATRIC HELP 5¢
THE DOCTOR IS IN
HELP 5¢
POP!
KLUNK!
THE DOCTOR IS IN
JUST RELAX, AND DON'T THINK SO MUCH, CHARLIE BROWN.. FIVE CENTS, PLEASE! OH, AND HERE'S SOME BUBBLE GUM WE'RE GIVING AWAY TODAY..
THE DOCTOR IS IN
SCHULZ

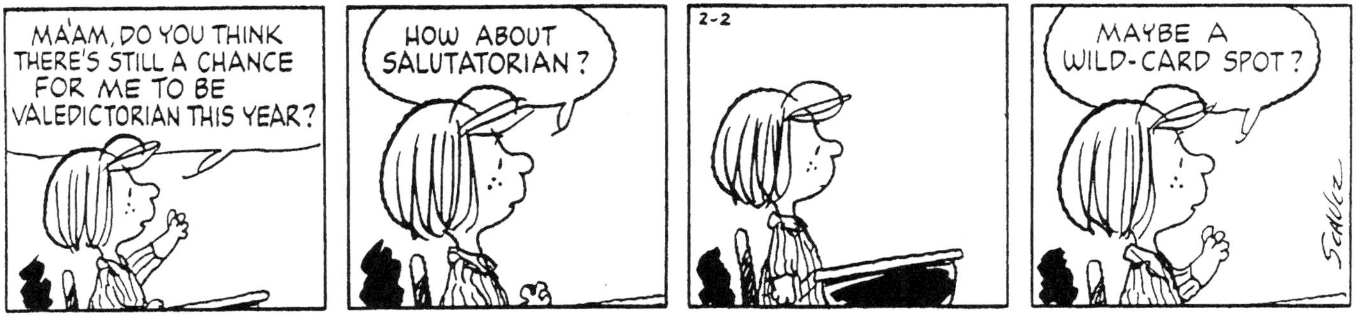
MA'AM, DO YOU THINK THERE'S STILL A CHANCE FOR ME TO BE VALEDICTORIAN THIS YEAR?
HOW ABOUT SALUTATORIAN?
2-2
MAYBE A WILD-CARD SPOT?

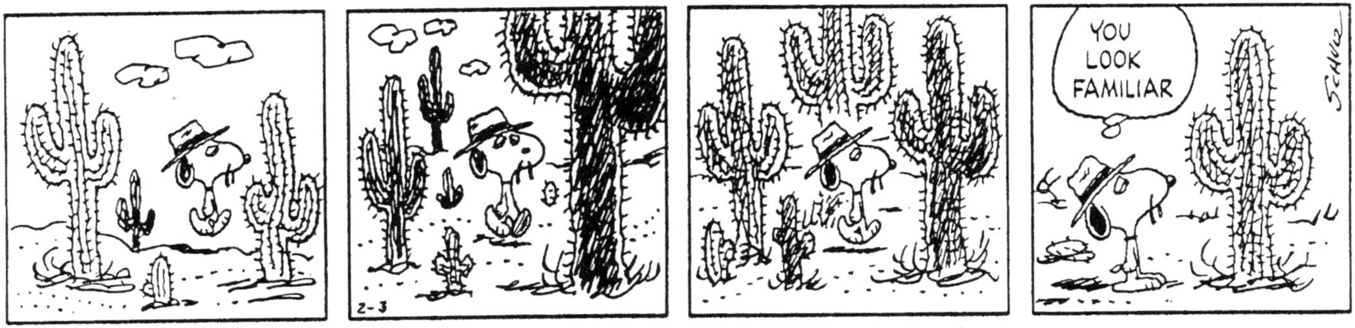
2-3
YOU LOOK FAMILIAR

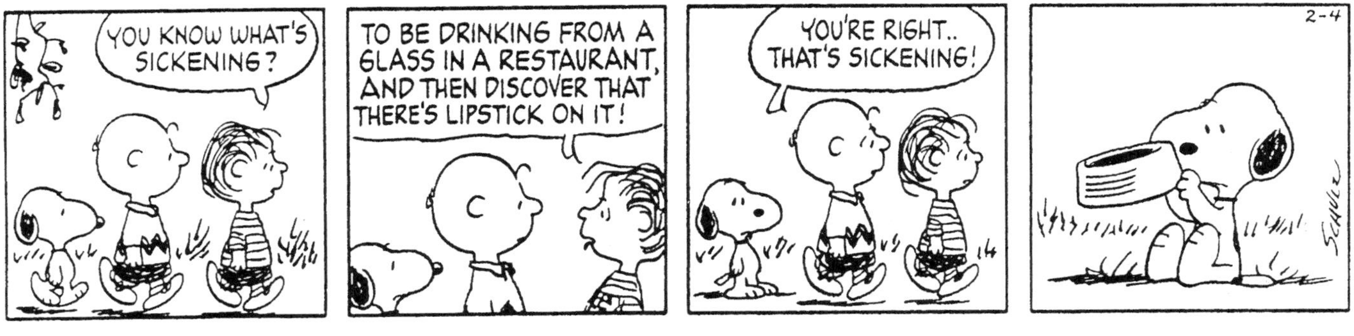
YOU KNOW WHAT'S SICKENING?
TO BE DRINKING FROM A GLASS IN A RESTAURANT, AND THEN DISCOVER THAT THERE'S LIPSTICK ON IT!
YOU'RE RIGHT.. THAT'S SICKENING!
2-4

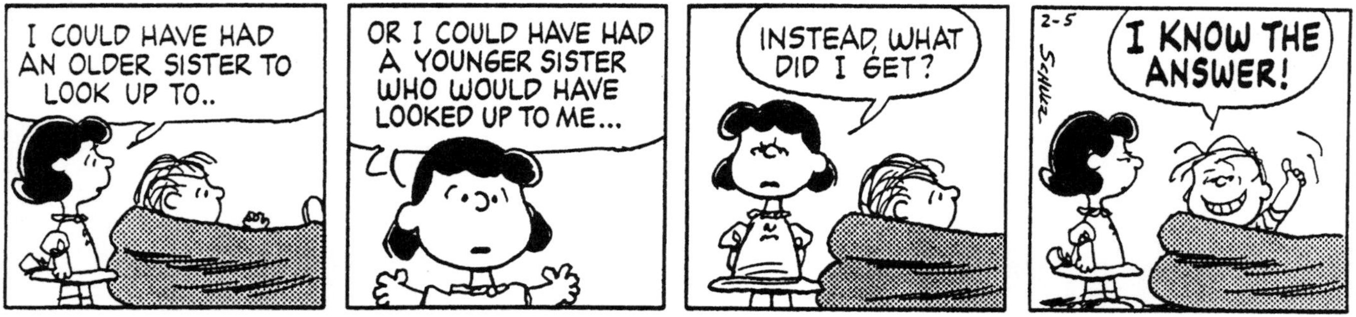
I COULD HAVE HAD AN OLDER SISTER TO LOOK UP TO..
OR I COULD HAVE HAD A YOUNGER SISTER WHO WOULD HAVE LOOKED UP TO ME...
INSTEAD, WHAT DID I GET?
2-5
I KNOW THE ANSWER!
SCHULZ

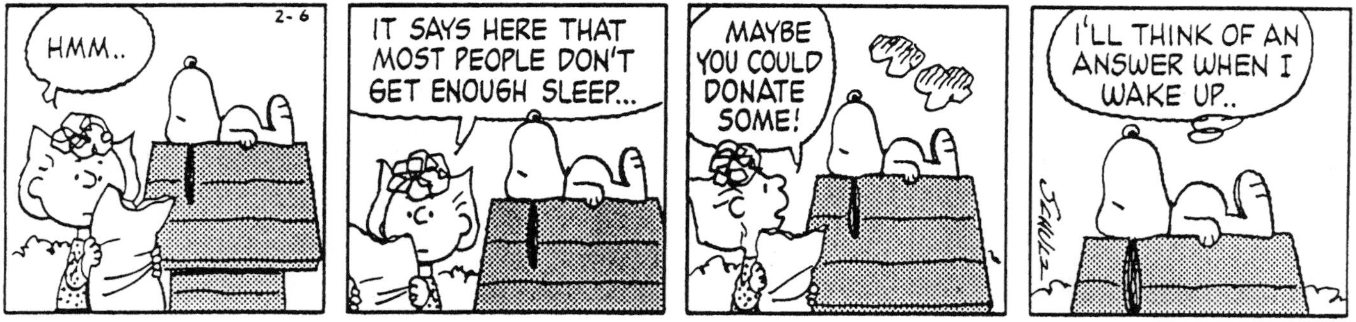
2-6
HMM..
IT SAYS HERE THAT MOST PEOPLE DON'T GET ENOUGH SLEEP...
MAYBE YOU COULD DONATE SOME!
I'LL THINK OF AN ANSWER WHEN I WAKE UP..
SCHULZ

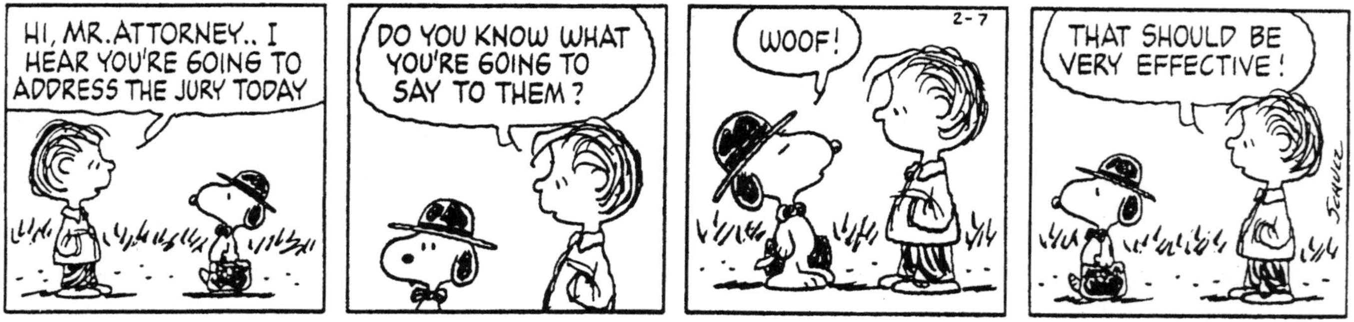
HI, MR. ATTORNEY.. I HEAR YOU'RE GOING TO ADDRESS THE JURY TODAY
DO YOU KNOW WHAT YOU'RE GOING TO SAY TO THEM?
2-7
WOOF!
THAT SHOULD BE VERY EFFECTIVE!
SCHULZ

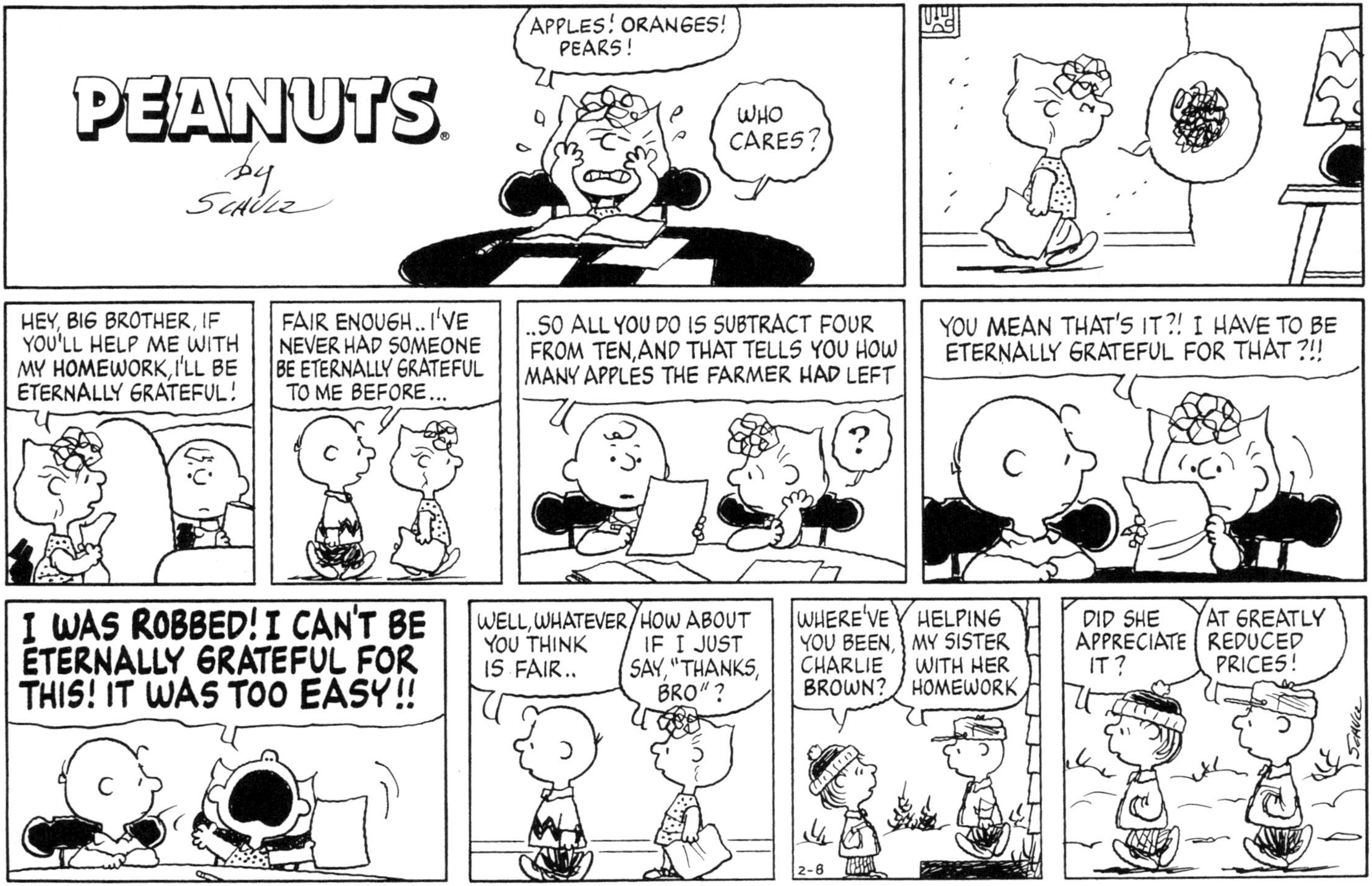
PEANUTS
by SCHULZ
APPLES! ORANGES! PEARS!
WHO CARES?
HEY, BIG BROTHER, IF YOU'LL HELP ME WITH MY HOMEWORK, I'LL BE ETERNALLY GRATEFUL!
FAIR ENOUGH.. I'VE NEVER HAD SOMEONE BE ETERNALLY GRATEFUL TO ME BEFORE...
..SO ALL YOU DO IS SUBTRACT FOUR FROM TEN, AND THAT TELLS YOU HOW MANY APPLES THE FARMER HAD LEFT
?
YOU MEAN THAT'S IT?! I HAVE TO BE ETERNALLY GRATEFUL FOR THAT?!!
I WAS ROBBED! I CAN'T BE ETERNALLY GRATEFUL FOR THIS! IT WAS TOO EASY!!
WELL, WHATEVER YOU THINK IS FAIR..
HOW ABOUT IF I JUST SAY, "THANKS, BRO"?
WHERE'VE YOU BEEN, CHARLIE BROWN?
HELPING MY SISTER WITH HER HOMEWORK
2-8
DID SHE APPRECIATE IT?
AT GREATLY REDUCED PRICES!
SCHULZ

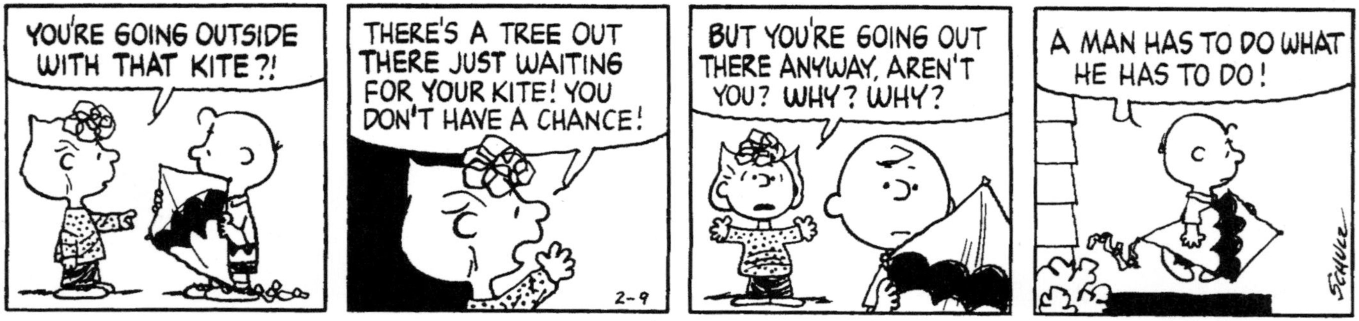
YOU'RE GOING OUTSIDE WITH THAT KITE?!
THERE'S A TREE OUT THERE JUST WAITING FOR YOUR KITE! YOU DON'T HAVE A CHANCE!
2-9
BUT YOU'RE GOING OUT THERE ANYWAY, AREN'T YOU? WHY? WHY?
A MAN HAS TO DO WHAT HE HAS TO DO!
SCHULZ

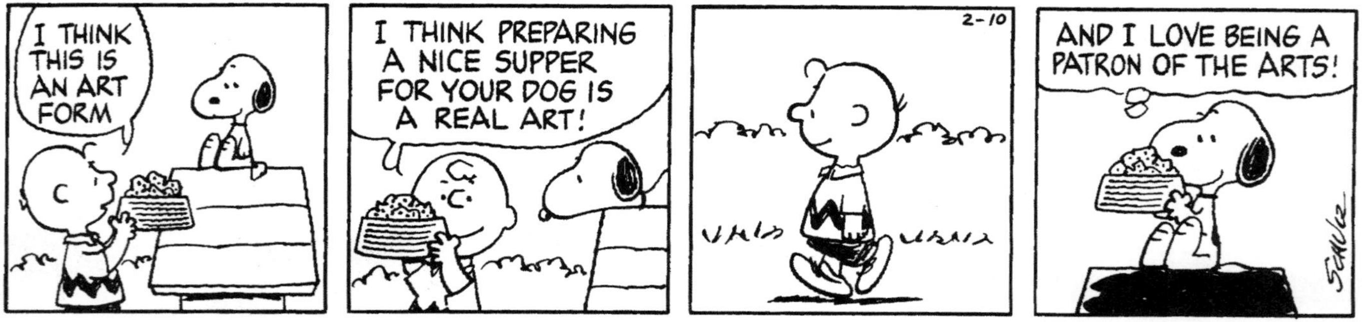
I THINK THIS IS AN ART FORM
I THINK PREPARING A NICE SUPPER FOR YOUR DOG IS A REAL ART!
2-10
AND I LOVE BEING A PATRON OF THE ARTS!
SCHULZ

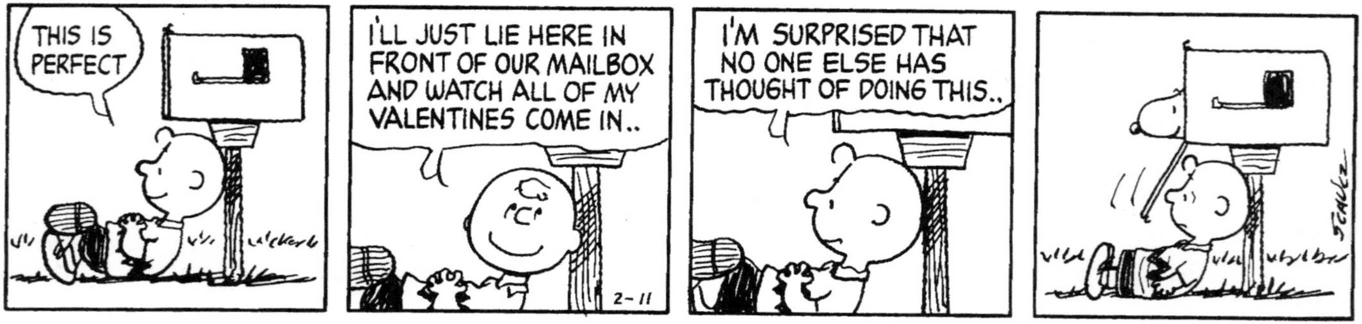
THIS IS PERFECT
I'LL JUST LIE HERE IN FRONT OF OUR MAILBOX AND WATCH ALL OF MY VALENTINES COME IN..
2-11
I'M SURPRISED THAT NO ONE ELSE HAS THOUGHT OF DOING THIS..
SCHULZ

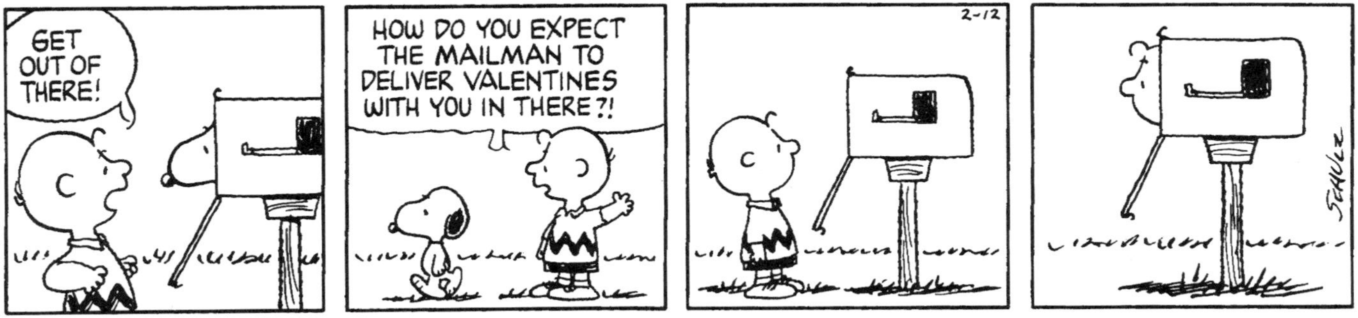
GET OUT OF THERE!
HOW DO YOU EXPECT THE MAILMAN TO DELIVER VALENTINES WITH YOU IN THERE?!
2-12
SCHULZ

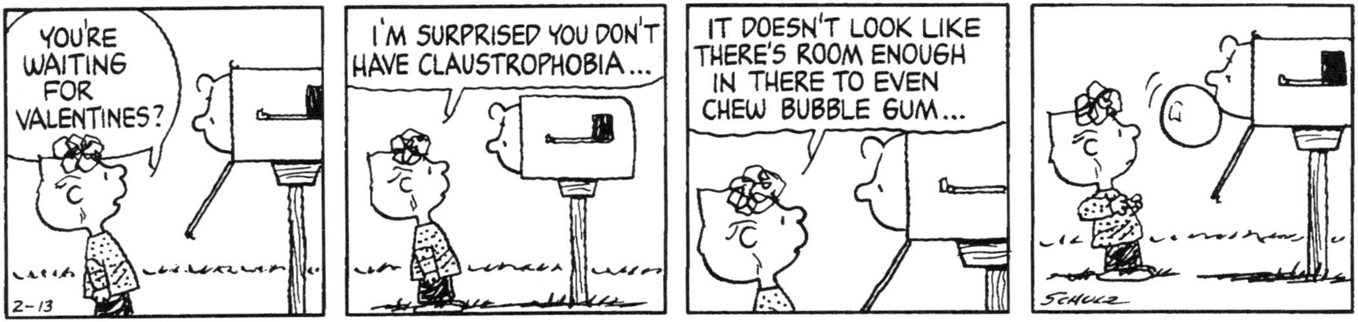
YOU'RE WAITING FOR VALENTINES?
2-13
I'M SURPRISED YOU DON'T HAVE CLAUSTROPHOBIA...
IT DOESN'T LOOK LIKE THERE'S ROOM ENOUGH IN THERE TO EVEN CHEW BUBBLE GUM...
SCHULZ

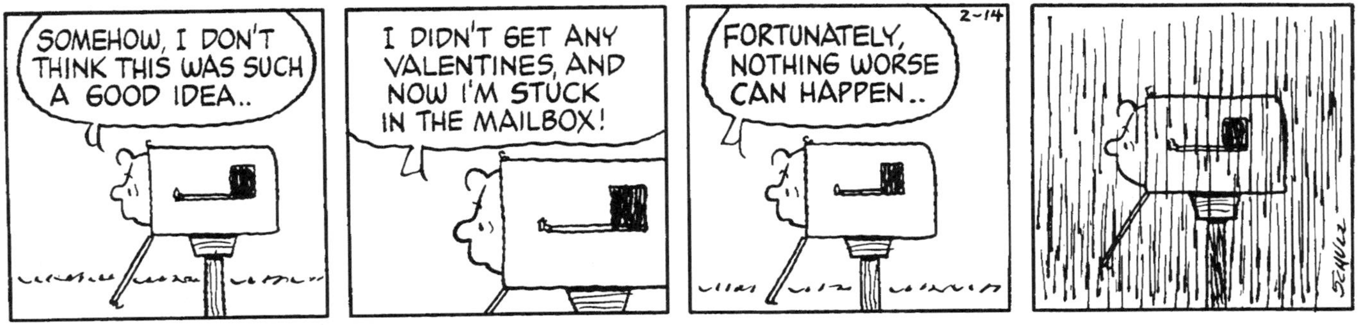
SOMEHOW, I DON'T THINK THIS WAS SUCH A GOOD IDEA..
I DIDN'T GET ANY VALENTINES, AND NOW I'M STUCK IN THE MAILBOX!
2-14
FORTUNATELY, NOTHING WORSE CAN HAPPEN..
SCHULZ

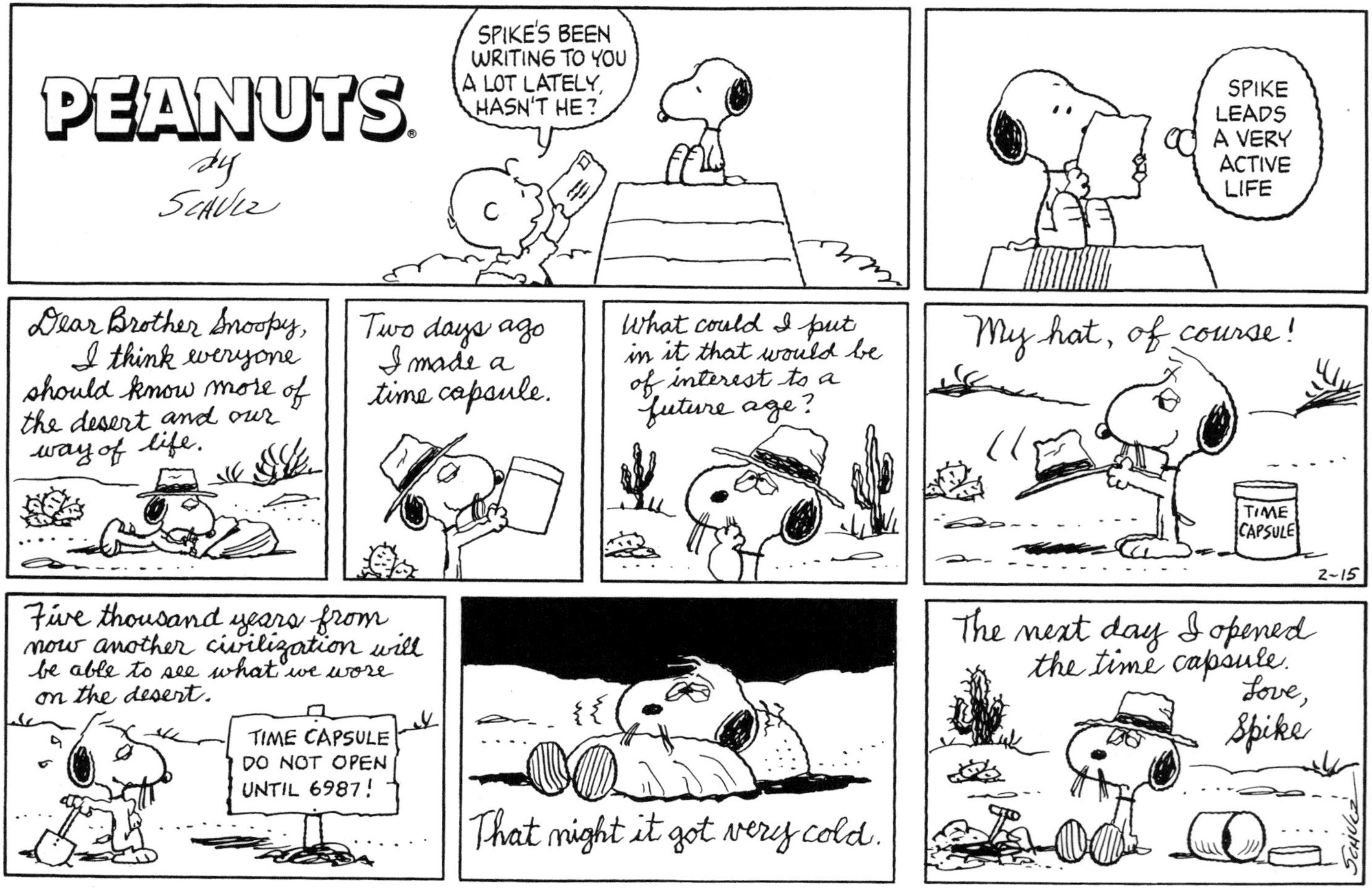
PEANUTS
by SCHULZ
SPIKE'S BEEN WRITING TO YOU A LOT LATELY, HASN'T HE?
SPIKE LEADS A VERY ACTIVE LIFE
Dear Brother Snoopy, I think everyone should know more of the desert and our way of life.
Two days ago I made a time capsule.
What could I put in it that would be of interest to a future age?
My hat, of course!
TIME CAPSULE
2-15
Five thousand years from now another civilization will be able to see what we wore on the desert.
TIME CAPSULE DO NOT OPEN UNTIL 6987!
That night it got very cold.
The next day I opened the time capsule. Love, Spike
SCHULZ

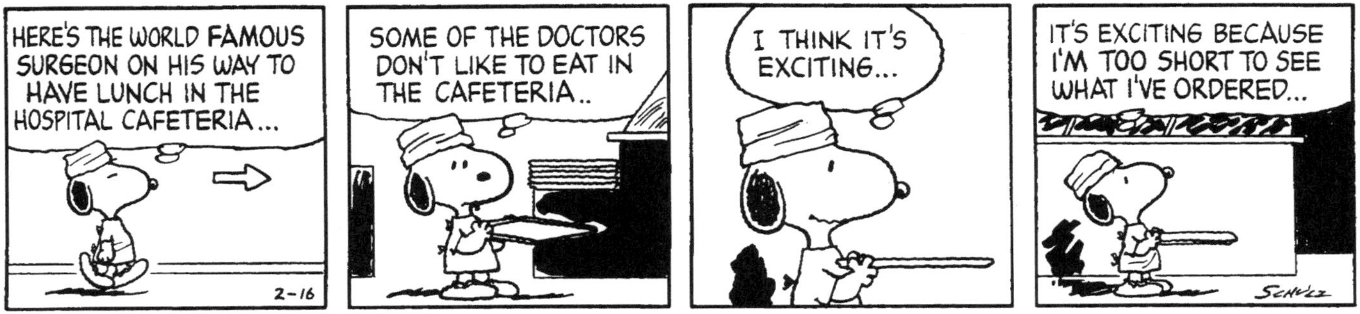
HERE'S THE WORLD FAMOUS SURGEON ON HIS WAY TO HAVE LUNCH IN THE HOSPITAL CAFETERIA...
2-16
SOME OF THE DOCTORS DON'T LIKE TO EAT IN THE CAFETERIA..
I THINK IT'S EXCITING...
IT'S EXCITING BECAUSE I'M TOO SHORT TO SEE WHAT I'VE ORDERED...
SCHULZ

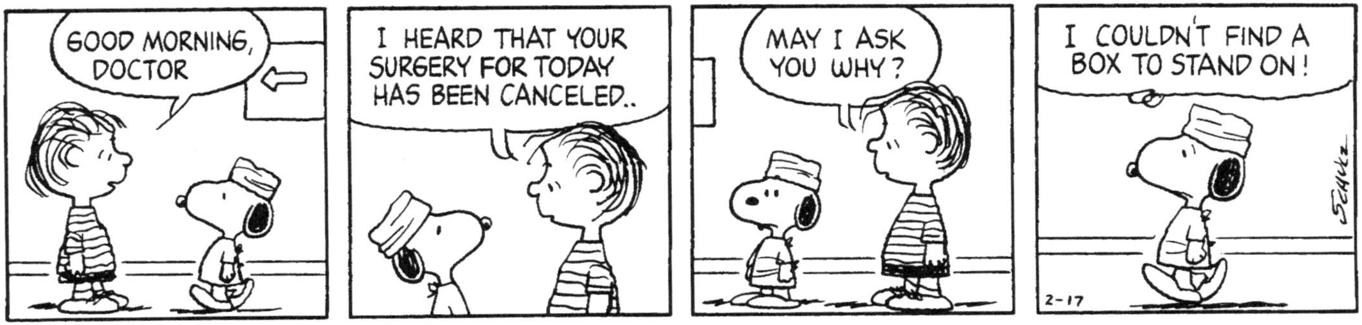
GOOD MORNING, DOCTOR
I HEARD THAT YOUR SURGERY FOR TODAY HAS BEEN CANCELED..
MAY I ASK YOU WHY?
I COULDN'T FIND A BOX TO STAND ON!
SCHULZ
2-17

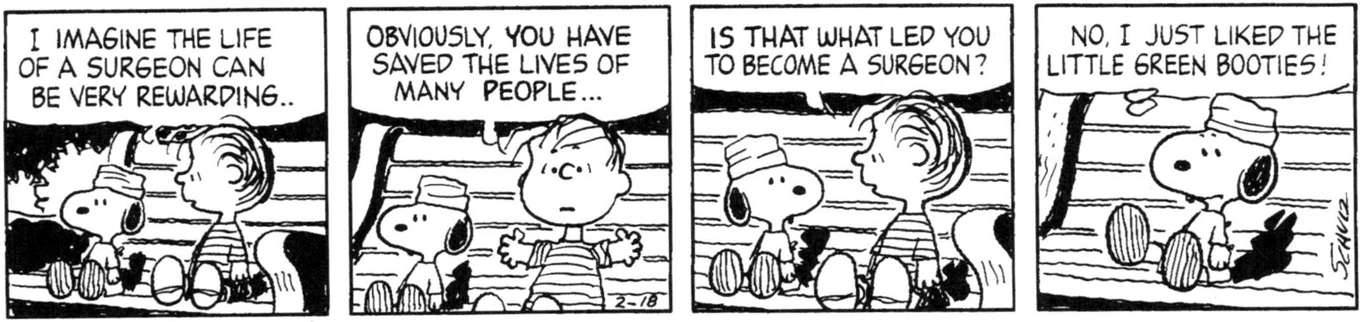
I IMAGINE THE LIFE OF A SURGEON CAN BE VERY REWARDING..
OBVIOUSLY, YOU HAVE SAVED THE LIVES OF MANY PEOPLE...
2-18
IS THAT WHAT LED YOU TO BECOME A SURGEON?
NO, I JUST LIKED THE LITTLE GREEN BOOTIES!
SCHULZ

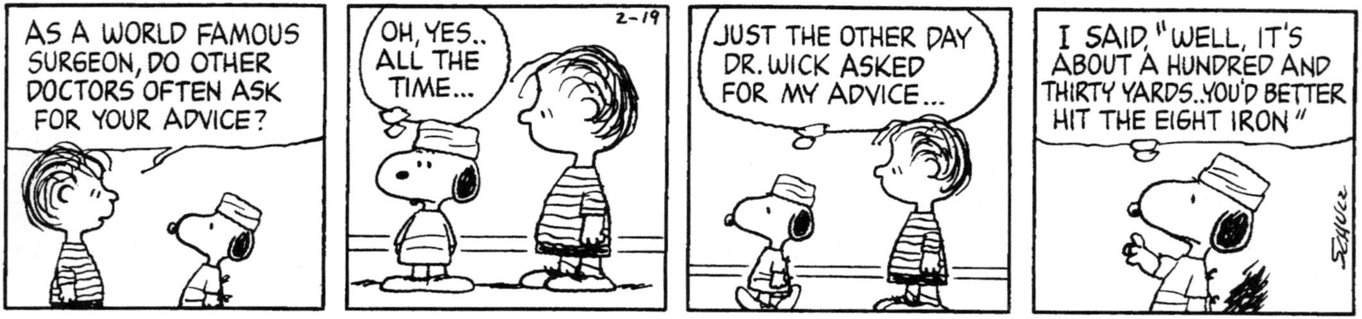
AS A WORLD FAMOUS SURGEON, DO OTHER DOCTORS OFTEN ASK FOR YOUR ADVICE?
2-19
OH, YES.. ALL THE TIME...
JUST THE OTHER DAY DR. WICK ASKED FOR MY ADVICE...
I SAID, "WELL, IT'S ABOUT A HUNDRED AND THIRTY YARDS..YOU'D BETTER HIT THE EIGHT IRON"
SCHULZ

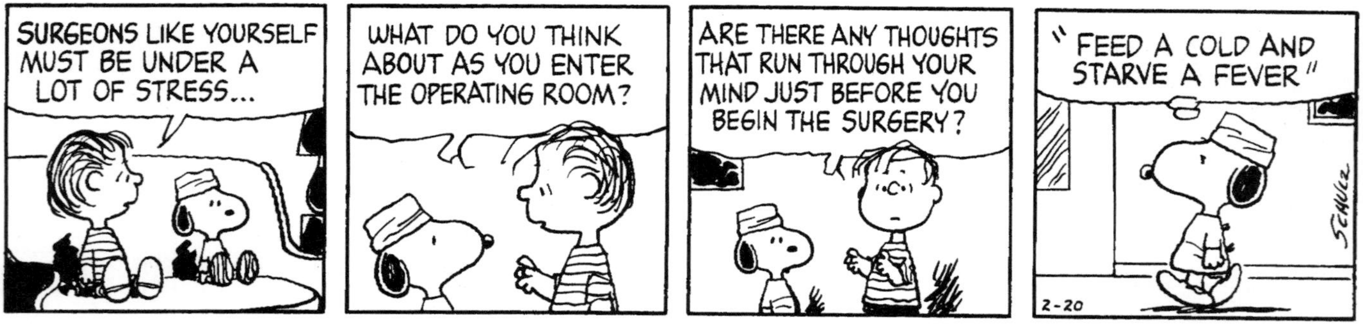
SURGEONS LIKE YOURSELF MUST BE UNDER A LOT OF STRESS...
WHAT DO YOU THINK ABOUT AS YOU ENTER THE OPERATING ROOM?
ARE THERE ANY THOUGHTS THAT RUN THROUGH YOUR MIND JUST BEFORE YOU BEGIN THE SURGERY?
"FEED A COLD AND STARVE A FEVER"
SCHULZ
2-20

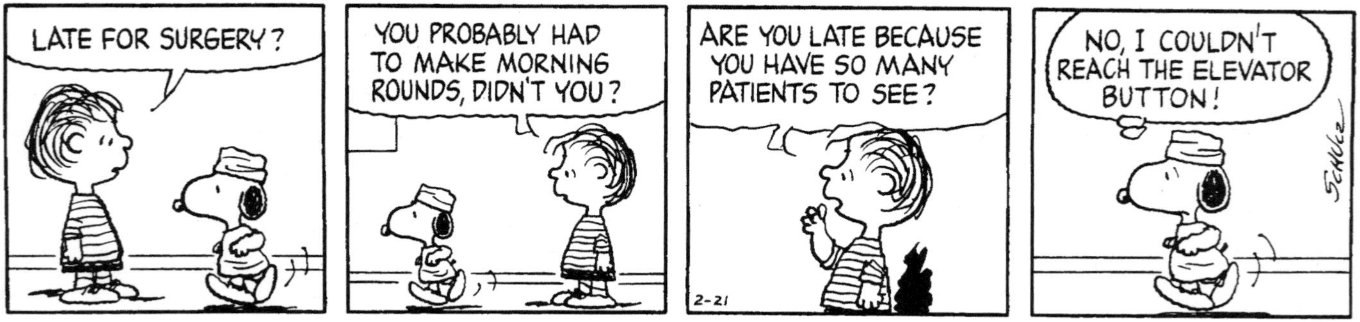
LATE FOR SURGERY?
YOU PROBABLY HAD TO MAKE MORNING ROUNDS, DIDN'T YOU?
ARE YOU LATE BECAUSE YOU HAVE SO MANY PATIENTS TO SEE?
2-21
NO, I COULDN'T REACH THE ELEVATOR BUTTON!
SCHULZ

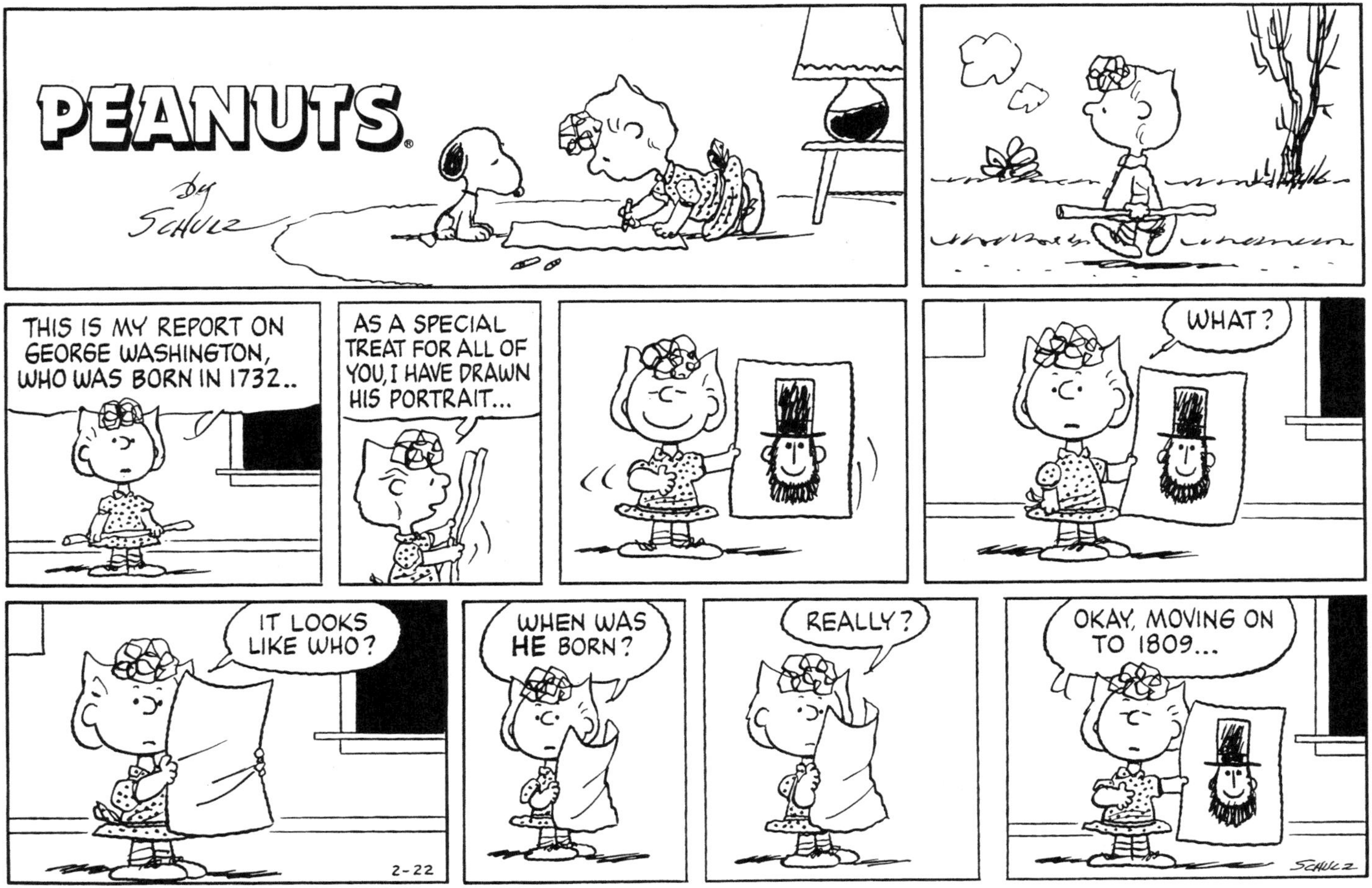
PEANUTS
by SCHULZ
THIS IS MY REPORT ON GEORGE WASHINGTON, WHO WAS BORN IN 1732..
AS A SPECIAL TREAT FOR ALL OF YOU, I HAVE DRAWN HIS PORTRAIT...
WHAT?
IT LOOKS LIKE WHO?
2-22
WHEN WAS HE BORN?
REALLY?
OKAY, MOVING ON TO 1809...
SCHULZ

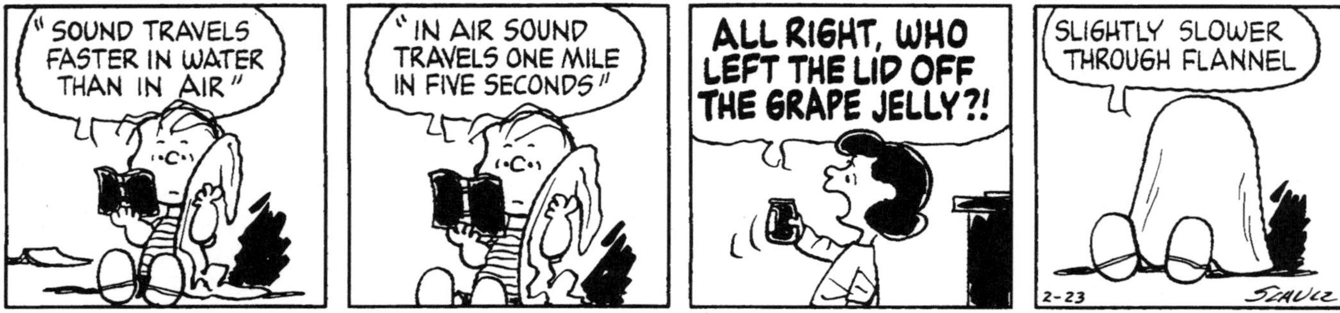
"SOUND TRAVELS FASTER IN WATER THAN IN AIR"
"IN AIR SOUND TRAVELS ONE MILE IN FIVE SECONDS"
ALL RIGHT, WHO LEFT THE LID OFF THE GRAPE JELLY?!
SLIGHTLY SLOWER THROUGH FLANNEL
2-23
SCHULZ

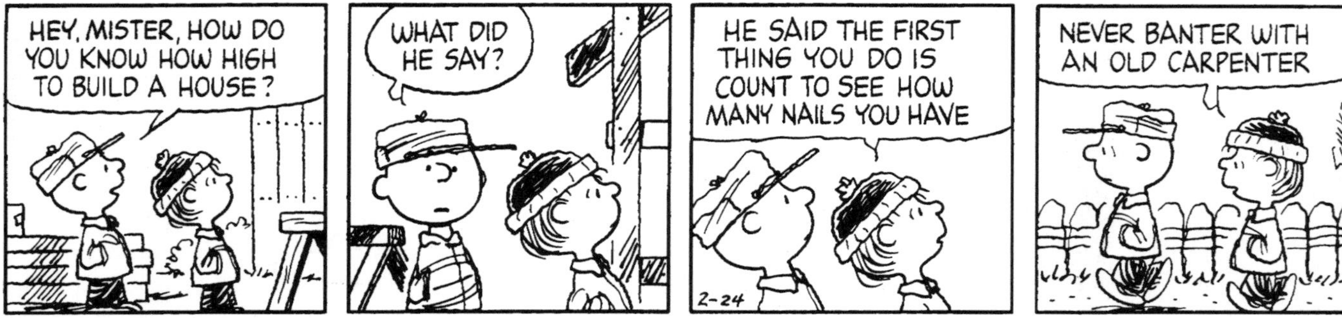
HEY, MISTER, HOW DO YOU KNOW HOW HIGH TO BUILD A HOUSE?
WHAT DID HE SAY?
HE SAID THE FIRST THING YOU DO IS COUNT TO SEE HOW MANY NAILS YOU HAVE
2-24
NEVER BANTER WITH AN OLD CARPENTER
SCHULZ

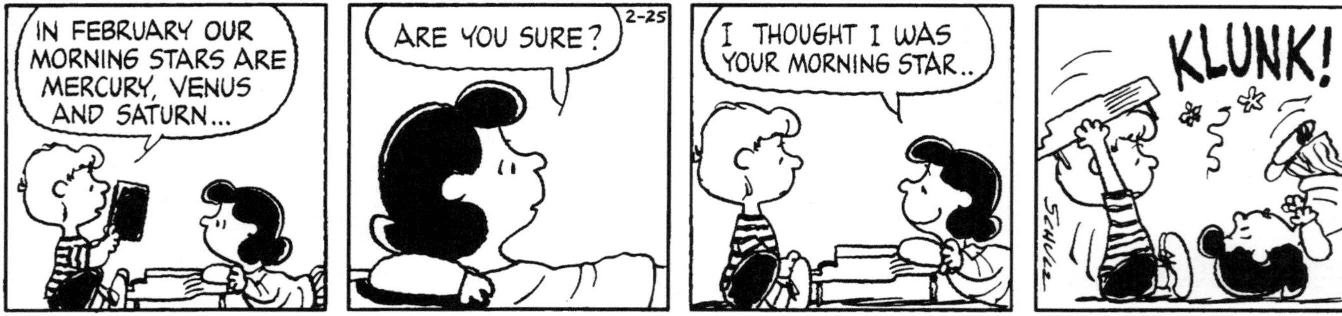
IN FEBRUARY OUR MORNING STARS ARE MERCURY, VENUS AND SATURN...
ARE YOU SURE?
2-25
I THOUGHT I WAS YOUR MORNING STAR..
KLUNK!
SCHULZ

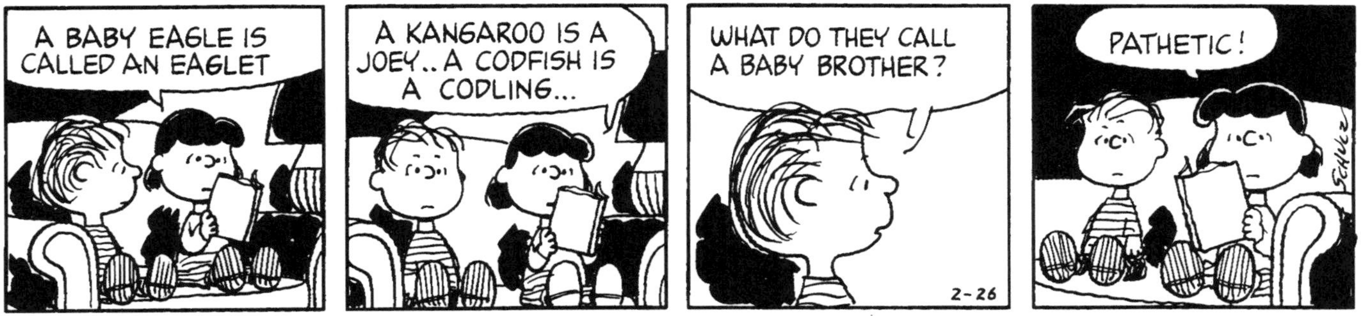
A BABY EAGLE IS CALLED AN EAGLET
A KANGAROO IS A JOEY.. A CODFISH IS A CODLING...
WHAT DO THEY CALL A BABY BROTHER?
2-26
PATHETIC!
SCHULZ

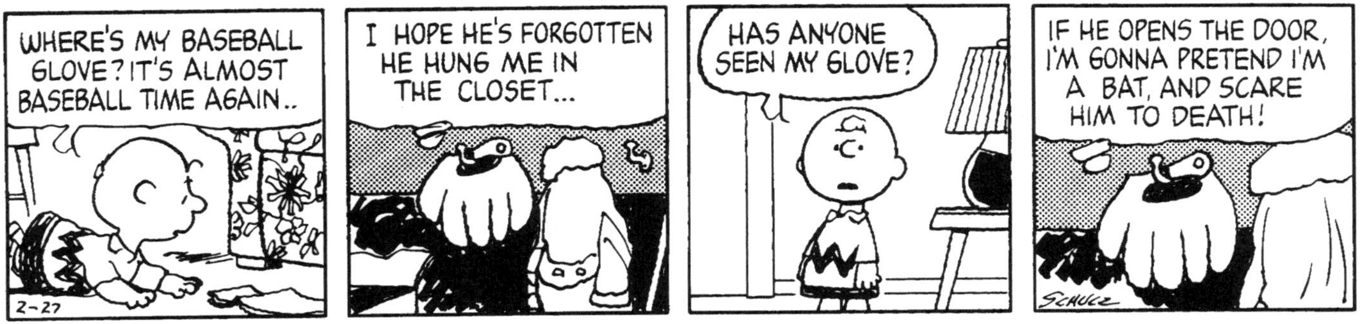
WHERE'S MY BASEBALL GLOVE? IT'S ALMOST BASEBALL TIME AGAIN..
2-27
I HOPE HE'S FORGOTTEN HE HUNG ME IN THE CLOSET...
HAS ANYONE SEEN MY GLOVE?
IF HE OPENS THE DOOR, I'M GONNA PRETEND I'M A BAT, AND SCARE HIM TO DEATH!
SCHULZ

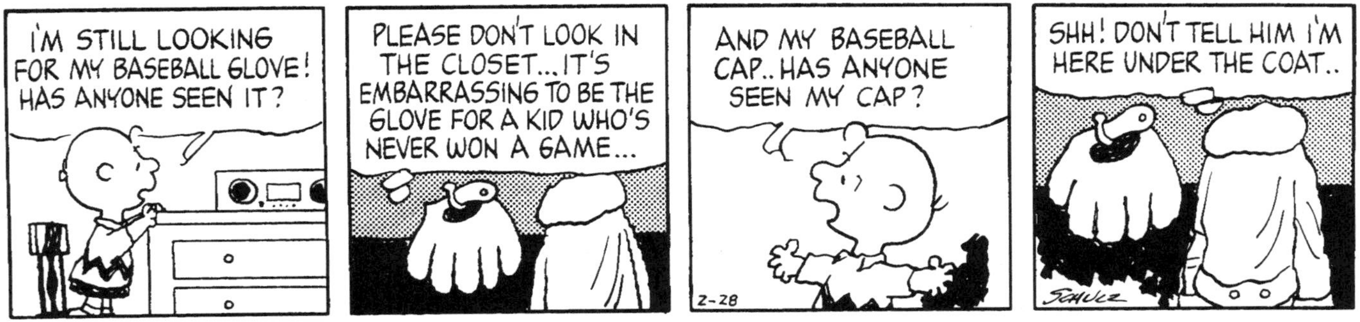
I'M STILL LOOKING FOR MY BASEBALL GLOVE! HAS ANYONE SEEN IT?
PLEASE DON'T LOOK IN THE CLOSET... IT'S EMBARRASSING TO BE THE GLOVE FOR A KID WHO'S NEVER WON A GAME...
AND MY BASEBALL CAP.. HAS ANYONE SEEN MY CAP?
2-28
SHH! DON'T TELL HIM I'M HERE UNDER THE COAT..
SCHULZ

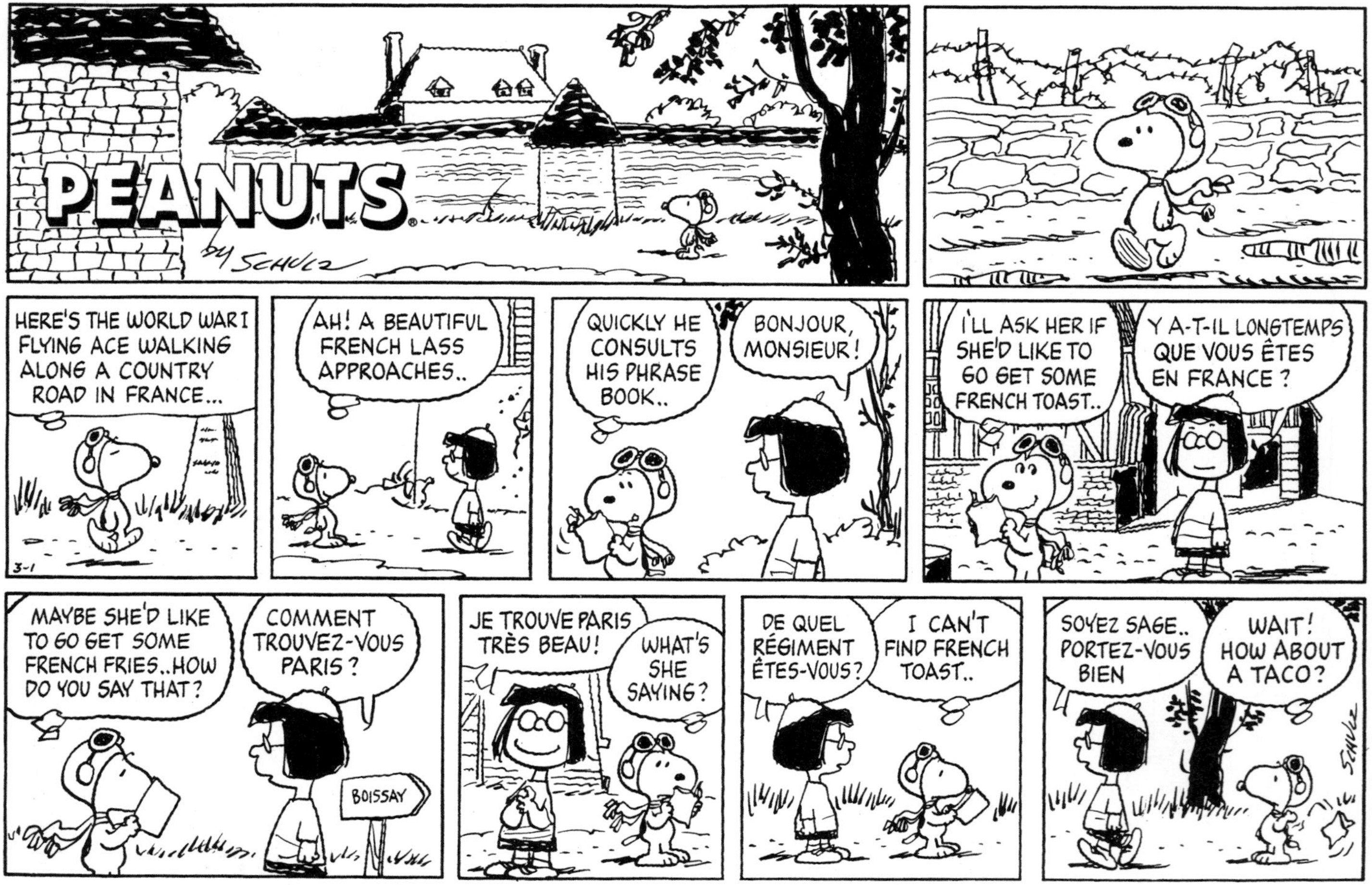
PEANUTS
by SCHULZ
3-1
HERE'S THE WORLD WAR I FLYING ACE WALKING ALONG A COUNTRY ROAD IN FRANCE...
AH! A BEAUTIFUL FRENCH LASS APPROACHES..
QUICKLY HE CONSULTS HIS PHRASE BOOK..
BONJOUR, MONSIEUR!
I'LL ASK HER IF SHE'D LIKE TO GO GET SOME FRENCH TOAST..
Y A-T-IL LONGTEMPS QUE VOUS ÊTES EN FRANCE?
MAYBE SHE'D LIKE TO GO GET SOME FRENCH FRIES..HOW DO YOU SAY THAT?
COMMENT TROUVEZ-VOUS PARIS?
BOISSAY
JE TROUVE PARIS TRÈS BEAU!
WHAT'S SHE SAYING?
DE QUEL RÉGIMENT ÊTES-VOUS?
I CAN'T FIND FRENCH TOAST..
SOYEZ SAGE.. PORTEZ-VOUS BIEN
WAIT! HOW ABOUT A TACO?
SCHULZ

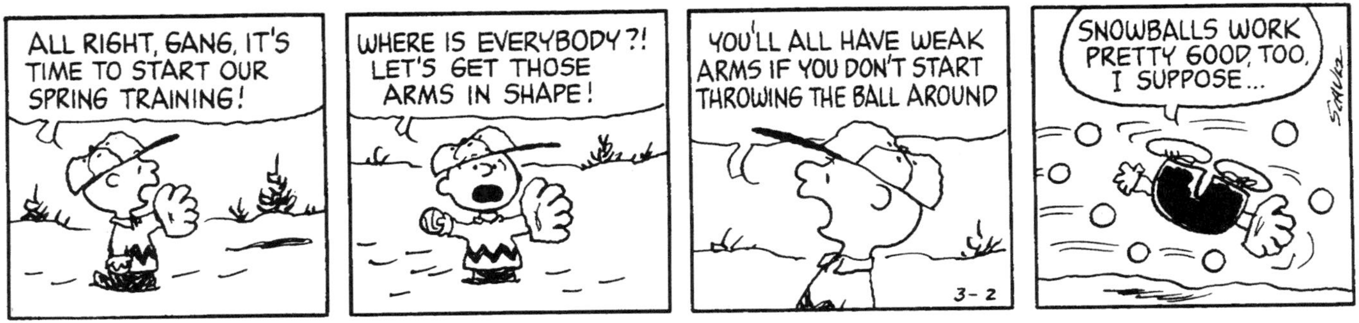
ALL RIGHT, GANG, IT'S TIME TO START OUR SPRING TRAINING!
WHERE IS EVERYBODY?! LET'S GET THOSE ARMS IN SHAPE!
YOU'LL ALL HAVE WEAK ARMS IF YOU DON'T START THROWING THE BALL AROUND
3-2
SNOWBALLS WORK PRETTY GOOD, TOO, I SUPPOSE...

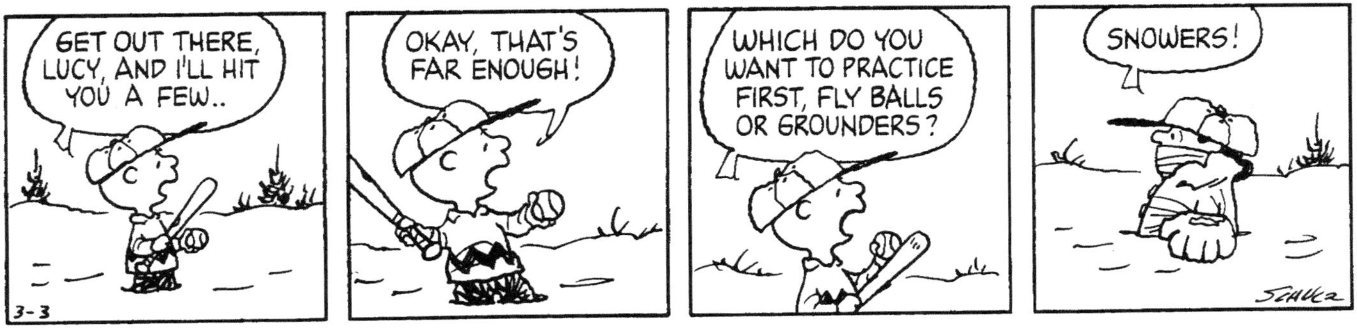
GET OUT THERE, LUCY, AND I'LL HIT YOU A FEW..
3-3
OKAY, THAT'S FAR ENOUGH!
WHICH DO YOU WANT TO PRACTICE FIRST, FLY BALLS OR GROUNDERS?
SNOWERS!

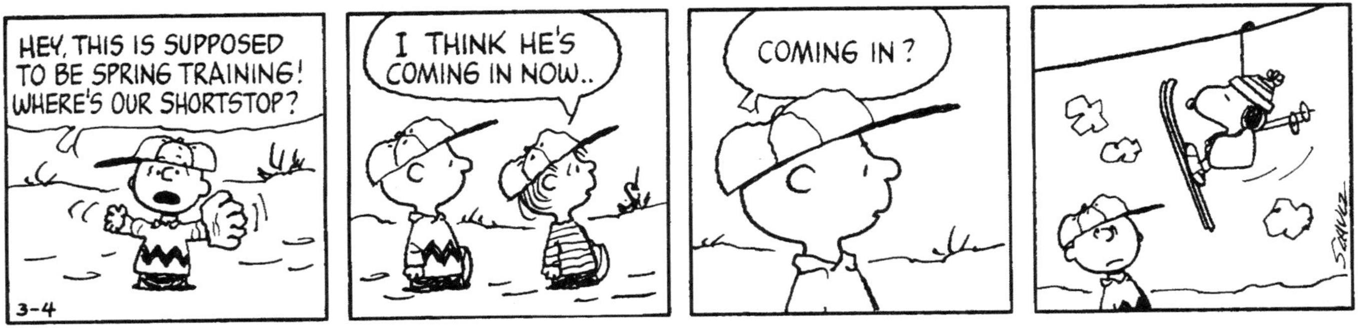
HEY, THIS IS SUPPOSED TO BE SPRING TRAINING! WHERE'S OUR SHORTSTOP?
3-4
I THINK HE'S COMING IN NOW..
COMING IN?

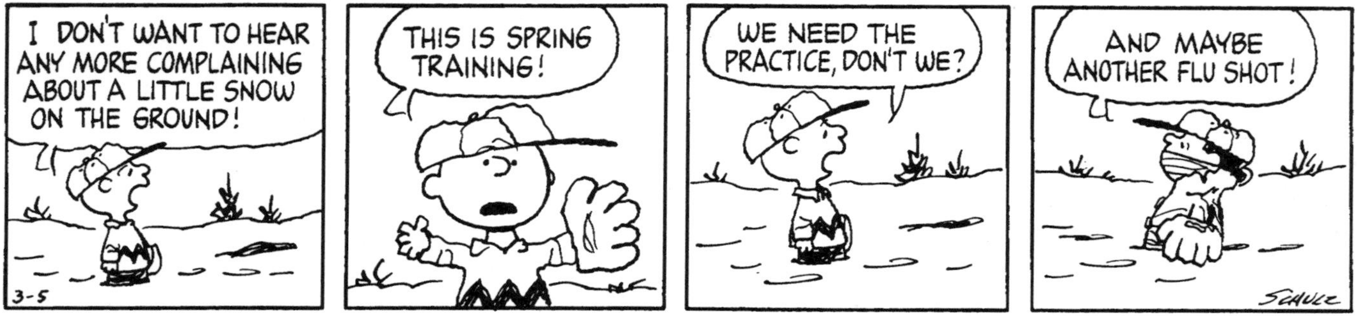
I DON'T WANT TO HEAR ANY MORE COMPLAINING ABOUT A LITTLE SNOW ON THE GROUND!
THIS IS SPRING TRAINING!
WE NEED THE PRACTICE, DON'T WE?
AND MAYBE ANOTHER FLU SHOT!

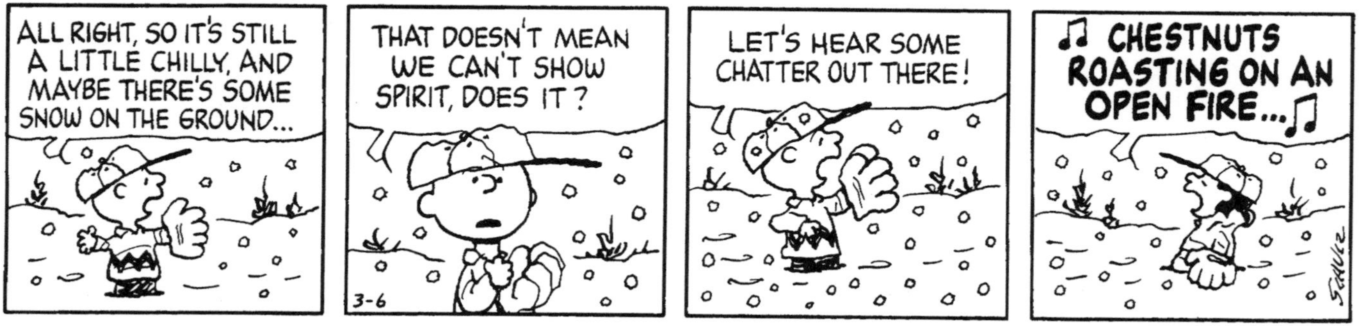
ALL RIGHT, SO IT'S STILL A LITTLE CHILLY, AND MAYBE THERE'S SOME SNOW ON THE GROUND...
THAT DOESN'T MEAN WE CAN'T SHOW SPIRIT, DOES IT?
LET'S HEAR SOME CHATTER OUT THERE!
♫ CHESTNUTS ROASTING ON AN OPEN FIRE...♫

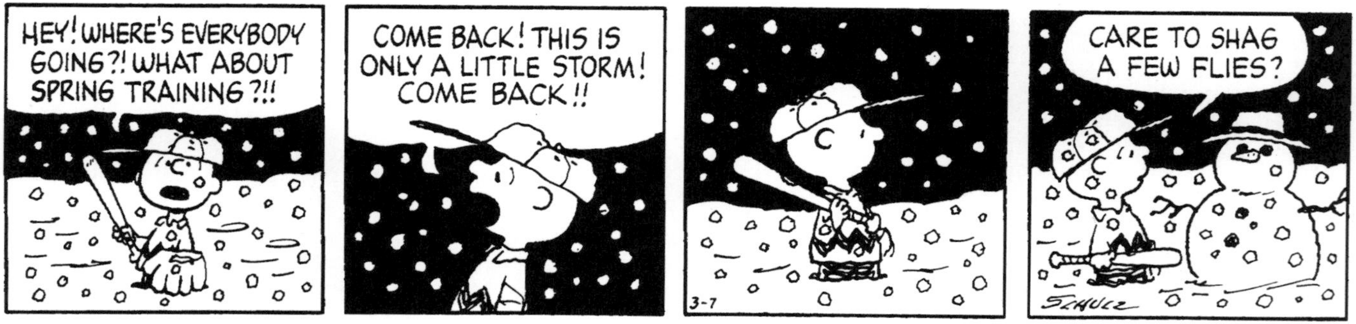
HEY! WHERE'S EVERYBODY GOING?! WHAT ABOUT SPRING TRAINING?!!
COME BACK! THIS IS ONLY A LITTLE STORM! COME BACK!!
CARE TO SHAG A FEW FLIES?

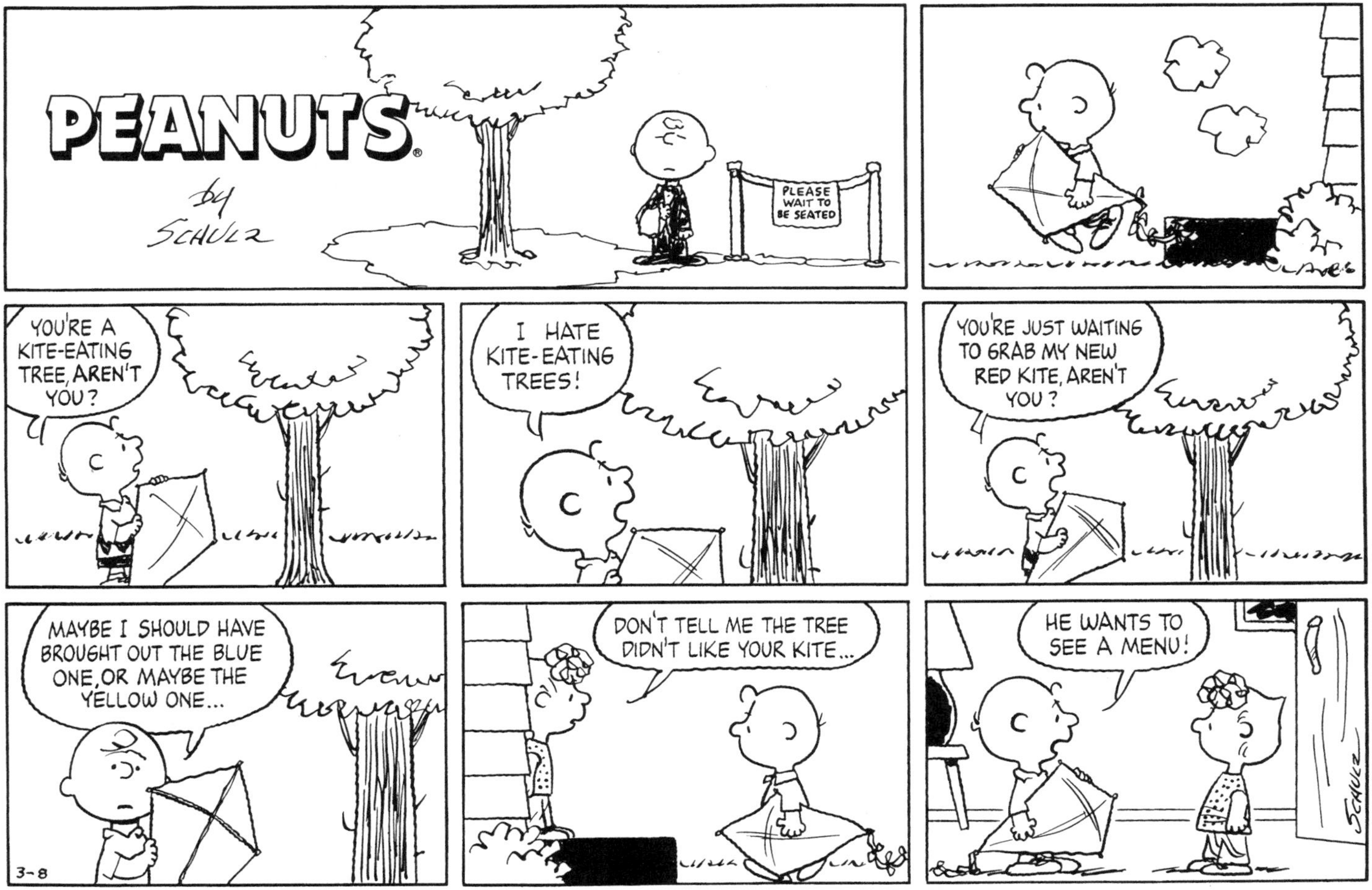
PEANUTS
by SCHULZ
PLEASE WAIT TO BE SEATED
YOU'RE A KITE-EATING TREE, AREN'T YOU?
I HATE KITE-EATING TREES!
YOU'RE JUST WAITING TO GRAB MY NEW RED KITE, AREN'T YOU?
MAYBE I SHOULD HAVE BROUGHT OUT THE BLUE ONE, OR MAYBE THE YELLOW ONE...
DON'T TELL ME THE TREE DIDN'T LIKE YOUR KITE...
HE WANTS TO SEE A MENU!
3-8
SCHULZ

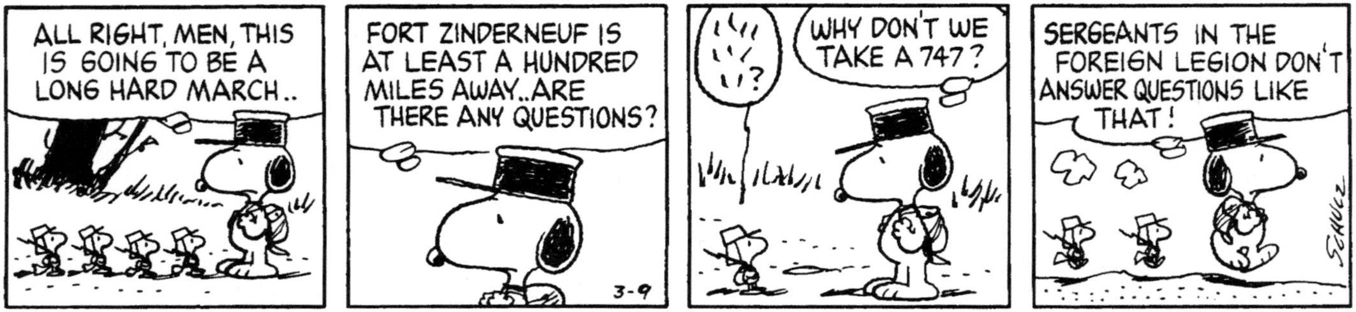
ALL RIGHT, MEN, THIS IS GOING TO BE A LONG HARD MARCH..
FORT ZINDERNEUF IS AT LEAST A HUNDRED MILES AWAY..ARE THERE ANY QUESTIONS?
3-9
WHY DON'T WE TAKE A 747?
SERGEANTS IN THE FOREIGN LEGION DON'T ANSWER QUESTIONS LIKE THAT!

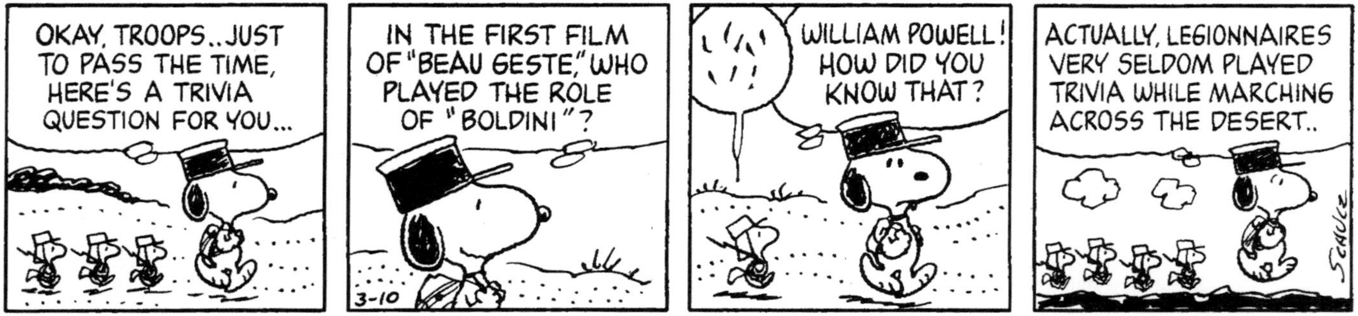
OKAY, TROOPS..JUST TO PASS THE TIME, HERE'S A TRIVIA QUESTION FOR YOU...
IN THE FIRST FILM OF "BEAU GESTE," WHO PLAYED THE ROLE OF "BOLDINI"?
3-10
WILLIAM POWELL! HOW DID YOU KNOW THAT?
ACTUALLY, LEGIONNAIRES VERY SELDOM PLAYED TRIVIA WHILE MARCHING ACROSS THE DESERT..

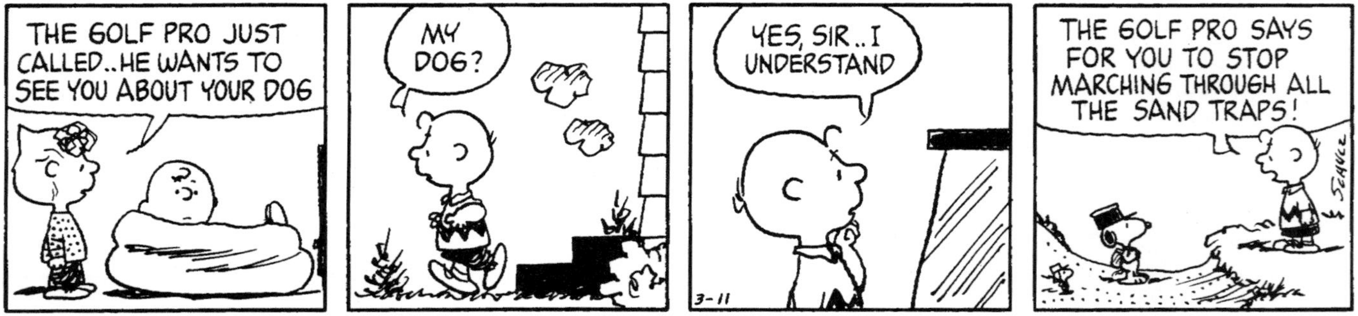
THE GOLF PRO JUST CALLED..HE WANTS TO SEE YOU ABOUT YOUR DOG
MY DOG?
YES, SIR..I UNDERSTAND
3-11
THE GOLF PRO SAYS FOR YOU TO STOP MARCHING THROUGH ALL THE SAND TRAPS!

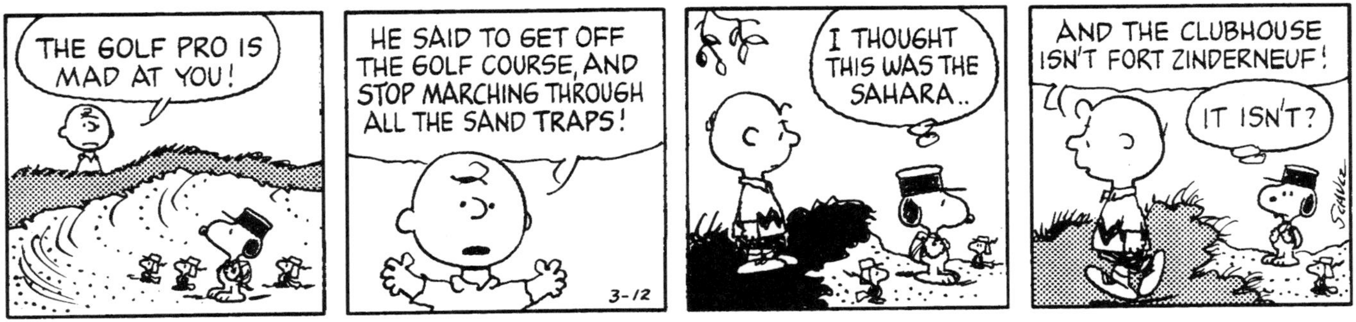
THE GOLF PRO IS MAD AT YOU!
HE SAID TO GET OFF THE GOLF COURSE, AND STOP MARCHING THROUGH ALL THE SAND TRAPS!
3-12
I THOUGHT THIS WAS THE SAHARA..
AND THE CLUBHOUSE ISN'T FORT ZINDERNEUF!
IT ISN'T?
SCHULZ

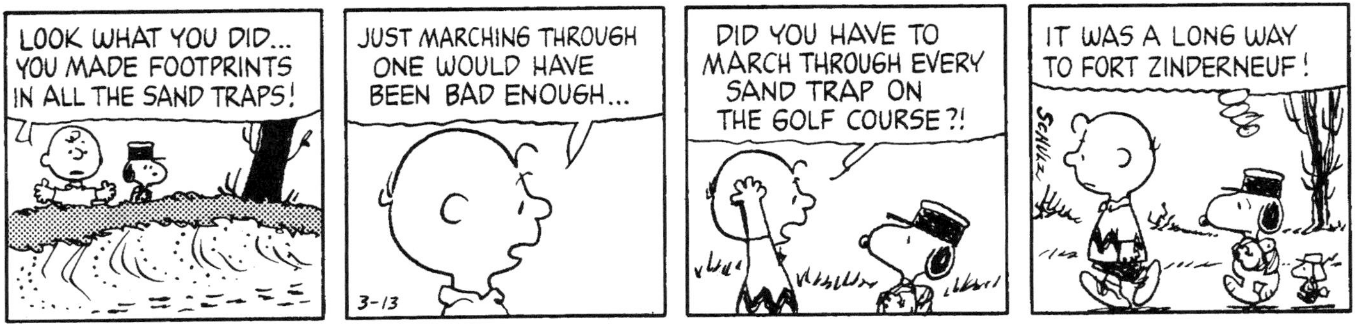
LOOK WHAT YOU DID... YOU MADE FOOTPRINTS IN ALL THE SAND TRAPS!
JUST MARCHING THROUGH ONE WOULD HAVE BEEN BAD ENOUGH...
3-13
DID YOU HAVE TO MARCH THROUGH EVERY SAND TRAP ON THE GOLF COURSE?!
IT WAS A LONG WAY TO FORT ZINDERNEUF!
SCHULZ

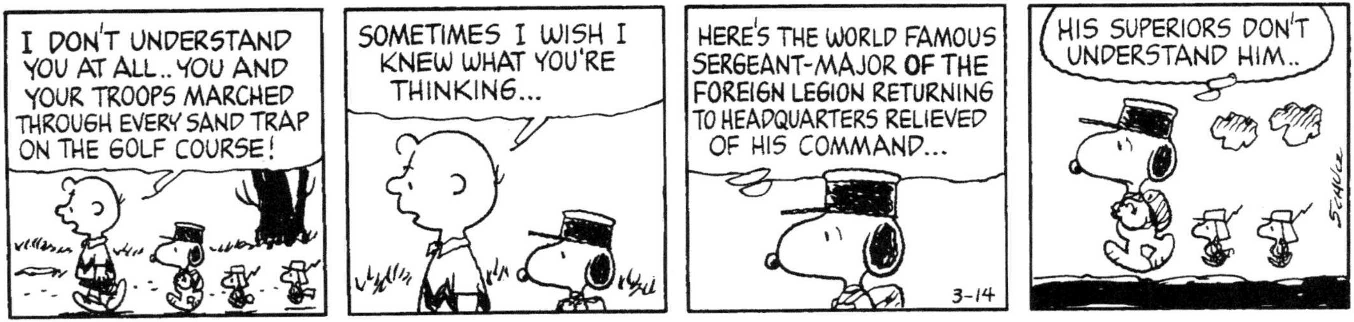
I DON'T UNDERSTAND YOU AT ALL.. YOU AND YOUR TROOPS MARCHED THROUGH EVERY SAND TRAP ON THE GOLF COURSE!
SOMETIMES I WISH I KNEW WHAT YOU'RE THINKING...
HERE'S THE WORLD FAMOUS SERGEANT-MAJOR OF THE FOREIGN LEGION RETURNING TO HEADQUARTERS RELIEVED OF HIS COMMAND...
3-14
HIS SUPERIORS DON'T UNDERSTAND HIM..
SCHULZ

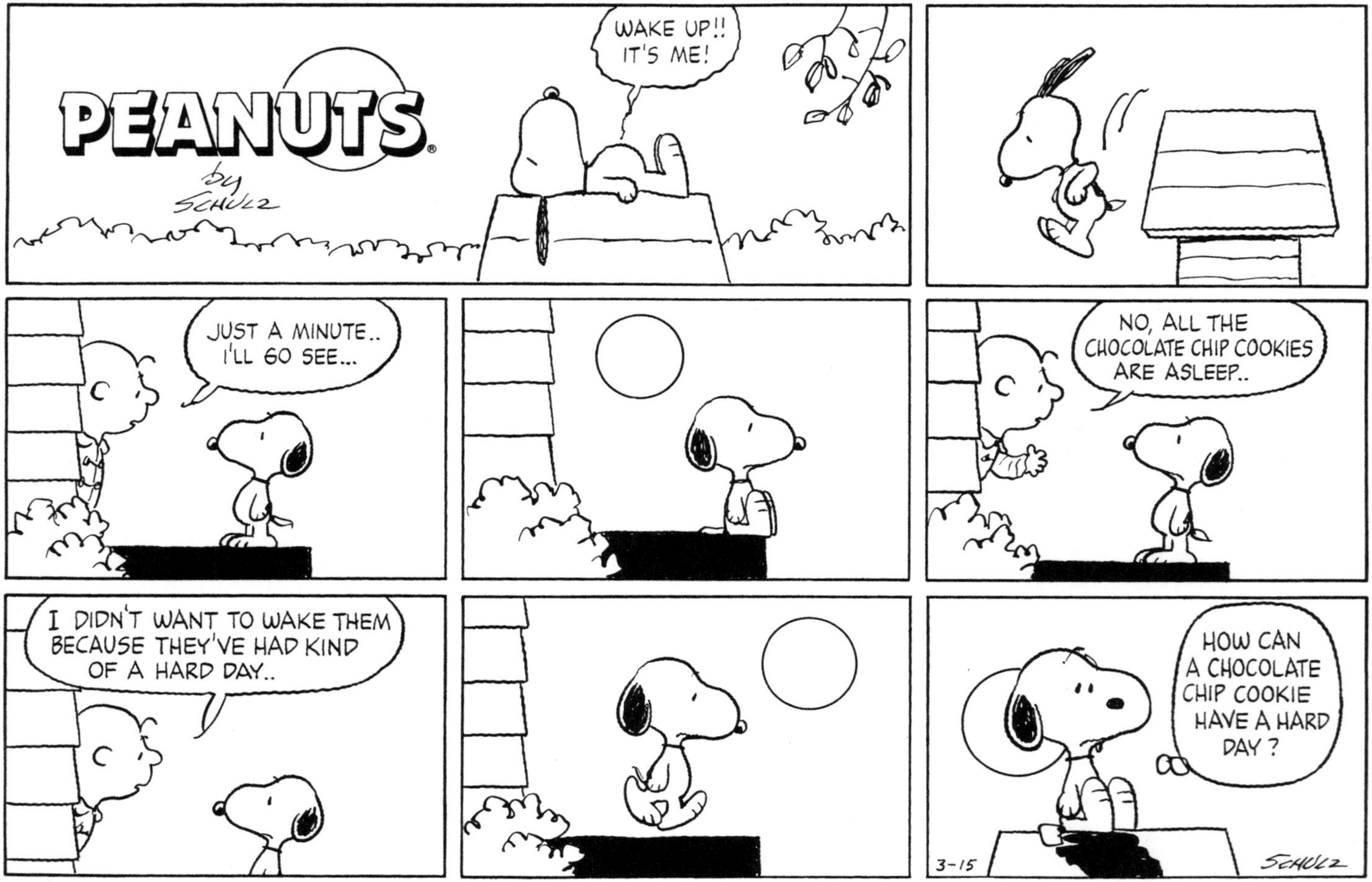
PEANUTS
by SCHULZ
WAKE UP!! IT'S ME!
JUST A MINUTE.. I'LL GO SEE...
NO, ALL THE CHOCOLATE CHIP COOKIES ARE ASLEEP..
I DIDN'T WANT TO WAKE THEM BECAUSE THEY'VE HAD KIND OF A HARD DAY..
HOW CAN A CHOCOLATE CHIP COOKIE HAVE A HARD DAY?
3-15
SCHULZ

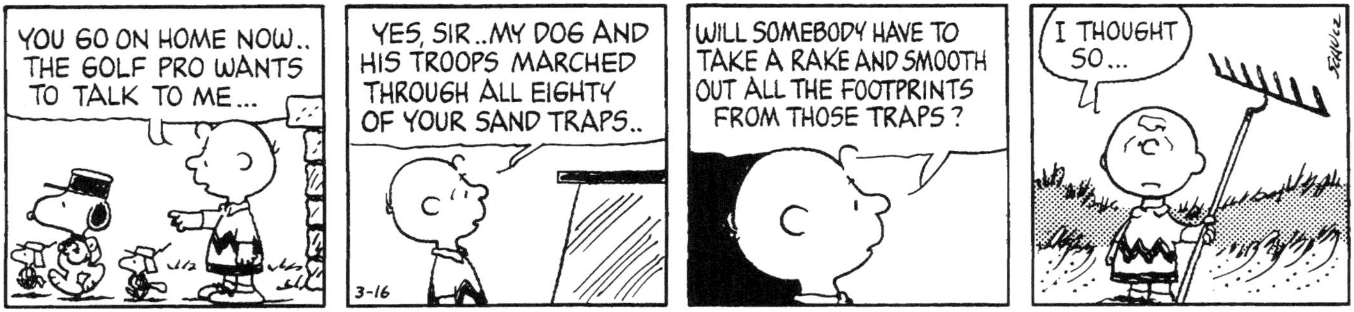
YOU GO ON HOME NOW.. THE GOLF PRO WANTS TO TALK TO ME...
YES, SIR..MY DOG AND HIS TROOPS MARCHED THROUGH ALL EIGHTY OF YOUR SAND TRAPS..
3-16
WILL SOMEBODY HAVE TO TAKE A RAKE AND SMOOTH OUT ALL THE FOOTPRINTS FROM THOSE TRAPS?
I THOUGHT SO...

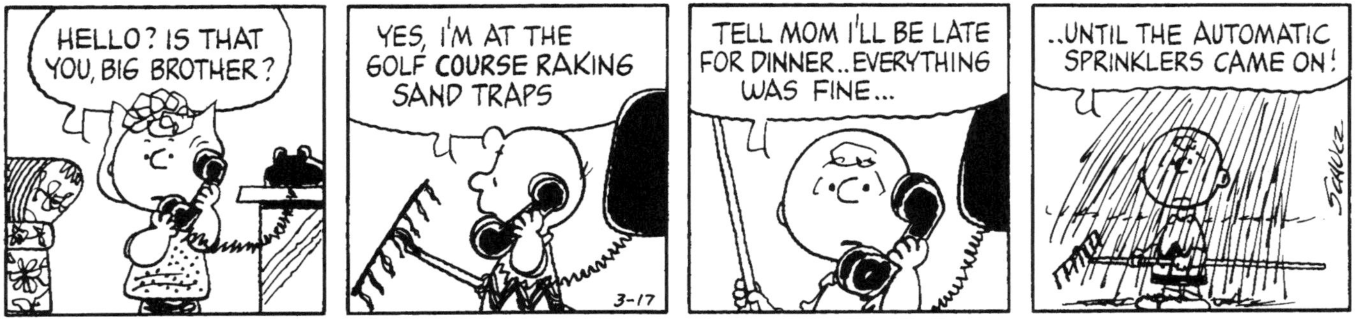
HELLO? IS THAT YOU, BIG BROTHER?
YES, I'M AT THE GOLF COURSE RAKING SAND TRAPS
3-17
TELL MOM I'LL BE LATE FOR DINNER..EVERYTHING WAS FINE...
..UNTIL THE AUTOMATIC SPRINKLERS CAME ON!

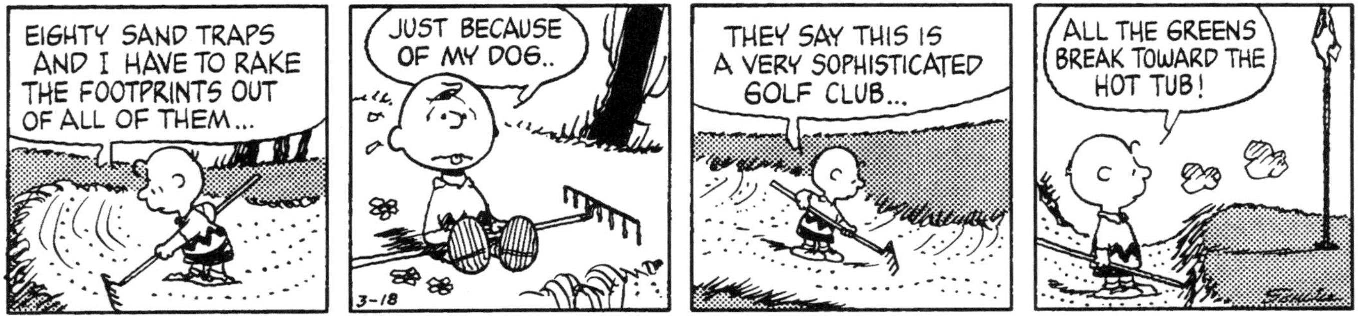
EIGHTY SAND TRAPS AND I HAVE TO RAKE THE FOOTPRINTS OUT OF ALL OF THEM...
JUST BECAUSE OF MY DOG..
3-18
THEY SAY THIS IS A VERY SOPHISTICATED GOLF CLUB...
ALL THE GREENS BREAK TOWARD THE HOT TUB!

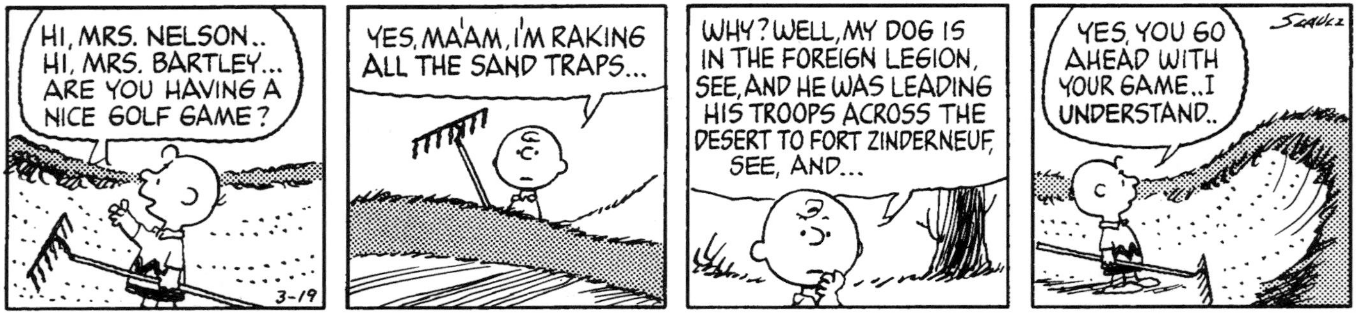
HI, MRS. NELSON.. HI, MRS. BARTLEY... ARE YOU HAVING A NICE GOLF GAME?
3-19
YES, MA'AM, I'M RAKING ALL THE SAND TRAPS...
WHY? WELL, MY DOG IS IN THE FOREIGN LEGION, SEE, AND HE WAS LEADING HIS TROOPS ACROSS THE DESERT TO FORT ZINDERNEUF, SEE, AND...
SCHULZ
YES, YOU GO AHEAD WITH YOUR GAME..I UNDERSTAND..

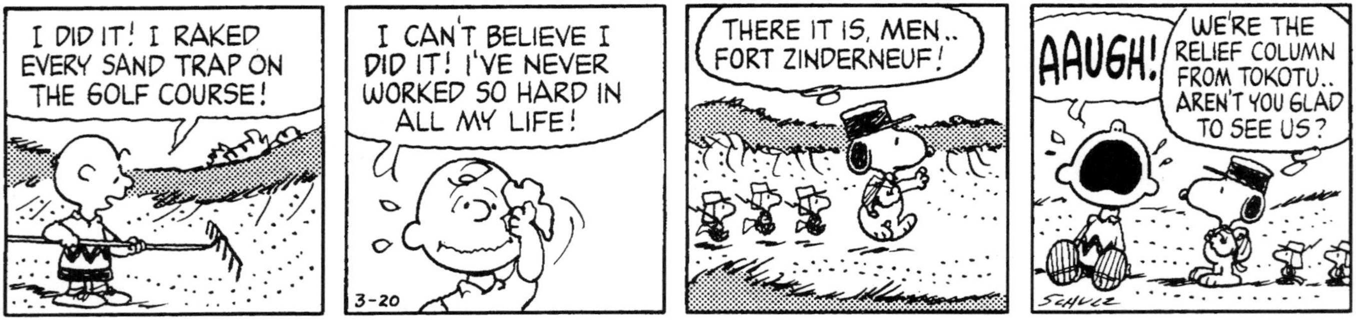
I DID IT! I RAKED EVERY SAND TRAP ON THE GOLF COURSE!
I CAN'T BELIEVE I DID IT! I'VE NEVER WORKED SO HARD IN ALL MY LIFE!
3-20
THERE IT IS, MEN.. FORT ZINDERNEUF!
AAUGH!
WE'RE THE RELIEF COLUMN FROM TOKOTU.. AREN'T YOU GLAD TO SEE US?
SCHULZ

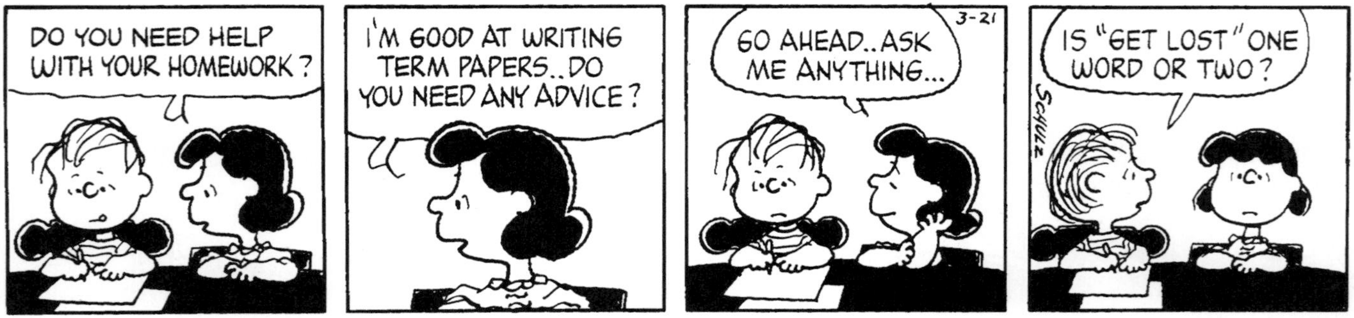
DO YOU NEED HELP WITH YOUR HOMEWORK?
I'M GOOD AT WRITING TERM PAPERS..DO YOU NEED ANY ADVICE?
3-21
GO AHEAD..ASK ME ANYTHING...
SCHULZ
IS "GET LOST" ONE WORD OR TWO?

PEANUTS®
by SCHULZ
!
3-22
?
WHAT ARE THESE?
THEY LOOK LIKE PINCUSHIONS, OR EARPLUGS, OR...
YES, RIGHT HERE..I FOUND THEM RIGHT HERE...
IS THAT WHAT THEY ARE?
WOODSTOCK'S "LEG WARMERS"
SCHULZ

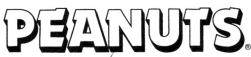

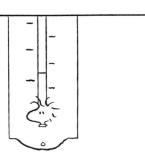

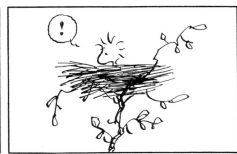

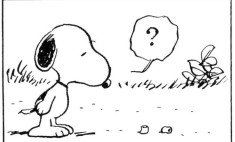

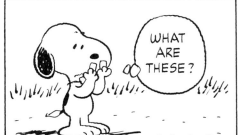

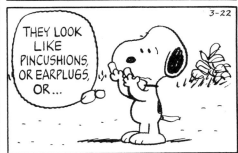

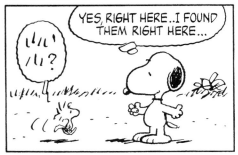

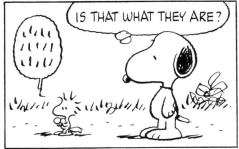

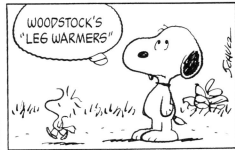

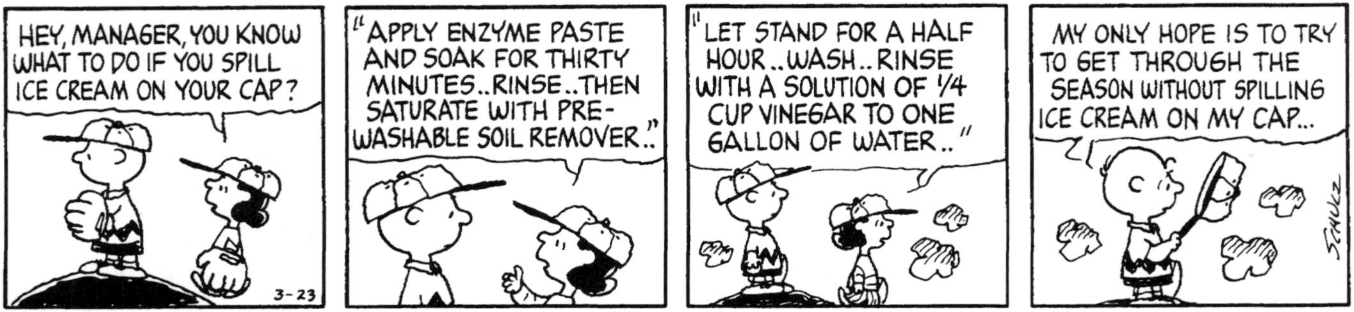
HEY, MANAGER, YOU KNOW WHAT TO DO IF YOU SPILL ICE CREAM ON YOUR CAP?
3-23
"APPLY ENZYME PASTE AND SOAK FOR THIRTY MINUTES..RINSE..THEN SATURATE WITH PRE-WASHABLE SOIL REMOVER.."
"LET STAND FOR A HALF HOUR..WASH..RINSE WITH A SOLUTION OF 1/4 CUP VINEGAR TO ONE GALLON OF WATER.."
MY ONLY HOPE IS TO TRY TO GET THROUGH THE SEASON WITHOUT SPILLING ICE CREAM ON MY CAP...
SCHULZ

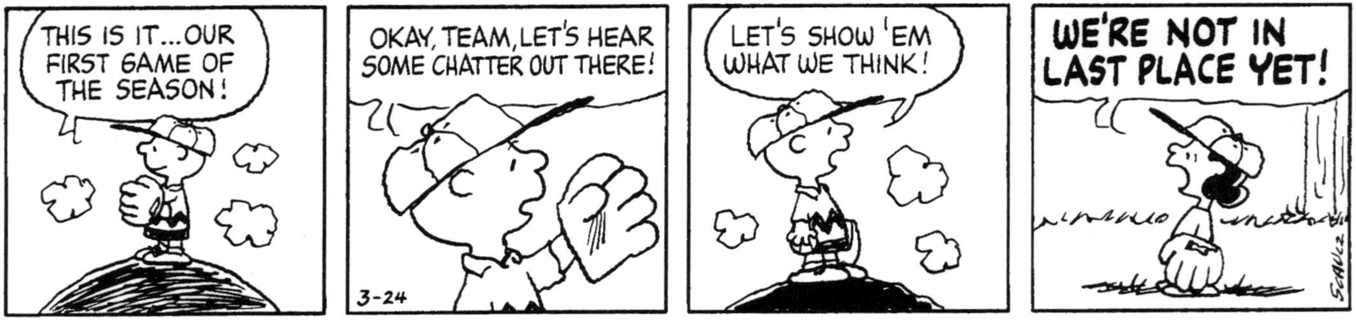
THIS IS IT...OUR FIRST GAME OF THE SEASON!
OKAY, TEAM, LET'S HEAR SOME CHATTER OUT THERE!
3-24
LET'S SHOW 'EM WHAT WE THINK!
WE'RE NOT IN LAST PLACE YET!
SCHULZ

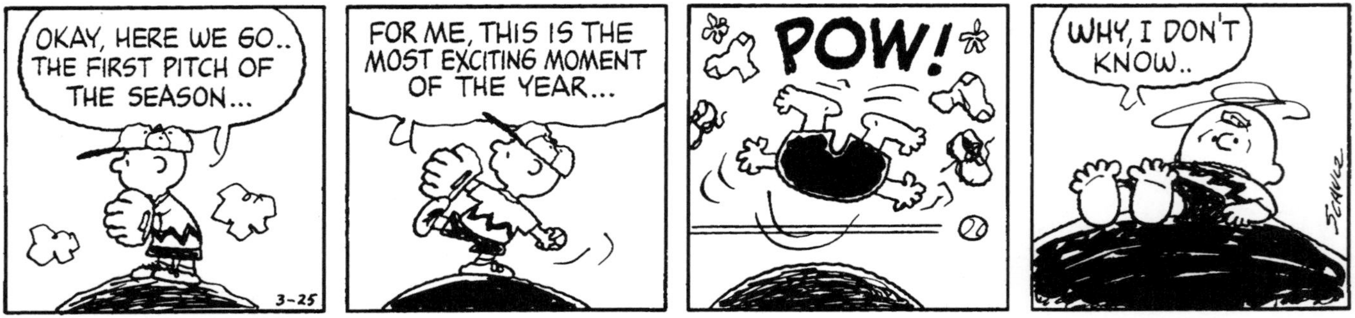
OKAY, HERE WE GO.. THE FIRST PITCH OF THE SEASON...
3-25
FOR ME, THIS IS THE MOST EXCITING MOMENT OF THE YEAR...
POW!
WHY, I DON'T KNOW..
SCHULZ

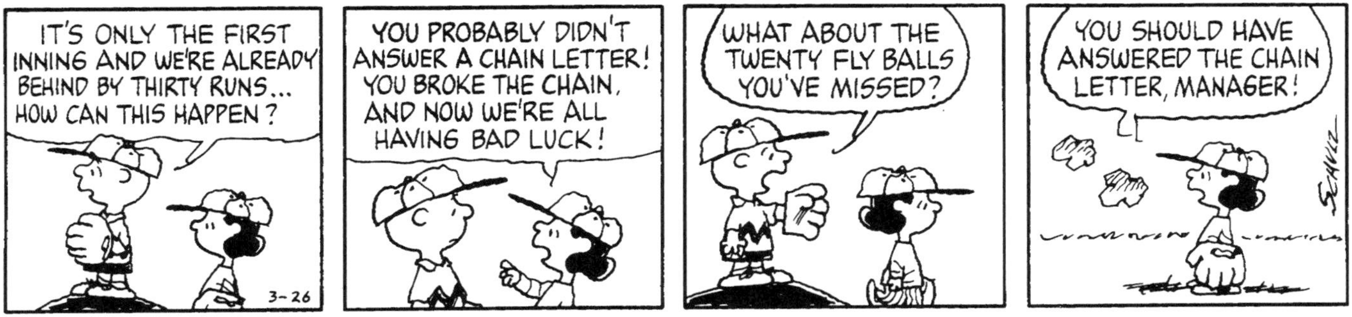
IT'S ONLY THE FIRST INNING AND WE'RE ALREADY BEHIND BY THIRTY RUNS... HOW CAN THIS HAPPEN?
3-26
YOU PROBABLY DIDN'T ANSWER A CHAIN LETTER! YOU BROKE THE CHAIN, AND NOW WE'RE ALL HAVING BAD LUCK!
WHAT ABOUT THE TWENTY FLY BALLS YOU'VE MISSED?
YOU SHOULD HAVE ANSWERED THE CHAIN LETTER, MANAGER!
SCHULZ

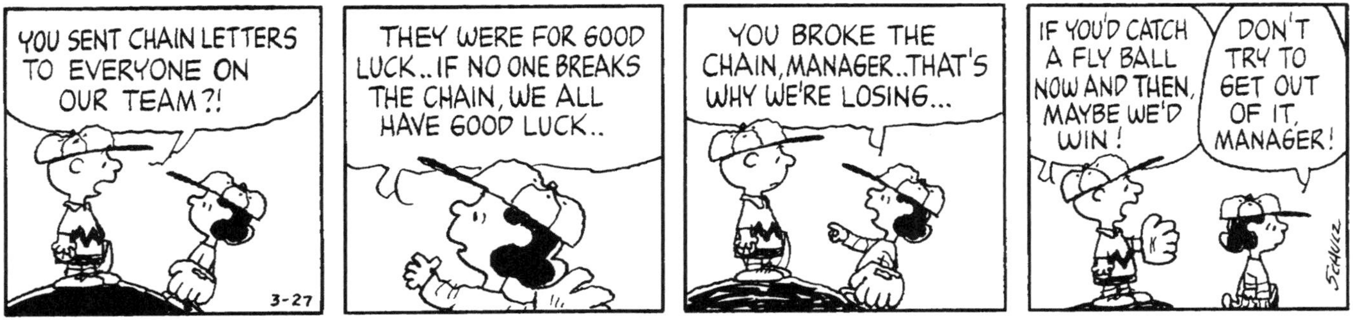
YOU SENT CHAIN LETTERS TO EVERYONE ON OUR TEAM?!
3-27
THEY WERE FOR GOOD LUCK.. IF NO ONE BREAKS THE CHAIN, WE ALL HAVE GOOD LUCK..
YOU BROKE THE CHAIN, MANAGER.. THAT'S WHY WE'RE LOSING...
IF YOU'D CATCH A FLY BALL NOW AND THEN, MAYBE WE'D WIN!
DON'T TRY TO GET OUT OF IT, MANAGER!
SCHULZ

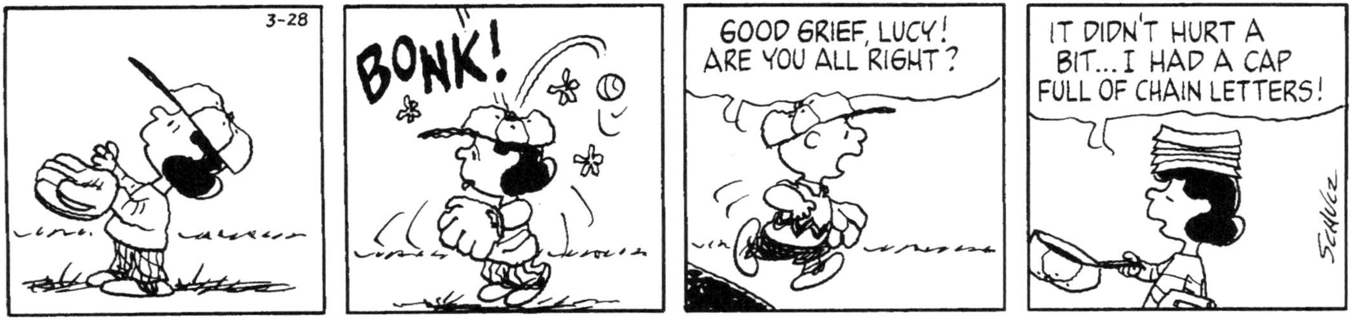
3-28
BONK!
GOOD GRIEF, LUCY! ARE YOU ALL RIGHT?
IT DIDN'T HURT A BIT... I HAD A CAP FULL OF CHAIN LETTERS!
SCHULZ

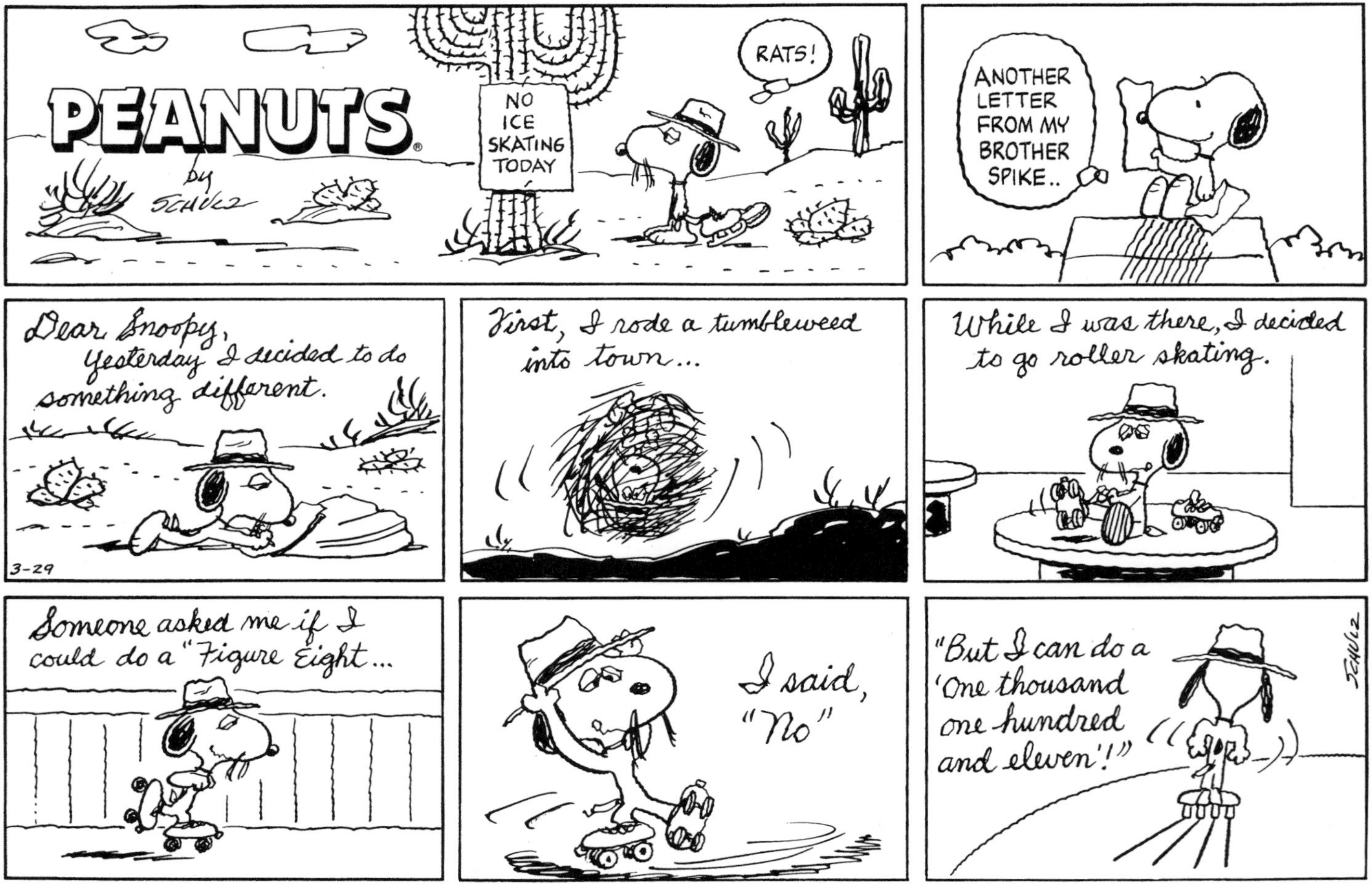
PEANUTS®
by SCHULZ
NO ICE SKATING TODAY
RATS!
ANOTHER LETTER FROM MY BROTHER SPIKE..
Dear Snoopy,
Yesterday I decided to do something different.
3-29
First, I rode a tumbleweed into town...
While I was there, I decided to go roller skating.
Someone asked me if I could do a "Figure Eight...
I said, "No"
"But I can do a 'One thousand one hundred and eleven'!"
SCHULZ

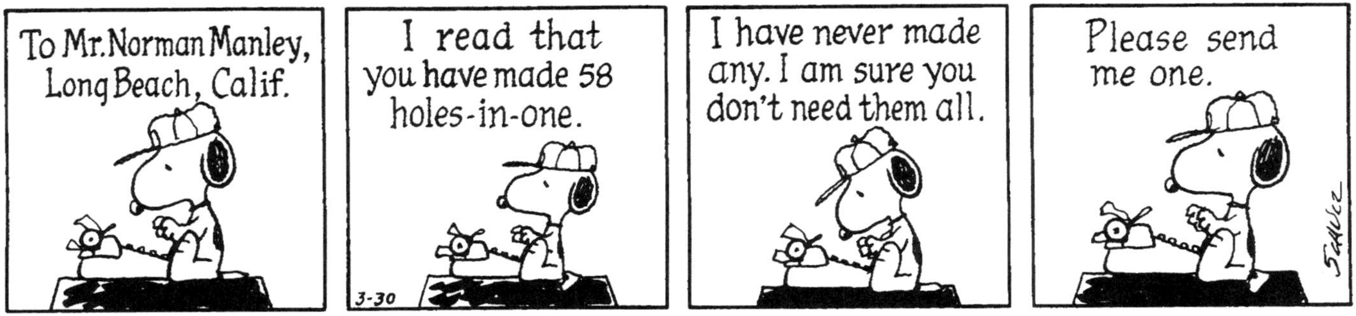
To Mr. Norman Manley, Long Beach, Calif.
I read that you have made 58 holes-in-one.
I have never made any. I am sure you don't need them all.
Please send me one.
3-30
SCHULZ

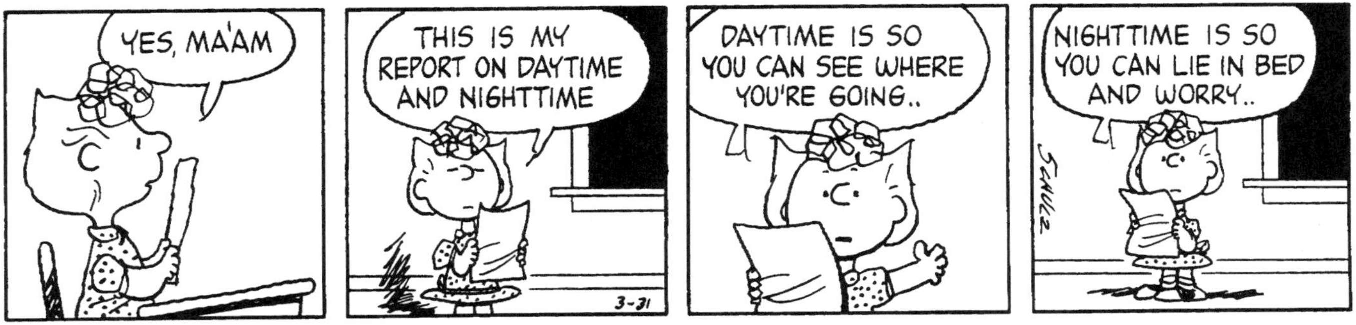
YES, MA'AM
THIS IS MY REPORT ON DAYTIME AND NIGHTTIME
DAYTIME IS SO YOU CAN SEE WHERE YOU'RE GOING..
NIGHTTIME IS SO YOU CAN LIE IN BED AND WORRY..
3-31
SCHULZ

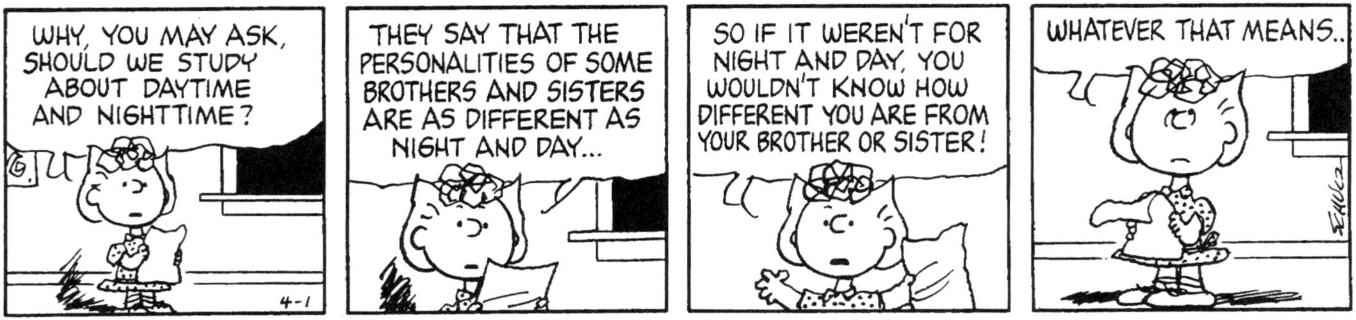
WHY, YOU MAY ASK, SHOULD WE STUDY ABOUT DAYTIME AND NIGHTTIME?
THEY SAY THAT THE PERSONALITIES OF SOME BROTHERS AND SISTERS ARE AS DIFFERENT AS NIGHT AND DAY...
SO IF IT WEREN'T FOR NIGHT AND DAY, YOU WOULDN'T KNOW HOW DIFFERENT YOU ARE FROM YOUR BROTHER OR SISTER!
WHATEVER THAT MEANS..
4-1
SCHULZ

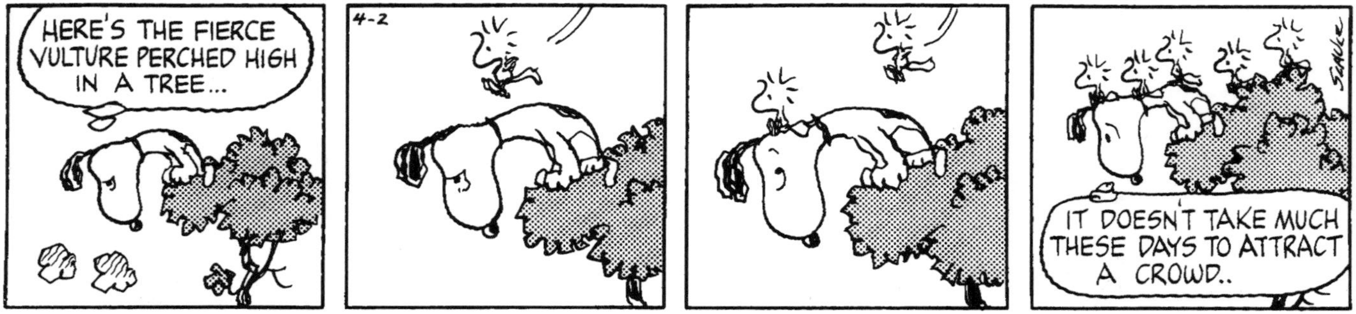
HERE'S THE FIERCE VULTURE PERCHED HIGH IN A TREE...
4-2
SCHULZ
IT DOESN'T TAKE MUCH THESE DAYS TO ATTRACT A CROWD..

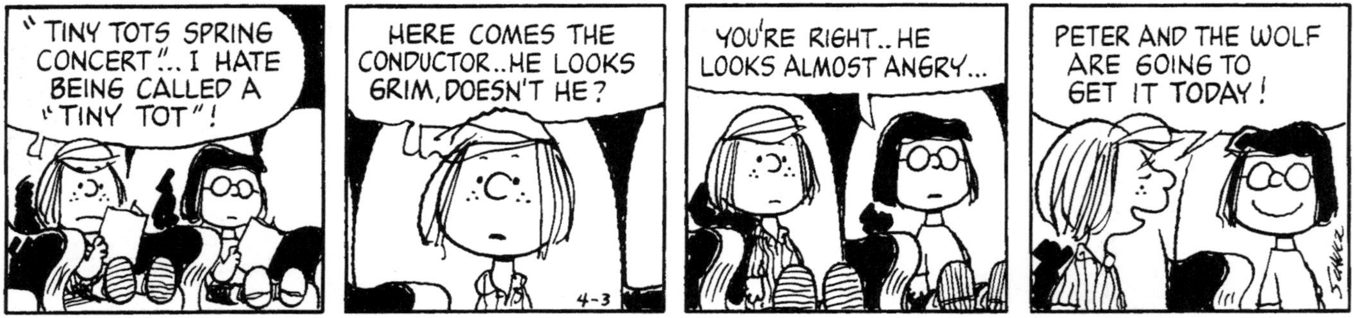
"TINY TOTS SPRING CONCERT"... I HATE BEING CALLED A "TINY TOT"!
HERE COMES THE CONDUCTOR.. HE LOOKS GRIM, DOESN'T HE?
4-3
YOU'RE RIGHT.. HE LOOKS ALMOST ANGRY...
PETER AND THE WOLF ARE GOING TO GET IT TODAY!
SCHULZ

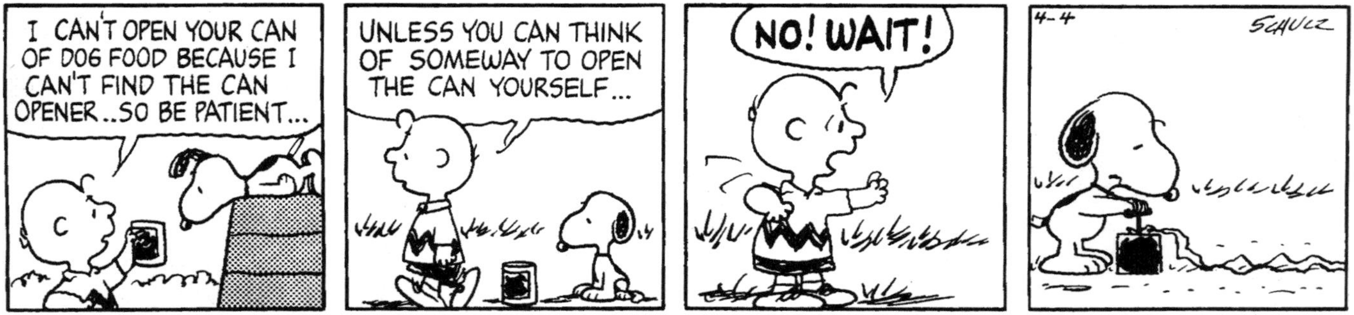
I CAN'T OPEN YOUR CAN OF DOG FOOD BECAUSE I CAN'T FIND THE CAN OPENER.. SO BE PATIENT...
UNLESS YOU CAN THINK OF SOMEWAY TO OPEN THE CAN YOURSELF...
NO! WAIT!
4-4
SCHULZ

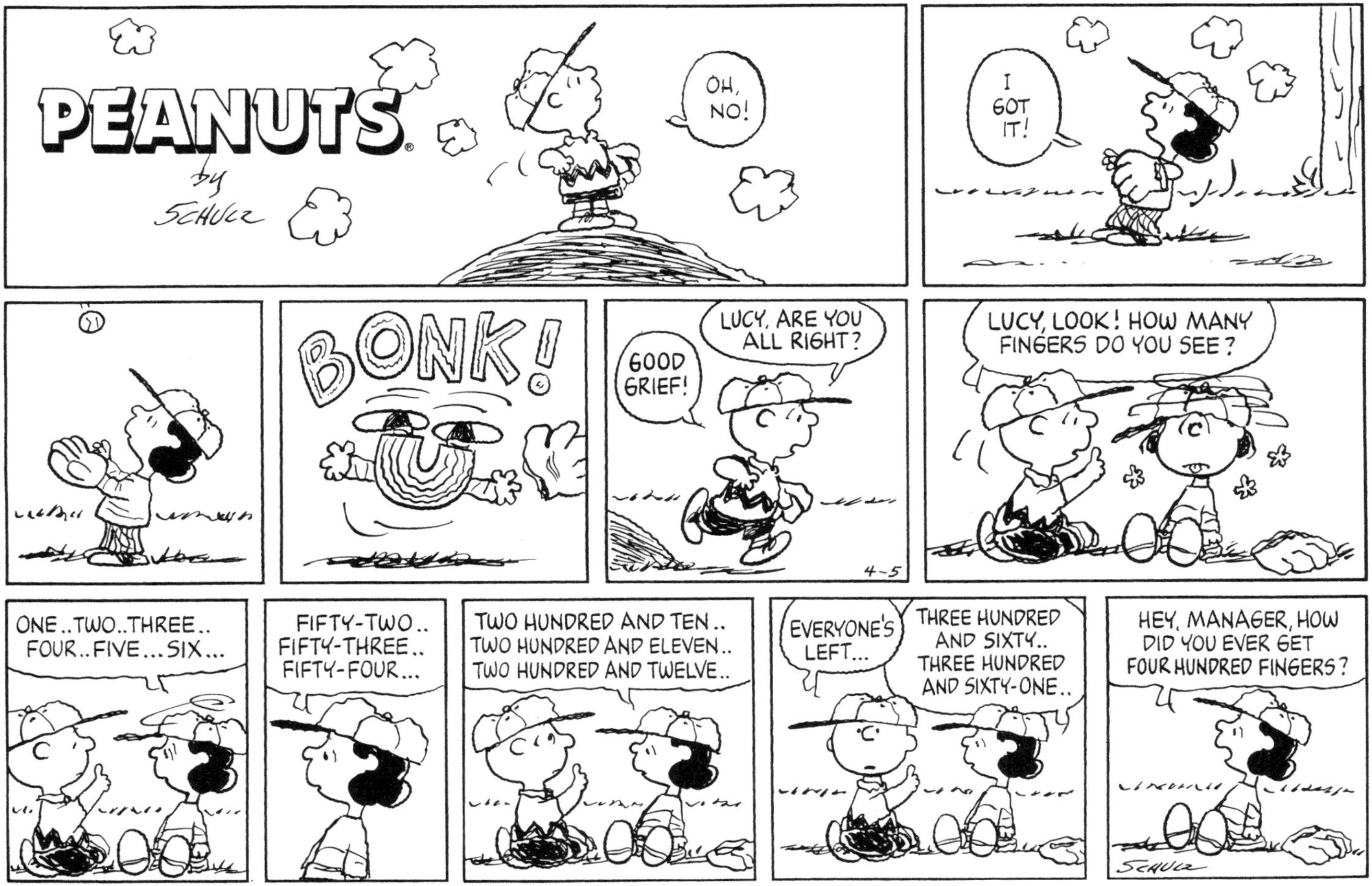
PEANUTS
by SCHULZ
OH, NO!
I GOT IT!
BONK!
GOOD GRIEF!
LUCY, ARE YOU ALL RIGHT?
4-5
LUCY, LOOK! HOW MANY FINGERS DO YOU SEE?
ONE..TWO..THREE.. FOUR..FIVE...SIX...
FIFTY-TWO.. FIFTY-THREE.. FIFTY-FOUR...
TWO HUNDRED AND TEN.. TWO HUNDRED AND ELEVEN.. TWO HUNDRED AND TWELVE..
EVERYONE'S LEFT...
THREE HUNDRED AND SIXTY.. THREE HUNDRED AND SIXTY-ONE..
HEY, MANAGER, HOW DID YOU EVER GET FOUR HUNDRED FINGERS?
SCHULZ

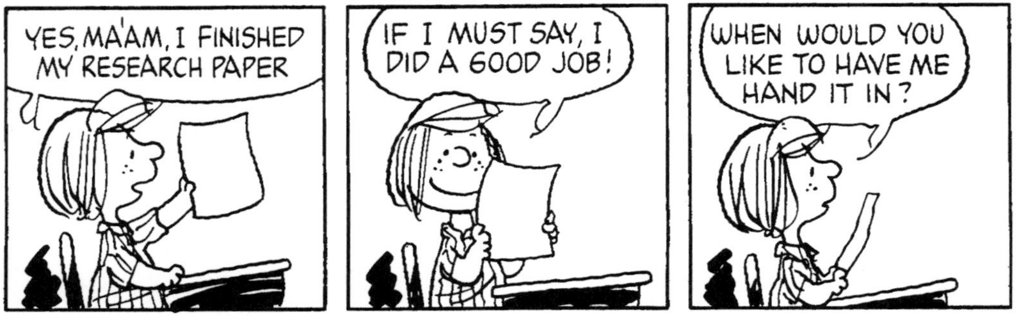
YES, MA'AM, I FINISHED MY RESEARCH PAPER
IF I MUST SAY, I DID A GOOD JOB!
WHEN WOULD YOU LIKE TO HAVE ME HAND IT IN?
LAST YEAR?
4-6

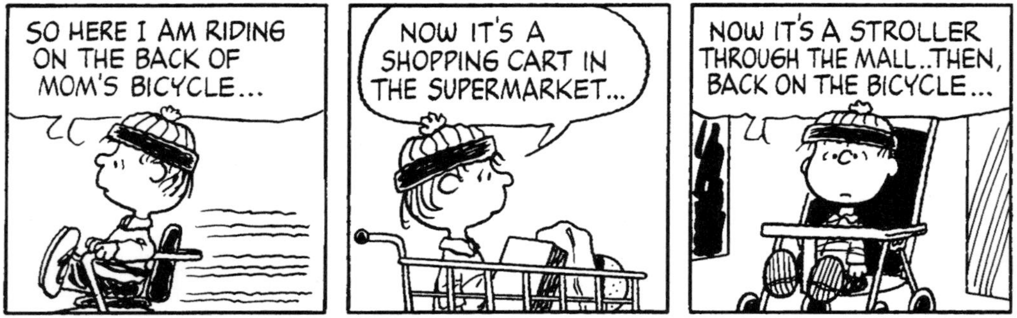
SO HERE I AM RIDING ON THE BACK OF MOM'S BICYCLE...
NOW IT'S A SHOPPING CART IN THE SUPERMARKET...
NOW IT'S A STROLLER THROUGH THE MALL..THEN, BACK ON THE BICYCLE...
SOMETIMES I GO A WHOLE DAY WITHOUT EVER TOUCHING THE GROUND!
4-7

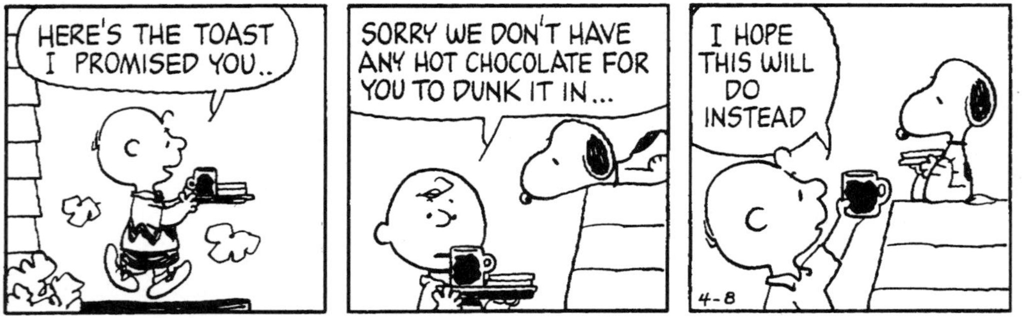
HERE'S THE TOAST I PROMISED YOU..
SORRY WE DON'T HAVE ANY HOT CHOCOLATE FOR YOU TO DUNK IT IN...
I HOPE THIS WILL DO INSTEAD
4-8
DUNKING TOAST IN ICE WATER TASTES TERRIBLE!

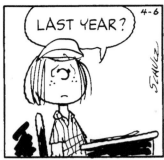

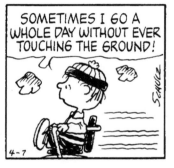

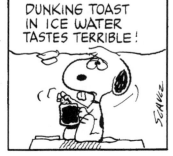

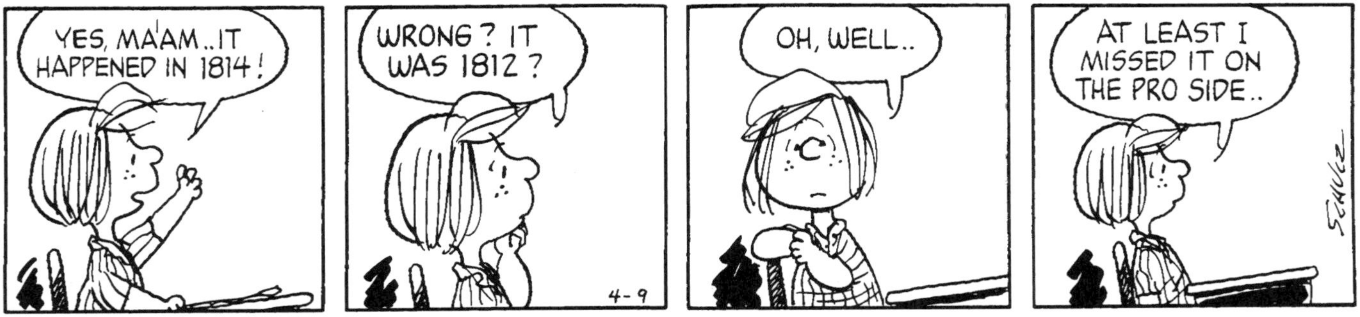
YES, MA'AM..IT HAPPENED IN 1814!
WRONG? IT WAS 1812?
4-9
OH, WELL..
AT LEAST I MISSED IT ON THE PRO SIDE..
SCHULZ

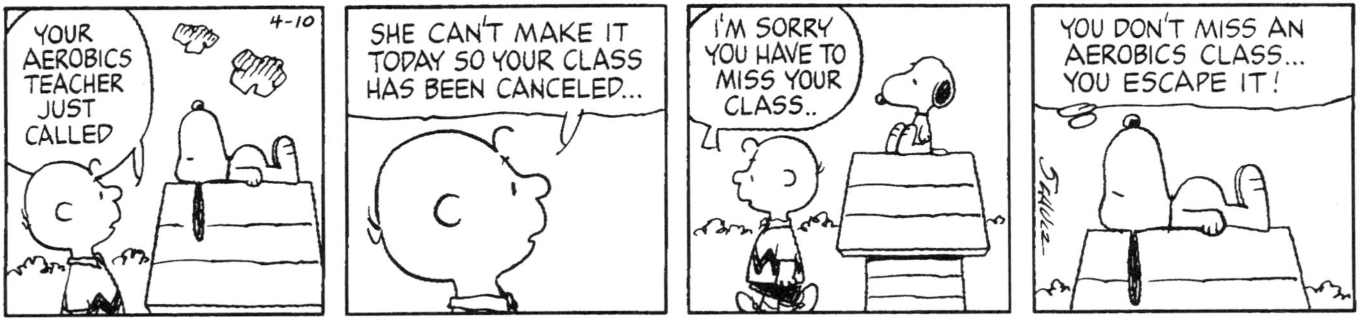
4-10
YOUR AEROBICS TEACHER JUST CALLED
SHE CAN'T MAKE IT TODAY SO YOUR CLASS HAS BEEN CANCELED...
I'M SORRY YOU HAVE TO MISS YOUR CLASS..
SCHULZ
YOU DON'T MISS AN AEROBICS CLASS... YOU ESCAPE IT!

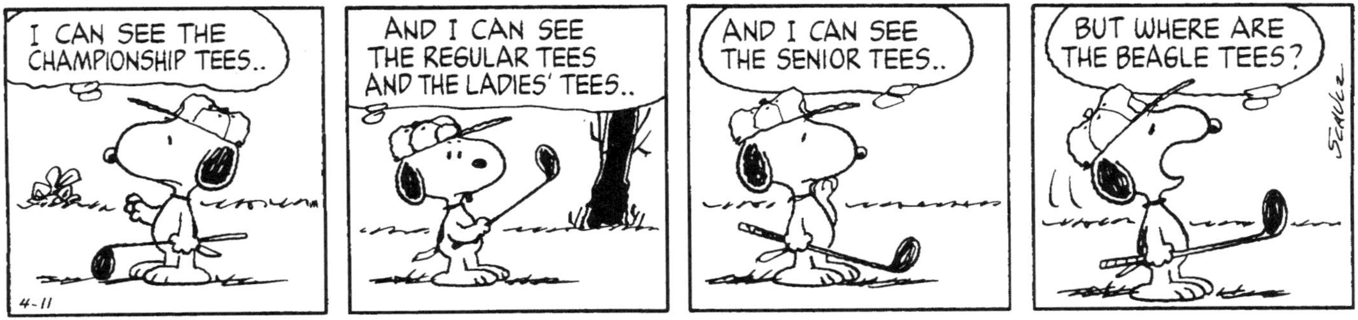
I CAN SEE THE CHAMPIONSHIP TEES..
4-11
AND I CAN SEE THE REGULAR TEES AND THE LADIES' TEES..
AND I CAN SEE THE SENIOR TEES..
BUT WHERE ARE THE BEAGLE TEES?
SCHULZ

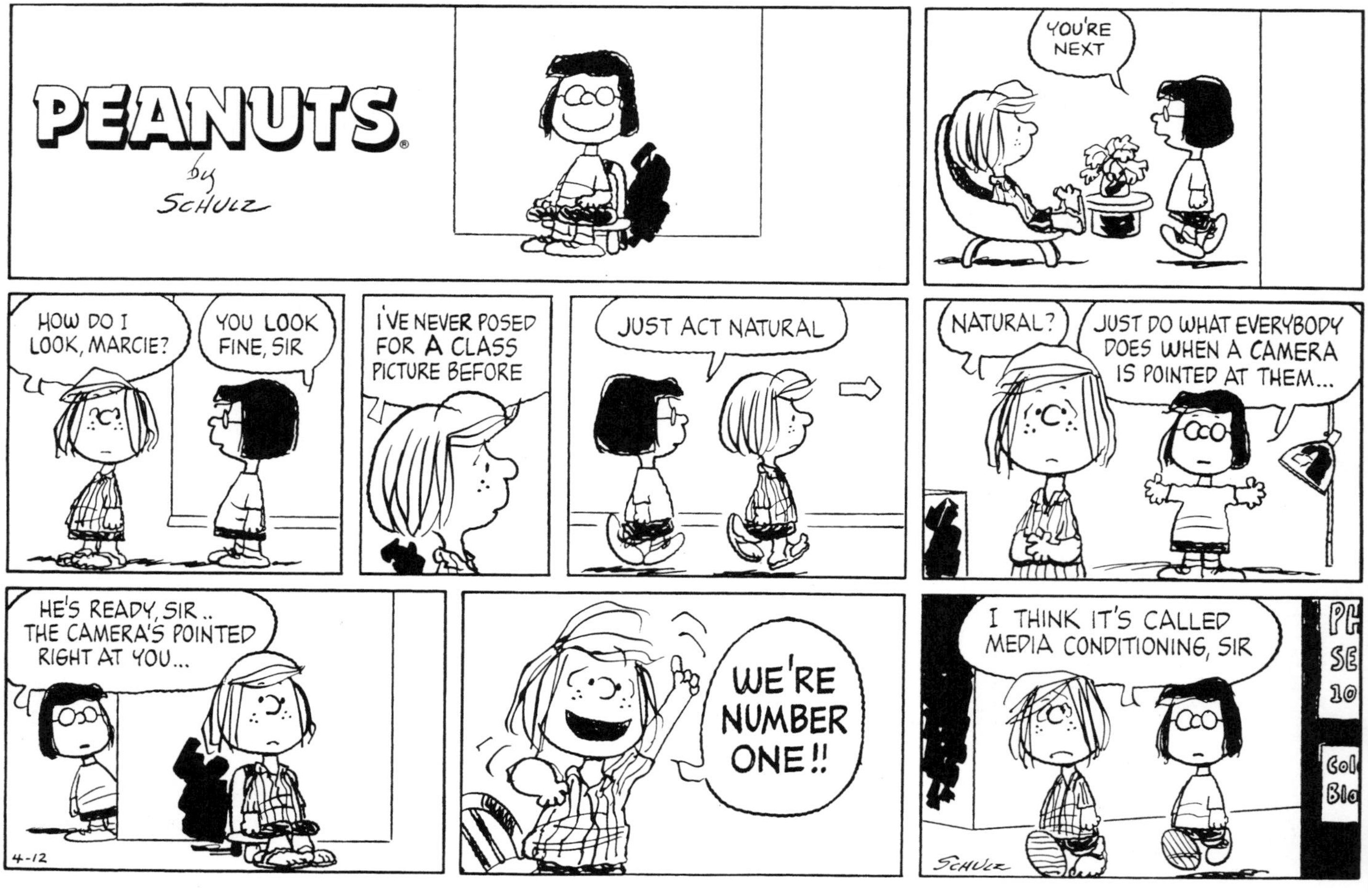
PEANUTS
by SCHULZ
YOU'RE NEXT
HOW DO I LOOK, MARCIE?
YOU LOOK FINE, SIR
I'VE NEVER POSED FOR A CLASS PICTURE BEFORE
JUST ACT NATURAL
NATURAL?
JUST DO WHAT EVERYBODY DOES WHEN A CAMERA IS POINTED AT THEM...
HE'S READY, SIR.. THE CAMERA'S POINTED RIGHT AT YOU...
4-12
WE'RE NUMBER ONE!!
I THINK IT'S CALLED MEDIA CONDITIONING, SIR
SCHULZ

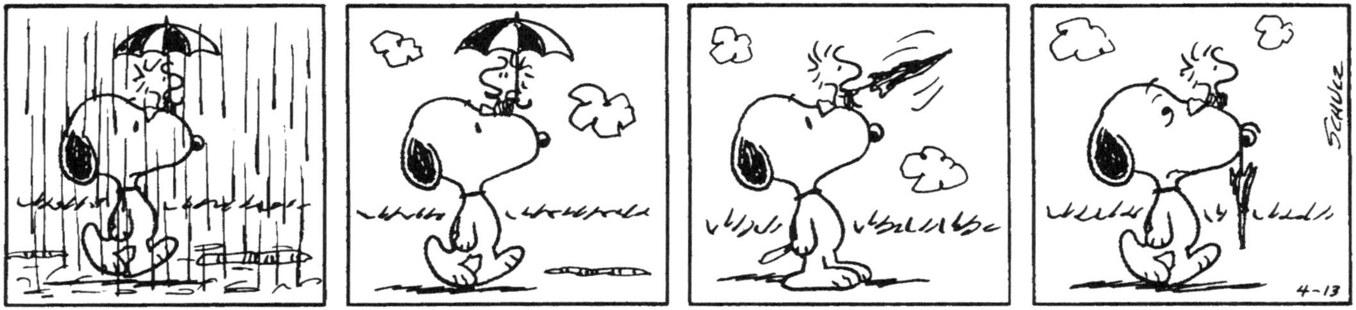

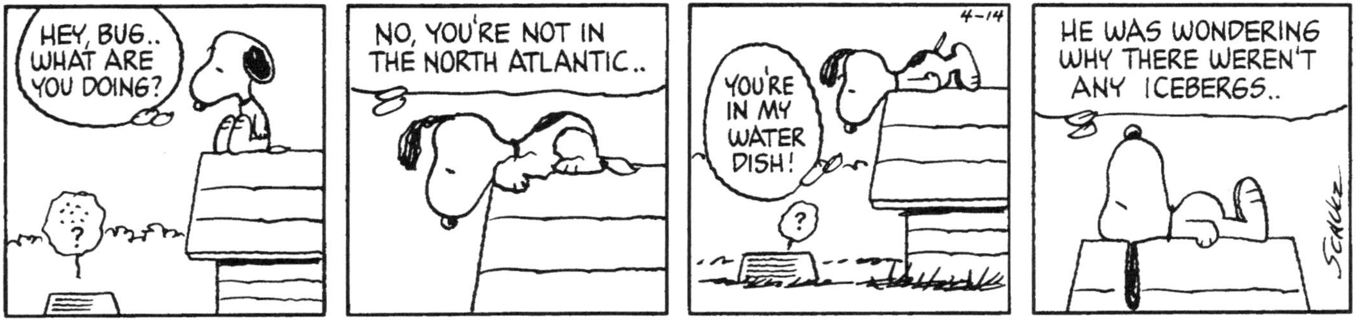
HEY, BUG.. WHAT ARE YOU DOING?
NO, YOU'RE NOT IN THE NORTH ATLANTIC..
YOU'RE IN MY WATER DISH!
HE WAS WONDERING WHY THERE WEREN'T ANY ICEBERGS..

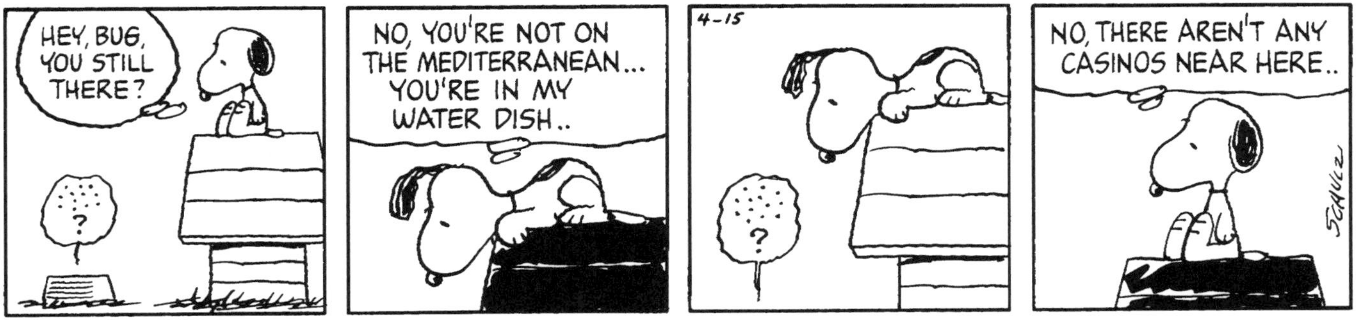
HEY, BUG, YOU STILL THERE?
NO, YOU'RE NOT ON THE MEDITERRANEAN... YOU'RE IN MY WATER DISH..
NO, THERE AREN'T ANY CASINOS NEAR HERE..

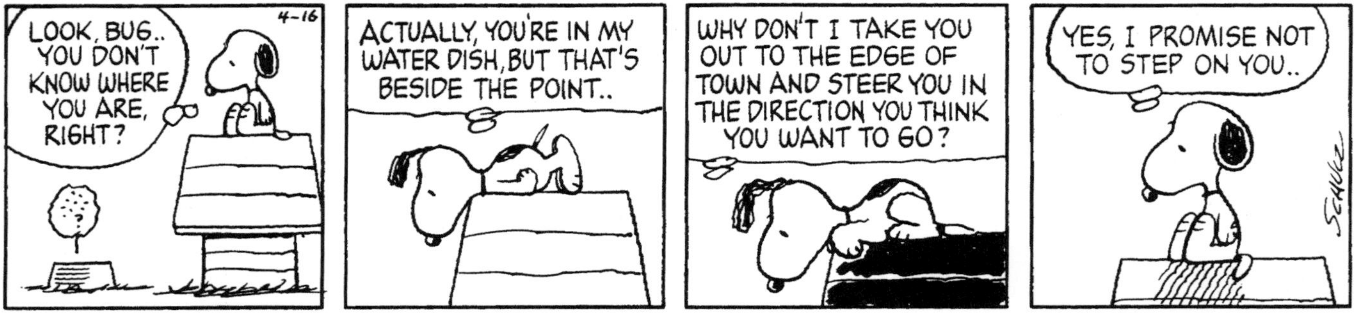
4-16
LOOK, BUG.. YOU DON'T KNOW WHERE YOU ARE, RIGHT?
ACTUALLY, YOU'RE IN MY WATER DISH, BUT THAT'S BESIDE THE POINT..
WHY DON'T I TAKE YOU OUT TO THE EDGE OF TOWN AND STEER YOU IN THE DIRECTION YOU THINK YOU WANT TO GO?
YES, I PROMISE NOT TO STEP ON YOU..
SCHULZ

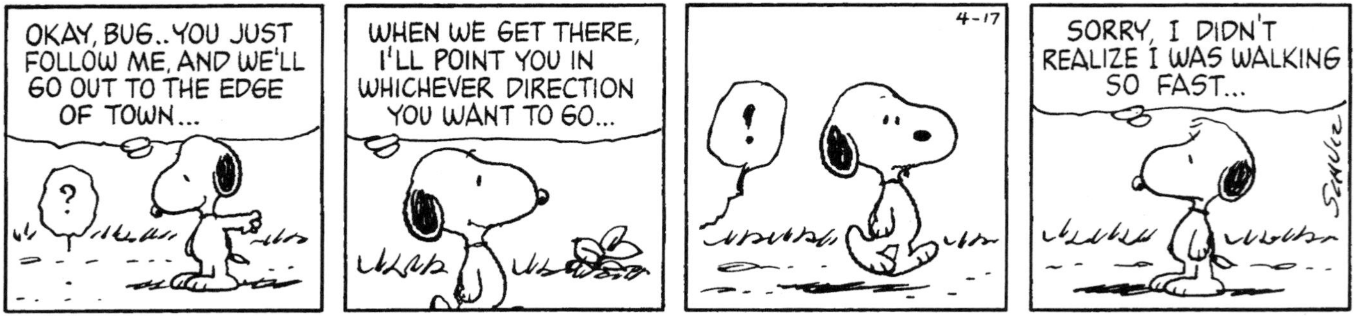
OKAY, BUG..YOU JUST FOLLOW ME, AND WE'LL GO OUT TO THE EDGE OF TOWN...
WHEN WE GET THERE, I'LL POINT YOU IN WHICHEVER DIRECTION YOU WANT TO GO...
4-17
SORRY, I DIDN'T REALIZE I WAS WALKING SO FAST...
SCHULZ

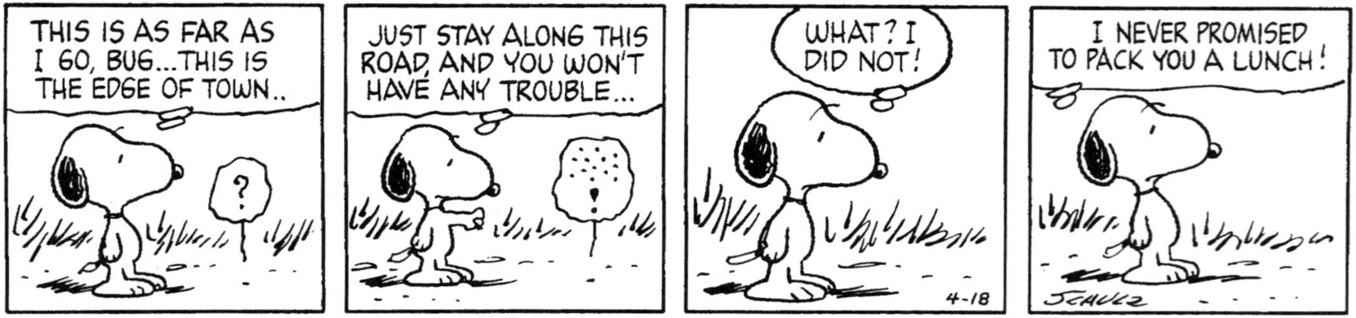
THIS IS AS FAR AS I GO, BUG...THIS IS THE EDGE OF TOWN..
JUST STAY ALONG THIS ROAD, AND YOU WON'T HAVE ANY TROUBLE...
WHAT? I DID NOT!
4-18
I NEVER PROMISED TO PACK YOU A LUNCH!
SCHULZ

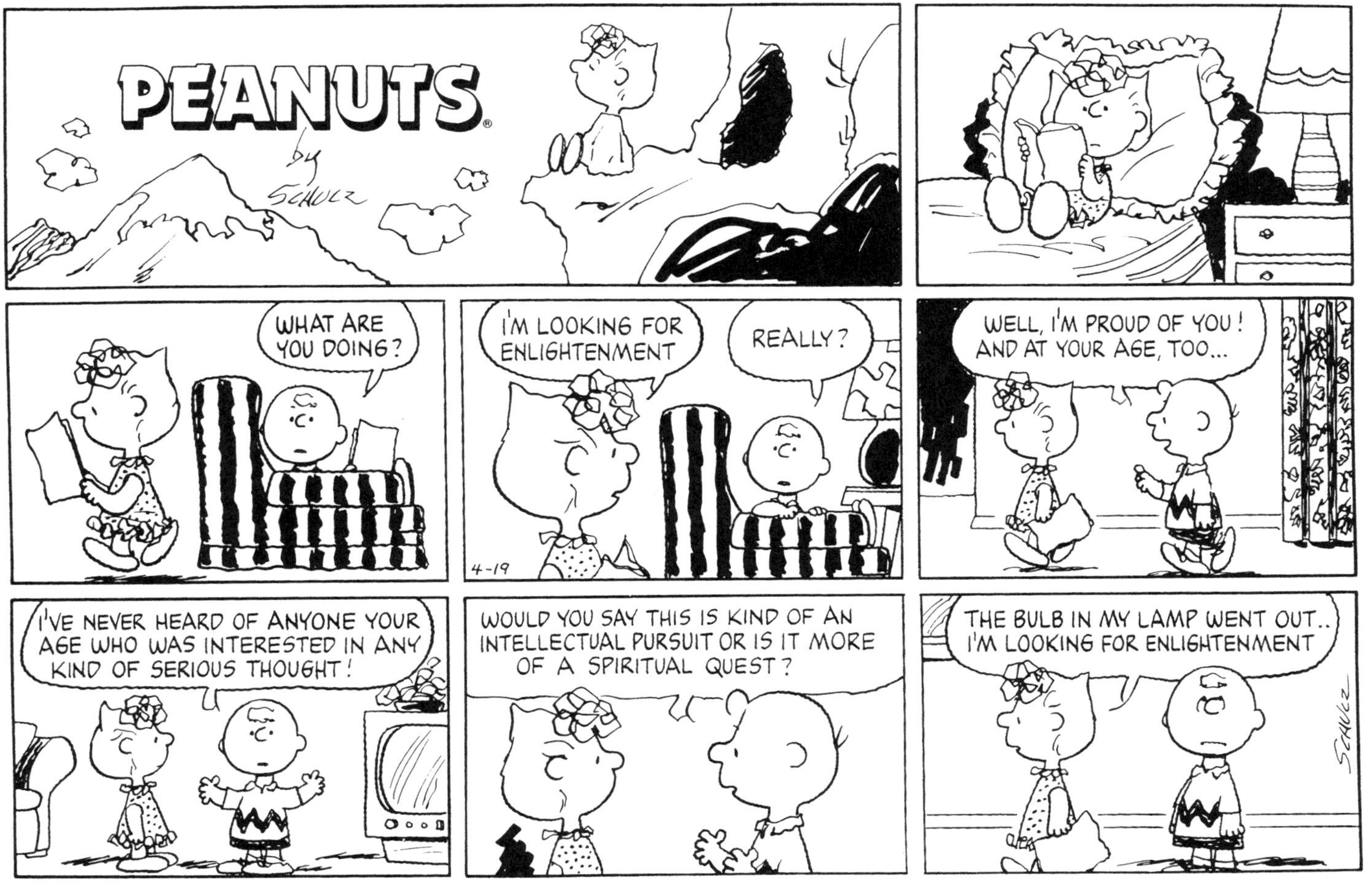
PEANUTS
by SCHULZ
WHAT ARE YOU DOING?
I'M LOOKING FOR ENLIGHTENMENT
REALLY?
4-19
WELL, I'M PROUD OF YOU! AND AT YOUR AGE, TOO...
I'VE NEVER HEARD OF ANYONE YOUR AGE WHO WAS INTERESTED IN ANY KIND OF SERIOUS THOUGHT!
WOULD YOU SAY THIS IS KIND OF AN INTELLECTUAL PURSUIT OR IS IT MORE OF A SPIRITUAL QUEST?
THE BULB IN MY LAMP WENT OUT.. I'M LOOKING FOR ENLIGHTENMENT
SCHULZ

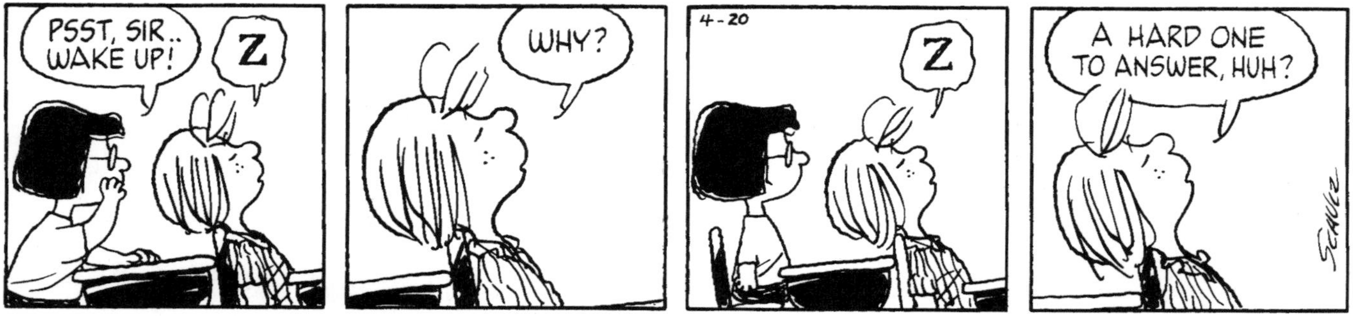
PSST, SIR..
WAKE UP!
Z
WHY?
4-20
Z
A HARD ONE
TO ANSWER, HUH?

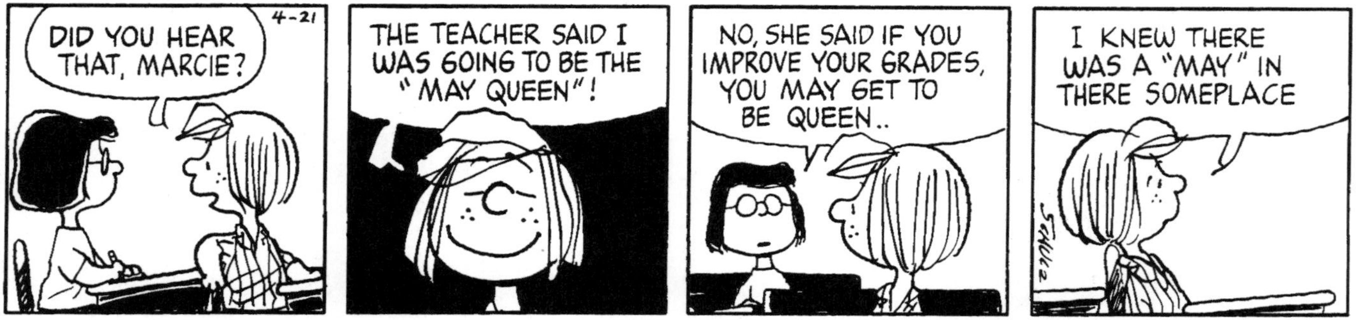
DID YOU HEAR
THAT, MARCIE?
4-21
THE TEACHER SAID I
WAS GOING TO BE THE
"MAY QUEEN"!
NO, SHE SAID IF YOU
IMPROVE YOUR GRADES,
YOU MAY GET TO
BE QUEEN..
I KNEW THERE
WAS A "MAY" IN
THERE SOMEPLACE

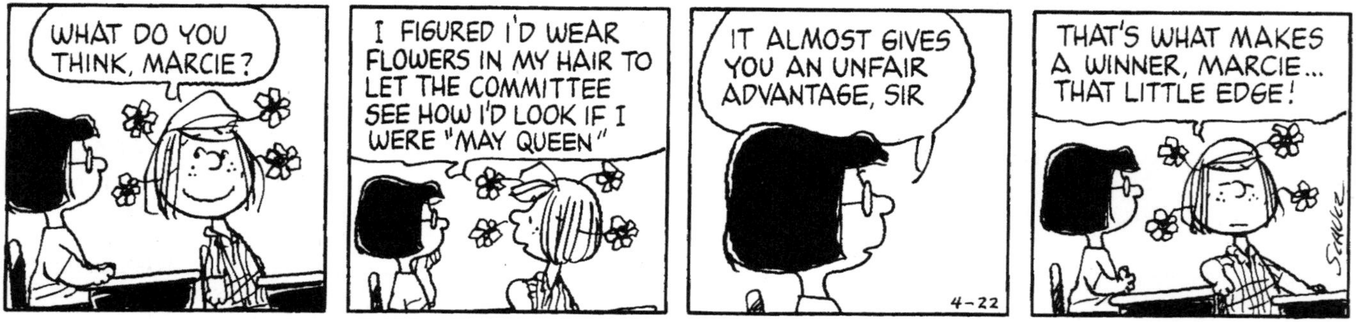
WHAT DO YOU
THINK, MARCIE?
I FIGURED I'D WEAR
FLOWERS IN MY HAIR TO
LET THE COMMITTEE
SEE HOW I'D LOOK IF I
WERE "MAY QUEEN"
IT ALMOST GIVES
YOU AN UNFAIR
ADVANTAGE, SIR
4-22
THAT'S WHAT MAKES
A WINNER, MARCIE...
THAT LITTLE EDGE!

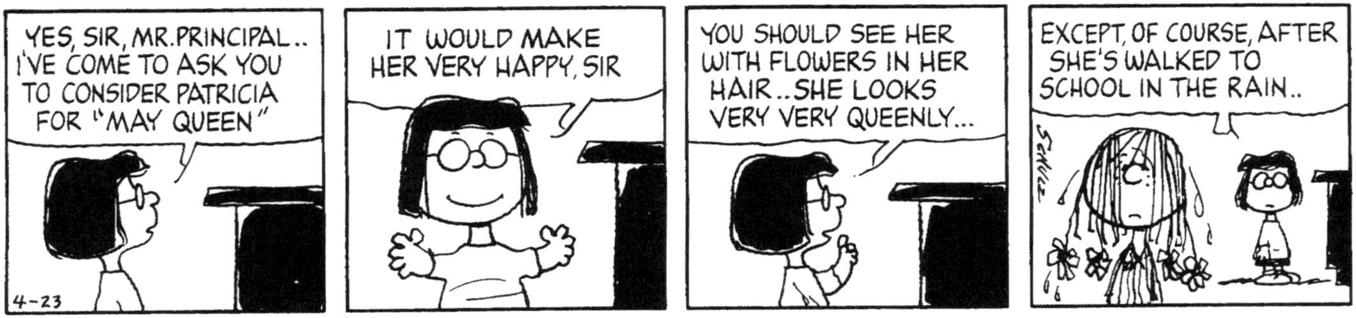
YES, SIR, MR. PRINCIPAL.. I'VE COME TO ASK YOU TO CONSIDER PATRICIA FOR "MAY QUEEN"
4-23
IT WOULD MAKE HER VERY HAPPY, SIR
YOU SHOULD SEE HER WITH FLOWERS IN HER HAIR..SHE LOOKS VERY VERY QUEENLY...
EXCEPT, OF COURSE, AFTER SHE'S WALKED TO SCHOOL IN THE RAIN..

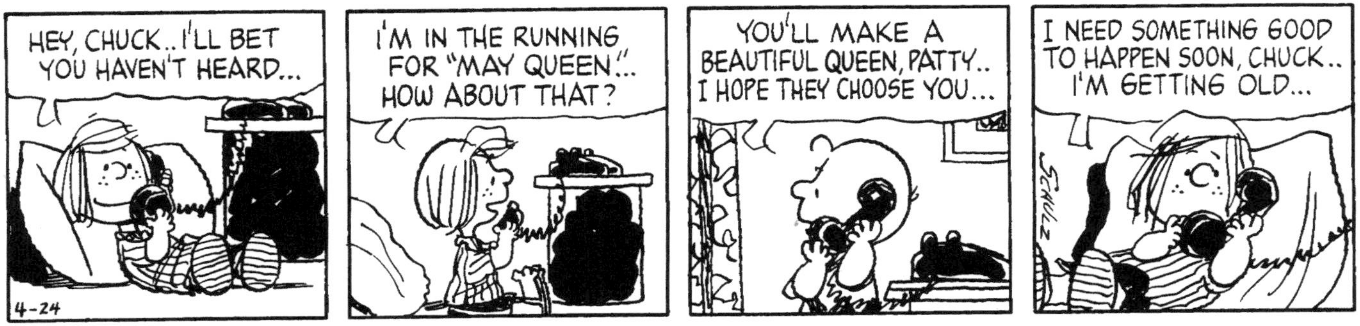
HEY, CHUCK.. I'LL BET YOU HAVEN'T HEARD...
4-24
I'M IN THE RUNNING FOR "MAY QUEEN"... HOW ABOUT THAT?
YOU'LL MAKE A BEAUTIFUL QUEEN, PATTY.. I HOPE THEY CHOOSE YOU...
I NEED SOMETHING GOOD TO HAPPEN SOON, CHUCK.. I'M GETTING OLD...

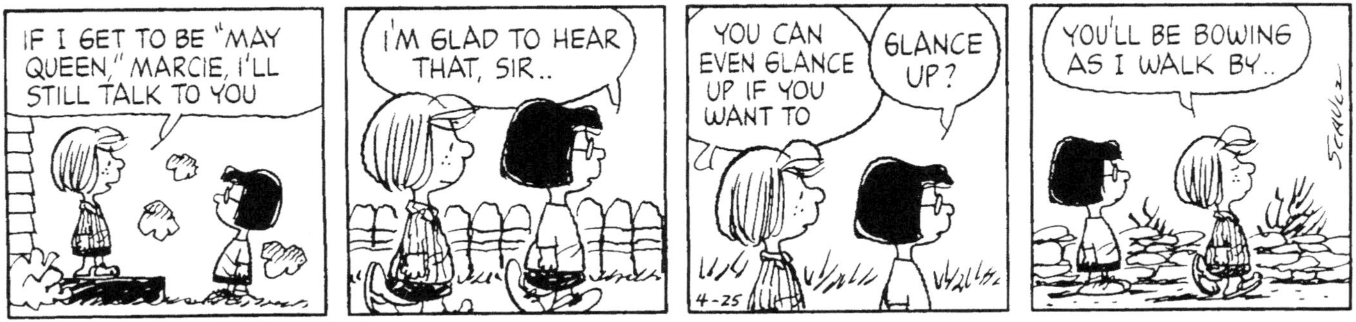
IF I GET TO BE "MAY QUEEN," MARCIE, I'LL STILL TALK TO YOU
I'M GLAD TO HEAR THAT, SIR..
YOU CAN EVEN GLANCE UP IF YOU WANT TO
GLANCE UP?
4-25
YOU'LL BE BOWING AS I WALK BY..

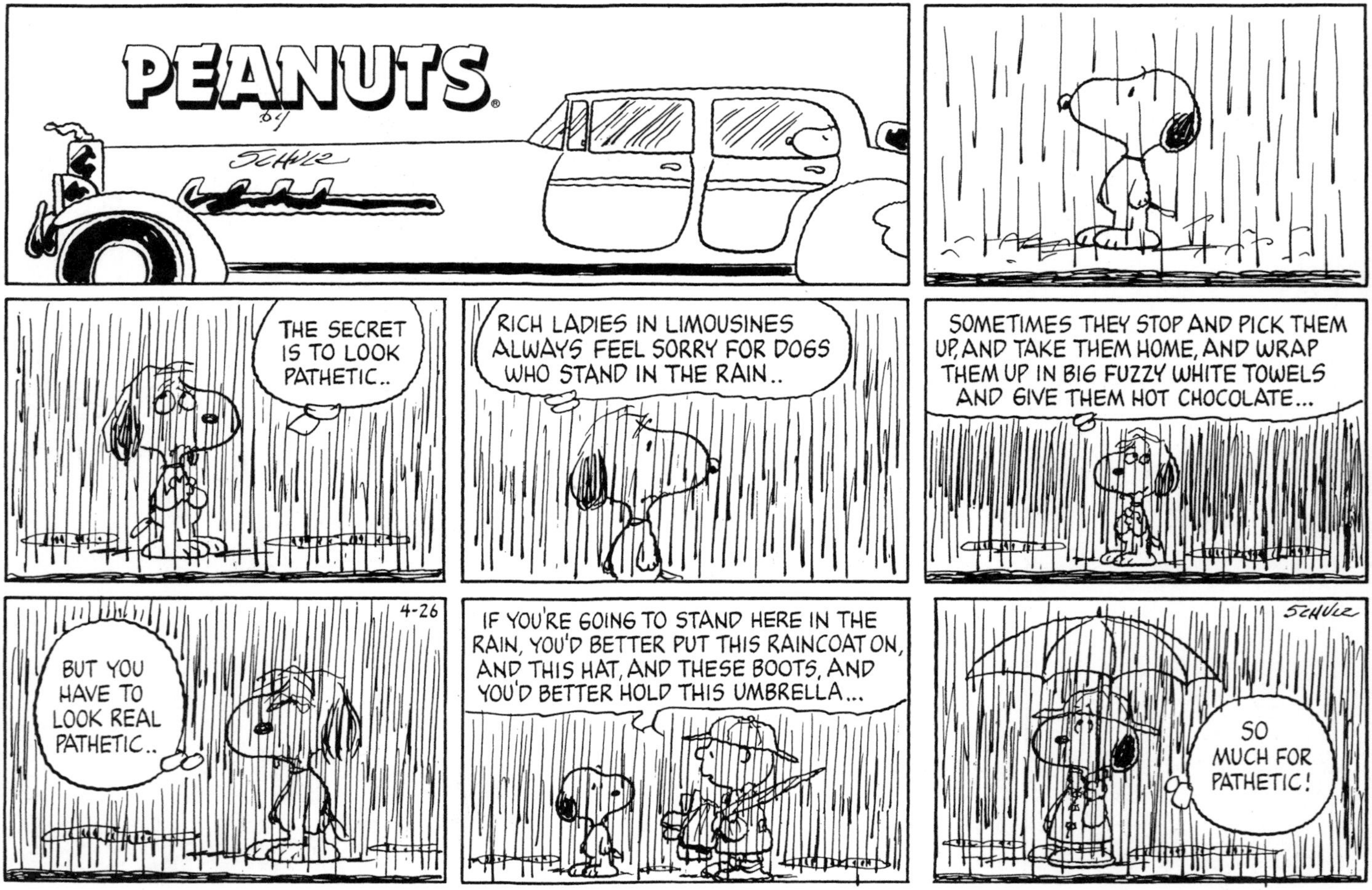
PEANUTS
SCHULZ
THE SECRET IS TO LOOK PATHETIC..
RICH LADIES IN LIMOUSINES ALWAYS FEEL SORRY FOR DOGS WHO STAND IN THE RAIN..
SOMETIMES THEY STOP AND PICK THEM UP, AND TAKE THEM HOME, AND WRAP THEM UP IN BIG FUZZY WHITE TOWELS AND GIVE THEM HOT CHOCOLATE...
4-26
BUT YOU HAVE TO LOOK REAL PATHETIC..
IF YOU'RE GOING TO STAND HERE IN THE RAIN, YOU'D BETTER PUT THIS RAINCOAT ON, AND THIS HAT, AND THESE BOOTS, AND YOU'D BETTER HOLD THIS UMBRELLA...
SCHULZ
SO MUCH FOR PATHETIC!

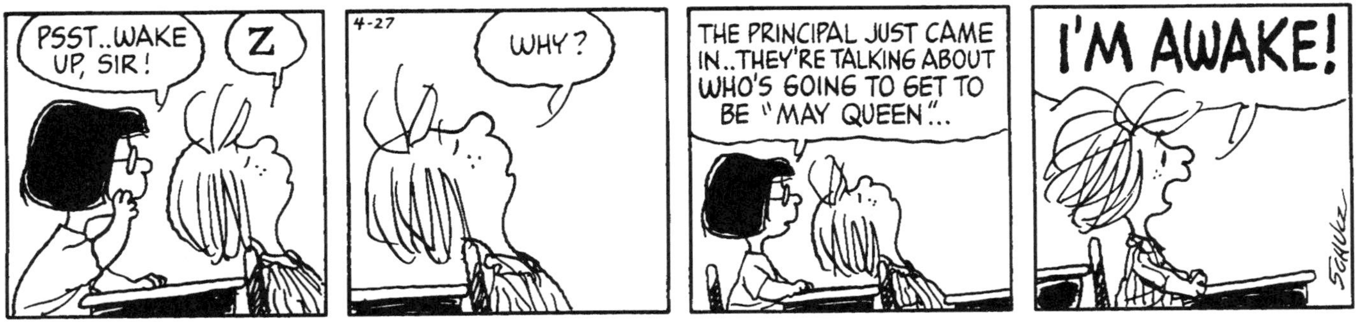
PSST..WAKE UP, SIR!
Z
4-27
WHY?
THE PRINCIPAL JUST CAME IN..THEY'RE TALKING ABOUT WHO'S GOING TO GET TO BE "MAY QUEEN"..
I'M AWAKE!
SCHULZ

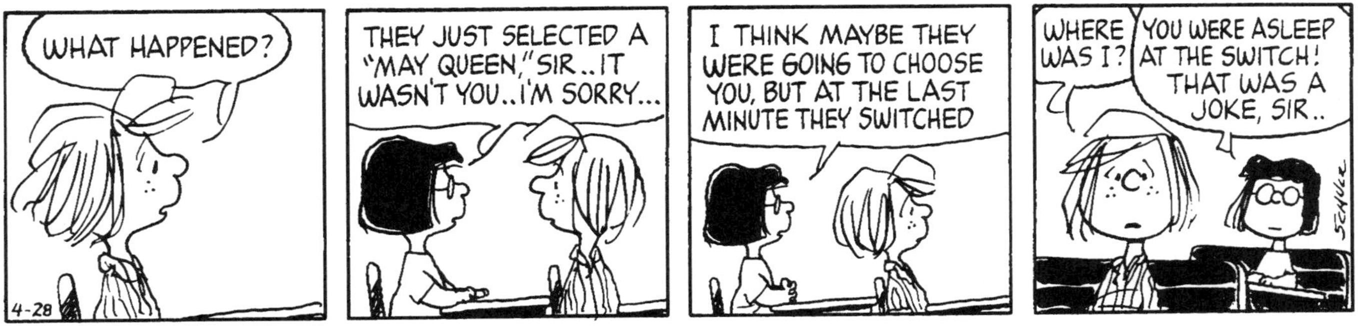
WHAT HAPPENED?
4-28
THEY JUST SELECTED A "MAY QUEEN," SIR..IT WASN'T YOU..I'M SORRY...
I THINK MAYBE THEY WERE GOING TO CHOOSE YOU, BUT AT THE LAST MINUTE THEY SWITCHED
WHERE WAS I?
YOU WERE ASLEEP AT THE SWITCH! THAT WAS A JOKE, SIR..
SCHULZ

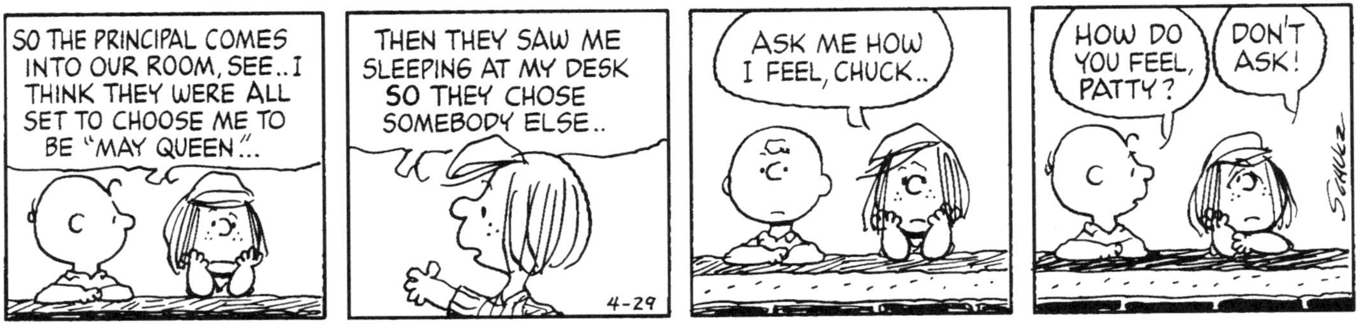
SO THE PRINCIPAL COMES INTO OUR ROOM, SEE..I THINK THEY WERE ALL SET TO CHOOSE ME TO BE "MAY QUEEN"..
THEN THEY SAW ME SLEEPING AT MY DESK SO THEY CHOSE SOMEBODY ELSE..
4-29
ASK ME HOW I FEEL, CHUCK..
HOW DO YOU FEEL, PATTY?
DON'T ASK!
SCHULZ

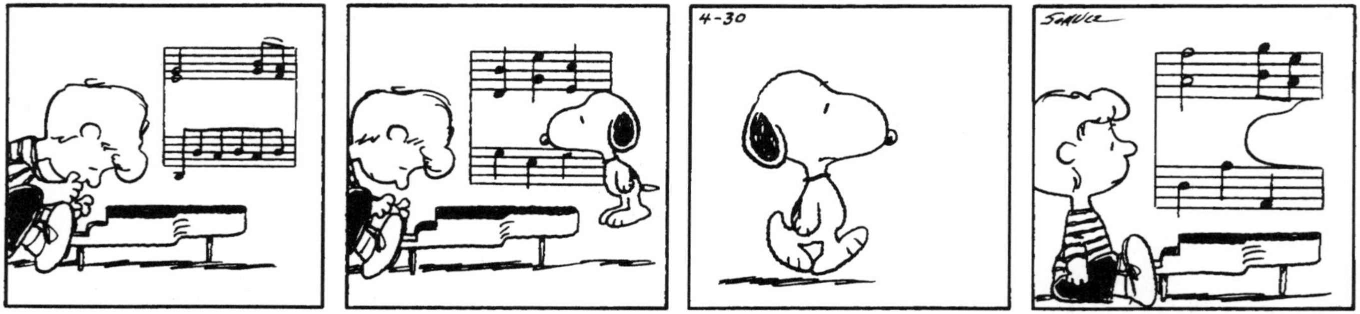
4-30

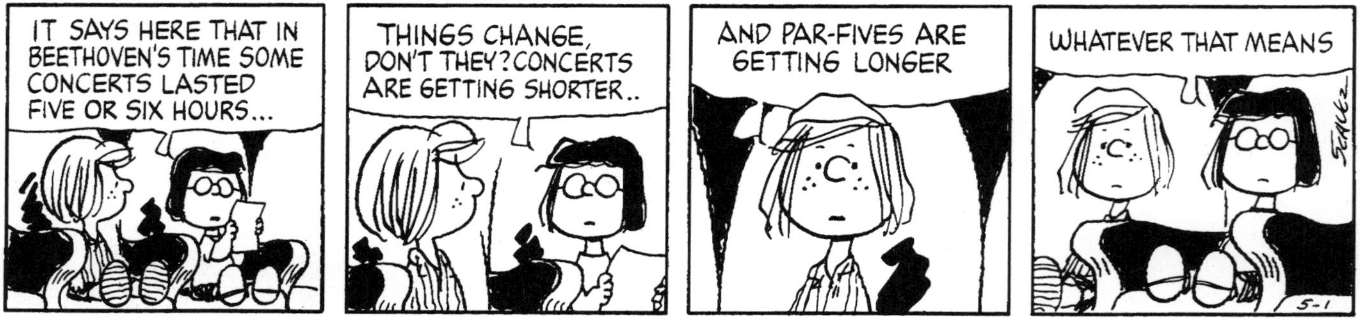
IT SAYS HERE THAT IN BEETHOVEN'S TIME SOME CONCERTS LASTED FIVE OR SIX HOURS...
THINGS CHANGE, DON'T THEY? CONCERTS ARE GETTING SHORTER..
AND PAR-FIVES ARE GETTING LONGER
WHATEVER THAT MEANS
5-1

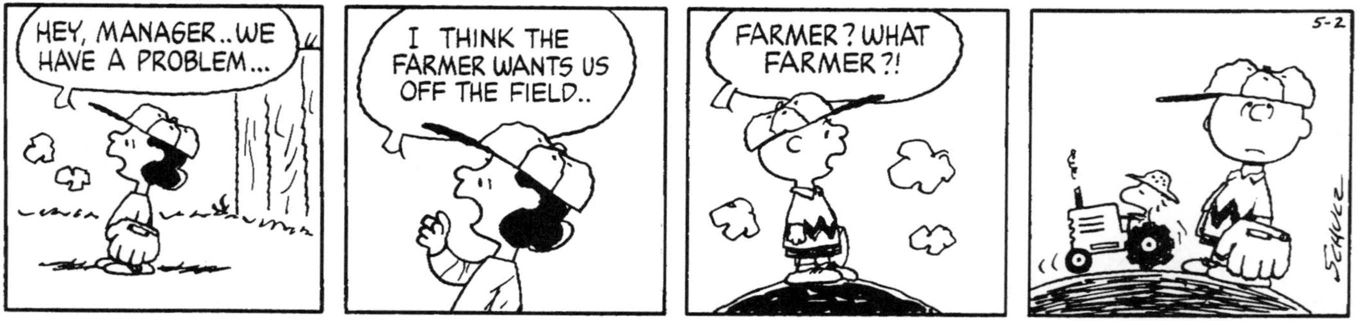
HEY, MANAGER..WE HAVE A PROBLEM...
I THINK THE FARMER WANTS US OFF THE FIELD..
FARMER? WHAT FARMER?!
5-2

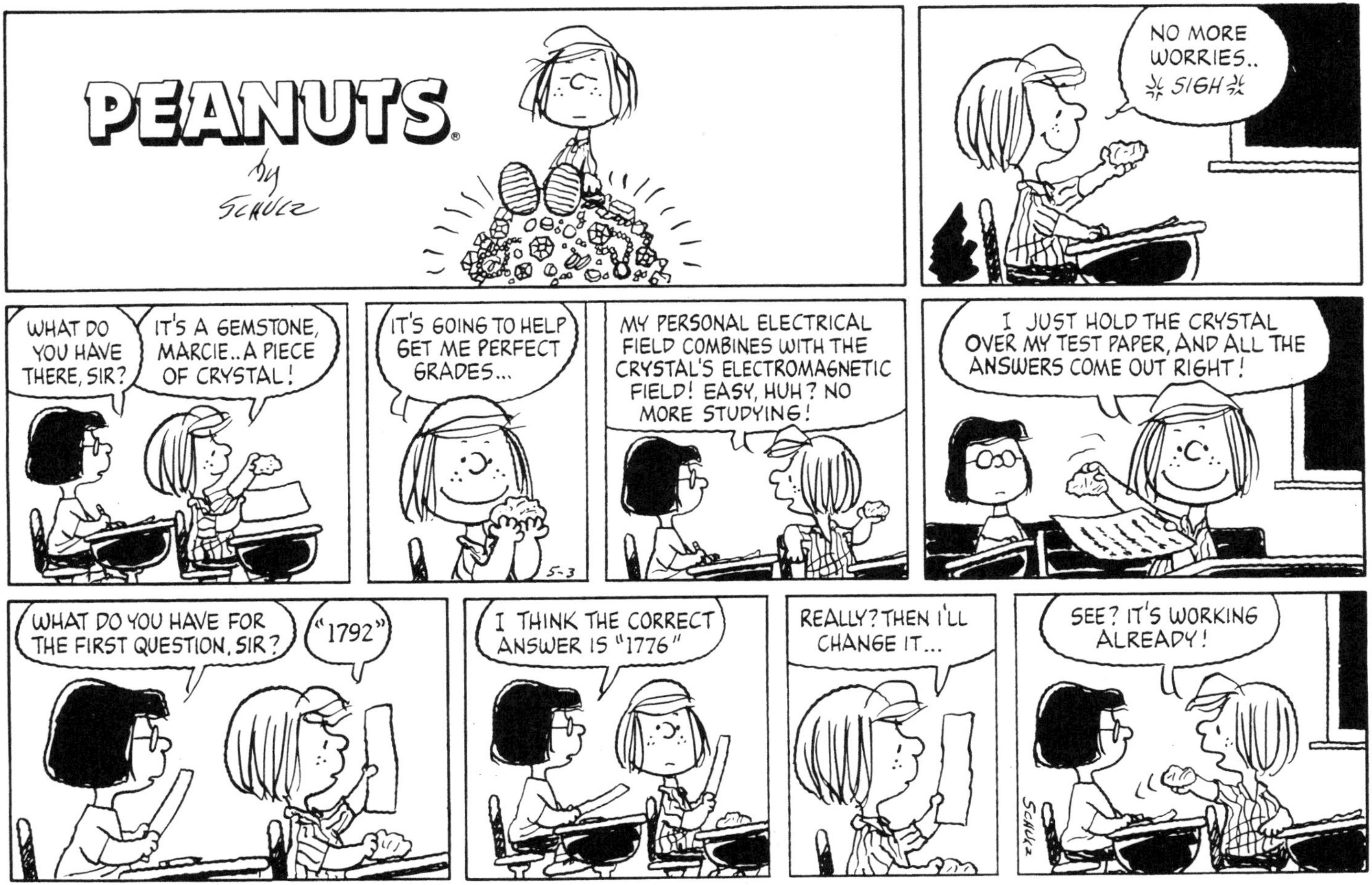
PEANUTS
by SCHULZ
NO MORE WORRIES.. SIGH
WHAT DO YOU HAVE THERE, SIR?
IT'S A GEMSTONE, MARCIE..A PIECE OF CRYSTAL!
IT'S GOING TO HELP GET ME PERFECT GRADES...
5-3
MY PERSONAL ELECTRICAL FIELD COMBINES WITH THE CRYSTAL'S ELECTROMAGNETIC FIELD! EASY, HUH? NO MORE STUDYING!
I JUST HOLD THE CRYSTAL OVER MY TEST PAPER, AND ALL THE ANSWERS COME OUT RIGHT!
WHAT DO YOU HAVE FOR THE FIRST QUESTION, SIR?
"1792"
I THINK THE CORRECT ANSWER IS "1776"
REALLY? THEN I'LL CHANGE IT...
SCHULZ
SEE? IT'S WORKING ALREADY!

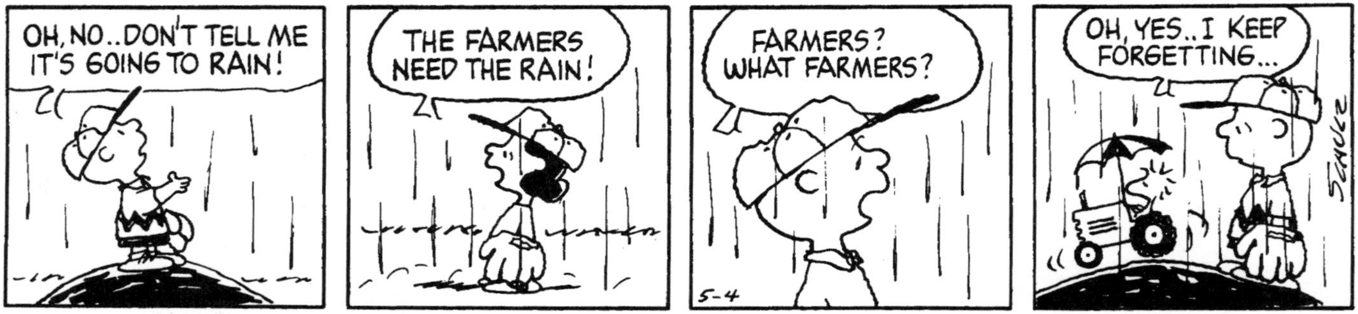
OH, NO..DON'T TELL ME IT'S GOING TO RAIN!
THE FARMERS NEED THE RAIN!
FARMERS? WHAT FARMERS?
5-4
OH, YES..I KEEP FORGETTING...

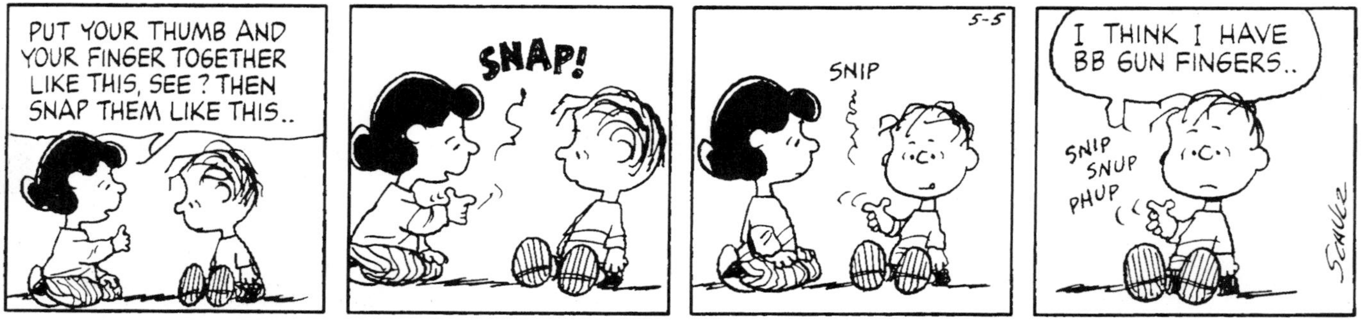
PUT YOUR THUMB AND YOUR FINGER TOGETHER LIKE THIS, SEE? THEN SNAP THEM LIKE THIS..
SNAP!
5-5
SNIP
I THINK I HAVE BB GUN FINGERS..
SNIP
SNUP
PHUP

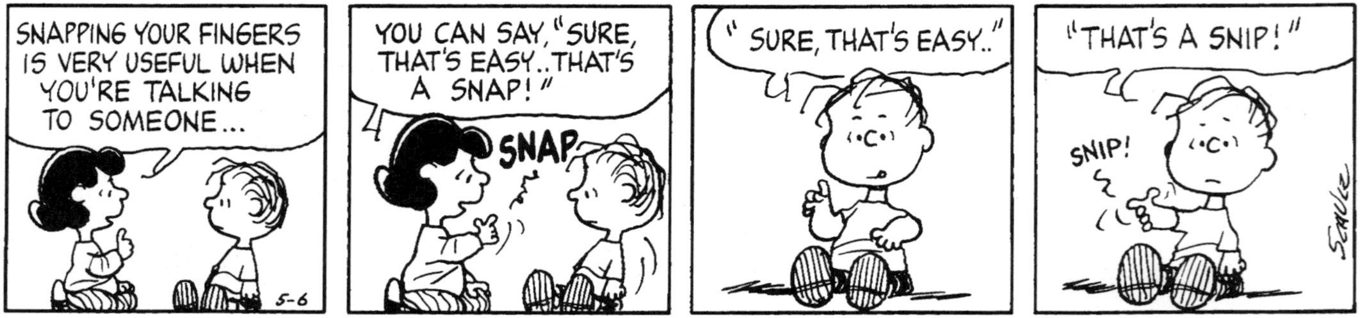
SNAPPING YOUR FINGERS IS VERY USEFUL WHEN YOU'RE TALKING TO SOMEONE...
5-6
YOU CAN SAY, "SURE, THAT'S EASY..THAT'S A SNAP!"
SNAP
" SURE, THAT'S EASY.."
"THAT'S A SNIP!"
SNIP!

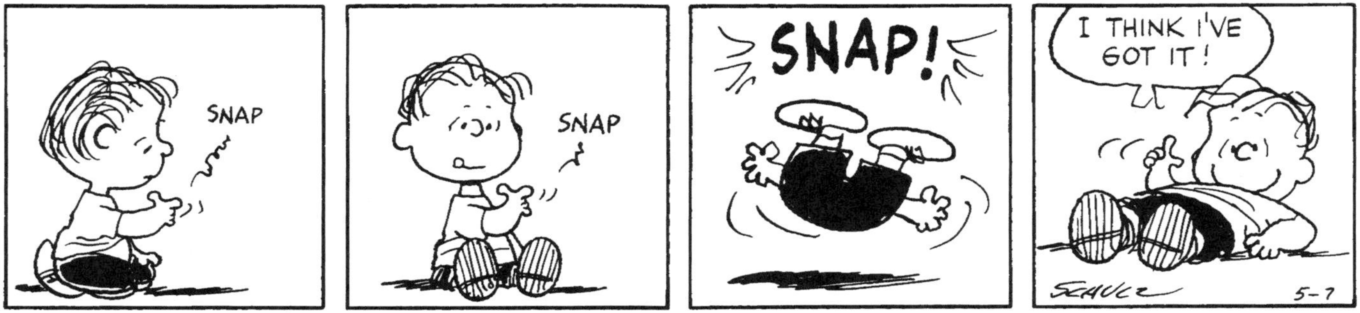
SNAP
SNAP
SNAP!
I THINK I'VE GOT IT!
5-7

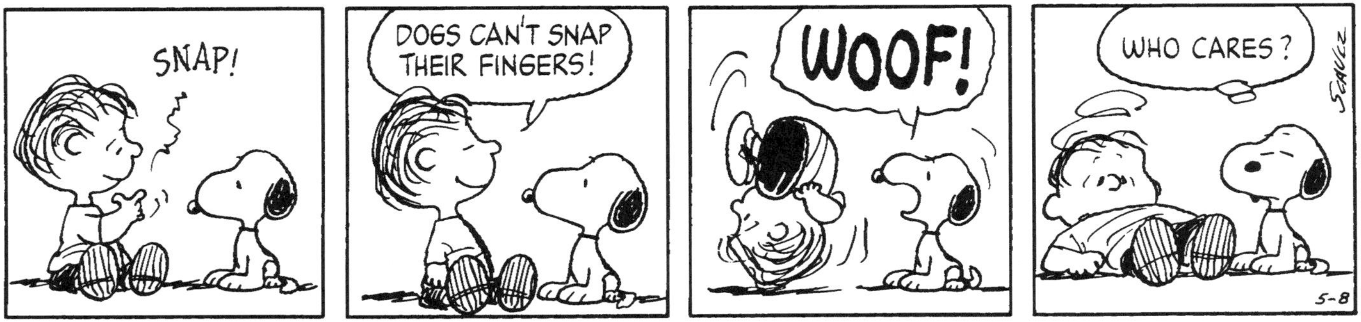
SNAP!
DOGS CAN'T SNAP THEIR FINGERS!
WOOF!
WHO CARES?
5-8

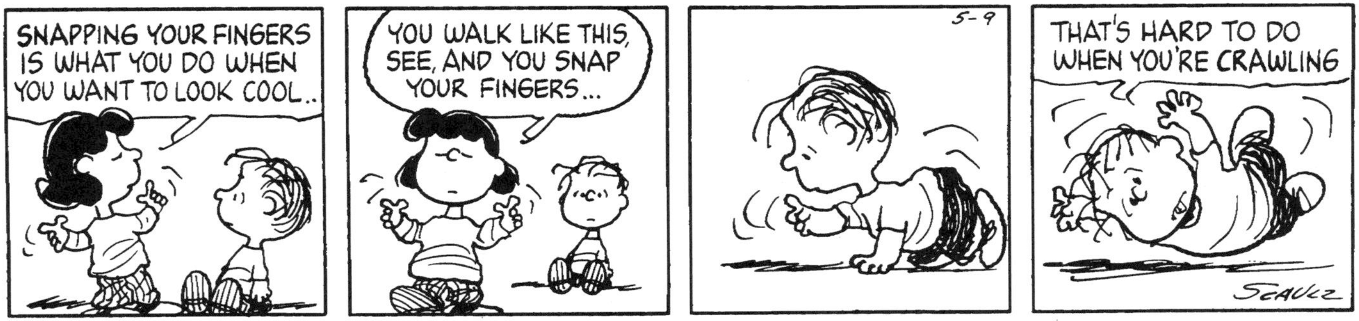
SNAPPING YOUR FINGERS IS WHAT YOU DO WHEN YOU WANT TO LOOK COOL..
YOU WALK LIKE THIS, SEE, AND YOU SNAP YOUR FINGERS...
5-9
THAT'S HARD TO DO WHEN YOU'RE CRAWLING

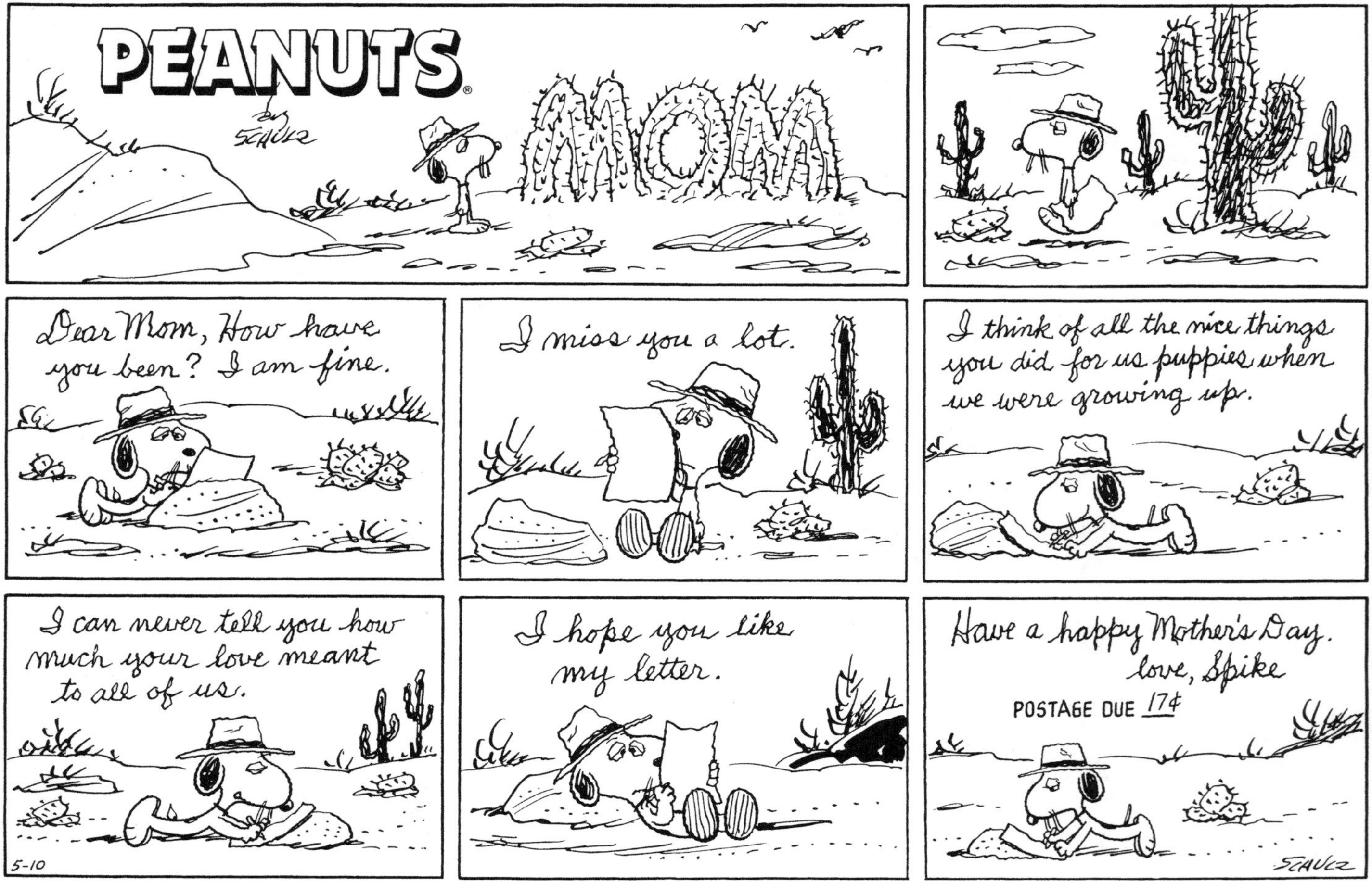
PEANUTS
by SCHULZ
MOM
Dear Mom, How have you been? I am fine.
I miss you a lot.
I think of all the nice things you did for us puppies when we were growing up.
I can never tell you how much your love meant to all of us.
I hope you like my letter.
Have a happy Mother's Day.
love, Spike
POSTAGE DUE 17¢
5-10
SCHULZ

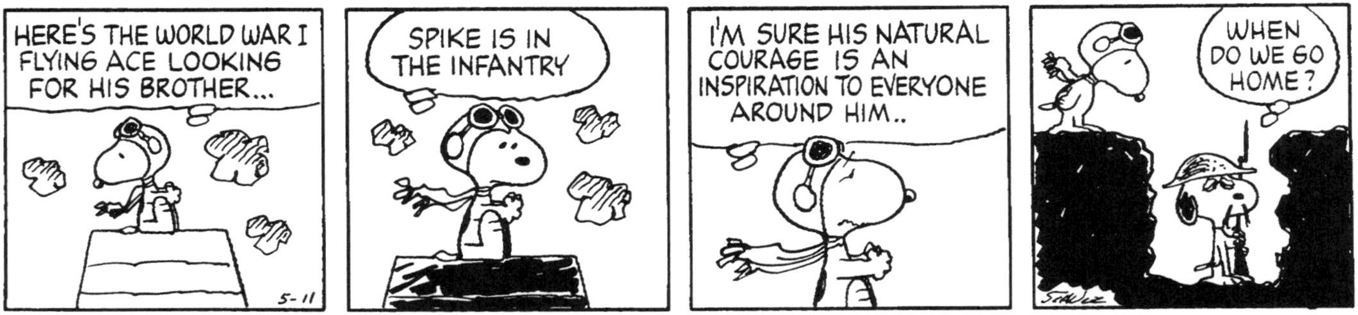
HERE'S THE WORLD WAR I FLYING ACE LOOKING FOR HIS BROTHER...
SPIKE IS IN THE INFANTRY
I'M SURE HIS NATURAL COURAGE IS AN INSPIRATION TO EVERYONE AROUND HIM..
WHEN DO WE GO HOME?

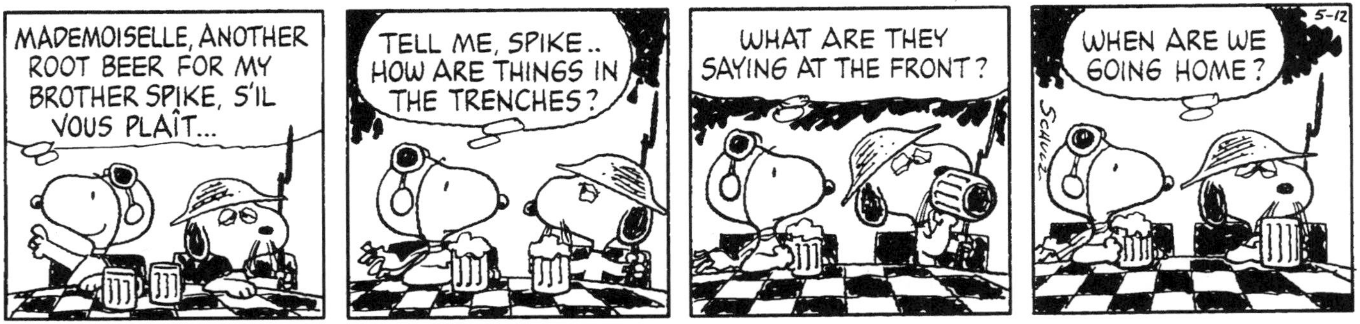
MADEMOISELLE, ANOTHER ROOT BEER FOR MY BROTHER SPIKE, S'IL VOUS PLAÎT...
TELL ME, SPIKE.. HOW ARE THINGS IN THE TRENCHES?
WHAT ARE THEY SAYING AT THE FRONT?
WHEN ARE WE GOING HOME?

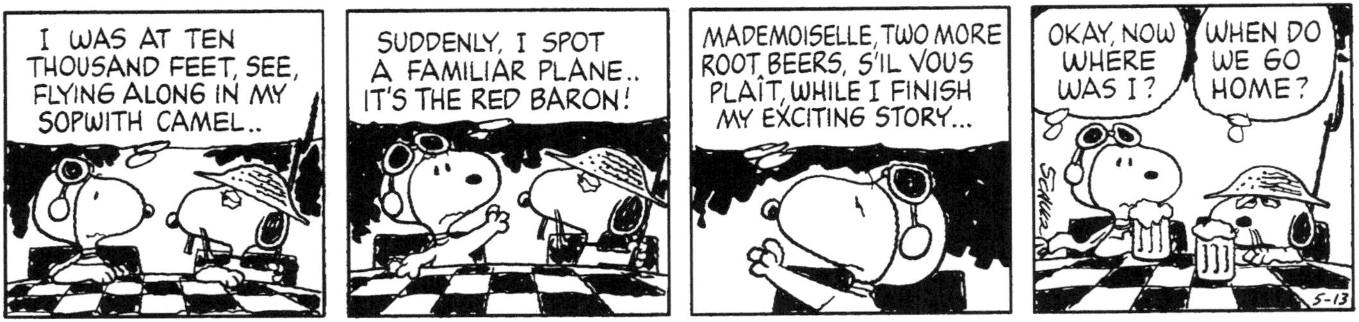
I WAS AT TEN THOUSAND FEET, SEE, FLYING ALONG IN MY SOPWITH CAMEL..
SUDDENLY, I SPOT A FAMILIAR PLANE.. IT'S THE RED BARON!
MADEMOISELLE, TWO MORE ROOT BEERS, S'IL VOUS PLAÎT, WHILE I FINISH MY EXCITING STORY...
OKAY, NOW WHERE WAS I?
WHEN DO WE GO HOME?

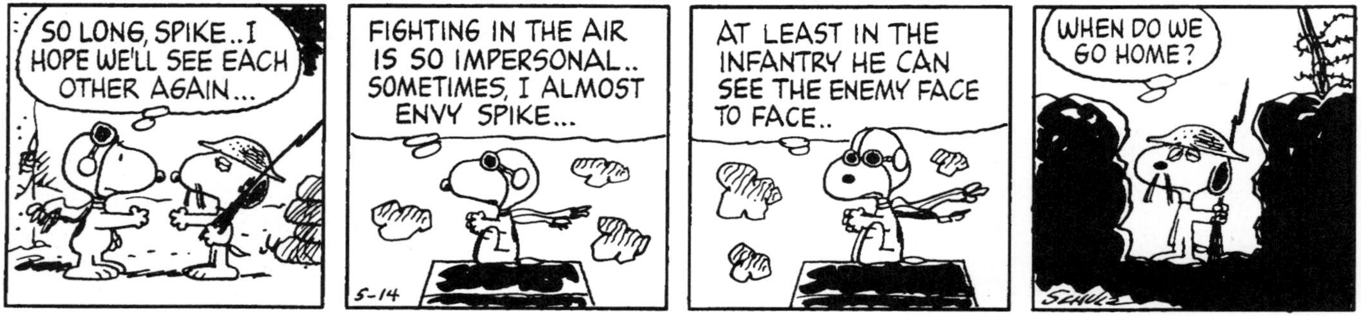
SO LONG, SPIKE..I HOPE WE'LL SEE EACH OTHER AGAIN...
FIGHTING IN THE AIR IS SO IMPERSONAL.. SOMETIMES, I ALMOST ENVY SPIKE...
5-14
AT LEAST IN THE INFANTRY HE CAN SEE THE ENEMY FACE TO FACE..
WHEN DO WE GO HOME?
SCHULZ

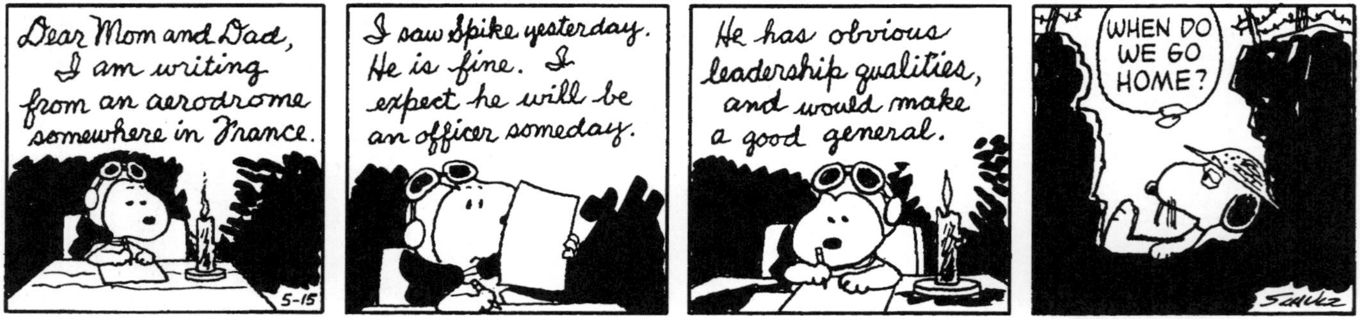
Dear Mom and Dad, I am writing from an aerodrome somewhere in France.
5-15
I saw Spike yesterday. He is fine. I expect he will be an officer someday.
He has obvious leadership qualities, and would make a good general.
WHEN DO WE GO HOME?
SCHULZ

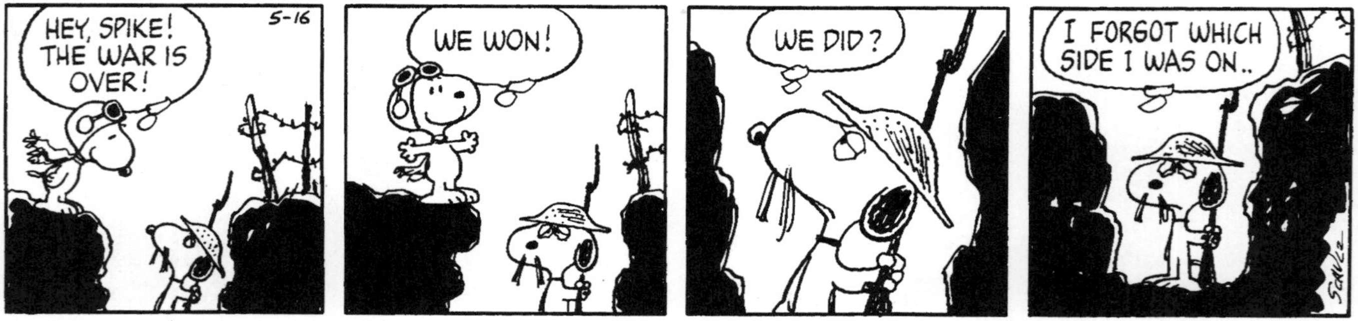
HEY, SPIKE! THE WAR IS OVER!
5-16
WE WON!
WE DID?
I FORGOT WHICH SIDE I WAS ON..
SCHULZ

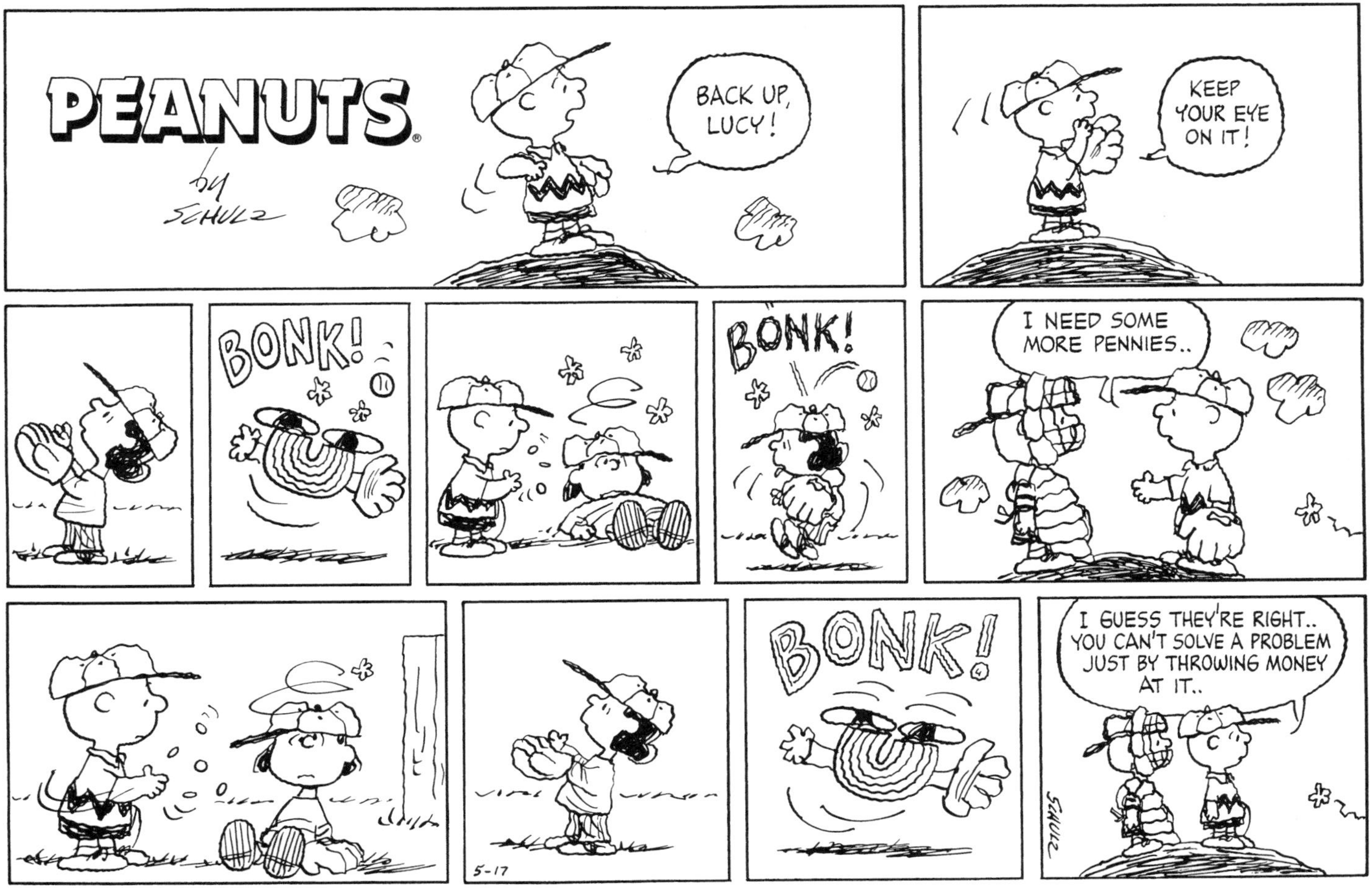
PEANUTS
by SCHULZ
BACK UP, LUCY!
KEEP YOUR EYE ON IT!
BONK!
BONK!
I NEED SOME MORE PENNIES..
BONK!
I GUESS THEY'RE RIGHT.. YOU CAN'T SOLVE A PROBLEM JUST BY THROWING MONEY AT IT..
5-17
SCHULZ

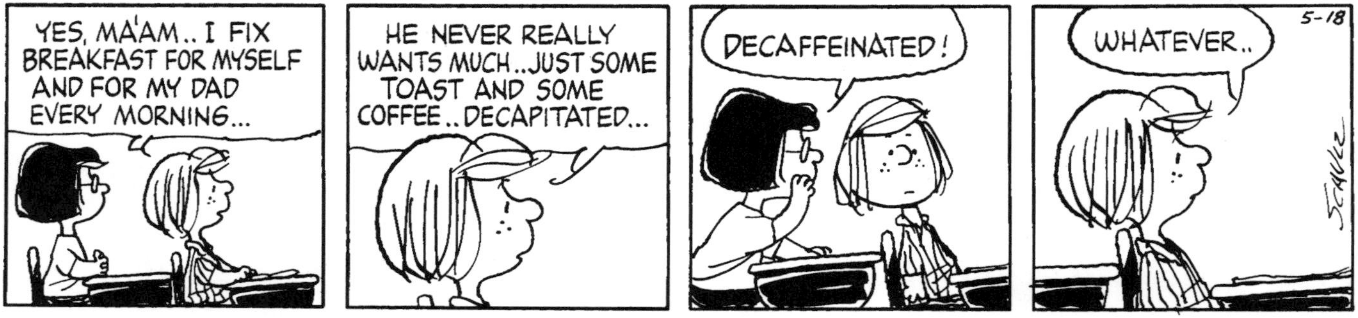
YES, MA'AM.. I FIX BREAKFAST FOR MYSELF AND FOR MY DAD EVERY MORNING...
HE NEVER REALLY WANTS MUCH..JUST SOME TOAST AND SOME COFFEE..DECAPITATED...
DECAFFEINATED!
WHATEVER..
5-18

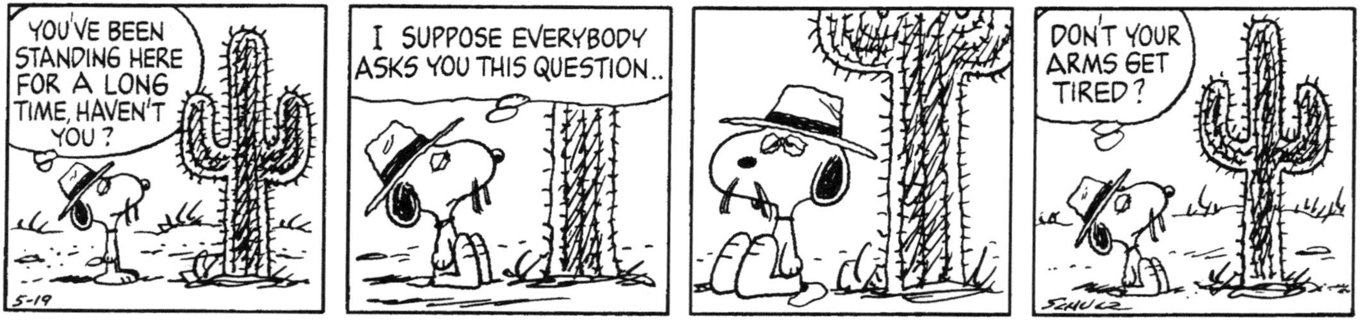
YOU'VE BEEN STANDING HERE FOR A LONG TIME, HAVEN'T YOU?
5-19
I SUPPOSE EVERYBODY ASKS YOU THIS QUESTION..
DON'T YOUR ARMS GET TIRED?

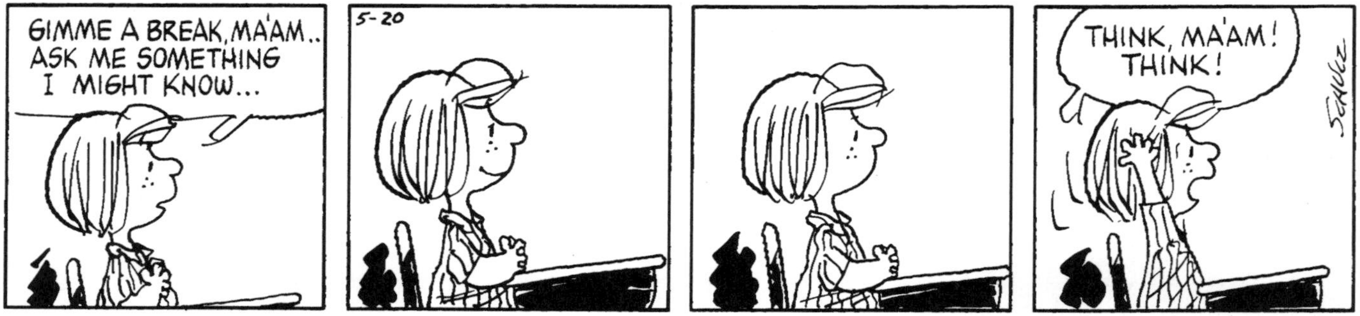
GIMME A BREAK, MA'AM.. ASK ME SOMETHING I MIGHT KNOW...
5-20
THINK, MA'AM! THINK!

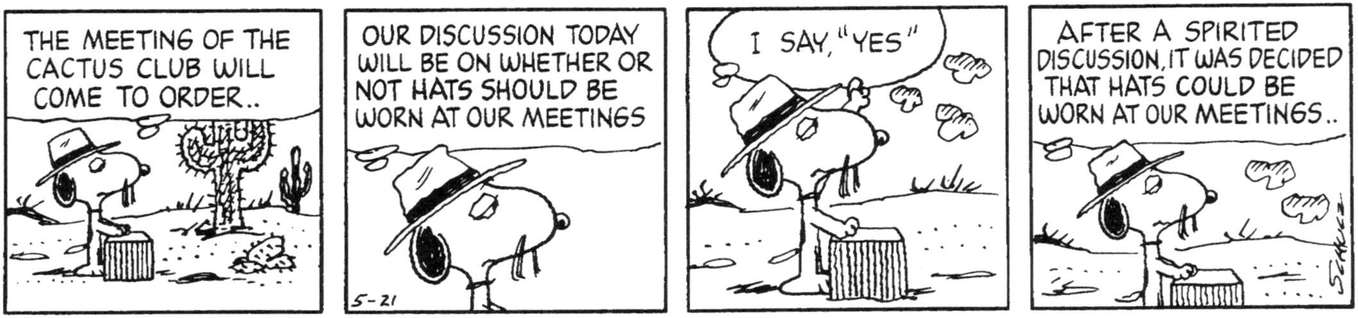
THE MEETING OF THE CACTUS CLUB WILL COME TO ORDER..
OUR DISCUSSION TODAY WILL BE ON WHETHER OR NOT HATS SHOULD BE WORN AT OUR MEETINGS
5-21
I SAY, "YES"
AFTER A SPIRITED DISCUSSION, IT WAS DECIDED THAT HATS COULD BE WORN AT OUR MEETINGS..
SCHULZ

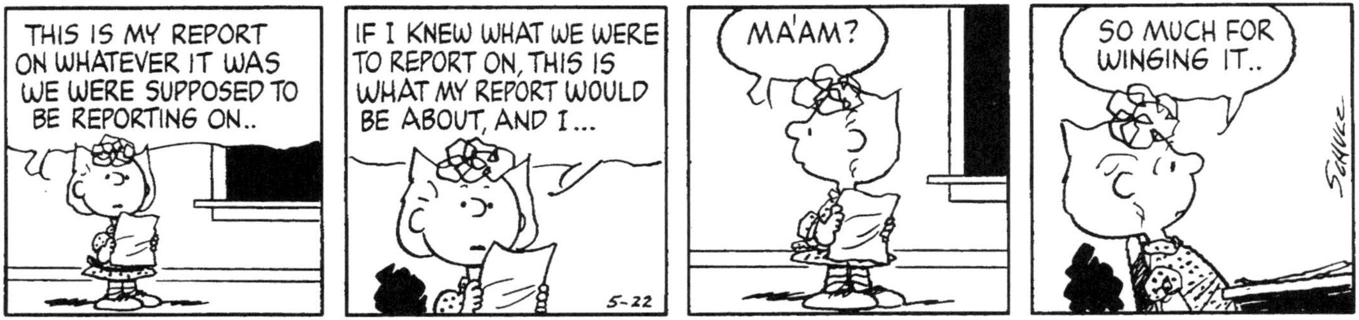
THIS IS MY REPORT ON WHATEVER IT WAS WE WERE SUPPOSED TO BE REPORTING ON..
IF I KNEW WHAT WE WERE TO REPORT ON, THIS IS WHAT MY REPORT WOULD BE ABOUT, AND I...
5-22
MA'AM?
SO MUCH FOR WINGING IT..
SCHULZ

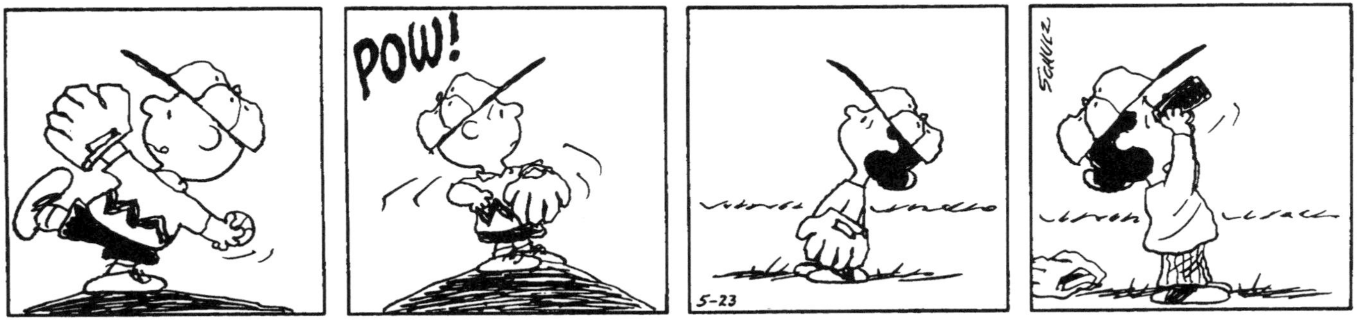
POW!
5-23
SCHULZ

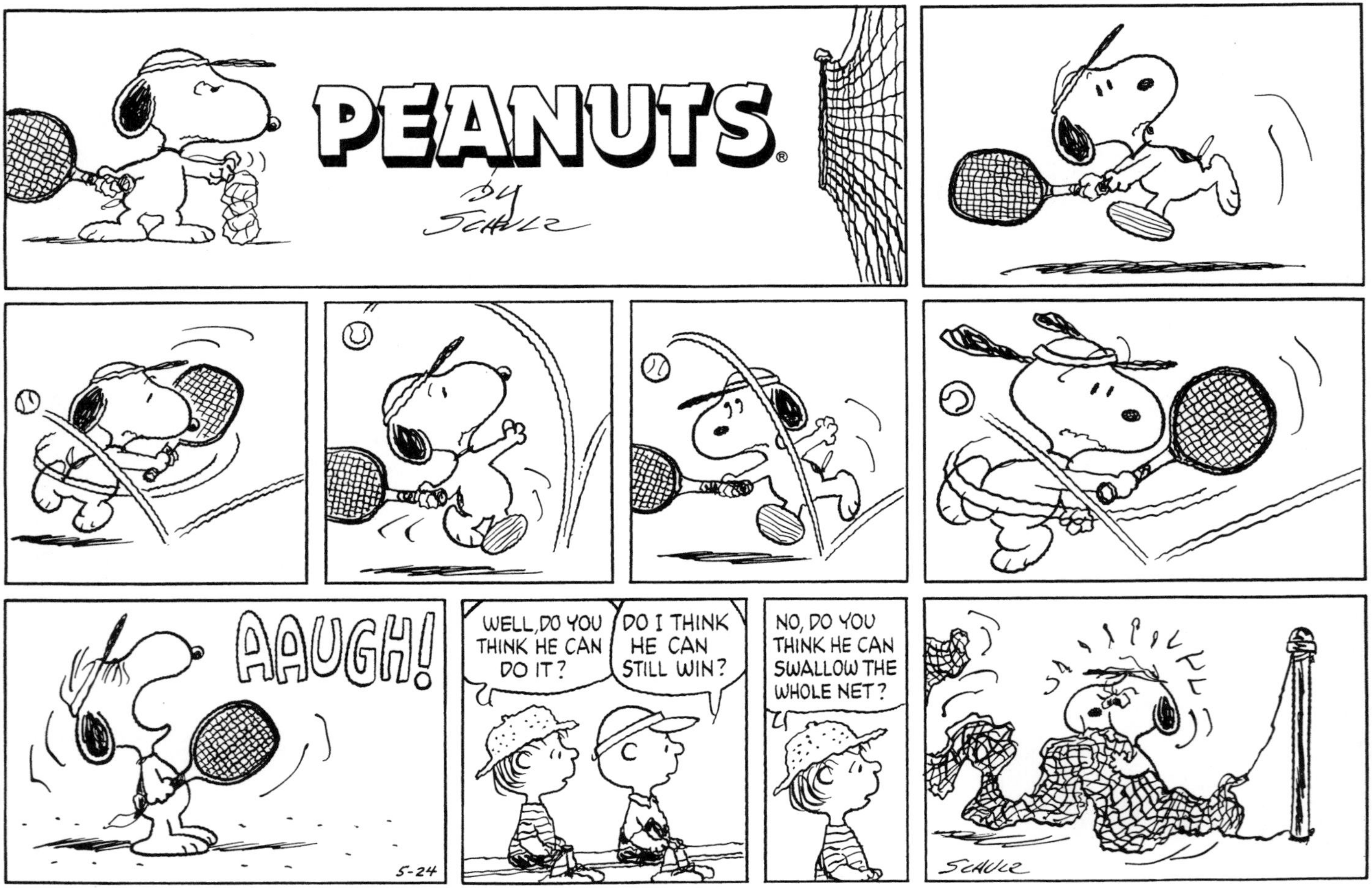
PEANUTS®
by Schulz
AAUGH!
5-24
WELL, DO YOU THINK HE CAN DO IT?
DO I THINK HE CAN STILL WIN?
NO, DO YOU THINK HE CAN SWALLOW THE WHOLE NET?
SCHULZ

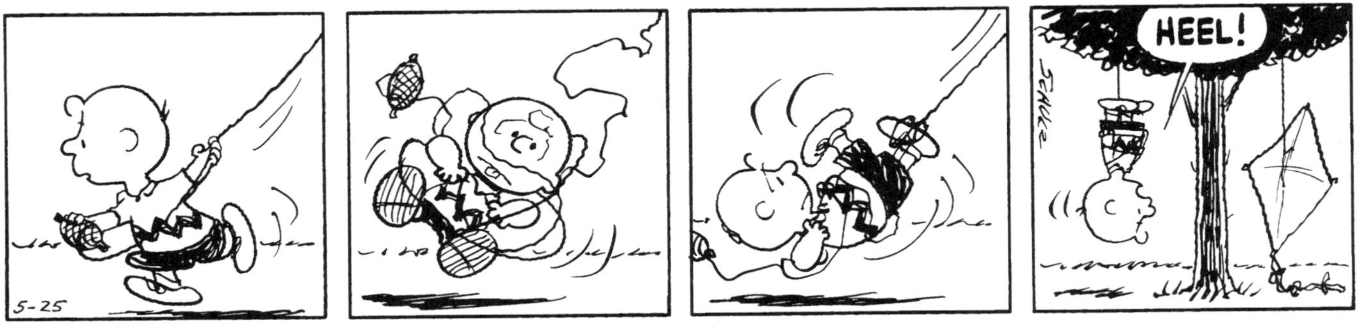
HEEL!

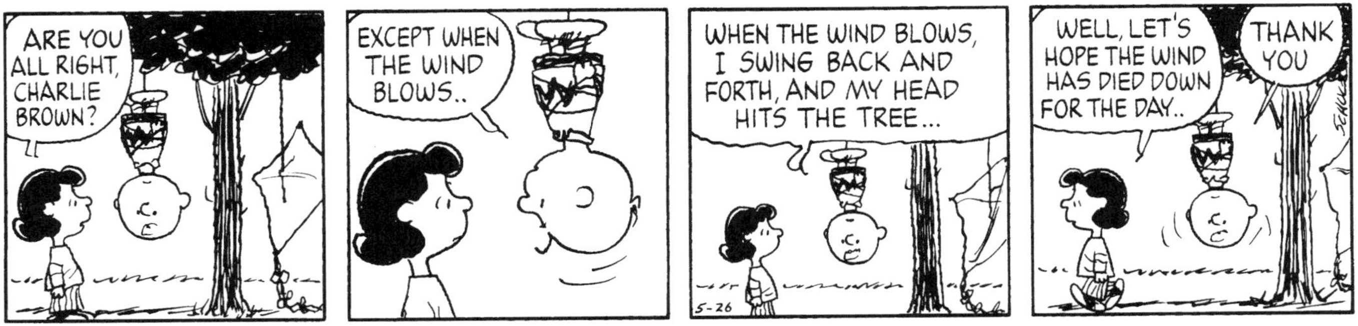
ARE YOU ALL RIGHT, CHARLIE BROWN?
EXCEPT WHEN THE WIND BLOWS..
WHEN THE WIND BLOWS, I SWING BACK AND FORTH, AND MY HEAD HITS THE TREE...
WELL, LET'S HOPE THE WIND HAS DIED DOWN FOR THE DAY..
THANK YOU

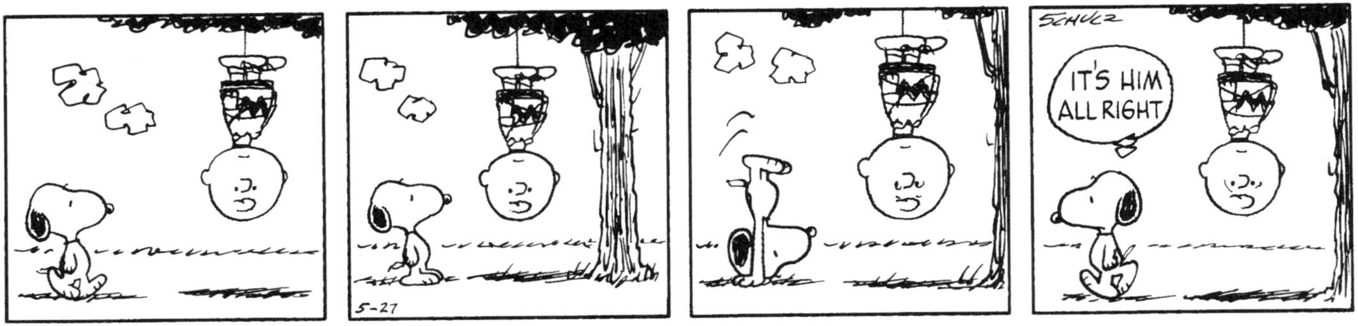
IT'S HIM ALL RIGHT

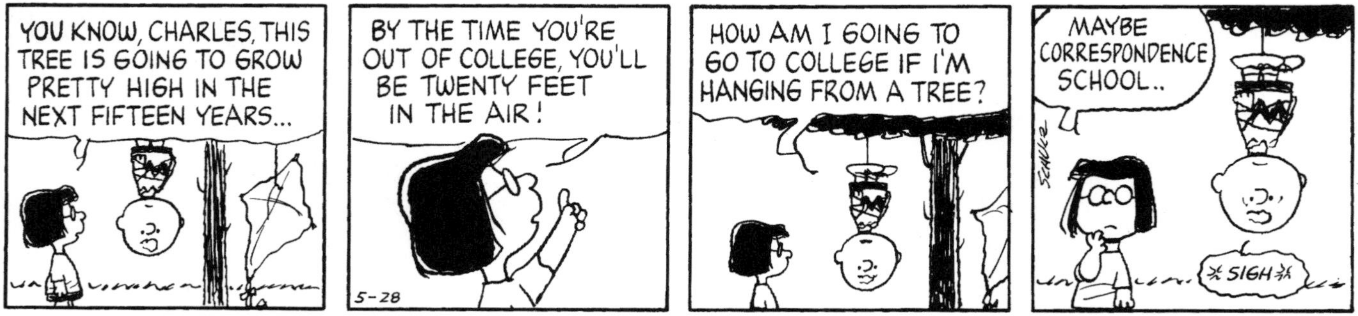
YOU KNOW, CHARLES, THIS TREE IS GOING TO GROW PRETTY HIGH IN THE NEXT FIFTEEN YEARS...
BY THE TIME YOU'RE OUT OF COLLEGE, YOU'LL BE TWENTY FEET IN THE AIR!
5-28
HOW AM I GOING TO GO TO COLLEGE IF I'M HANGING FROM A TREE?
MAYBE CORRESPONDENCE SCHOOL..
SCHULZ
SIGH

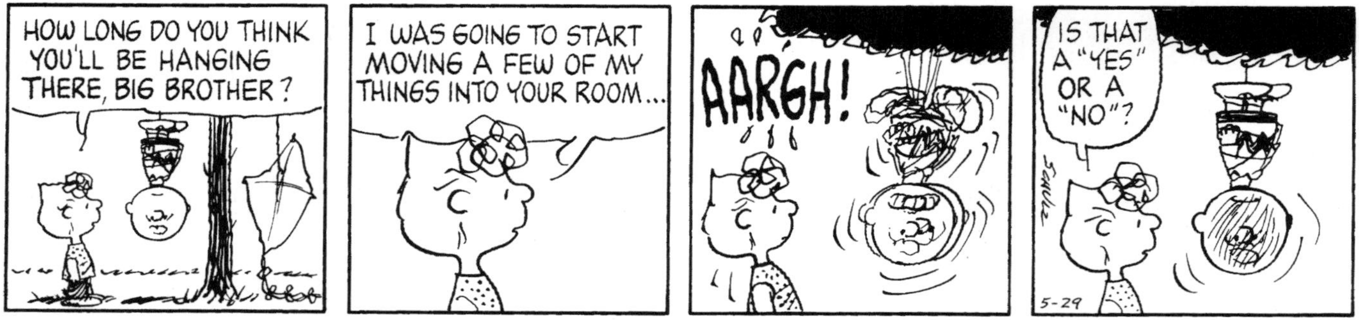
HOW LONG DO YOU THINK YOU'LL BE HANGING THERE, BIG BROTHER?
I WAS GOING TO START MOVING A FEW OF MY THINGS INTO YOUR ROOM...
AARGH!
IS THAT A "YES" OR A "NO"?
SCHULZ
5-29

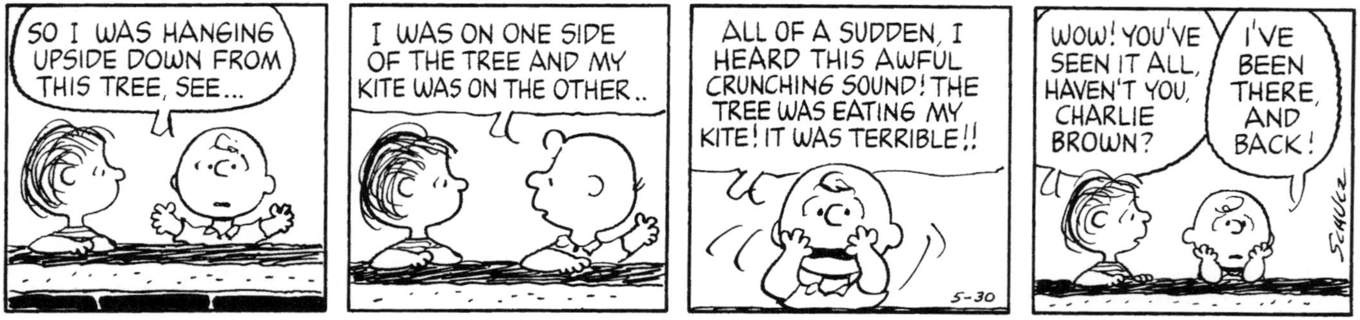
SO I WAS HANGING UPSIDE DOWN FROM THIS TREE, SEE...
I WAS ON ONE SIDE OF THE TREE AND MY KITE WAS ON THE OTHER..
ALL OF A SUDDEN, I HEARD THIS AWFUL CRUNCHING SOUND! THE TREE WAS EATING MY KITE! IT WAS TERRIBLE!!
5-30
WOW! YOU'VE SEEN IT ALL, HAVEN'T YOU, CHARLIE BROWN?
I'VE BEEN THERE, AND BACK!
SCHULZ

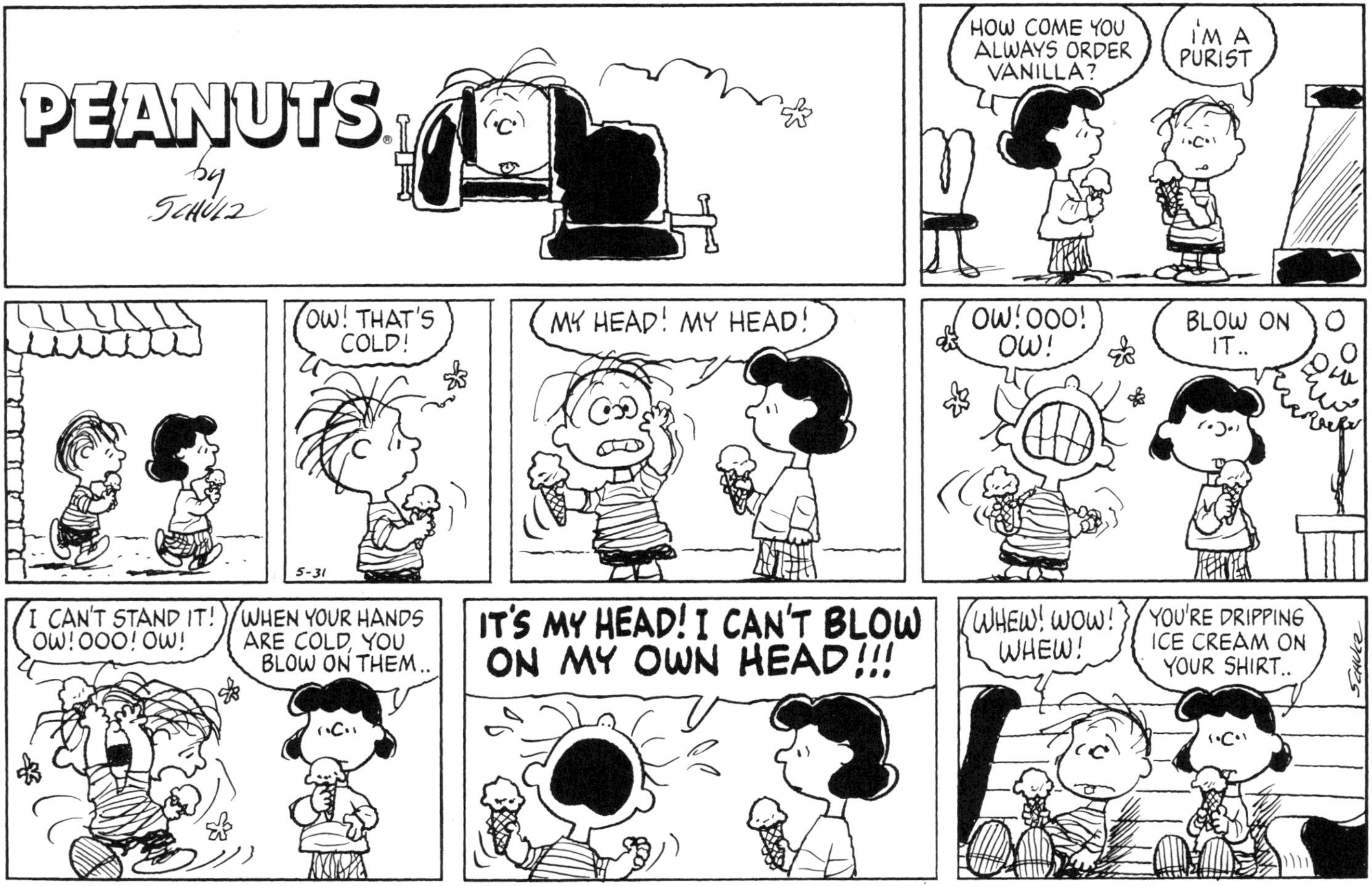
PEANUTS
by SCHULZ
HOW COME YOU ALWAYS ORDER VANILLA?
I'M A PURIST
OW! THAT'S COLD!
5-31
MY HEAD! MY HEAD!
OW! OOO! OW!
BLOW ON IT..
I CAN'T STAND IT! OW! OOO! OW!
WHEN YOUR HANDS ARE COLD, YOU BLOW ON THEM..
IT'S MY HEAD! I CAN'T BLOW ON MY OWN HEAD!!!
WHEW! WOW! WHEW!
YOU'RE DRIPPING ICE CREAM ON YOUR SHIRT..
SCHULZ

PSYCHIATRIC HELP 5¢

THE DOCTOR IS IN

LET ME GET THIS STRAIGHT..

YOU WERE HANGING UPSIDE DOWN FROM A TREE, AND YOU SAW THE TREE EAT YOUR KITE...

THE DOCTOR

IT WAS A KITE-EATING TREE

6-1

I'D BETTER TAKE NOTES.. THIS CASE COULD MAKE ME FAMOUS!

THE DOCTOR IS IN

PSYCHIATRIC HELP 5¢

THE DOCTOR IS IN

TELL ME THIS..

HOW CAN A TREE EAT A KITE IF IT DOESN'T HAVE ANY TEETH?

AND HOW CAN A TREE SWALLOW A KITE IF IT DOESN'T HAVE A STOMACH?

THE DOCTOR

YOU'RE JUST LEADING UP TO CHARGING ME MORE, AREN'T YOU?

THE DOCTOR IS IN

6-2

SO A TREE DOESN'T HAVE A STOMACH.. IT HAS LIMBS, BUT THAT DOESN'T MAKE IT A TRACK STAR, DOES IT?

THE DOCTOR IS IN

AND IF A TREE HAS A TRUNK, DOES THAT MAKE IT AN ELEPHANT? AND IF IT HAS BARK, DOES THAT MAKE IT A DOG?

6-3

HA HA HA HA!

THE DOCTOR IS IN

"DURING INTERVIEW PATIENT SUDDENLY BECAME HYSTERICAL.."

THE DOCTOR IS IN

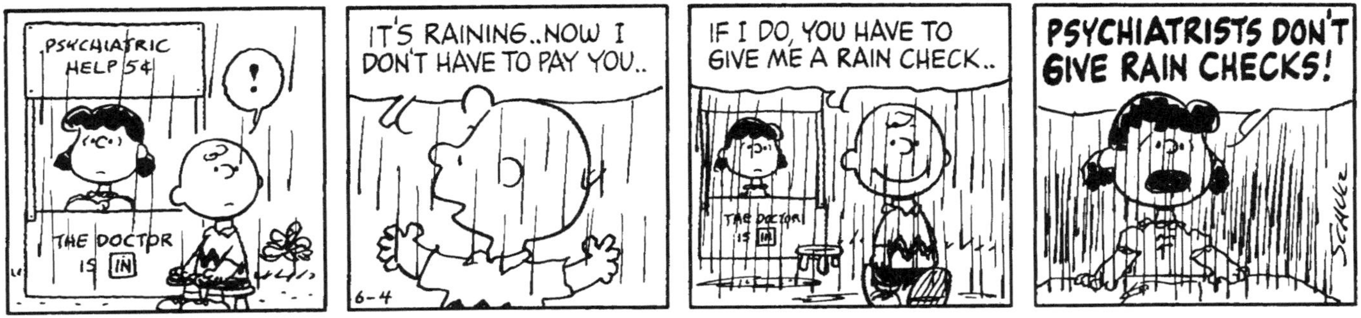
PSYCHIATRIC HELP 5¢
THE DOCTOR IS IN
!
IT'S RAINING..NOW I DON'T HAVE TO PAY YOU..
6-4
IF I DO, YOU HAVE TO GIVE ME A RAIN CHECK..
THE DOCTOR IS IN
PSYCHIATRISTS DON'T GIVE RAIN CHECKS!
SCHULZ

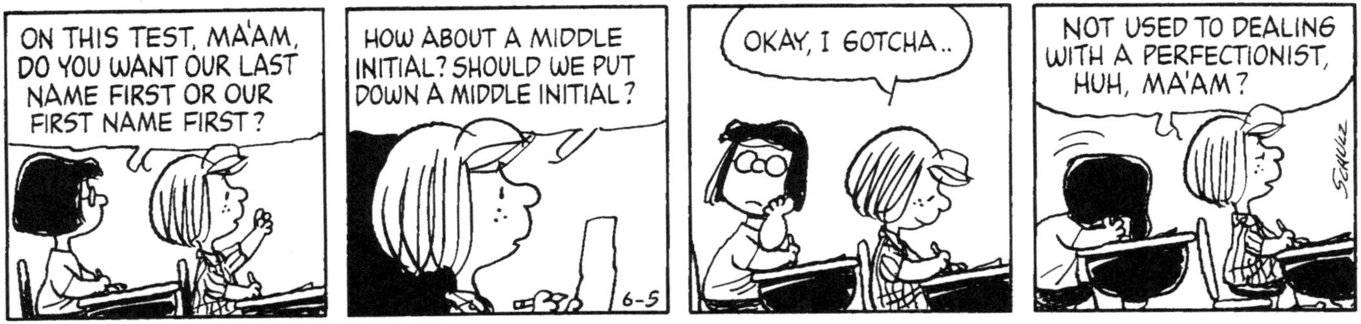
ON THIS TEST, MA'AM, DO YOU WANT OUR LAST NAME FIRST OR OUR FIRST NAME FIRST?
HOW ABOUT A MIDDLE INITIAL? SHOULD WE PUT DOWN A MIDDLE INITIAL?
6-5
OKAY, I GOTCHA..
NOT USED TO DEALING WITH A PERFECTIONIST, HUH, MA'AM?
SCHULZ

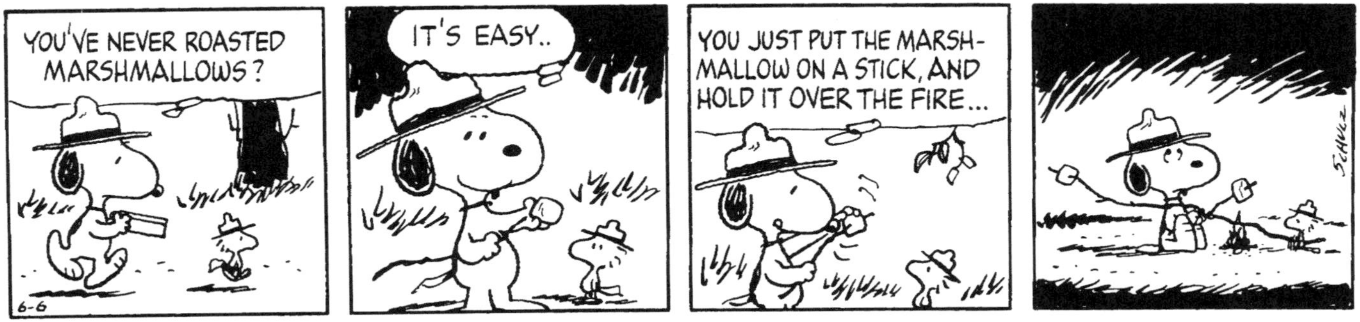
YOU'VE NEVER ROASTED MARSHMALLOWS?
6-6
IT'S EASY..
YOU JUST PUT THE MARSH-MALLOW ON A STICK, AND HOLD IT OVER THE FIRE...
SCHULZ

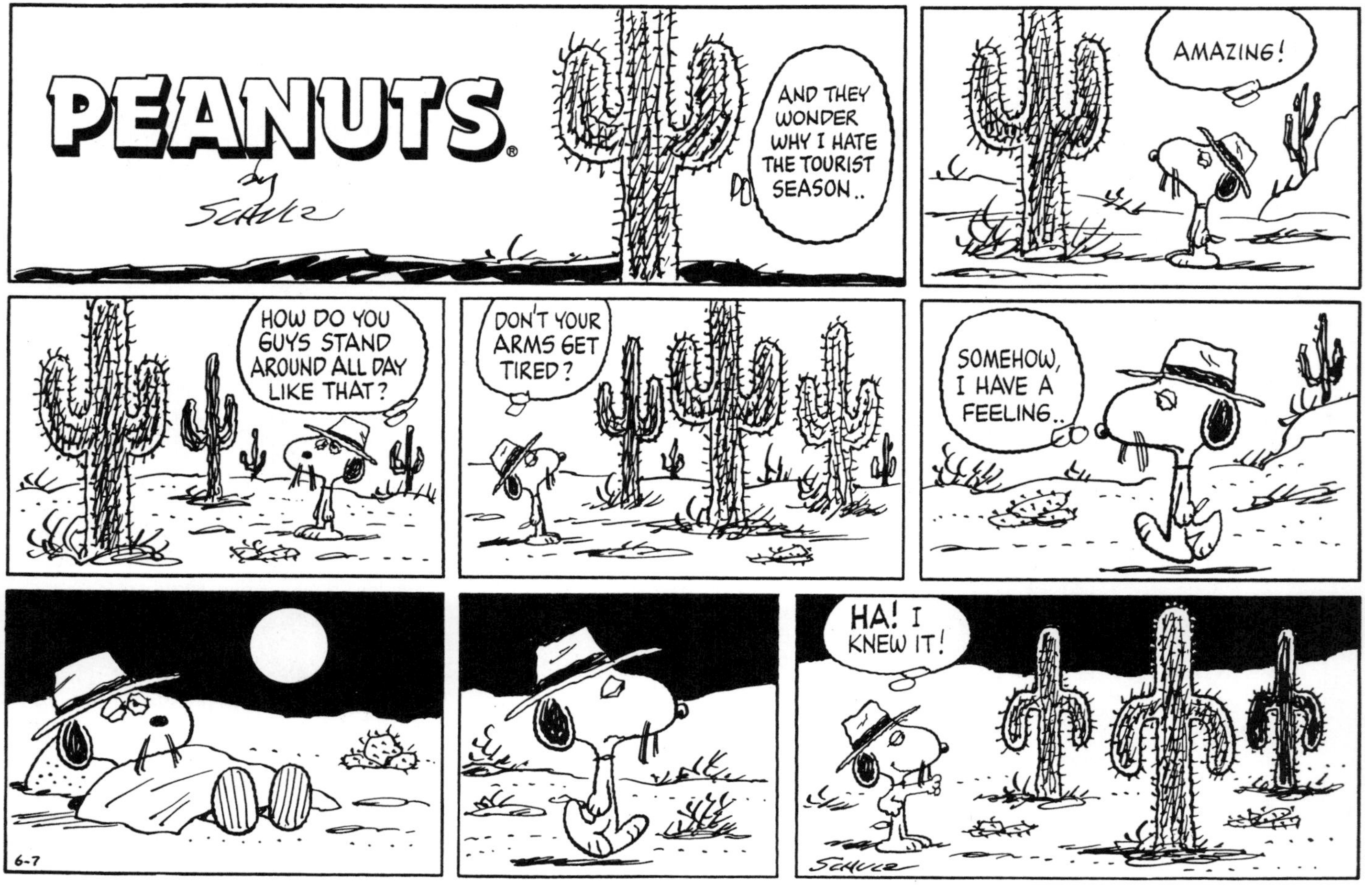
PEANUTS
by SCHULZ
AND THEY WONDER WHY I HATE THE TOURIST SEASON..
AMAZING!
HOW DO YOU GUYS STAND AROUND ALL DAY LIKE THAT?
DON'T YOUR ARMS GET TIRED?
SOMEHOW, I HAVE A FEELING..
6-7
HA! I KNEW IT!
SCHULZ

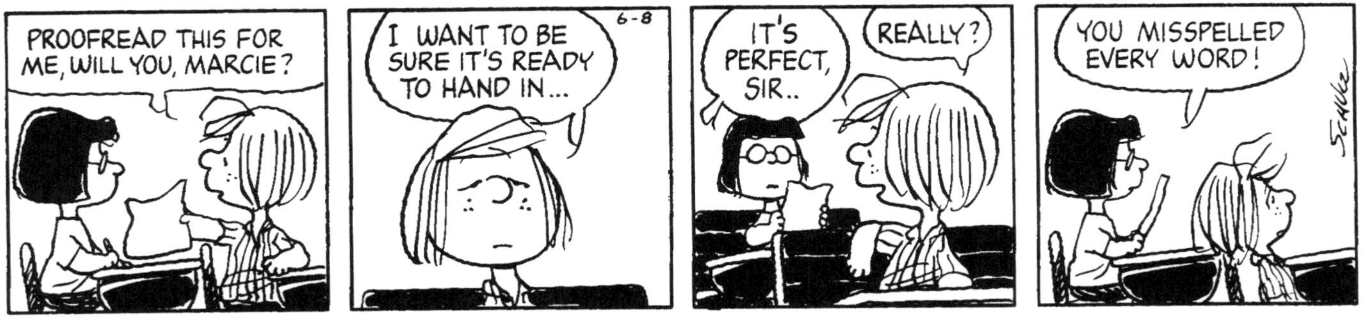
PROOFREAD THIS FOR ME, WILL YOU, MARCIE?
I WANT TO BE SURE IT'S READY TO HAND IN...
IT'S PERFECT, SIR..
REALLY?
YOU MISSPELLED EVERY WORD!

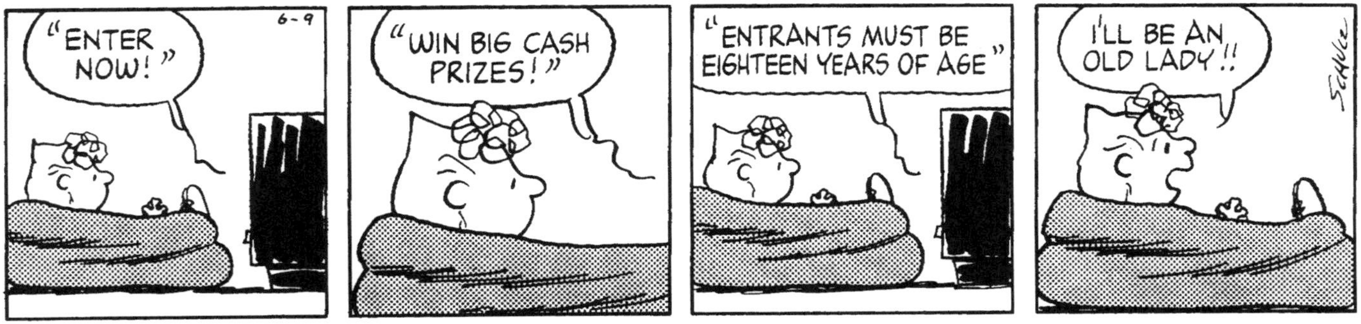
"ENTER NOW!"
"WIN BIG CASH PRIZES!"
"ENTRANTS MUST BE EIGHTEEN YEARS OF AGE"
I'LL BE AN OLD LADY!!

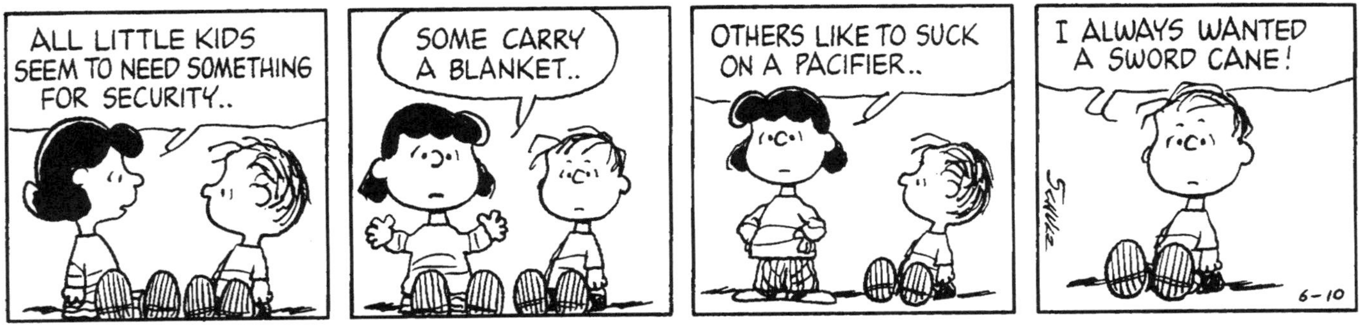
ALL LITTLE KIDS SEEM TO NEED SOMETHING FOR SECURITY..
SOME CARRY A BLANKET..
OTHERS LIKE TO SUCK ON A PACIFIER..
I ALWAYS WANTED A SWORD CANE!

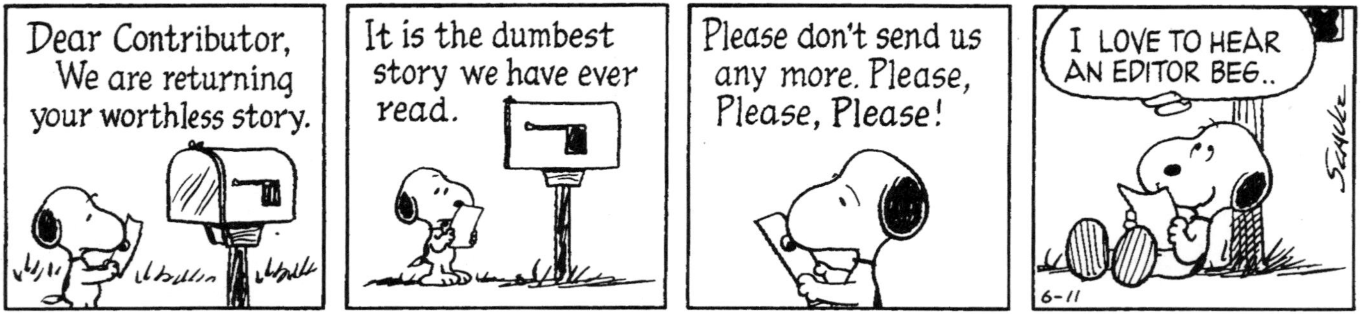
Dear Contributor,
We are returning your worthless story.
It is the dumbest story we have ever read.
Please don't send us any more. Please, Please, Please!
I LOVE TO HEAR AN EDITOR BEG..
6-11

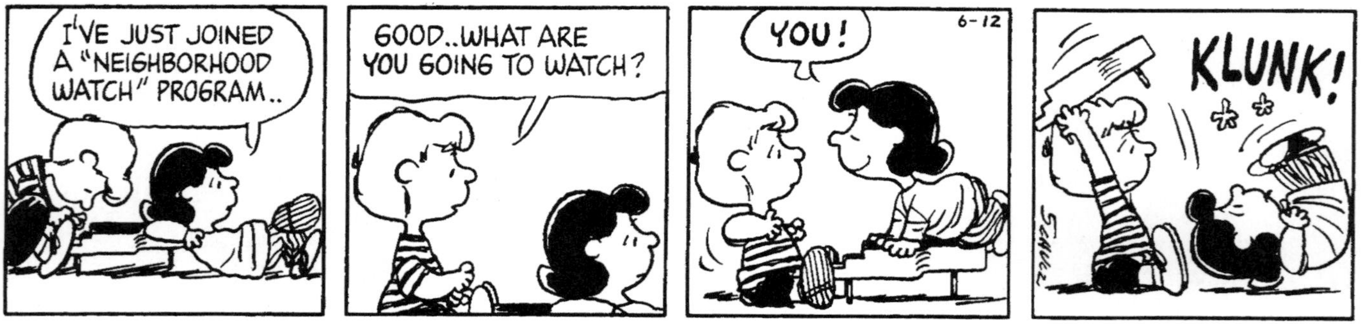
I'VE JUST JOINED A "NEIGHBORHOOD WATCH" PROGRAM..
GOOD..WHAT ARE YOU GOING TO WATCH?
YOU!
6-12
KLUNK!

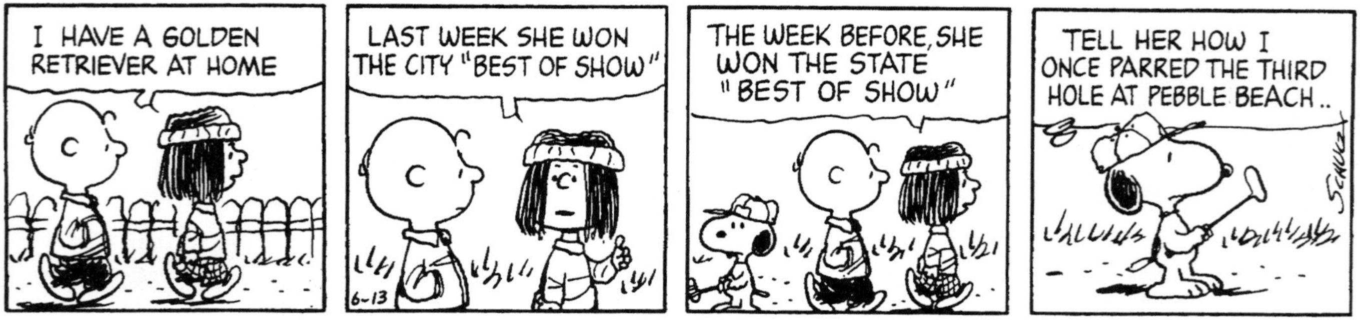
I HAVE A GOLDEN RETRIEVER AT HOME
LAST WEEK SHE WON THE CITY "BEST OF SHOW"
6-13
THE WEEK BEFORE, SHE WON THE STATE "BEST OF SHOW"
TELL HER HOW I ONCE PARRED THE THIRD HOLE AT PEBBLE BEACH..

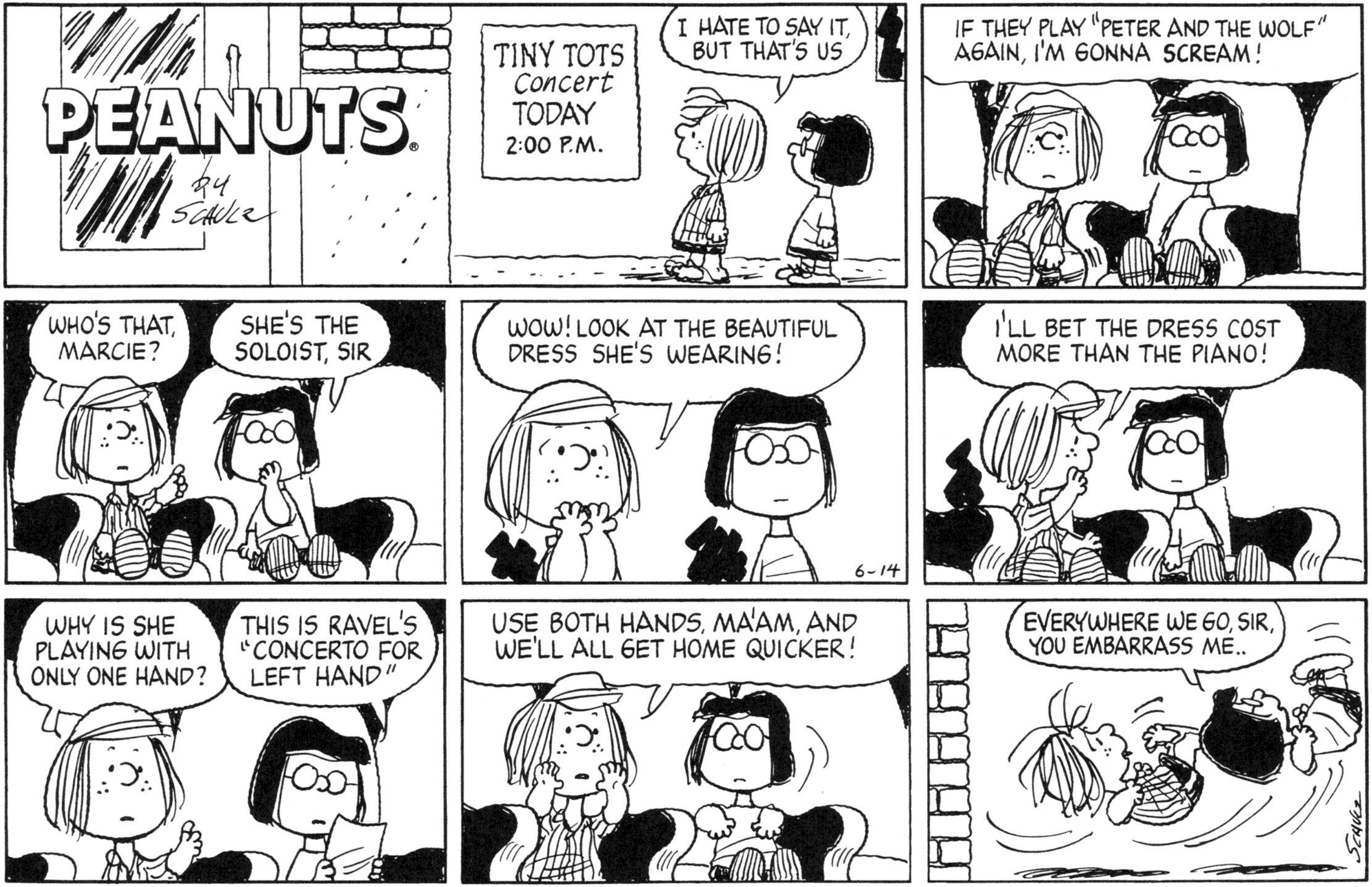
PEANUTS
TINY TOTS Concert TODAY 2:00 P.M.
I HATE TO SAY IT, BUT THAT'S US
IF THEY PLAY "PETER AND THE WOLF" AGAIN, I'M GONNA SCREAM!
WHO'S THAT, MARCIE?
SHE'S THE SOLOIST, SIR
WOW! LOOK AT THE BEAUTIFUL DRESS SHE'S WEARING!
I'LL BET THE DRESS COST MORE THAN THE PIANO!
WHY IS SHE PLAYING WITH ONLY ONE HAND?
THIS IS RAVEL'S "CONCERTO FOR LEFT HAND"
USE BOTH HANDS, MA'AM, AND WE'LL ALL GET HOME QUICKER!
EVERYWHERE WE GO, SIR, YOU EMBARRASS ME..

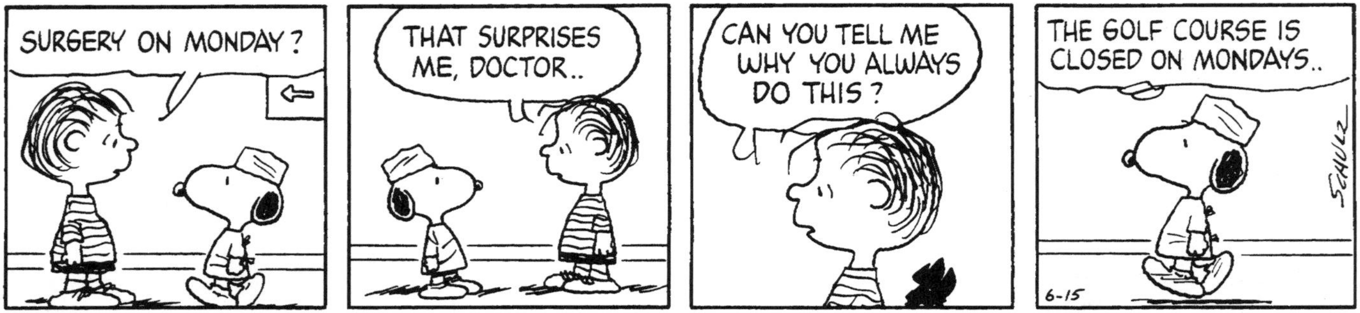
SURGERY ON MONDAY?
THAT SURPRISES ME, DOCTOR..
CAN YOU TELL ME WHY YOU ALWAYS DO THIS?
THE GOLF COURSE IS CLOSED ON MONDAYS..
SCHULZ
6-15

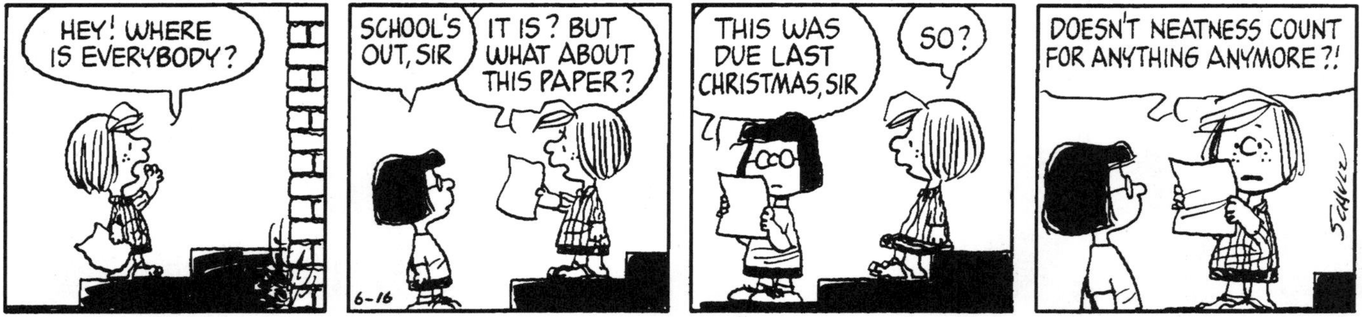
HEY! WHERE IS EVERYBODY?
SCHOOL'S OUT, SIR
IT IS? BUT WHAT ABOUT THIS PAPER?
6-16
THIS WAS DUE LAST CHRISTMAS, SIR
SO?
DOESN'T NEATNESS COUNT FOR ANYTHING ANYMORE?!
SCHULZ

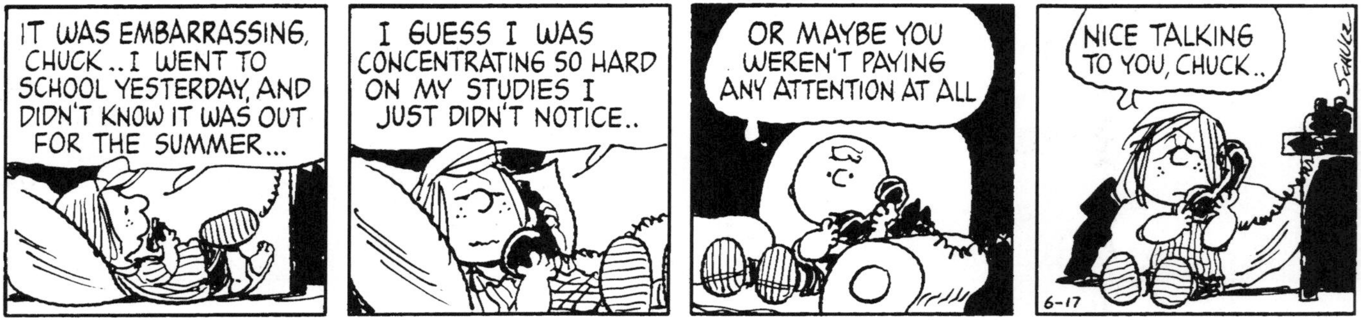
IT WAS EMBARRASSING, CHUCK..I WENT TO SCHOOL YESTERDAY, AND DIDN'T KNOW IT WAS OUT FOR THE SUMMER...
I GUESS I WAS CONCENTRATING SO HARD ON MY STUDIES I JUST DIDN'T NOTICE..
OR MAYBE YOU WEREN'T PAYING ANY ATTENTION AT ALL
NICE TALKING TO YOU, CHUCK..
SCHULZ
6-17

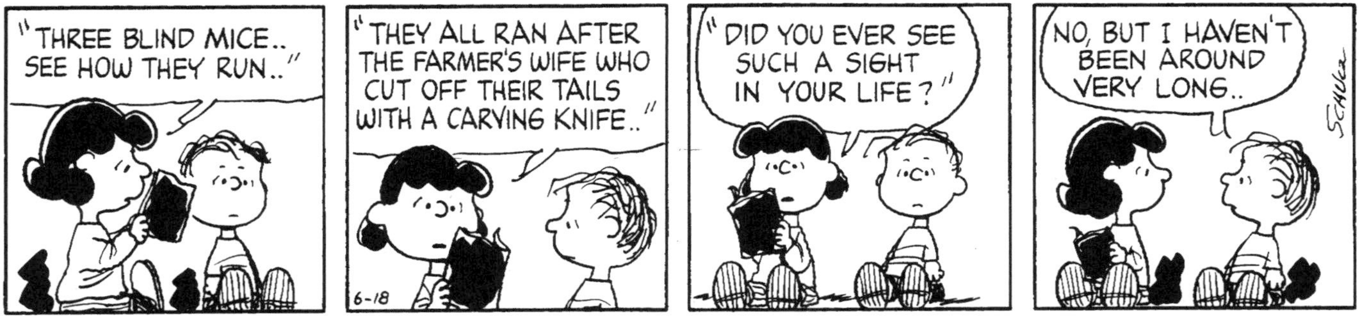
"THREE BLIND MICE.. SEE HOW THEY RUN.."
"THEY ALL RAN AFTER THE FARMER'S WIFE WHO CUT OFF THEIR TAILS WITH A CARVING KNIFE.."
6-18
"DID YOU EVER SEE SUCH A SIGHT IN YOUR LIFE?"
NO, BUT I HAVEN'T BEEN AROUND VERY LONG..
SCHULZ

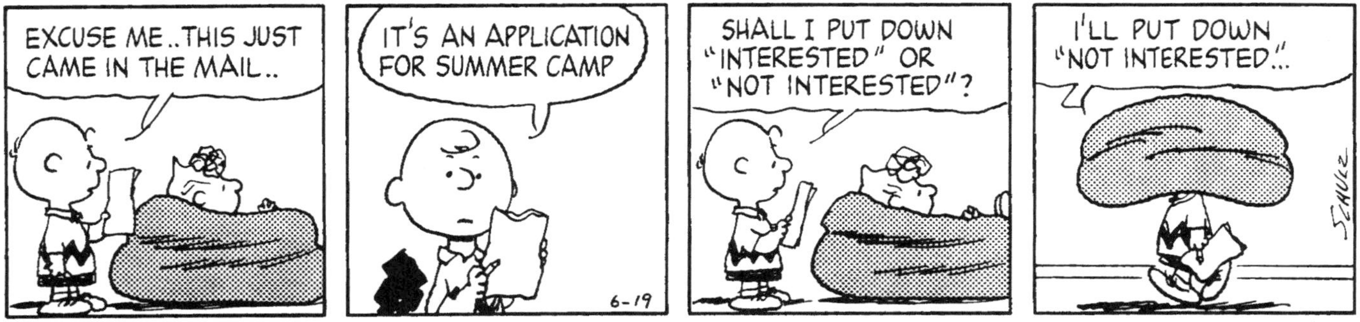
EXCUSE ME..THIS JUST CAME IN THE MAIL..
IT'S AN APPLICATION FOR SUMMER CAMP
6-19
SHALL I PUT DOWN "INTERESTED" OR "NOT INTERESTED"?
I'LL PUT DOWN "NOT INTERESTED"..
SCHULZ

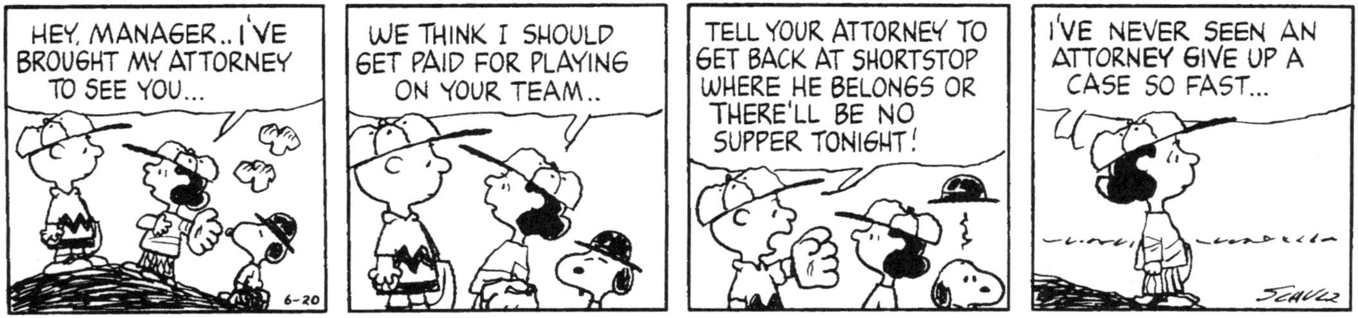
HEY, MANAGER.. I'VE BROUGHT MY ATTORNEY TO SEE YOU...
6-20
WE THINK I SHOULD GET PAID FOR PLAYING ON YOUR TEAM..
TELL YOUR ATTORNEY TO GET BACK AT SHORTSTOP WHERE HE BELONGS OR THERE'LL BE NO SUPPER TONIGHT!
I'VE NEVER SEEN AN ATTORNEY GIVE UP A CASE SO FAST...
SCHULZ

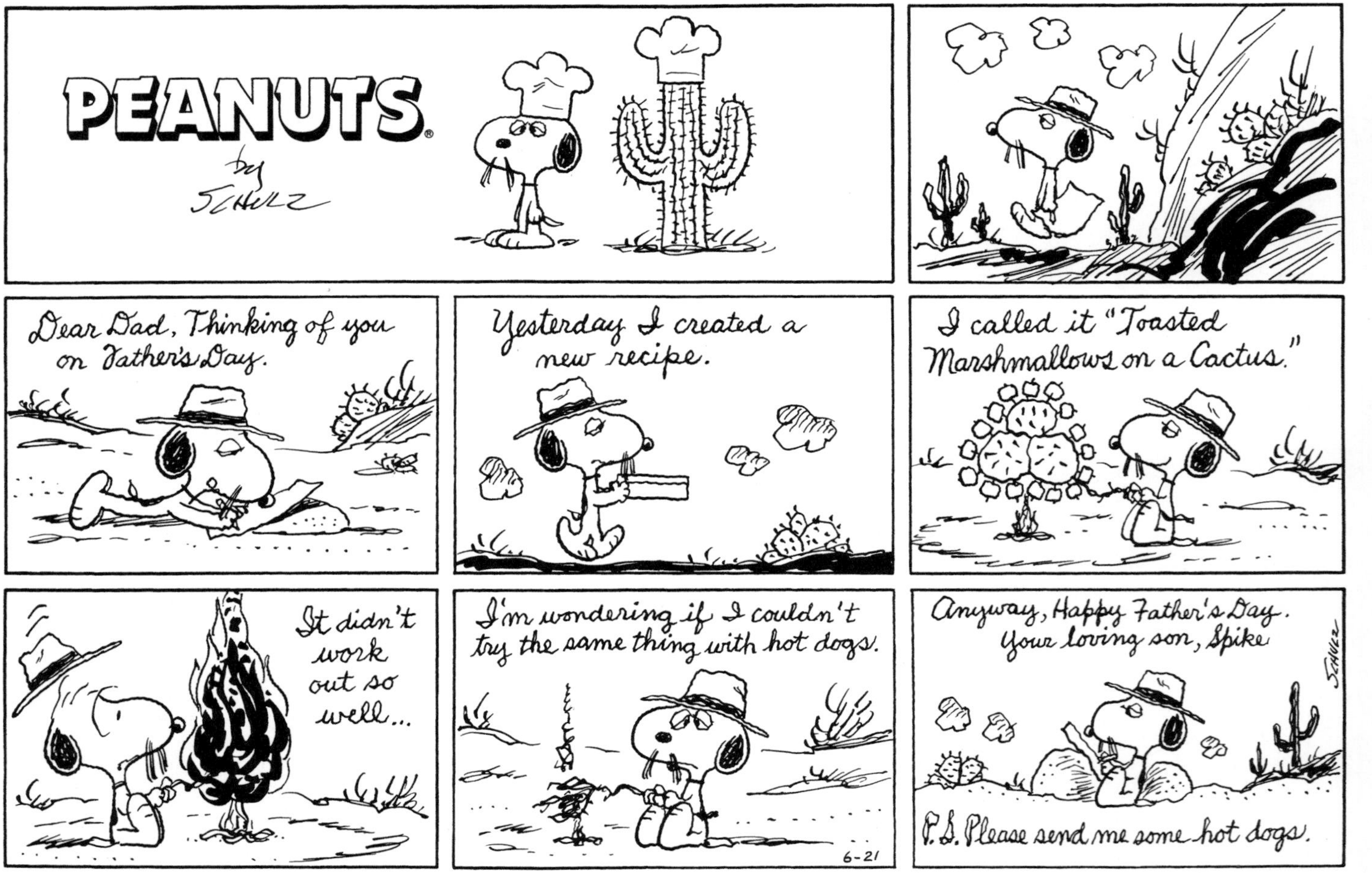
PEANUTS
by Schulz
Dear Dad, Thinking of you on Father's Day.
Yesterday I created a new recipe.
I called it "Toasted Marshmallows on a Cactus."
It didn't work out so well...
I'm wondering if I couldn't try the same thing with hot dogs.
Anyway, Happy Father's Day. Your loving son, Spike
P.S. Please send me some hot dogs.
6-21

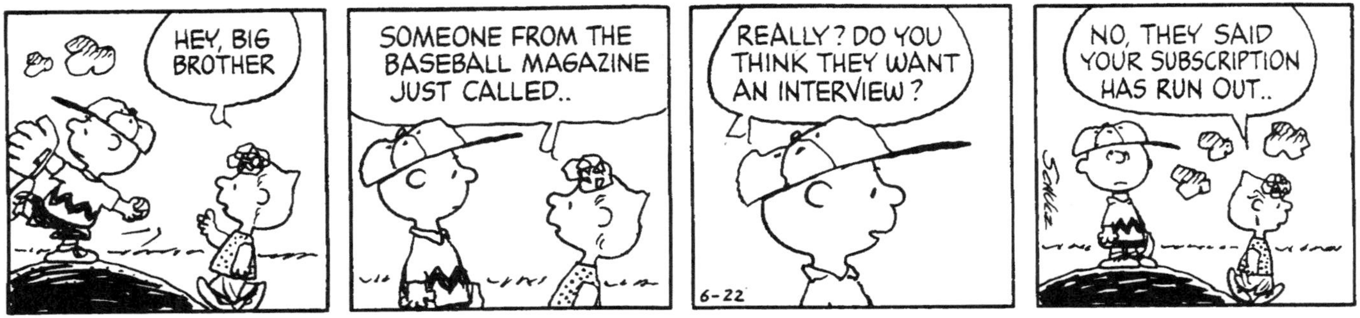
HEY, BIG BROTHER
SOMEONE FROM THE BASEBALL MAGAZINE JUST CALLED..
REALLY? DO YOU THINK THEY WANT AN INTERVIEW?
6-22
NO, THEY SAID YOUR SUBSCRIPTION HAS RUN OUT..
SCHULZ

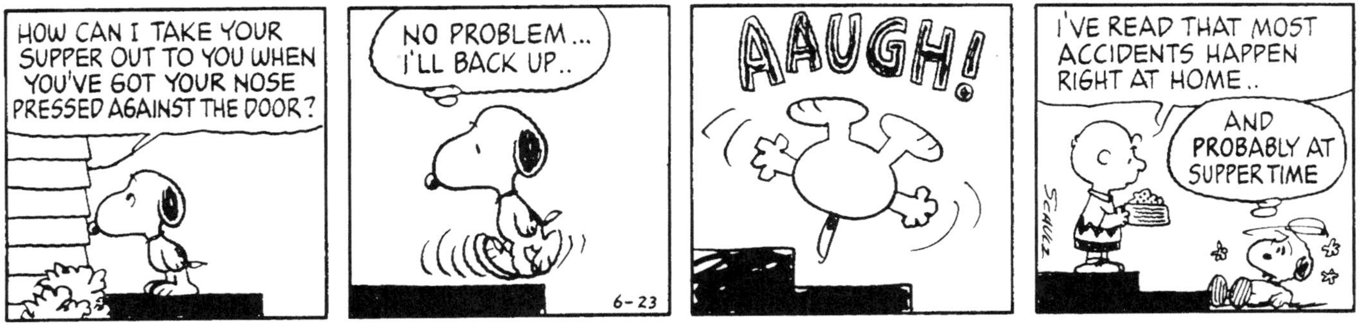
HOW CAN I TAKE YOUR SUPPER OUT TO YOU WHEN YOU'VE GOT YOUR NOSE PRESSED AGAINST THE DOOR?
NO PROBLEM... I'LL BACK UP..
6-23
AAUGH!
I'VE READ THAT MOST ACCIDENTS HAPPEN RIGHT AT HOME..
AND PROBABLY AT SUPPERTIME
SCHULZ

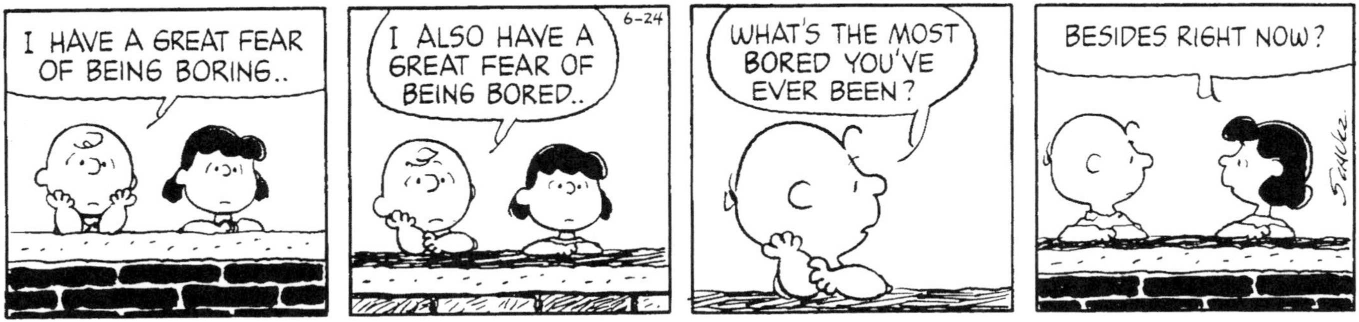
I HAVE A GREAT FEAR OF BEING BORING..
6-24
I ALSO HAVE A GREAT FEAR OF BEING BORED..
WHAT'S THE MOST BORED YOU'VE EVER BEEN?
BESIDES RIGHT NOW?
SCHULZ

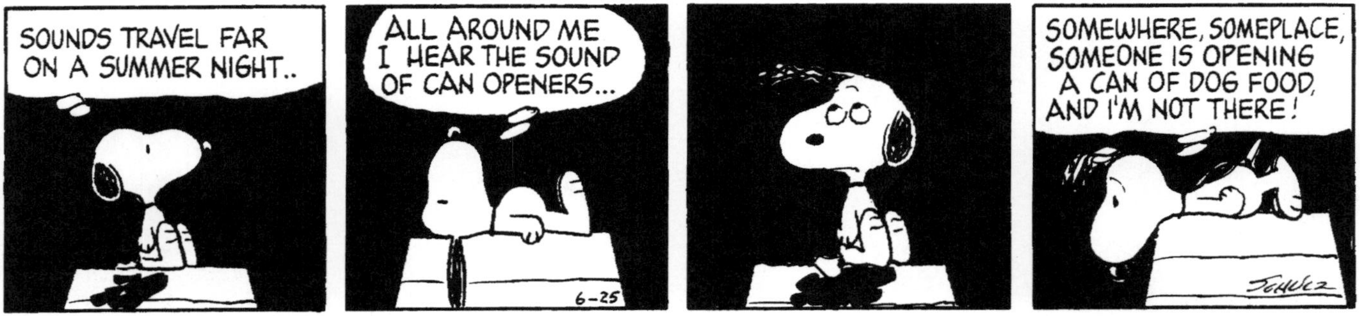
SOUNDS TRAVEL FAR ON A SUMMER NIGHT..
ALL AROUND ME I HEAR THE SOUND OF CAN OPENERS...
6-25
SOMEWHERE, SOMEPLACE, SOMEONE IS OPENING A CAN OF DOG FOOD, AND I'M NOT THERE!

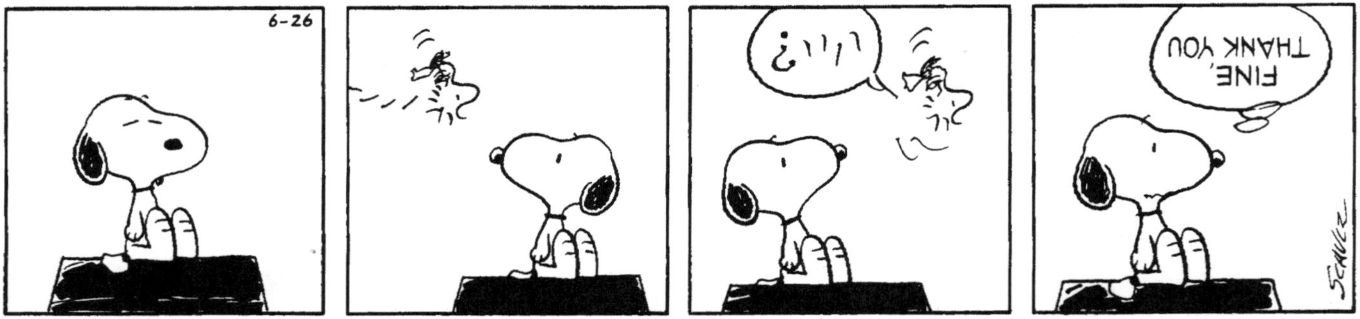
6-26
FINE, THANK YOU

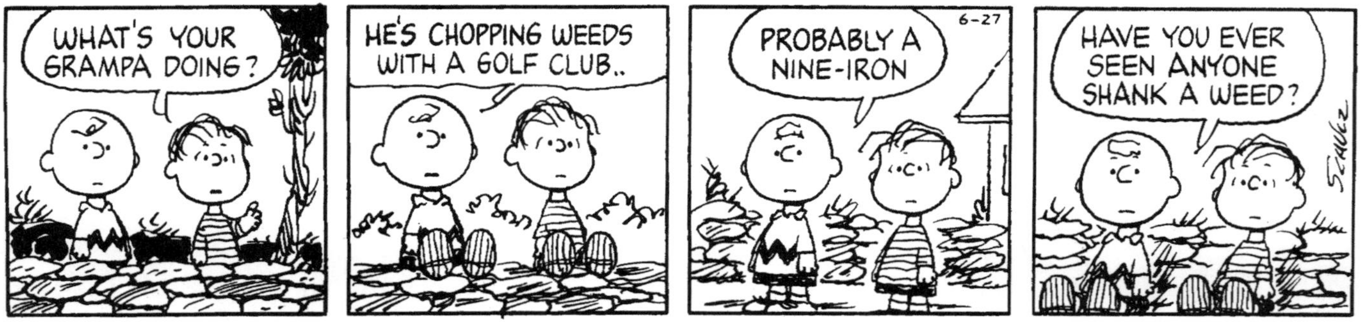
WHAT'S YOUR GRAMPA DOING?
HE'S CHOPPING WEEDS WITH A GOLF CLUB..
6-27
PROBABLY A NINE-IRON
HAVE YOU EVER SEEN ANYONE SHANK A WEED?

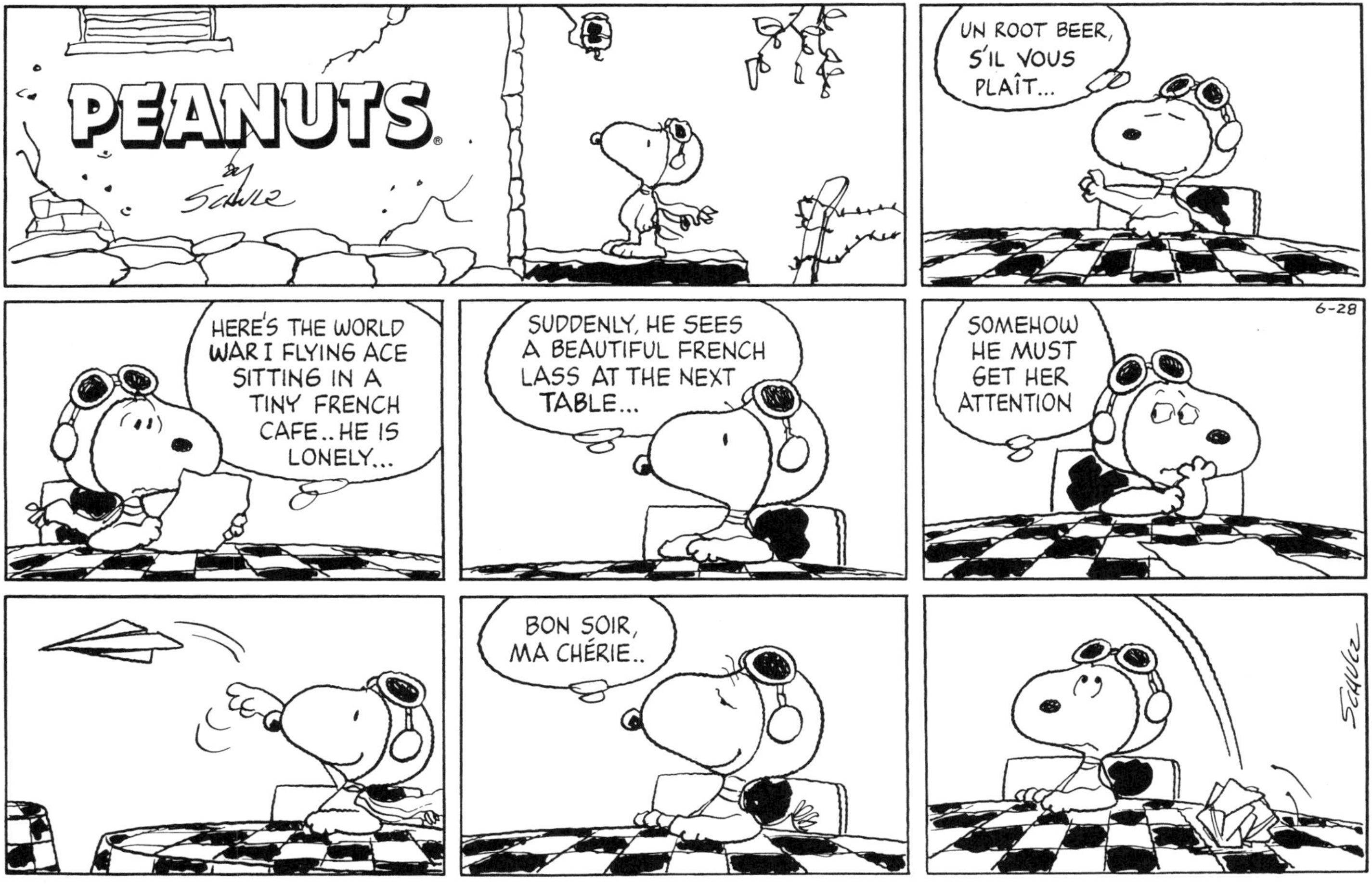
PEANUTS®
by SCHULZ
UN ROOT BEER, S'IL VOUS PLAÎT...
6-28
HERE'S THE WORLD WAR I FLYING ACE SITTING IN A TINY FRENCH CAFE.. HE IS LONELY...
SUDDENLY, HE SEES A BEAUTIFUL FRENCH LASS AT THE NEXT TABLE...
SOMEHOW HE MUST GET HER ATTENTION
BON SOIR, MA CHÉRIE..
SCHULZ

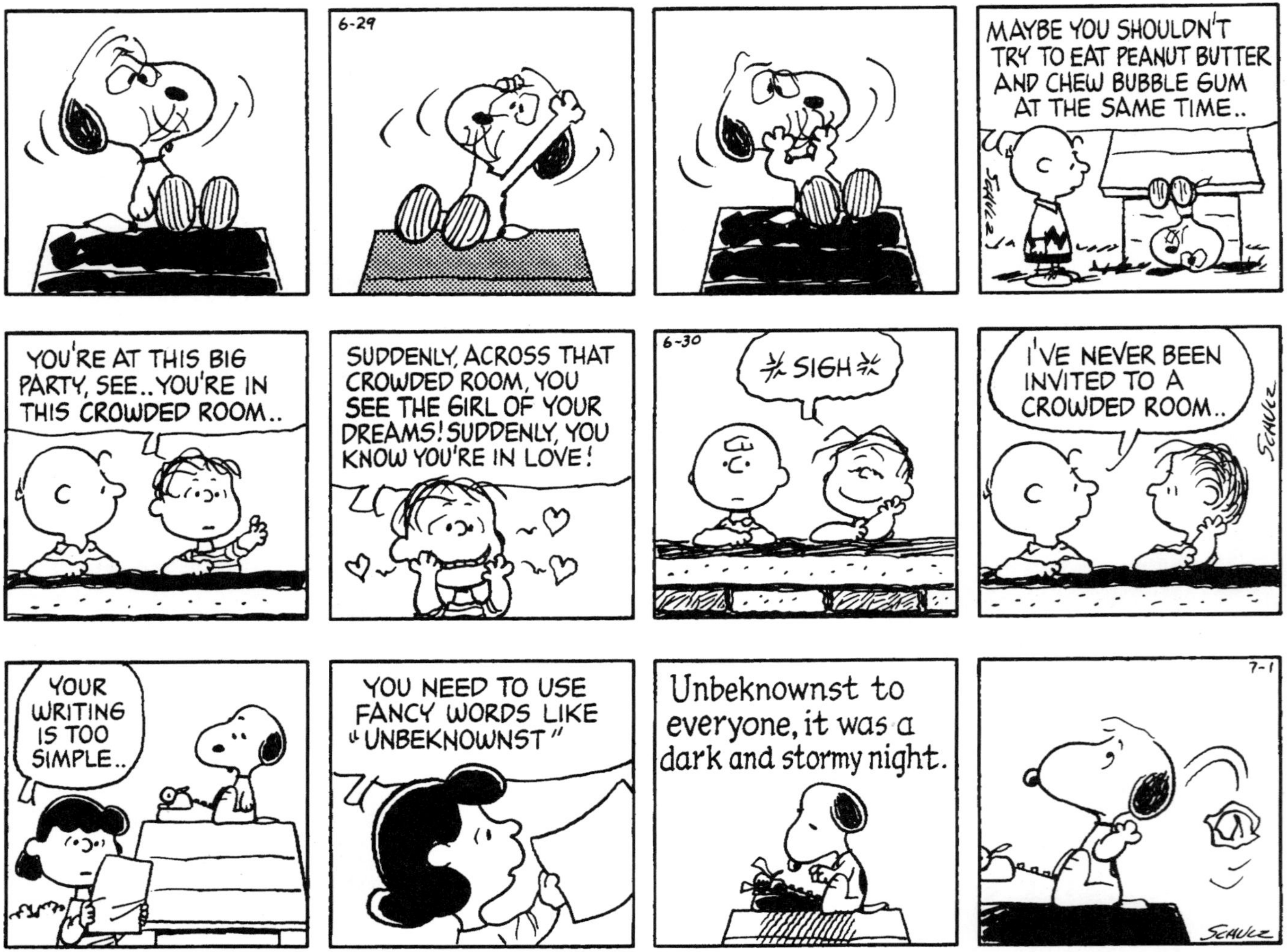
6-29
MAYBE YOU SHOULDN'T TRY TO EAT PEANUT BUTTER AND CHEW BUBBLE GUM AT THE SAME TIME..
YOU'RE AT THIS BIG PARTY, SEE..YOU'RE IN THIS CROWDED ROOM..
SUDDENLY, ACROSS THAT CROWDED ROOM, YOU SEE THE GIRL OF YOUR DREAMS! SUDDENLY, YOU KNOW YOU'RE IN LOVE!
6-30
SIGH
I'VE NEVER BEEN INVITED TO A CROWDED ROOM..
YOUR WRITING IS TOO SIMPLE..
YOU NEED TO USE FANCY WORDS LIKE "UNBEKNOWNST"
Unbeknownst to everyone, it was a dark and stormy night.
7-1

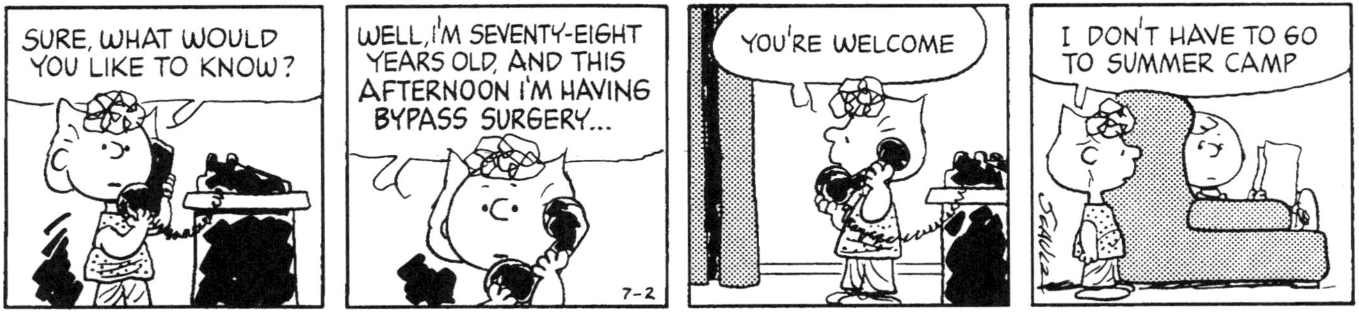
SURE, WHAT WOULD YOU LIKE TO KNOW?
WELL, I'M SEVENTY-EIGHT YEARS OLD, AND THIS AFTERNOON I'M HAVING BYPASS SURGERY...
YOU'RE WELCOME
I DON'T HAVE TO GO TO SUMMER CAMP

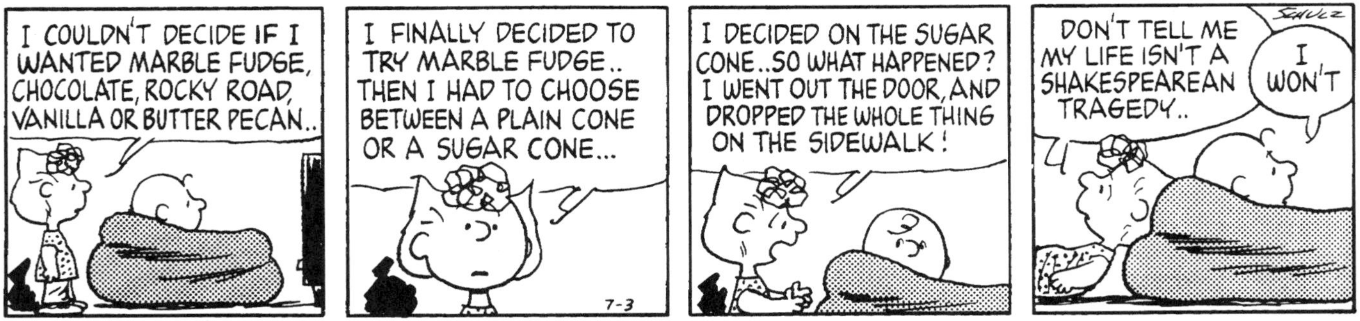
I COULDN'T DECIDE IF I WANTED MARBLE FUDGE, CHOCOLATE, ROCKY ROAD, VANILLA OR BUTTER PECAN..
I FINALLY DECIDED TO TRY MARBLE FUDGE.. THEN I HAD TO CHOOSE BETWEEN A PLAIN CONE OR A SUGAR CONE...
I DECIDED ON THE SUGAR CONE..SO WHAT HAPPENED? I WENT OUT THE DOOR, AND DROPPED THE WHOLE THING ON THE SIDEWALK!
DON'T TELL ME MY LIFE ISN'T A SHAKESPEAREAN TRAGEDY..
I WON'T

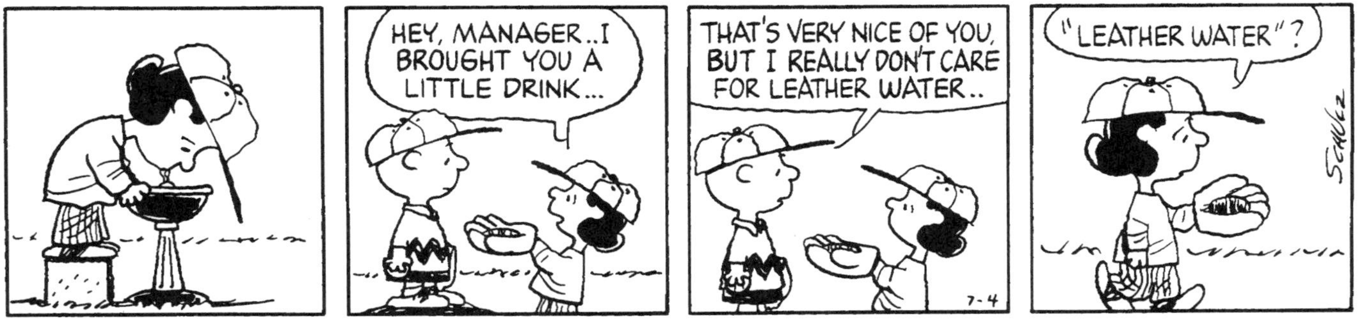
HEY, MANAGER..I BROUGHT YOU A LITTLE DRINK...
THAT'S VERY NICE OF YOU, BUT I REALLY DON'T CARE FOR LEATHER WATER..
"LEATHER WATER"?

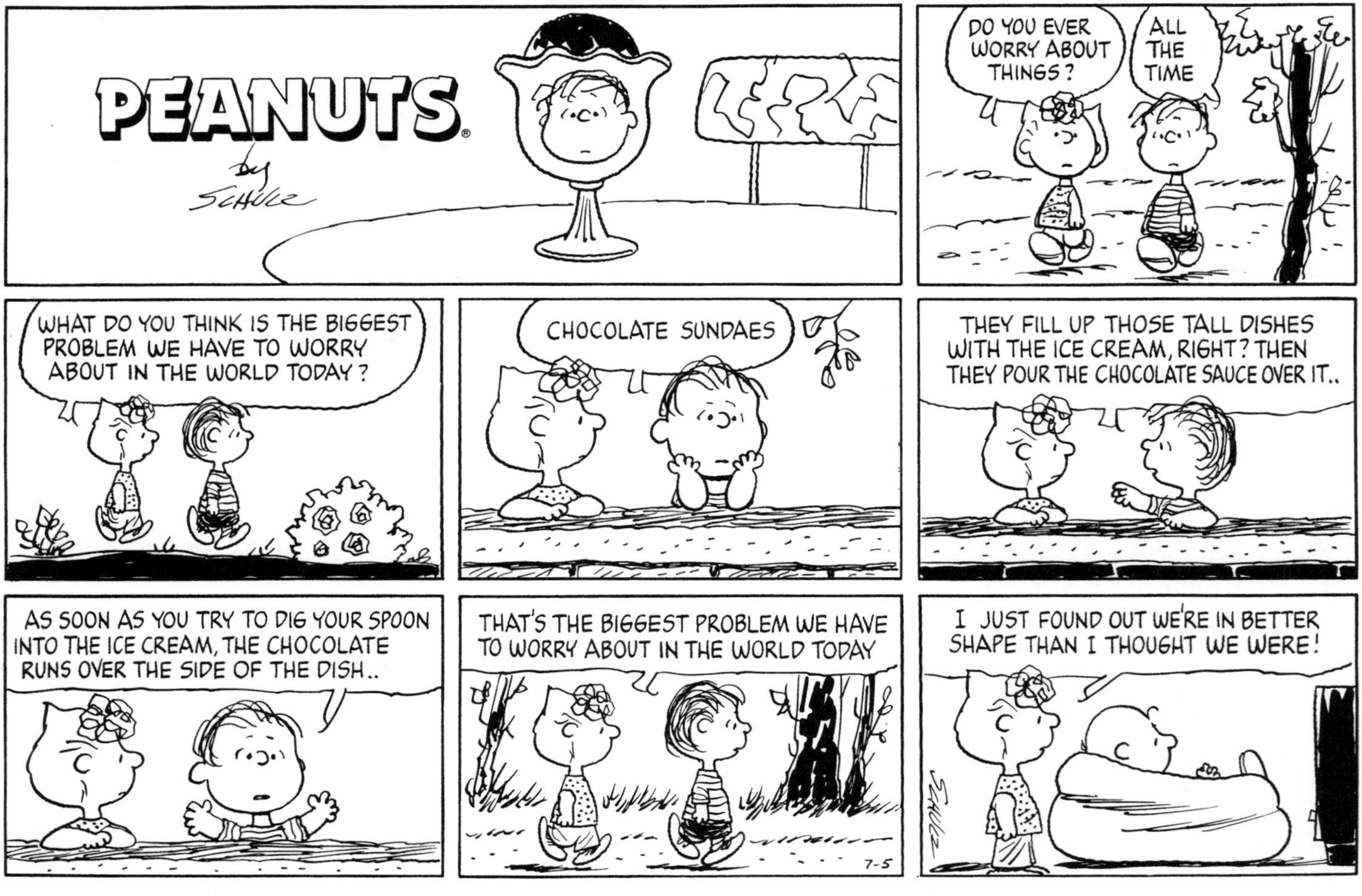
PEANUTS
by SCHULZ
DO YOU EVER WORRY ABOUT THINGS?
ALL THE TIME
WHAT DO YOU THINK IS THE BIGGEST PROBLEM WE HAVE TO WORRY ABOUT IN THE WORLD TODAY?
CHOCOLATE SUNDAES
THEY FILL UP THOSE TALL DISHES WITH THE ICE CREAM, RIGHT? THEN THEY POUR THE CHOCOLATE SAUCE OVER IT..
AS SOON AS YOU TRY TO DIG YOUR SPOON INTO THE ICE CREAM, THE CHOCOLATE RUNS OVER THE SIDE OF THE DISH..
THAT'S THE BIGGEST PROBLEM WE HAVE TO WORRY ABOUT IN THE WORLD TODAY
7-5
I JUST FOUND OUT WE'RE IN BETTER SHAPE THAN I THOUGHT WE WERE!
SCHULZ

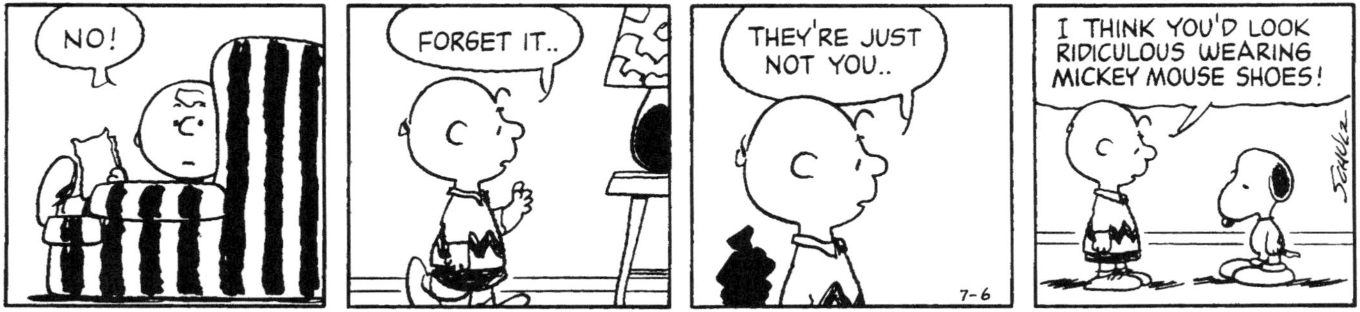
NO!
FORGET IT..
THEY'RE JUST NOT YOU..
I THINK YOU'D LOOK RIDICULOUS WEARING MICKEY MOUSE SHOES!
7-6
SCHULZ

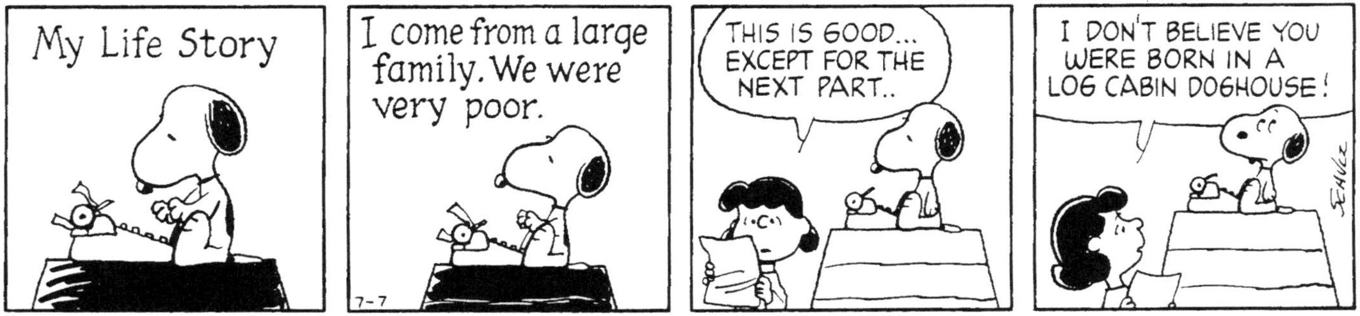
My Life Story
I come from a large family. We were very poor.
7-7
THIS IS GOOD... EXCEPT FOR THE NEXT PART..
I DON'T BELIEVE YOU WERE BORN IN A LOG CABIN DOGHOUSE!
SCHULZ

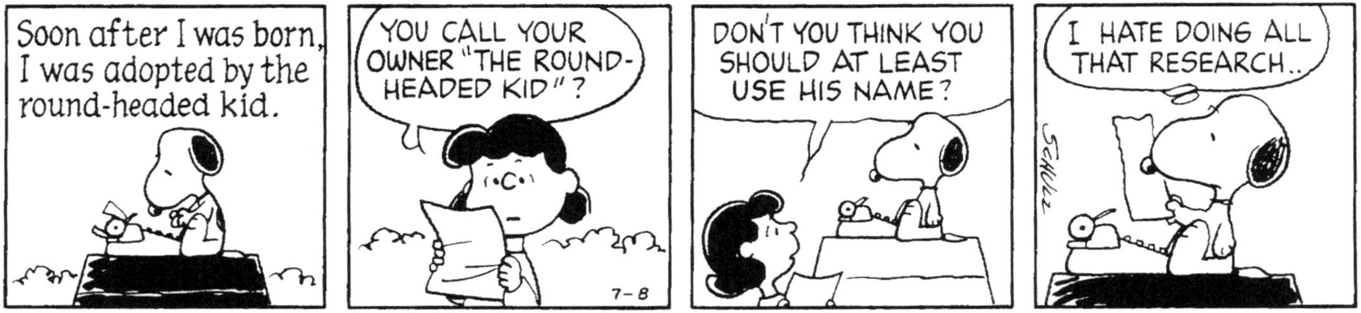
Soon after I was born, I was adopted by the round-headed kid.
YOU CALL YOUR OWNER "THE ROUND-HEADED KID"?
7-8
DON'T YOU THINK YOU SHOULD AT LEAST USE HIS NAME?
SCHULZ
I HATE DOING ALL THAT RESEARCH..

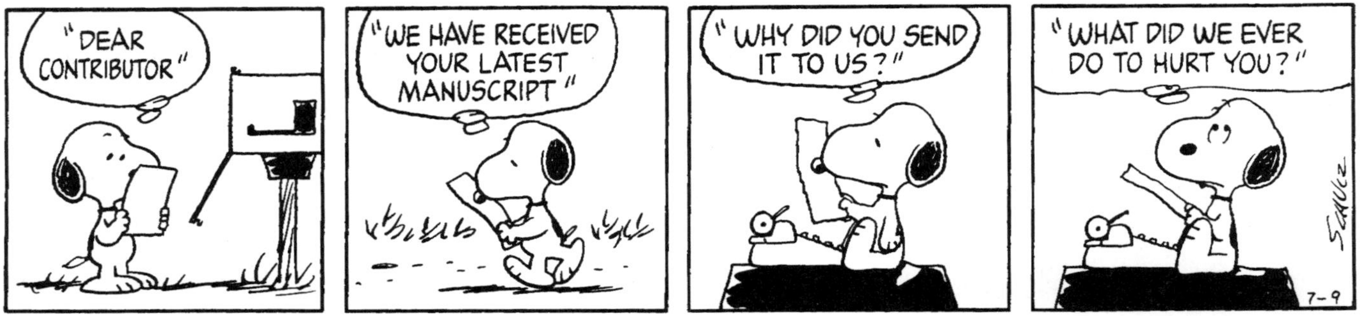
"DEAR CONTRIBUTOR"
"WE HAVE RECEIVED YOUR LATEST MANUSCRIPT"
"WHY DID YOU SEND IT TO US?"
"WHAT DID WE EVER DO TO HURT YOU?"

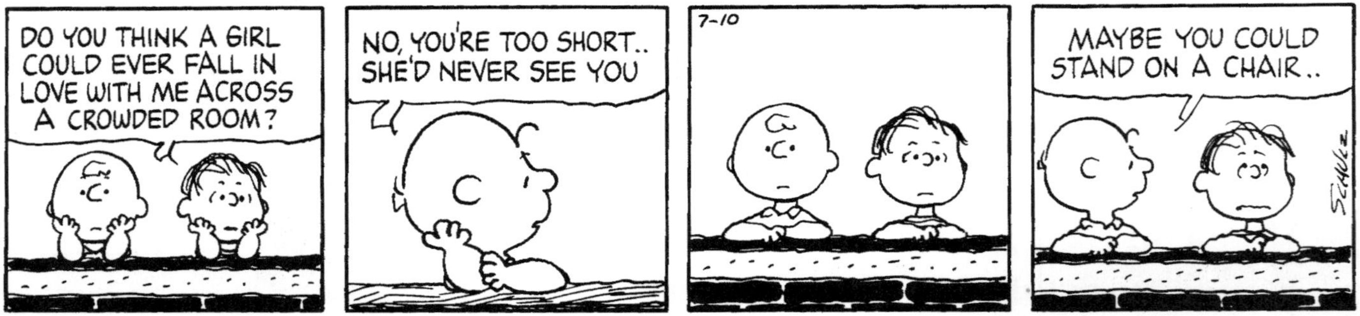
DO YOU THINK A GIRL COULD EVER FALL IN LOVE WITH ME ACROSS A CROWDED ROOM?
NO, YOU'RE TOO SHORT.. SHE'D NEVER SEE YOU
MAYBE YOU COULD STAND ON A CHAIR..

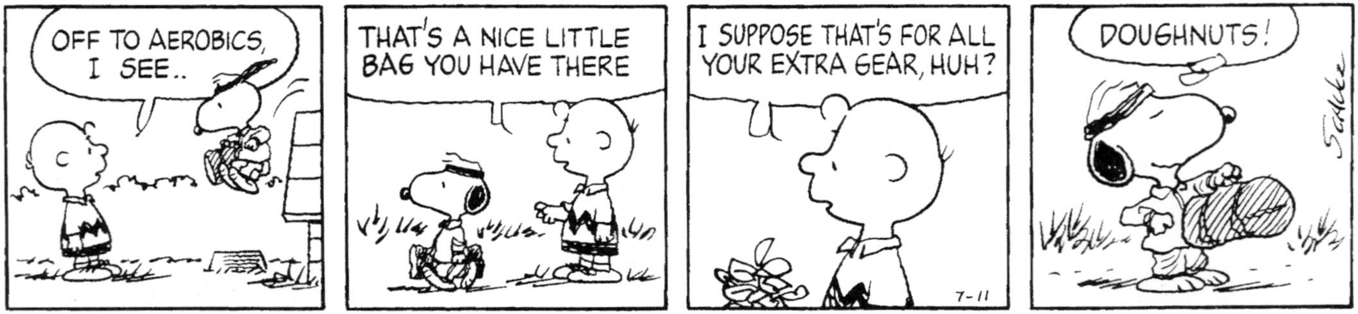
OFF TO AEROBICS, I SEE..
THAT'S A NICE LITTLE BAG YOU HAVE THERE
I SUPPOSE THAT'S FOR ALL YOUR EXTRA GEAR, HUH?
DOUGHNUTS!

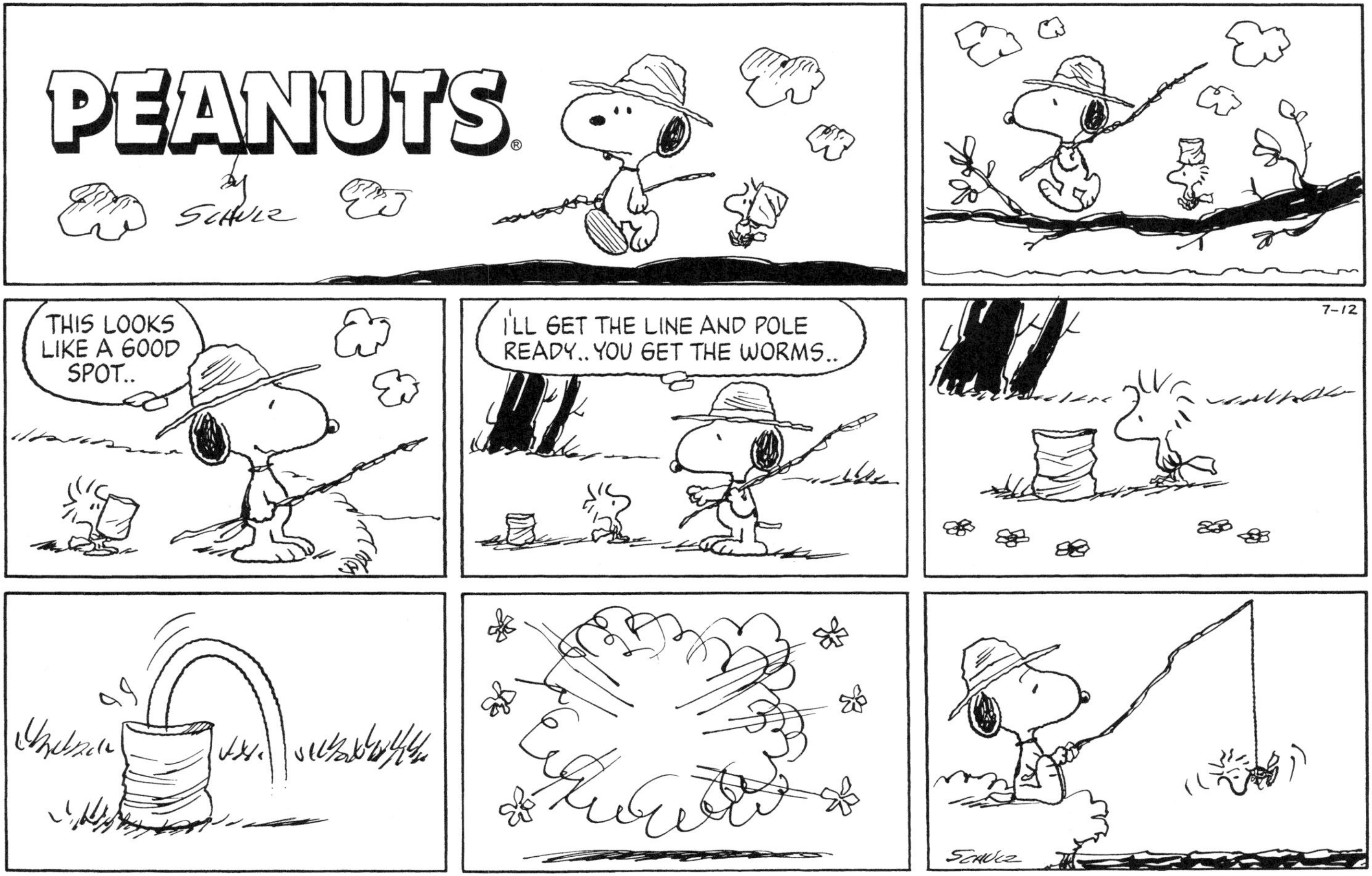
PEANUTS
by SCHULZ
THIS LOOKS LIKE A GOOD SPOT..
I'LL GET THE LINE AND POLE READY.. YOU GET THE WORMS..
7-12
SCHULZ

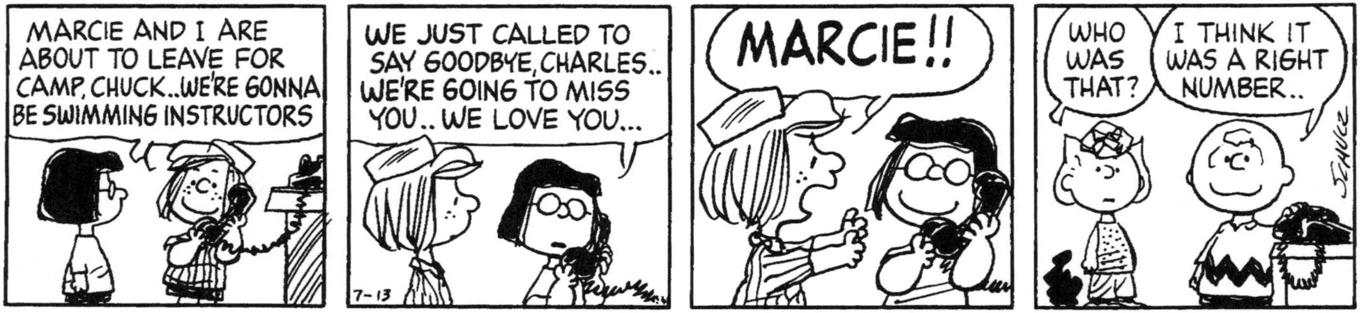
MARCIE AND I ARE ABOUT TO LEAVE FOR CAMP, CHUCK..WE'RE GONNA BE SWIMMING INSTRUCTORS
WE JUST CALLED TO SAY GOODBYE, CHARLES.. WE'RE GOING TO MISS YOU.. WE LOVE YOU...
7-13
MARCIE!!
WHO WAS THAT?
I THINK IT WAS A RIGHT NUMBER..

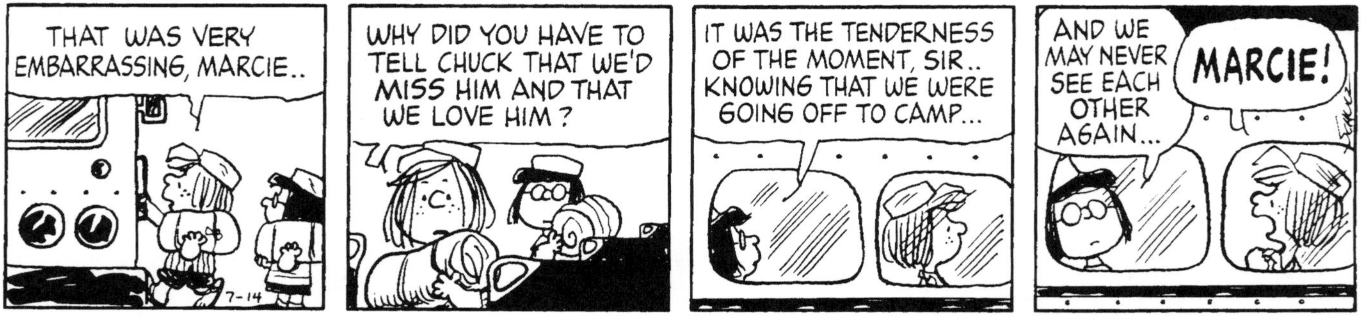
THAT WAS VERY EMBARRASSING, MARCIE..
7-14
WHY DID YOU HAVE TO TELL CHUCK THAT WE'D MISS HIM AND THAT WE LOVE HIM?
IT WAS THE TENDERNESS OF THE MOMENT, SIR.. KNOWING THAT WE WERE GOING OFF TO CAMP...
AND WE MAY NEVER SEE EACH OTHER AGAIN...
MARCIE!

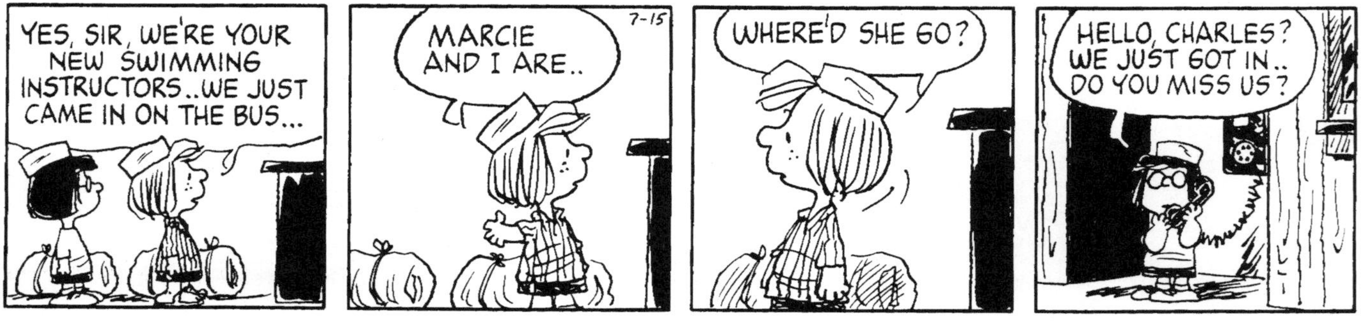
YES, SIR, WE'RE YOUR NEW SWIMMING INSTRUCTORS..WE JUST CAME IN ON THE BUS...
7-15
MARCIE AND I ARE..
WHERE'D SHE GO?
HELLO, CHARLES? WE JUST GOT IN.. DO YOU MISS US?

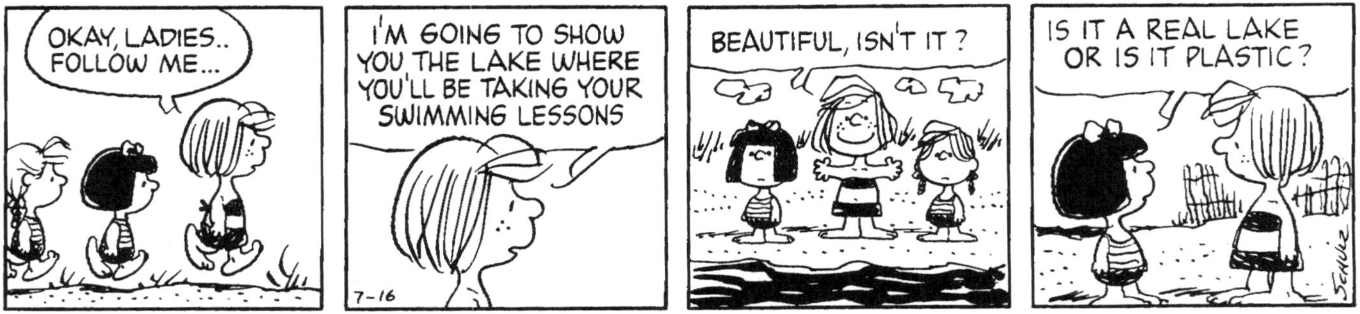
OKAY, LADIES.. FOLLOW ME...
I'M GOING TO SHOW YOU THE LAKE WHERE YOU'LL BE TAKING YOUR SWIMMING LESSONS
7-16
BEAUTIFUL, ISN'T IT ?
IS IT A REAL LAKE OR IS IT PLASTIC ?
SCHULZ

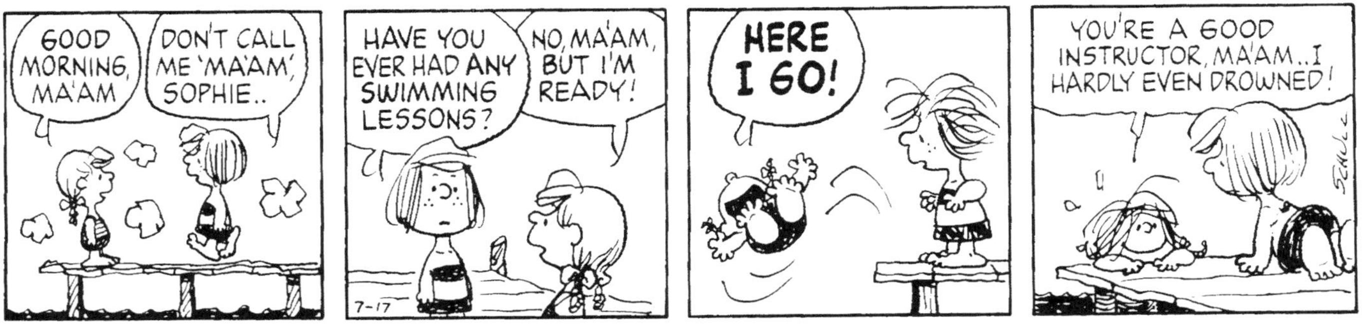
GOOD MORNING, MA'AM
DON'T CALL ME 'MA'AM', SOPHIE..
HAVE YOU EVER HAD ANY SWIMMING LESSONS ?
NO, MA'AM, BUT I'M READY !
7-17
HERE I GO!
YOU'RE A GOOD INSTRUCTOR, MA'AM..I HARDLY EVEN DROWNED !
SCHULZ

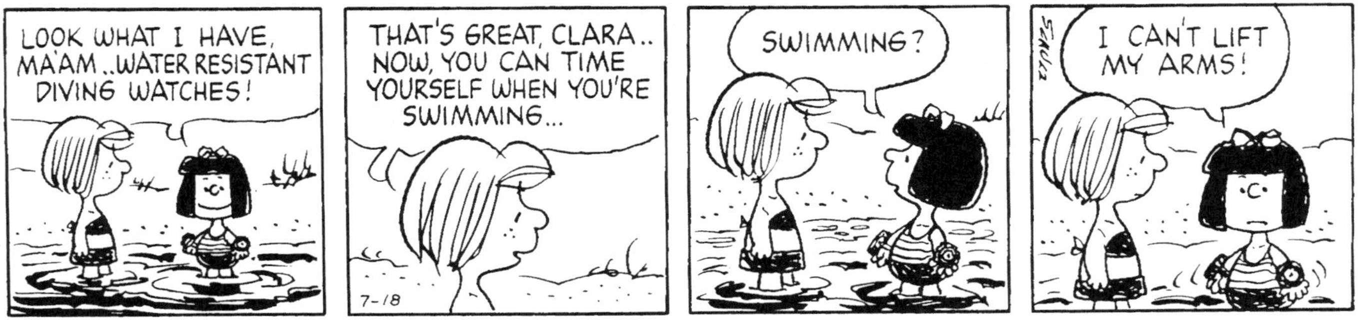
LOOK WHAT I HAVE, MA'AM..WATER RESISTANT DIVING WATCHES !
THAT'S GREAT, CLARA.. NOW, YOU CAN TIME YOURSELF WHEN YOU'RE SWIMMING...
7-18
SWIMMING ?
SCHULZ
I CAN'T LIFT MY ARMS !

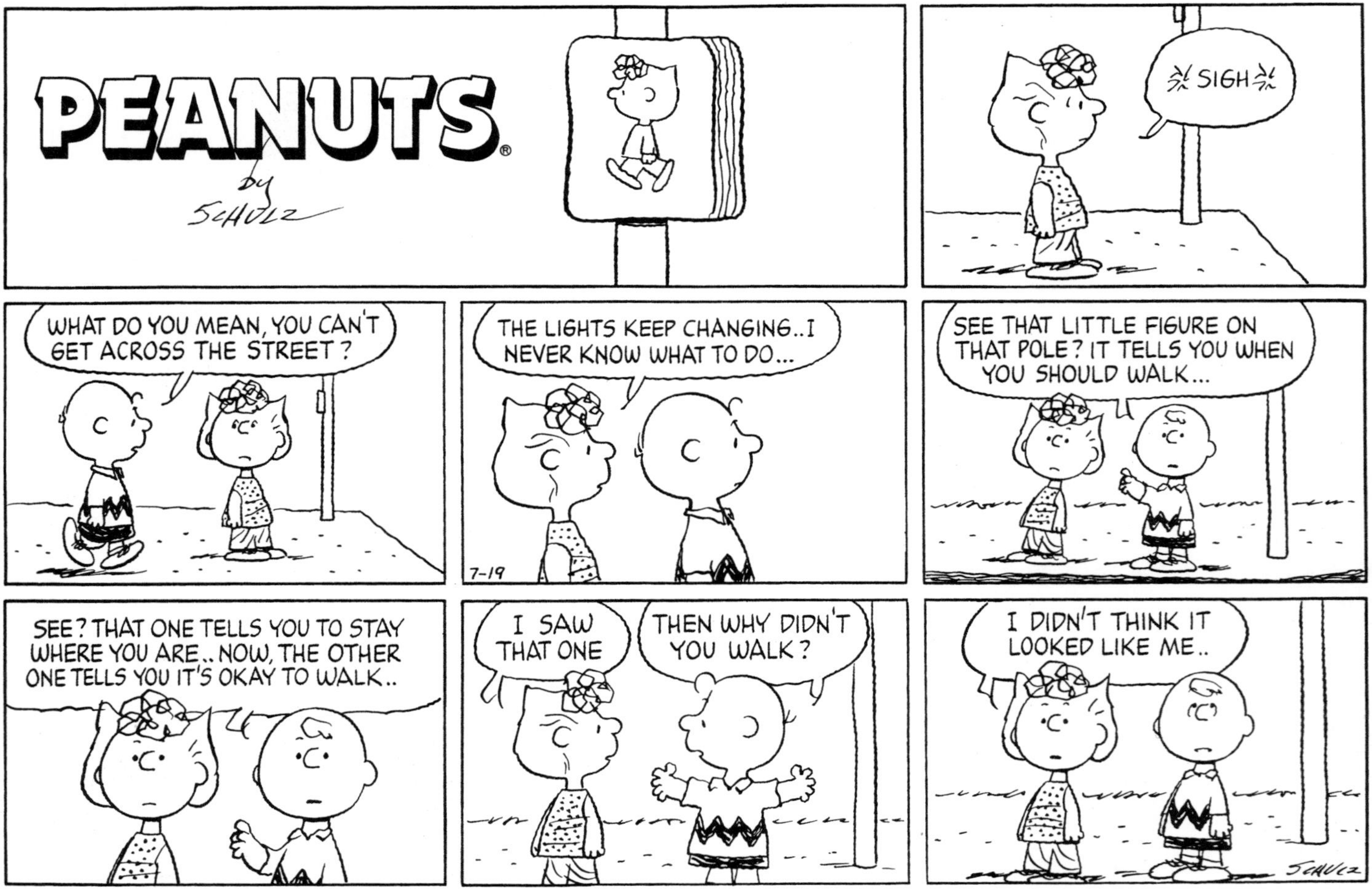
PEANUTS®
by SCHULZ
SIGH
WHAT DO YOU MEAN, YOU CAN'T GET ACROSS THE STREET?
THE LIGHTS KEEP CHANGING.. I NEVER KNOW WHAT TO DO...
7-19
SEE THAT LITTLE FIGURE ON THAT POLE? IT TELLS YOU WHEN YOU SHOULD WALK...
SEE? THAT ONE TELLS YOU TO STAY WHERE YOU ARE.. NOW, THE OTHER ONE TELLS YOU IT'S OKAY TO WALK..
I SAW THAT ONE
THEN WHY DIDN'T YOU WALK?
I DIDN'T THINK IT LOOKED LIKE ME..
SCHULZ

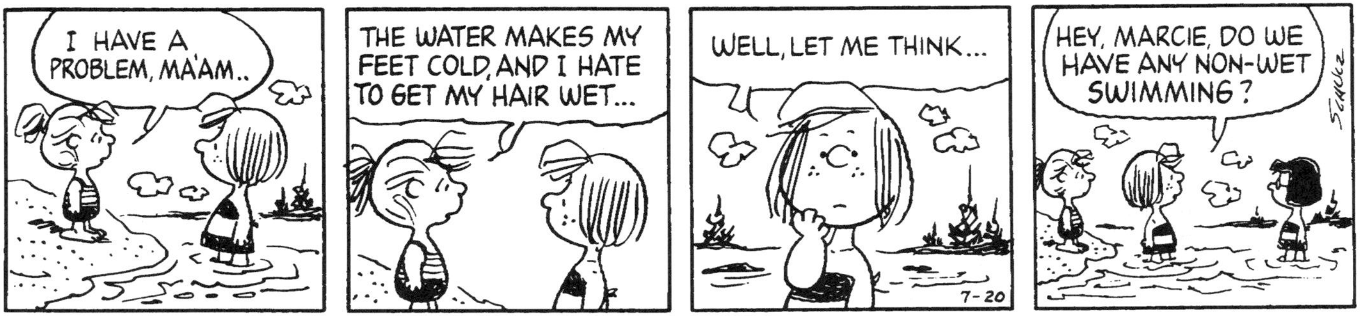
I HAVE A PROBLEM, MA'AM..
THE WATER MAKES MY FEET COLD, AND I HATE TO GET MY HAIR WET...
WELL, LET ME THINK...
7-20
HEY, MARCIE, DO WE HAVE ANY NON-WET SWIMMING?

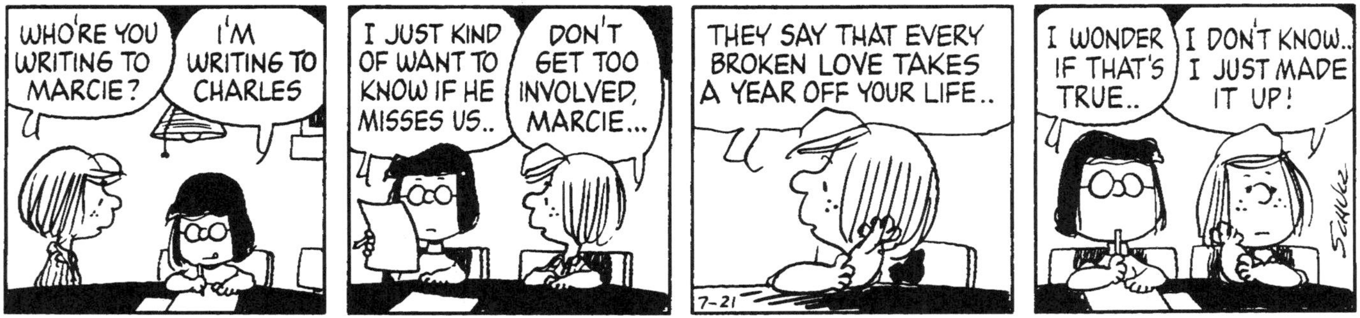
WHO'RE YOU WRITING TO MARCIE?
I'M WRITING TO CHARLES
I JUST KIND OF WANT TO KNOW IF HE MISSES US..
DON'T GET TOO INVOLVED, MARCIE...
THEY SAY THAT EVERY BROKEN LOVE TAKES A YEAR OFF YOUR LIFE..
7-21
I WONDER IF THAT'S TRUE..
I DON'T KNOW.. I JUST MADE IT UP!

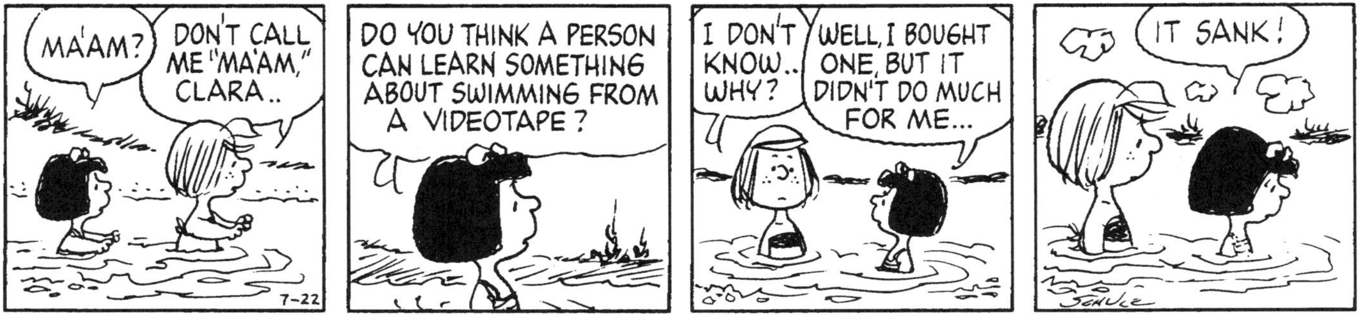
MA'AM?
DON'T CALL ME "MA'AM," CLARA..
7-22
DO YOU THINK A PERSON CAN LEARN SOMETHING ABOUT SWIMMING FROM A VIDEOTAPE?
I DON'T KNOW.. WHY?
WELL, I BOUGHT ONE, BUT IT DIDN'T DO MUCH FOR ME...
IT SANK!

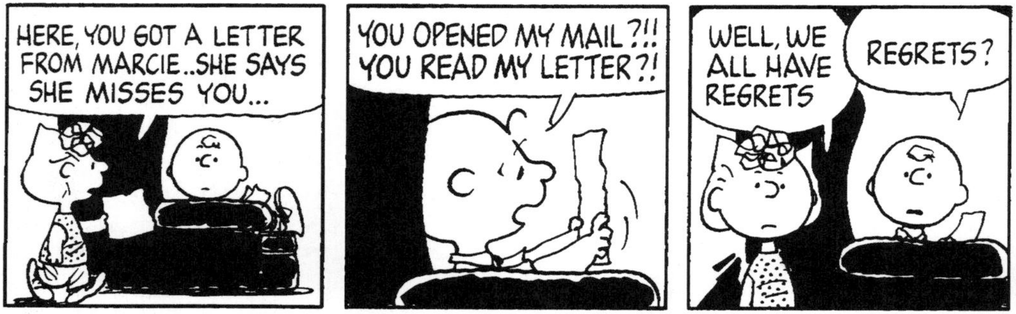
HERE, YOU GOT A LETTER FROM MARCIE..SHE SAYS SHE MISSES YOU...
YOU OPENED MY MAIL?!! YOU READ MY LETTER?!
WELL, WE ALL HAVE REGRETS
REGRETS?
I KNEW IF I DIDN'T READ IT, I'D REGRET IT FOR THE REST OF MY LIFE..
7-23

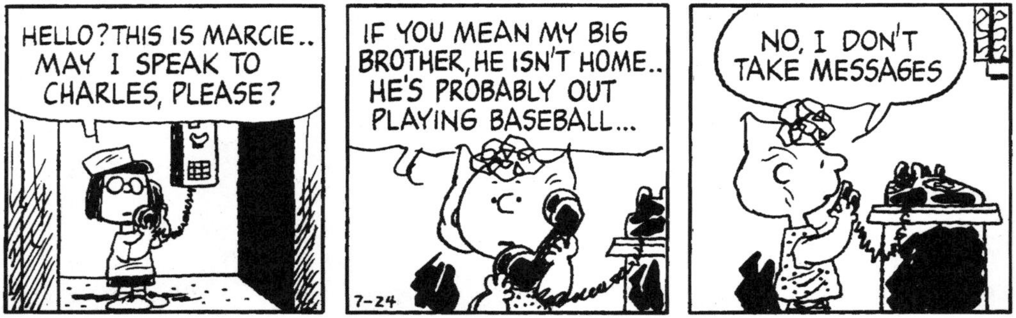
HELLO? THIS IS MARCIE.. MAY I SPEAK TO CHARLES, PLEASE?
IF YOU MEAN MY BIG BROTHER, HE ISN'T HOME.. HE'S PROBABLY OUT PLAYING BASEBALL...
7-24
NO, I DON'T TAKE MESSAGES
I HAVE BETTER THINGS TO DO..

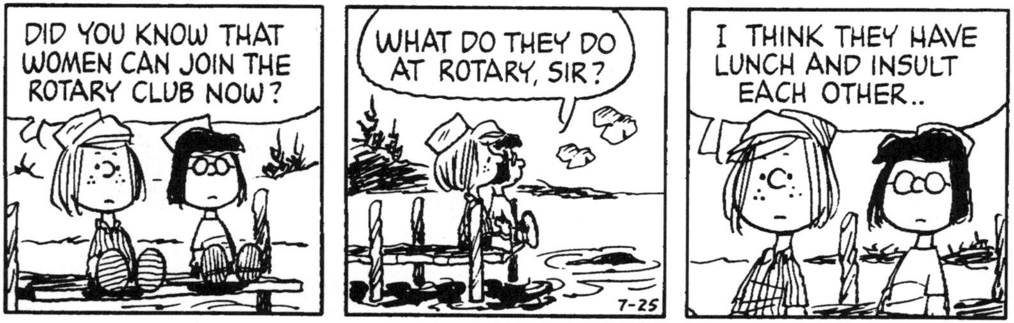
DID YOU KNOW THAT WOMEN CAN JOIN THE ROTARY CLUB NOW?
WHAT DO THEY DO AT ROTARY, SIR?
7-25
I THINK THEY HAVE LUNCH AND INSULT EACH OTHER..
WE'D FIT RIGHT IN, WOULDN'T WE, SIR?

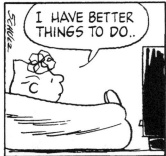

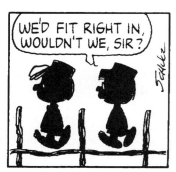

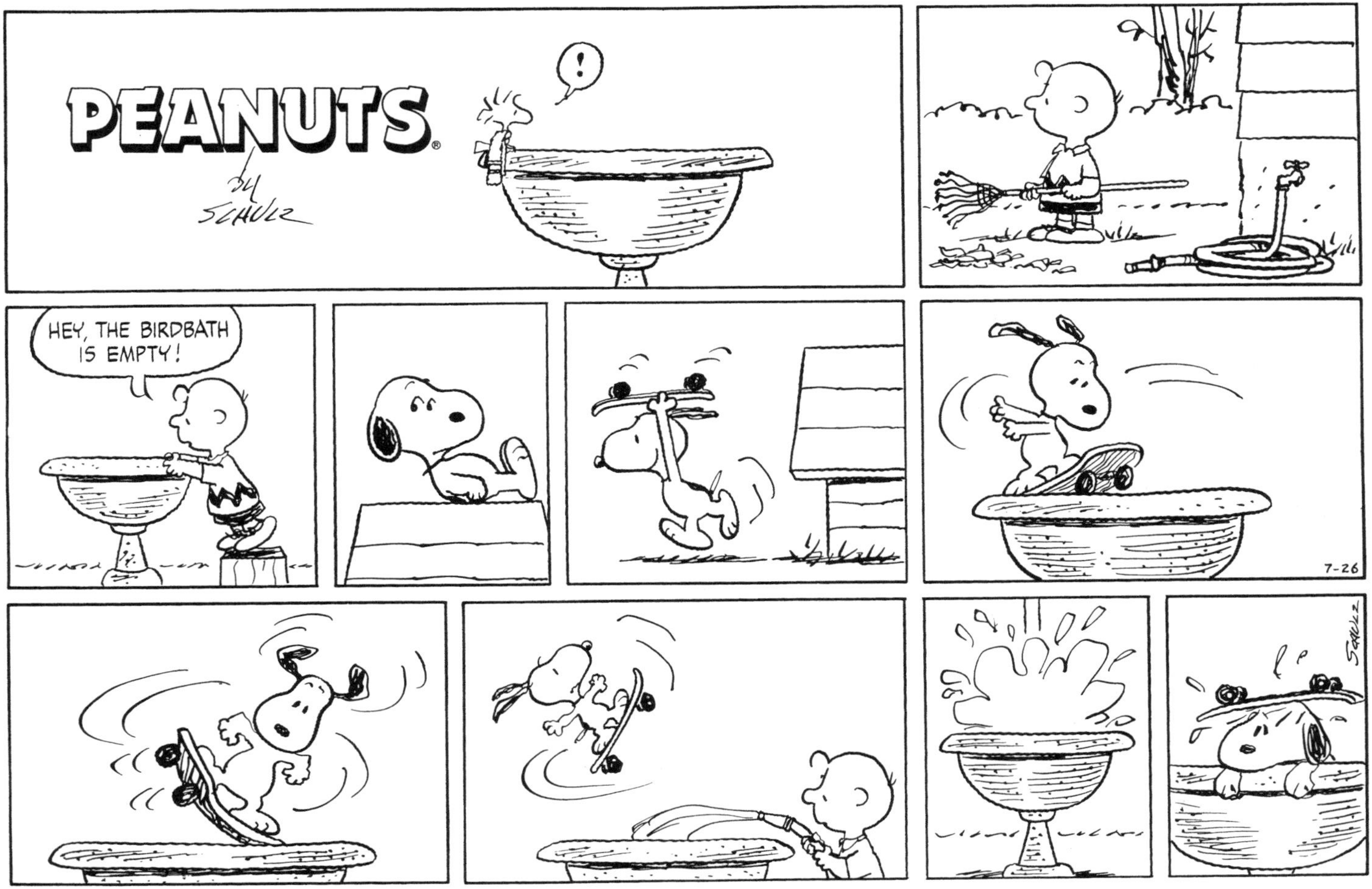
PEANUTS
!
HEY, THE BIRDBATH IS EMPTY!
7-26

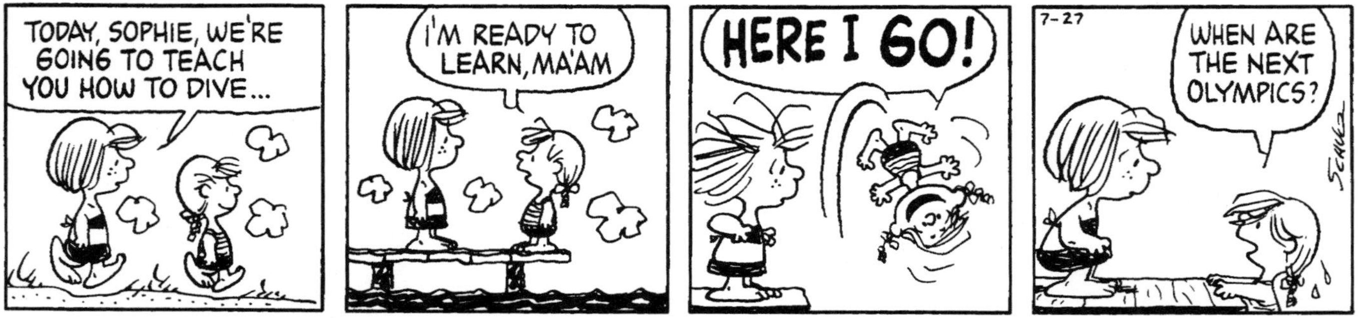
TODAY, SOPHIE, WE'RE GOING TO TEACH YOU HOW TO DIVE...
I'M READY TO LEARN, MA'AM
HERE I GO!
7-27
WHEN ARE THE NEXT OLYMPICS?

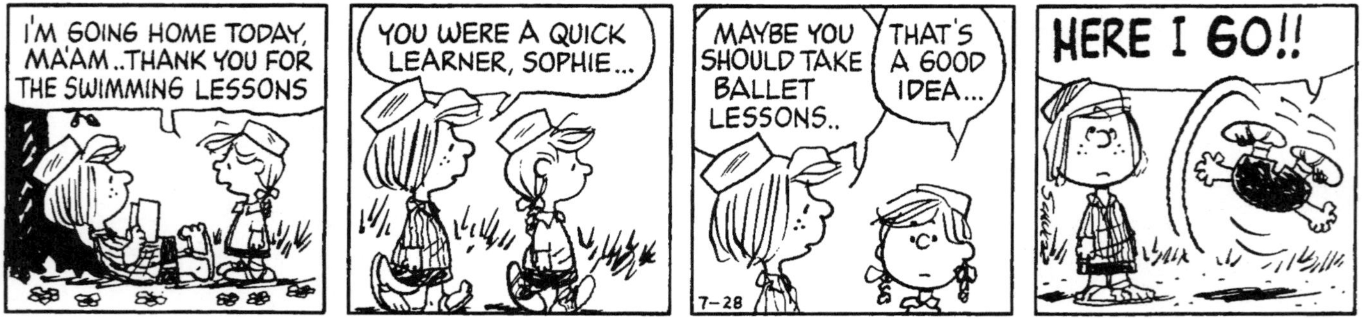
I'M GOING HOME TODAY, MA'AM..THANK YOU FOR THE SWIMMING LESSONS
YOU WERE A QUICK LEARNER, SOPHIE...
MAYBE YOU SHOULD TAKE BALLET LESSONS..
THAT'S A GOOD IDEA...
7-28
HERE I GO!!

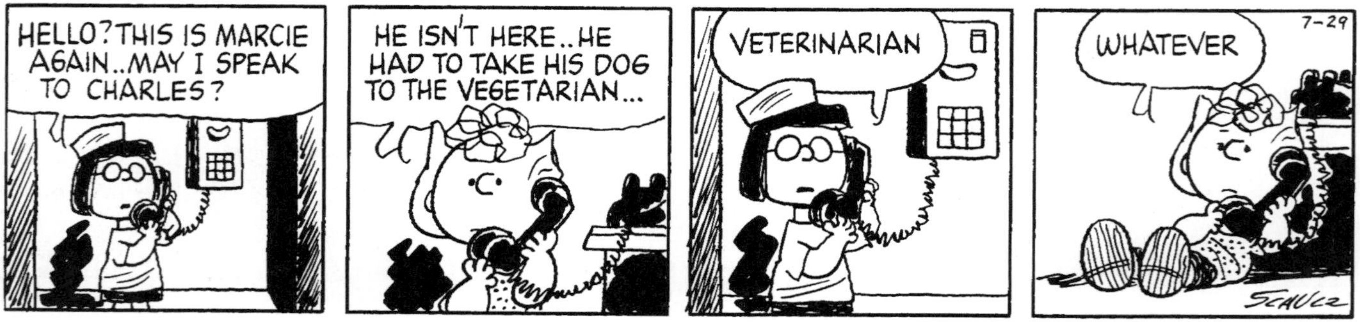
HELLO? THIS IS MARCIE AGAIN..MAY I SPEAK TO CHARLES?
HE ISN'T HERE..HE HAD TO TAKE HIS DOG TO THE VEGETARIAN...
VETERINARIAN
WHATEVER
7-29

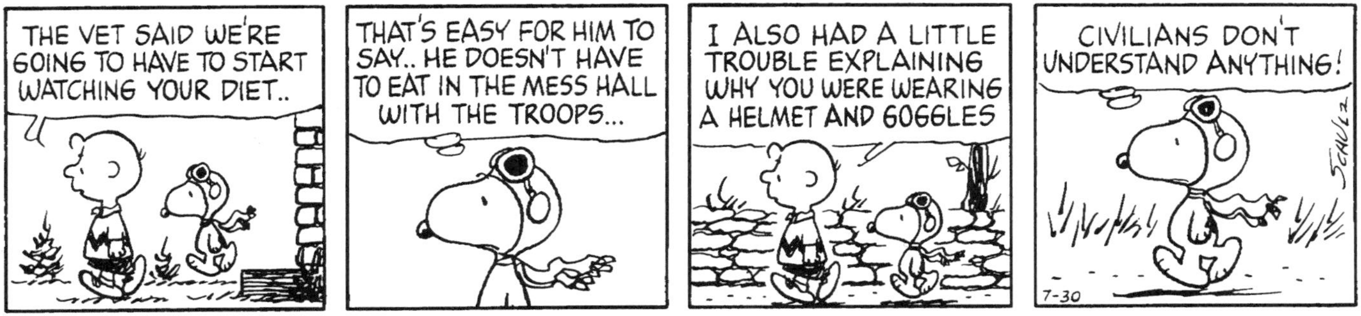
THE VET SAID WE'RE GOING TO HAVE TO START WATCHING YOUR DIET..
THAT'S EASY FOR HIM TO SAY.. HE DOESN'T HAVE TO EAT IN THE MESS HALL WITH THE TROOPS...
I ALSO HAD A LITTLE TROUBLE EXPLAINING WHY YOU WERE WEARING A HELMET AND GOGGLES
CIVILIANS DON'T UNDERSTAND ANYTHING!
SCHULZ
7-30

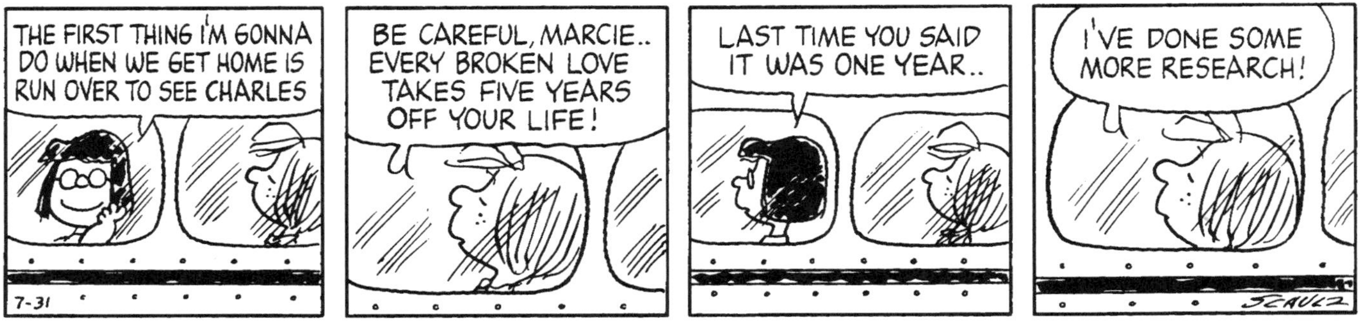
THE FIRST THING I'M GONNA DO WHEN WE GET HOME IS RUN OVER TO SEE CHARLES
7-31
BE CAREFUL, MARCIE.. EVERY BROKEN LOVE TAKES FIVE YEARS OFF YOUR LIFE!
LAST TIME YOU SAID IT WAS ONE YEAR..
I'VE DONE SOME MORE RESEARCH!
SCHULZ

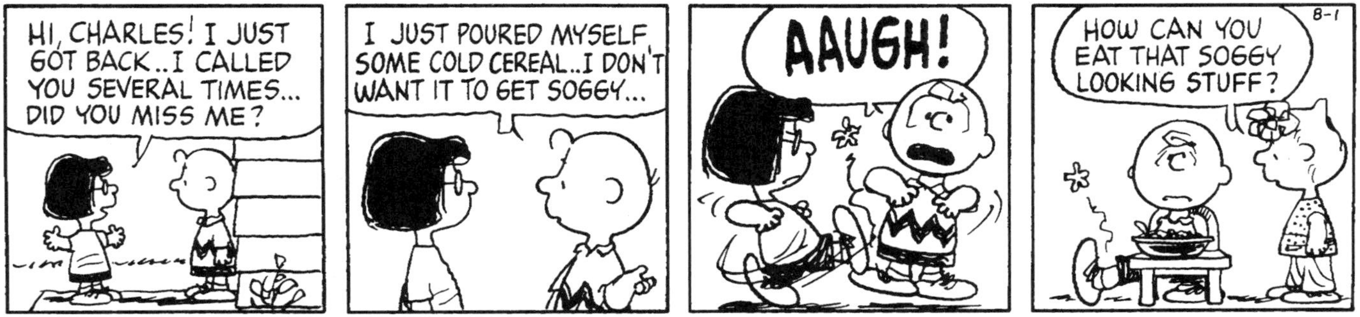
HI, CHARLES! I JUST GOT BACK..I CALLED YOU SEVERAL TIMES... DID YOU MISS ME?
I JUST POURED MYSELF SOME COLD CEREAL..I DON'T WANT IT TO GET SOGGY...
AAUGH!
8-1
HOW CAN YOU EAT THAT SOGGY LOOKING STUFF?

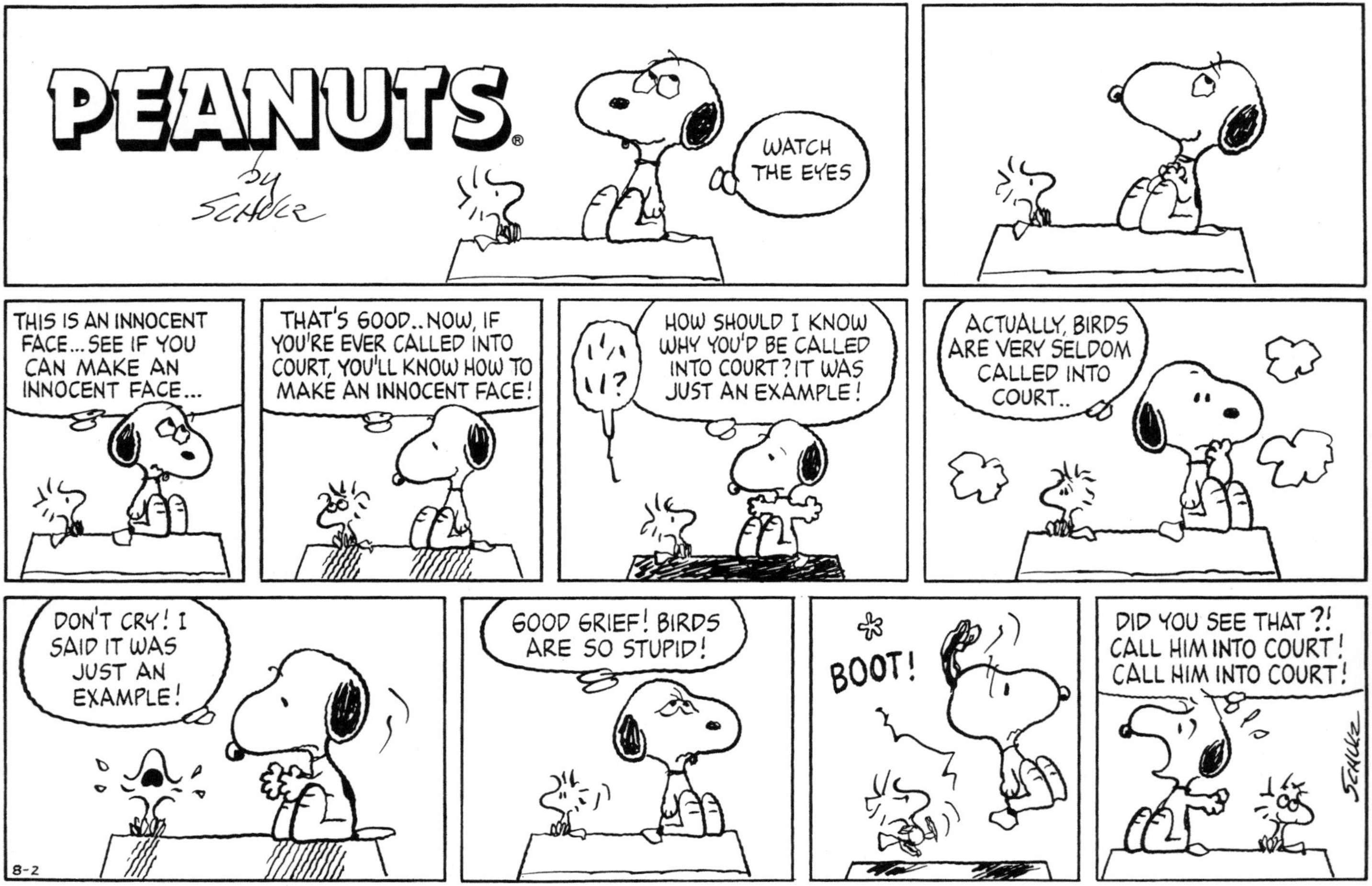
PEANUTS
by SCHULZ
WATCH THE EYES
THIS IS AN INNOCENT FACE... SEE IF YOU CAN MAKE AN INNOCENT FACE...
THAT'S GOOD..NOW, IF YOU'RE EVER CALLED INTO COURT, YOU'LL KNOW HOW TO MAKE AN INNOCENT FACE!
?
HOW SHOULD I KNOW WHY YOU'D BE CALLED INTO COURT? IT WAS JUST AN EXAMPLE!
ACTUALLY, BIRDS ARE VERY SELDOM CALLED INTO COURT..
DON'T CRY! I SAID IT WAS JUST AN EXAMPLE!
8-2
GOOD GRIEF! BIRDS ARE SO STUPID!
BOOT!
DID YOU SEE THAT?! CALL HIM INTO COURT! CALL HIM INTO COURT!
SCHULZ

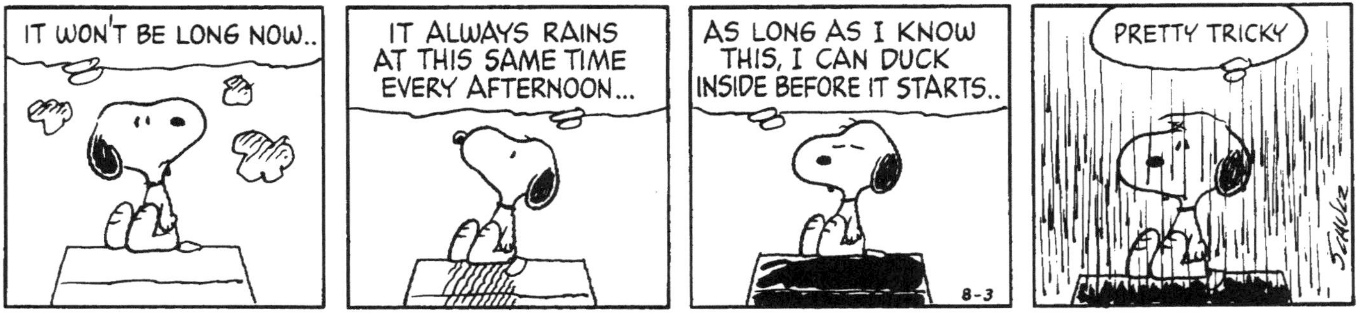
IT WON'T BE LONG NOW..
IT ALWAYS RAINS AT THIS SAME TIME EVERY AFTERNOON...
AS LONG AS I KNOW THIS, I CAN DUCK INSIDE BEFORE IT STARTS..
8-3
PRETTY TRICKY
SCHULZ

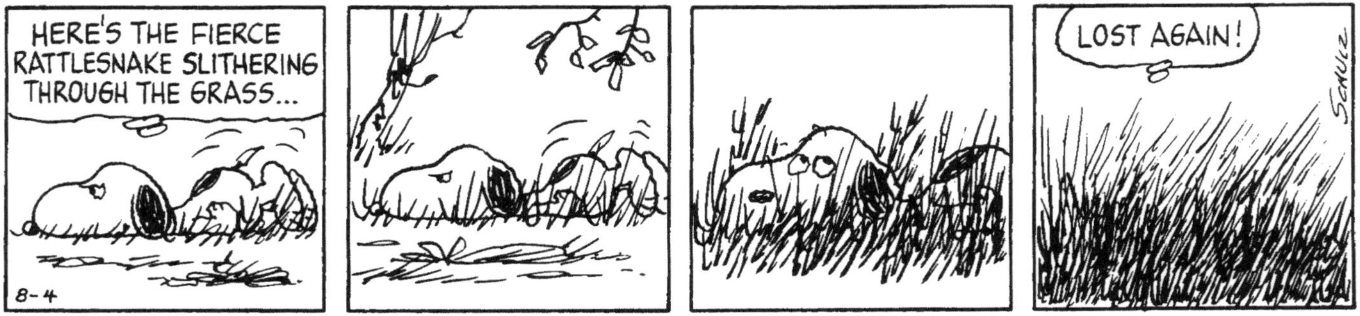
HERE'S THE FIERCE RATTLESNAKE SLITHERING THROUGH THE GRASS...
8-4
LOST AGAIN!
SCHULZ

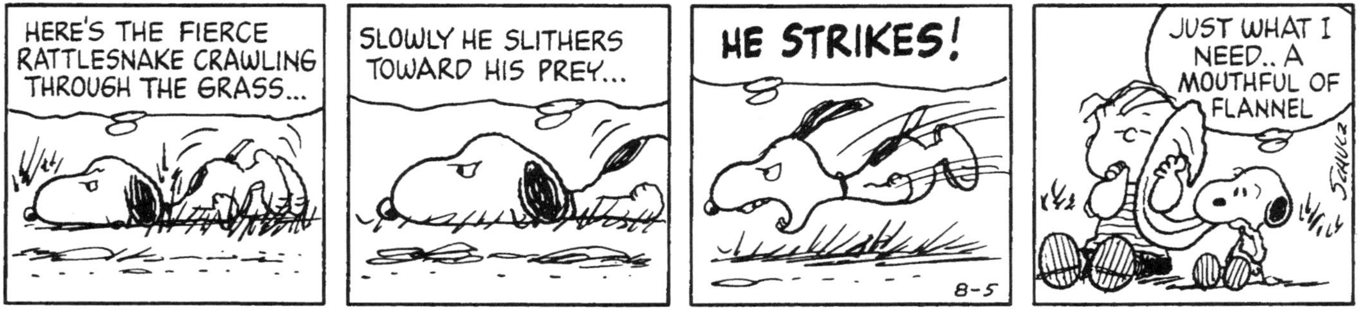
HERE'S THE FIERCE RATTLESNAKE CRAWLING THROUGH THE GRASS...
SLOWLY HE SLITHERS TOWARD HIS PREY...
HE STRIKES!
8-5
JUST WHAT I NEED.. A MOUTHFUL OF FLANNEL
SCHULZ

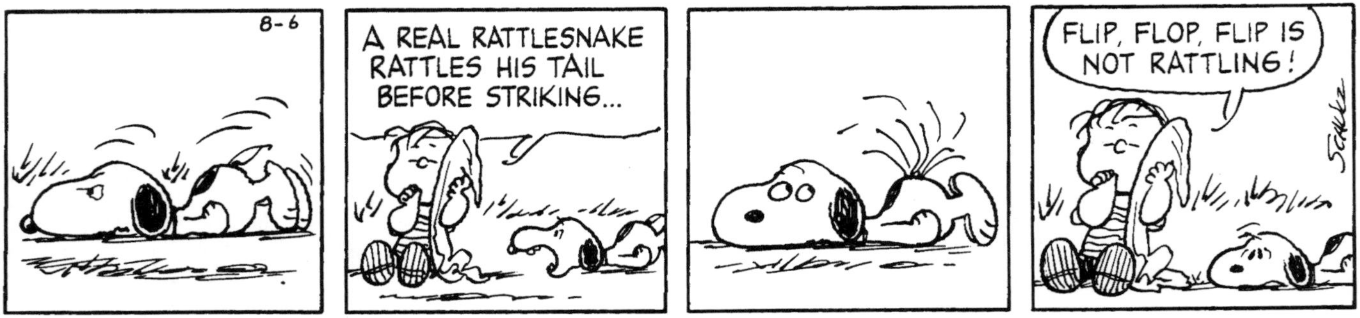
8-6
A REAL RATTLESNAKE RATTLES HIS TAIL BEFORE STRIKING...
FLIP, FLOP, FLIP IS NOT RATTLING!

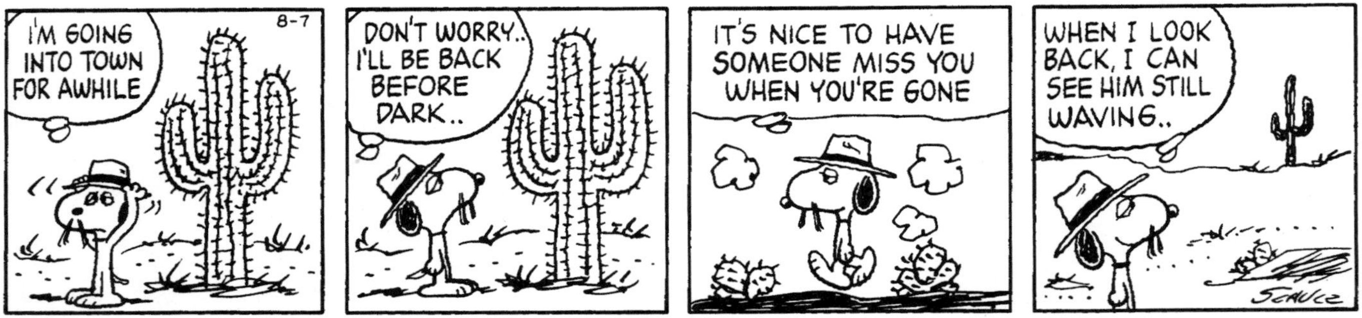
8-7
I'M GOING INTO TOWN FOR AWHILE
DON'T WORRY.. I'LL BE BACK BEFORE DARK..
IT'S NICE TO HAVE SOMEONE MISS YOU WHEN YOU'RE GONE
WHEN I LOOK BACK, I CAN SEE HIM STILL WAVING..

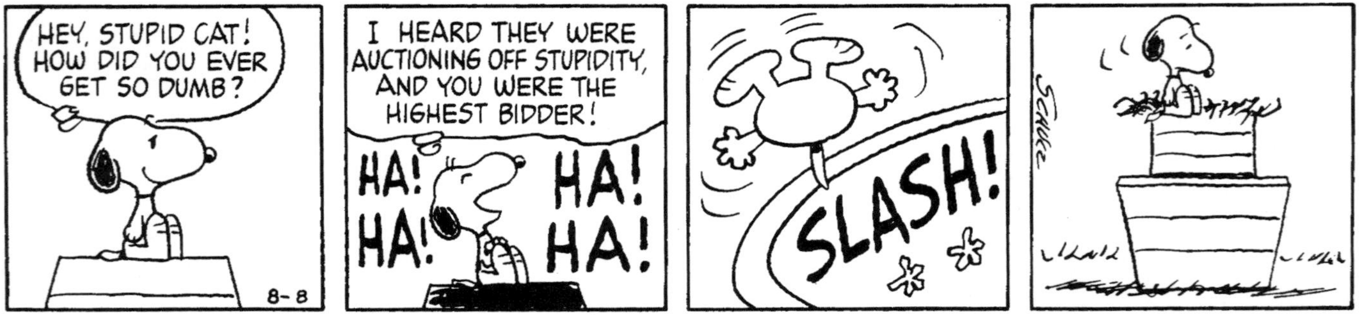
HEY, STUPID CAT! HOW DID YOU EVER GET SO DUMB?
8-8
I HEARD THEY WERE AUCTIONING OFF STUPIDITY, AND YOU WERE THE HIGHEST BIDDER!
HA! HA! HA! HA!
SLASH!

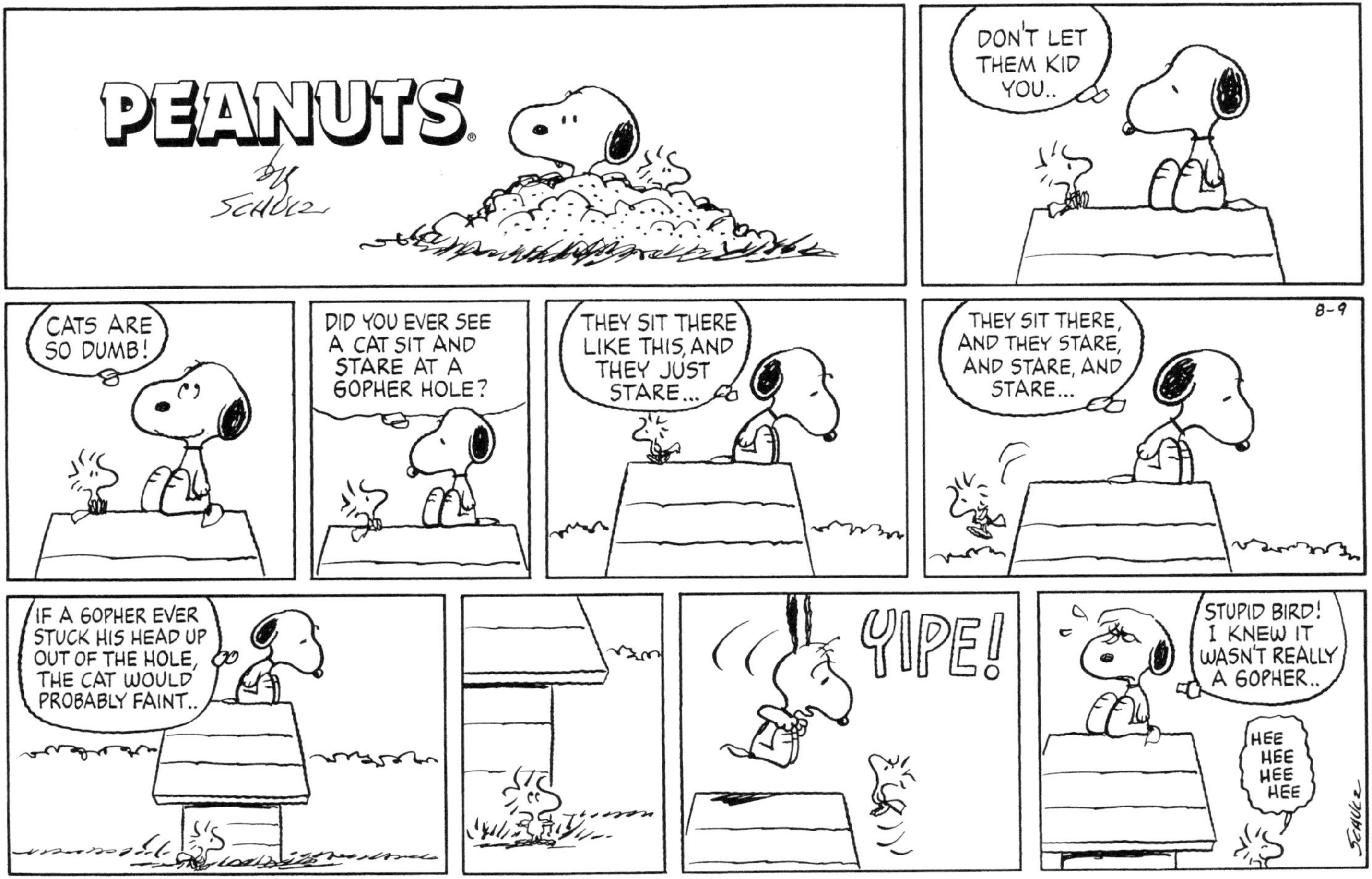
PEANUTS
SCHULZ
DON'T LET THEM KID YOU..
CATS ARE SO DUMB!
DID YOU EVER SEE A CAT SIT AND STARE AT A GOPHER HOLE?
THEY SIT THERE LIKE THIS, AND THEY JUST STARE...
THEY SIT THERE, AND THEY STARE, AND STARE, AND STARE...
8-9
IF A GOPHER EVER STUCK HIS HEAD UP OUT OF THE HOLE, THE CAT WOULD PROBABLY FAINT..
YIPE!
STUPID BIRD! I KNEW IT WASN'T REALLY A GOPHER..
HEE HEE HEE HEE
SCHULZ

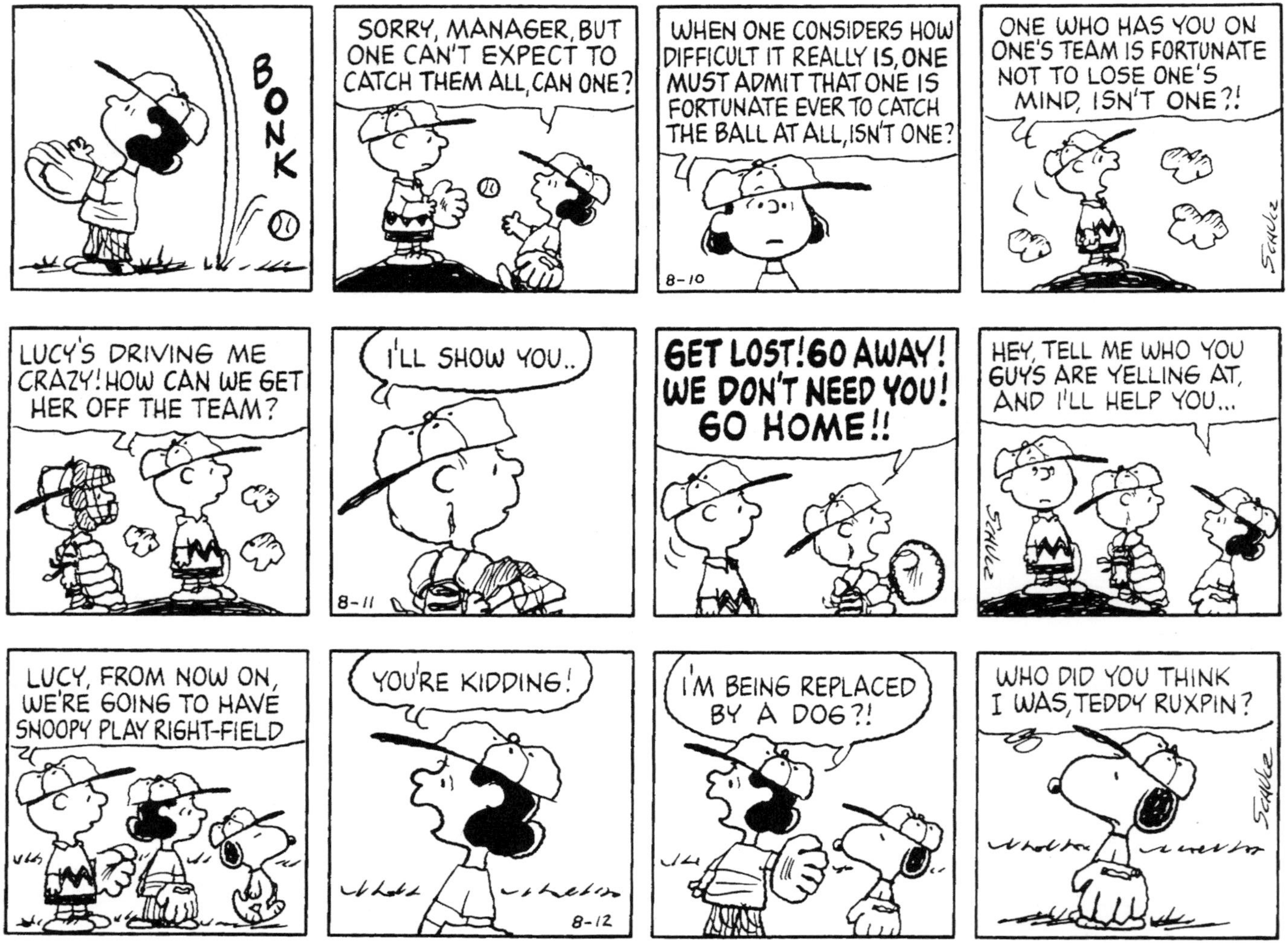
BONK
SORRY, MANAGER, BUT ONE CAN'T EXPECT TO CATCH THEM ALL, CAN ONE?
WHEN ONE CONSIDERS HOW DIFFICULT IT REALLY IS, ONE MUST ADMIT THAT ONE IS FORTUNATE EVER TO CATCH THE BALL AT ALL, ISN'T ONE?
8-10
ONE WHO HAS YOU ON ONE'S TEAM IS FORTUNATE NOT TO LOSE ONE'S MIND, ISN'T ONE?!
SCHULZ
LUCY'S DRIVING ME CRAZY! HOW CAN WE GET HER OFF THE TEAM?
I'LL SHOW YOU..
8-11
GET LOST! GO AWAY! WE DON'T NEED YOU! GO HOME!!
HEY, TELL ME WHO YOU GUYS ARE YELLING AT, AND I'LL HELP YOU...
SCHULZ
LUCY, FROM NOW ON, WE'RE GOING TO HAVE SNOOPY PLAY RIGHT-FIELD
YOU'RE KIDDING!
8-12
I'M BEING REPLACED BY A DOG?!
WHO DID YOU THINK I WAS, TEDDY RUXPIN?
SCHULZ

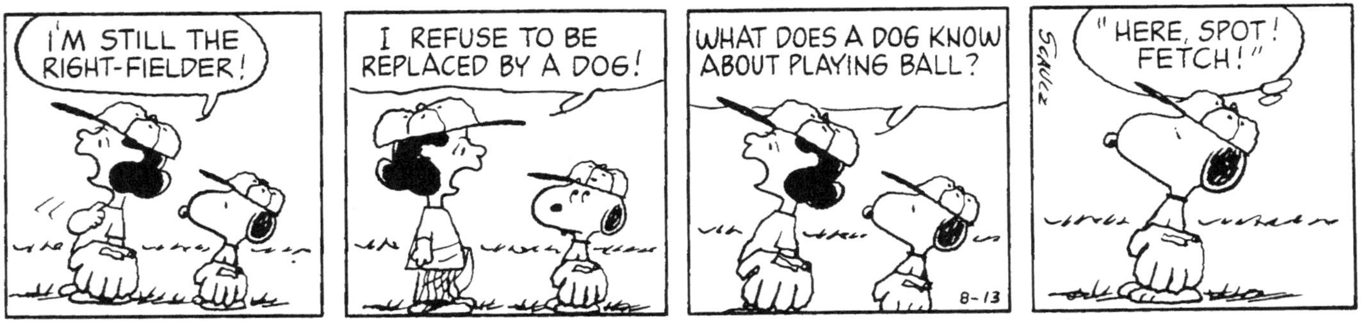
I'M STILL THE RIGHT-FIELDER!
I REFUSE TO BE REPLACED BY A DOG!
WHAT DOES A DOG KNOW ABOUT PLAYING BALL?
8-13
SCHULZ
"HERE, SPOT! FETCH!"

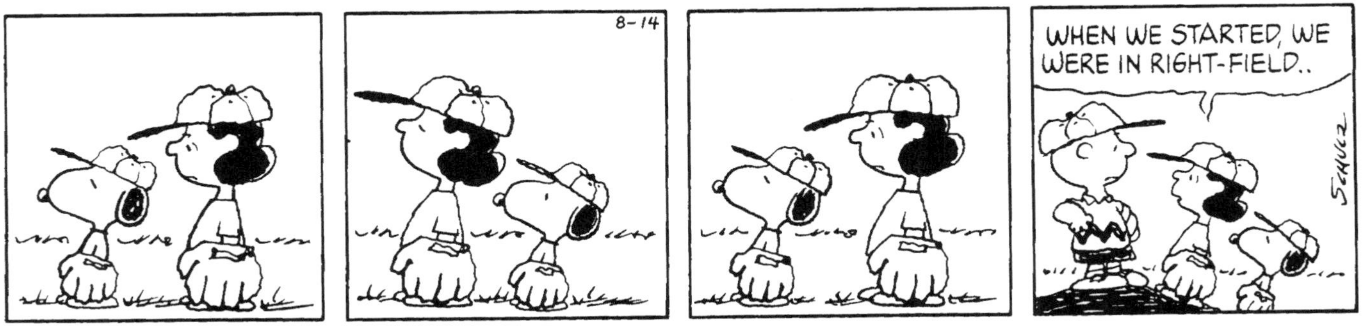
8-14
WHEN WE STARTED, WE WERE IN RIGHT-FIELD..
SCHULZ

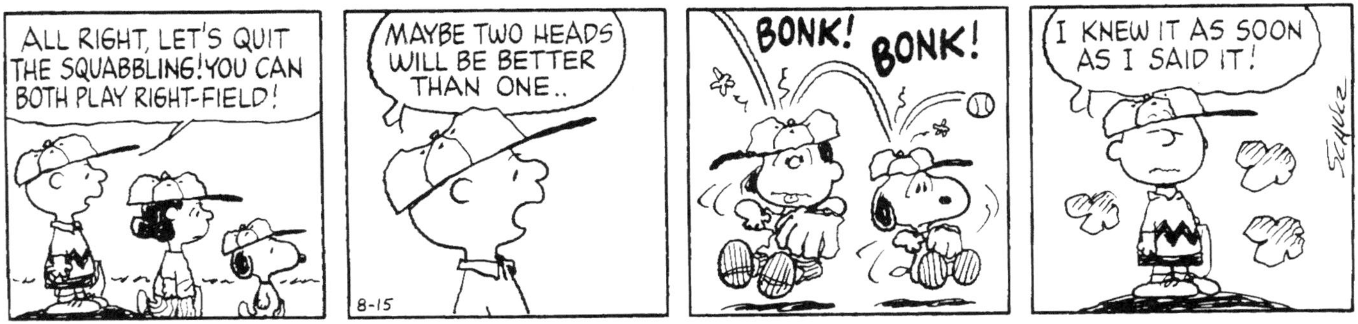
ALL RIGHT, LET'S QUIT THE SQUABBLING! YOU CAN BOTH PLAY RIGHT-FIELD!
MAYBE TWO HEADS WILL BE BETTER THAN ONE..
8-15
BONK!
BONK!
I KNEW IT AS SOON AS I SAID IT!
SCHULZ

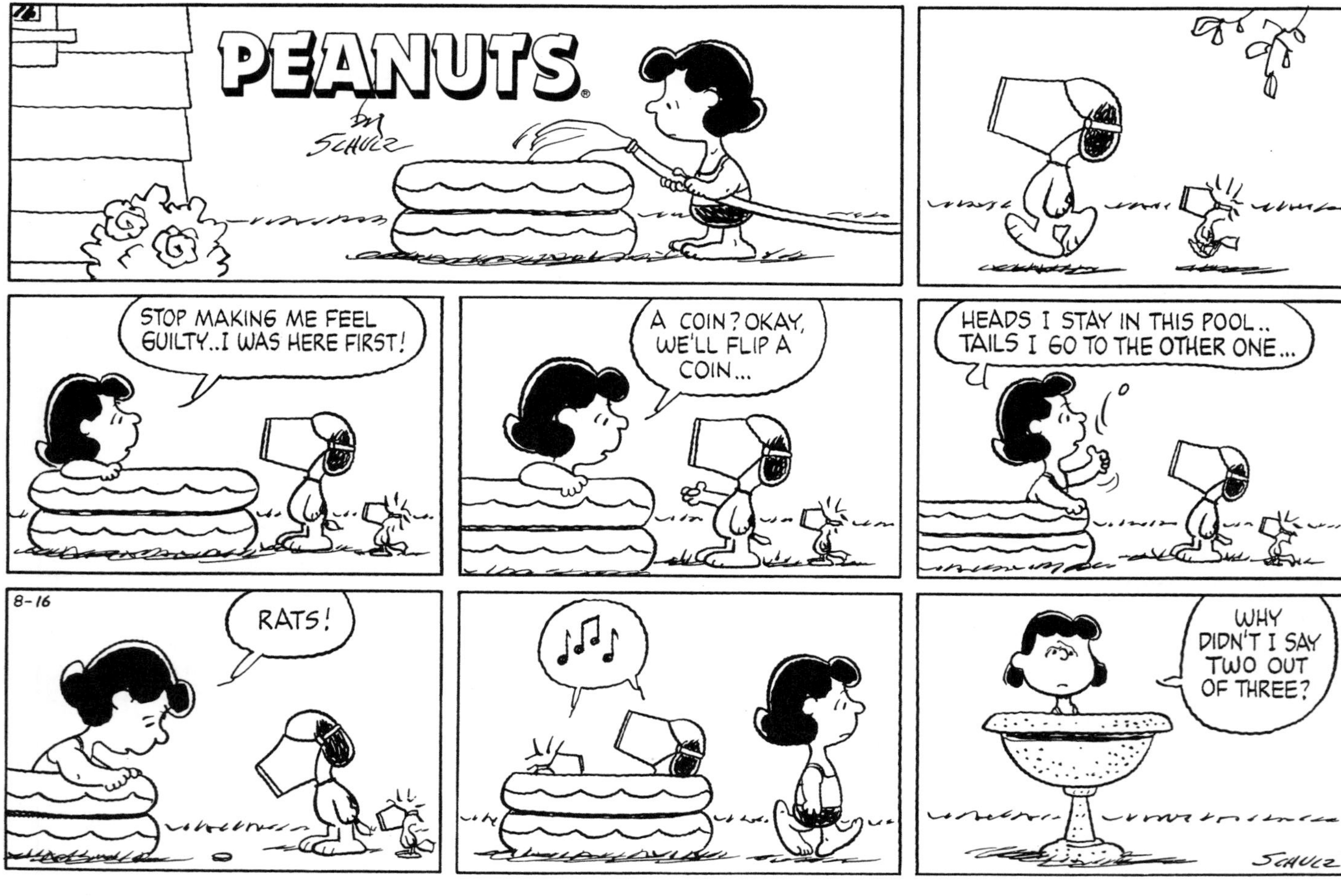
PEANUTS
by SCHULZ
STOP MAKING ME FEEL GUILTY..I WAS HERE FIRST!
A COIN? OKAY, WE'LL FLIP A COIN...
HEADS I STAY IN THIS POOL.. TAILS I GO TO THE OTHER ONE...
8-16
RATS!
WHY DIDN'T I SAY TWO OUT OF THREE?
SCHULZ

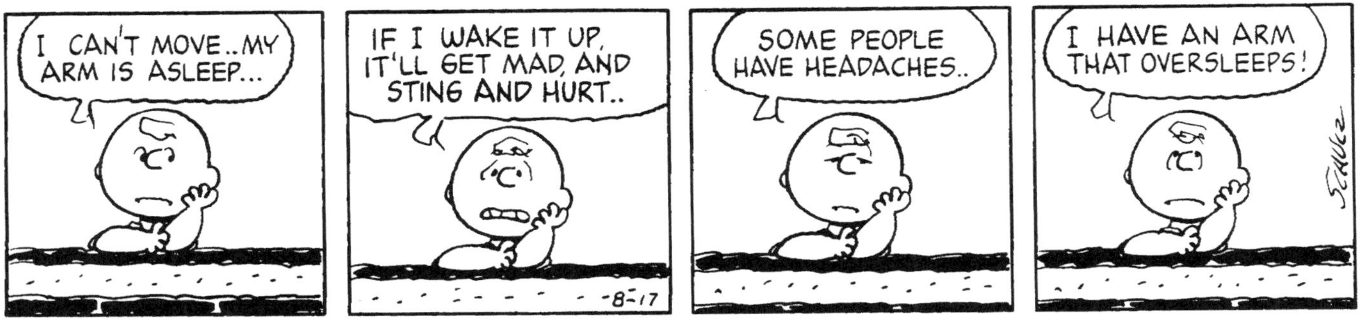
I CAN'T MOVE..MY ARM IS ASLEEP...
IF I WAKE IT UP, IT'LL GET MAD, AND STING AND HURT..
8-17
SOME PEOPLE HAVE HEADACHES..
I HAVE AN ARM THAT OVERSLEEPS!
SCHULZ

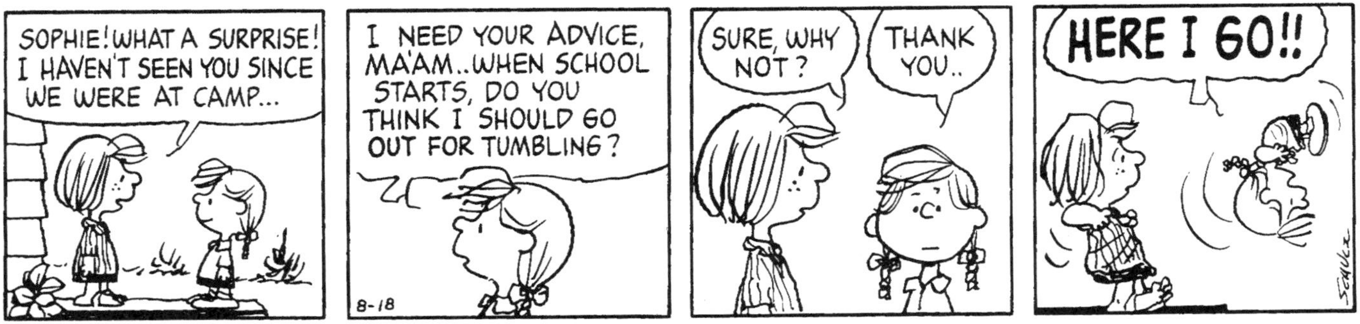
SOPHIE! WHAT A SURPRISE! I HAVEN'T SEEN YOU SINCE WE WERE AT CAMP...
I NEED YOUR ADVICE, MA'AM..WHEN SCHOOL STARTS, DO YOU THINK I SHOULD GO OUT FOR TUMBLING?
8-18
SURE, WHY NOT?
THANK YOU..
HERE I GO!!
SCHULZ

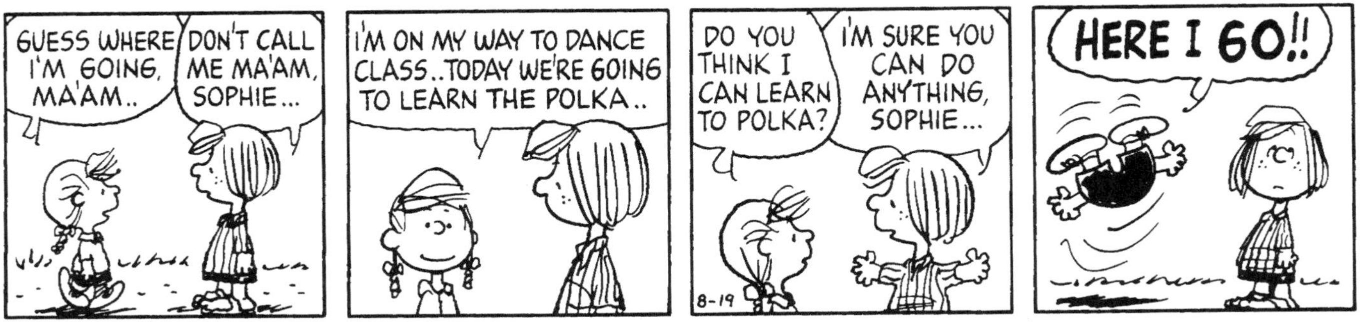
GUESS WHERE I'M GOING, MA'AM..
DON'T CALL ME MA'AM, SOPHIE...
I'M ON MY WAY TO DANCE CLASS..TODAY WE'RE GOING TO LEARN THE POLKA..
DO YOU THINK I CAN LEARN TO POLKA?
I'M SURE YOU CAN DO ANYTHING, SOPHIE...
8-19
HERE I GO!!

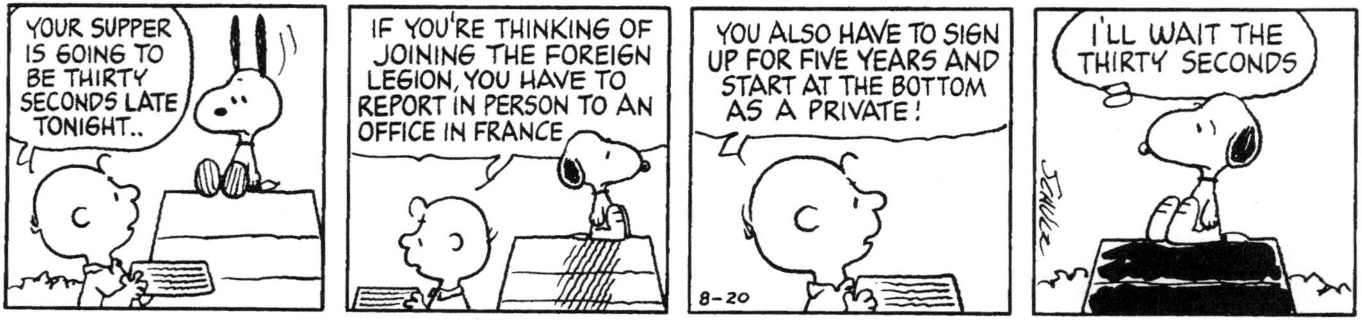
YOUR SUPPER IS GOING TO BE THIRTY SECONDS LATE TONIGHT..
IF YOU'RE THINKING OF JOINING THE FOREIGN LEGION, YOU HAVE TO REPORT IN PERSON TO AN OFFICE IN FRANCE
YOU ALSO HAVE TO SIGN UP FOR FIVE YEARS AND START AT THE BOTTOM AS A PRIVATE!
8-20
I'LL WAIT THE THIRTY SECONDS
SCHULZ

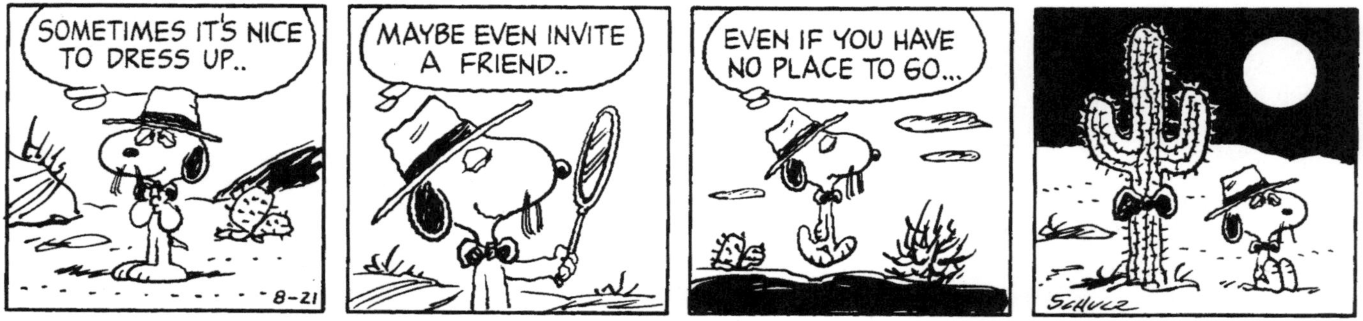
SOMETIMES IT'S NICE TO DRESS UP..
8-21
MAYBE EVEN INVITE A FRIEND..
EVEN IF YOU HAVE NO PLACE TO GO...
SCHULZ

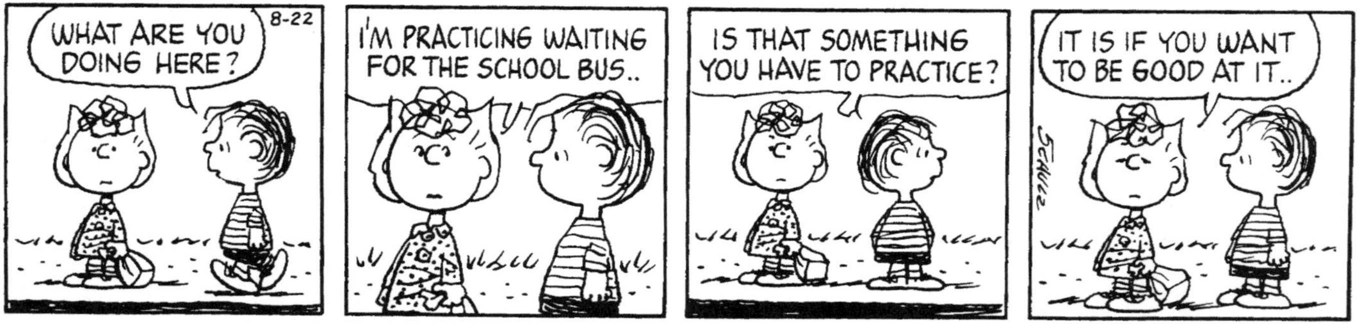
WHAT ARE YOU DOING HERE?
8-22
I'M PRACTICING WAITING FOR THE SCHOOL BUS..
IS THAT SOMETHING YOU HAVE TO PRACTICE?
IT IS IF YOU WANT TO BE GOOD AT IT..
SCHULZ

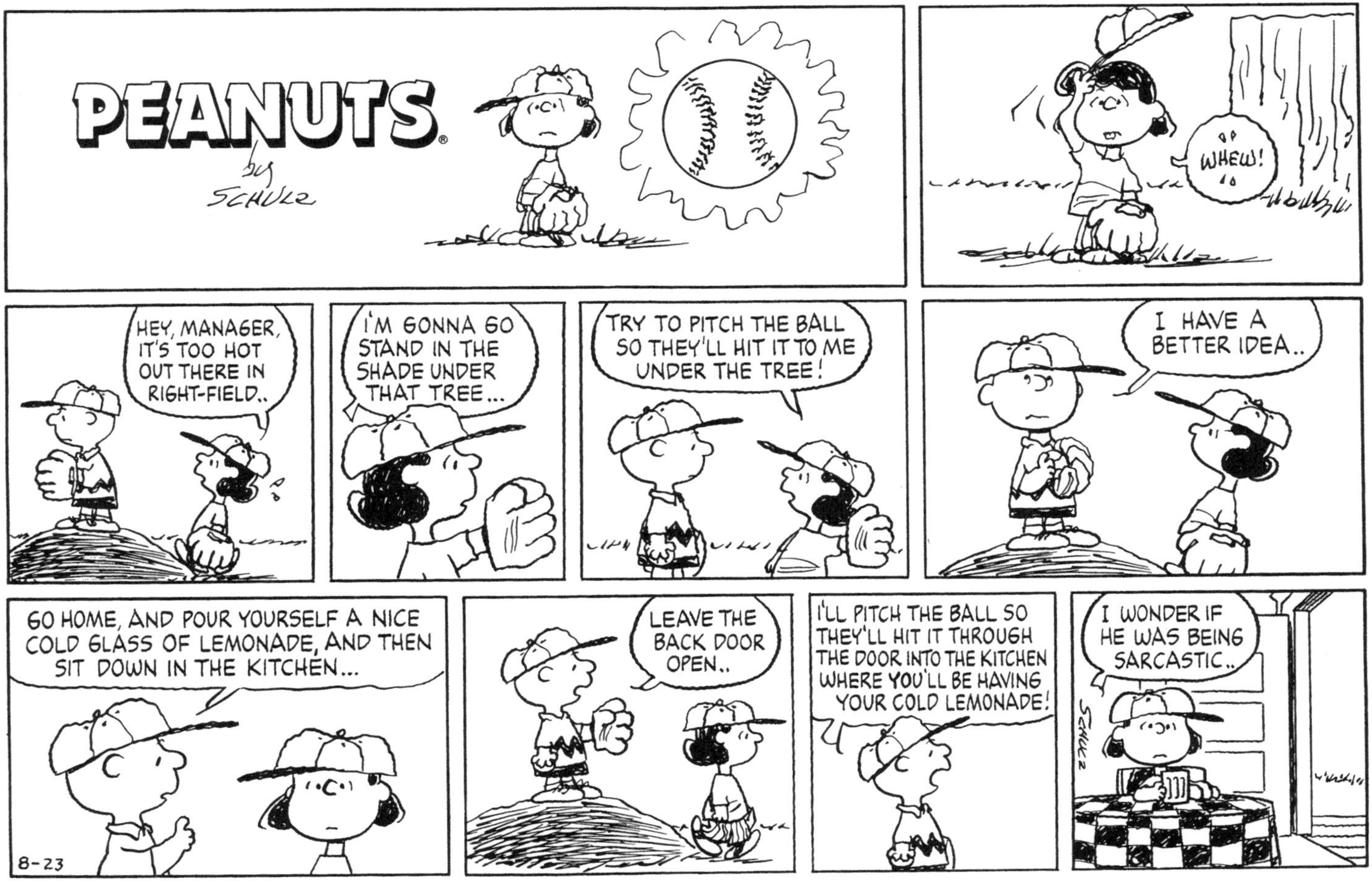
PEANUTS
by SCHULZ
WHEW!
HEY, MANAGER, IT'S TOO HOT OUT THERE IN RIGHT-FIELD..
I'M GONNA GO STAND IN THE SHADE UNDER THAT TREE...
TRY TO PITCH THE BALL SO THEY'LL HIT IT TO ME UNDER THE TREE!
I HAVE A BETTER IDEA..
GO HOME, AND POUR YOURSELF A NICE COLD GLASS OF LEMONADE, AND THEN SIT DOWN IN THE KITCHEN...
8-23
LEAVE THE BACK DOOR OPEN..
I'LL PITCH THE BALL SO THEY'LL HIT IT THROUGH THE DOOR INTO THE KITCHEN WHERE YOU'LL BE HAVING YOUR COLD LEMONADE!
SCHULZ
I WONDER IF HE WAS BEING SARCASTIC..

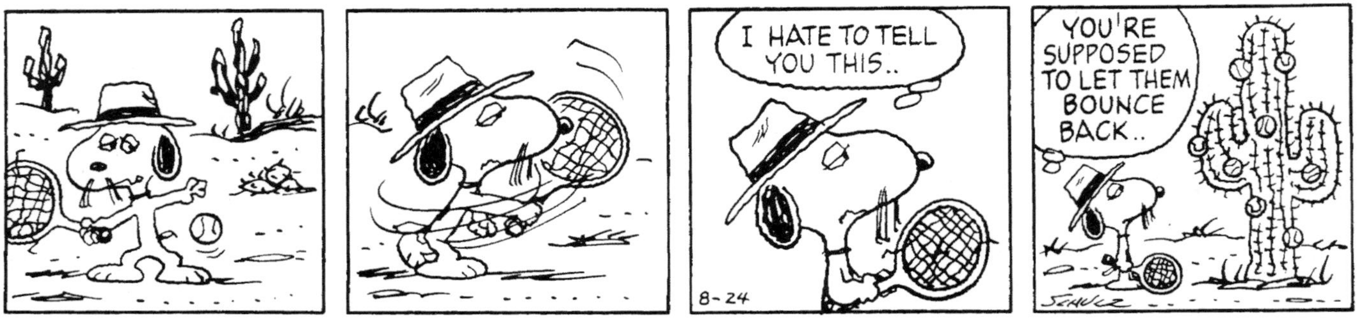
I HATE TO TELL YOU THIS..
YOU'RE SUPPOSED TO LET THEM BOUNCE BACK..
8-24
SCHULZ

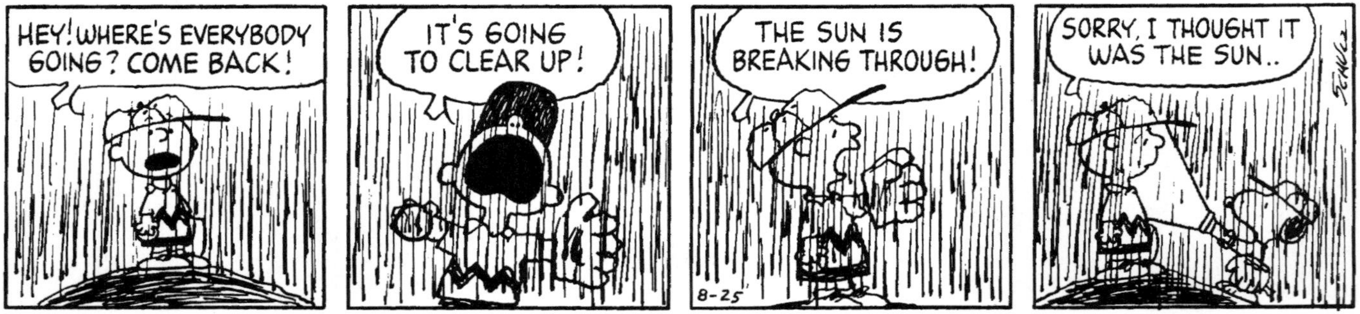
HEY! WHERE'S EVERYBODY GOING? COME BACK!
IT'S GOING TO CLEAR UP!
THE SUN IS BREAKING THROUGH!
SORRY, I THOUGHT IT WAS THE SUN..
8-25
SCHULZ

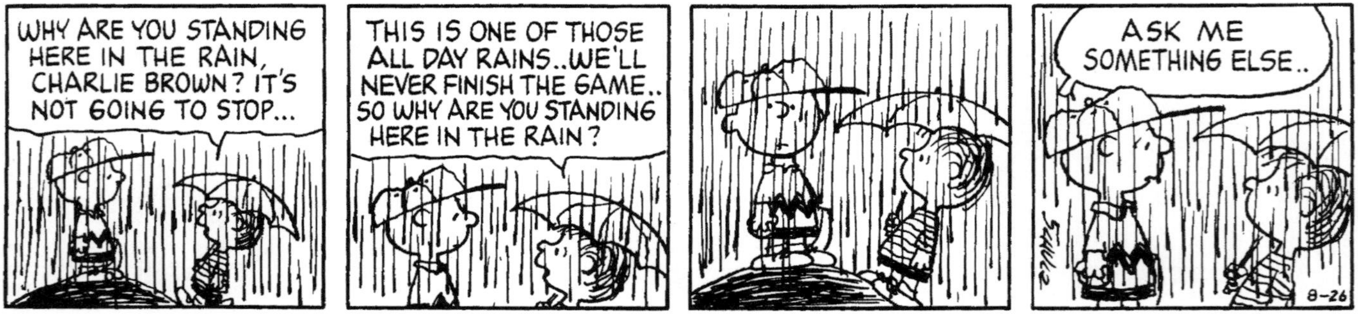
WHY ARE YOU STANDING HERE IN THE RAIN, CHARLIE BROWN? IT'S NOT GOING TO STOP...
THIS IS ONE OF THOSE ALL DAY RAINS..WE'LL NEVER FINISH THE GAME.. SO WHY ARE YOU STANDING HERE IN THE RAIN?
ASK ME SOMETHING ELSE..
SCHULZ
8-26

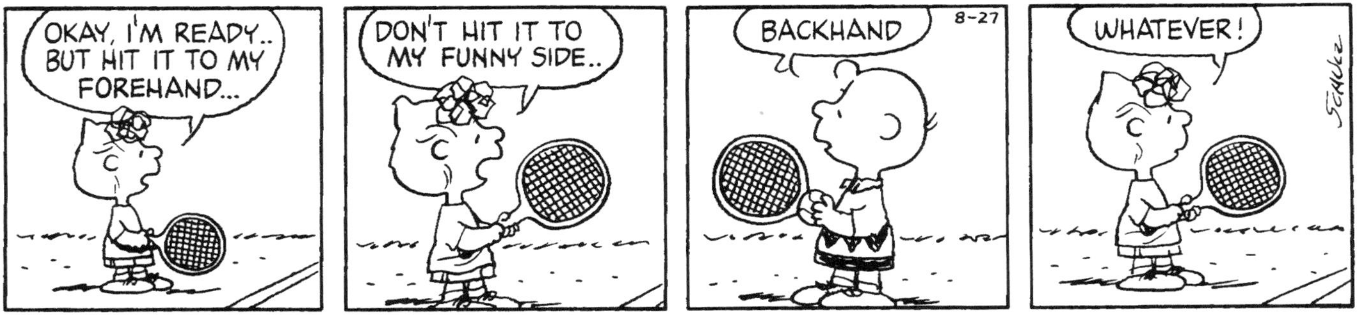
OKAY, I'M READY.. BUT HIT IT TO MY FOREHAND...
DON'T HIT IT TO MY FUNNY SIDE..
BACKHAND
8-27
WHATEVER!
SCHULZ

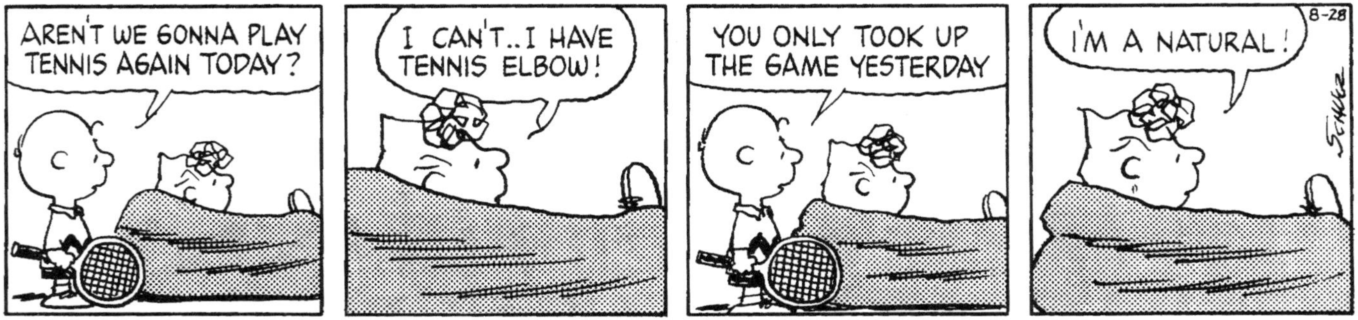
AREN'T WE GONNA PLAY TENNIS AGAIN TODAY?
I CAN'T..I HAVE TENNIS ELBOW!
YOU ONLY TOOK UP THE GAME YESTERDAY
8-28
I'M A NATURAL!
SCHULZ

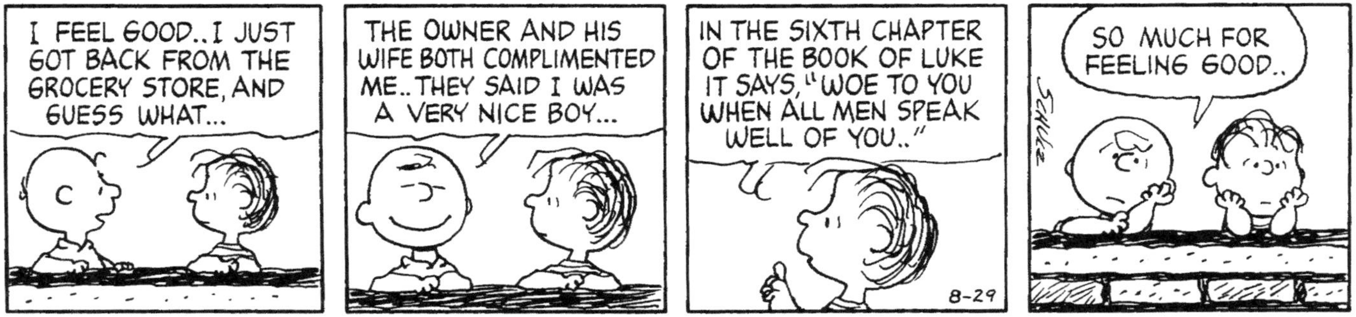
I FEEL GOOD..I JUST GOT BACK FROM THE GROCERY STORE, AND GUESS WHAT...
THE OWNER AND HIS WIFE BOTH COMPLIMENTED ME..THEY SAID I WAS A VERY NICE BOY...
IN THE SIXTH CHAPTER OF THE BOOK OF LUKE IT SAYS, "WOE TO YOU WHEN ALL MEN SPEAK WELL OF YOU.."
8-29
SCHULZ
SO MUCH FOR FEELING GOOD..

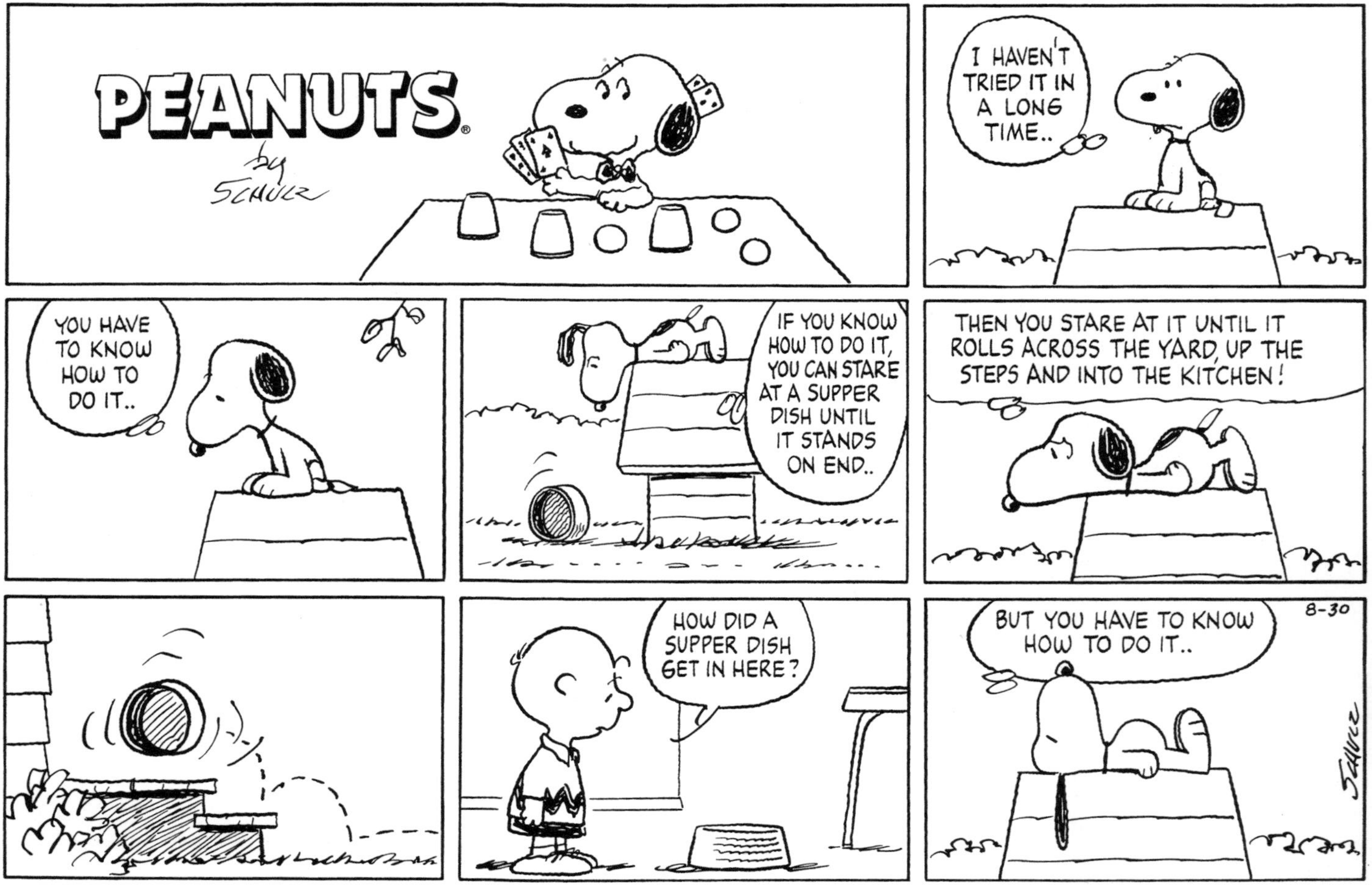
PEANUTS®
by SCHULZ
I HAVEN'T TRIED IT IN A LONG TIME..
YOU HAVE TO KNOW HOW TO DO IT..
IF YOU KNOW HOW TO DO IT, YOU CAN STARE AT A SUPPER DISH UNTIL IT STANDS ON END..
THEN YOU STARE AT IT UNTIL IT ROLLS ACROSS THE YARD, UP THE STEPS AND INTO THE KITCHEN!
HOW DID A SUPPER DISH GET IN HERE?
8-30
BUT YOU HAVE TO KNOW HOW TO DO IT..
SCHULZ

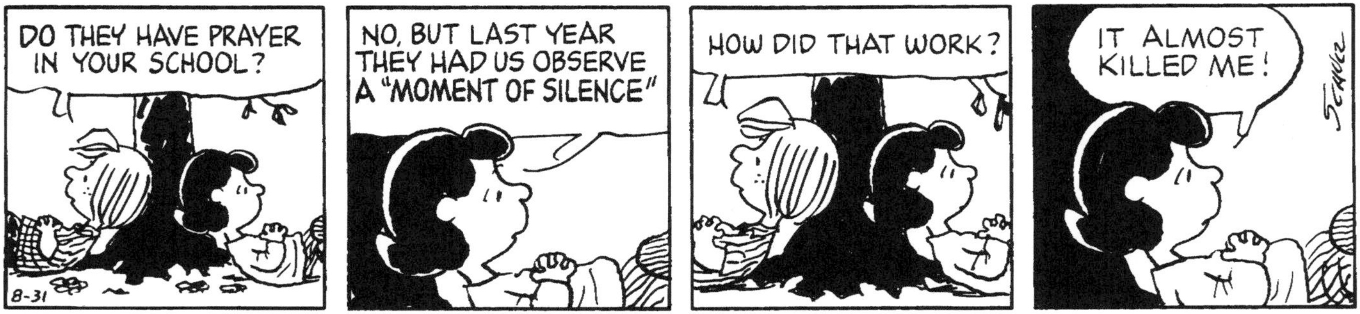
DO THEY HAVE PRAYER IN YOUR SCHOOL?
8-31
NO, BUT LAST YEAR THEY HAD US OBSERVE A "MOMENT OF SILENCE"
HOW DID THAT WORK?
IT ALMOST KILLED ME!
SCHULZ

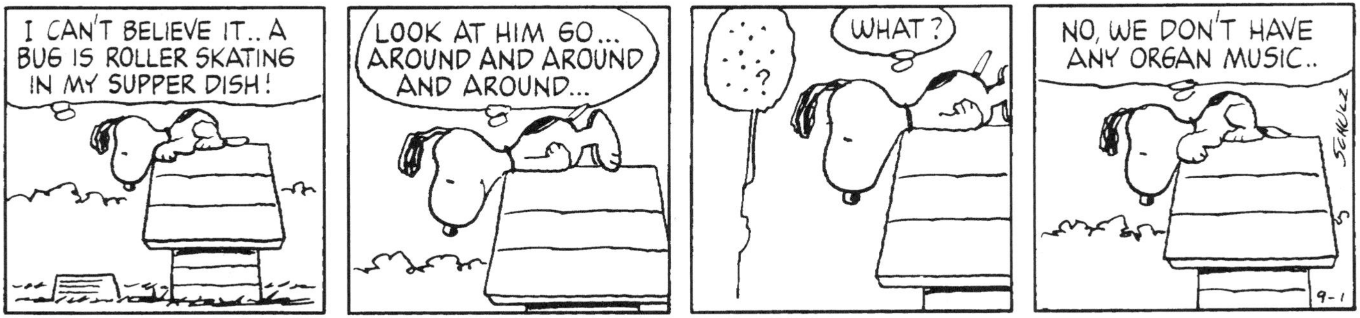
I CAN'T BELIEVE IT.. A BUG IS ROLLER SKATING IN MY SUPPER DISH!
LOOK AT HIM GO... AROUND AND AROUND AND AROUND...
?
WHAT?
NO, WE DON'T HAVE ANY ORGAN MUSIC..
SCHULZ
9-1

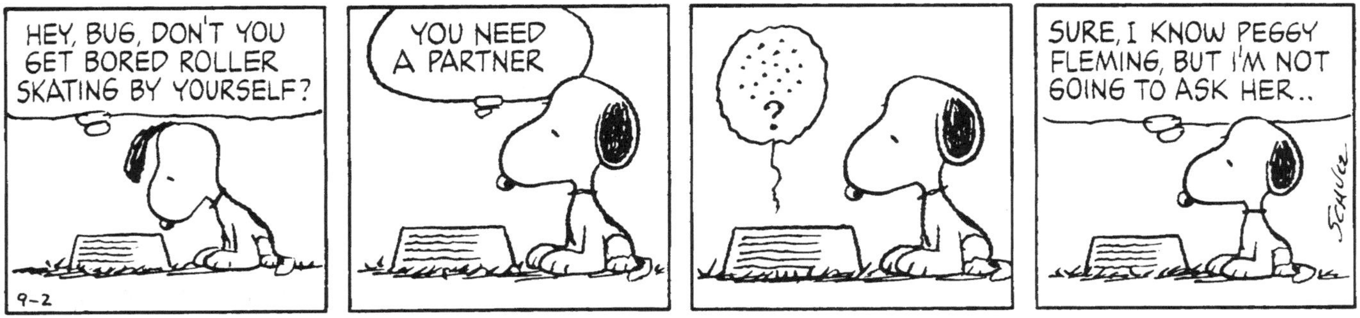
HEY, BUG, DON'T YOU GET BORED ROLLER SKATING BY YOURSELF?
9-2
YOU NEED A PARTNER
?
SURE, I KNOW PEGGY FLEMING, BUT I'M NOT GOING TO ASK HER..
SCHULZ

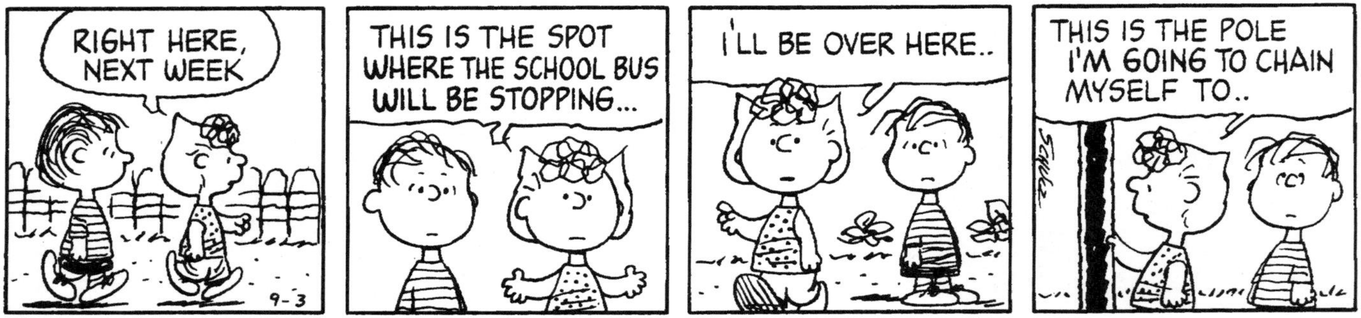
RIGHT HERE, NEXT WEEK
THIS IS THE SPOT WHERE THE SCHOOL BUS WILL BE STOPPING...
I'LL BE OVER HERE..
THIS IS THE POLE I'M GOING TO CHAIN MYSELF TO..

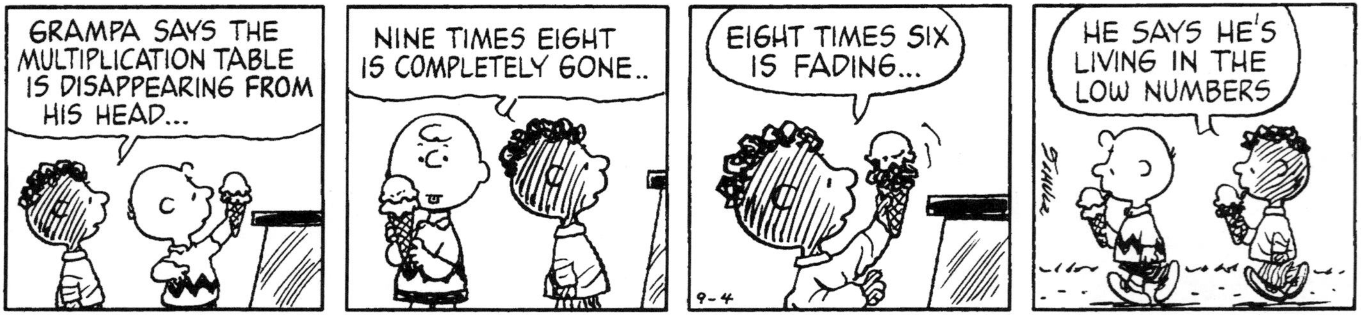
GRAMPA SAYS THE MULTIPLICATION TABLE IS DISAPPEARING FROM HIS HEAD...
NINE TIMES EIGHT IS COMPLETELY GONE..
EIGHT TIMES SIX IS FADING...
HE SAYS HE'S LIVING IN THE LOW NUMBERS

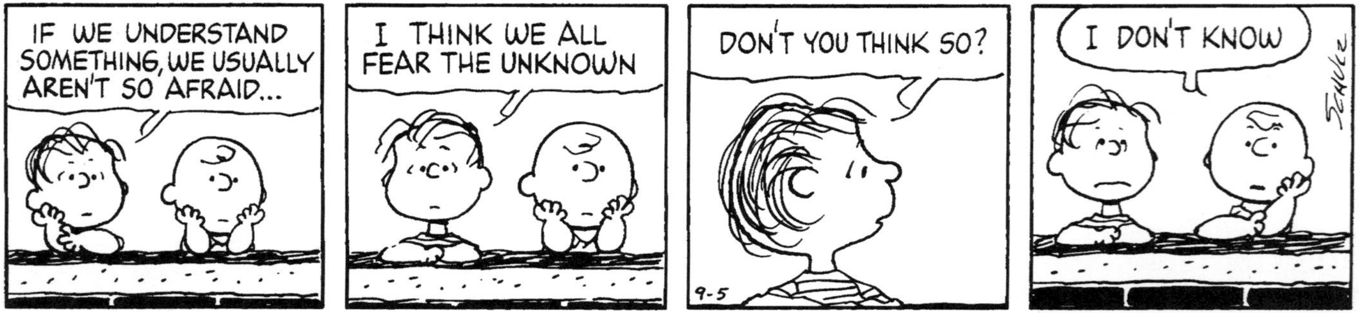
IF WE UNDERSTAND SOMETHING, WE USUALLY AREN'T SO AFRAID...
I THINK WE ALL FEAR THE UNKNOWN
DON'T YOU THINK SO?
I DON'T KNOW

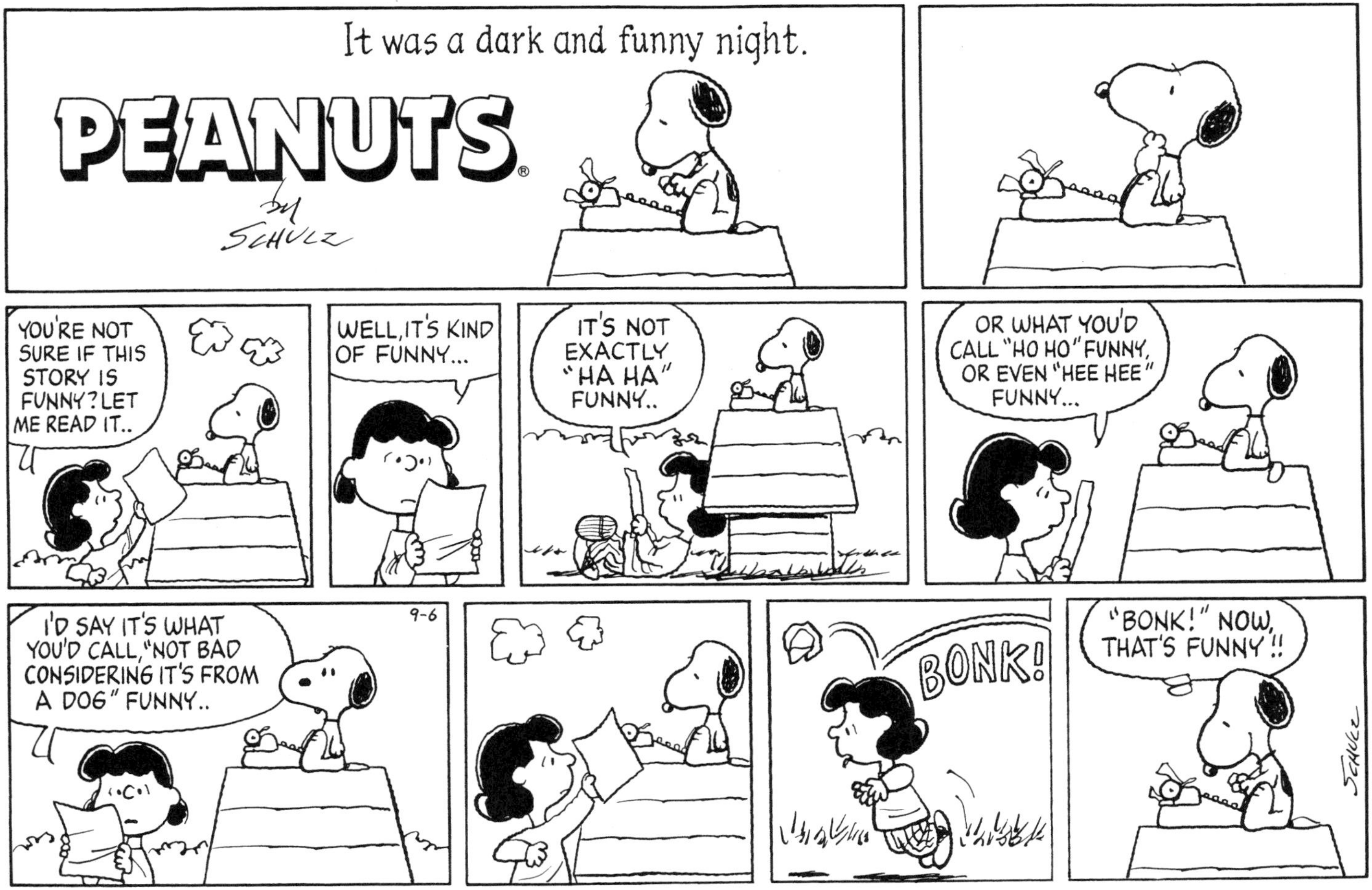
It was a dark and funny night.
PEANUTS
by SCHULZ
YOU'RE NOT SURE IF THIS STORY IS FUNNY? LET ME READ IT..
WELL, IT'S KIND OF FUNNY...
IT'S NOT EXACTLY "HA HA" FUNNY..
OR WHAT YOU'D CALL "HO HO" FUNNY, OR EVEN "HEE HEE" FUNNY...
I'D SAY IT'S WHAT YOU'D CALL, "NOT BAD CONSIDERING IT'S FROM A DOG" FUNNY..
9-6
BONK!
"BONK!" NOW, THAT'S FUNNY!!
SCHULZ

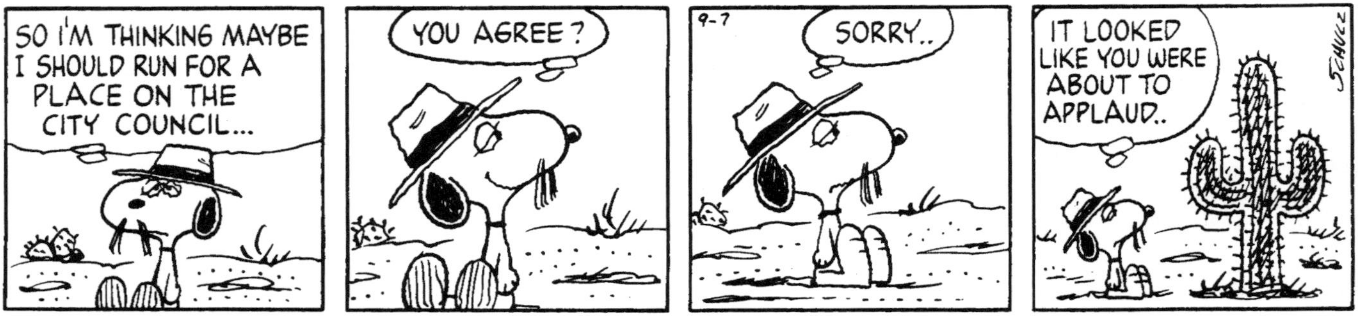
SO I'M THINKING MAYBE I SHOULD RUN FOR A PLACE ON THE CITY COUNCIL...
YOU AGREE?
9-7
SORRY..
IT LOOKED LIKE YOU WERE ABOUT TO APPLAUD..

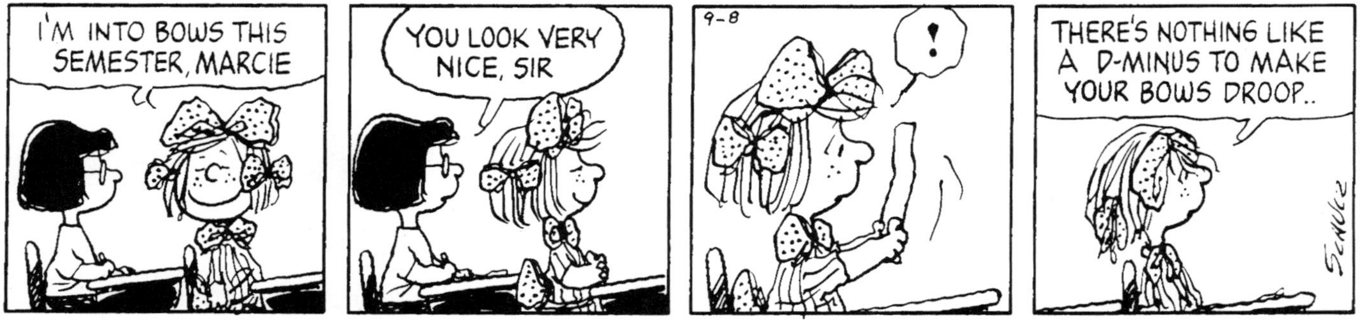
I'M INTO BOWS THIS SEMESTER, MARCIE
YOU LOOK VERY NICE, SIR
9-8
!
THERE'S NOTHING LIKE A D-MINUS TO MAKE YOUR BOWS DROOP..

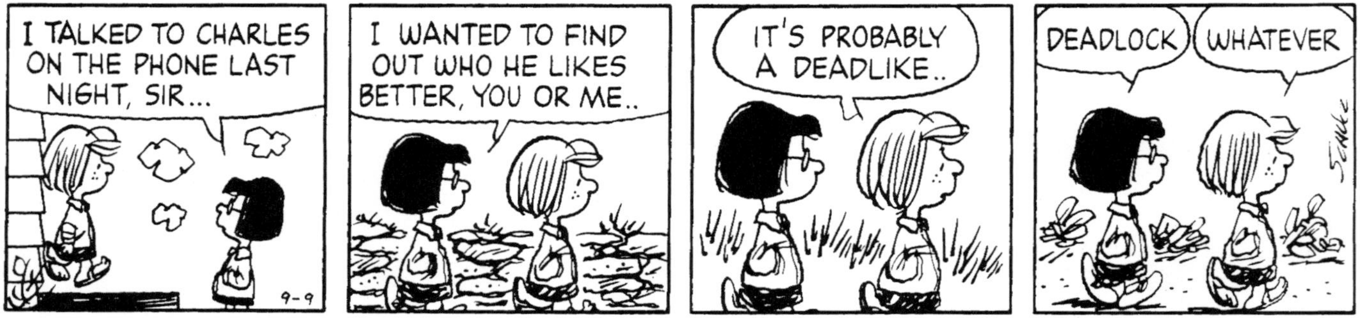
I TALKED TO CHARLES ON THE PHONE LAST NIGHT, SIR...
9-9
I WANTED TO FIND OUT WHO HE LIKES BETTER, YOU OR ME..
IT'S PROBABLY A DEADLIKE..
DEADLOCK
WHATEVER

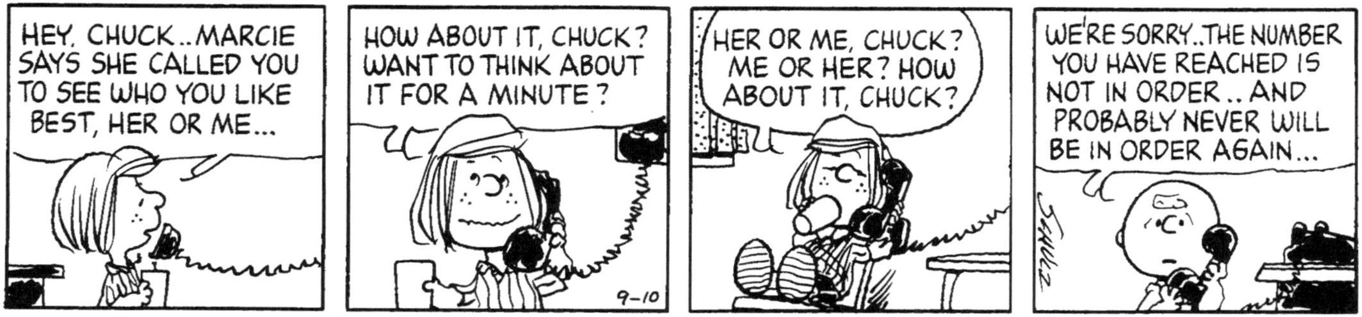
HEY, CHUCK..MARCIE SAYS SHE CALLED YOU TO SEE WHO YOU LIKE BEST, HER OR ME...
HOW ABOUT IT, CHUCK? WANT TO THINK ABOUT IT FOR A MINUTE?
9-10
HER OR ME, CHUCK? ME OR HER? HOW ABOUT IT, CHUCK?
WE'RE SORRY..THE NUMBER YOU HAVE REACHED IS NOT IN ORDER.. AND PROBABLY NEVER WILL BE IN ORDER AGAIN...
SCHULZ

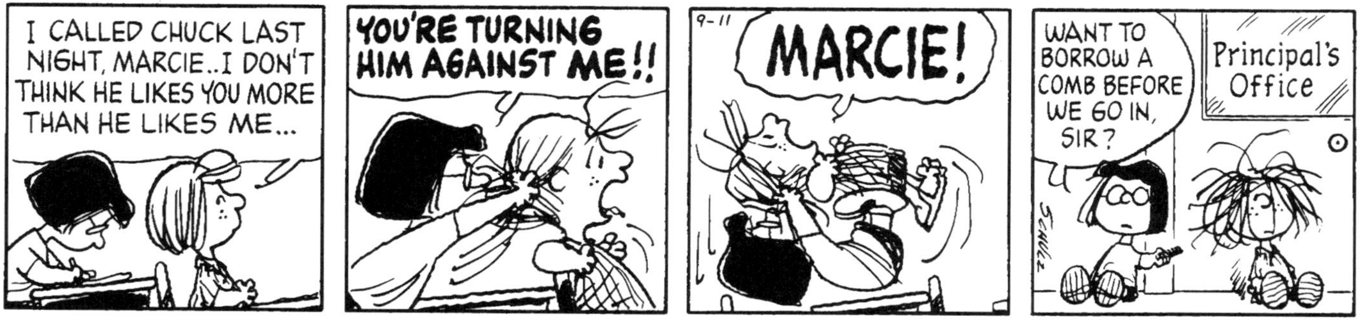
I CALLED CHUCK LAST NIGHT, MARCIE..I DON'T THINK HE LIKES YOU MORE THAN HE LIKES ME...
YOU'RE TURNING HIM AGAINST ME!!
9-11
MARCIE!
WANT TO BORROW A COMB BEFORE WE GO IN, SIR?
Principal's Office
SCHULZ

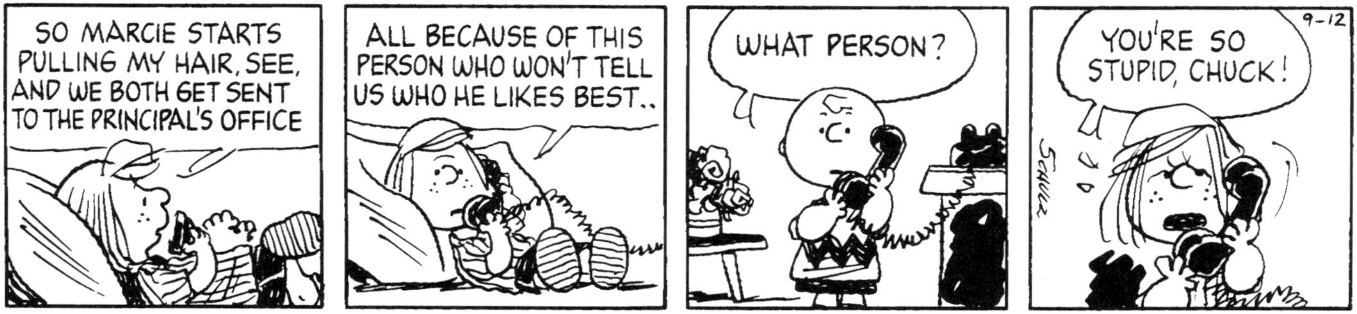
SO MARCIE STARTS PULLING MY HAIR, SEE, AND WE BOTH GET SENT TO THE PRINCIPAL'S OFFICE
ALL BECAUSE OF THIS PERSON WHO WON'T TELL US WHO HE LIKES BEST..
WHAT PERSON?
9-12
YOU'RE SO STUPID, CHUCK!
SCHULZ

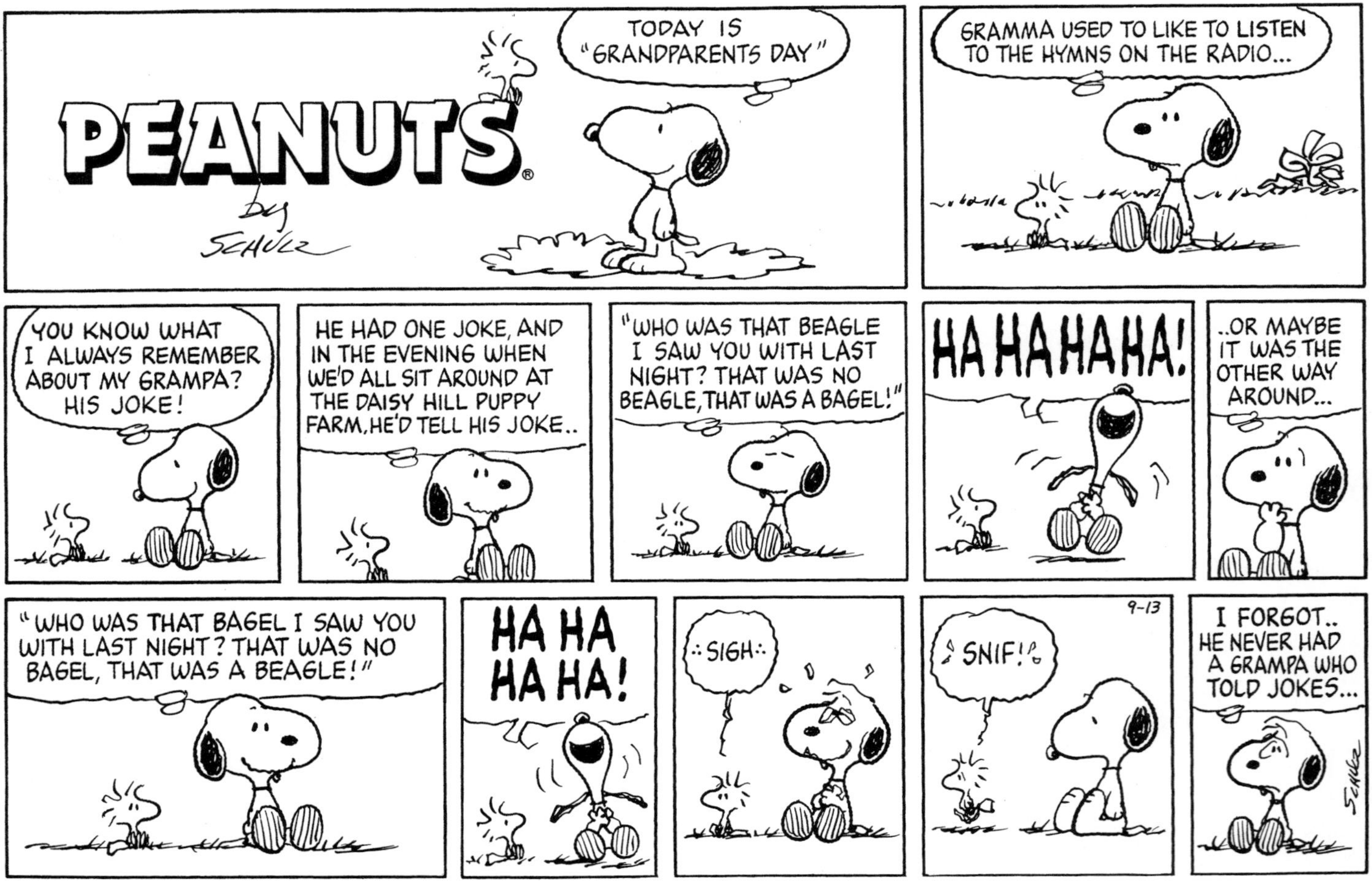
PEANUTS
by SCHULZ
TODAY IS "GRANDPARENTS DAY"
GRAMMA USED TO LIKE TO LISTEN TO THE HYMNS ON THE RADIO...
YOU KNOW WHAT I ALWAYS REMEMBER ABOUT MY GRAMPA? HIS JOKE!
HE HAD ONE JOKE, AND IN THE EVENING WHEN WE'D ALL SIT AROUND AT THE DAISY HILL PUPPY FARM, HE'D TELL HIS JOKE..
"WHO WAS THAT BEAGLE I SAW YOU WITH LAST NIGHT? THAT WAS NO BEAGLE, THAT WAS A BAGEL!"
HA HA HA HA HA!
..OR MAYBE IT WAS THE OTHER WAY AROUND...
"WHO WAS THAT BAGEL I SAW YOU WITH LAST NIGHT? THAT WAS NO BAGEL, THAT WAS A BEAGLE!"
HA HA HA HA!
SIGH
9-13
SNIF!
I FORGOT.. HE NEVER HAD A GRAMPA WHO TOLD JOKES...
SCHULZ

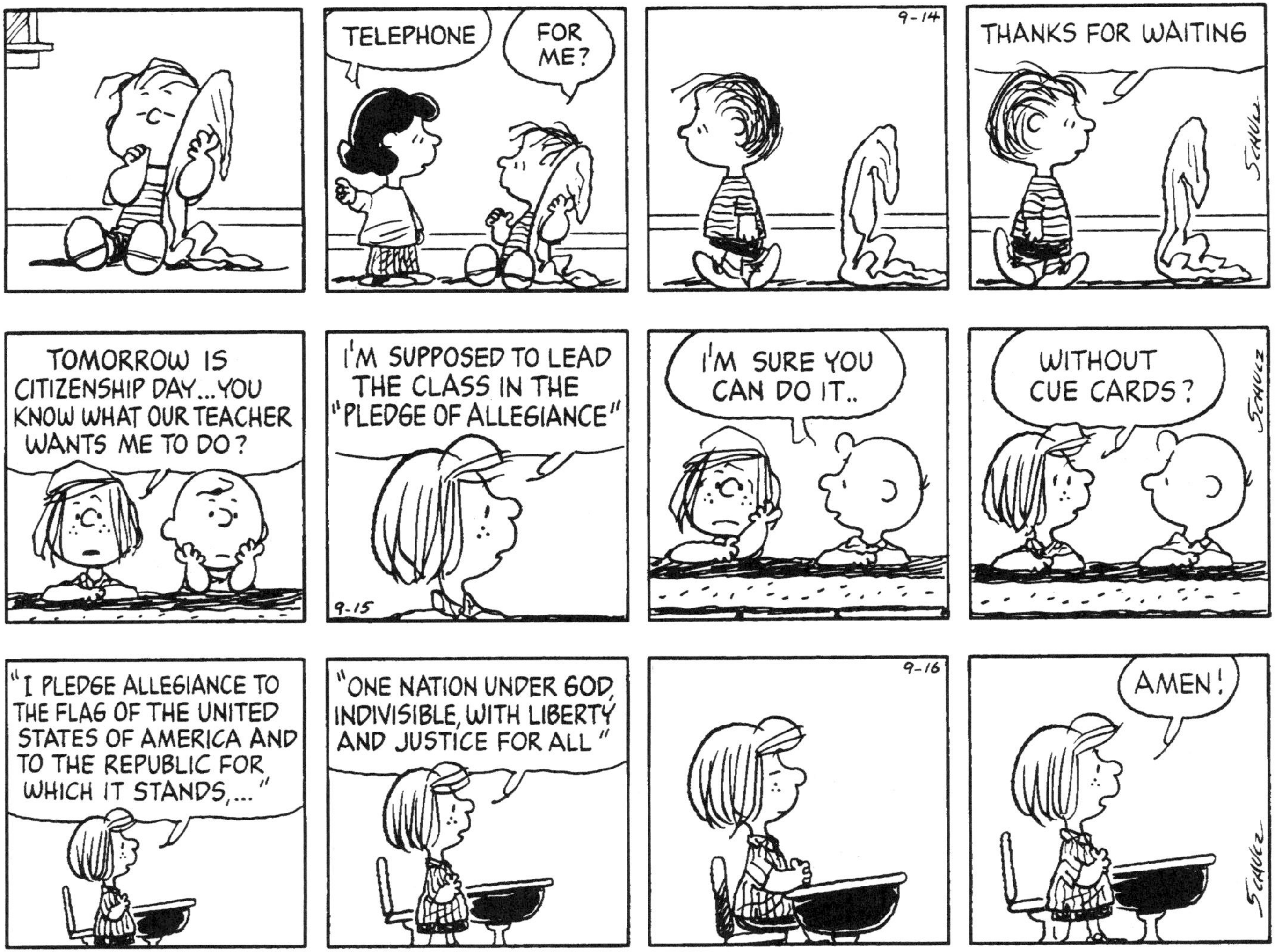
TELEPHONE
FOR ME?
9-14
THANKS FOR WAITING
SCHULZ
TOMORROW IS CITIZENSHIP DAY...YOU KNOW WHAT OUR TEACHER WANTS ME TO DO?
I'M SUPPOSED TO LEAD THE CLASS IN THE "PLEDGE OF ALLEGIANCE"
9-15
I'M SURE YOU CAN DO IT..
WITHOUT CUE CARDS?
SCHULZ
"I PLEDGE ALLEGIANCE TO THE FLAG OF THE UNITED STATES OF AMERICA AND TO THE REPUBLIC FOR WHICH IT STANDS,..."
"ONE NATION UNDER GOD, INDIVISIBLE, WITH LIBERTY AND JUSTICE FOR ALL"
9-16
AMEN!
SCHULZ

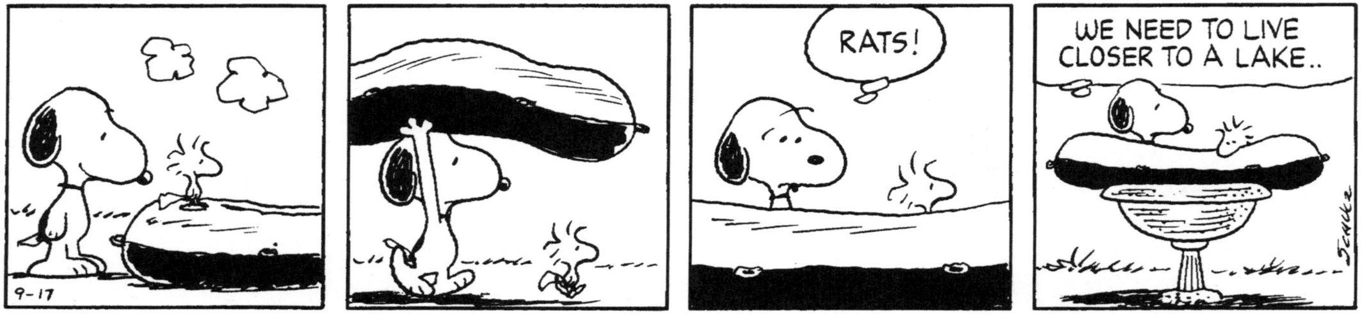
9-17
RATS!
WE NEED TO LIVE CLOSER TO A LAKE..

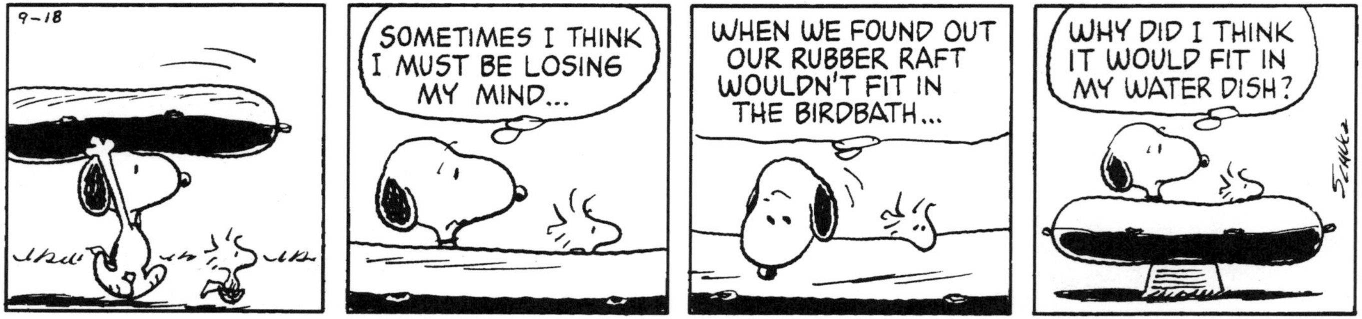
9-18
SOMETIMES I THINK I MUST BE LOSING MY MIND...
WHEN WE FOUND OUT OUR RUBBER RAFT WOULDN'T FIT IN THE BIRDBATH...
WHY DID I THINK IT WOULD FIT IN MY WATER DISH?

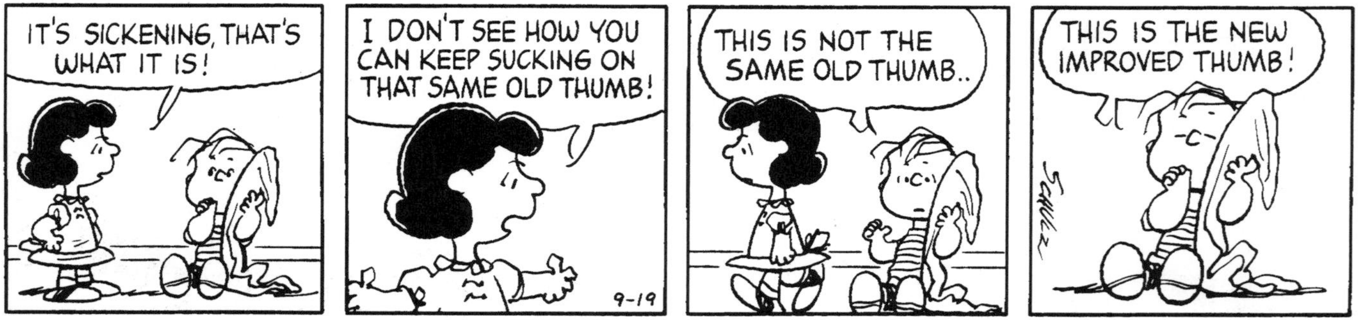
IT'S SICKENING, THAT'S WHAT IT IS!
I DON'T SEE HOW YOU CAN KEEP SUCKING ON THAT SAME OLD THUMB!
9-19
THIS IS NOT THE SAME OLD THUMB..
THIS IS THE NEW IMPROVED THUMB!

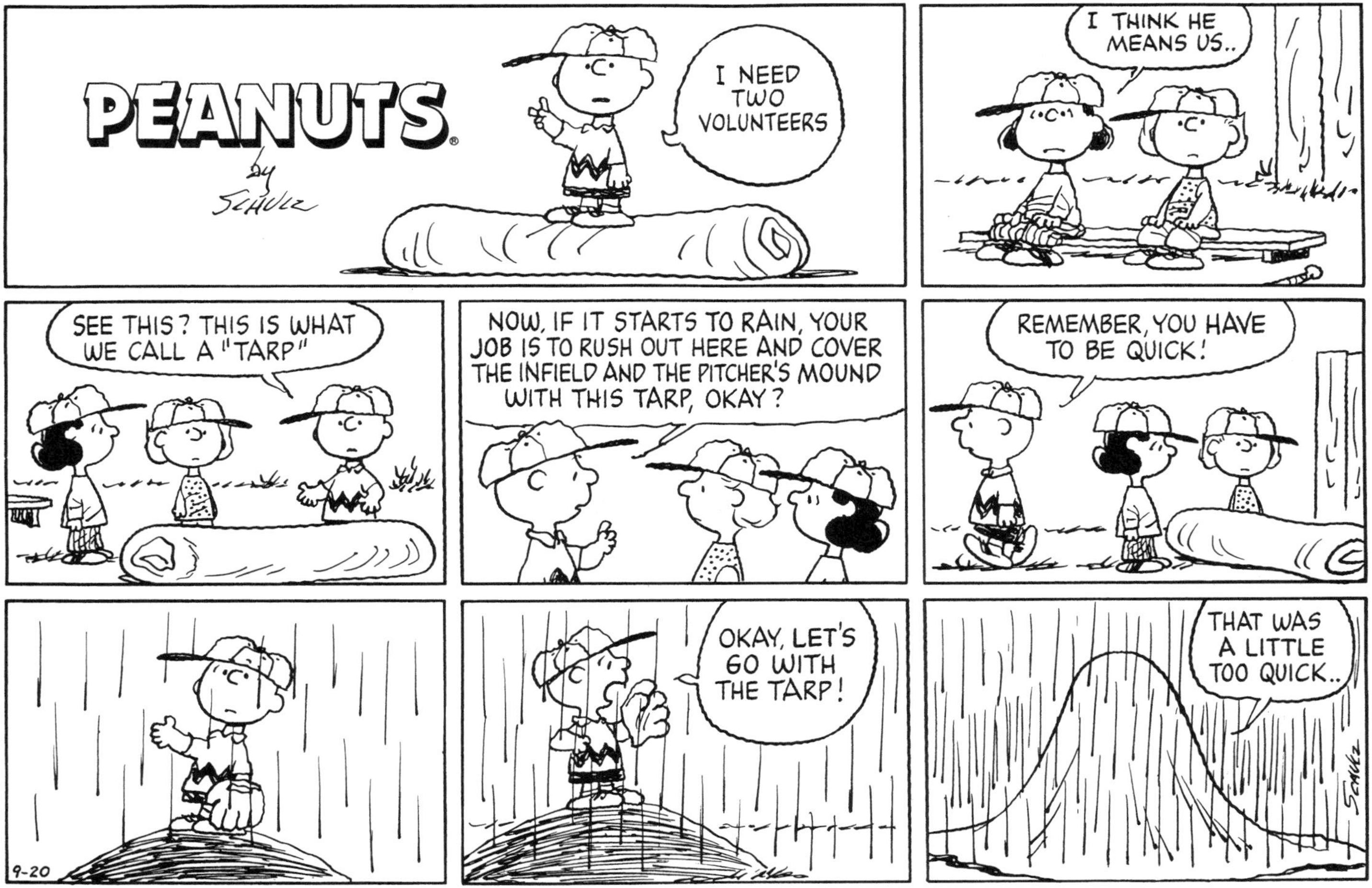
PEANUTS
by SCHULZ
I NEED TWO VOLUNTEERS
I THINK HE MEANS US..
SEE THIS? THIS IS WHAT WE CALL A "TARP"
NOW, IF IT STARTS TO RAIN, YOUR JOB IS TO RUSH OUT HERE AND COVER THE INFIELD AND THE PITCHER'S MOUND WITH THIS TARP, OKAY?
REMEMBER, YOU HAVE TO BE QUICK!
9-20
OKAY, LET'S GO WITH THE TARP!
THAT WAS A LITTLE TOO QUICK..
SCHULZ

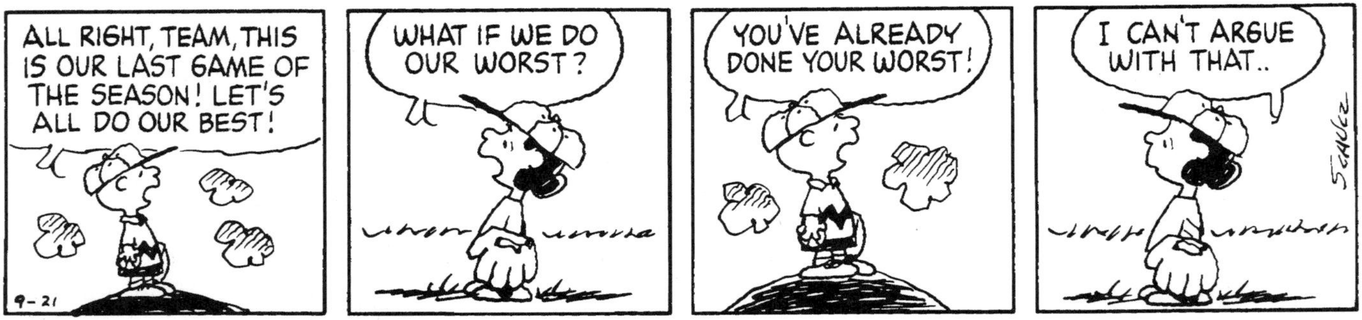
ALL RIGHT, TEAM, THIS IS OUR LAST GAME OF THE SEASON! LET'S ALL DO OUR BEST!
9-21
WHAT IF WE DO OUR WORST?
YOU'VE ALREADY DONE YOUR WORST!
I CAN'T ARGUE WITH THAT..

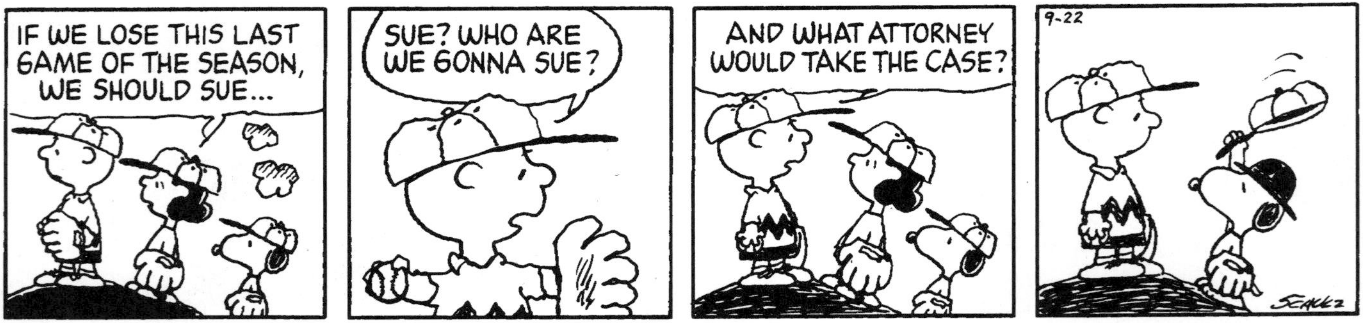
IF WE LOSE THIS LAST GAME OF THE SEASON, WE SHOULD SUE...
SUE? WHO ARE WE GONNA SUE?
AND WHAT ATTORNEY WOULD TAKE THE CASE?
9-22

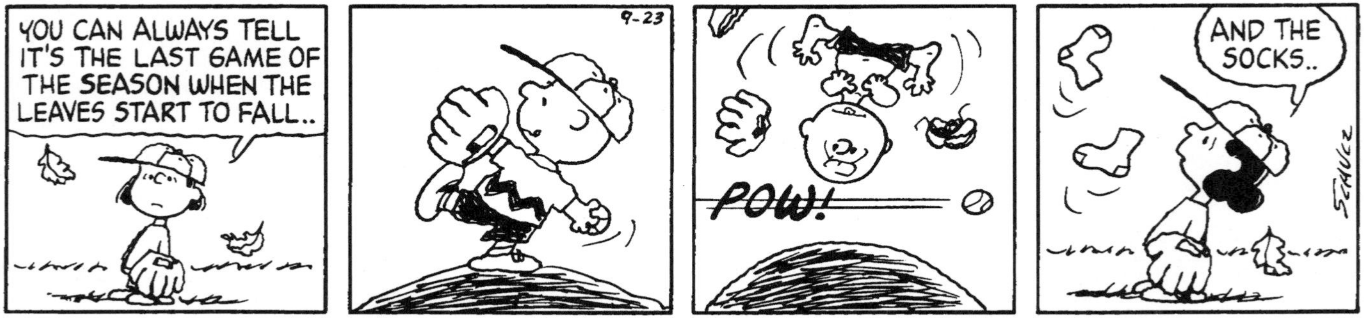
YOU CAN ALWAYS TELL IT'S THE LAST GAME OF THE SEASON WHEN THE LEAVES START TO FALL..
9-23
POW!
AND THE SOCKS..

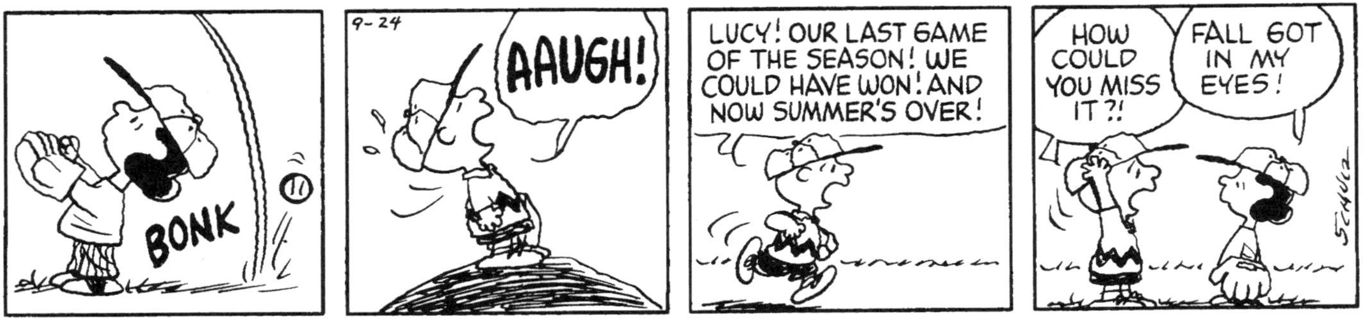
BONK
9-24
AAUGH!
LUCY! OUR LAST GAME OF THE SEASON! WE COULD HAVE WON! AND NOW SUMMER'S OVER!
HOW COULD YOU MISS IT?!
FALL GOT IN MY EYES!
SCHULZ

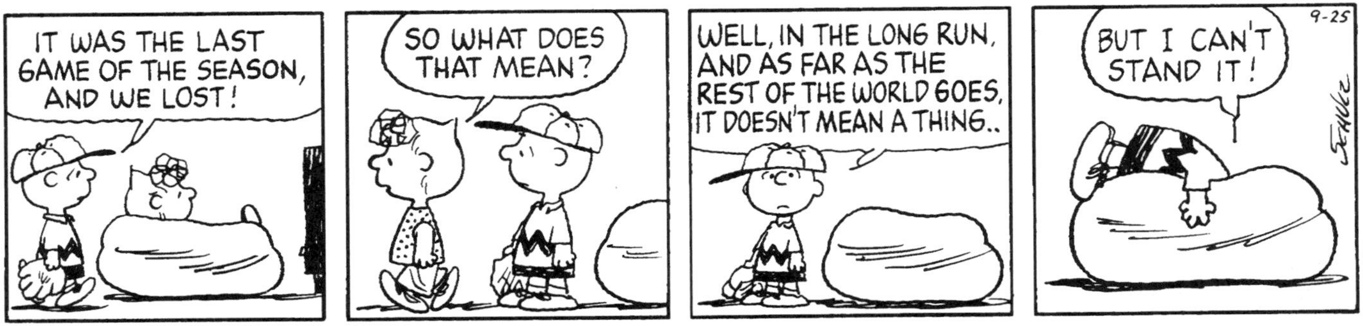
IT WAS THE LAST GAME OF THE SEASON, AND WE LOST!
SO WHAT DOES THAT MEAN?
WELL, IN THE LONG RUN, AND AS FAR AS THE REST OF THE WORLD GOES, IT DOESN'T MEAN A THING..
9-25
BUT I CAN'T STAND IT!
SCHULZ

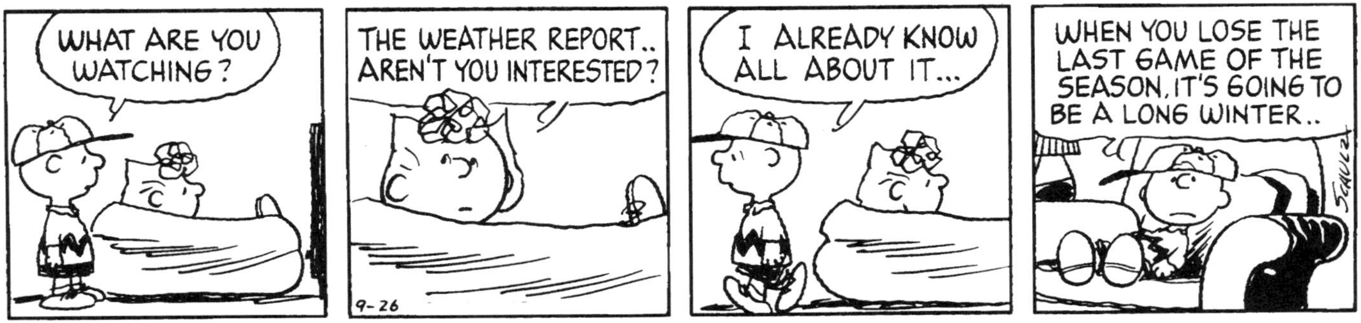
WHAT ARE YOU WATCHING?
THE WEATHER REPORT.. AREN'T YOU INTERESTED?
9-26
I ALREADY KNOW ALL ABOUT IT...
WHEN YOU LOSE THE LAST GAME OF THE SEASON, IT'S GOING TO BE A LONG WINTER..
SCHULZ

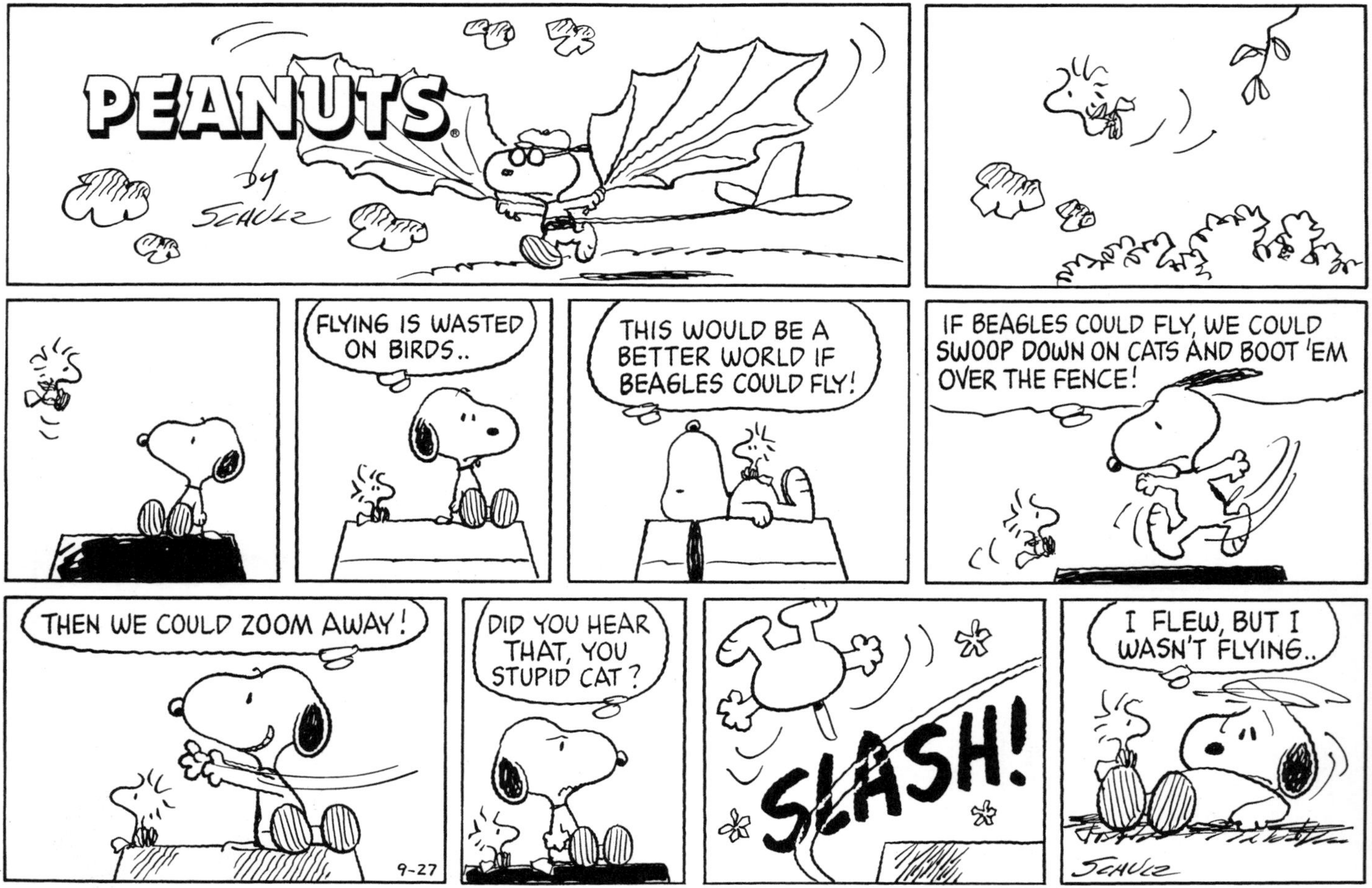
PEANUTS®
by SCHULZ
FLYING IS WASTED ON BIRDS..
THIS WOULD BE A BETTER WORLD IF BEAGLES COULD FLY!
IF BEAGLES COULD FLY, WE COULD SWOOP DOWN ON CATS AND BOOT 'EM OVER THE FENCE!
THEN WE COULD ZOOM AWAY!
9-27
DID YOU HEAR THAT, YOU STUPID CAT?
SLASH!
I FLEW, BUT I WASN'T FLYING..
SCHULZ

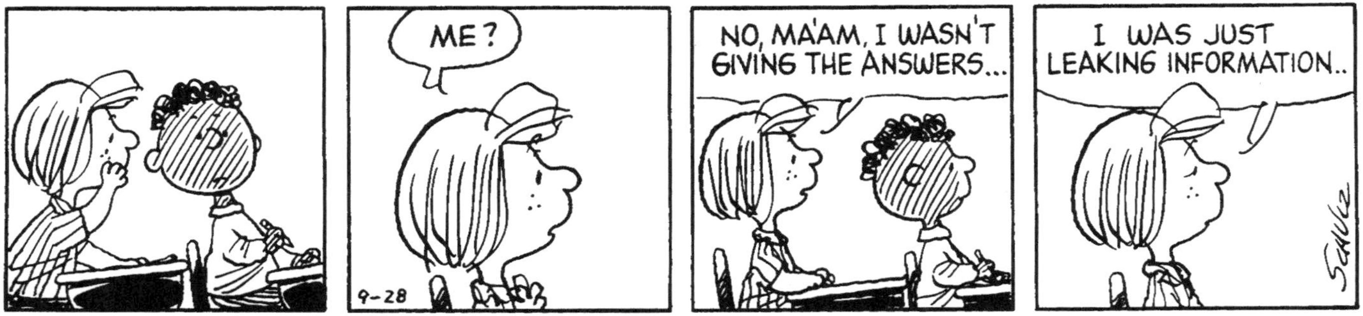
ME?
NO, MA'AM, I WASN'T GIVING THE ANSWERS...
I WAS JUST LEAKING INFORMATION..

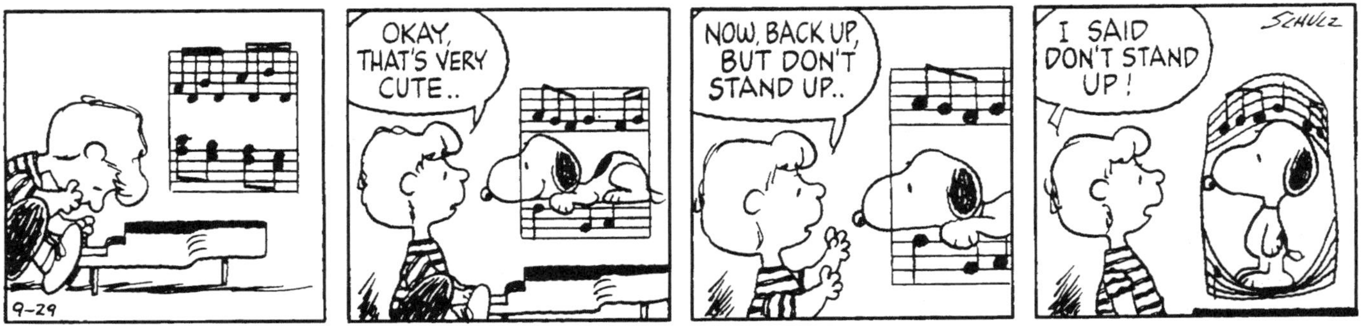
OKAY, THAT'S VERY CUTE..
NOW, BACK UP, BUT DON'T STAND UP..
I SAID DON'T STAND UP!

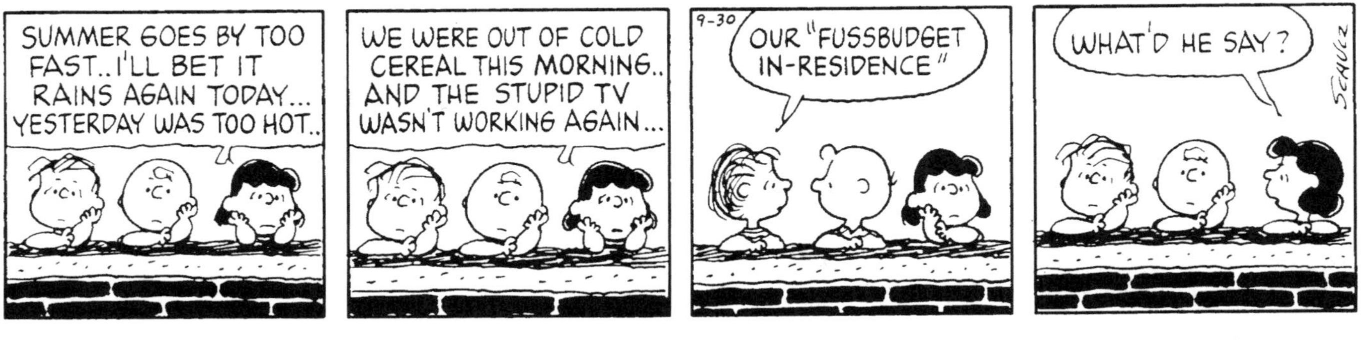
SUMMER GOES BY TOO FAST.. I'LL BET IT RAINS AGAIN TODAY... YESTERDAY WAS TOO HOT..
WE WERE OUT OF COLD CEREAL THIS MORNING.. AND THE STUPID TV WASN'T WORKING AGAIN...
OUR "FUSSBUDGET IN-RESIDENCE"
WHAT'D HE SAY?

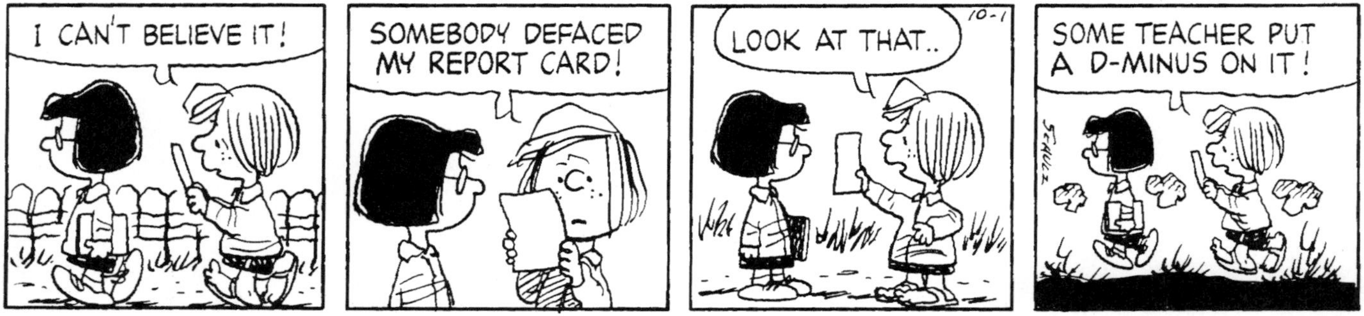
I CAN'T BELIEVE IT!
SOMEBODY DEFACED MY REPORT CARD!
LOOK AT THAT..
10-1
SOME TEACHER PUT A D-MINUS ON IT!

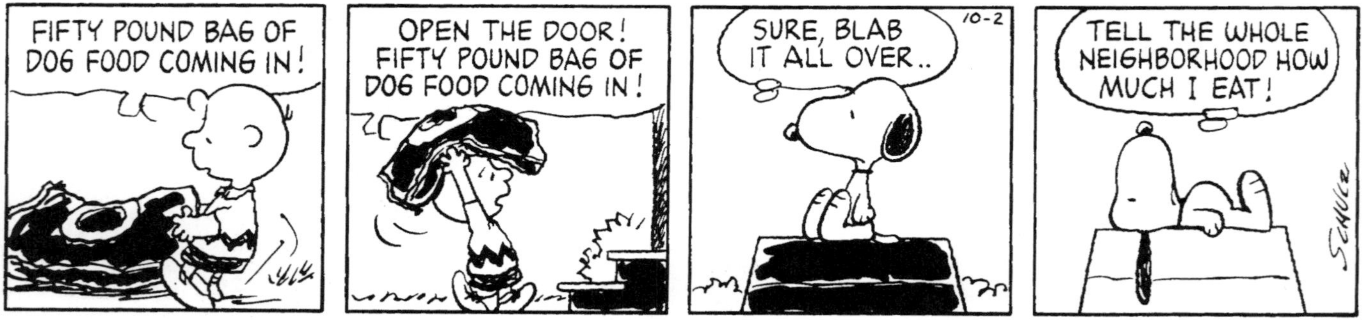
FIFTY POUND BAG OF DOG FOOD COMING IN!
OPEN THE DOOR! FIFTY POUND BAG OF DOG FOOD COMING IN!
SURE, BLAB IT ALL OVER..
10-2
TELL THE WHOLE NEIGHBORHOOD HOW MUCH I EAT!

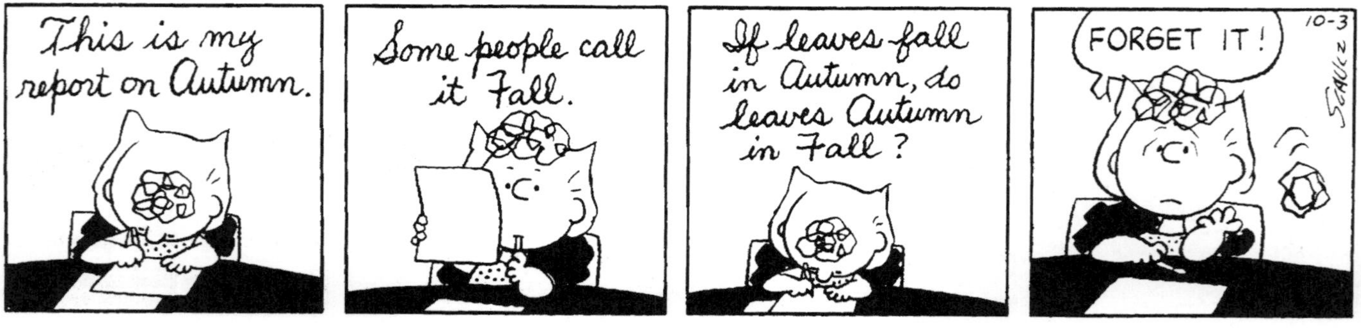
This is my report on Autumn.
Some people call it Fall.
If leaves fall in Autumn, do leaves Autumn in Fall?
FORGET IT!
10-3

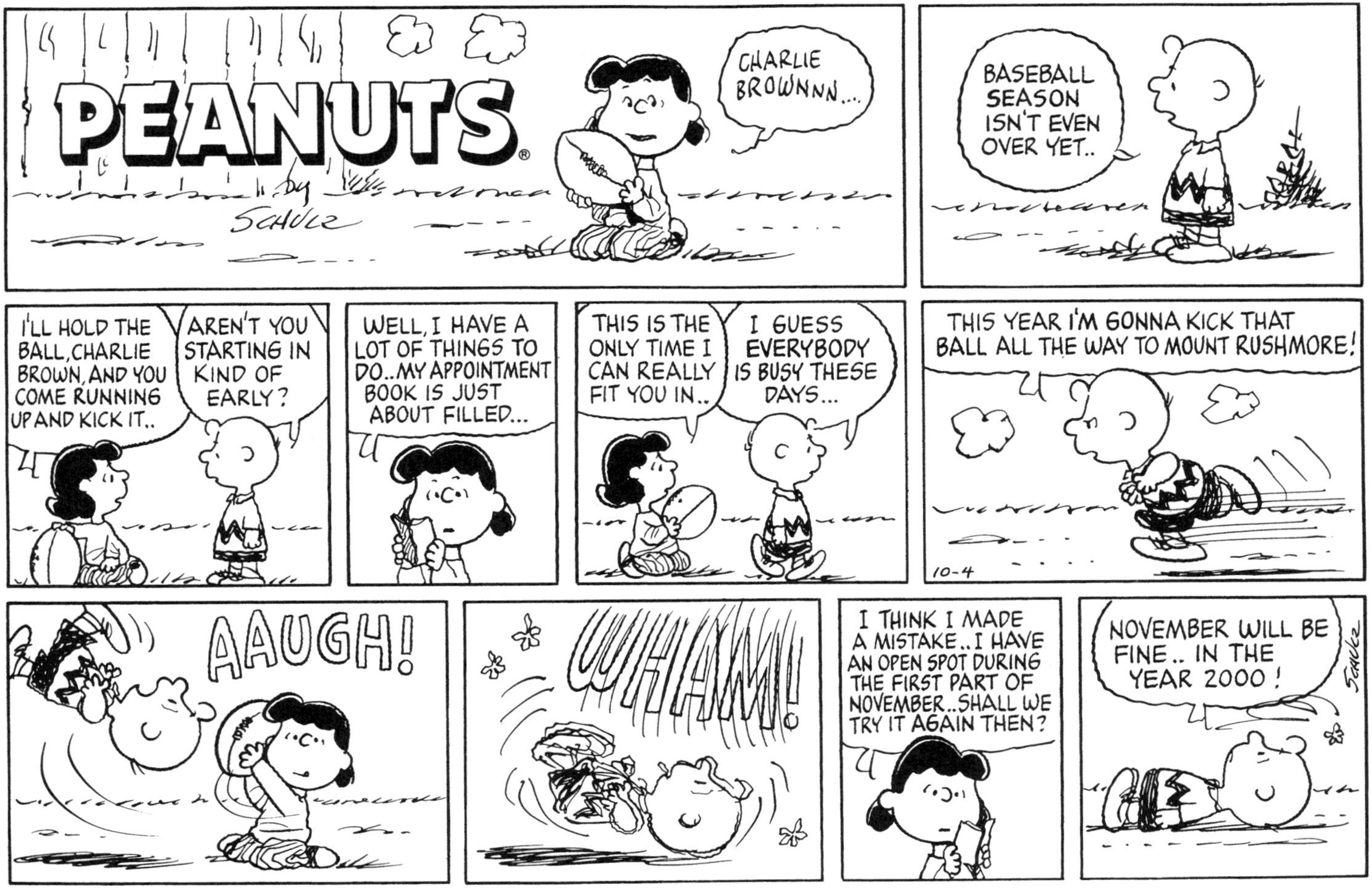
PEANUTS
CHARLIE BROWNNN....
BASEBALL SEASON ISN'T EVEN OVER YET..
I'LL HOLD THE BALL, CHARLIE BROWN, AND YOU COME RUNNING UP AND KICK IT..
AREN'T YOU STARTING IN KIND OF EARLY?
WELL, I HAVE A LOT OF THINGS TO DO..MY APPOINTMENT BOOK IS JUST ABOUT FILLED...
THIS IS THE ONLY TIME I CAN REALLY FIT YOU IN..
I GUESS EVERYBODY IS BUSY THESE DAYS...
THIS YEAR I'M GONNA KICK THAT BALL ALL THE WAY TO MOUNT RUSHMORE!
10-4
AAUGH!
WHAM!
I THINK I MADE A MISTAKE..I HAVE AN OPEN SPOT DURING THE FIRST PART OF NOVEMBER..SHALL WE TRY IT AGAIN THEN?
NOVEMBER WILL BE FINE.. IN THE YEAR 2000!

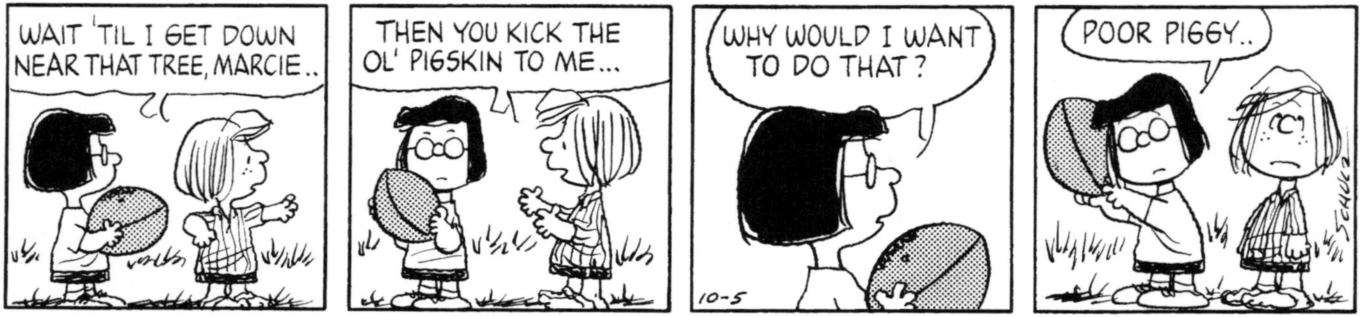
WAIT 'TIL I GET DOWN NEAR THAT TREE, MARCIE..
THEN YOU KICK THE OL' PIGSKIN TO ME...
WHY WOULD I WANT TO DO THAT?
10-5
POOR PIGGY..
SCHULZ

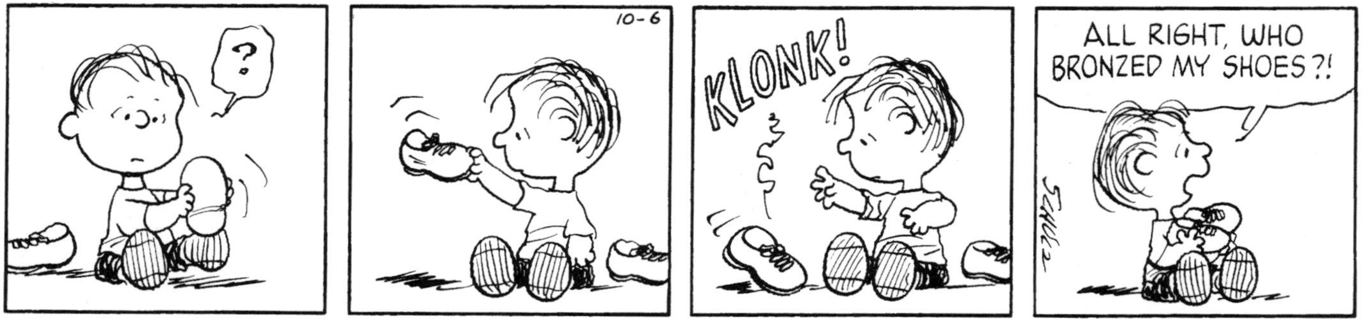
?
10-6
KLONK!
ALL RIGHT, WHO BRONZED MY SHOES?!
SCHULZ

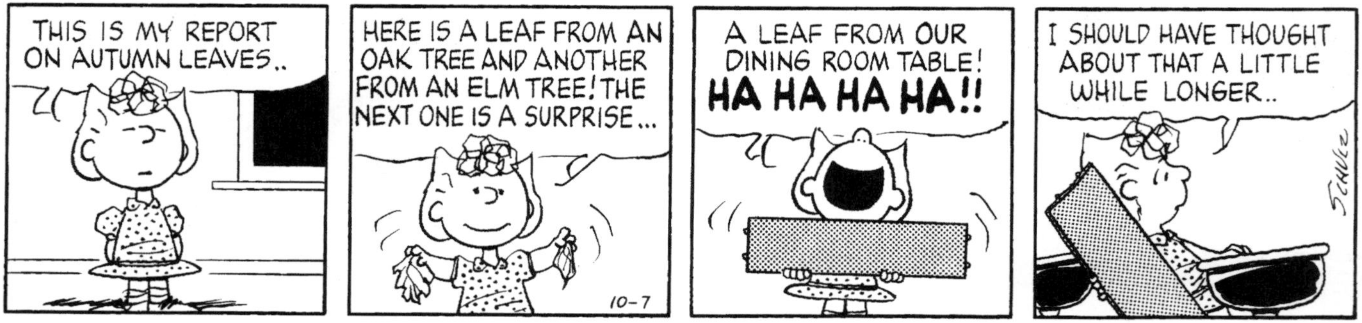
THIS IS MY REPORT ON AUTUMN LEAVES..
HERE IS A LEAF FROM AN OAK TREE AND ANOTHER FROM AN ELM TREE! THE NEXT ONE IS A SURPRISE...
10-7
A LEAF FROM OUR DINING ROOM TABLE! HA HA HA HA!!
I SHOULD HAVE THOUGHT ABOUT THAT A LITTLE WHILE LONGER..
SCHULZ

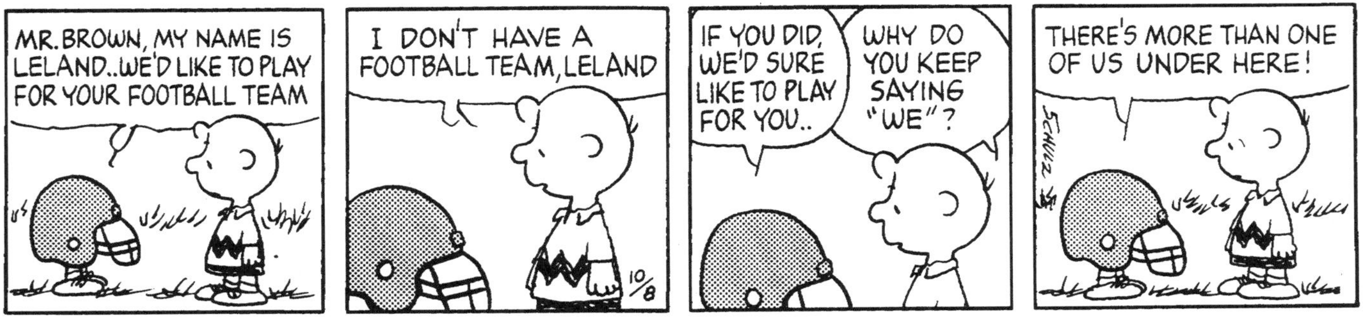
MR. BROWN, MY NAME IS LELAND..WE'D LIKE TO PLAY FOR YOUR FOOTBALL TEAM
I DON'T HAVE A FOOTBALL TEAM, LELAND
10/8
IF YOU DID, WE'D SURE LIKE TO PLAY FOR YOU..
WHY DO YOU KEEP SAYING "WE"?
SCHULZ
THERE'S MORE THAN ONE OF US UNDER HERE!

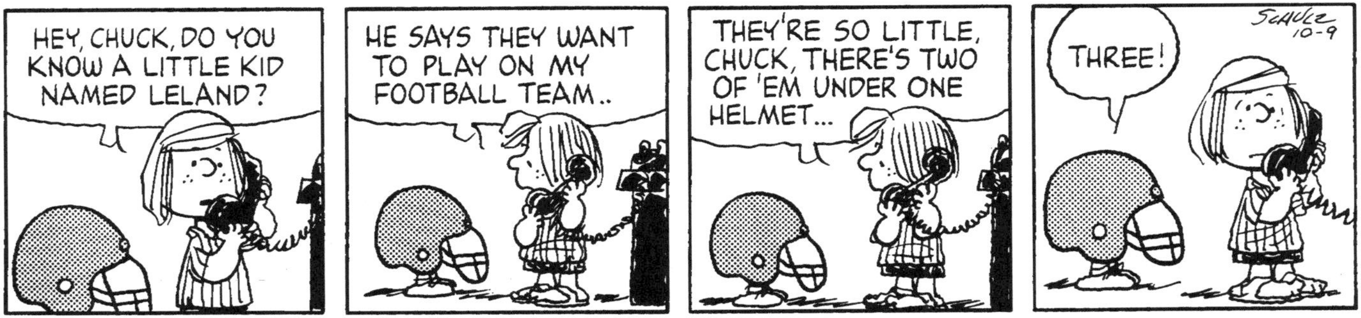
HEY, CHUCK, DO YOU KNOW A LITTLE KID NAMED LELAND?
HE SAYS THEY WANT TO PLAY ON MY FOOTBALL TEAM..
THEY'RE SO LITTLE, CHUCK, THERE'S TWO OF 'EM UNDER ONE HELMET...
SCHULZ
10-9
THREE!

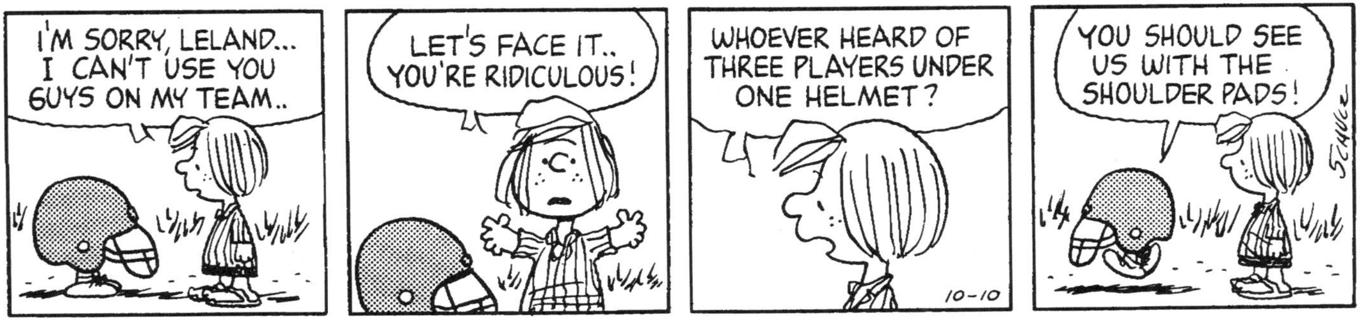
I'M SORRY, LELAND... I CAN'T USE YOU GUYS ON MY TEAM..
LET'S FACE IT.. YOU'RE RIDICULOUS!
WHOEVER HEARD OF THREE PLAYERS UNDER ONE HELMET?
10-10
YOU SHOULD SEE US WITH THE SHOULDER PADS!
SCHULZ

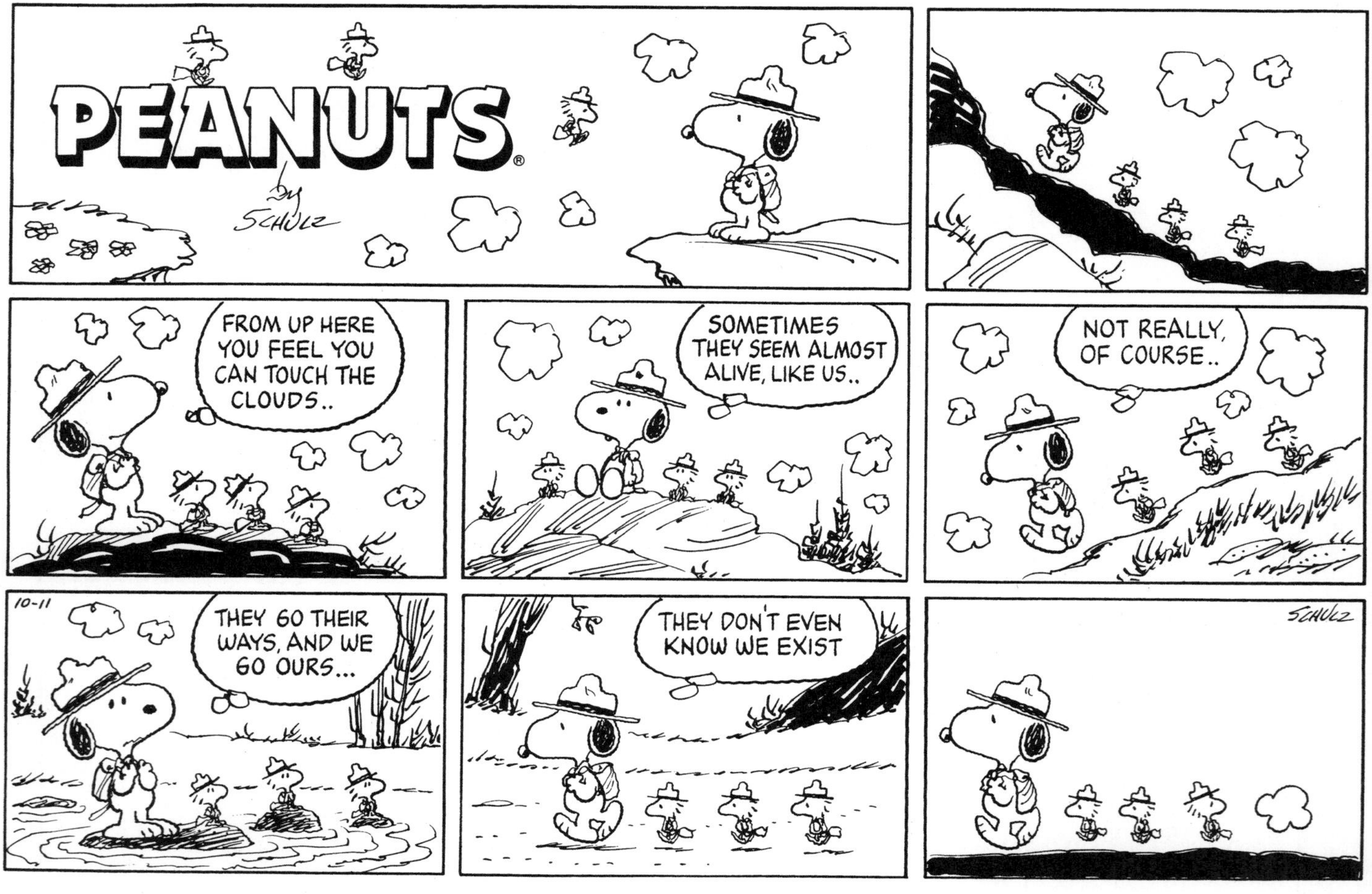
PEANUTS®
by SCHULZ
FROM UP HERE YOU FEEL YOU CAN TOUCH THE CLOUDS..
SOMETIMES THEY SEEM ALMOST ALIVE, LIKE US..
NOT REALLY, OF COURSE..
10-11
THEY GO THEIR WAYS, AND WE GO OURS...
THEY DON'T EVEN KNOW WE EXIST
SCHULZ

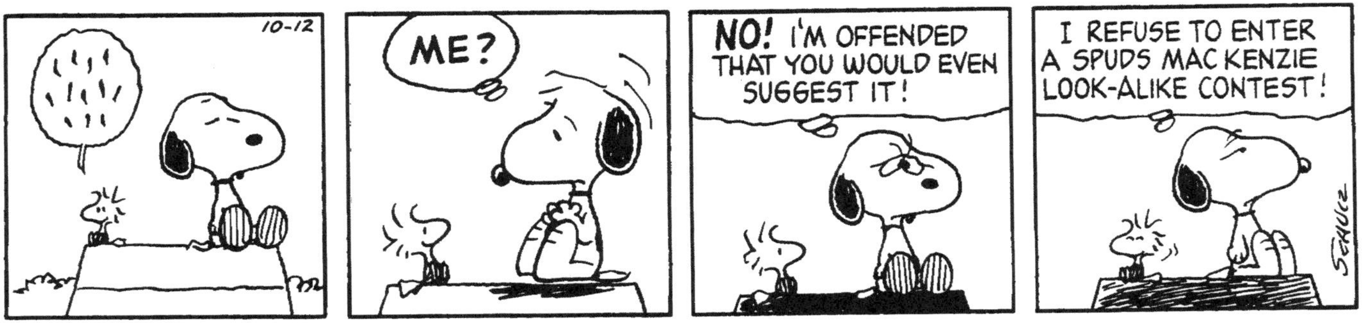
10-12
ME?
NO! I'M OFFENDED THAT YOU WOULD EVEN SUGGEST IT!
I REFUSE TO ENTER A SPUDS MAC KENZIE LOOK-ALIKE CONTEST!
SCHULZ

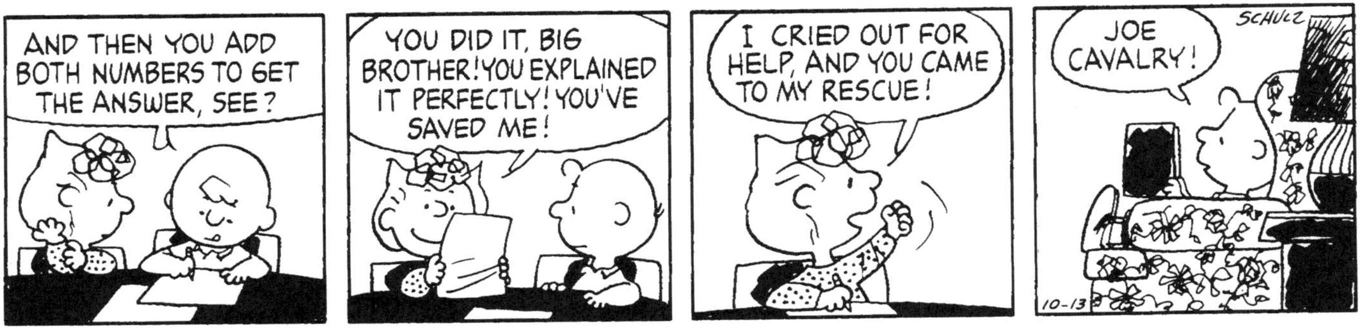
AND THEN YOU ADD BOTH NUMBERS TO GET THE ANSWER, SEE?
YOU DID IT, BIG BROTHER! YOU EXPLAINED IT PERFECTLY! YOU'VE SAVED ME!
I CRIED OUT FOR HELP, AND YOU CAME TO MY RESCUE!
JOE CAVALRY!
SCHULZ
10-13

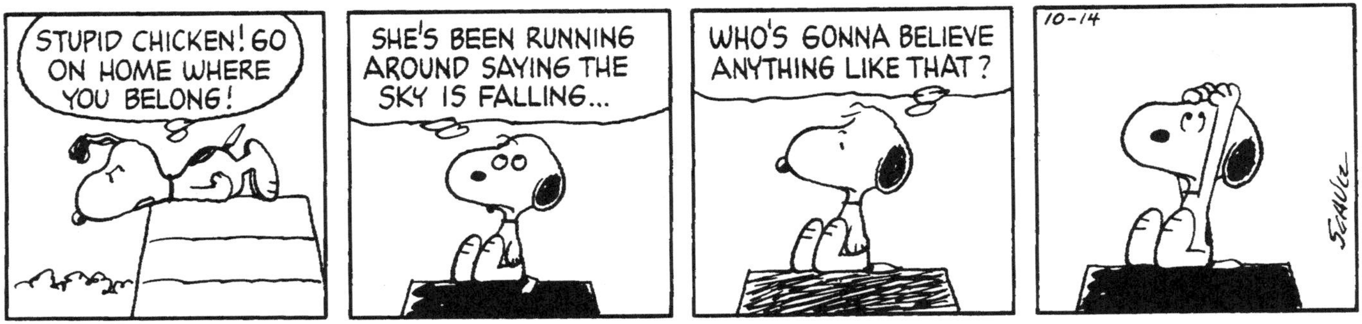
STUPID CHICKEN! GO ON HOME WHERE YOU BELONG!
SHE'S BEEN RUNNING AROUND SAYING THE SKY IS FALLING...
WHO'S GONNA BELIEVE ANYTHING LIKE THAT?
10-14
SCHULZ

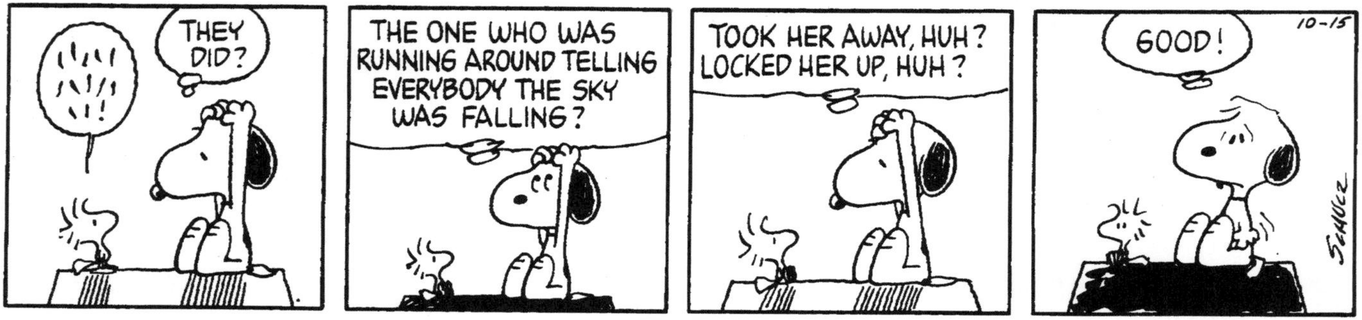
THEY DID?
THE ONE WHO WAS RUNNING AROUND TELLING EVERYBODY THE SKY WAS FALLING?
TOOK HER AWAY, HUH? LOCKED HER UP, HUH?
GOOD!
10-15

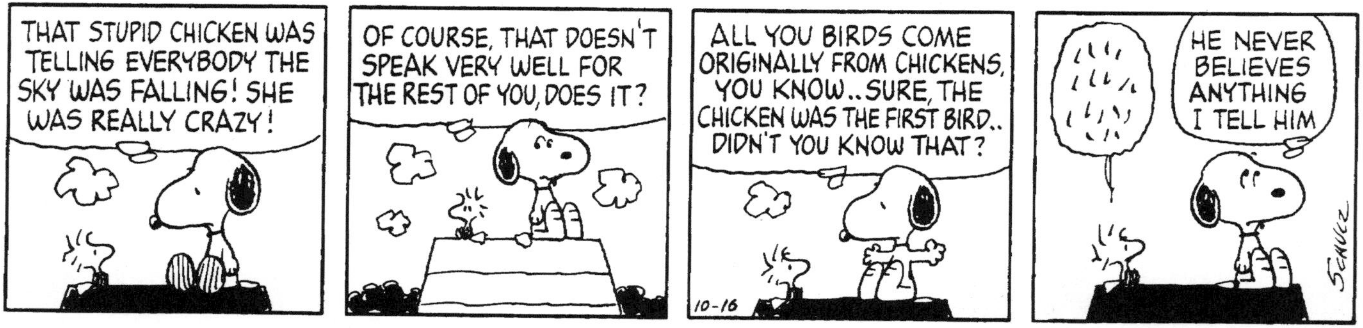
THAT STUPID CHICKEN WAS TELLING EVERYBODY THE SKY WAS FALLING! SHE WAS REALLY CRAZY!
OF COURSE, THAT DOESN'T SPEAK VERY WELL FOR THE REST OF YOU, DOES IT?
ALL YOU BIRDS COME ORIGINALLY FROM CHICKENS, YOU KNOW.. SURE, THE CHICKEN WAS THE FIRST BIRD.. DIDN'T YOU KNOW THAT?
10-16
HE NEVER BELIEVES ANYTHING I TELL HIM

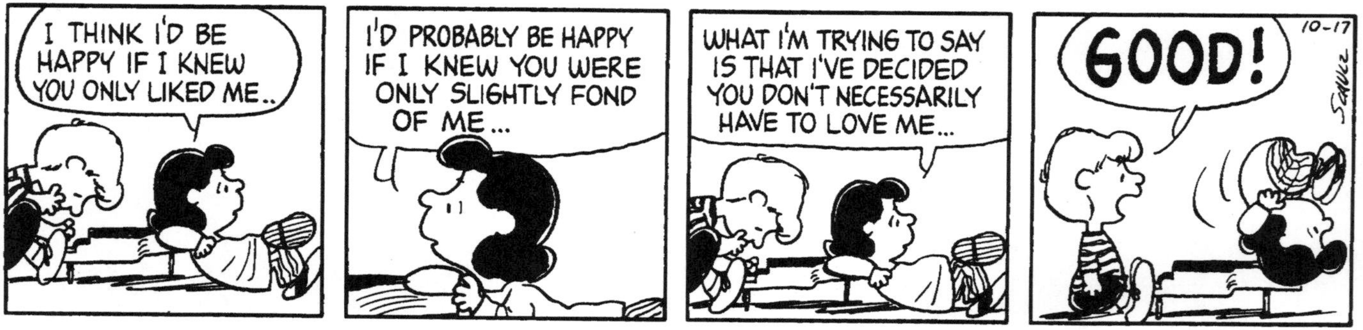
I THINK I'D BE HAPPY IF I KNEW YOU ONLY LIKED ME..
I'D PROBABLY BE HAPPY IF I KNEW YOU WERE ONLY SLIGHTLY FOND OF ME...
WHAT I'M TRYING TO SAY IS THAT I'VE DECIDED YOU DON'T NECESSARILY HAVE TO LOVE ME...
GOOD!
10-17

PEANUTS.
by SCHULZ

HOW NICE.. A POST CARD FROM MY DOG AT GOLF CAMP...

On our first day here, all we did was a little putting.

Today we worked on the short irons.

HE DOESN'T SAY ANYTHING ABOUT EATING OR SLEEPING..

10-18

I WONDER WHERE YOU SLEEP WHEN YOU'RE AT GOLF CAMP..

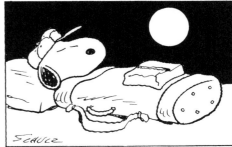

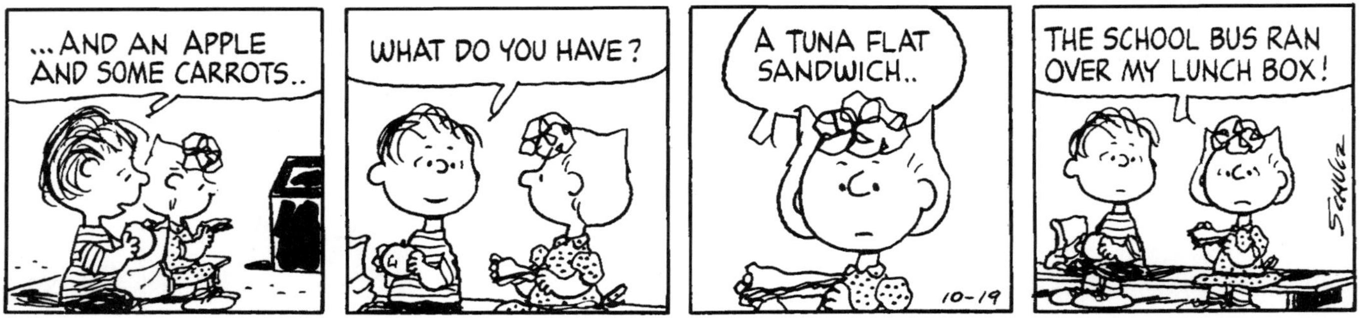
...AND AN APPLE AND SOME CARROTS..
WHAT DO YOU HAVE?
A TUNA FLAT SANDWICH..
THE SCHOOL BUS RAN OVER MY LUNCH BOX!
10-19

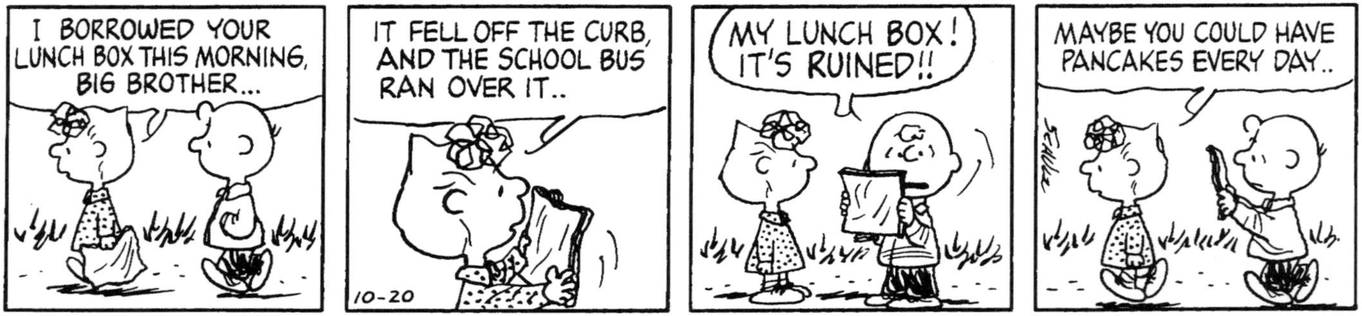
I BORROWED YOUR LUNCH BOX THIS MORNING, BIG BROTHER...
IT FELL OFF THE CURB, AND THE SCHOOL BUS RAN OVER IT..
10-20
MY LUNCH BOX! IT'S RUINED!!
MAYBE YOU COULD HAVE PANCAKES EVERY DAY..

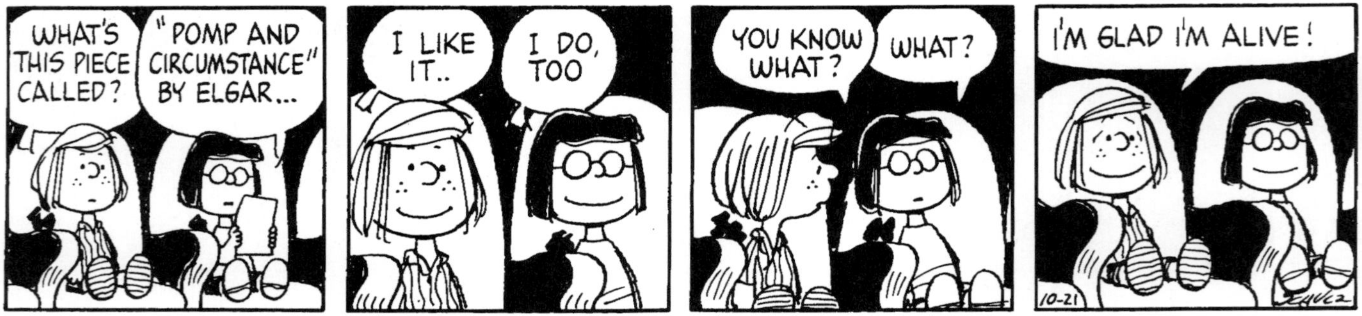
WHAT'S THIS PIECE CALLED?
"POMP AND CIRCUMSTANCE" BY ELGAR...
I LIKE IT..
I DO, TOO
YOU KNOW WHAT?
WHAT?
I'M GLAD I'M ALIVE!
10-21

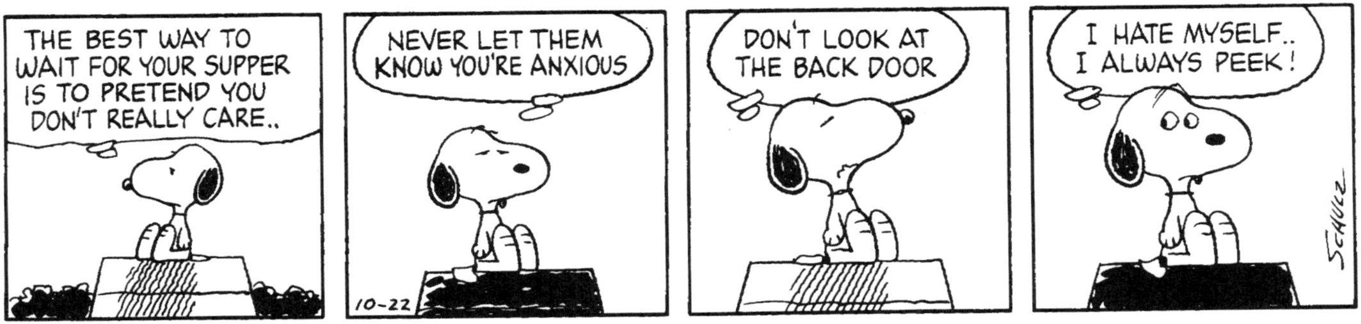
THE BEST WAY TO WAIT FOR YOUR SUPPER IS TO PRETEND YOU DON'T REALLY CARE..
NEVER LET THEM KNOW YOU'RE ANXIOUS
DON'T LOOK AT THE BACK DOOR
I HATE MYSELF.. I ALWAYS PEEK!
10-22
SCHULZ

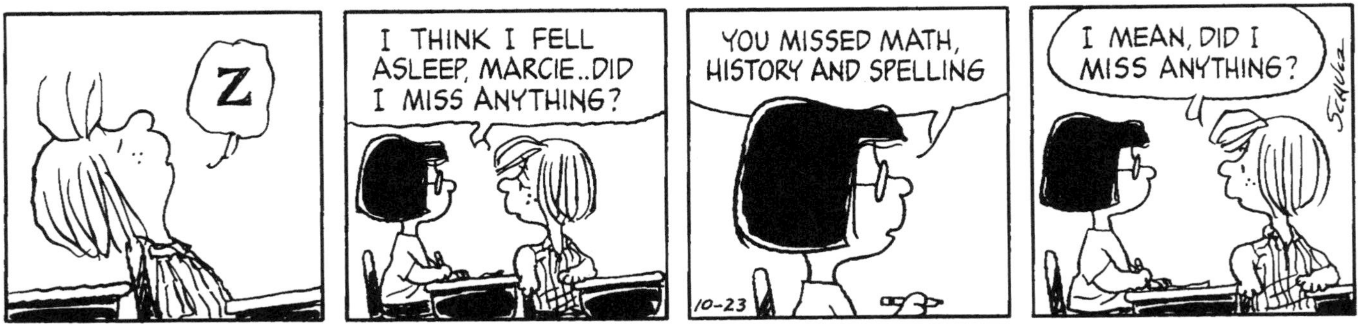
Z
I THINK I FELL ASLEEP, MARCIE..DID I MISS ANYTHING?
YOU MISSED MATH, HISTORY AND SPELLING
I MEAN, DID I MISS ANYTHING?
10-23
SCHULZ

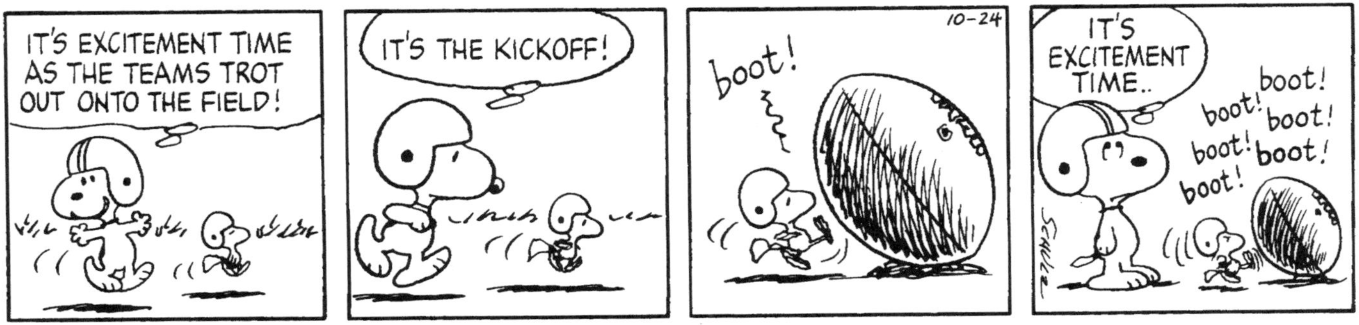
IT'S EXCITEMENT TIME AS THE TEAMS TROT OUT ONTO THE FIELD!
IT'S THE KICKOFF!
boot!
10-24
IT'S EXCITEMENT TIME..
boot! boot! boot! boot! boot! boot!
SCHULZ

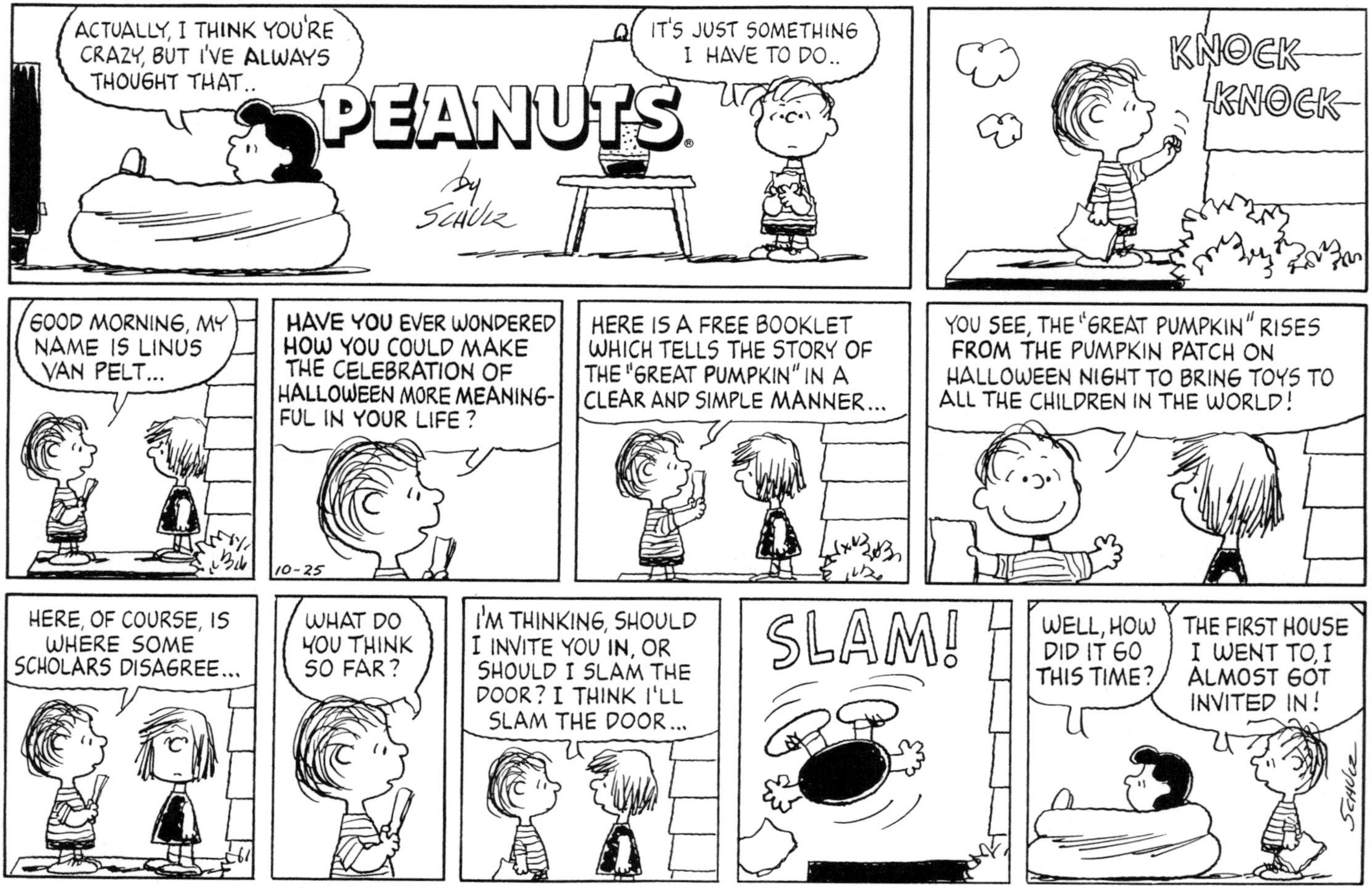
ACTUALLY, I THINK YOU'RE CRAZY, BUT I'VE ALWAYS THOUGHT THAT..
PEANUTS
by SCHULZ
IT'S JUST SOMETHING I HAVE TO DO..
KNOCK KNOCK
GOOD MORNING, MY NAME IS LINUS VAN PELT...
HAVE YOU EVER WONDERED HOW YOU COULD MAKE THE CELEBRATION OF HALLOWEEN MORE MEANING-FUL IN YOUR LIFE?
10-25
HERE IS A FREE BOOKLET WHICH TELLS THE STORY OF THE "GREAT PUMPKIN" IN A CLEAR AND SIMPLE MANNER...
YOU SEE, THE "GREAT PUMPKIN" RISES FROM THE PUMPKIN PATCH ON HALLOWEEN NIGHT TO BRING TOYS TO ALL THE CHILDREN IN THE WORLD!
HERE, OF COURSE, IS WHERE SOME SCHOLARS DISAGREE...
WHAT DO YOU THINK SO FAR?
I'M THINKING, SHOULD I INVITE YOU IN, OR SHOULD I SLAM THE DOOR? I THINK I'LL SLAM THE DOOR...
SLAM!
WELL, HOW DID IT GO THIS TIME?
THE FIRST HOUSE I WENT TO, I ALMOST GOT INVITED IN!
SCHULZ

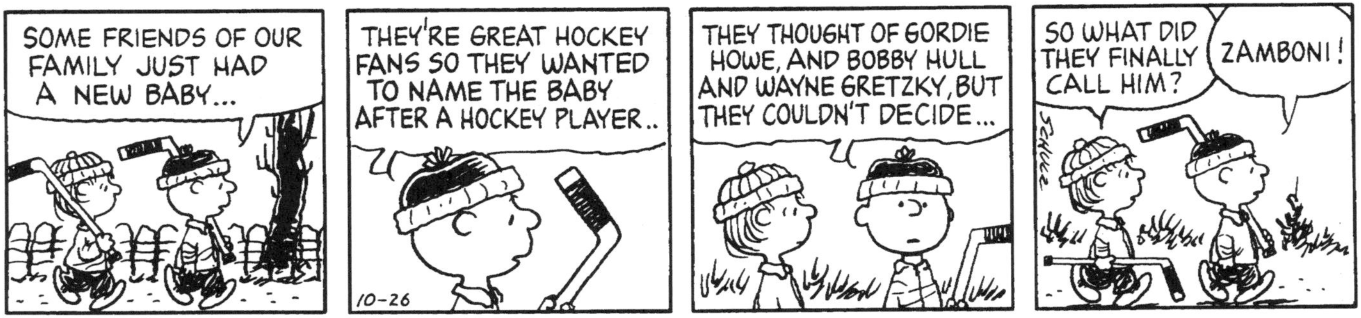
SOME FRIENDS OF OUR FAMILY JUST HAD A NEW BABY...
THEY'RE GREAT HOCKEY FANS SO THEY WANTED TO NAME THE BABY AFTER A HOCKEY PLAYER..
10-26
THEY THOUGHT OF GORDIE HOWE, AND BOBBY HULL AND WAYNE GRETZKY, BUT THEY COULDN'T DECIDE...
SO WHAT DID THEY FINALLY CALL HIM?
ZAMBONI!
SCHULZ

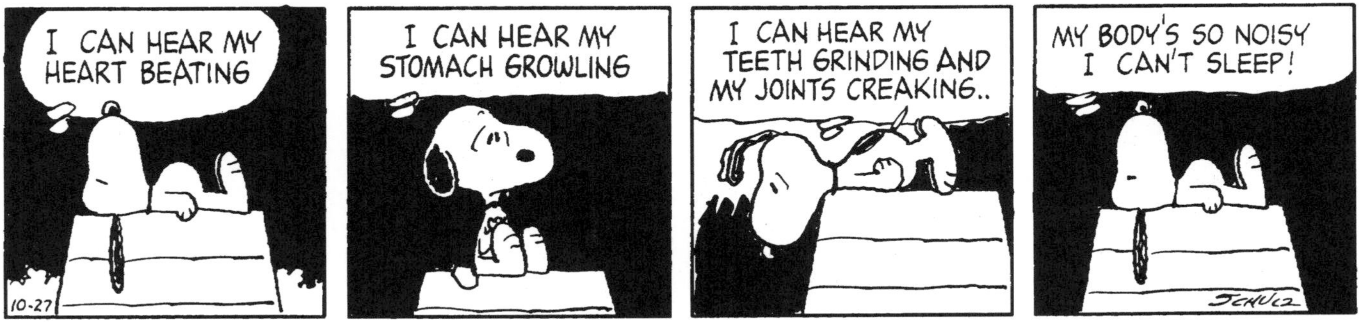
I CAN HEAR MY HEART BEATING
10-27
I CAN HEAR MY STOMACH GROWLING
I CAN HEAR MY TEETH GRINDING AND MY JOINTS CREAKING..
MY BODY'S SO NOISY I CAN'T SLEEP!
SCHULZ

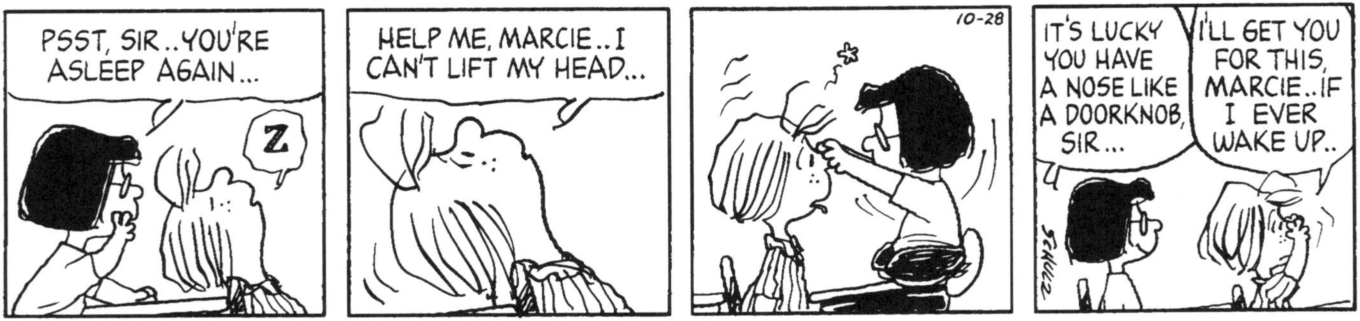
PSST, SIR..YOU'RE ASLEEP AGAIN...
Z
HELP ME, MARCIE..I CAN'T LIFT MY HEAD...
10-28
IT'S LUCKY YOU HAVE A NOSE LIKE A DOORKNOB, SIR...
I'LL GET YOU FOR THIS, MARCIE..IF I EVER WAKE UP..
SCHULZ

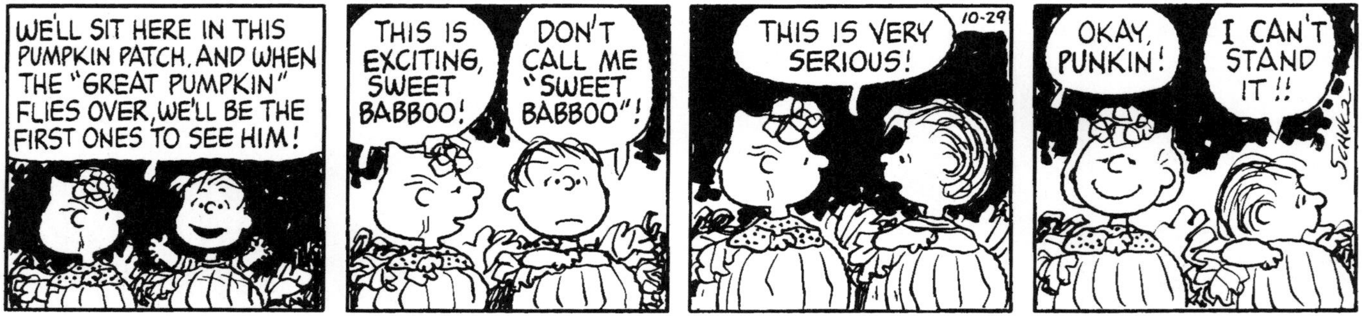
WE'LL SIT HERE IN THIS PUMPKIN PATCH, AND WHEN THE "GREAT PUMPKIN" FLIES OVER, WE'LL BE THE FIRST ONES TO SEE HIM!
THIS IS EXCITING, SWEET BABBOO!
DON'T CALL ME "SWEET BABBOO"!
10-29
THIS IS VERY SERIOUS!
OKAY, PUNKIN!
I CAN'T STAND IT!!
SCHULZ

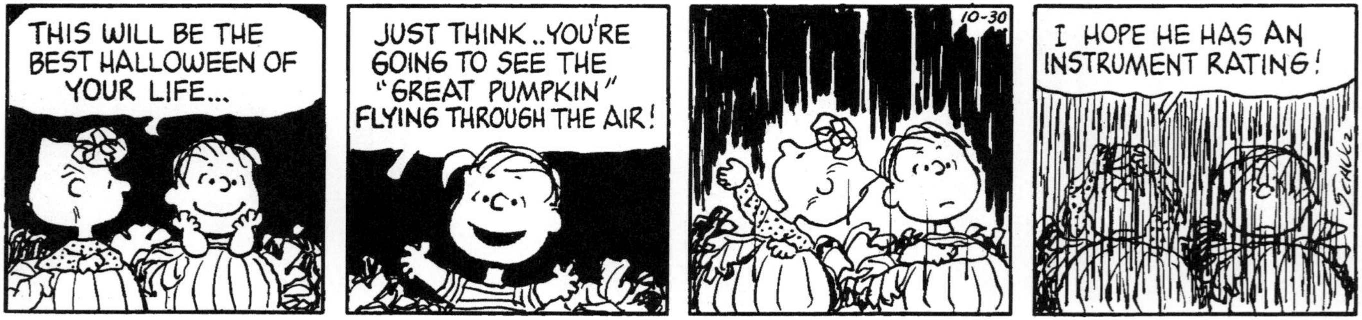
THIS WILL BE THE BEST HALLOWEEN OF YOUR LIFE...
JUST THINK..YOU'RE GOING TO SEE THE "GREAT PUMPKIN" FLYING THROUGH THE AIR!
10-30
I HOPE HE HAS AN INSTRUMENT RATING!
SCHULZ

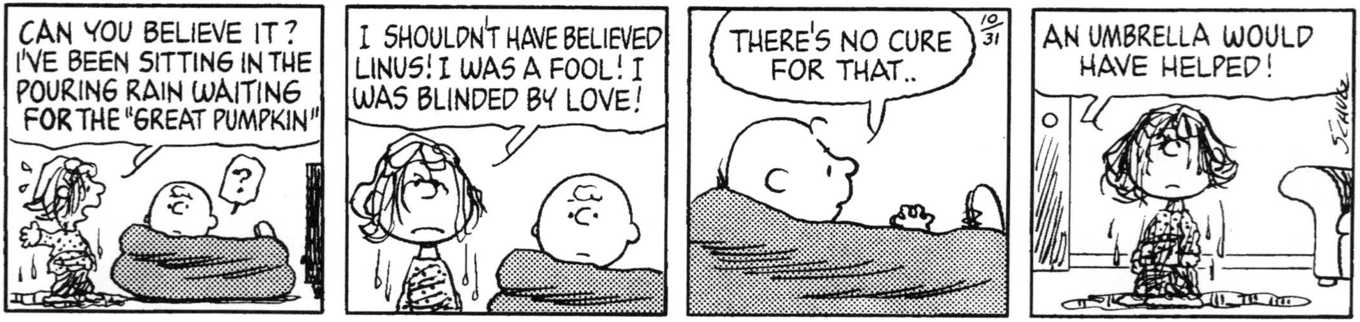
CAN YOU BELIEVE IT? I'VE BEEN SITTING IN THE POURING RAIN WAITING FOR THE "GREAT PUMPKIN"
?
I SHOULDN'T HAVE BELIEVED LINUS! I WAS A FOOL! I WAS BLINDED BY LOVE!
10/31
THERE'S NO CURE FOR THAT..
AN UMBRELLA WOULD HAVE HELPED!
SCHULZ

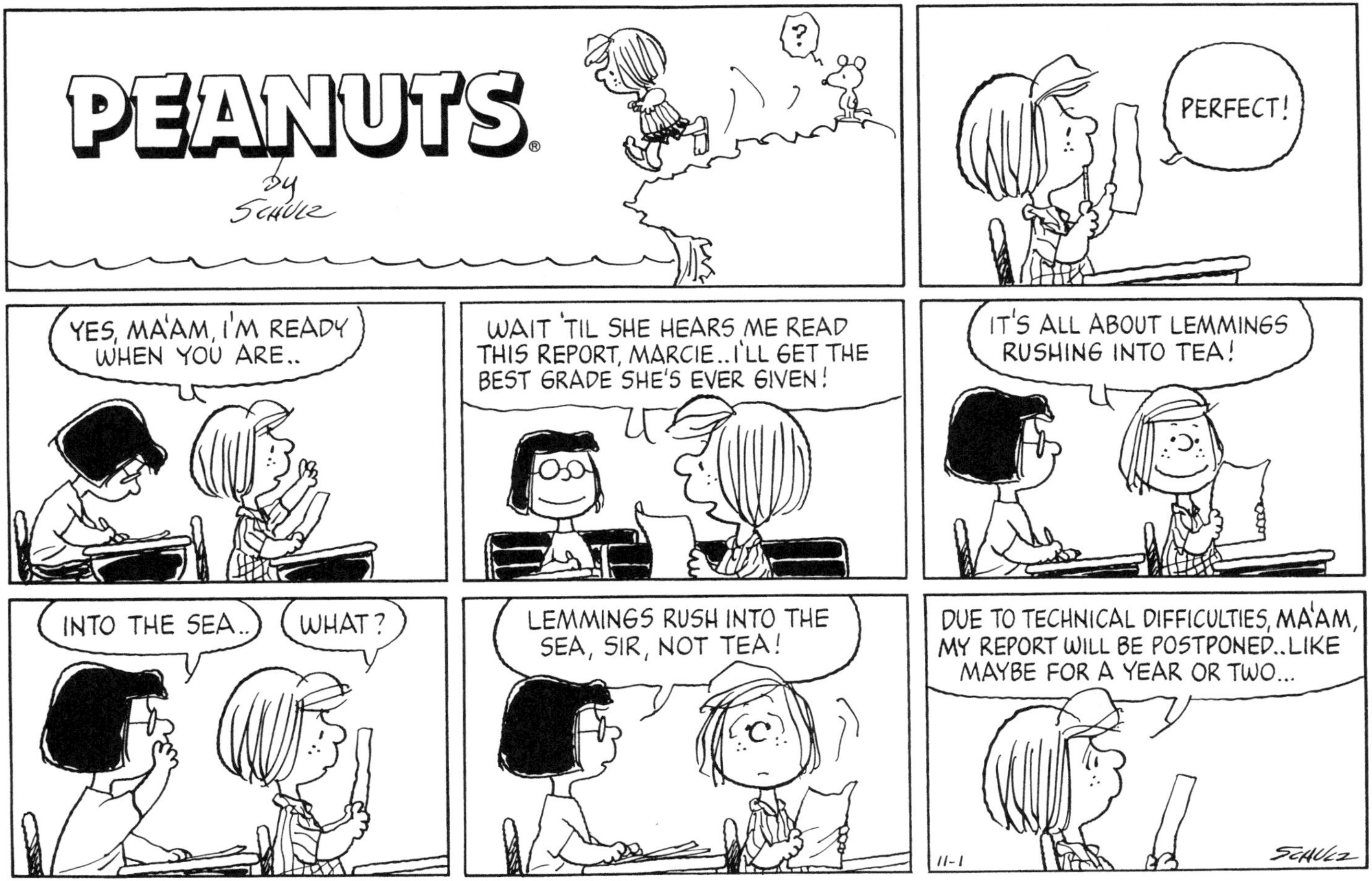
PEANUTS®
by SCHULZ
?
PERFECT!
YES, MA'AM, I'M READY WHEN YOU ARE..
WAIT 'TIL SHE HEARS ME READ THIS REPORT, MARCIE..I'LL GET THE BEST GRADE SHE'S EVER GIVEN!
IT'S ALL ABOUT LEMMINGS RUSHING INTO TEA!
INTO THE SEA..
WHAT?
LEMMINGS RUSH INTO THE SEA, SIR, NOT TEA!
DUE TO TECHNICAL DIFFICULTIES, MA'AM, MY REPORT WILL BE POSTPONED..LIKE MAYBE FOR A YEAR OR TWO...
11-1
SCHULZ

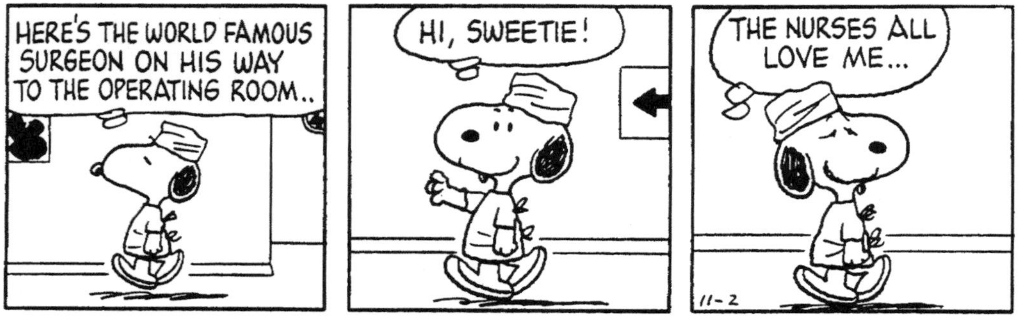
HERE'S THE WORLD FAMOUS SURGEON ON HIS WAY TO THE OPERATING ROOM..
HI, SWEETIE!
THE NURSES ALL LOVE ME...
11-2
AND I LOVE ME!
SCHULZ

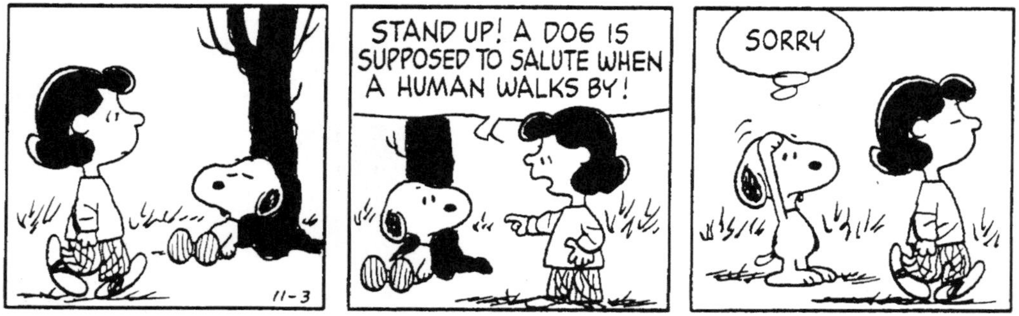
11-3
STAND UP! A DOG IS SUPPOSED TO SALUTE WHEN A HUMAN WALKS BY!
SORRY
I THOUGHT YOU WEREN'T REQUIRED TO SALUTE IF YOU WEREN'T IN UNIFORM...
SCHULZ

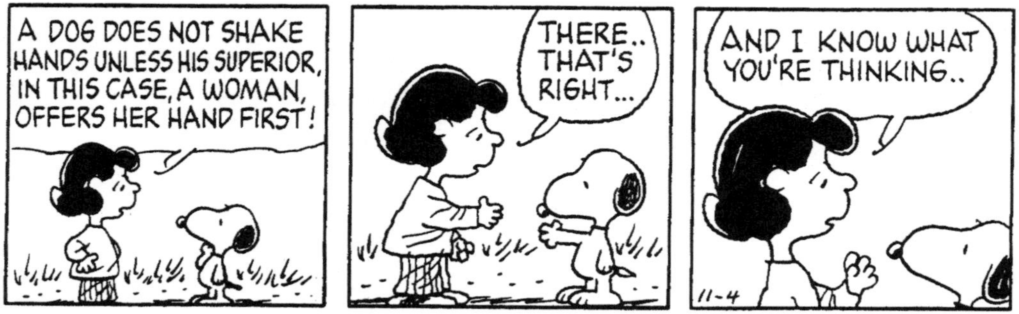
A DOG DOES NOT SHAKE HANDS UNLESS HIS SUPERIOR, IN THIS CASE, A WOMAN, OFFERS HER HAND FIRST!
THERE.. THAT'S RIGHT...
AND I KNOW WHAT YOU'RE THINKING..
11-4
YOU DON'T STICK OUT YOUR TONGUE UNTIL AFTER SHE LEAVES!
RATS!
SCHULZ

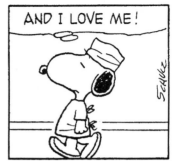

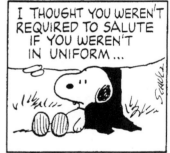

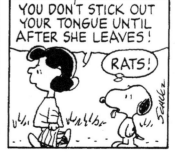

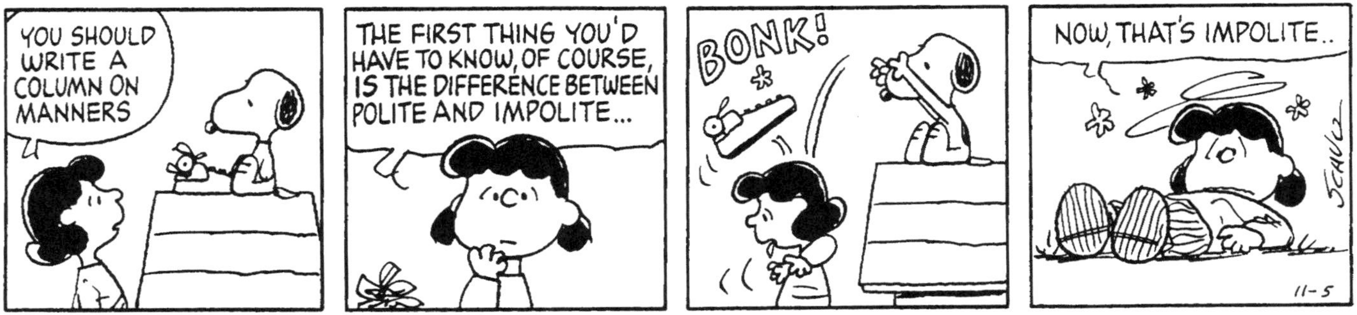
YOU SHOULD WRITE A COLUMN ON MANNERS
THE FIRST THING YOU'D HAVE TO KNOW, OF COURSE, IS THE DIFFERENCE BETWEEN POLITE AND IMPOLITE...
BONK!
NOW, THAT'S IMPOLITE..
SCHULZ
11-5

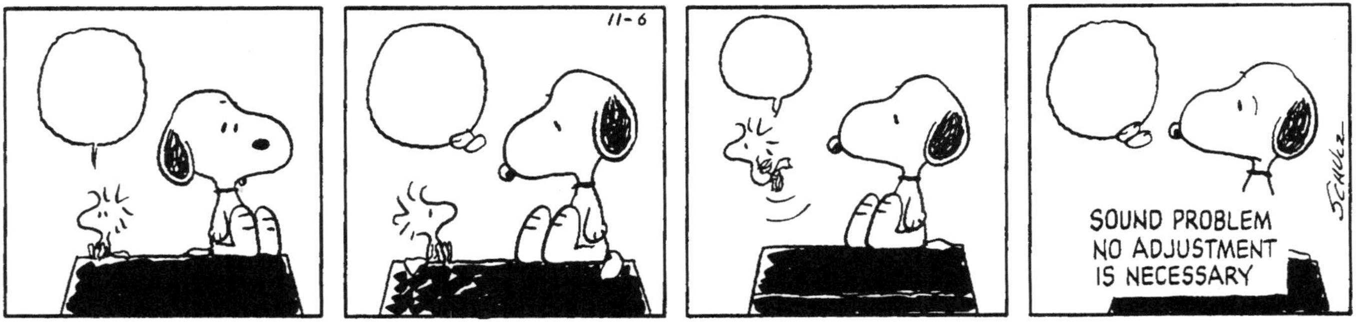
11-6
SOUND PROBLEM NO ADJUSTMENT IS NECESSARY
SCHULZ

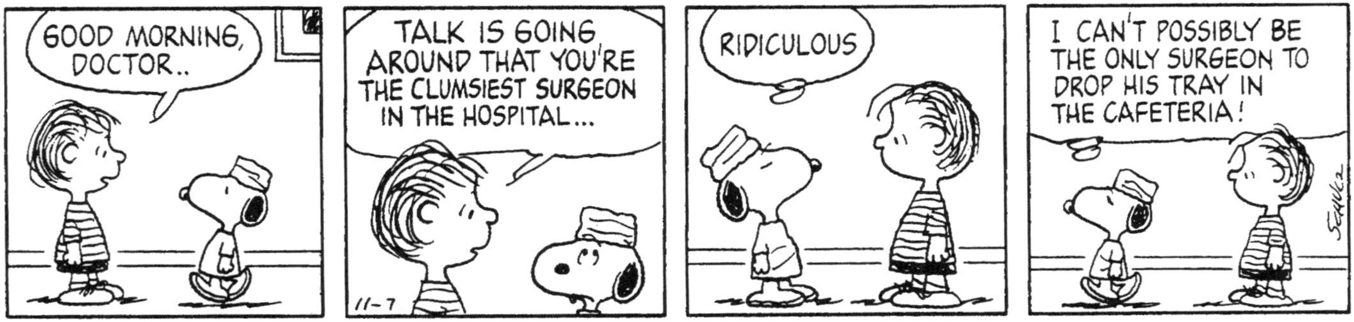
GOOD MORNING, DOCTOR..
TALK IS GOING AROUND THAT YOU'RE THE CLUMSIEST SURGEON IN THE HOSPITAL...
11-7
RIDICULOUS
I CAN'T POSSIBLY BE THE ONLY SURGEON TO DROP HIS TRAY IN THE CAFETERIA!
SCHULZ

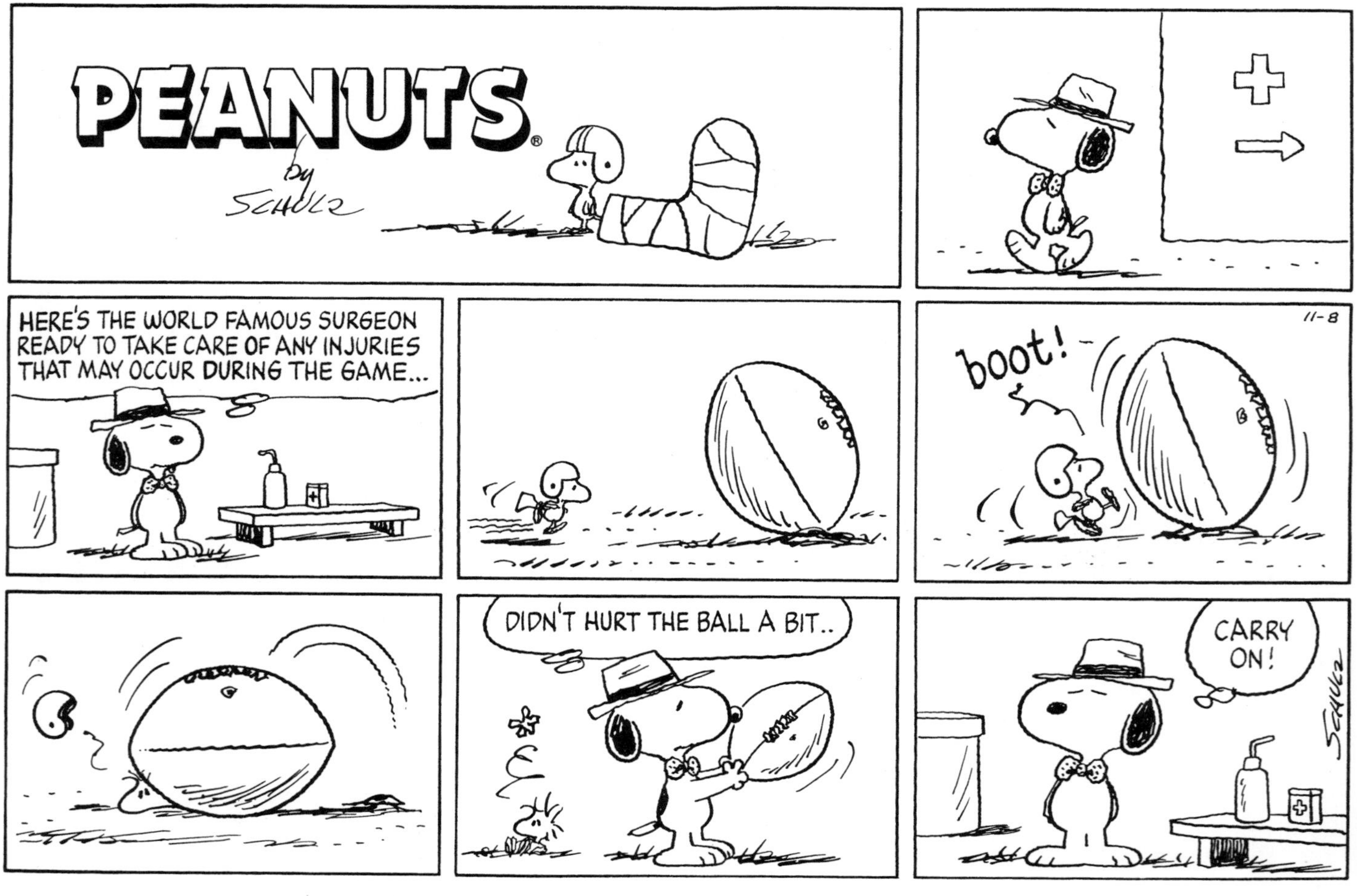
PEANUTS®
by SCHULZ
HERE'S THE WORLD FAMOUS SURGEON READY TO TAKE CARE OF ANY INJURIES THAT MAY OCCUR DURING THE GAME...
11-8
boot!
DIDN'T HURT THE BALL A BIT..
CARRY ON!
SCHULZ

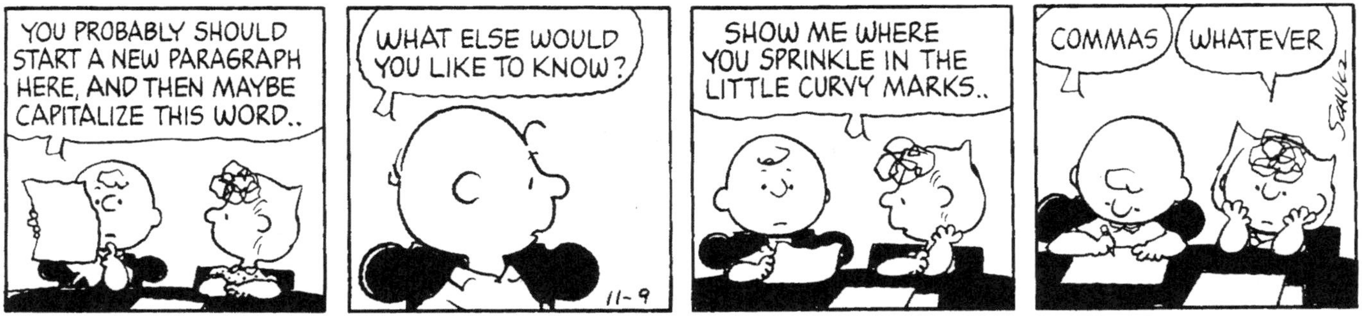
YOU PROBABLY SHOULD START A NEW PARAGRAPH HERE, AND THEN MAYBE CAPITALIZE THIS WORD..
WHAT ELSE WOULD YOU LIKE TO KNOW?
11-9
SHOW ME WHERE YOU SPRINKLE IN THE LITTLE CURVY MARKS..
COMMAS
WHATEVER
SCHULZ

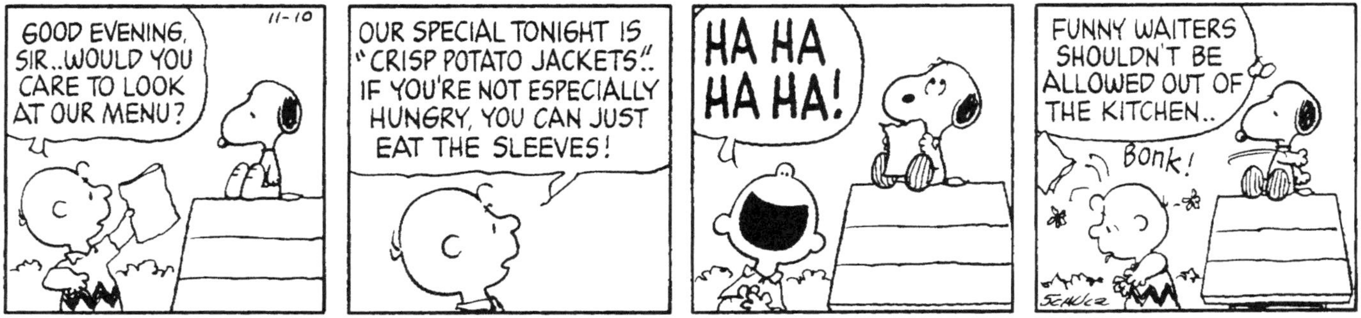
11-10
GOOD EVENING, SIR..WOULD YOU CARE TO LOOK AT OUR MENU?
OUR SPECIAL TONIGHT IS "CRISP POTATO JACKETS".. IF YOU'RE NOT ESPECIALLY HUNGRY, YOU CAN JUST EAT THE SLEEVES!
HA HA HA HA!
FUNNY WAITERS SHOULDN'T BE ALLOWED OUT OF THE KITCHEN..
Bonk!
SCHULZ

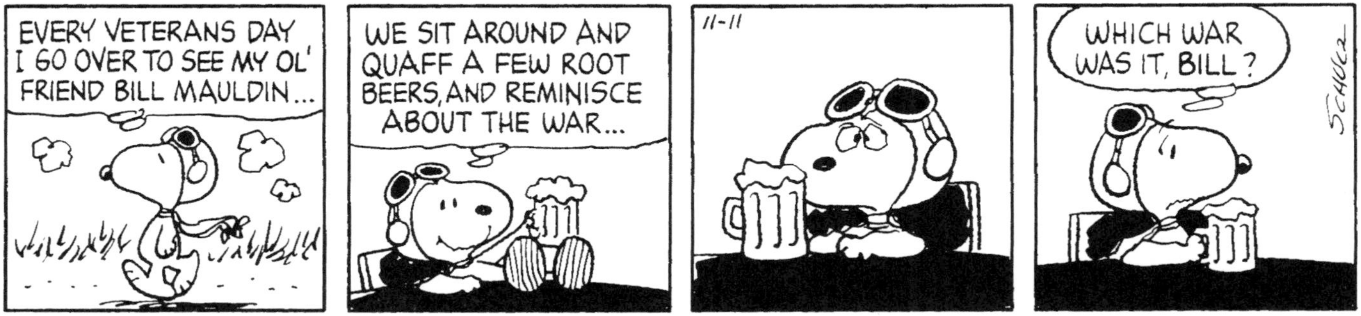
EVERY VETERANS DAY I GO OVER TO SEE MY OL' FRIEND BILL MAULDIN...
WE SIT AROUND AND QUAFF A FEW ROOT BEERS, AND REMINISCE ABOUT THE WAR...
11-11
WHICH WAR WAS IT, BILL?
SCHULZ

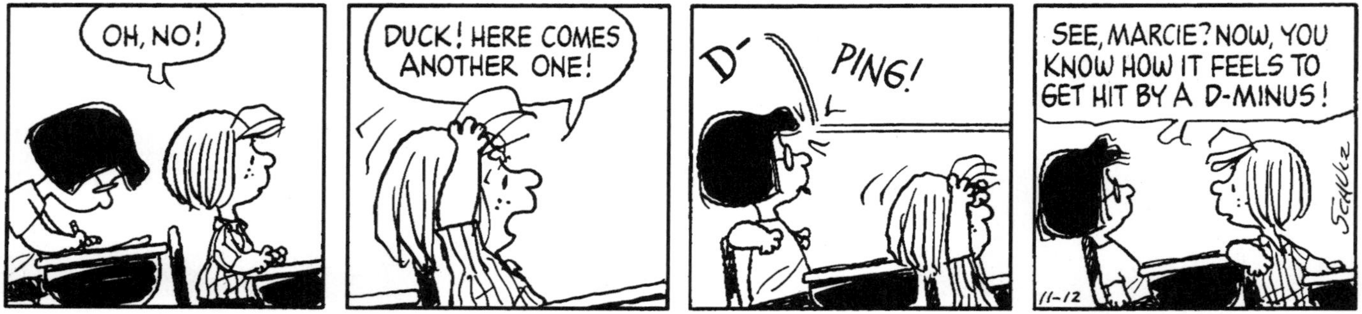
OH, NO!
DUCK! HERE COMES ANOTHER ONE!
D-
PING!
SEE, MARCIE? NOW, YOU KNOW HOW IT FEELS TO GET HIT BY A D-MINUS!
SCHULZ
11-12

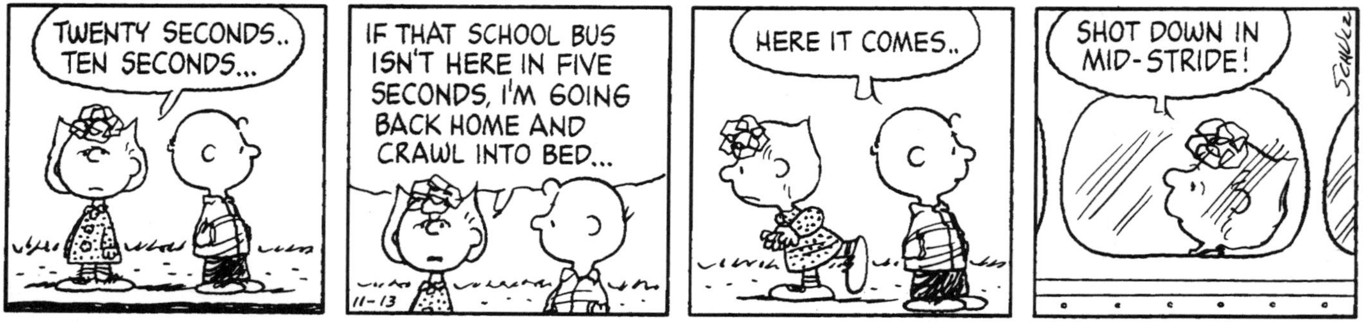
TWENTY SECONDS.. TEN SECONDS...
IF THAT SCHOOL BUS ISN'T HERE IN FIVE SECONDS, I'M GOING BACK HOME AND CRAWL INTO BED...
11-13
HERE IT COMES..
SHOT DOWN IN MID-STRIDE!
SCHULZ

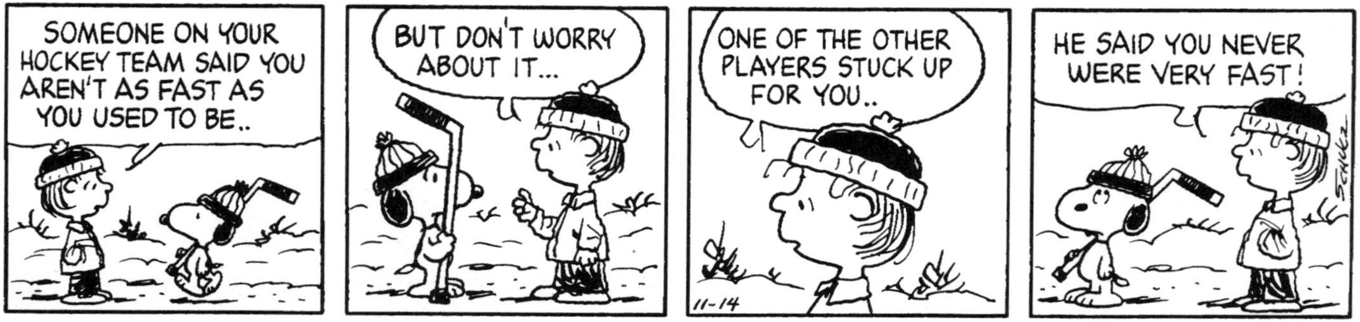
SOMEONE ON YOUR HOCKEY TEAM SAID YOU AREN'T AS FAST AS YOU USED TO BE..
BUT DON'T WORRY ABOUT IT...
ONE OF THE OTHER PLAYERS STUCK UP FOR YOU..
11-14
HE SAID YOU NEVER WERE VERY FAST!
SCHULZ

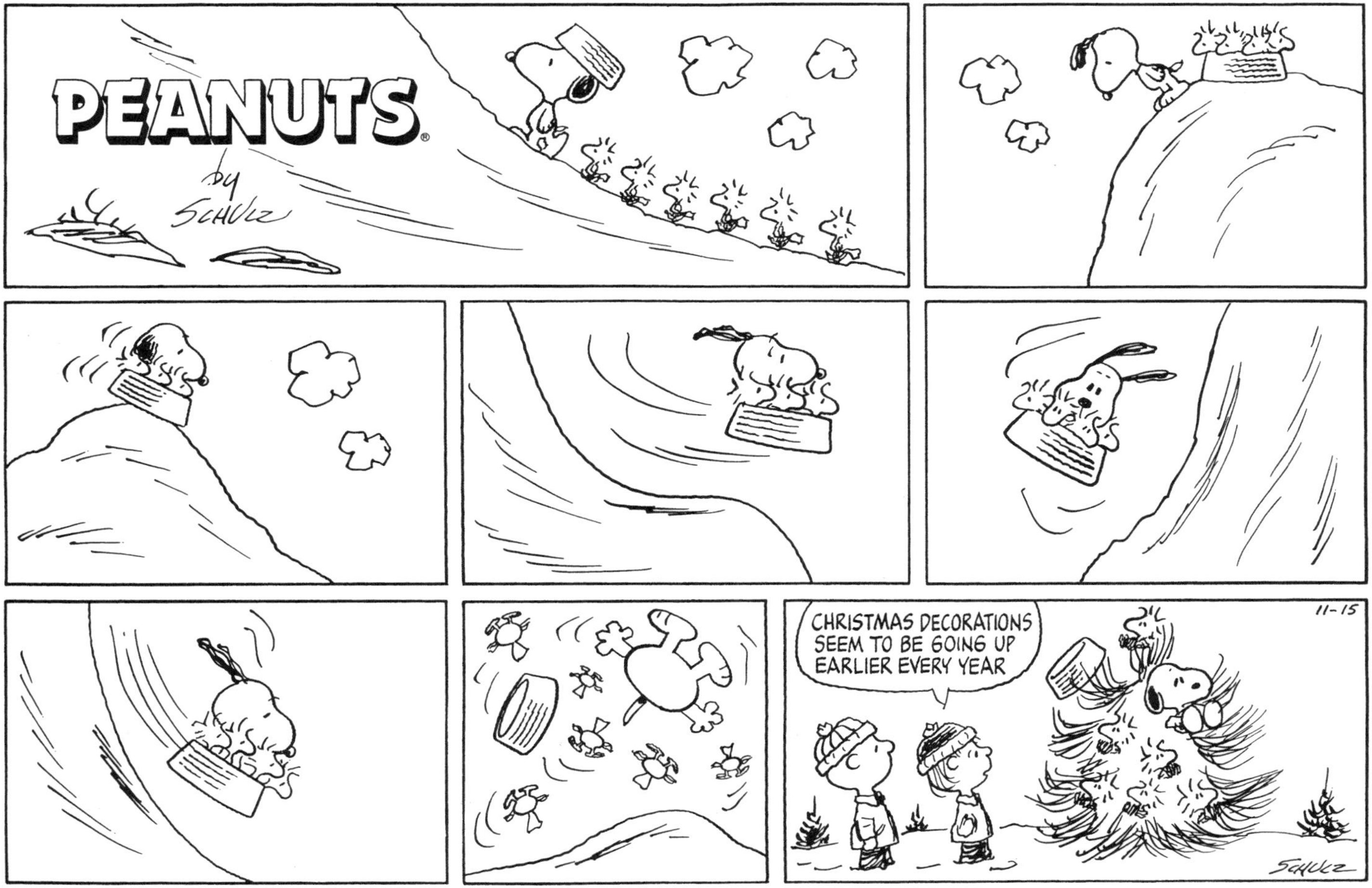
PEANUTS®
by SCHULZ
11-15
CHRISTMAS DECORATIONS SEEM TO BE GOING UP EARLIER EVERY YEAR
SCHULZ

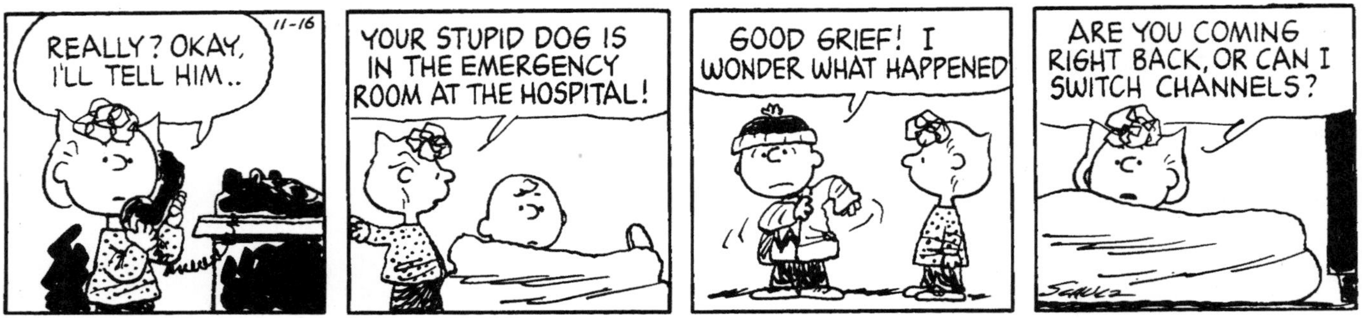
11-16
REALLY? OKAY, I'LL TELL HIM..
YOUR STUPID DOG IS IN THE EMERGENCY ROOM AT THE HOSPITAL!
GOOD GRIEF! I WONDER WHAT HAPPENED
ARE YOU COMING RIGHT BACK, OR CAN I SWITCH CHANNELS?
SCHULZ

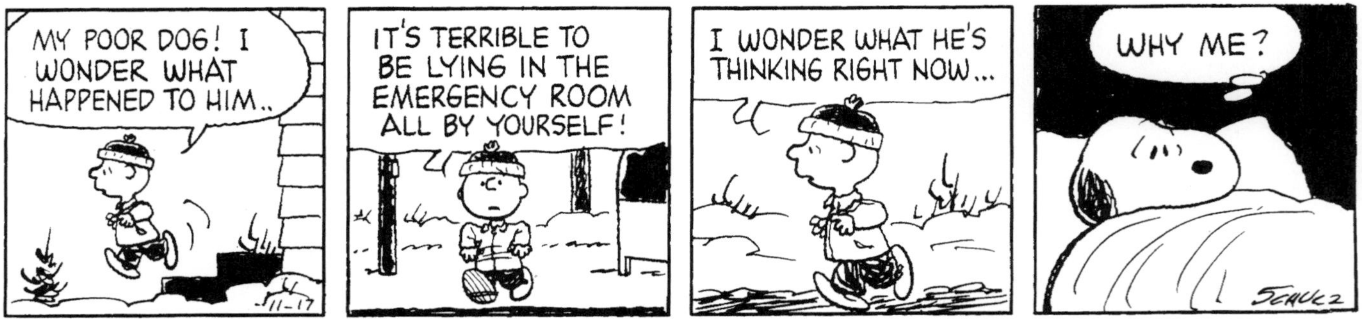
MY POOR DOG! I WONDER WHAT HAPPENED TO HIM..
11-17
IT'S TERRIBLE TO BE LYING IN THE EMERGENCY ROOM ALL BY YOURSELF!
I WONDER WHAT HE'S THINKING RIGHT NOW...
WHY ME?
SCHULZ

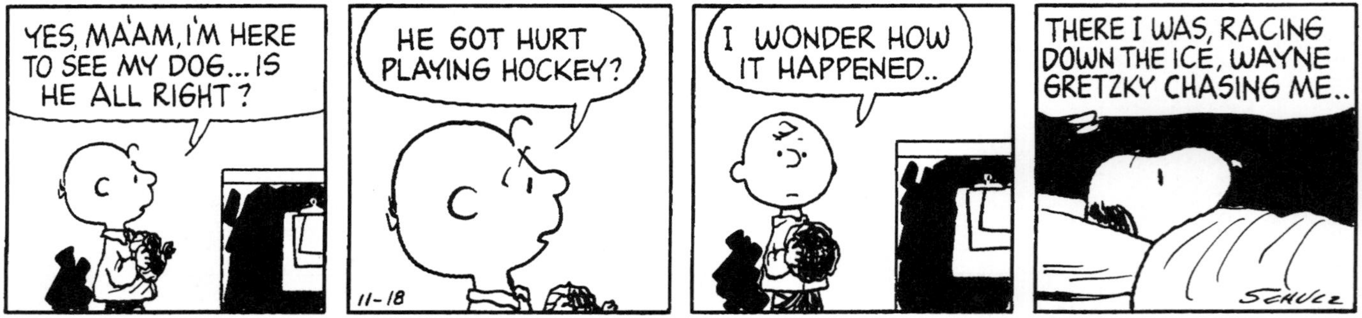
YES, MA'AM, I'M HERE TO SEE MY DOG... IS HE ALL RIGHT?
HE GOT HURT PLAYING HOCKEY?
11-18
I WONDER HOW IT HAPPENED..
THERE I WAS, RACING DOWN THE ICE, WAYNE GRETZKY CHASING ME..
SCHULZ

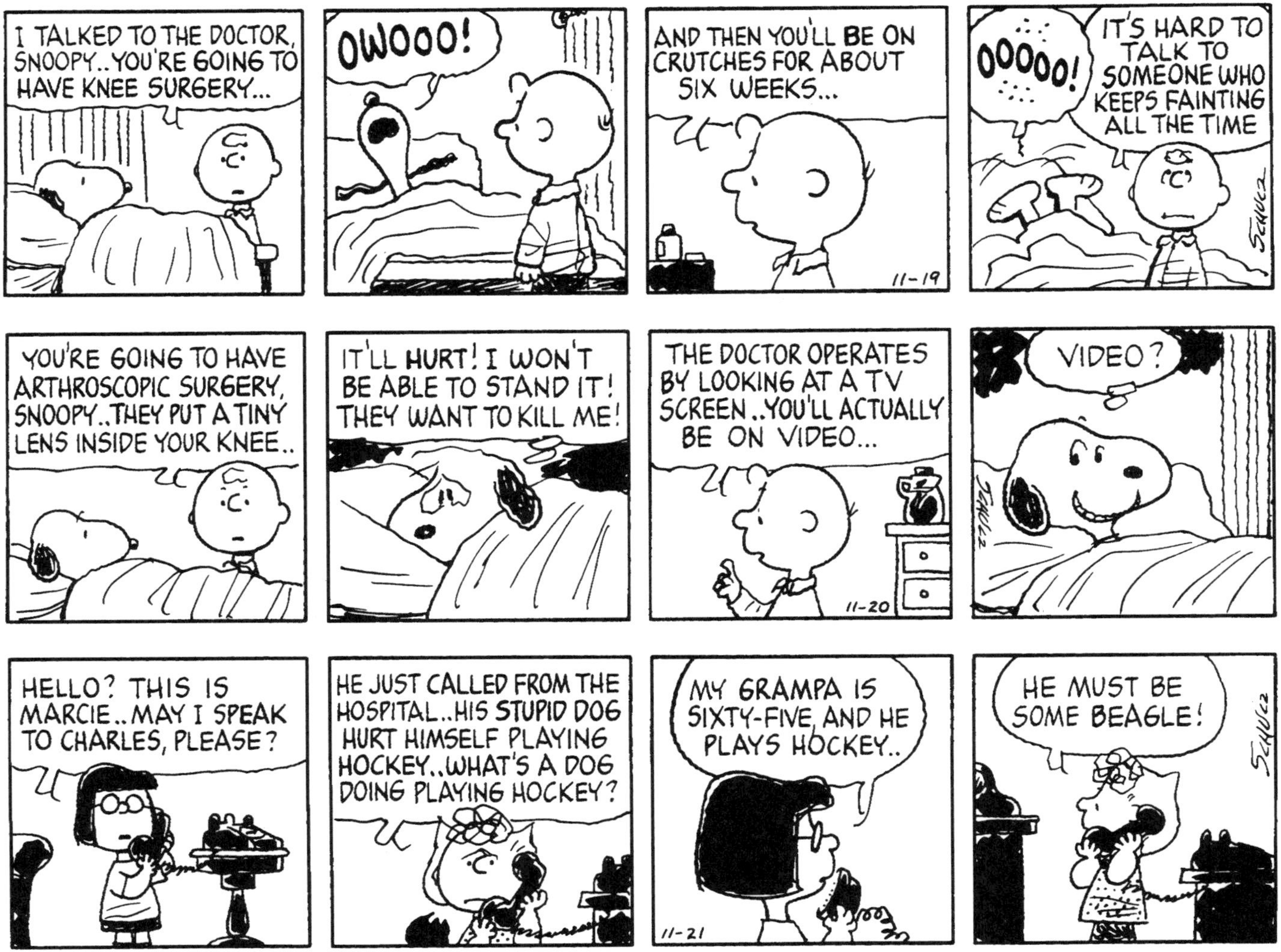
I TALKED TO THE DOCTOR, SNOOPY..YOU'RE GOING TO HAVE KNEE SURGERY...
OWOOO!
AND THEN YOU'LL BE ON CRUTCHES FOR ABOUT SIX WEEKS...
11-19
OOOOO!
IT'S HARD TO TALK TO SOMEONE WHO KEEPS FAINTING ALL THE TIME
SCHULZ
YOU'RE GOING TO HAVE ARTHROSCOPIC SURGERY, SNOOPY..THEY PUT A TINY LENS INSIDE YOUR KNEE..
IT'LL HURT! I WON'T BE ABLE TO STAND IT! THEY WANT TO KILL ME!
THE DOCTOR OPERATES BY LOOKING AT A TV SCREEN..YOU'LL ACTUALLY BE ON VIDEO...
11-20
VIDEO?
SCHULZ
HELLO? THIS IS MARCIE..MAY I SPEAK TO CHARLES, PLEASE?
HE JUST CALLED FROM THE HOSPITAL..HIS STUPID DOG HURT HIMSELF PLAYING HOCKEY..WHAT'S A DOG DOING PLAYING HOCKEY?
11-21
MY GRAMPA IS SIXTY-FIVE, AND HE PLAYS HOCKEY..
HE MUST BE SOME BEAGLE!
SCHULZ

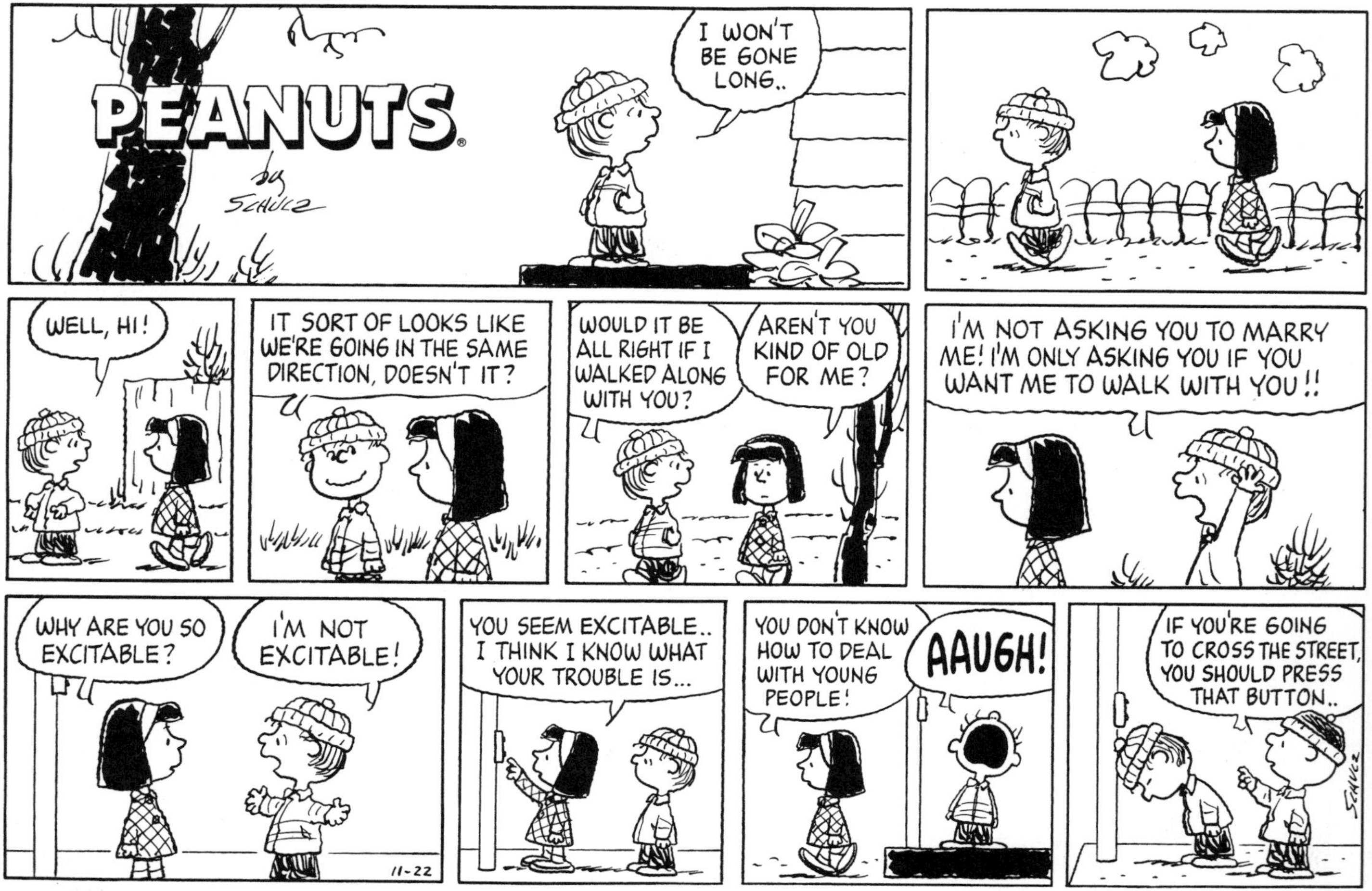
PEANUTS
by SCHULZ
I WON'T BE GONE LONG..
WELL, HI!
IT SORT OF LOOKS LIKE WE'RE GOING IN THE SAME DIRECTION, DOESN'T IT?
WOULD IT BE ALL RIGHT IF I WALKED ALONG WITH YOU?
AREN'T YOU KIND OF OLD FOR ME?
I'M NOT ASKING YOU TO MARRY ME! I'M ONLY ASKING YOU IF YOU WANT ME TO WALK WITH YOU!!
WHY ARE YOU SO EXCITABLE?
I'M NOT EXCITABLE!
11-22
YOU SEEM EXCITABLE.. I THINK I KNOW WHAT YOUR TROUBLE IS...
YOU DON'T KNOW HOW TO DEAL WITH YOUNG PEOPLE!
AAUGH!
IF YOU'RE GOING TO CROSS THE STREET, YOU SHOULD PRESS THAT BUTTON..
SCHULZ

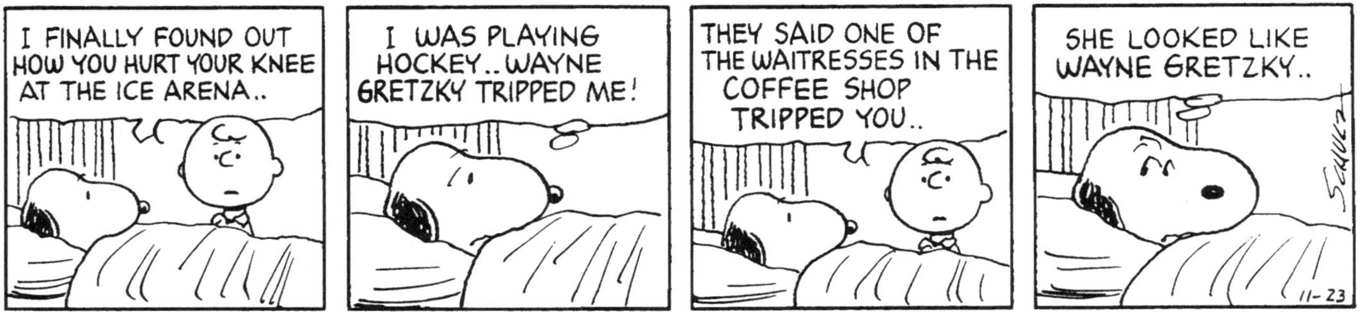
I FINALLY FOUND OUT HOW YOU HURT YOUR KNEE AT THE ICE ARENA..
I WAS PLAYING HOCKEY.. WAYNE GRETZKY TRIPPED ME!
THEY SAID ONE OF THE WAITRESSES IN THE COFFEE SHOP TRIPPED YOU..
SHE LOOKED LIKE WAYNE GRETZKY..
SCHULZ
11-23

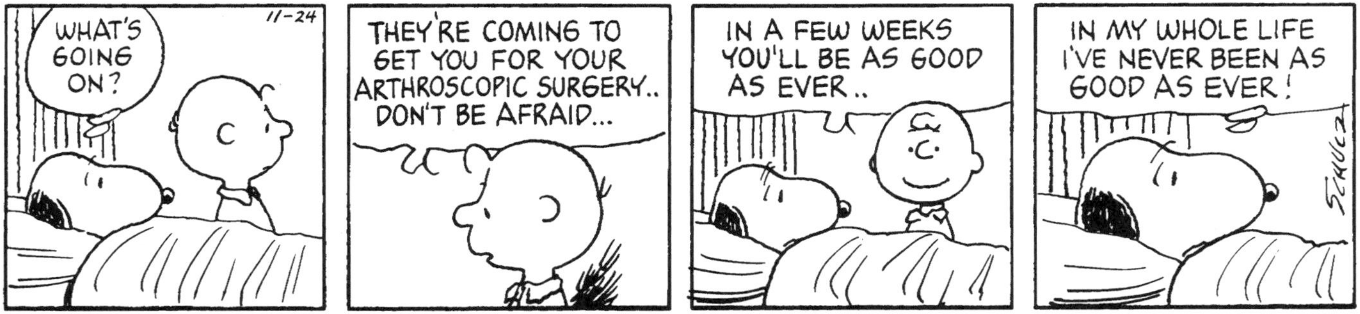
11-24
WHAT'S GOING ON?
THEY'RE COMING TO GET YOU FOR YOUR ARTHROSCOPIC SURGERY.. DON'T BE AFRAID...
IN A FEW WEEKS YOU'LL BE AS GOOD AS EVER..
IN MY WHOLE LIFE I'VE NEVER BEEN AS GOOD AS EVER!
SCHULZ

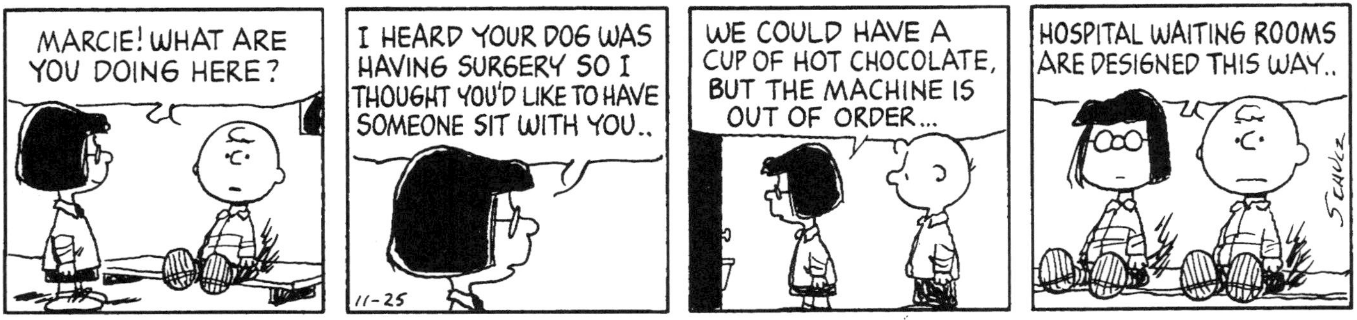
MARCIE! WHAT ARE YOU DOING HERE?
I HEARD YOUR DOG WAS HAVING SURGERY SO I THOUGHT YOU'D LIKE TO HAVE SOMEONE SIT WITH YOU..
11-25
WE COULD HAVE A CUP OF HOT CHOCOLATE, BUT THE MACHINE IS OUT OF ORDER...
HOSPITAL WAITING ROOMS ARE DESIGNED THIS WAY..
SCHULZ

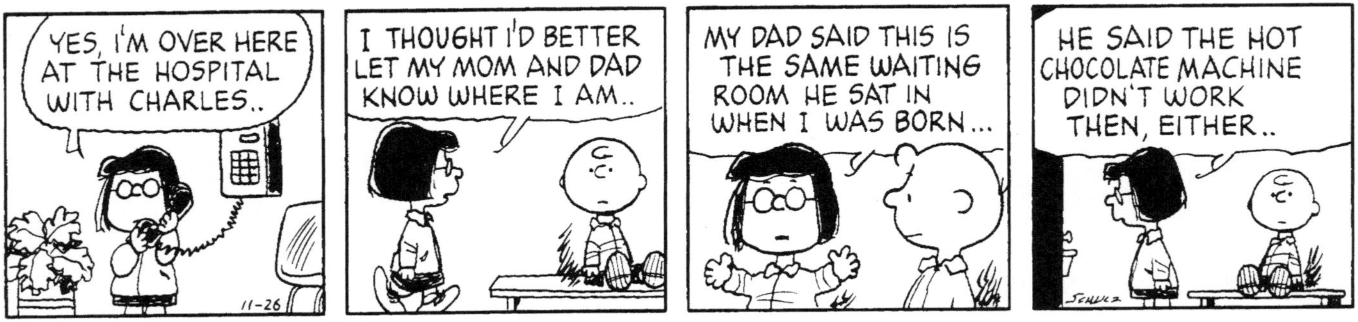
YES, I'M OVER HERE AT THE HOSPITAL WITH CHARLES..
I THOUGHT I'D BETTER LET MY MOM AND DAD KNOW WHERE I AM..
MY DAD SAID THIS IS THE SAME WAITING ROOM HE SAT IN WHEN I WAS BORN...
HE SAID THE HOT CHOCOLATE MACHINE DIDN'T WORK THEN, EITHER..

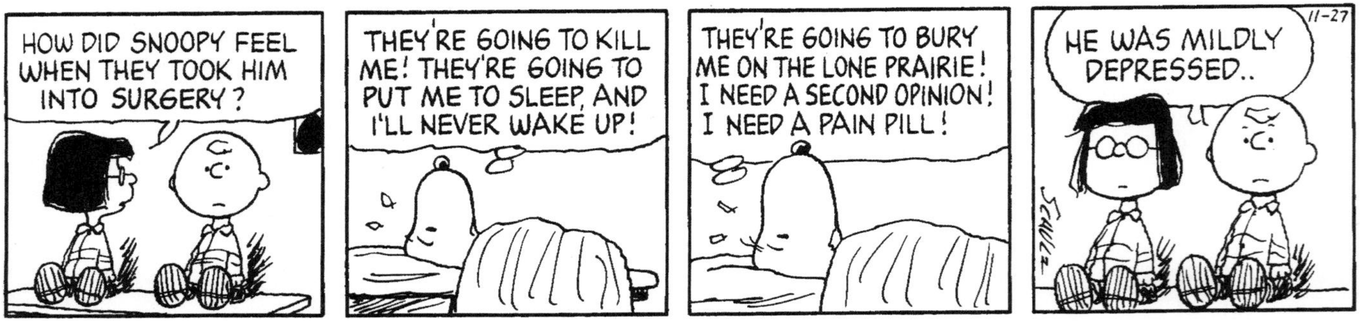
HOW DID SNOOPY FEEL WHEN THEY TOOK HIM INTO SURGERY?
THEY'RE GOING TO KILL ME! THEY'RE GOING TO PUT ME TO SLEEP, AND I'LL NEVER WAKE UP!
THEY'RE GOING TO BURY ME ON THE LONE PRAIRIE! I NEED A SECOND OPINION! I NEED A PAIN PILL!
HE WAS MILDLY DEPRESSED..

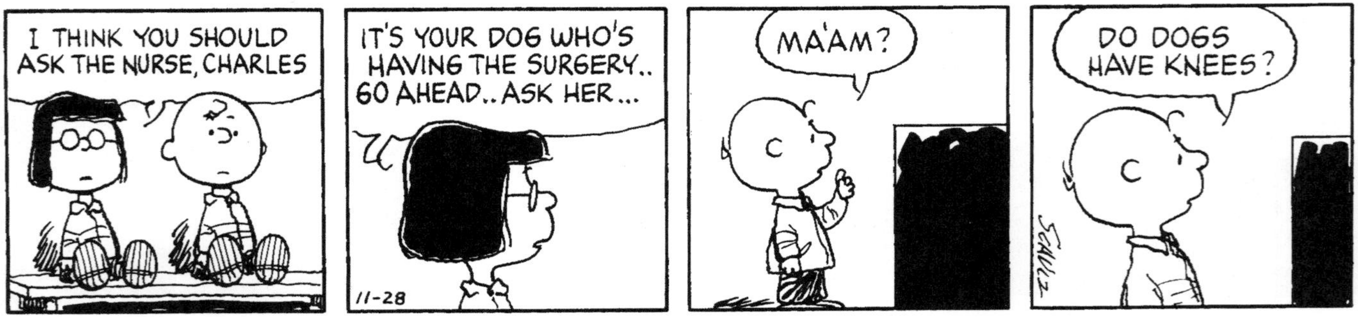
I THINK YOU SHOULD ASK THE NURSE, CHARLES
IT'S YOUR DOG WHO'S HAVING THE SURGERY.. GO AHEAD.. ASK HER...
MA'AM?
DO DOGS HAVE KNEES?

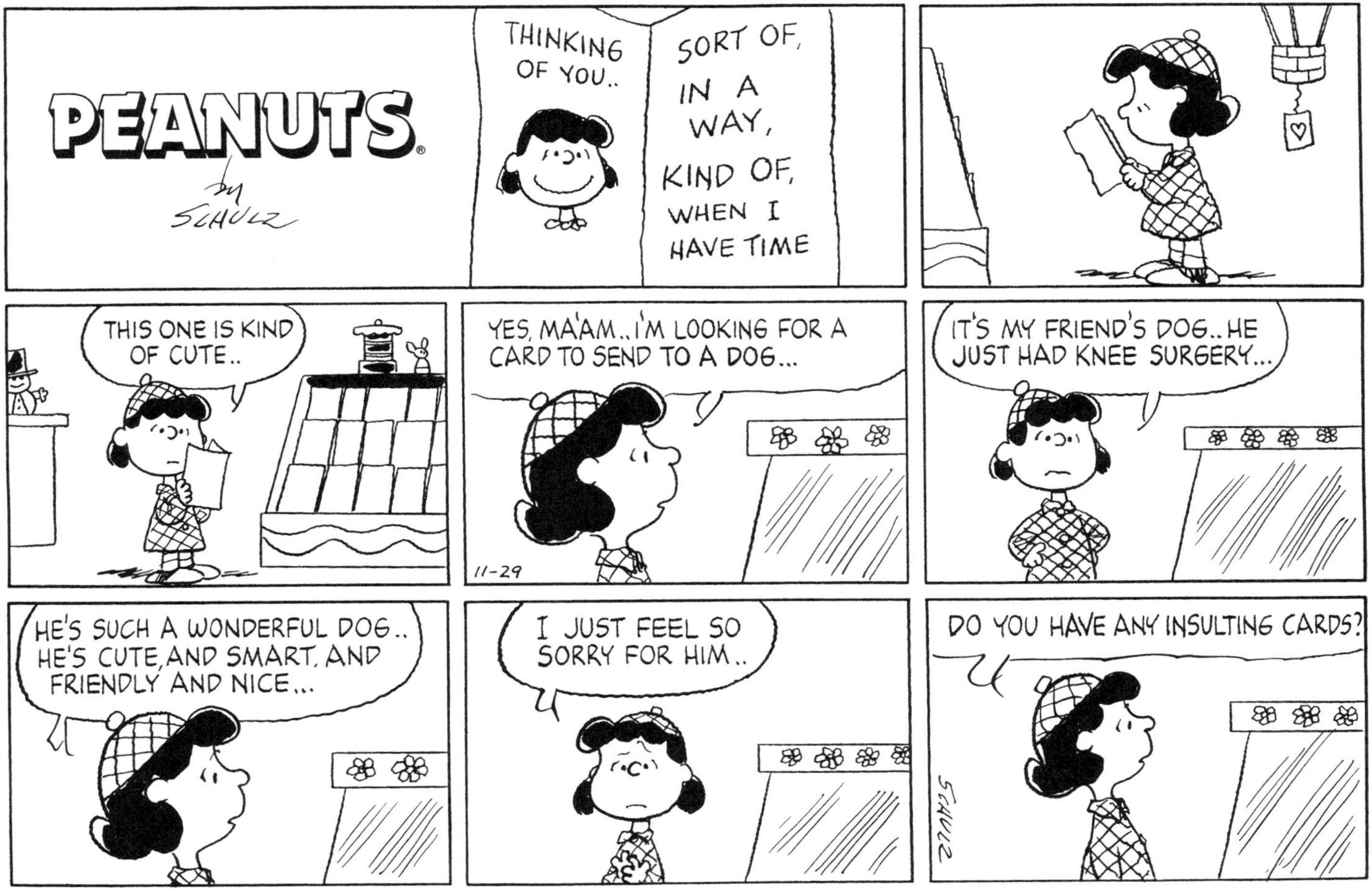
PEANUTS
by SCHULZ
THINKING OF YOU..
SORT OF, IN A WAY, KIND OF, WHEN I HAVE TIME
THIS ONE IS KIND OF CUTE..
YES, MA'AM.. I'M LOOKING FOR A CARD TO SEND TO A DOG...
11-29
IT'S MY FRIEND'S DOG.. HE JUST HAD KNEE SURGERY...
HE'S SUCH A WONDERFUL DOG.. HE'S CUTE, AND SMART, AND FRIENDLY AND NICE...
I JUST FEEL SO SORRY FOR HIM..
DO YOU HAVE ANY INSULTING CARDS?
SCHULZ

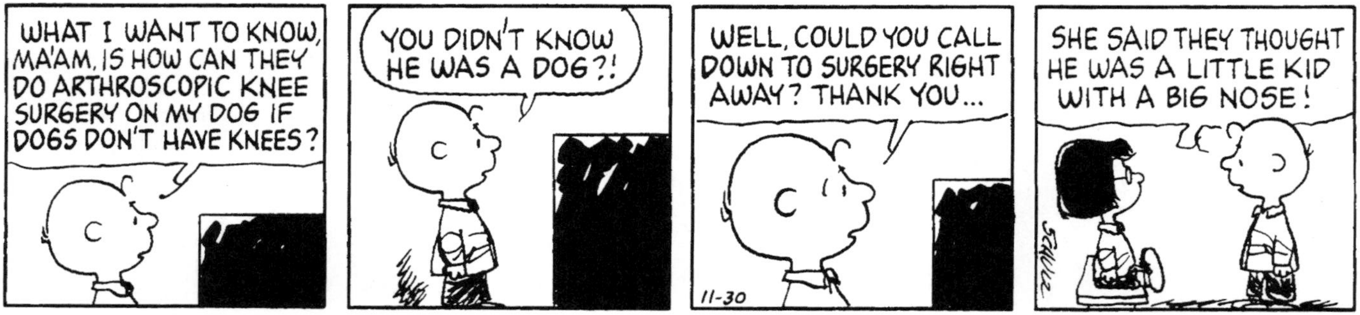
WHAT I WANT TO KNOW, MA'AM, IS HOW CAN THEY DO ARTHROSCOPIC KNEE SURGERY ON MY DOG IF DOGS DON'T HAVE KNEES?
YOU DIDN'T KNOW HE WAS A DOG?!
WELL, COULD YOU CALL DOWN TO SURGERY RIGHT AWAY? THANK YOU...
11-30
SHE SAID THEY THOUGHT HE WAS A LITTLE KID WITH A BIG NOSE!
SCHULZ

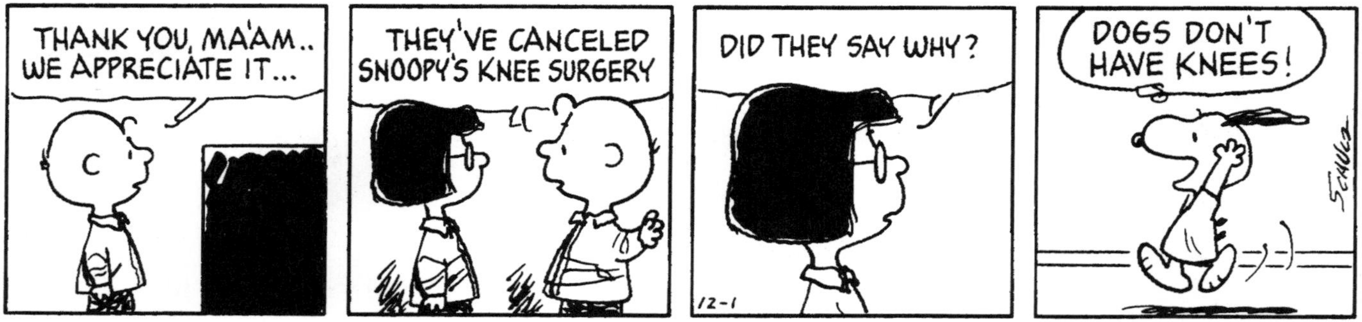
THANK YOU, MA'AM.. WE APPRECIATE IT...
THEY'VE CANCELED SNOOPY'S KNEE SURGERY
DID THEY SAY WHY?
12-1
DOGS DON'T HAVE KNEES!
SCHULZ

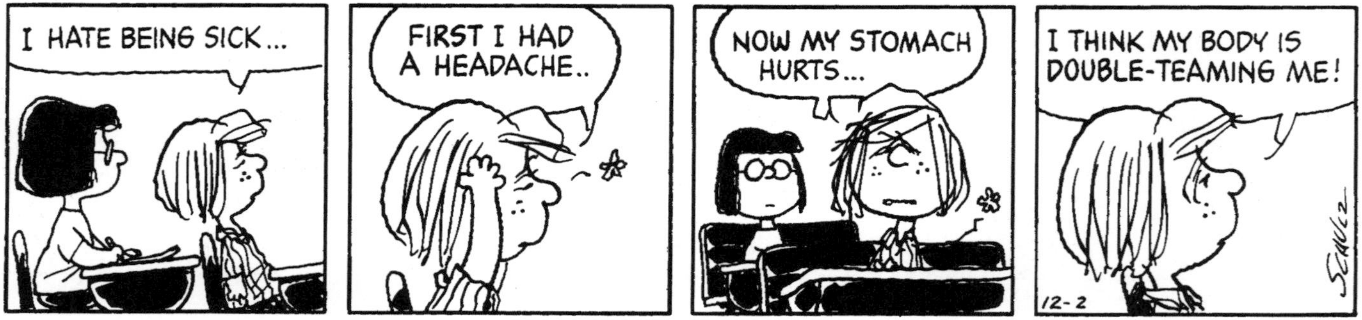
I HATE BEING SICK...
FIRST I HAD A HEADACHE..
NOW MY STOMACH HURTS...
I THINK MY BODY IS DOUBLE-TEAMING ME!
12-2
SCHULZ

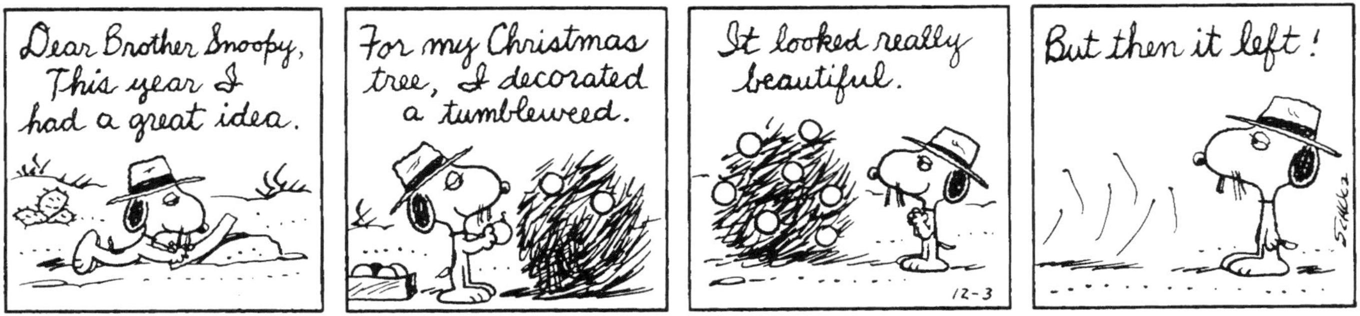
Dear Brother Snoopy, This year I had a great idea.
For my Christmas tree, I decorated a tumbleweed.
It looked really beautiful.
12-3
But then it left!

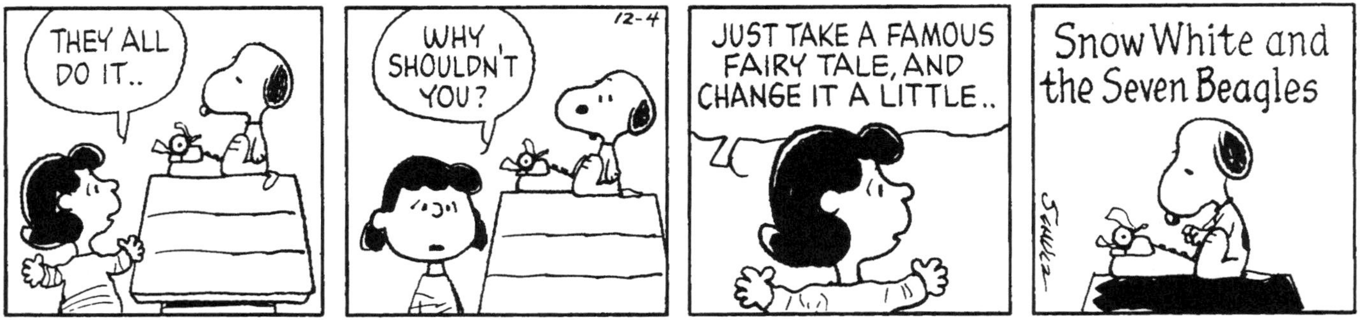
THEY ALL DO IT..
12-4
WHY SHOULDN'T YOU?
JUST TAKE A FAMOUS FAIRY TALE, AND CHANGE IT A LITTLE..
Snow White and the Seven Beagles

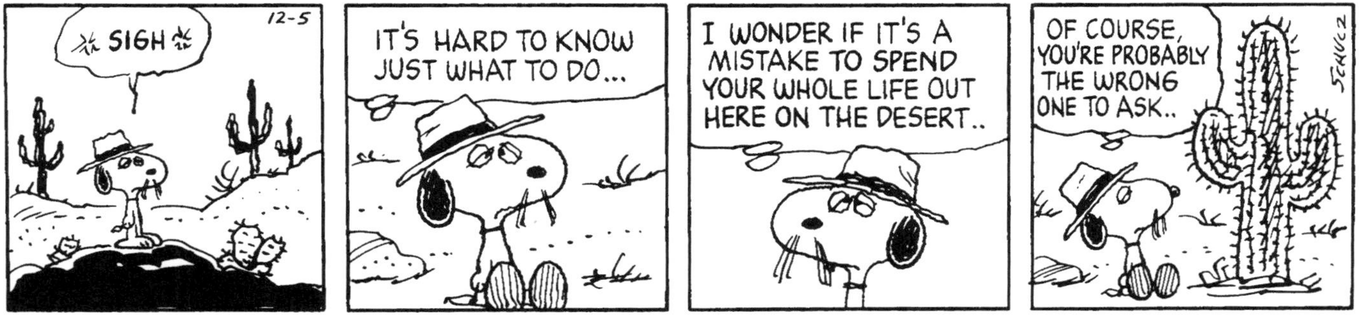
12-5
SIGH
IT'S HARD TO KNOW JUST WHAT TO DO...
I WONDER IF IT'S A MISTAKE TO SPEND YOUR WHOLE LIFE OUT HERE ON THE DESERT..
OF COURSE, YOU'RE PROBABLY THE WRONG ONE TO ASK..

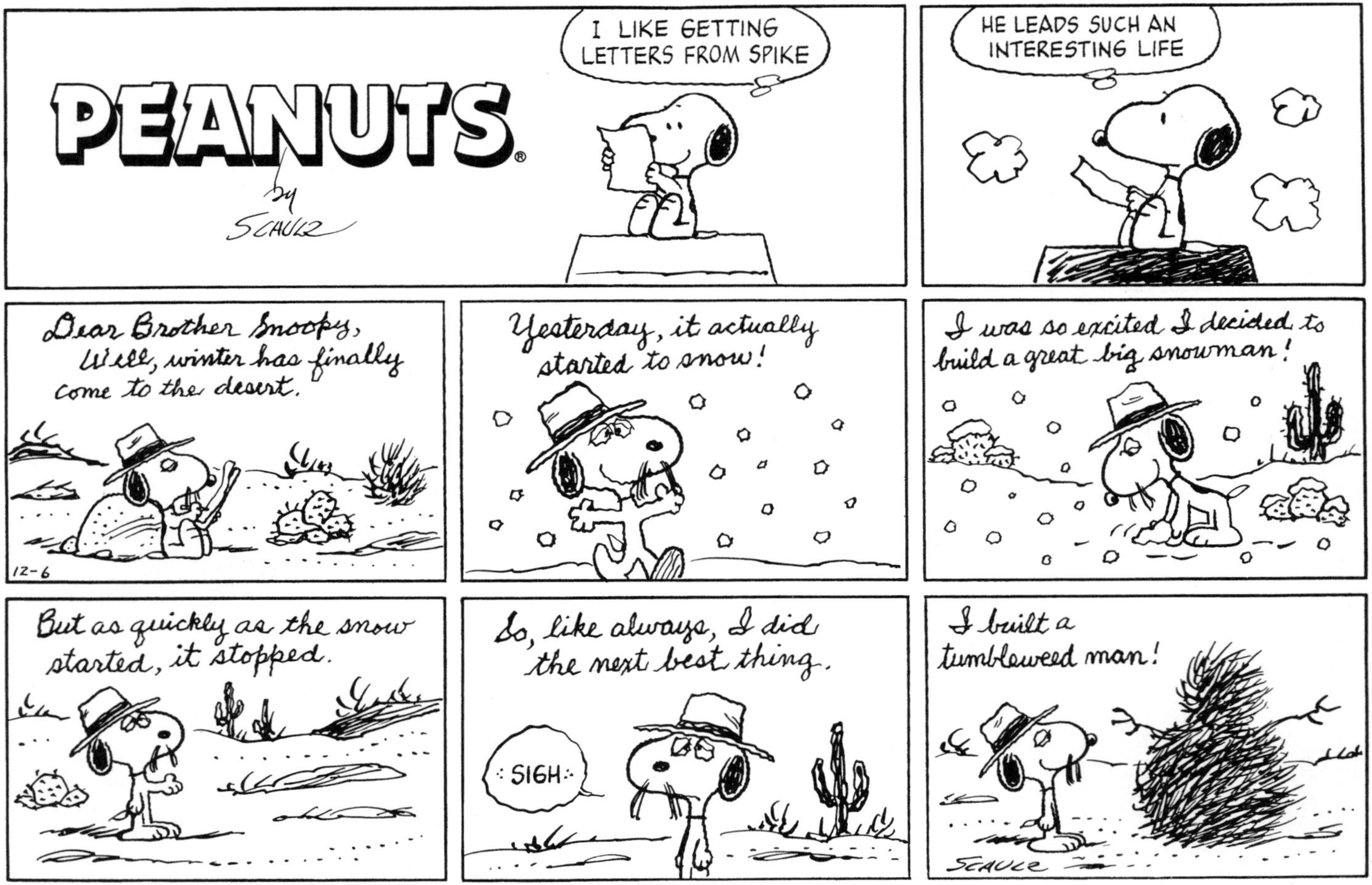
PEANUTS
by SCHULZ
I LIKE GETTING LETTERS FROM SPIKE
HE LEADS SUCH AN INTERESTING LIFE
Dear Brother Snoopy, Well, winter has finally come to the desert.
12-6
Yesterday, it actually started to snow!
I was so excited I decided to build a great big snowman!
But as quickly as the snow started, it stopped.
So, like always, I did the next best thing.
SIGH
I built a tumbleweed man!
SCHULZ

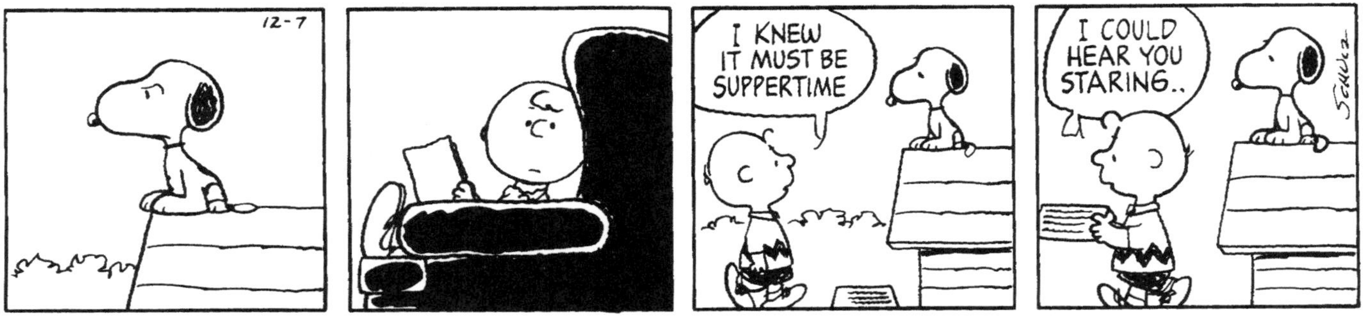
12-7
I KNEW IT MUST BE SUPPERTIME
I COULD HEAR YOU STARING..

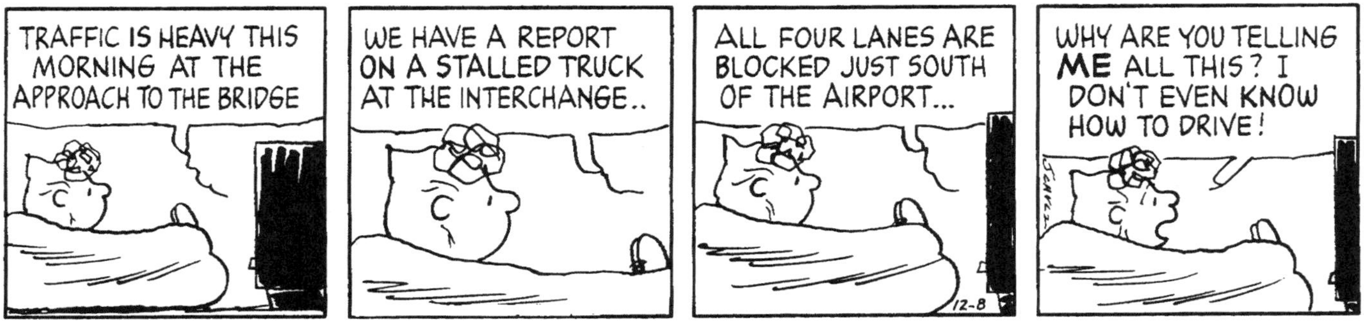
TRAFFIC IS HEAVY THIS MORNING AT THE APPROACH TO THE BRIDGE
WE HAVE A REPORT ON A STALLED TRUCK AT THE INTERCHANGE..
ALL FOUR LANES ARE BLOCKED JUST SOUTH OF THE AIRPORT...
12-8
WHY ARE YOU TELLING ME ALL THIS? I DON'T EVEN KNOW HOW TO DRIVE!

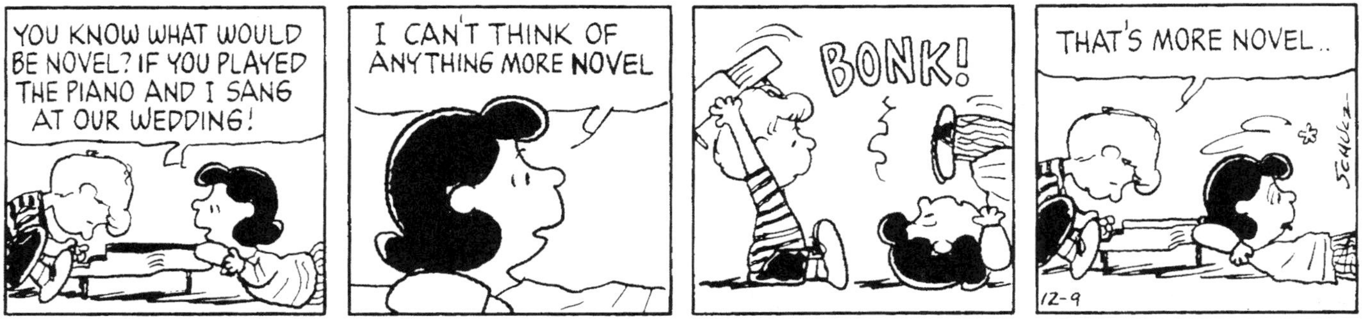
YOU KNOW WHAT WOULD BE NOVEL? IF YOU PLAYED THE PIANO AND I SANG AT OUR WEDDING!
I CAN'T THINK OF ANYTHING MORE NOVEL
BONK!
12-9
THAT'S MORE NOVEL..

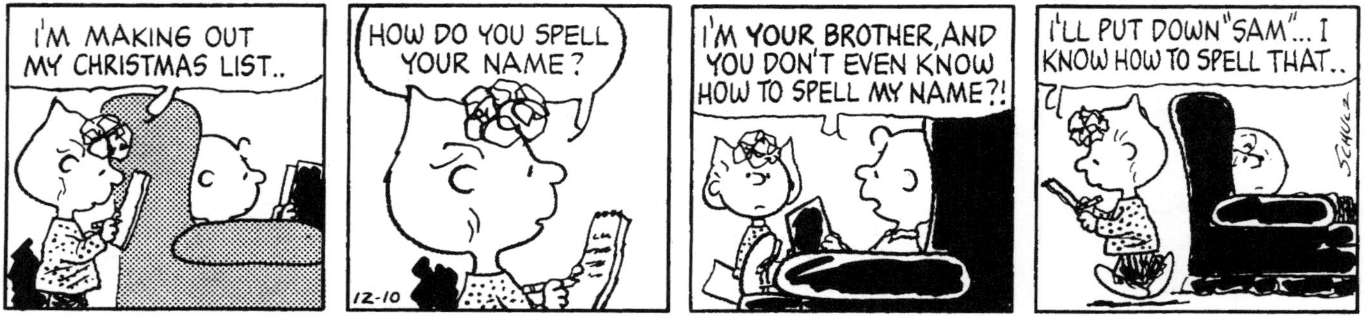
I'M MAKING OUT MY CHRISTMAS LIST..
HOW DO YOU SPELL YOUR NAME?
I'M YOUR BROTHER, AND YOU DON'T EVEN KNOW HOW TO SPELL MY NAME?!
I'LL PUT DOWN "SAM"... I KNOW HOW TO SPELL THAT..

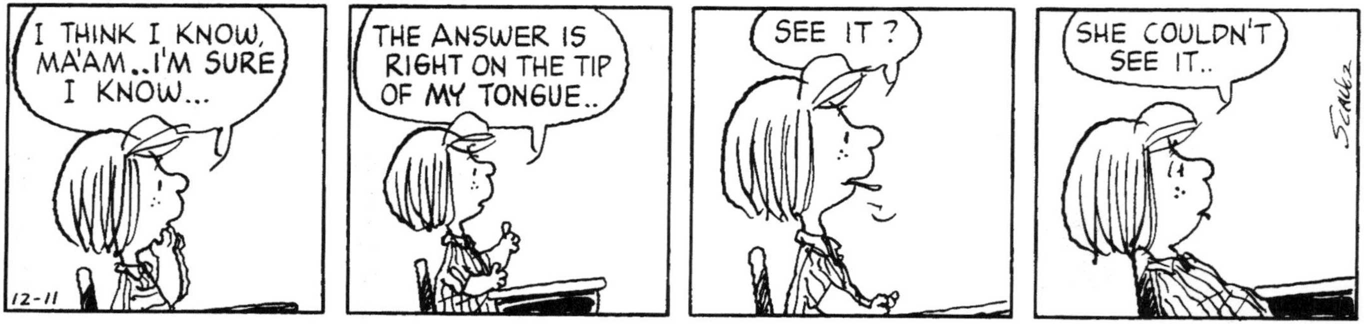
I THINK I KNOW, MA'AM..I'M SURE I KNOW...
THE ANSWER IS RIGHT ON THE TIP OF MY TONGUE..
SEE IT?
SHE COULDN'T SEE IT..

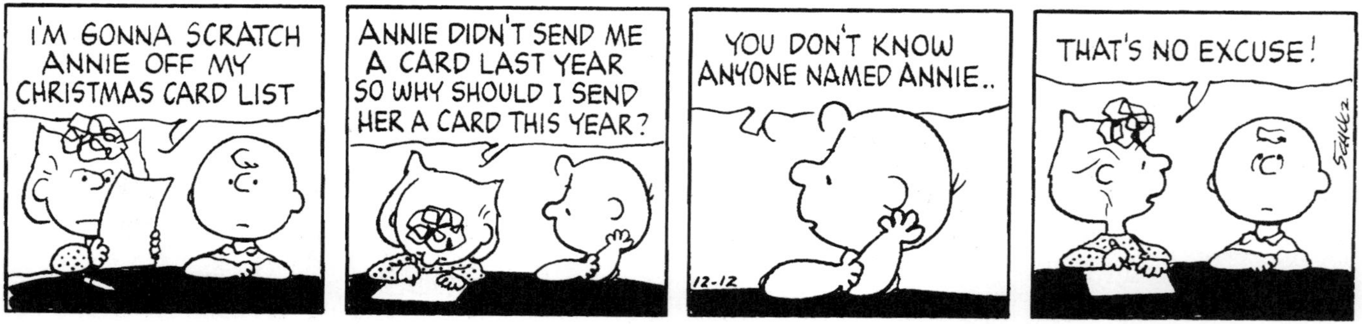
I'M GONNA SCRATCH ANNIE OFF MY CHRISTMAS CARD LIST
ANNIE DIDN'T SEND ME A CARD LAST YEAR SO WHY SHOULD I SEND HER A CARD THIS YEAR?
YOU DON'T KNOW ANYONE NAMED ANNIE..
THAT'S NO EXCUSE!

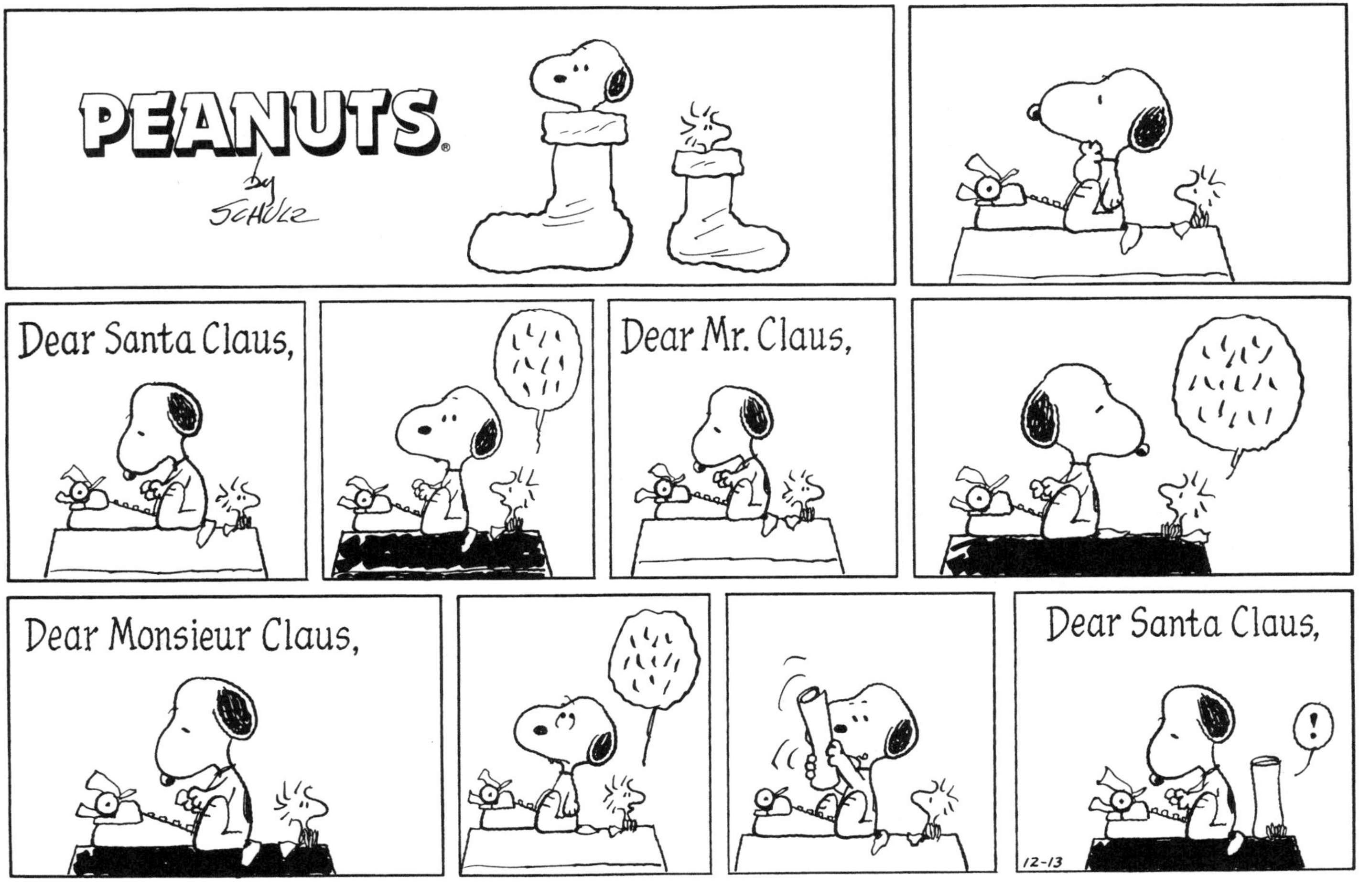
PEANUTS
by SCHULZ
Dear Santa Claus,
Dear Mr. Claus,
Dear Monsieur Claus,
Dear Santa Claus,
!
12-13

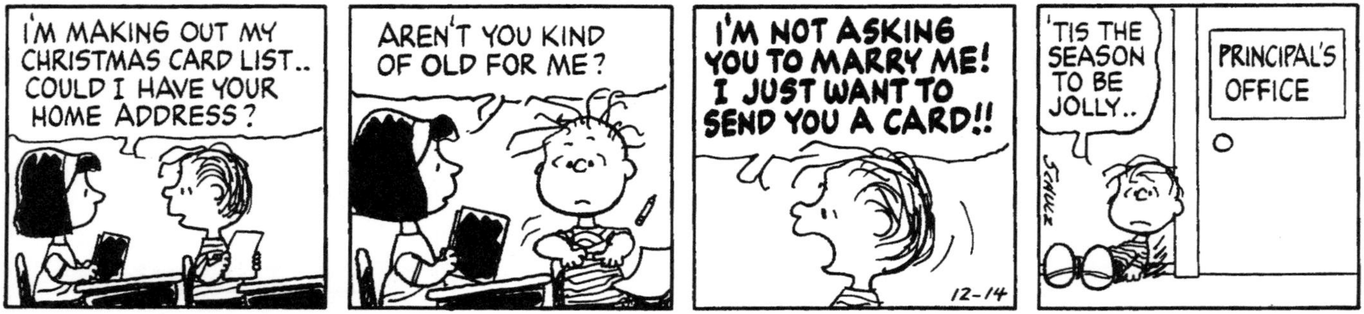
I'M MAKING OUT MY CHRISTMAS CARD LIST.. COULD I HAVE YOUR HOME ADDRESS?
AREN'T YOU KIND OF OLD FOR ME?
I'M NOT ASKING YOU TO MARRY ME! I JUST WANT TO SEND YOU A CARD!!
12-14
'TIS THE SEASON TO BE JOLLY..
PRINCIPAL'S OFFICE
SCHULZ

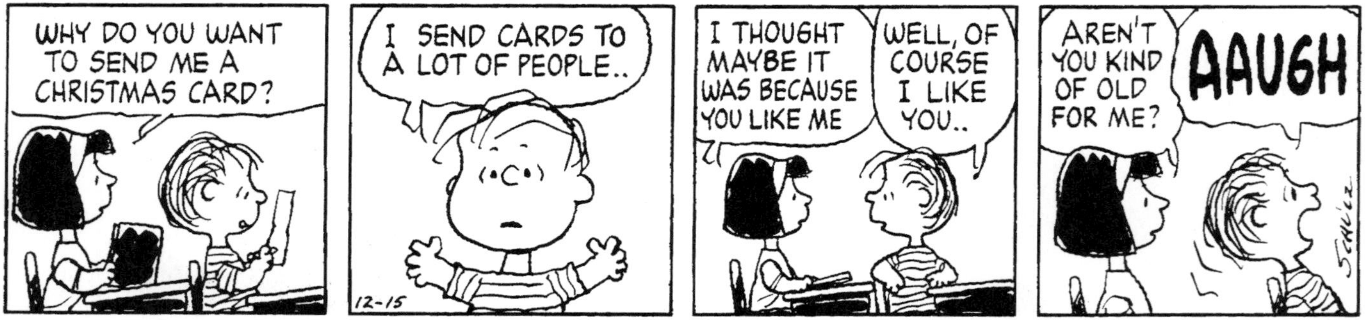
WHY DO YOU WANT TO SEND ME A CHRISTMAS CARD?
I SEND CARDS TO A LOT OF PEOPLE..
12-15
I THOUGHT MAYBE IT WAS BECAUSE YOU LIKE ME
WELL, OF COURSE I LIKE YOU..
AREN'T YOU KIND OF OLD FOR ME?
AAUGH
SCHULZ

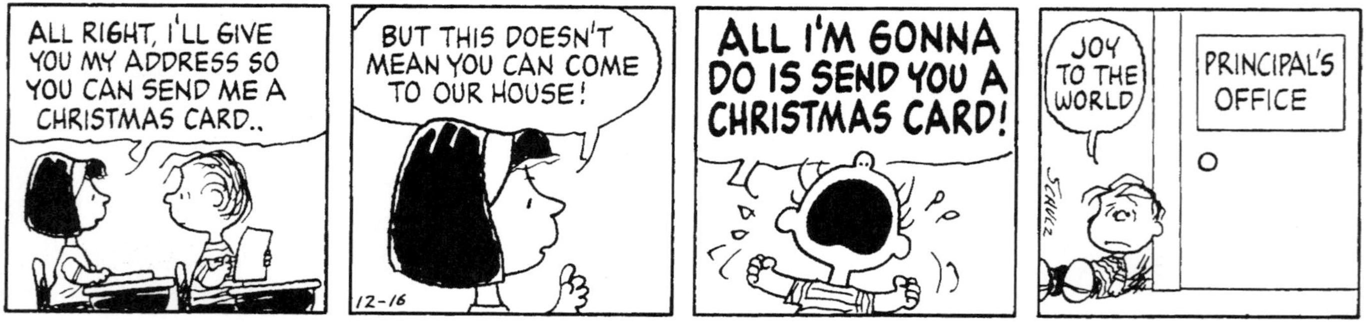
ALL RIGHT, I'LL GIVE YOU MY ADDRESS SO YOU CAN SEND ME A CHRISTMAS CARD..
BUT THIS DOESN'T MEAN YOU CAN COME TO OUR HOUSE!
12-16
ALL I'M GONNA DO IS SEND YOU A CHRISTMAS CARD!
JOY TO THE WORLD
PRINCIPAL'S OFFICE
SCHULZ

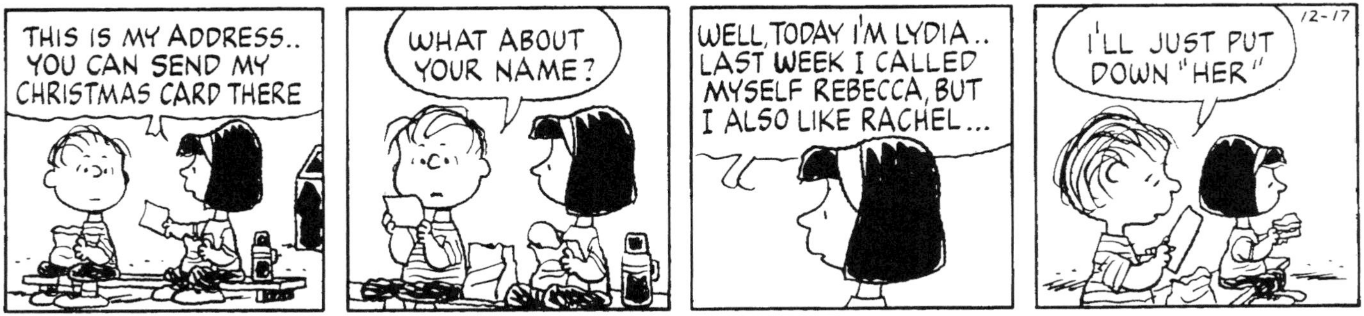
THIS IS MY ADDRESS.. YOU CAN SEND MY CHRISTMAS CARD THERE
WHAT ABOUT YOUR NAME?
WELL, TODAY I'M LYDIA.. LAST WEEK I CALLED MYSELF REBECCA, BUT I ALSO LIKE RACHEL...
I'LL JUST PUT DOWN "HER"
12-17
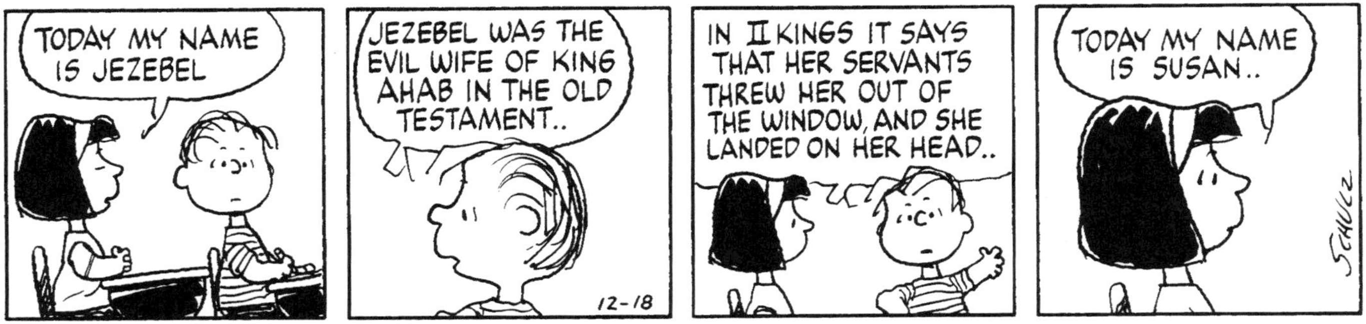
TODAY MY NAME IS JEZEBEL
JEZEBEL WAS THE EVIL WIFE OF KING AHAB IN THE OLD TESTAMENT..
12-18
IN II KINGS IT SAYS THAT HER SERVANTS THREW HER OUT OF THE WINDOW, AND SHE LANDED ON HER HEAD..
TODAY MY NAME IS SUSAN..
SCHULZ
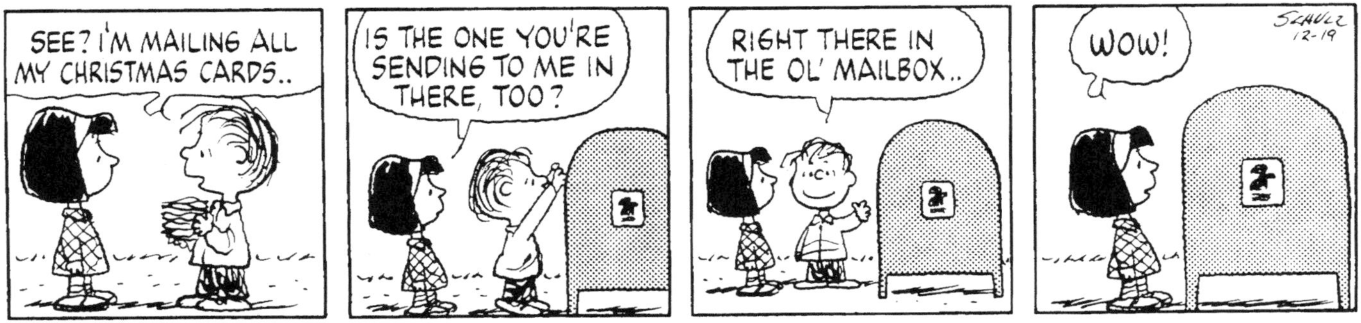
SEE? I'M MAILING ALL MY CHRISTMAS CARDS..
IS THE ONE YOU'RE SENDING TO ME IN THERE, TOO?
RIGHT THERE IN THE OL' MAILBOX..
WOW!
SCHULZ
12-19

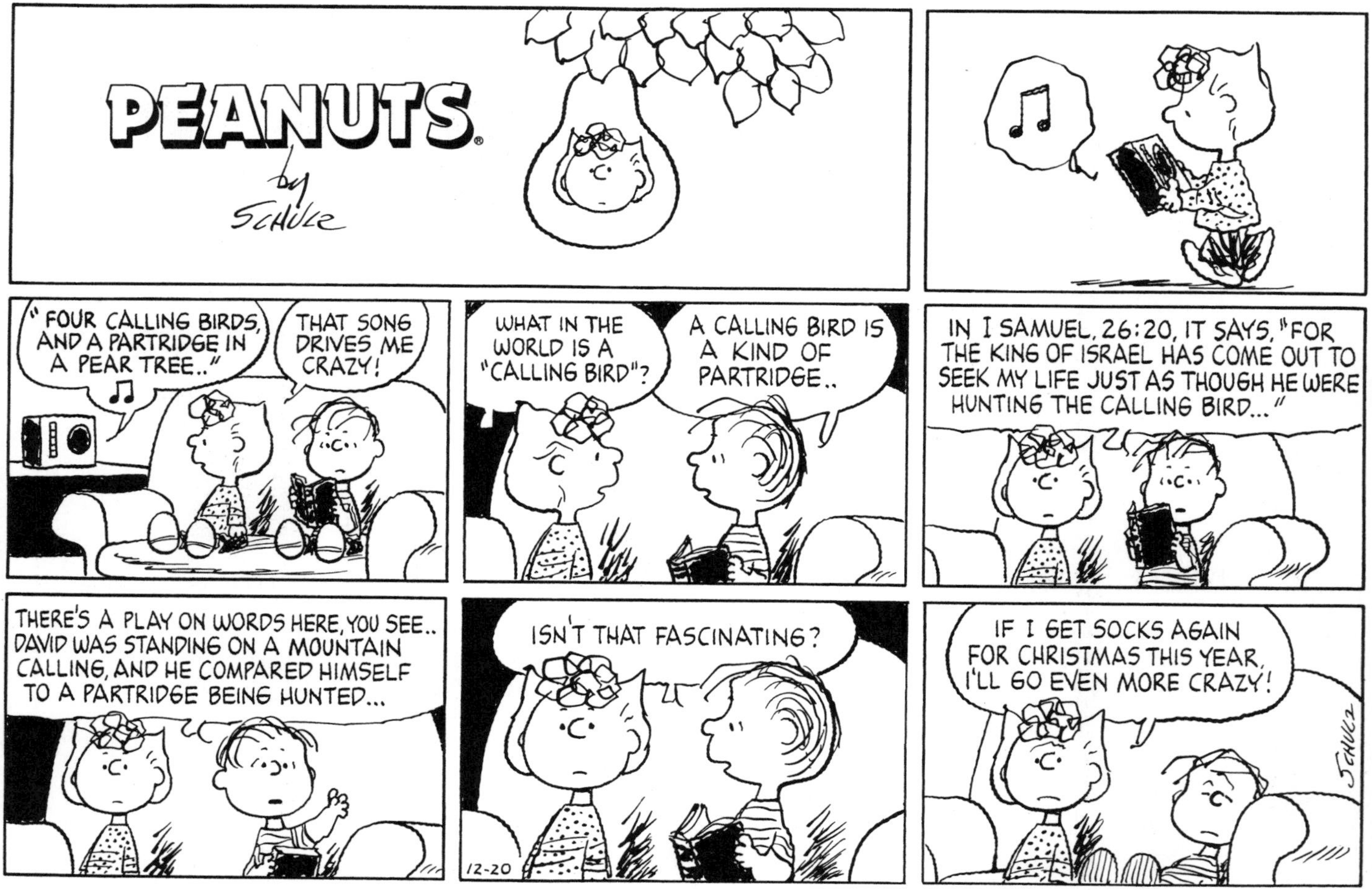
PEANUTS
by SCHULZ
♫
"FOUR CALLING BIRDS, AND A PARTRIDGE IN A PEAR TREE.." ♫
THAT SONG DRIVES ME CRAZY!
WHAT IN THE WORLD IS A "CALLING BIRD"?
A CALLING BIRD IS A KIND OF PARTRIDGE..
IN I SAMUEL, 26:20, IT SAYS, "FOR THE KING OF ISRAEL HAS COME OUT TO SEEK MY LIFE JUST AS THOUGH HE WERE HUNTING THE CALLING BIRD..."
THERE'S A PLAY ON WORDS HERE, YOU SEE.. DAVID WAS STANDING ON A MOUNTAIN CALLING, AND HE COMPARED HIMSELF TO A PARTRIDGE BEING HUNTED...
ISN'T THAT FASCINATING?
12-20
IF I GET SOCKS AGAIN FOR CHRISTMAS THIS YEAR, I'LL GO EVEN MORE CRAZY!
SCHULZ

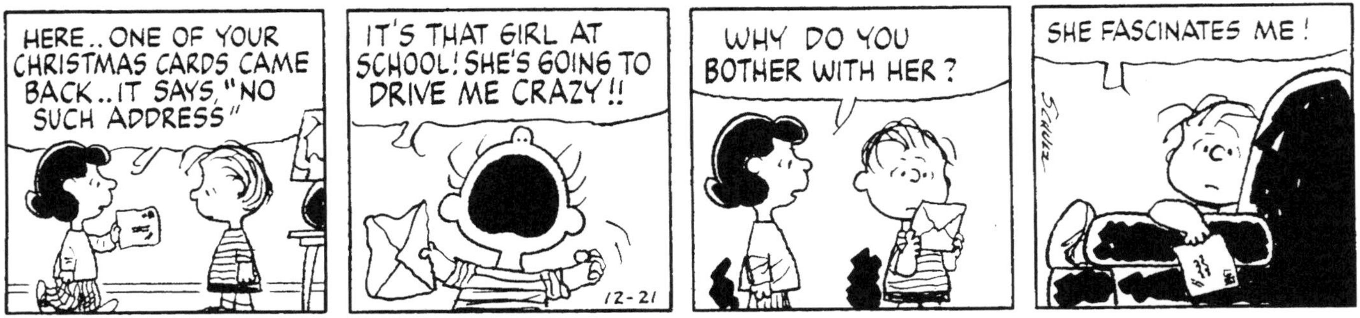
HERE..ONE OF YOUR CHRISTMAS CARDS CAME BACK..IT SAYS, "NO SUCH ADDRESS"
IT'S THAT GIRL AT SCHOOL! SHE'S GOING TO DRIVE ME CRAZY!!
12-21
WHY DO YOU BOTHER WITH HER?
SHE FASCINATES ME!
SCHULZ

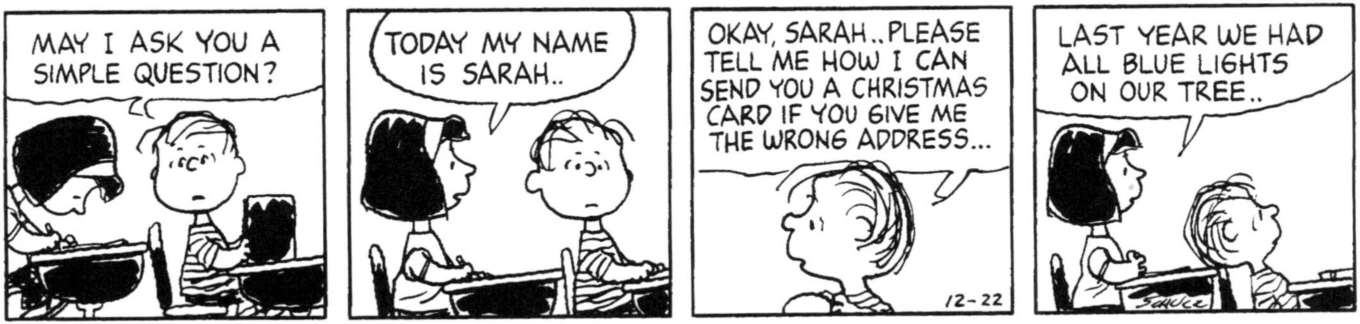
MAY I ASK YOU A SIMPLE QUESTION?
TODAY MY NAME IS SARAH..
OKAY, SARAH..PLEASE TELL ME HOW I CAN SEND YOU A CHRISTMAS CARD IF YOU GIVE ME THE WRONG ADDRESS...
12-22
LAST YEAR WE HAD ALL BLUE LIGHTS ON OUR TREE..
SCHULZ

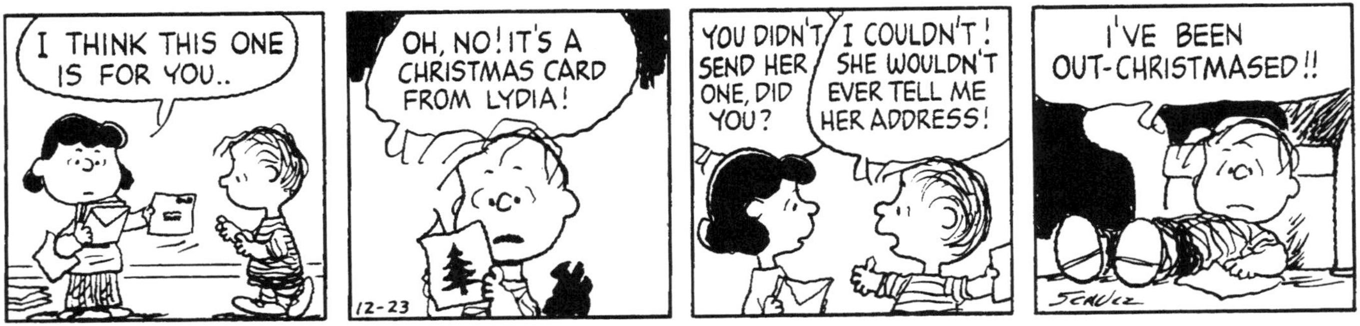
I THINK THIS ONE IS FOR YOU..
OH, NO! IT'S A CHRISTMAS CARD FROM LYDIA!
12-23
YOU DIDN'T SEND HER ONE, DID YOU?
I COULDN'T! SHE WOULDN'T EVER TELL ME HER ADDRESS!
I'VE BEEN OUT-CHRISTMASED!!
SCHULZ

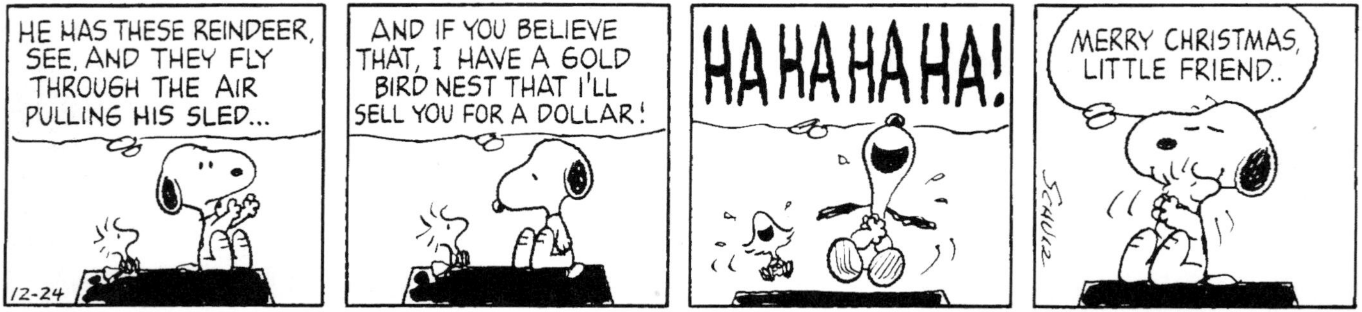
HE HAS THESE REINDEER, SEE, AND THEY FLY THROUGH THE AIR PULLING HIS SLED...
12-24
AND IF YOU BELIEVE THAT, I HAVE A GOLD BIRD NEST THAT I'LL SELL YOU FOR A DOLLAR!
HA HA HA HA HA!
MERRY CHRISTMAS, LITTLE FRIEND..
SCHULZ

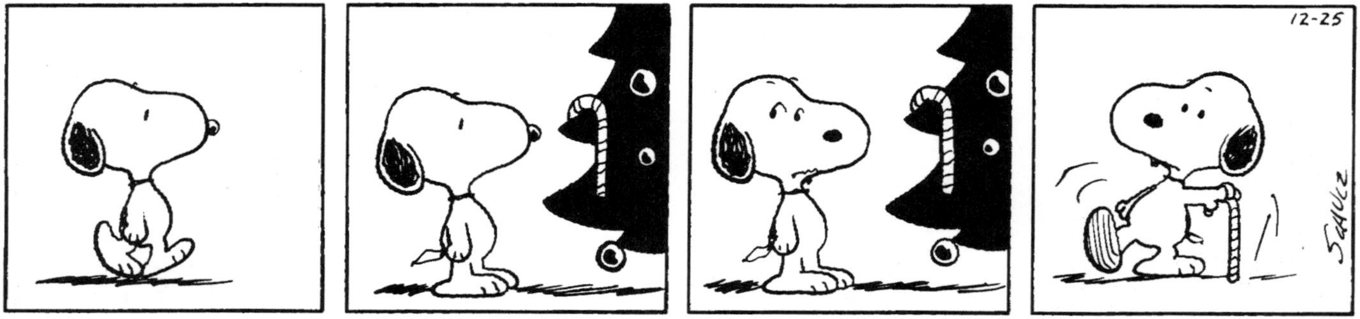
12-25
SCHULZ

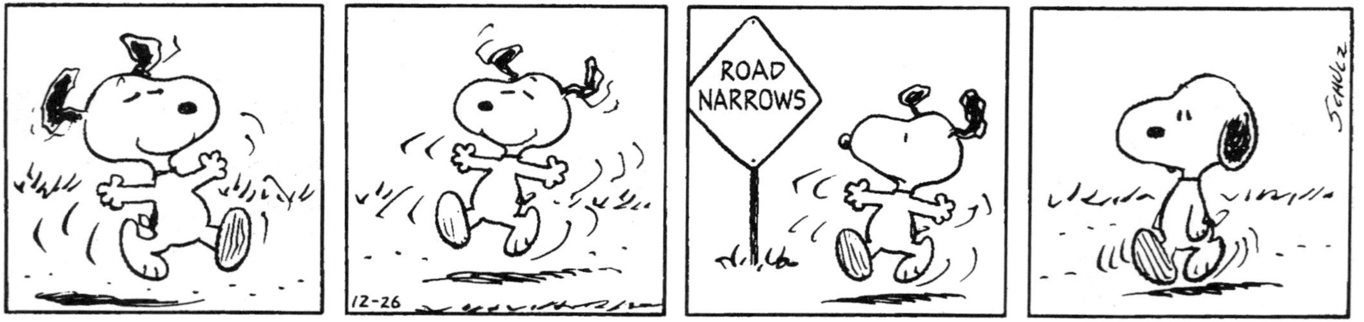
12-26
ROAD NARROWS
SCHULZ

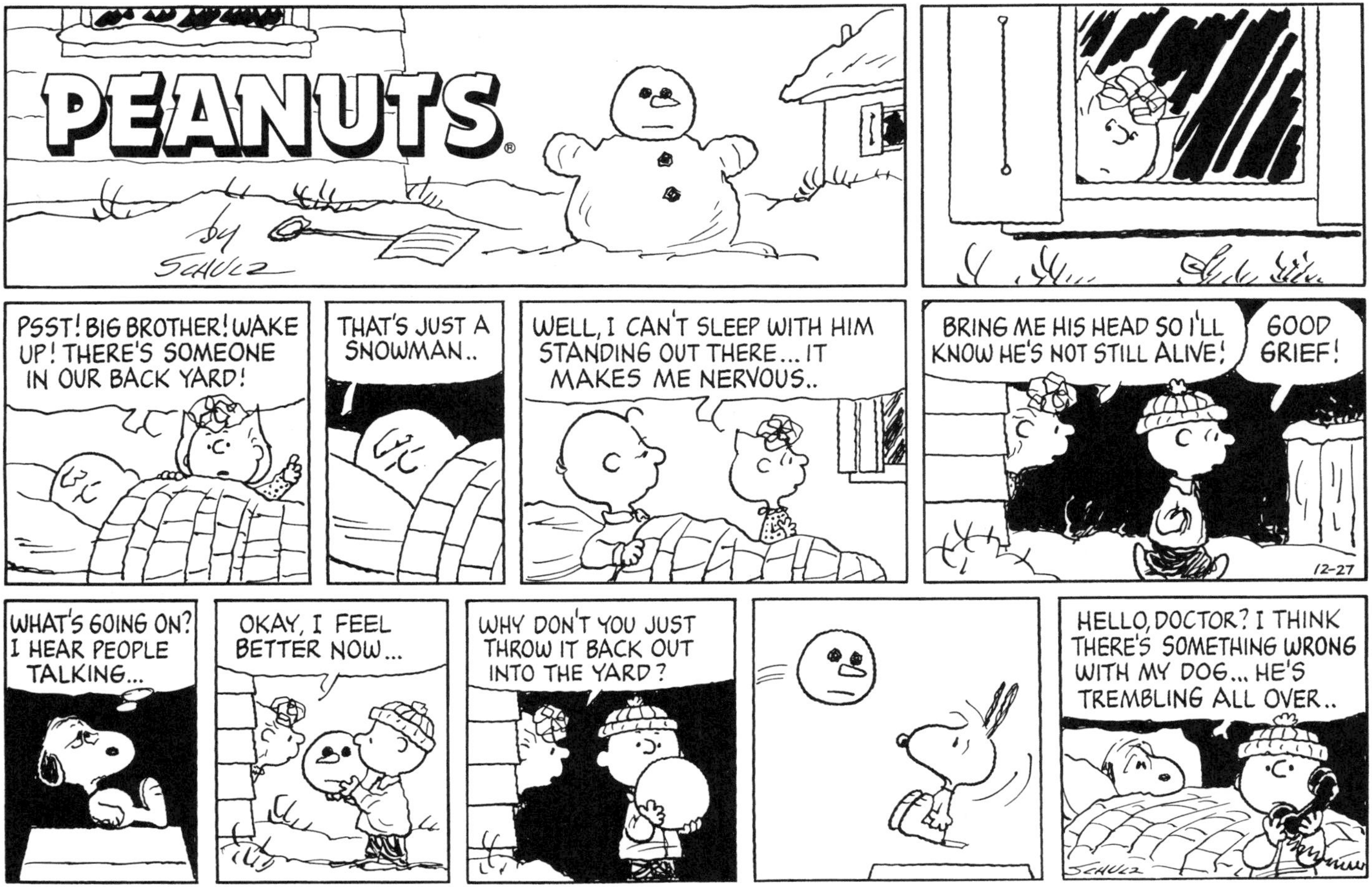
PEANUTS
by SCHULZ
PSST! BIG BROTHER! WAKE UP! THERE'S SOMEONE IN OUR BACK YARD!
THAT'S JUST A SNOWMAN..
WELL, I CAN'T SLEEP WITH HIM STANDING OUT THERE... IT MAKES ME NERVOUS..
BRING ME HIS HEAD SO I'LL KNOW HE'S NOT STILL ALIVE!
GOOD GRIEF!
12-27
WHAT'S GOING ON? I HEAR PEOPLE TALKING...
OKAY, I FEEL BETTER NOW...
WHY DON'T YOU JUST THROW IT BACK OUT INTO THE YARD?
HELLO, DOCTOR? I THINK THERE'S SOMETHING WRONG WITH MY DOG... HE'S TREMBLING ALL OVER..
SCHULZ

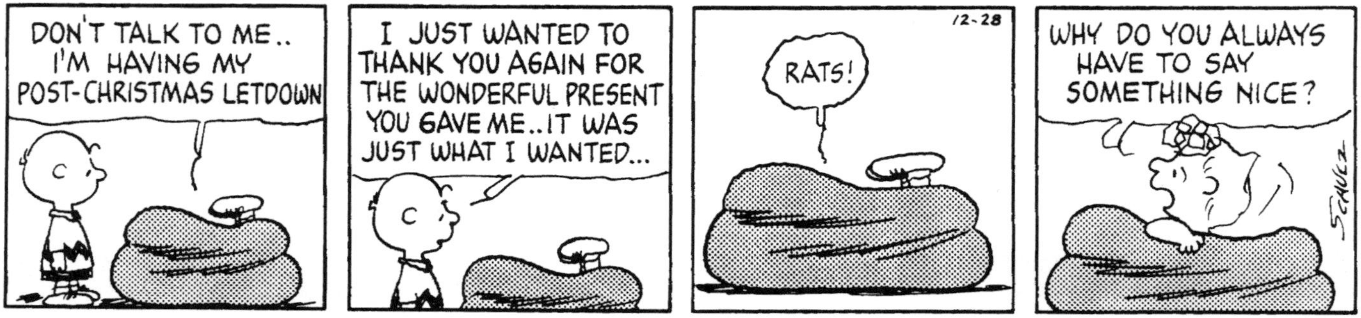
DON'T TALK TO ME.. I'M HAVING MY POST-CHRISTMAS LETDOWN
I JUST WANTED TO THANK YOU AGAIN FOR THE WONDERFUL PRESENT YOU GAVE ME..IT WAS JUST WHAT I WANTED...
12-28
RATS!
WHY DO YOU ALWAYS HAVE TO SAY SOMETHING NICE?
SCHULZ

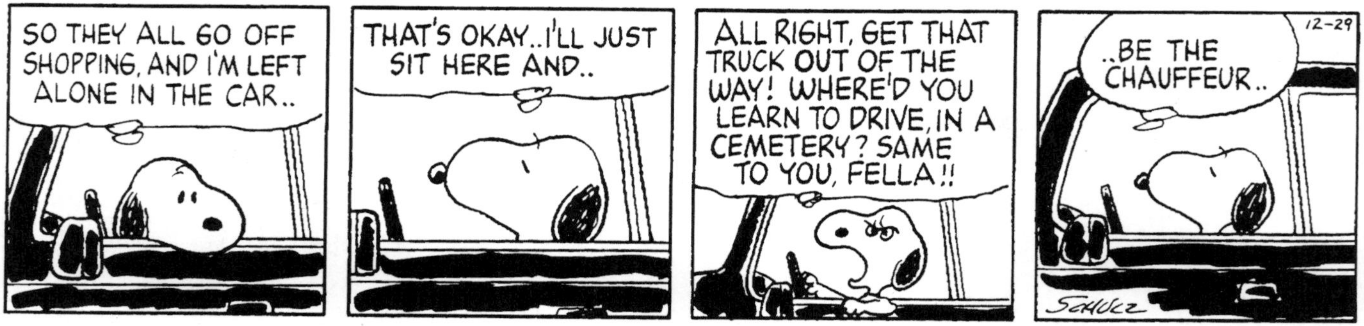
SO THEY ALL GO OFF SHOPPING, AND I'M LEFT ALONE IN THE CAR..
THAT'S OKAY..I'LL JUST SIT HERE AND..
ALL RIGHT, GET THAT TRUCK OUT OF THE WAY! WHERE'D YOU LEARN TO DRIVE, IN A CEMETERY? SAME TO YOU, FELLA!!
12-29
..BE THE CHAUFFEUR..
SCHULZ

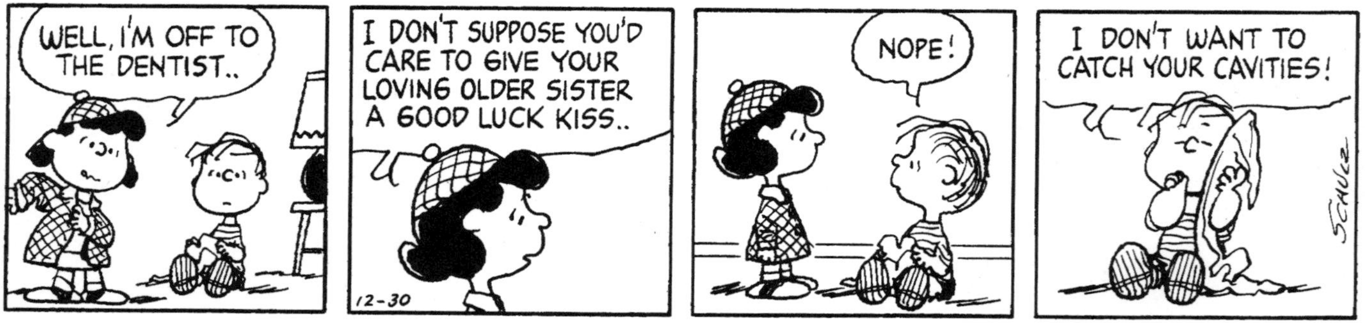
WELL, I'M OFF TO THE DENTIST..
I DON'T SUPPOSE YOU'D CARE TO GIVE YOUR LOVING OLDER SISTER A GOOD LUCK KISS..
12-30
NOPE!
I DON'T WANT TO CATCH YOUR CAVITIES!
SCHULZ

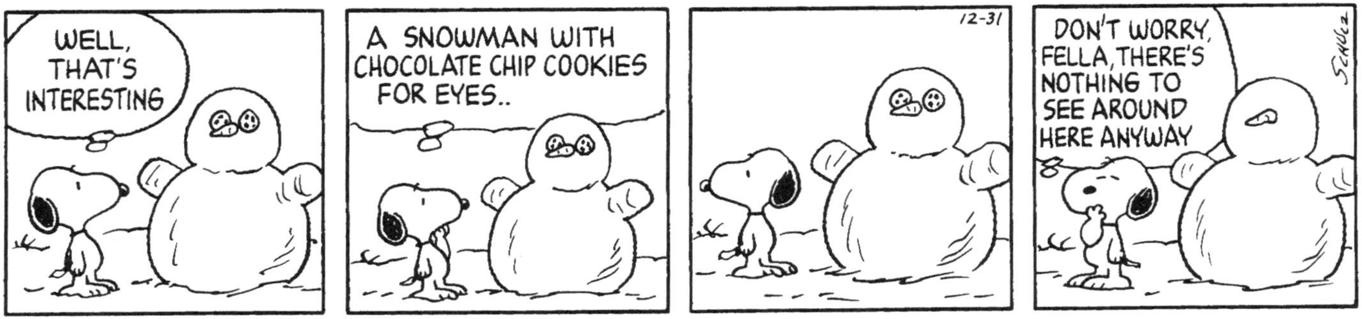
WELL, THAT'S INTERESTING
A SNOWMAN WITH CHOCOLATE CHIP COOKIES FOR EYES..
12-31
DON'T WORRY, FELLA, THERE'S NOTHING TO SEE AROUND HERE ANYWAY
SCHULZ

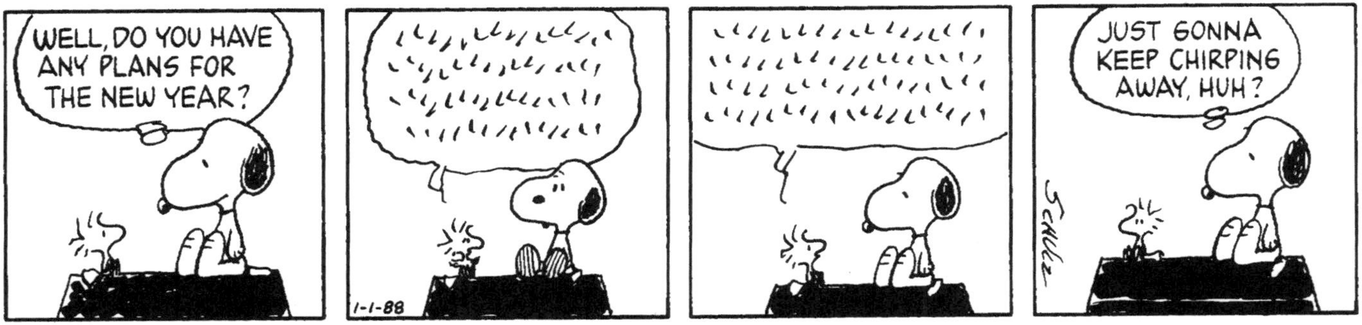
WELL, DO YOU HAVE ANY PLANS FOR THE NEW YEAR?
1-1-88
JUST GONNA KEEP CHIRPING AWAY, HUH?
SCHULZ

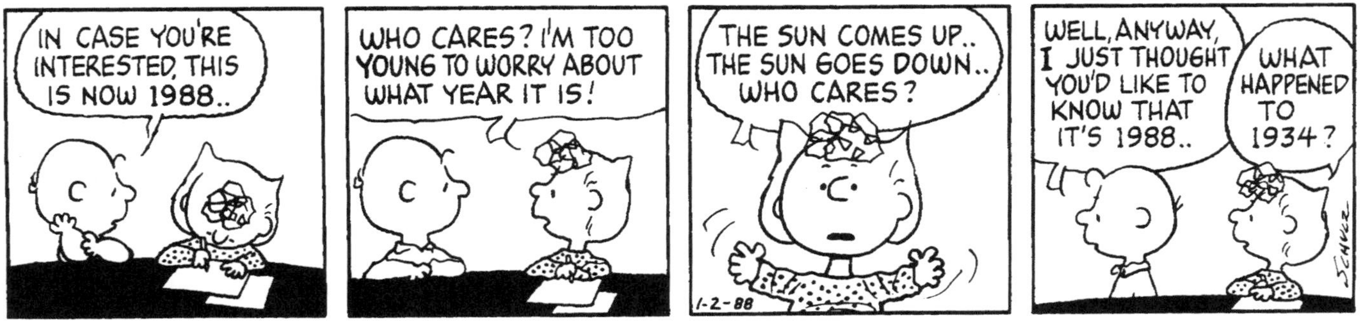
IN CASE YOU'RE INTERESTED, THIS IS NOW 1988..
WHO CARES? I'M TOO YOUNG TO WORRY ABOUT WHAT YEAR IT IS!
THE SUN COMES UP.. THE SUN GOES DOWN.. WHO CARES?
1-2-88
WELL, ANYWAY, I JUST THOUGHT YOU'D LIKE TO KNOW THAT IT'S 1988..
WHAT HAPPENED TO 1934?
SCHULZ

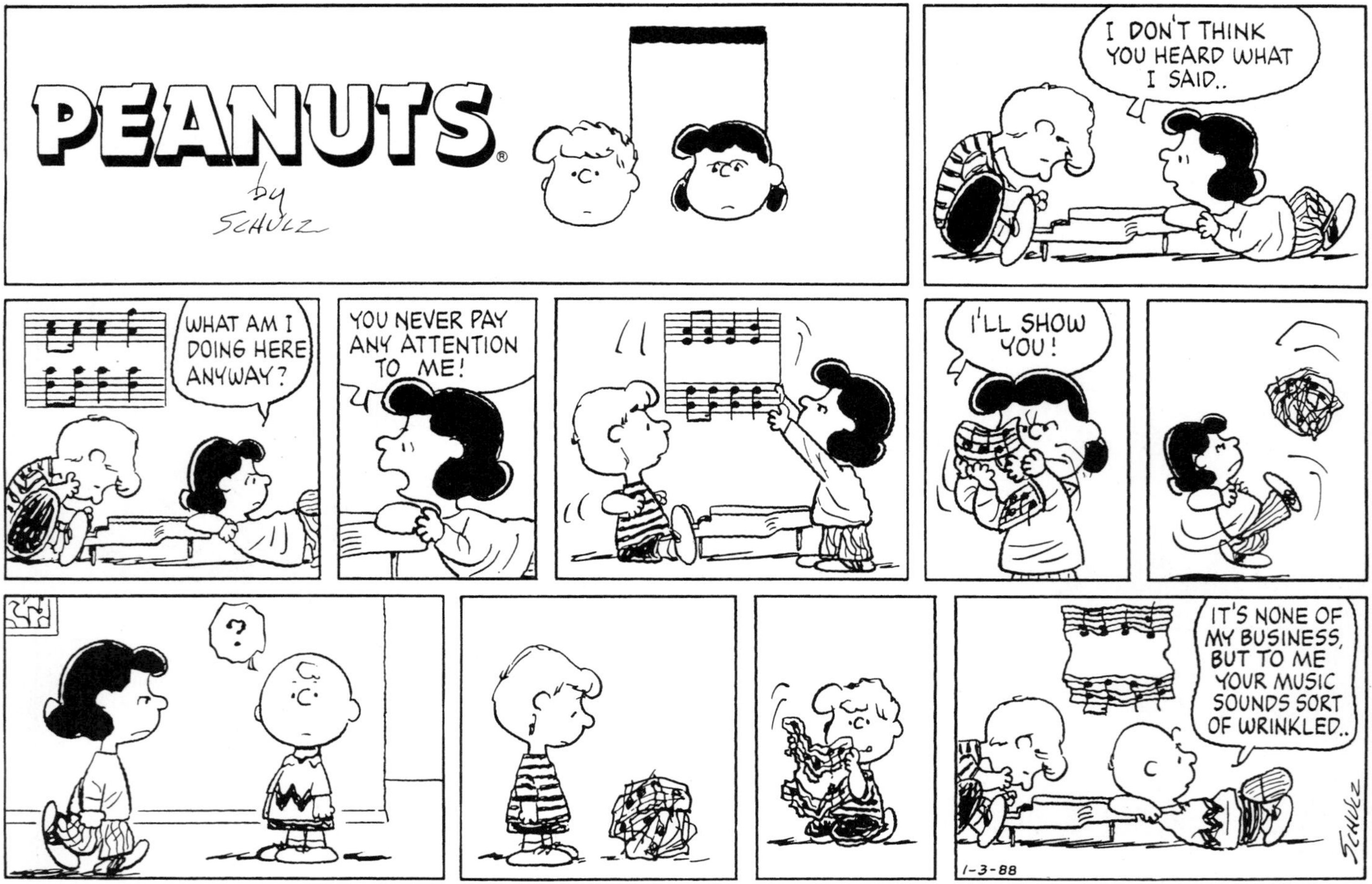
PEANUTS
by SCHULZ
I DON'T THINK YOU HEARD WHAT I SAID..
WHAT AM I DOING HERE ANYWAY?
YOU NEVER PAY ANY ATTENTION TO ME!
I'LL SHOW YOU!
?
IT'S NONE OF MY BUSINESS, BUT TO ME YOUR MUSIC SOUNDS SORT OF WRINKLED..
SCHULZ
1-3-88

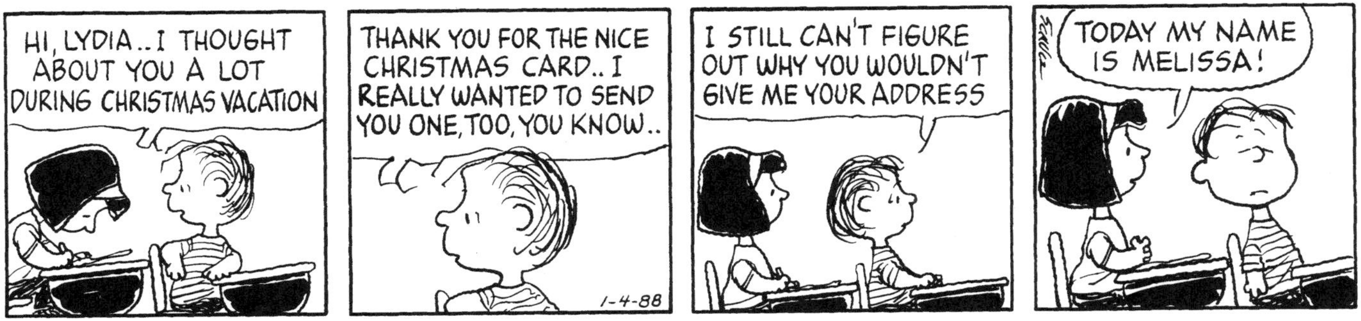
HI, LYDIA.. I THOUGHT ABOUT YOU A LOT DURING CHRISTMAS VACATION
THANK YOU FOR THE NICE CHRISTMAS CARD.. I REALLY WANTED TO SEND YOU ONE, TOO, YOU KNOW..
1-4-88
I STILL CAN'T FIGURE OUT WHY YOU WOULDN'T GIVE ME YOUR ADDRESS
TODAY MY NAME IS MELISSA!

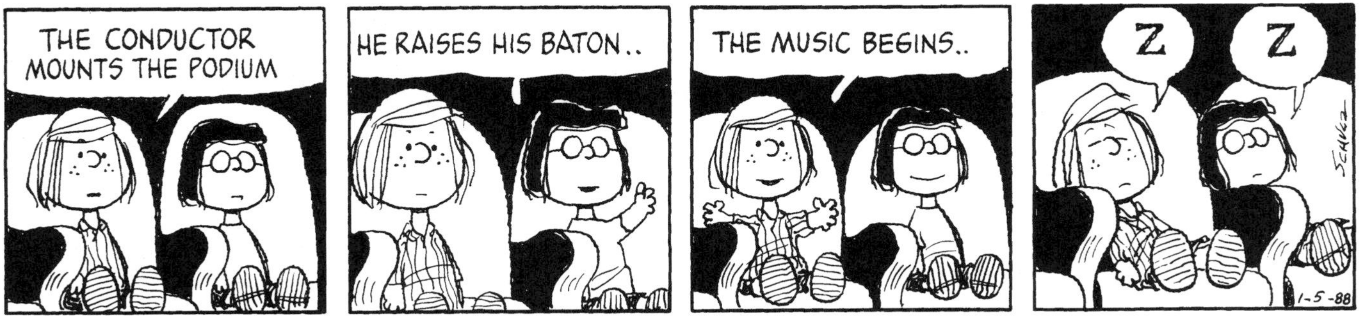
THE CONDUCTOR MOUNTS THE PODIUM
HE RAISES HIS BATON..
THE MUSIC BEGINS..
Z
Z
SCHULZ
1-5-88

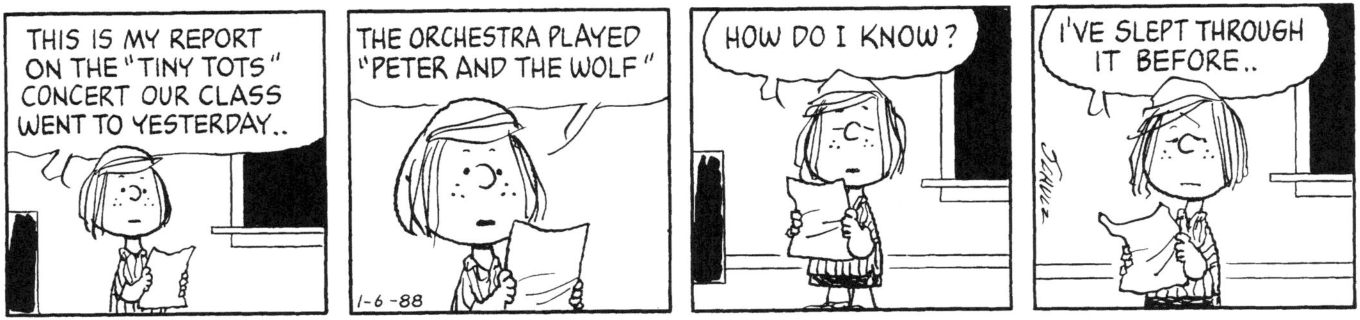
THIS IS MY REPORT ON THE "TINY TOTS" CONCERT OUR CLASS WENT TO YESTERDAY..
THE ORCHESTRA PLAYED "PETER AND THE WOLF"
1-6-88
HOW DO I KNOW?
I'VE SLEPT THROUGH IT BEFORE..

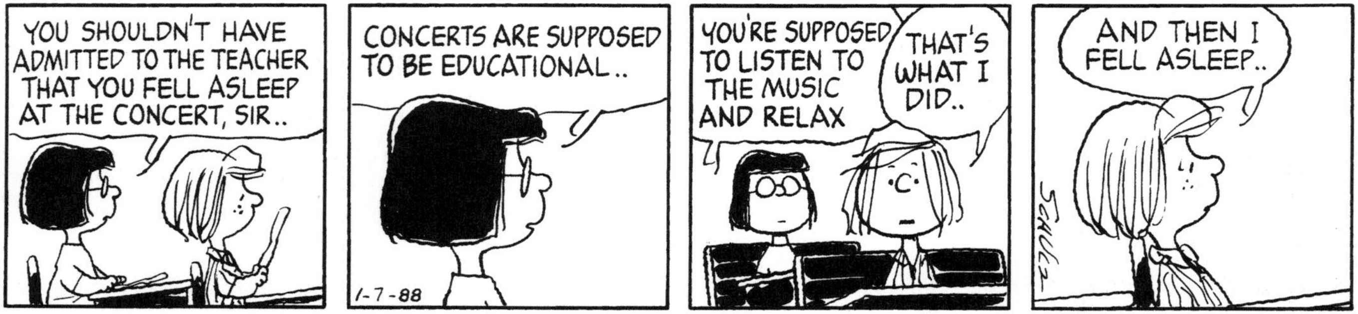
YOU SHOULDN'T HAVE ADMITTED TO THE TEACHER THAT YOU FELL ASLEEP AT THE CONCERT, SIR..
CONCERTS ARE SUPPOSED TO BE EDUCATIONAL..
1-7-88
YOU'RE SUPPOSED TO LISTEN TO THE MUSIC AND RELAX
THAT'S WHAT I DID..
AND THEN I FELL ASLEEP..

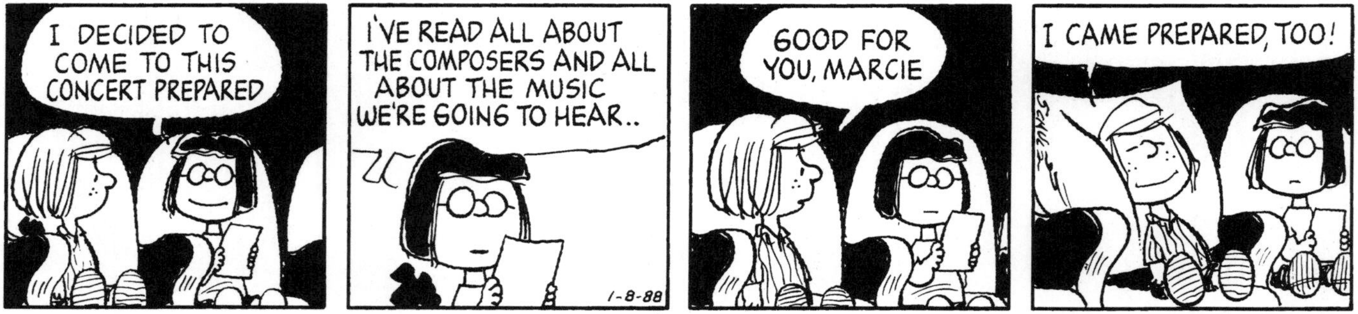
I DECIDED TO COME TO THIS CONCERT PREPARED
I'VE READ ALL ABOUT THE COMPOSERS AND ALL ABOUT THE MUSIC WE'RE GOING TO HEAR..
1-8-88
GOOD FOR YOU, MARCIE
I CAME PREPARED, TOO!

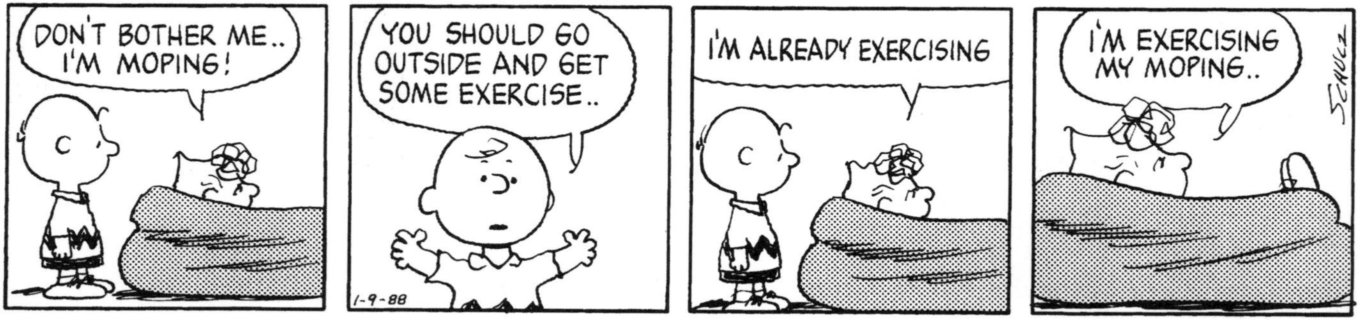
DON'T BOTHER ME.. I'M MOPING!
YOU SHOULD GO OUTSIDE AND GET SOME EXERCISE..
1-9-88
I'M ALREADY EXERCISING
I'M EXERCISING MY MOPING..

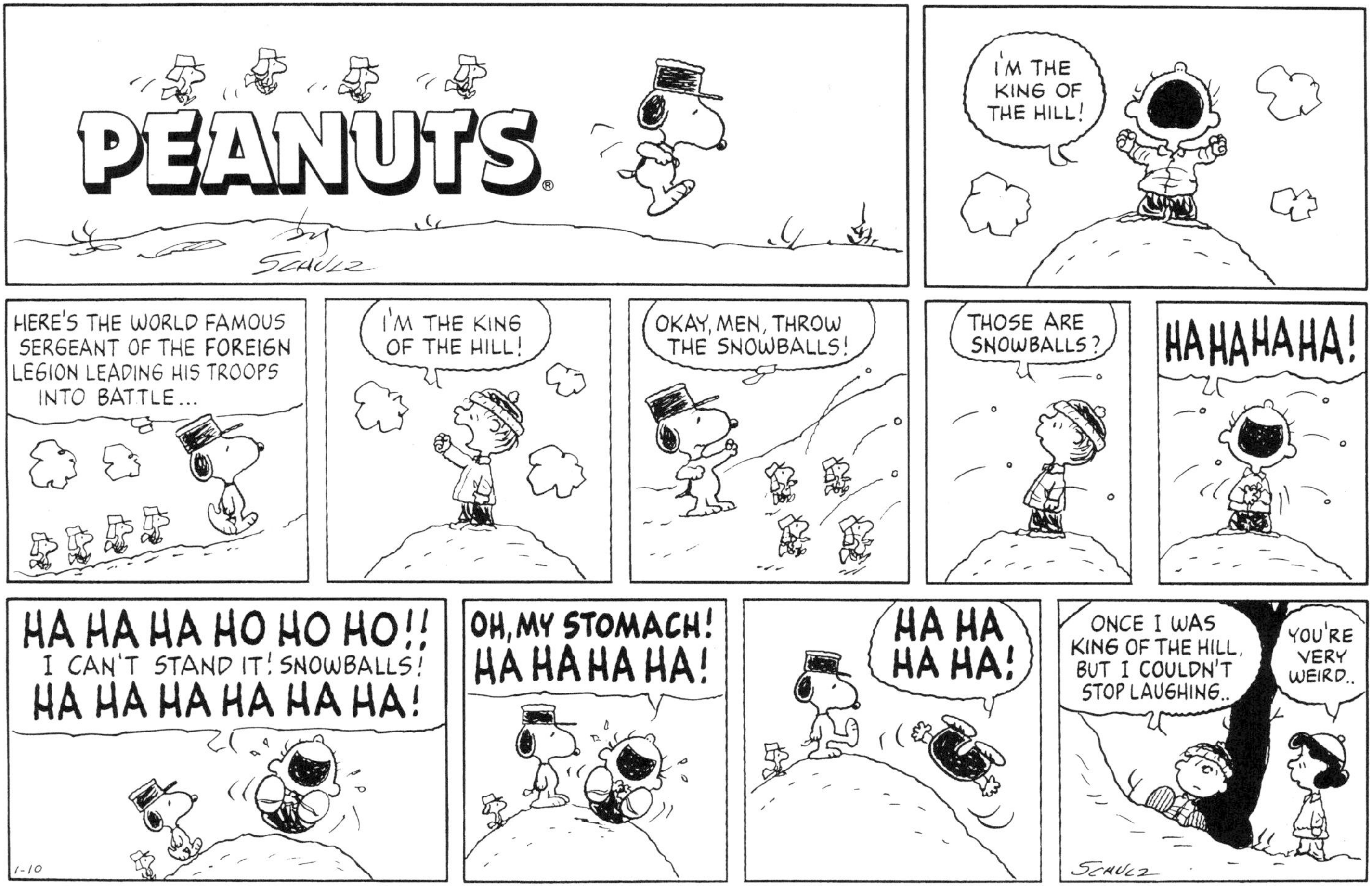
PEANUTS®
SCHULZ
I'M THE KING OF THE HILL!
HERE'S THE WORLD FAMOUS SERGEANT OF THE FOREIGN LEGION LEADING HIS TROOPS INTO BATTLE...
I'M THE KING OF THE HILL!
OKAY, MEN, THROW THE SNOWBALLS!
THOSE ARE SNOWBALLS?
HAHAHAHA!
HA HA HA HO HO HO!! I CAN'T STAND IT! SNOWBALLS! HA HA HA HA HA HA!
1-10
OH, MY STOMACH! HA HA HA HA!
HA HA HA HA!
ONCE I WAS KING OF THE HILL, BUT I COULDN'T STOP LAUGHING..
YOU'RE VERY WEIRD..
SCHULZ

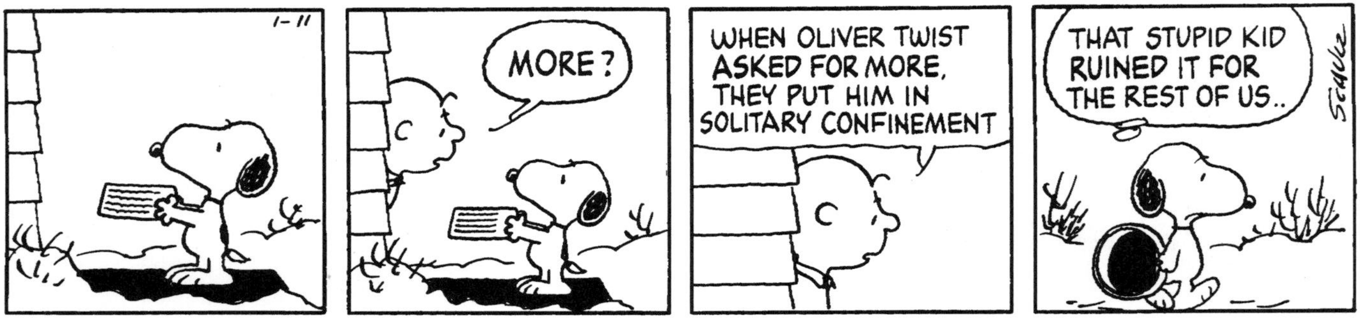
1-11
MORE?
WHEN OLIVER TWIST ASKED FOR MORE, THEY PUT HIM IN SOLITARY CONFINEMENT
THAT STUPID KID RUINED IT FOR THE REST OF US..

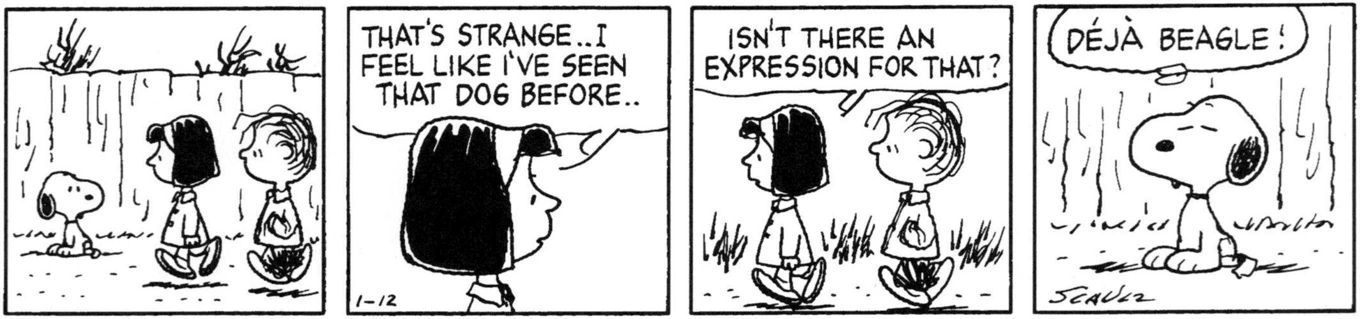
THAT'S STRANGE..I FEEL LIKE I'VE SEEN THAT DOG BEFORE..
1-12
ISN'T THERE AN EXPRESSION FOR THAT?
DÉJÀ BEAGLE!

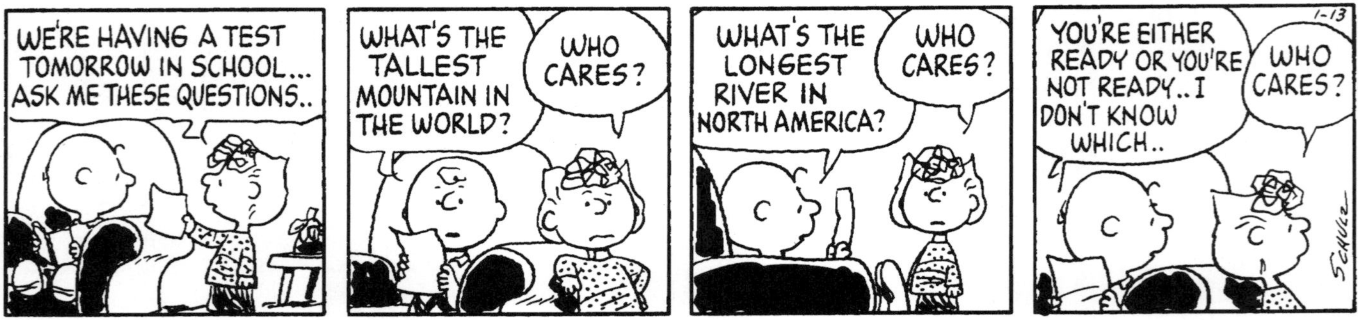
WE'RE HAVING A TEST TOMORROW IN SCHOOL... ASK ME THESE QUESTIONS..
WHAT'S THE TALLEST MOUNTAIN IN THE WORLD?
WHO CARES?
WHAT'S THE LONGEST RIVER IN NORTH AMERICA?
WHO CARES?
1-13
YOU'RE EITHER READY OR YOU'RE NOT READY..I DON'T KNOW WHICH..
WHO CARES?

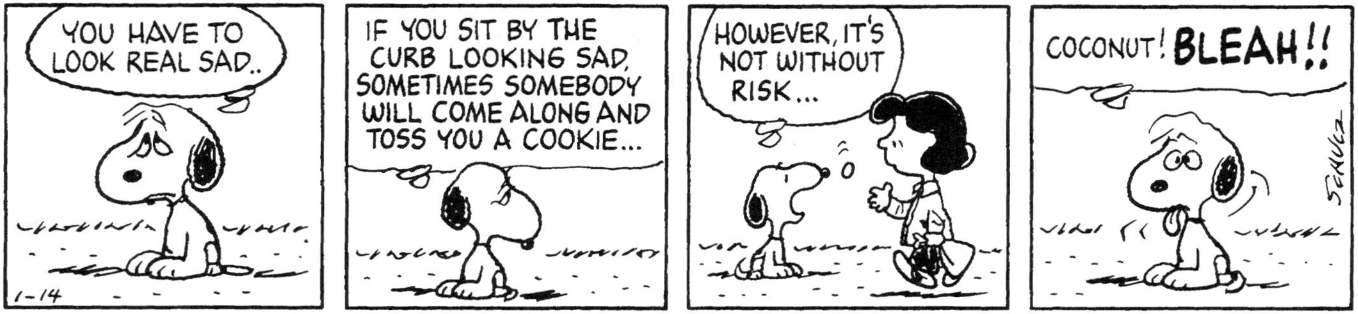
YOU HAVE TO LOOK REAL SAD..
1-14
IF YOU SIT BY THE CURB LOOKING SAD, SOMETIMES SOMEBODY WILL COME ALONG AND TOSS YOU A COOKIE...
HOWEVER, IT'S NOT WITHOUT RISK...
COCONUT! BLEAH!!

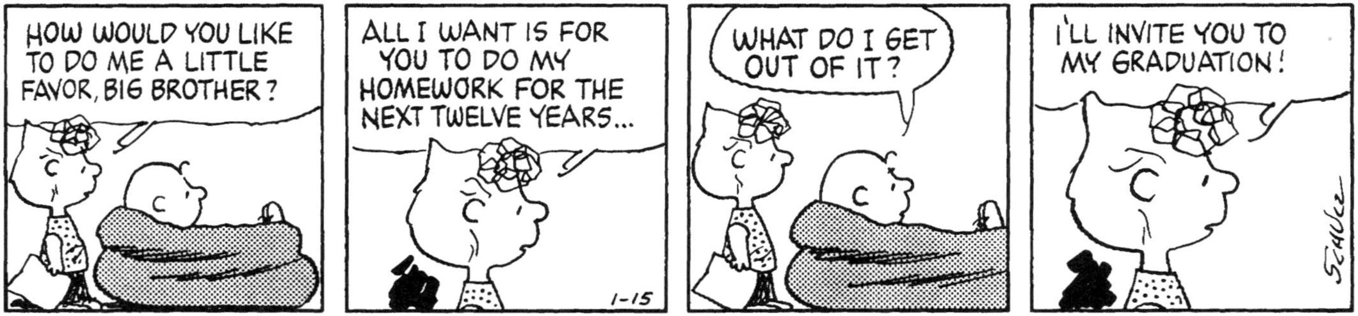
HOW WOULD YOU LIKE TO DO ME A LITTLE FAVOR, BIG BROTHER?
ALL I WANT IS FOR YOU TO DO MY HOMEWORK FOR THE NEXT TWELVE YEARS...
1-15
WHAT DO I GET OUT OF IT?
I'LL INVITE YOU TO MY GRADUATION!

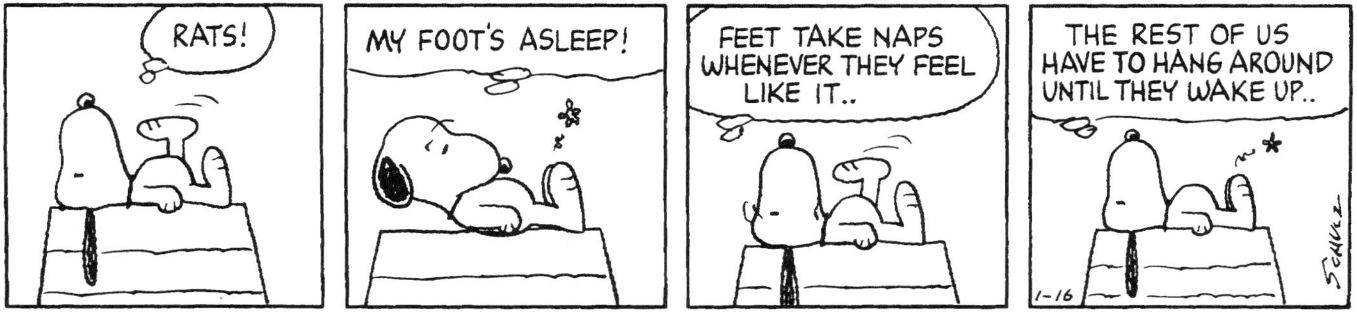
RATS!
MY FOOT'S ASLEEP!
FEET TAKE NAPS WHENEVER THEY FEEL LIKE IT..
THE REST OF US HAVE TO HANG AROUND UNTIL THEY WAKE UP..
1-16

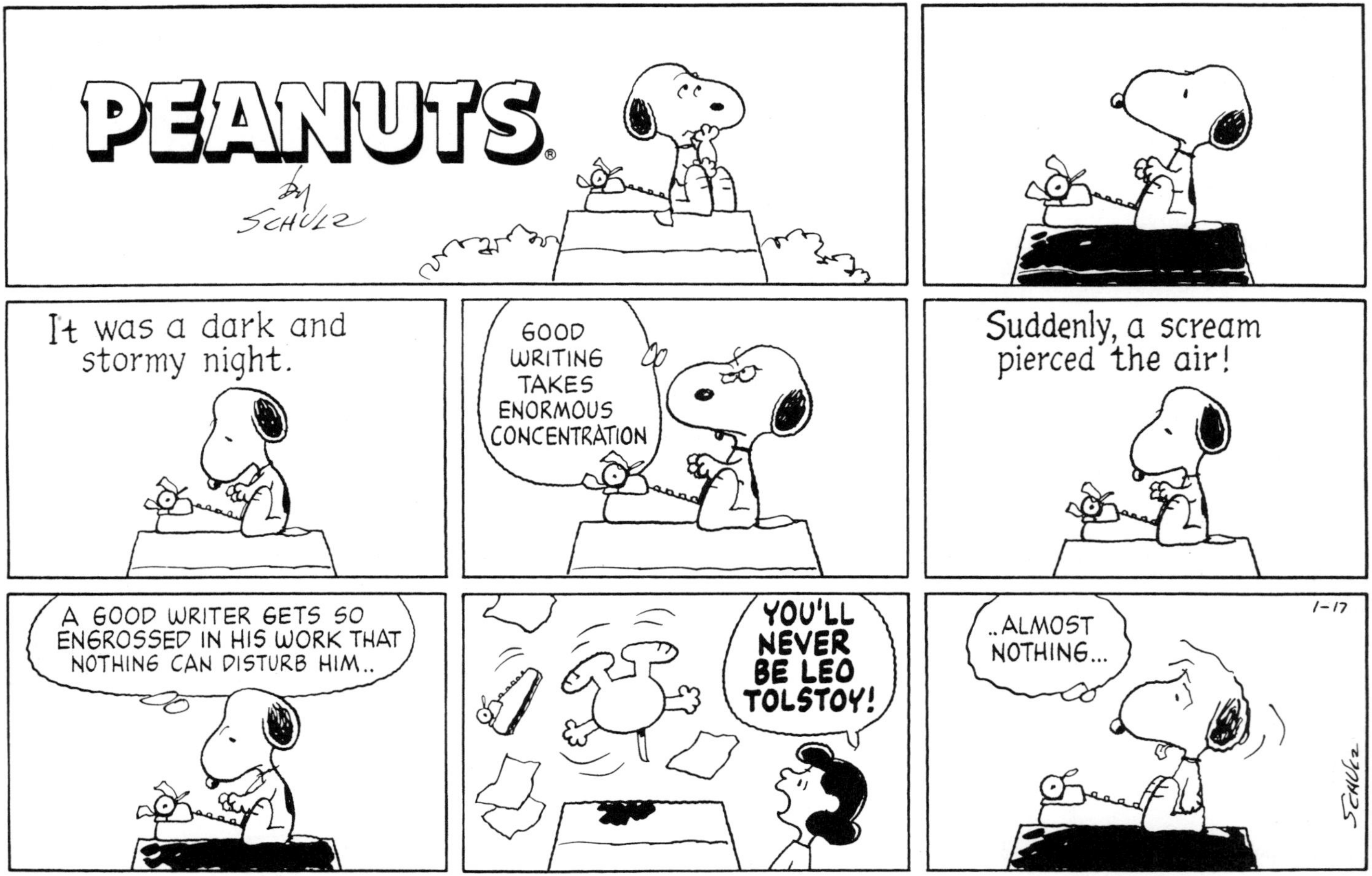
PEANUTS®
by SCHULZ
It was a dark and stormy night.
GOOD WRITING TAKES ENORMOUS CONCENTRATION
Suddenly, a scream pierced the air!
A GOOD WRITER GETS SO ENGROSSED IN HIS WORK THAT NOTHING CAN DISTURB HIM..
YOU'LL NEVER BE LEO TOLSTOY!
1-17
..ALMOST NOTHING...
SCHULZ

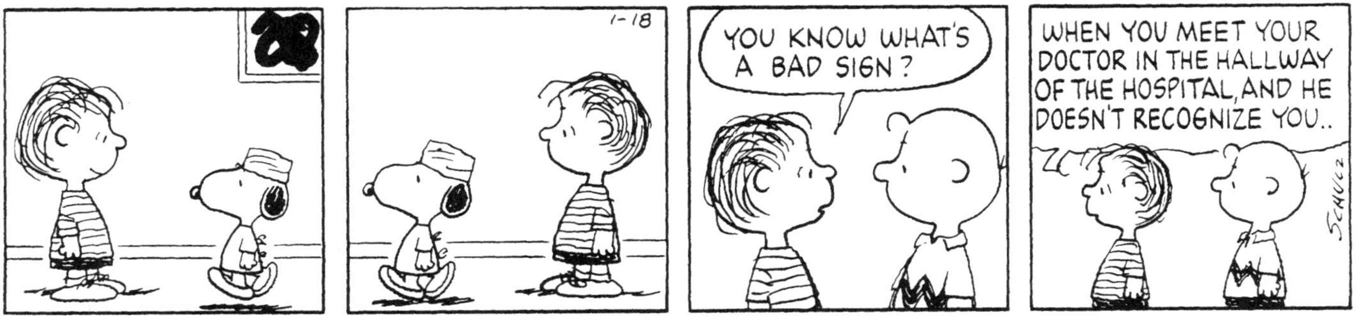
1-18
YOU KNOW WHAT'S A BAD SIGN?
WHEN YOU MEET YOUR DOCTOR IN THE HALLWAY OF THE HOSPITAL, AND HE DOESN'T RECOGNIZE YOU..

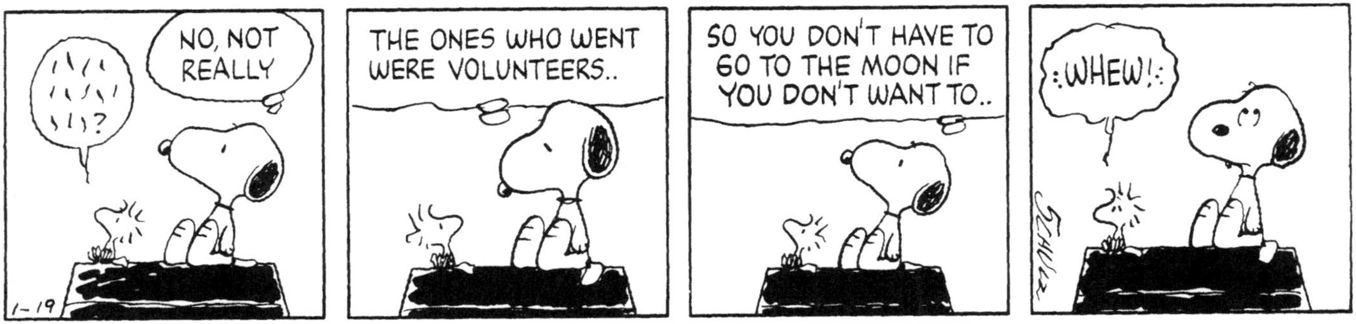
NO, NOT REALLY
1-19
THE ONES WHO WENT WERE VOLUNTEERS..
SO YOU DON'T HAVE TO GO TO THE MOON IF YOU DON'T WANT TO..
WHEW!

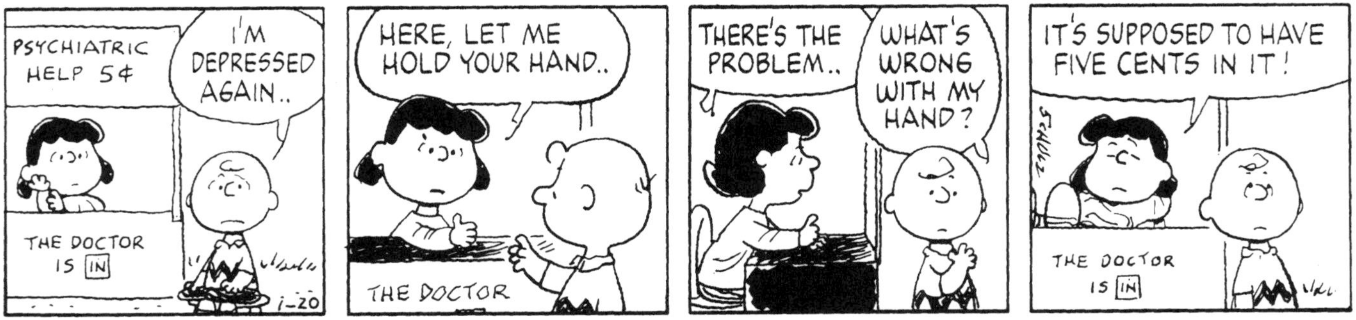
PSYCHIATRIC HELP 5¢
THE DOCTOR IS IN
I'M DEPRESSED AGAIN..
1-20
HERE, LET ME HOLD YOUR HAND..
THE DOCTOR
THERE'S THE PROBLEM..
WHAT'S WRONG WITH MY HAND?
IT'S SUPPOSED TO HAVE FIVE CENTS IN IT!
THE DOCTOR IS IN

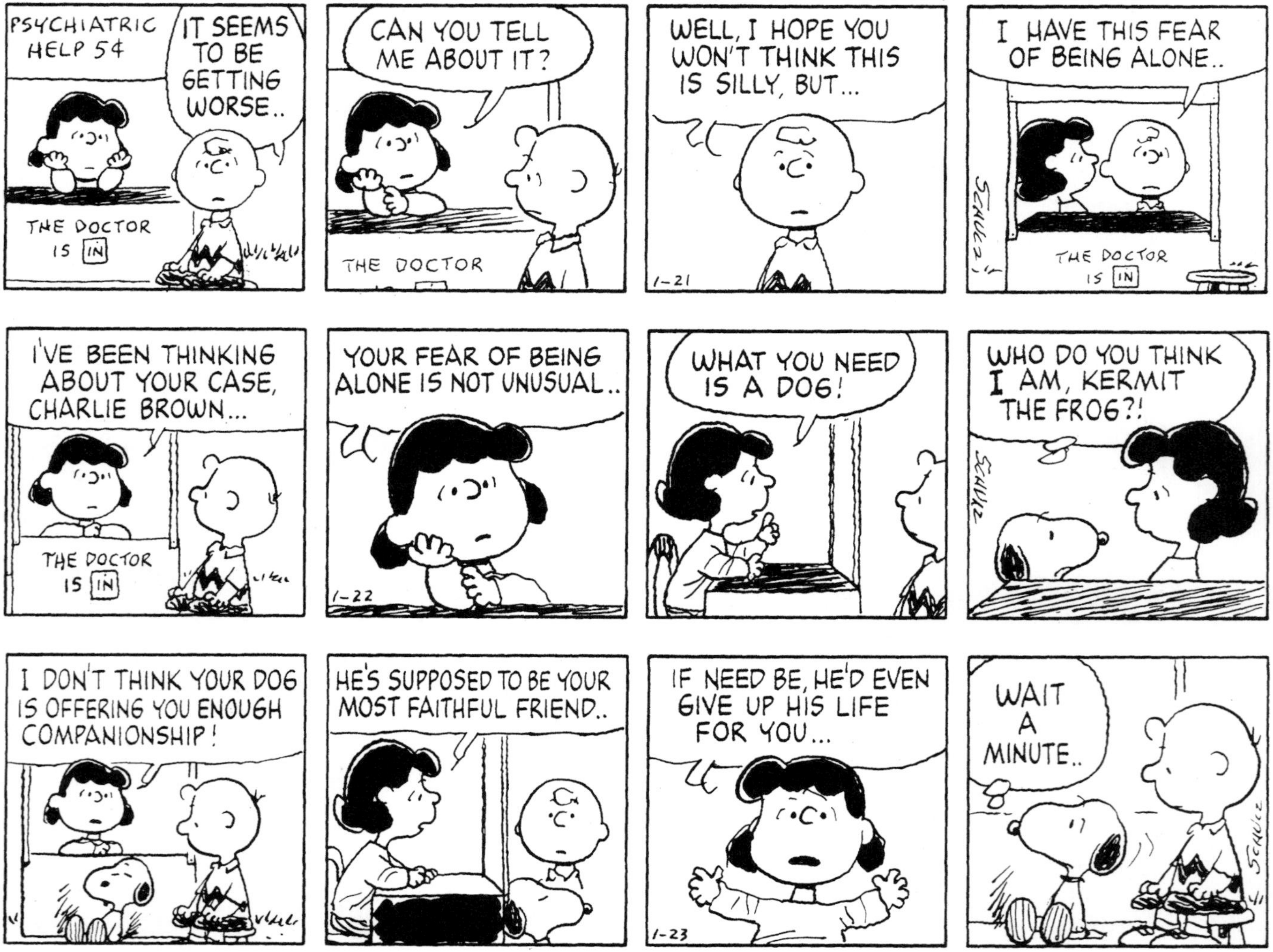
PSYCHIATRIC HELP 5¢
IT SEEMS TO BE GETTING WORSE..
THE DOCTOR IS IN
CAN YOU TELL ME ABOUT IT?
THE DOCTOR
WELL, I HOPE YOU WON'T THINK THIS IS SILLY, BUT...
1-21
I HAVE THIS FEAR OF BEING ALONE..
THE DOCTOR IS IN
I'VE BEEN THINKING ABOUT YOUR CASE, CHARLIE BROWN...
THE DOCTOR IS IN
YOUR FEAR OF BEING ALONE IS NOT UNUSUAL..
1-22
WHAT YOU NEED IS A DOG!
WHO DO YOU THINK I AM, KERMIT THE FROG?!
I DON'T THINK YOUR DOG IS OFFERING YOU ENOUGH COMPANIONSHIP!
HE'S SUPPOSED TO BE YOUR MOST FAITHFUL FRIEND..
IF NEED BE, HE'D EVEN GIVE UP HIS LIFE FOR YOU...
1-23
WAIT A MINUTE..

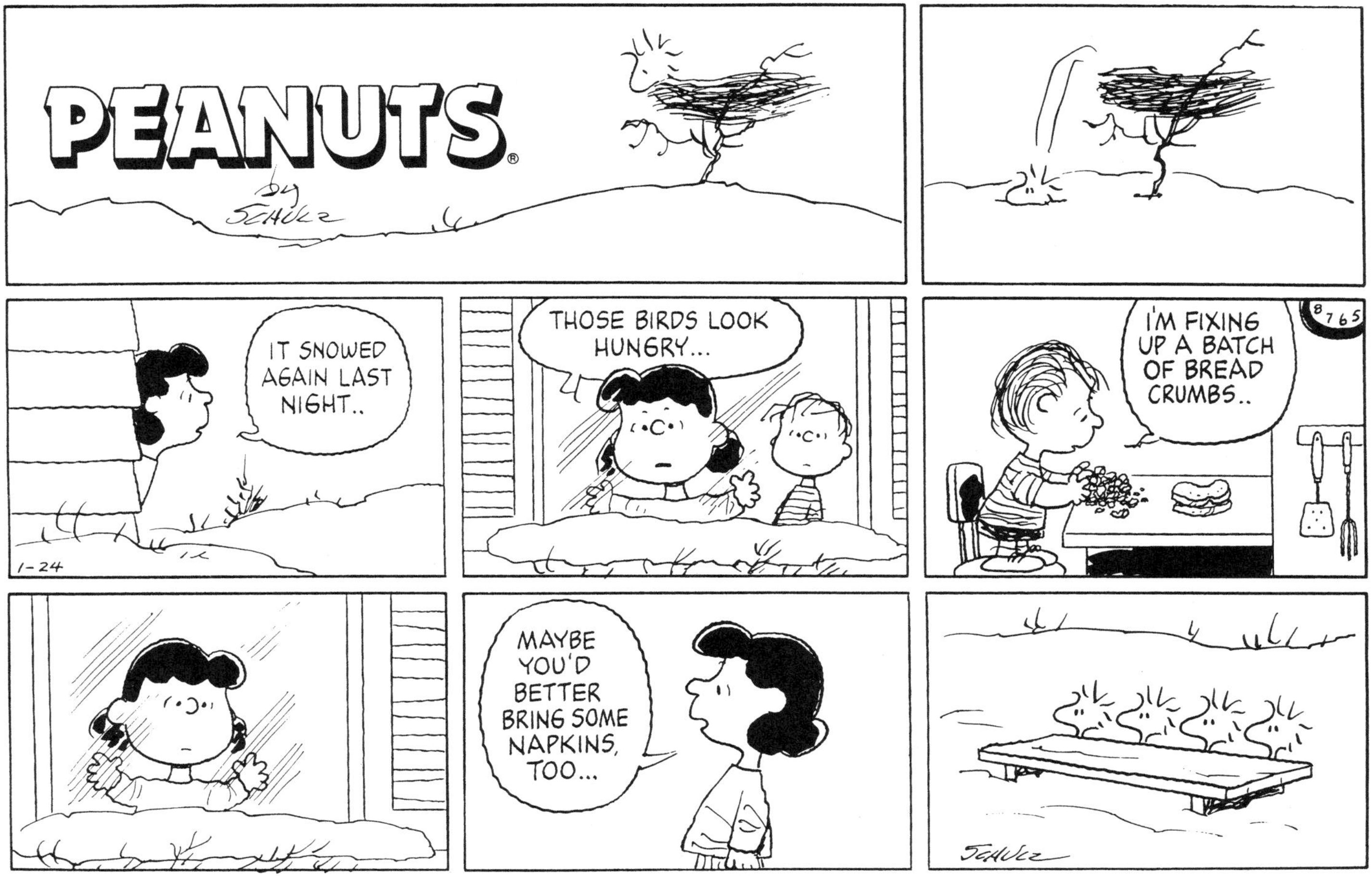
PEANUTS
by SCHULZ
1-24
IT SNOWED AGAIN LAST NIGHT..
THOSE BIRDS LOOK HUNGRY...
I'M FIXING UP A BATCH OF BREAD CRUMBS..
MAYBE YOU'D BETTER BRING SOME NAPKINS, TOO...
SCHULZ

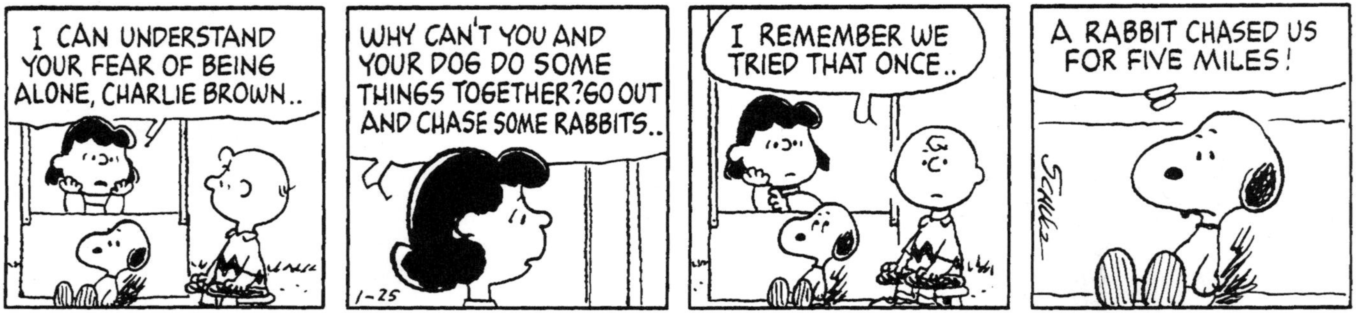
I CAN UNDERSTAND YOUR FEAR OF BEING ALONE, CHARLIE BROWN..
WHY CAN'T YOU AND YOUR DOG DO SOME THINGS TOGETHER? GO OUT AND CHASE SOME RABBITS..
1-25
I REMEMBER WE TRIED THAT ONCE..
A RABBIT CHASED US FOR FIVE MILES!
SCHULZ

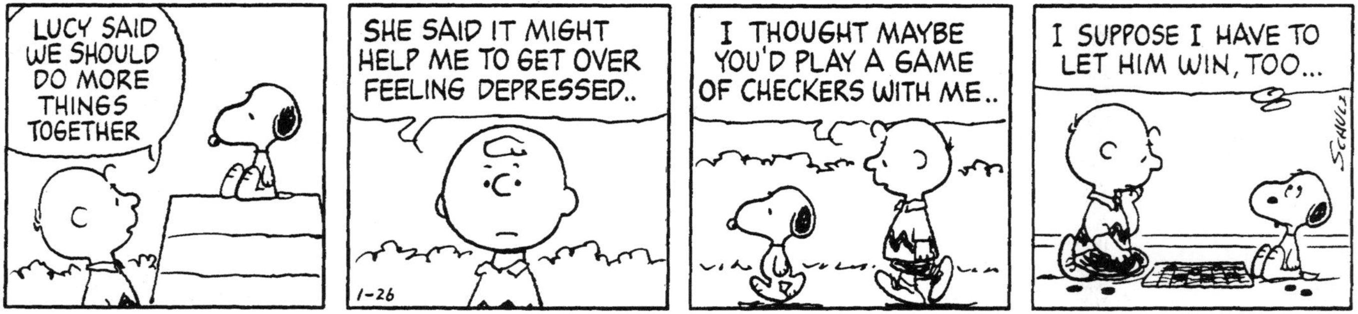
LUCY SAID WE SHOULD DO MORE THINGS TOGETHER
SHE SAID IT MIGHT HELP ME TO GET OVER FEELING DEPRESSED..
1-26
I THOUGHT MAYBE YOU'D PLAY A GAME OF CHECKERS WITH ME..
I SUPPOSE I HAVE TO LET HIM WIN, TOO...
SCHULZ

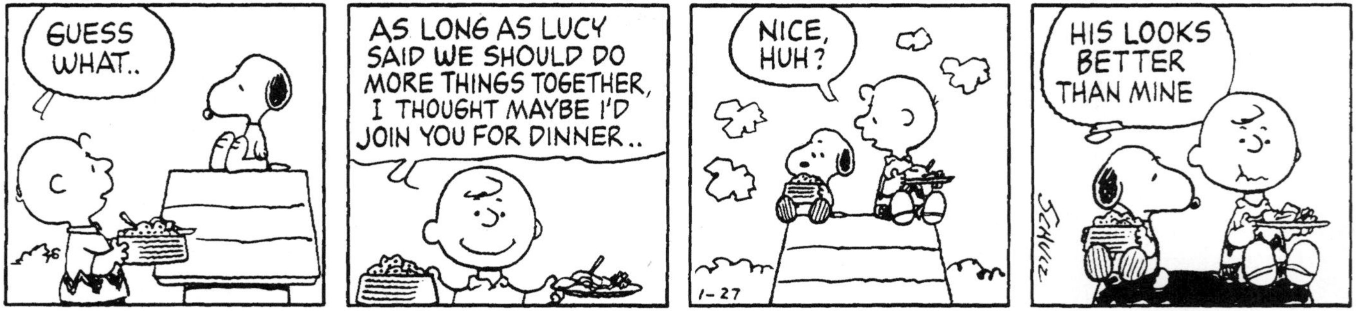
GUESS WHAT..
AS LONG AS LUCY SAID WE SHOULD DO MORE THINGS TOGETHER, I THOUGHT MAYBE I'D JOIN YOU FOR DINNER..
NICE, HUH?
1-27
HIS LOOKS BETTER THAN MINE
SCHULZ

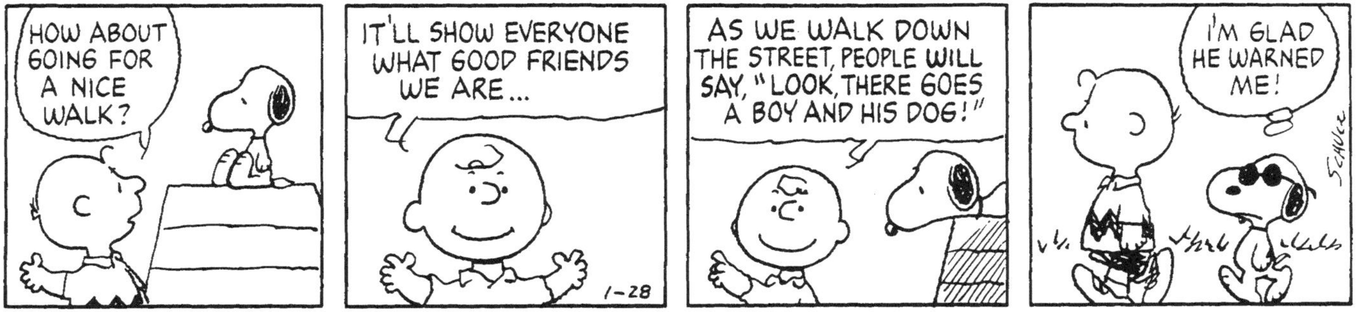
HOW ABOUT GOING FOR A NICE WALK?
IT'LL SHOW EVERYONE WHAT GOOD FRIENDS WE ARE...
1-28
AS WE WALK DOWN THE STREET, PEOPLE WILL SAY, "LOOK, THERE GOES A BOY AND HIS DOG!"
I'M GLAD HE WARNED ME!

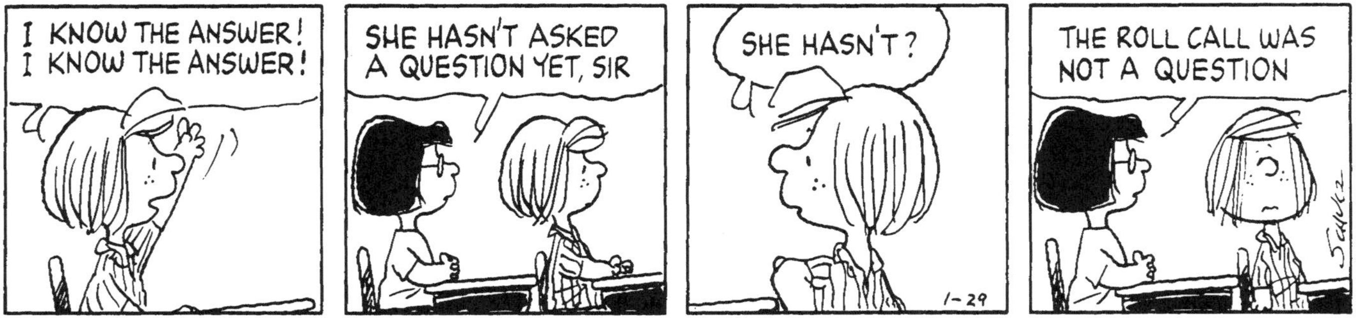
I KNOW THE ANSWER! I KNOW THE ANSWER!
SHE HASN'T ASKED A QUESTION YET, SIR
SHE HASN'T?
1-29
THE ROLL CALL WAS NOT A QUESTION

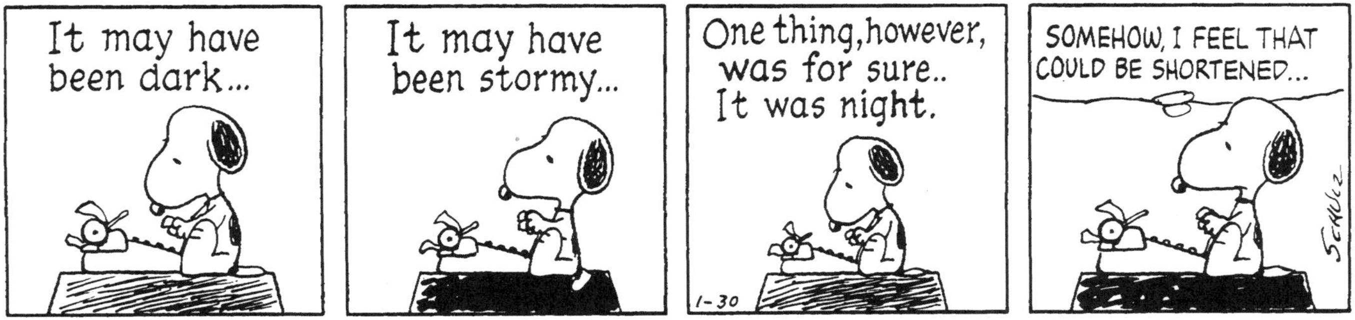
It may have been dark...
It may have been stormy...
One thing, however, was for sure.. It was night.
1-30
SOMEHOW, I FEEL THAT COULD BE SHORTENED...

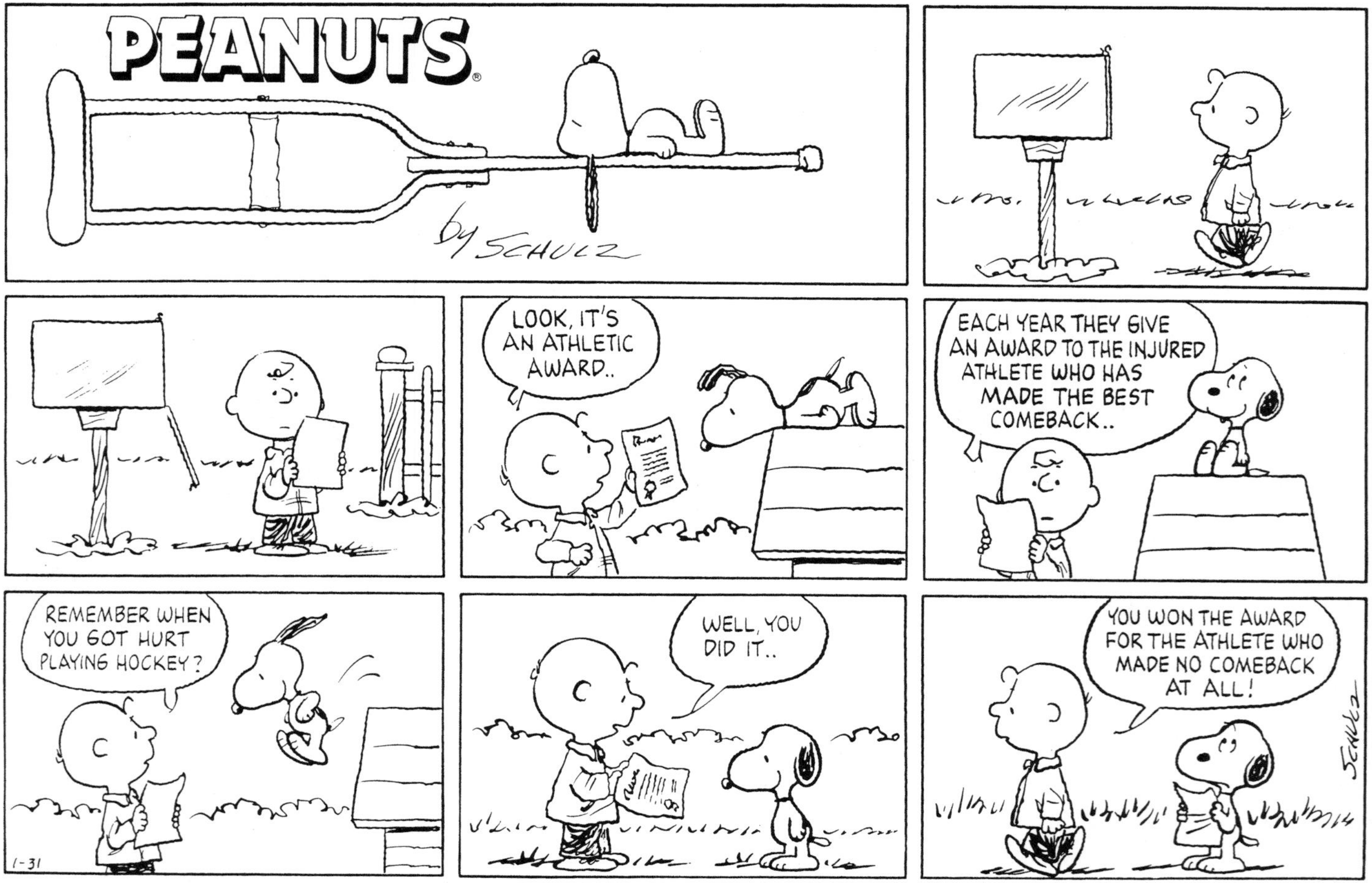
PEANUTS
by SCHULZ
LOOK, IT'S AN ATHLETIC AWARD..
EACH YEAR THEY GIVE AN AWARD TO THE INJURED ATHLETE WHO HAS MADE THE BEST COMEBACK..
REMEMBER WHEN YOU GOT HURT PLAYING HOCKEY?
1-31
WELL, YOU DID IT..
YOU WON THE AWARD FOR THE ATHLETE WHO MADE NO COMEBACK AT ALL!
SCHULZ

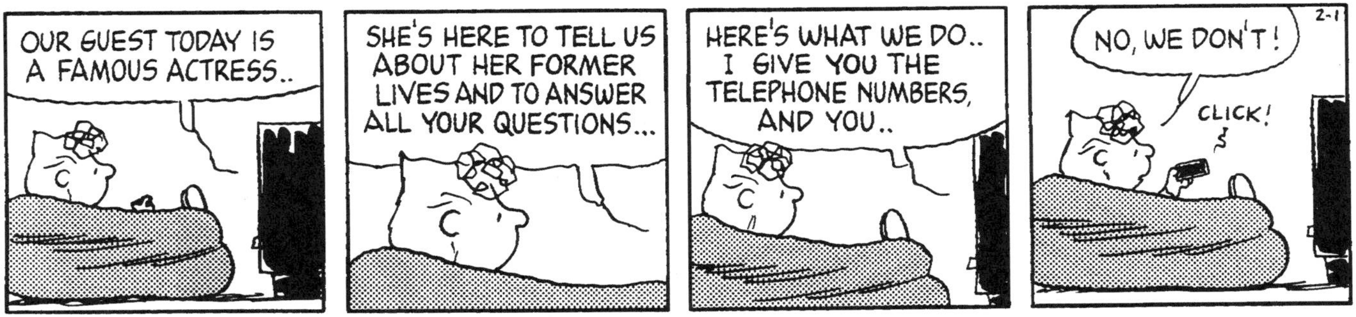
OUR GUEST TODAY IS A FAMOUS ACTRESS..
SHE'S HERE TO TELL US ABOUT HER FORMER LIVES AND TO ANSWER ALL YOUR QUESTIONS...
HERE'S WHAT WE DO.. I GIVE YOU THE TELEPHONE NUMBERS, AND YOU..
2-1
NO, WE DON'T!
CLICK!

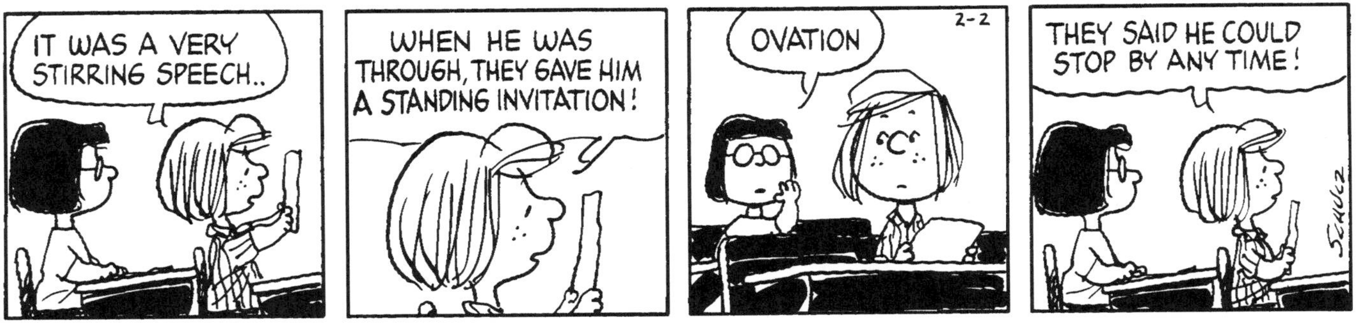
IT WAS A VERY STIRRING SPEECH..
WHEN HE WAS THROUGH, THEY GAVE HIM A STANDING INVITATION!
2-2
OVATION
THEY SAID HE COULD STOP BY ANY TIME!
SCHULZ

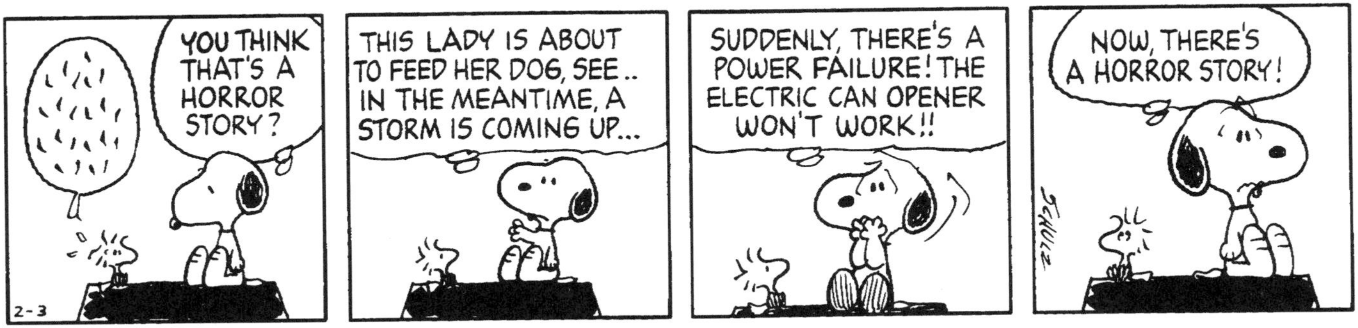
YOU THINK THAT'S A HORROR STORY?
2-3
THIS LADY IS ABOUT TO FEED HER DOG, SEE.. IN THE MEANTIME, A STORM IS COMING UP...
SUDDENLY, THERE'S A POWER FAILURE! THE ELECTRIC CAN OPENER WON'T WORK!!
SCHULZ
NOW, THERE'S A HORROR STORY!

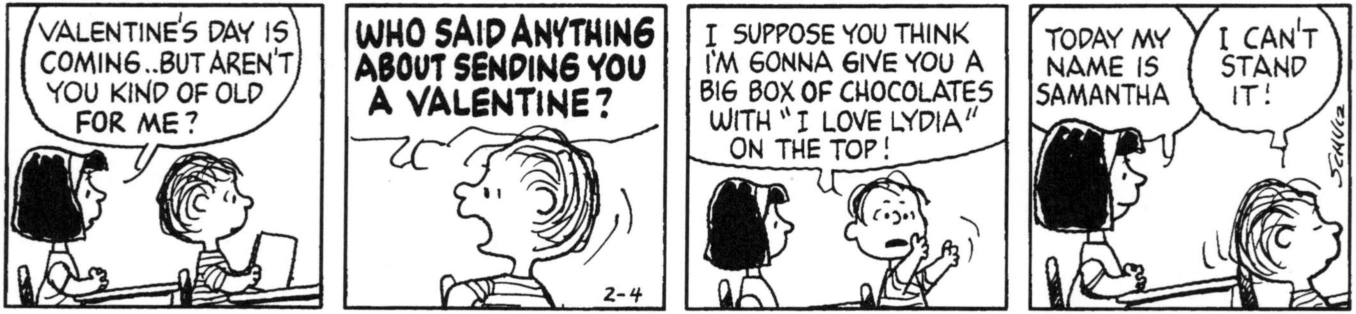
VALENTINE'S DAY IS COMING..BUT AREN'T YOU KIND OF OLD FOR ME?
WHO SAID ANYTHING ABOUT SENDING YOU A VALENTINE?
2-4
I SUPPOSE YOU THINK I'M GONNA GIVE YOU A BIG BOX OF CHOCOLATES WITH "I LOVE LYDIA" ON THE TOP!
TODAY MY NAME IS SAMANTHA
I CAN'T STAND IT!
SCHULZ

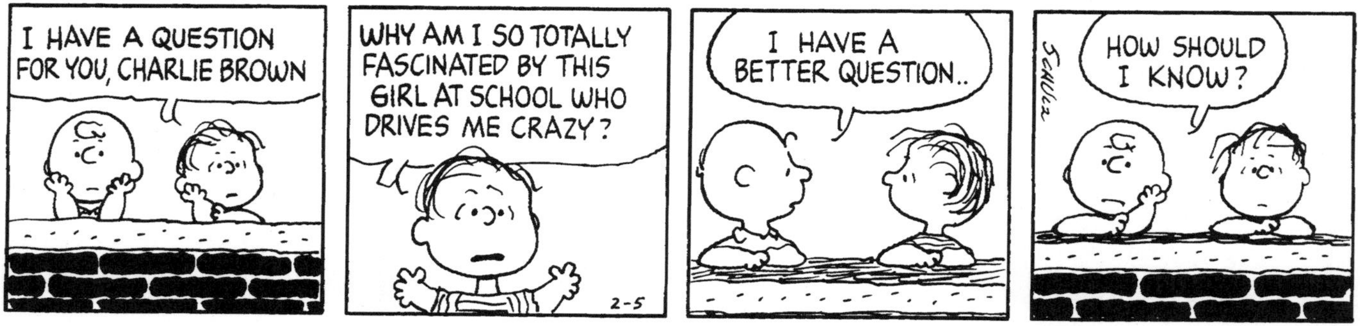
I HAVE A QUESTION FOR YOU, CHARLIE BROWN
WHY AM I SO TOTALLY FASCINATED BY THIS GIRL AT SCHOOL WHO DRIVES ME CRAZY?
2-5
I HAVE A BETTER QUESTION..
SCHULZ
HOW SHOULD I KNOW?

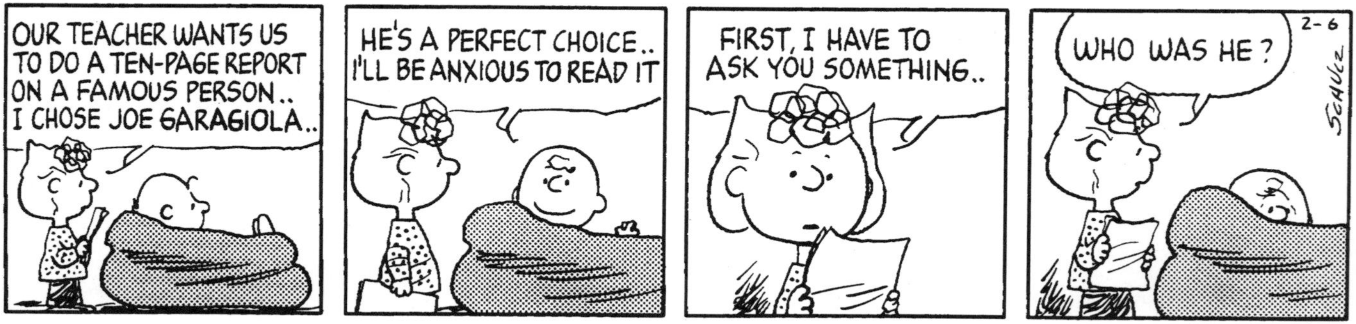
OUR TEACHER WANTS US TO DO A TEN-PAGE REPORT ON A FAMOUS PERSON.. I CHOSE JOE GARAGIOLA..
HE'S A PERFECT CHOICE.. I'LL BE ANXIOUS TO READ IT
FIRST, I HAVE TO ASK YOU SOMETHING..
2-6
WHO WAS HE?
SCHULZ

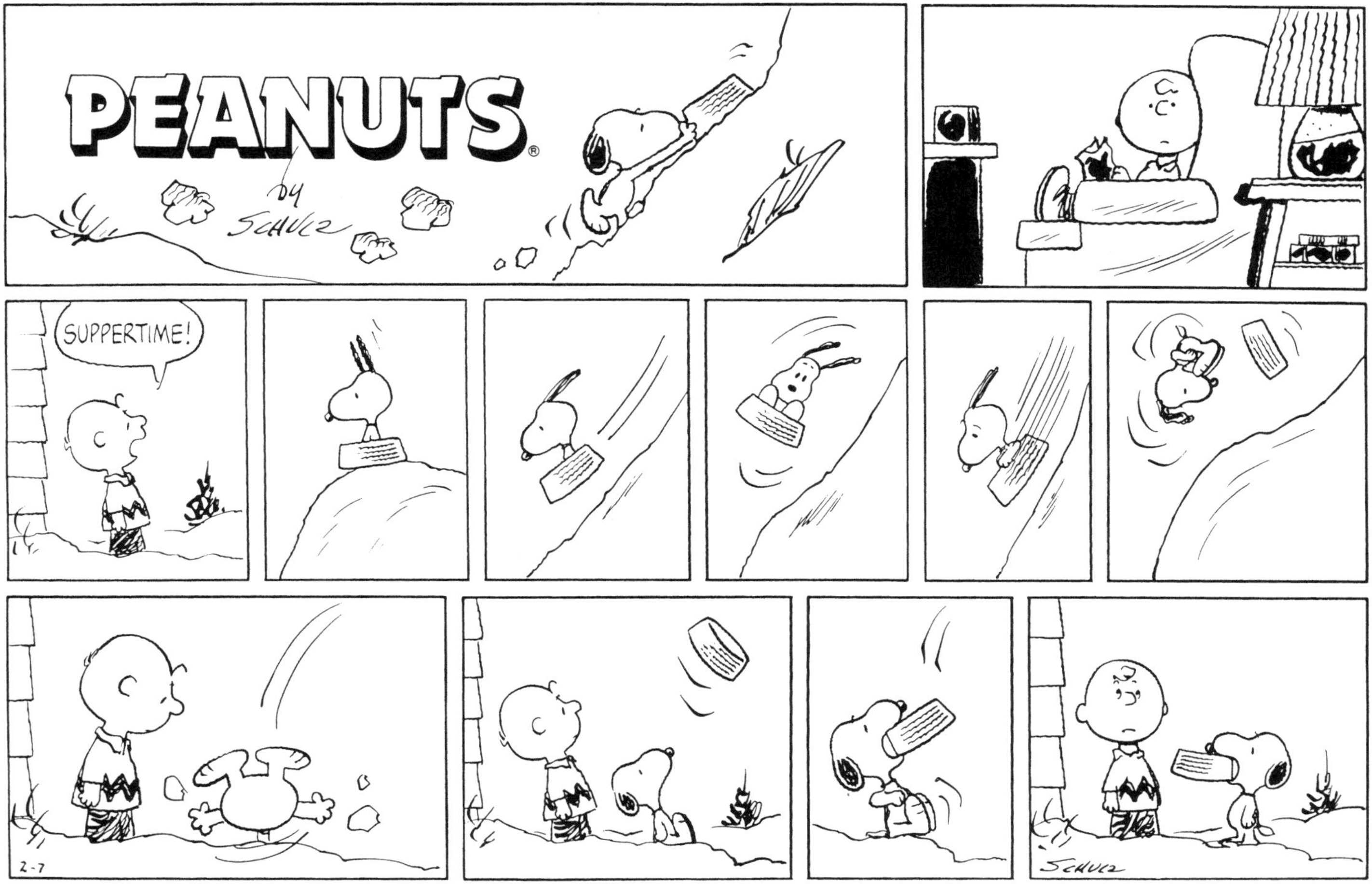
PEANUTS
by Schulz
SUPPERTIME!
2-7
Schulz

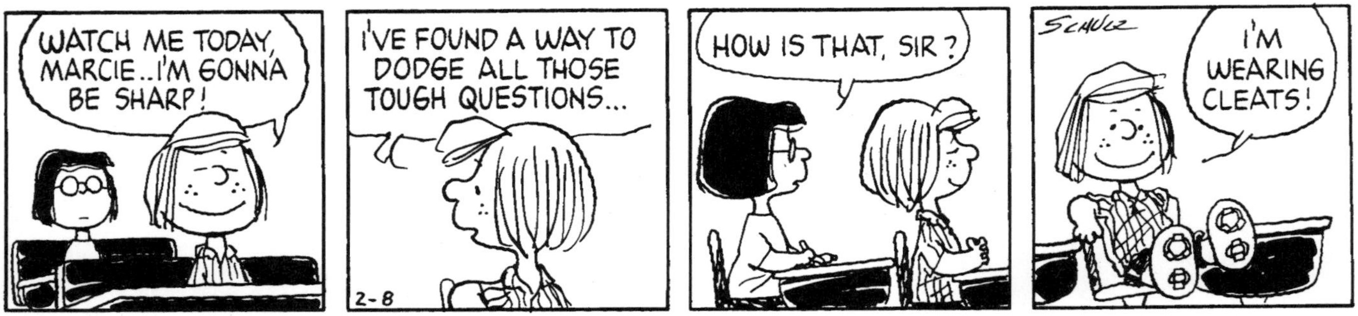
WATCH ME TODAY, MARCIE..I'M GONNA BE SHARP!
I'VE FOUND A WAY TO DODGE ALL THOSE TOUGH QUESTIONS...
2-8
HOW IS THAT, SIR?
SCHULZ
I'M WEARING CLEATS!

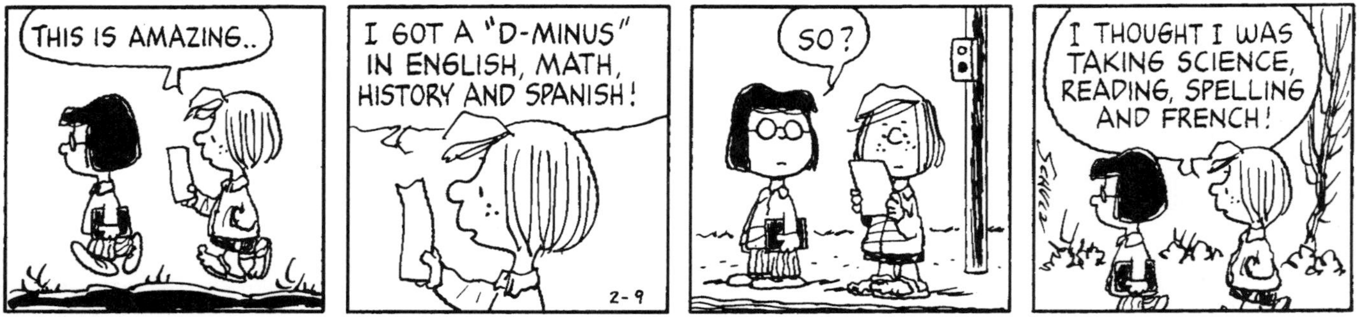
THIS IS AMAZING..
I GOT A "D-MINUS" IN ENGLISH, MATH, HISTORY AND SPANISH!
2-9
SO?
SCHULZ
I THOUGHT I WAS TAKING SCIENCE, READING, SPELLING AND FRENCH!

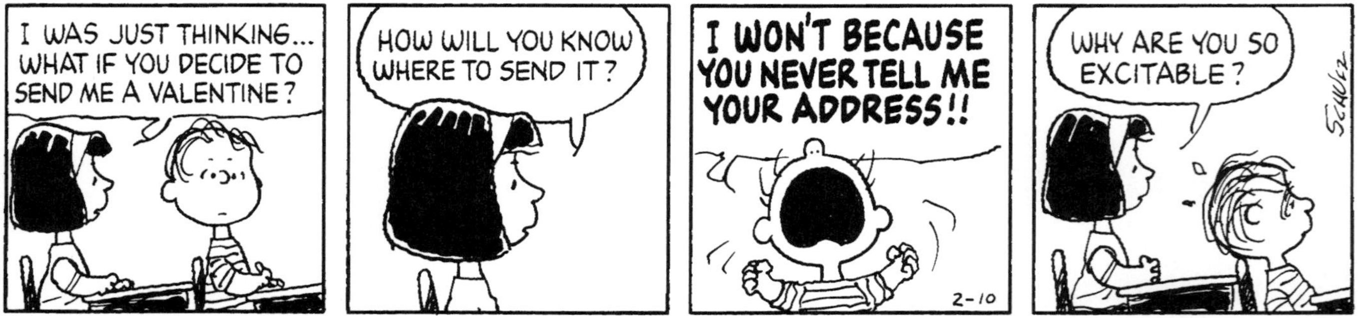
I WAS JUST THINKING... WHAT IF YOU DECIDE TO SEND ME A VALENTINE?
HOW WILL YOU KNOW WHERE TO SEND IT?
I WON'T BECAUSE YOU NEVER TELL ME YOUR ADDRESS!!
2-10
WHY ARE YOU SO EXCITABLE?
SCHULZ

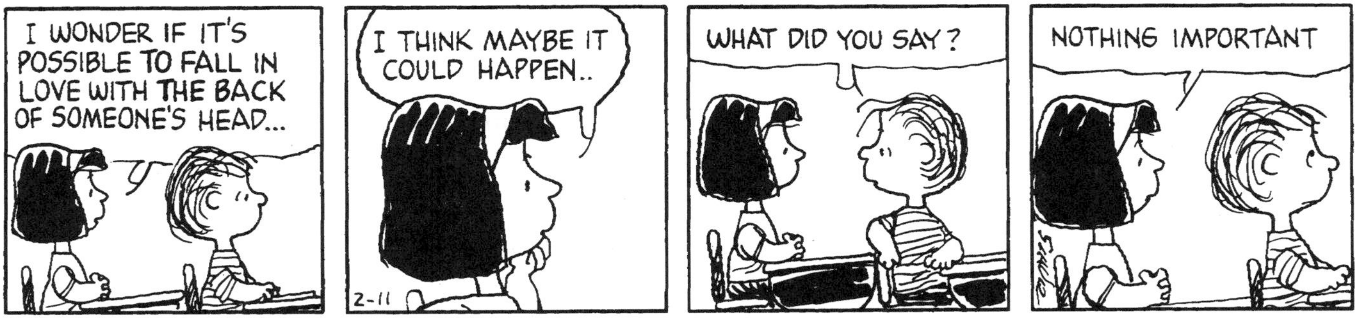
I WONDER IF IT'S POSSIBLE TO FALL IN LOVE WITH THE BACK OF SOMEONE'S HEAD...
I THINK MAYBE IT COULD HAPPEN..
2-11
WHAT DID YOU SAY?
NOTHING IMPORTANT

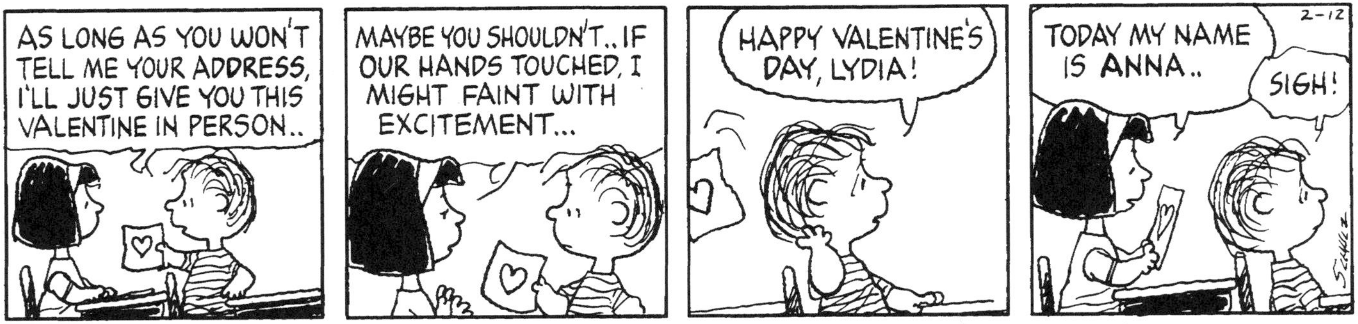
AS LONG AS YOU WON'T TELL ME YOUR ADDRESS, I'LL JUST GIVE YOU THIS VALENTINE IN PERSON..
MAYBE YOU SHOULDN'T.. IF OUR HANDS TOUCHED, I MIGHT FAINT WITH EXCITEMENT...
HAPPY VALENTINE'S DAY, LYDIA!
2-12
TODAY MY NAME IS ANNA..
SIGH!

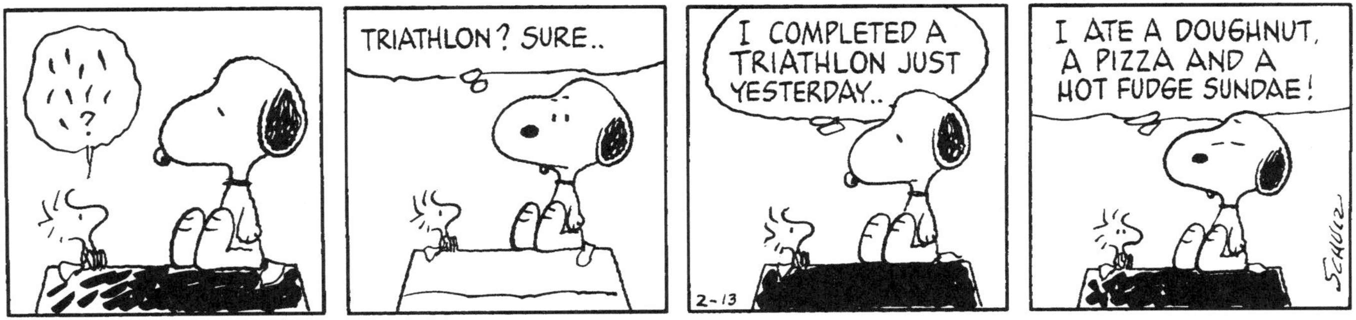
TRIATHLON? SURE..
I COMPLETED A TRIATHLON JUST YESTERDAY..
2-13
I ATE A DOUGHNUT, A PIZZA AND A HOT FUDGE SUNDAE!

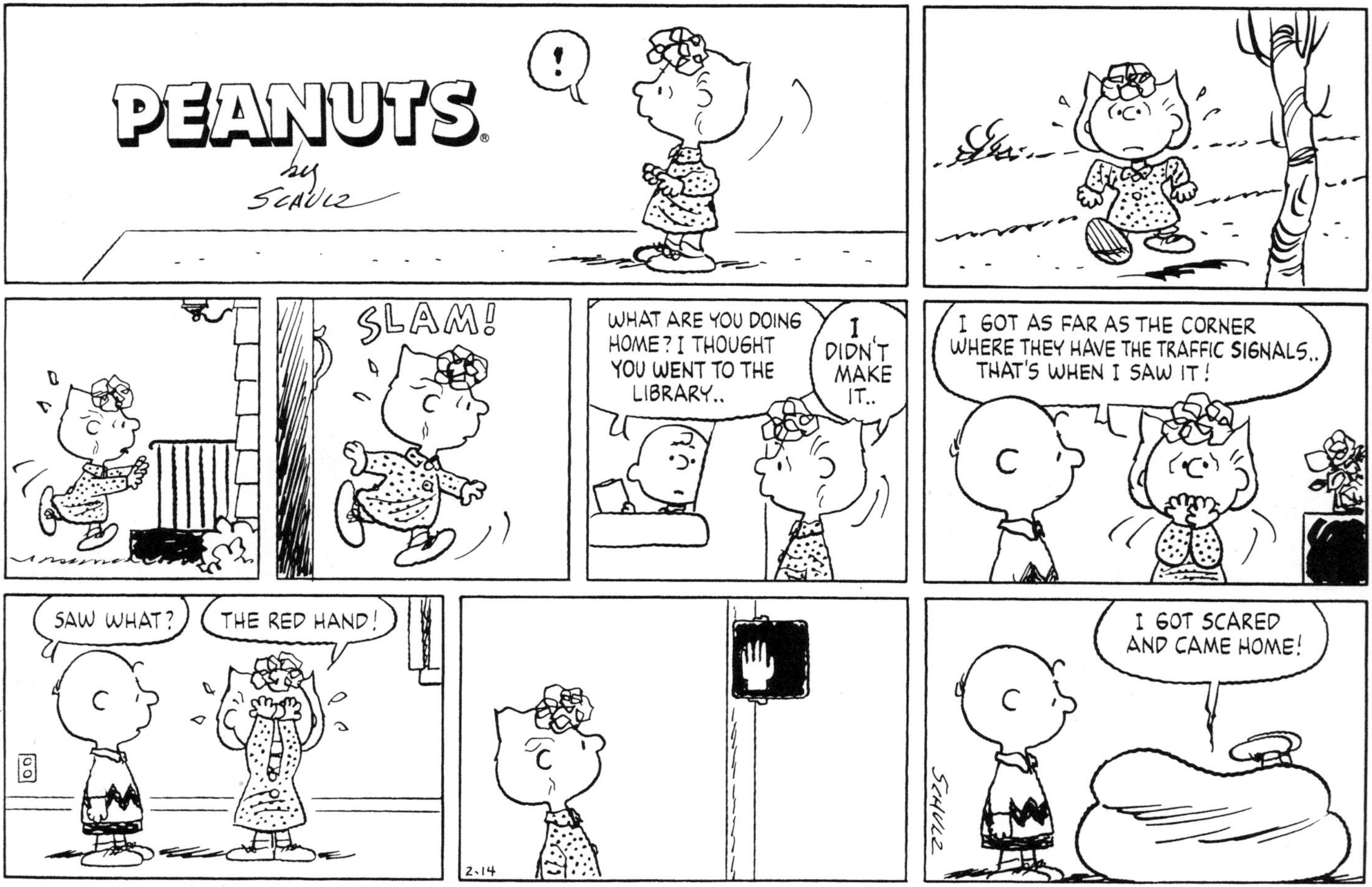
PEANUTS
by SCHULZ
!
SLAM!
WHAT ARE YOU DOING HOME? I THOUGHT YOU WENT TO THE LIBRARY..
I DIDN'T MAKE IT..
I GOT AS FAR AS THE CORNER WHERE THEY HAVE THE TRAFFIC SIGNALS.. THAT'S WHEN I SAW IT!
SAW WHAT?
THE RED HAND!
2-14
I GOT SCARED AND CAME HOME!
SCHULZ

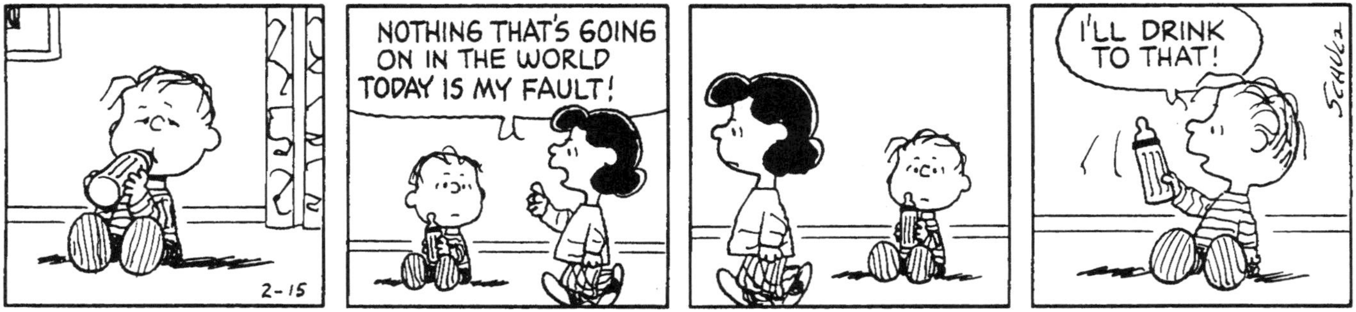
2-15
NOTHING THAT'S GOING ON IN THE WORLD TODAY IS MY FAULT!
I'LL DRINK TO THAT!

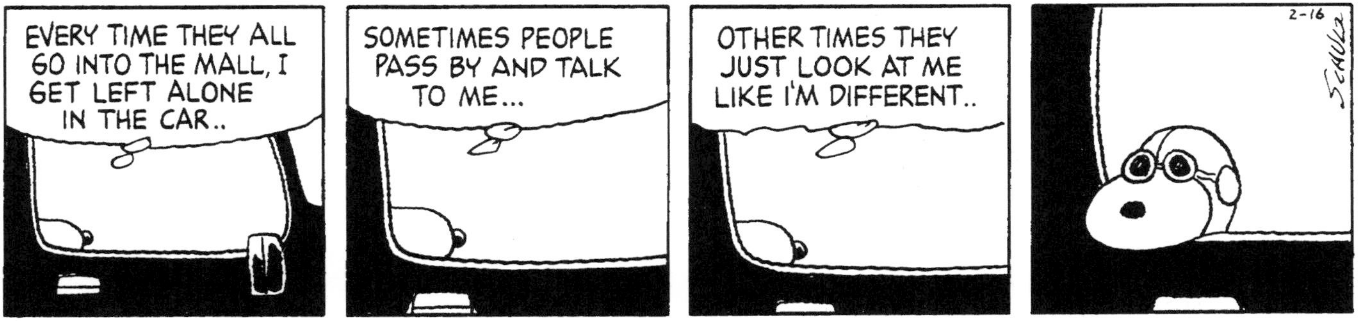
EVERY TIME THEY ALL GO INTO THE MALL, I GET LEFT ALONE IN THE CAR..
SOMETIMES PEOPLE PASS BY AND TALK TO ME...
OTHER TIMES THEY JUST LOOK AT ME LIKE I'M DIFFERENT..
2-16

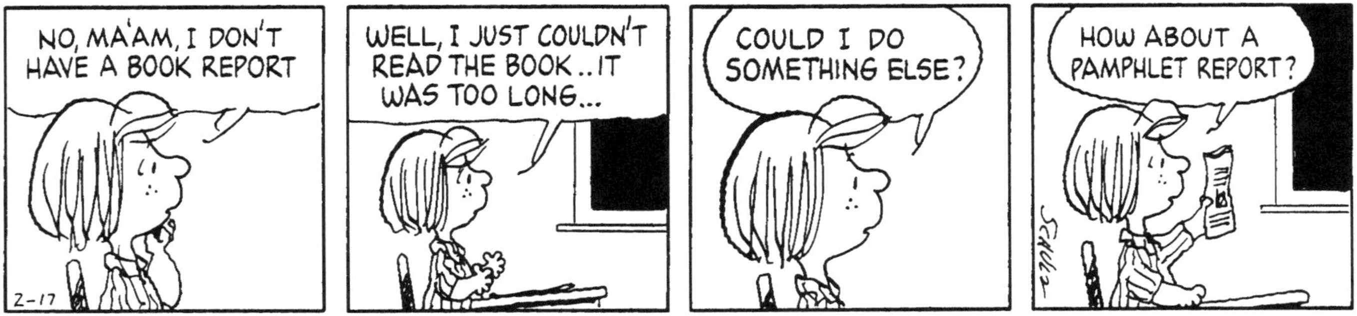
NO, MA'AM, I DON'T HAVE A BOOK REPORT
2-17
WELL, I JUST COULDN'T READ THE BOOK..IT WAS TOO LONG...
COULD I DO SOMETHING ELSE?
HOW ABOUT A PAMPHLET REPORT?

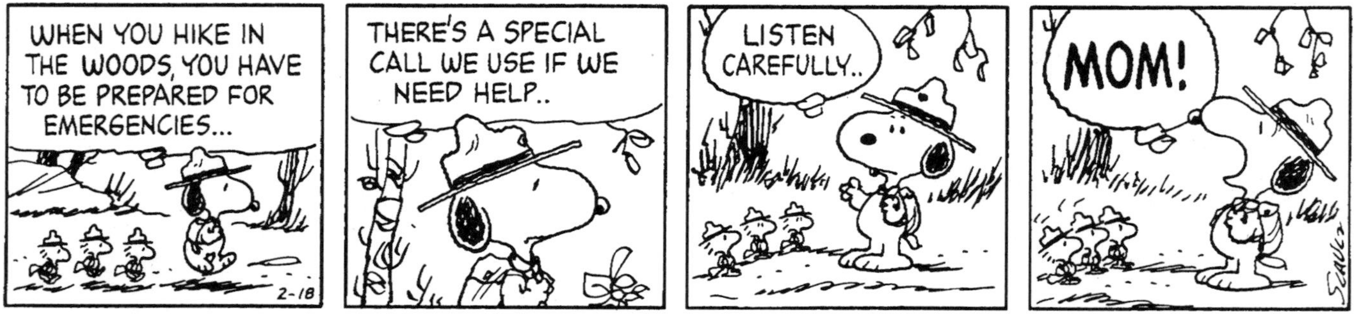
WHEN YOU HIKE IN THE WOODS, YOU HAVE TO BE PREPARED FOR EMERGENCIES...
2-18
THERE'S A SPECIAL CALL WE USE IF WE NEED HELP..
LISTEN CAREFULLY..
MOM!
SCHULZ

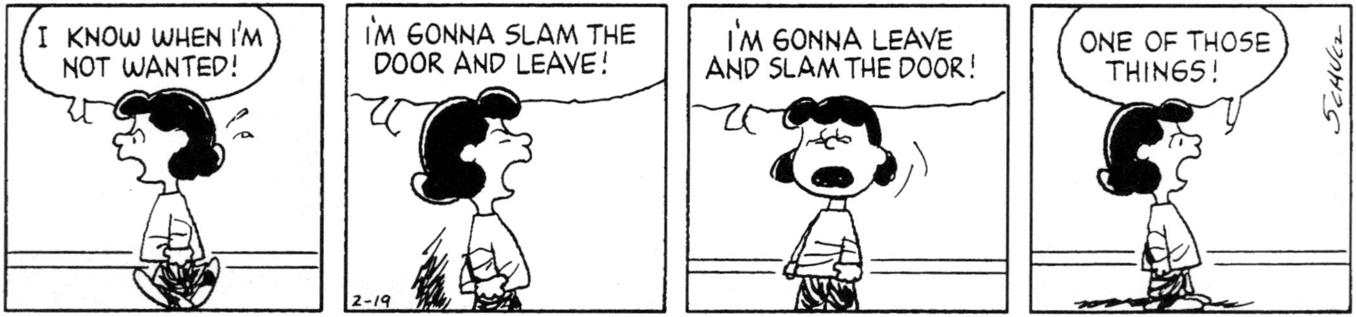
I KNOW WHEN I'M NOT WANTED!
I'M GONNA SLAM THE DOOR AND LEAVE!
2-19
I'M GONNA LEAVE AND SLAM THE DOOR!
ONE OF THOSE THINGS!
SCHULZ

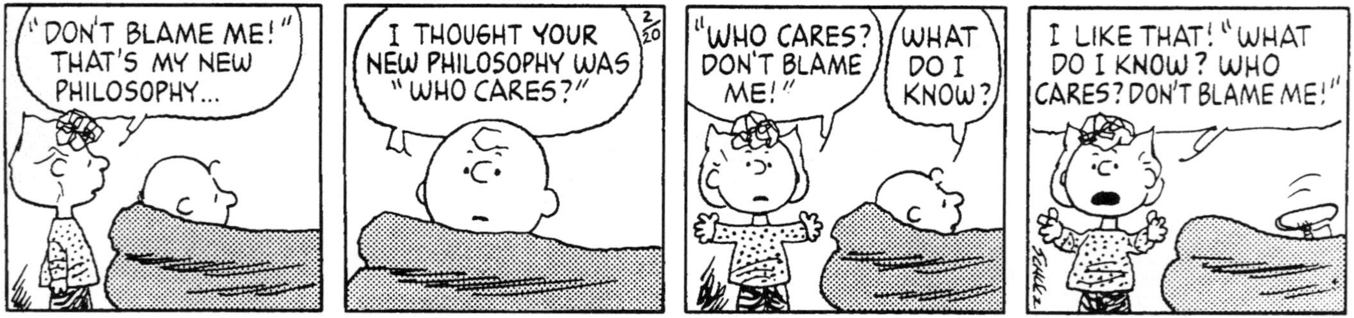
"DON'T BLAME ME!" THAT'S MY NEW PHILOSOPHY...
I THOUGHT YOUR NEW PHILOSOPHY WAS "WHO CARES?"
2/20
"WHO CARES? DON'T BLAME ME!"
WHAT DO I KNOW?
SCHULZ
I LIKE THAT! "WHAT DO I KNOW? WHO CARES? DON'T BLAME ME!"

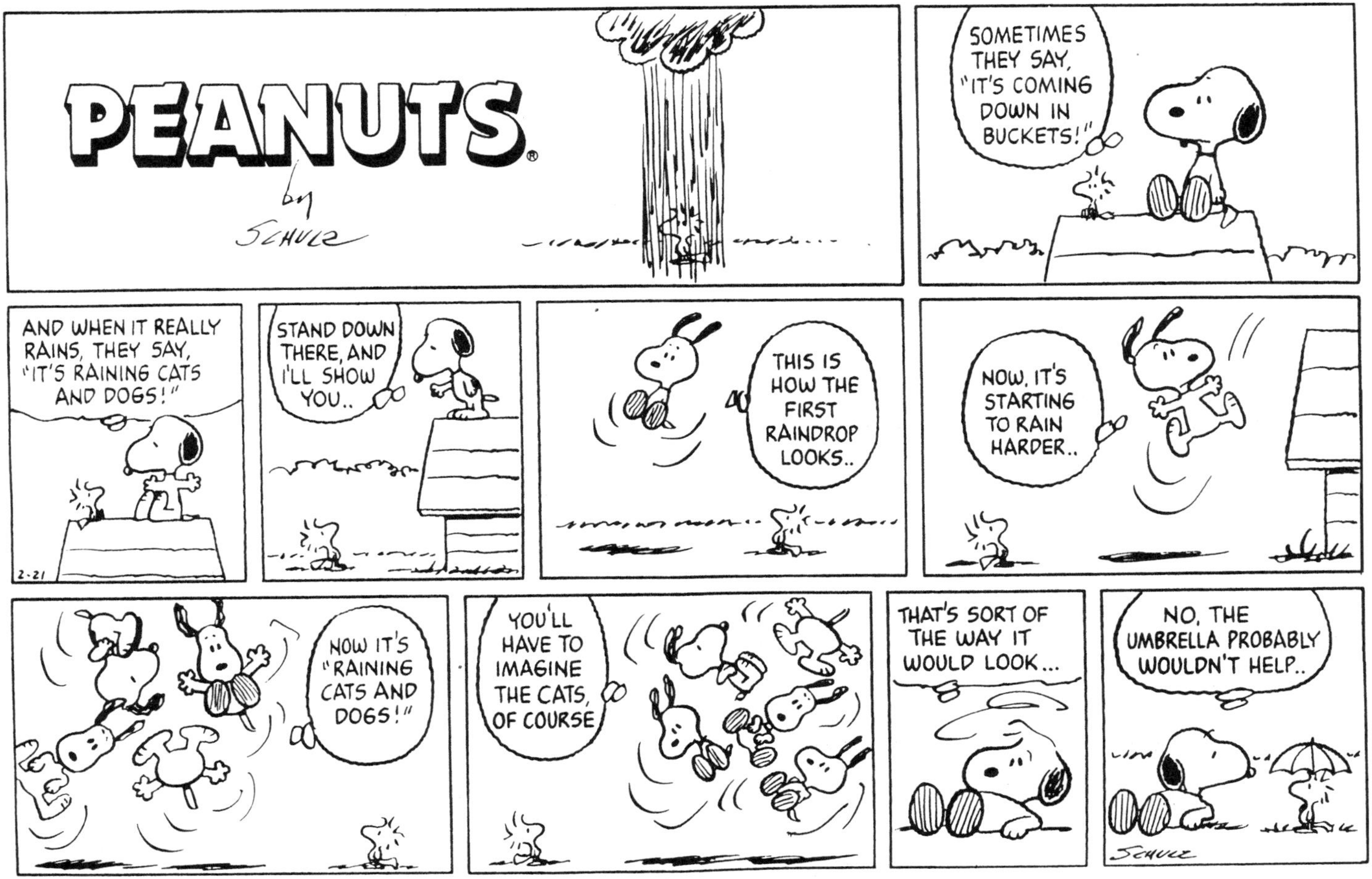
PEANUTS®
by SCHULZ
SOMETIMES THEY SAY, "IT'S COMING DOWN IN BUCKETS!"
AND WHEN IT REALLY RAINS, THEY SAY, "IT'S RAINING CATS AND DOGS!"
2-21
STAND DOWN THERE, AND I'LL SHOW YOU..
THIS IS HOW THE FIRST RAINDROP LOOKS..
NOW, IT'S STARTING TO RAIN HARDER..
NOW IT'S "RAINING CATS AND DOGS!"
YOU'LL HAVE TO IMAGINE THE CATS, OF COURSE
THAT'S SORT OF THE WAY IT WOULD LOOK...
NO, THE UMBRELLA PROBABLY WOULDN'T HELP..
SCHULZ

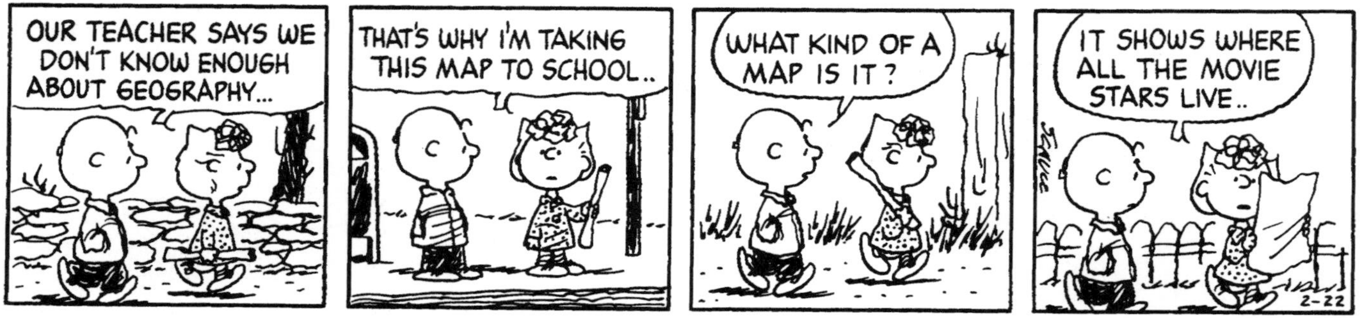
OUR TEACHER SAYS WE DON'T KNOW ENOUGH ABOUT GEOGRAPHY...
THAT'S WHY I'M TAKING THIS MAP TO SCHOOL..
WHAT KIND OF A MAP IS IT?
IT SHOWS WHERE ALL THE MOVIE STARS LIVE..
SCHULZ
2-22

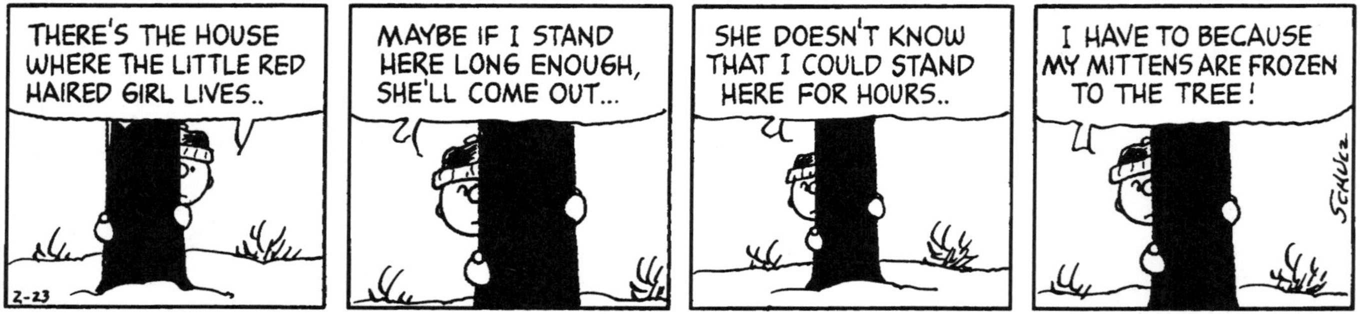
THERE'S THE HOUSE WHERE THE LITTLE RED HAIRED GIRL LIVES..
2-23
MAYBE IF I STAND HERE LONG ENOUGH, SHE'LL COME OUT...
SHE DOESN'T KNOW THAT I COULD STAND HERE FOR HOURS..
I HAVE TO BECAUSE MY MITTENS ARE FROZEN TO THE TREE!
SCHULZ

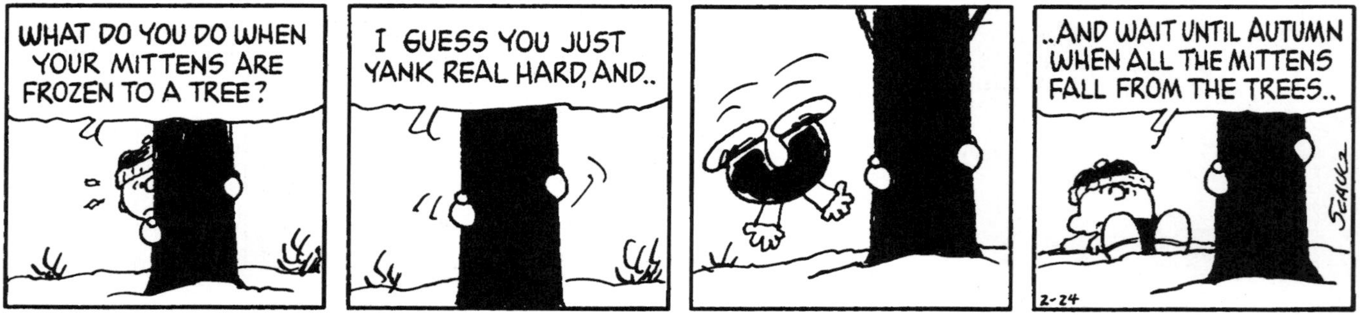
WHAT DO YOU DO WHEN YOUR MITTENS ARE FROZEN TO A TREE?
I GUESS YOU JUST YANK REAL HARD, AND..
..AND WAIT UNTIL AUTUMN WHEN ALL THE MITTENS FALL FROM THE TREES..
SCHULZ
2-24

Panel 1: SHE'S COMING OUT OF THE HOUSE! THAT LITTLE RED-HAIRED GIRL IS COMING OUT OF THE HOUSE!

Panel 2: SHE'S GOING TO SEE MY MITTENS FROZEN ON THE TREE!

Panel 3: SHE DID! SHE'S LOOKING AT THEM! SHE'S TAKING THEM OFF THE TREE! SHE'S HOLDING MY MITTENS IN HER HAND!

Panel 4: MY MITTENS ARE DOING BETTER THAN I AM!

2-25

Panel 5: SHE'S HOLDING MY MITTENS IN HER HAND..

Panel 6: NOW, SHE'S DROPPING THEM IN THE SNOW, AND WALKING AWAY...

2-26

Panel 8: SORRY, GUYS.. I KNOW JUST HOW YOU FEEL..

Panel 9: GUESS WHAT, BIG BROTHER..

Panel 10: IF YOU'LL HELP ME WITH MY HOMEWORK, I'LL TELL EVERYONE IN THE WORLD WHAT A WONDERFUL PERSON YOU ARE!

2-27

Panel 11: IF YOU DON'T HELP ME, YOU CAN'T IMAGINE WHAT I'LL TELL THEM..

Panel 12: HOW COULD YOU IMAGINE WHAT I WAS GOING TO TELL THEM?

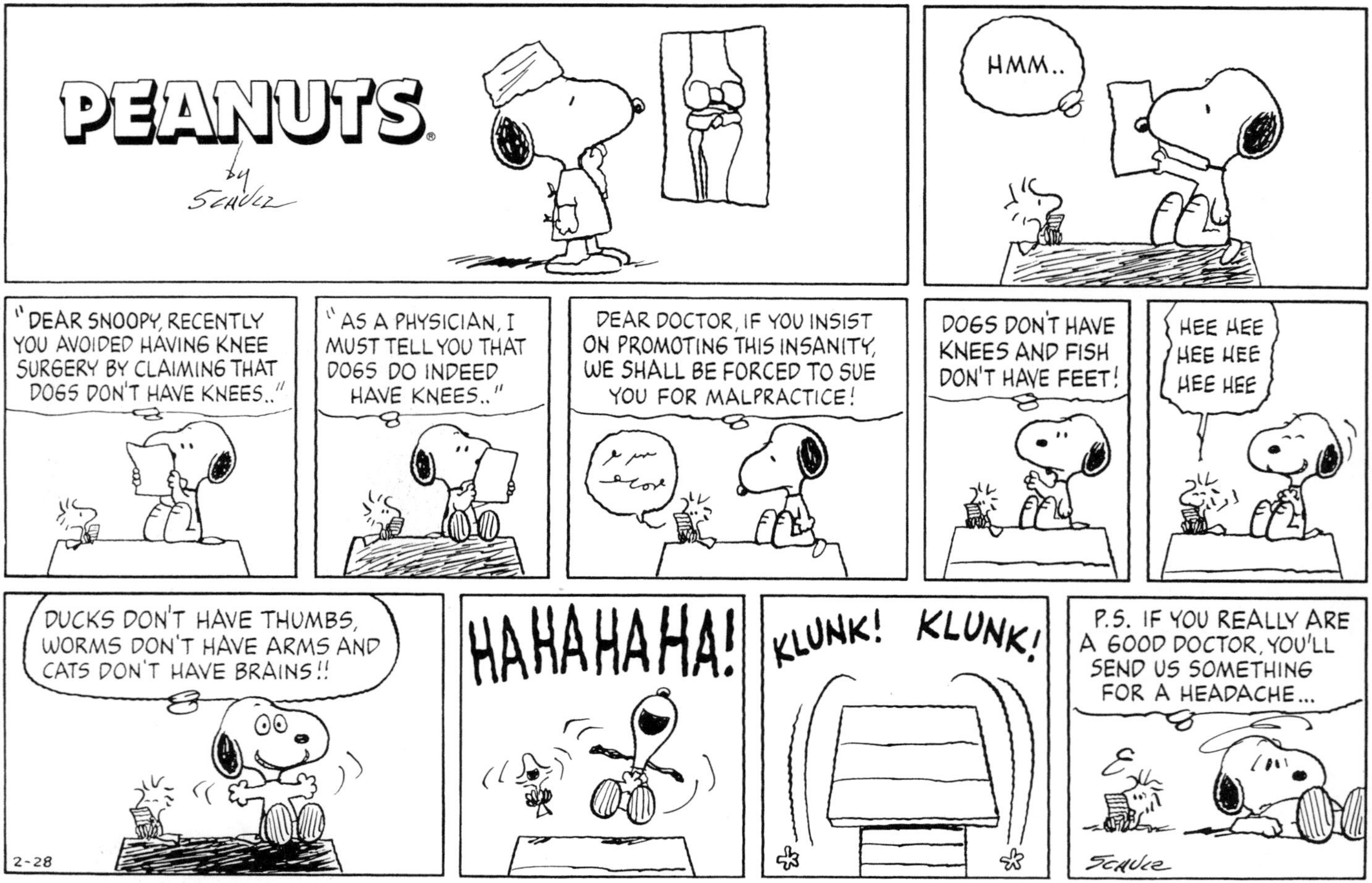
PEANUTS®
by SCHULZ
HMM..
"DEAR SNOOPY, RECENTLY YOU AVOIDED HAVING KNEE SURGERY BY CLAIMING THAT DOGS DON'T HAVE KNEES.."
"AS A PHYSICIAN, I MUST TELL YOU THAT DOGS DO INDEED HAVE KNEES.."
DEAR DOCTOR, IF YOU INSIST ON PROMOTING THIS INSANITY, WE SHALL BE FORCED TO SUE YOU FOR MALPRACTICE!
DOGS DON'T HAVE KNEES AND FISH DON'T HAVE FEET!
HEE HEE HEE HEE HEE HEE
DUCKS DON'T HAVE THUMBS, WORMS DON'T HAVE ARMS AND CATS DON'T HAVE BRAINS!!
2-28
HAHAHAHA!
KLUNK! KLUNK!
P.S. IF YOU REALLY ARE A GOOD DOCTOR, YOU'LL SEND US SOMETHING FOR A HEADACHE...
SCHULZ

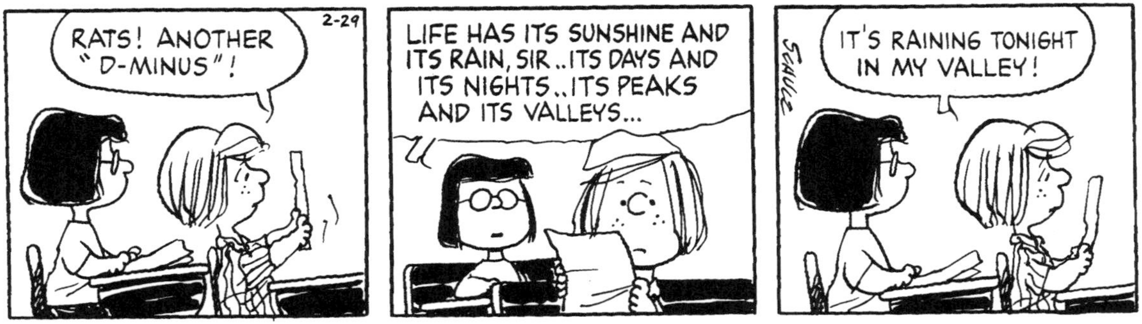
2-29
RATS! ANOTHER "D-MINUS"!
LIFE HAS ITS SUNSHINE AND ITS RAIN, SIR..ITS DAYS AND ITS NIGHTS..ITS PEAKS AND ITS VALLEYS...
IT'S RAINING TONIGHT IN MY VALLEY!
SCHULZ

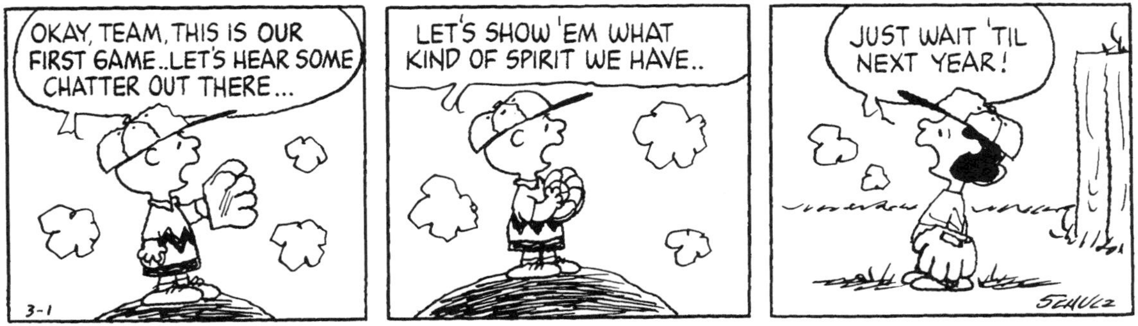
OKAY, TEAM, THIS IS OUR FIRST GAME..LET'S HEAR SOME CHATTER OUT THERE...
3-1
LET'S SHOW 'EM WHAT KIND OF SPIRIT WE HAVE..
JUST WAIT 'TIL NEXT YEAR!
SCHULZ

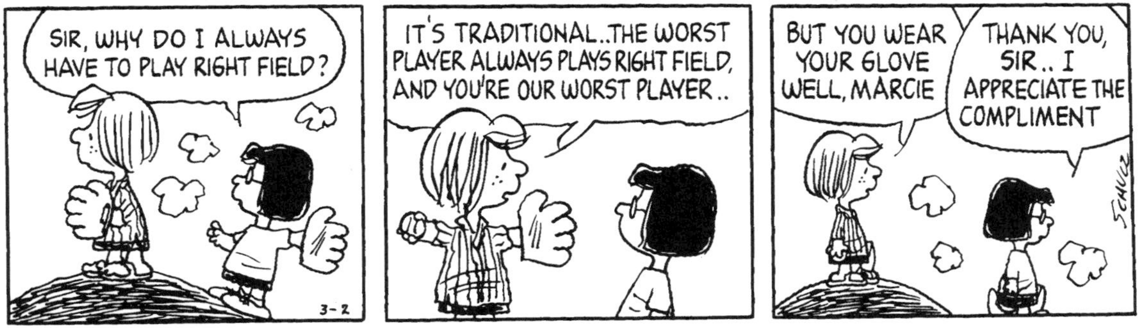
SIR, WHY DO I ALWAYS HAVE TO PLAY RIGHT FIELD?
3-2
IT'S TRADITIONAL..THE WORST PLAYER ALWAYS PLAYS RIGHT FIELD, AND YOU'RE OUR WORST PLAYER..
BUT YOU WEAR YOUR GLOVE WELL, MARCIE
THANK YOU, SIR.. I APPRECIATE THE COMPLIMENT
SCHULZ

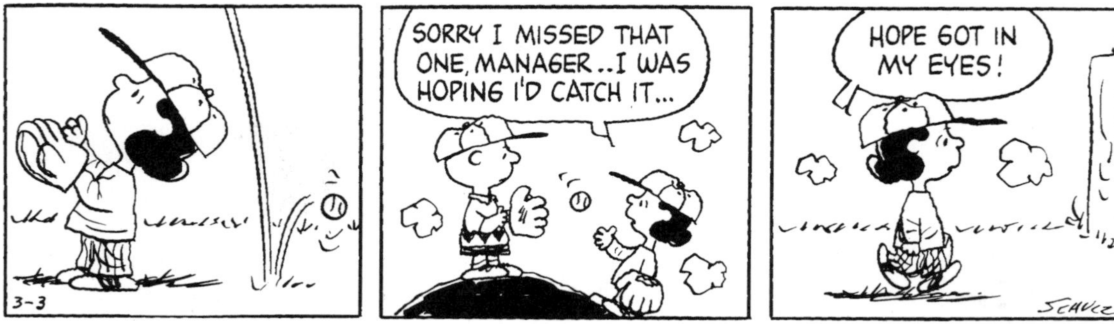
3-3
SORRY I MISSED THAT ONE, MANAGER..I WAS HOPING I'D CATCH IT...
HOPE GOT IN MY EYES!

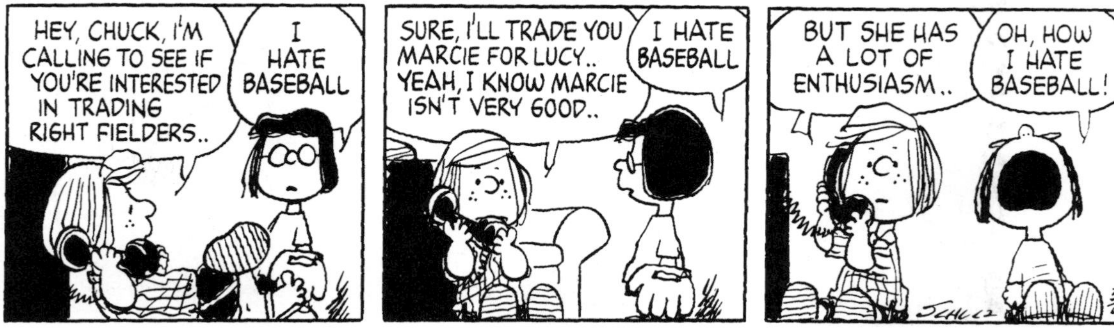
HEY, CHUCK, I'M CALLING TO SEE IF YOU'RE INTERESTED IN TRADING RIGHT FIELDERS..
I HATE BASEBALL
SURE, I'LL TRADE YOU MARCIE FOR LUCY.. YEAH, I KNOW MARCIE ISN'T VERY GOOD..
I HATE BASEBALL
BUT SHE HAS A LOT OF ENTHUSIASM..
OH, HOW I HATE BASEBALL!
3/4

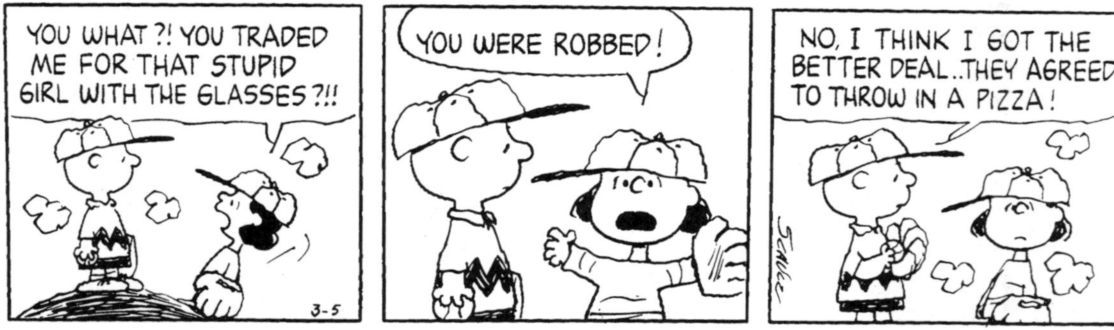
YOU WHAT?! YOU TRADED ME FOR THAT STUPID GIRL WITH THE GLASSES?!!
3-5
YOU WERE ROBBED!
NO, I THINK I GOT THE BETTER DEAL..THEY AGREED TO THROW IN A PIZZA!

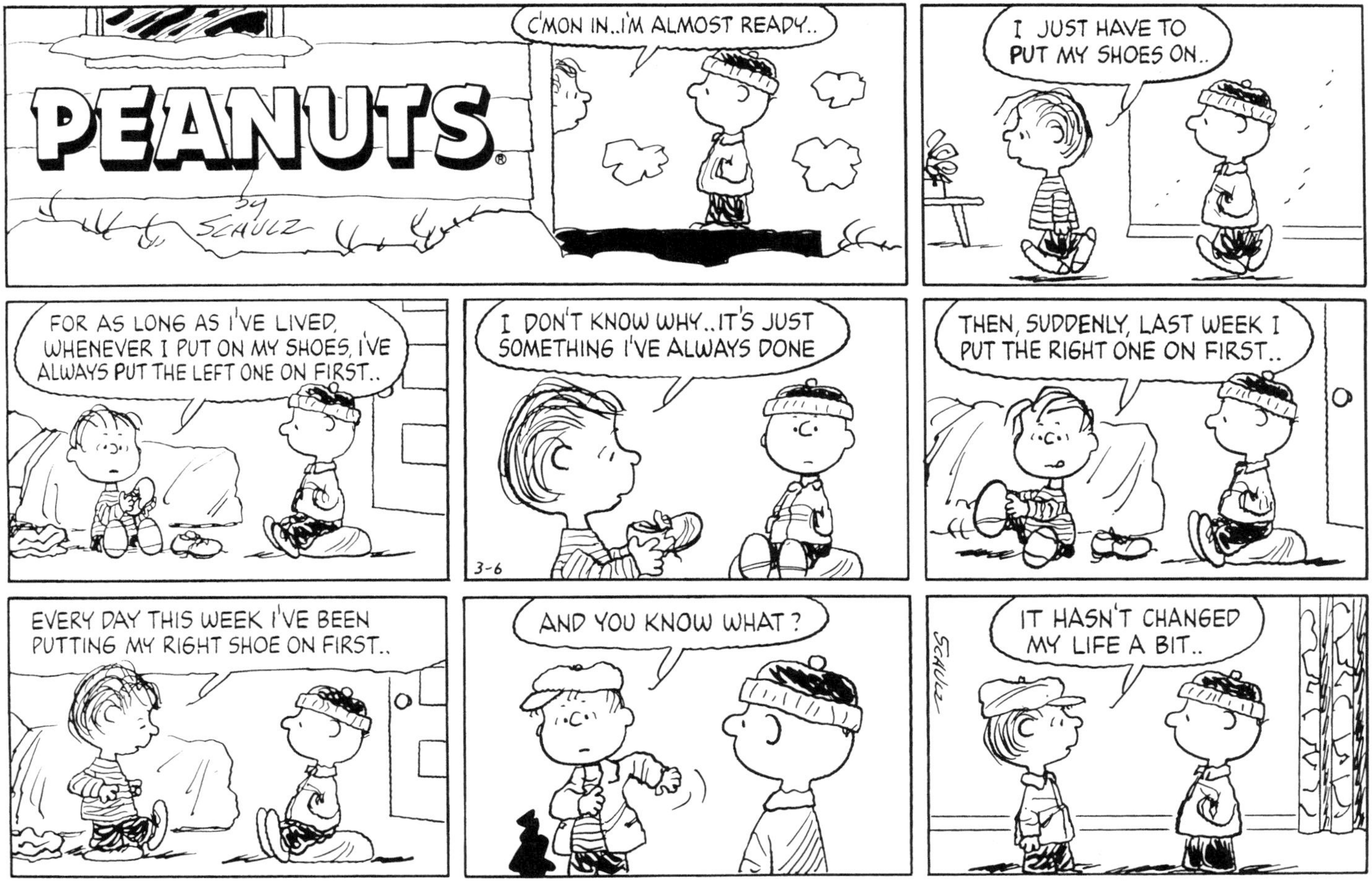
PEANUTS
by SCHULZ
C'MON IN..I'M ALMOST READY..
I JUST HAVE TO PUT MY SHOES ON..
FOR AS LONG AS I'VE LIVED, WHENEVER I PUT ON MY SHOES, I'VE ALWAYS PUT THE LEFT ONE ON FIRST..
I DON'T KNOW WHY..IT'S JUST SOMETHING I'VE ALWAYS DONE
3-6
THEN, SUDDENLY, LAST WEEK I PUT THE RIGHT ONE ON FIRST..
EVERY DAY THIS WEEK I'VE BEEN PUTTING MY RIGHT SHOE ON FIRST..
AND YOU KNOW WHAT ?
SCHULZ
IT HASN'T CHANGED MY LIFE A BIT..

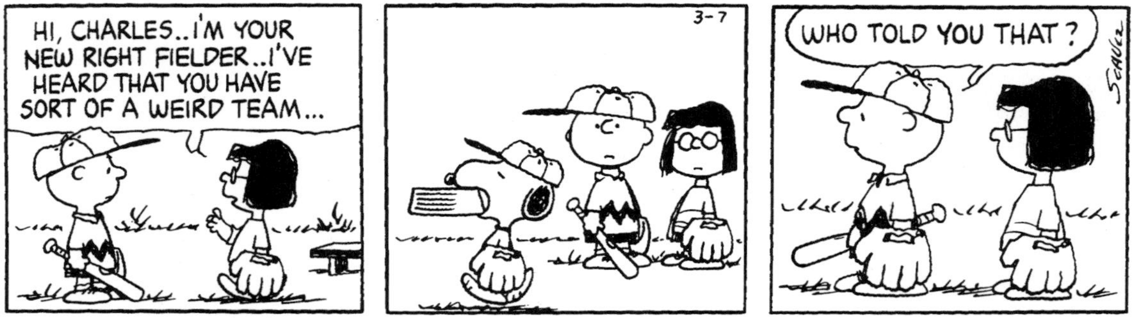
HI, CHARLES..I'M YOUR NEW RIGHT FIELDER..I'VE HEARD THAT YOU HAVE SORT OF A WEIRD TEAM...
WHO TOLD YOU THAT?

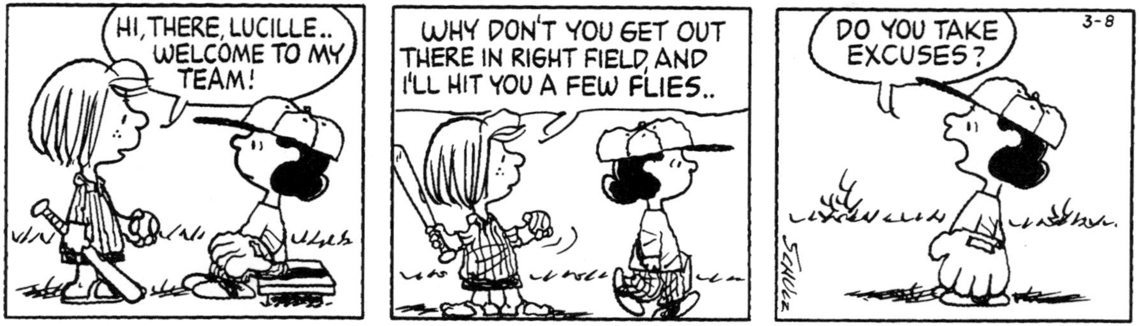
HI, THERE, LUCILLE.. WELCOME TO MY TEAM!
WHY DON'T YOU GET OUT THERE IN RIGHT FIELD, AND I'LL HIT YOU A FEW FLIES..
DO YOU TAKE EXCUSES?

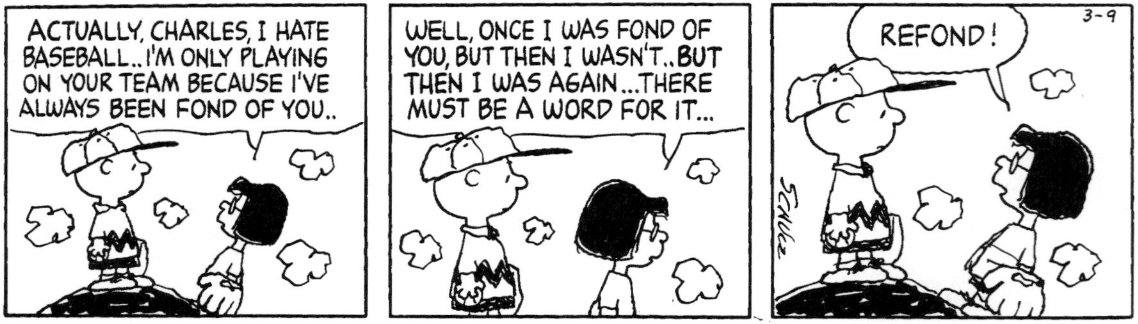
ACTUALLY, CHARLES, I HATE BASEBALL..I'M ONLY PLAYING ON YOUR TEAM BECAUSE I'VE ALWAYS BEEN FOND OF YOU..
WELL, ONCE I WAS FOND OF YOU, BUT THEN I WASN'T..BUT THEN I WAS AGAIN...THERE MUST BE A WORD FOR IT...
REFOND!

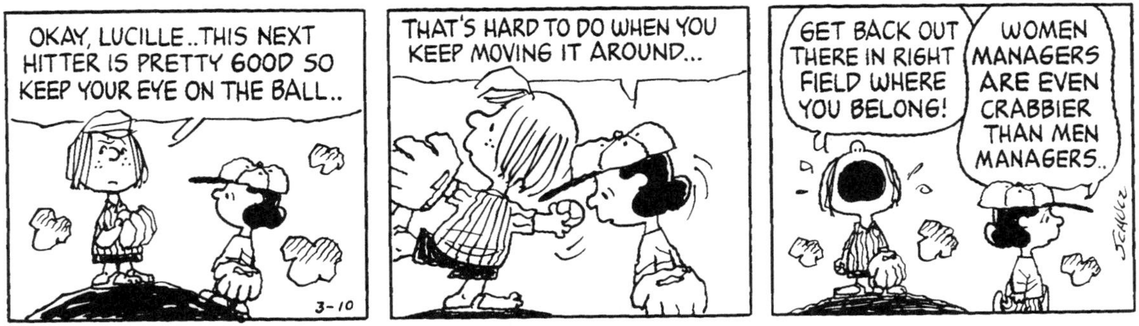
OKAY, LUCILLE..THIS NEXT HITTER IS PRETTY GOOD SO KEEP YOUR EYE ON THE BALL..
3-10
THAT'S HARD TO DO WHEN YOU KEEP MOVING IT AROUND...
GET BACK OUT THERE IN RIGHT FIELD WHERE YOU BELONG!
WOMEN MANAGERS ARE EVEN CRABBIER THAN MEN MANAGERS..

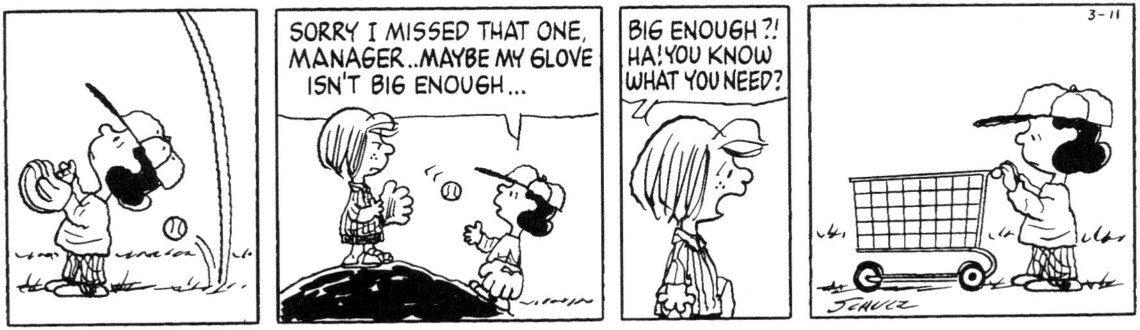
SORRY I MISSED THAT ONE, MANAGER..MAYBE MY GLOVE ISN'T BIG ENOUGH...
BIG ENOUGH?! HA! YOU KNOW WHAT YOU NEED?
3-11

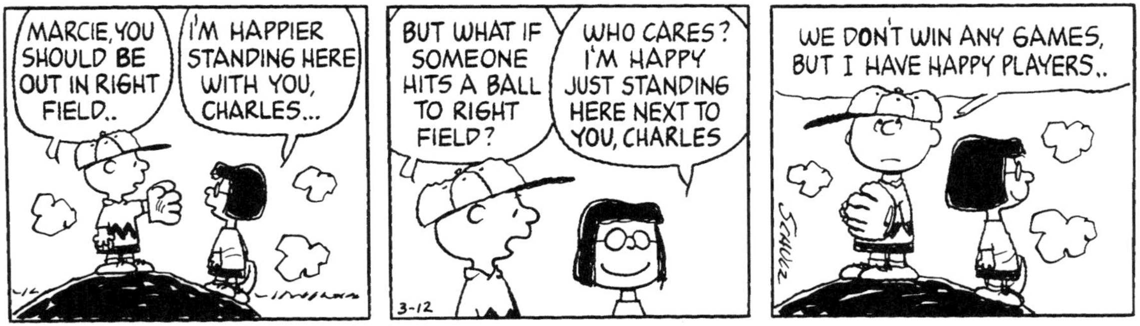
MARCIE, YOU SHOULD BE OUT IN RIGHT FIELD..
I'M HAPPIER STANDING HERE WITH YOU, CHARLES...
BUT WHAT IF SOMEONE HITS A BALL TO RIGHT FIELD?
WHO CARES? I'M HAPPY JUST STANDING HERE NEXT TO YOU, CHARLES
3-12
WE DON'T WIN ANY GAMES, BUT I HAVE HAPPY PLAYERS..

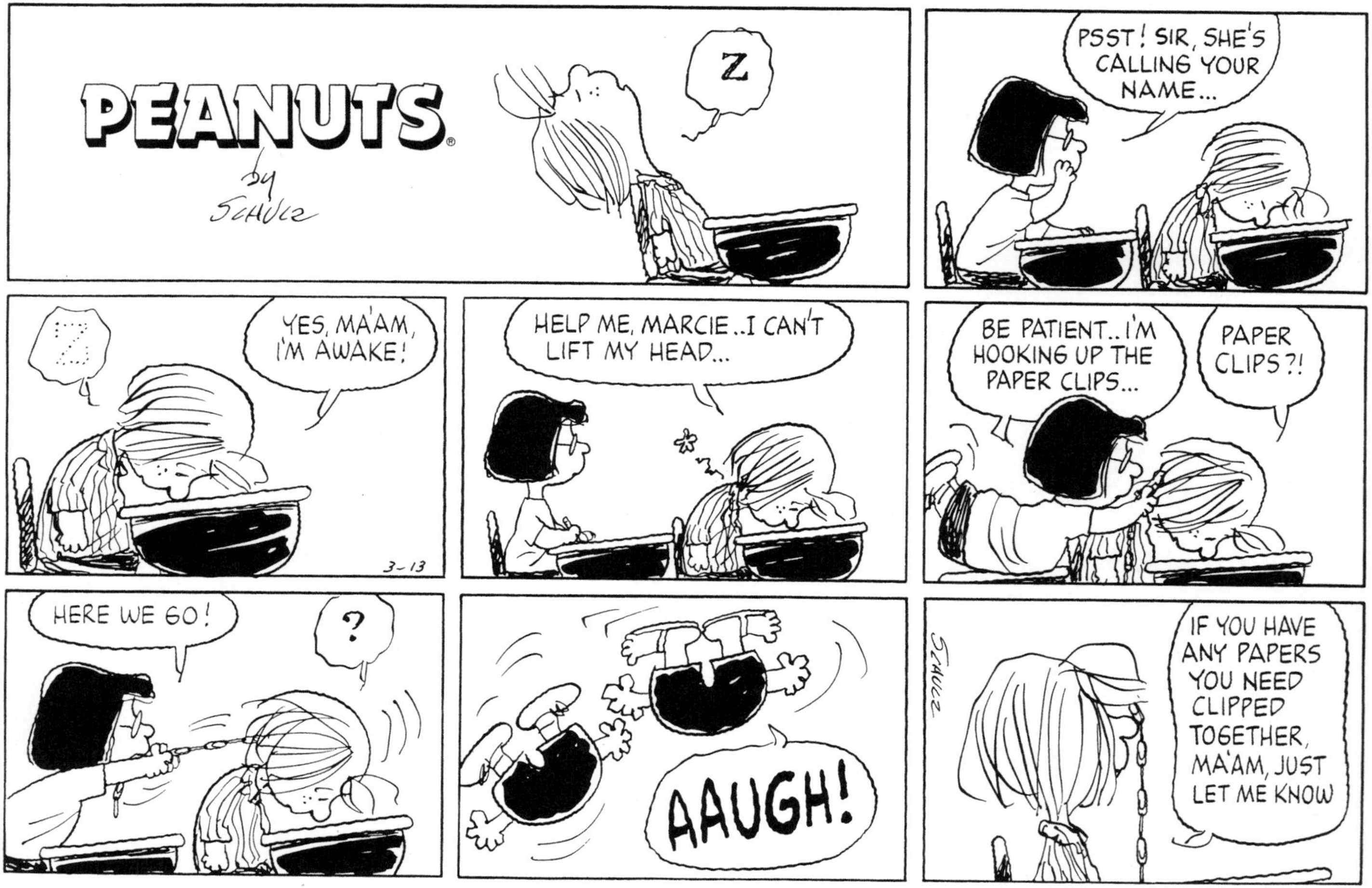
PEANUTS
by Schulz
Z
PSST! SIR, SHE'S CALLING YOUR NAME...
Z
YES, MA'AM, I'M AWAKE!
3-13
HELP ME, MARCIE..I CAN'T LIFT MY HEAD...
BE PATIENT..I'M HOOKING UP THE PAPER CLIPS...
PAPER CLIPS?!
HERE WE GO!
?
AAUGH!
Schulz
IF YOU HAVE ANY PAPERS YOU NEED CLIPPED TOGETHER, MA'AM, JUST LET ME KNOW

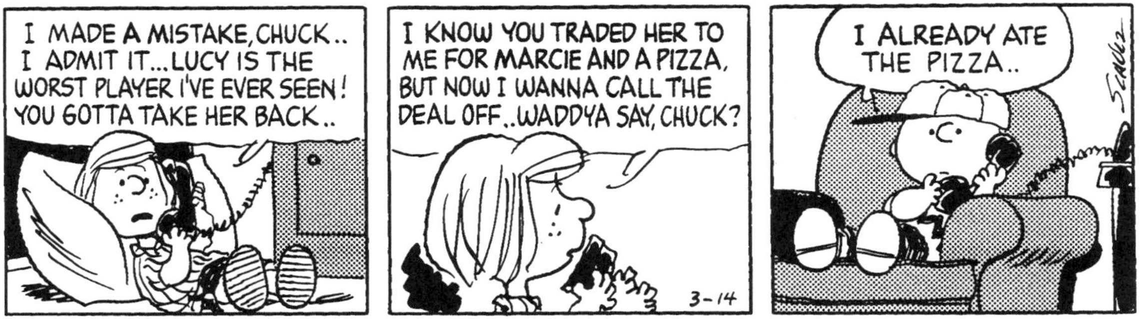
I MADE A MISTAKE, CHUCK.. I ADMIT IT...LUCY IS THE WORST PLAYER I'VE EVER SEEN! YOU GOTTA TAKE HER BACK..
I KNOW YOU TRADED HER TO ME FOR MARCIE AND A PIZZA, BUT NOW I WANNA CALL THE DEAL OFF..WADDYA SAY, CHUCK?
3-14
I ALREADY ATE THE PIZZA..

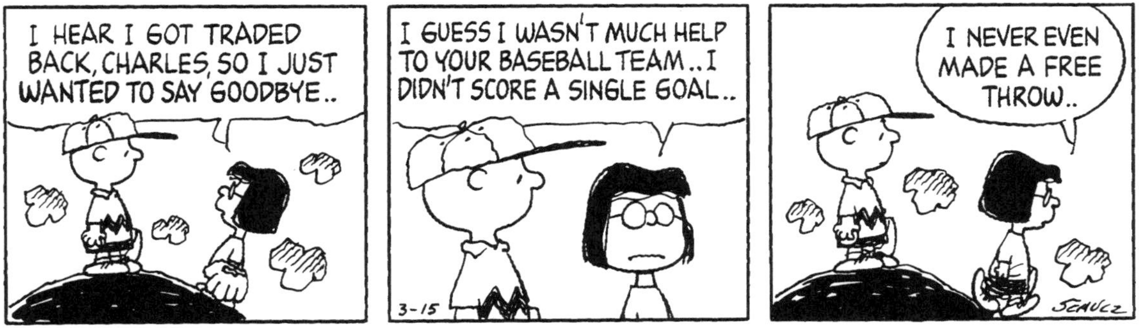
I HEAR I GOT TRADED BACK, CHARLES, SO I JUST WANTED TO SAY GOODBYE..
I GUESS I WASN'T MUCH HELP TO YOUR BASEBALL TEAM..I DIDN'T SCORE A SINGLE GOAL..
3-15
I NEVER EVEN MADE A FREE THROW..

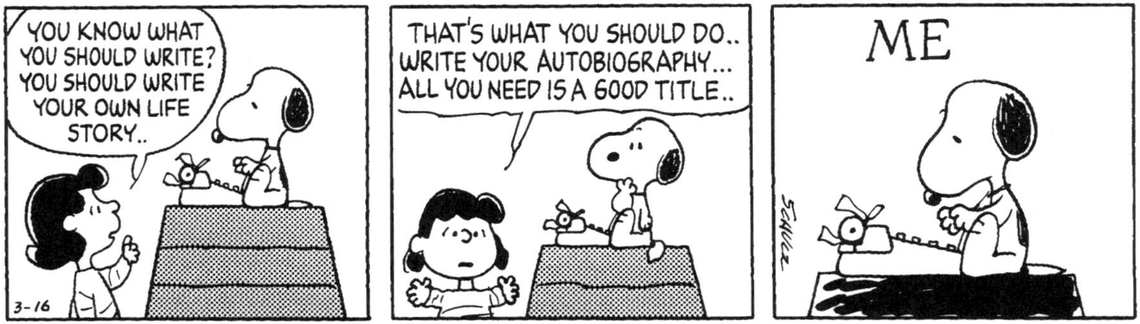
YOU KNOW WHAT YOU SHOULD WRITE? YOU SHOULD WRITE YOUR OWN LIFE STORY..
3-16
THAT'S WHAT YOU SHOULD DO.. WRITE YOUR AUTOBIOGRAPHY... ALL YOU NEED IS A GOOD TITLE..
ME

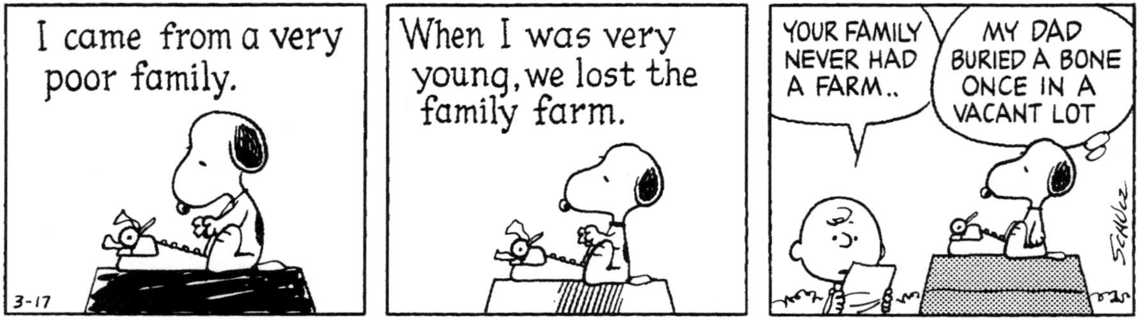
I came from a very poor family.
3-17
When I was very young, we lost the family farm.
YOUR FAMILY NEVER HAD A FARM..
MY DAD BURIED A BONE ONCE IN A VACANT LOT
SCHULZ

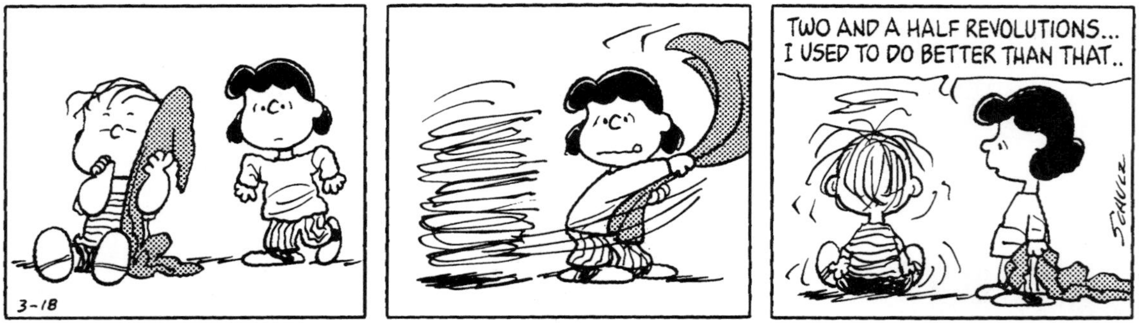
3-18
TWO AND A HALF REVOLUTIONS... I USED TO DO BETTER THAN THAT..
SCHULZ

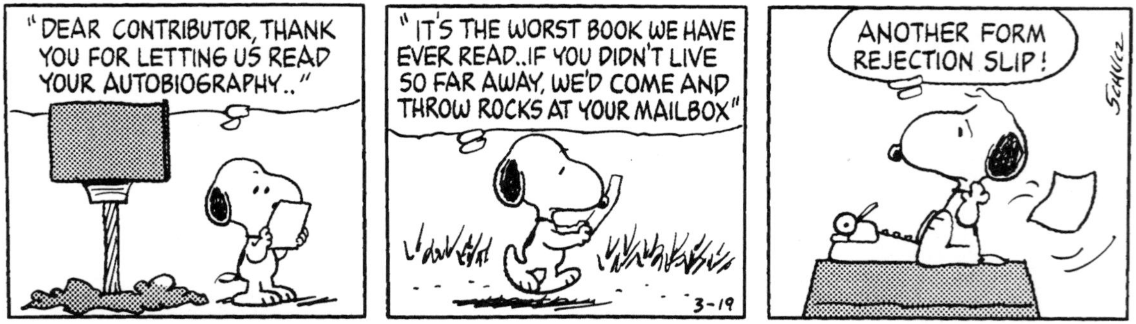
"DEAR CONTRIBUTOR, THANK YOU FOR LETTING US READ YOUR AUTOBIOGRAPHY.."
"IT'S THE WORST BOOK WE HAVE EVER READ..IF YOU DIDN'T LIVE SO FAR AWAY, WE'D COME AND THROW ROCKS AT YOUR MAILBOX"
3-19
ANOTHER FORM REJECTION SLIP!
SCHULZ

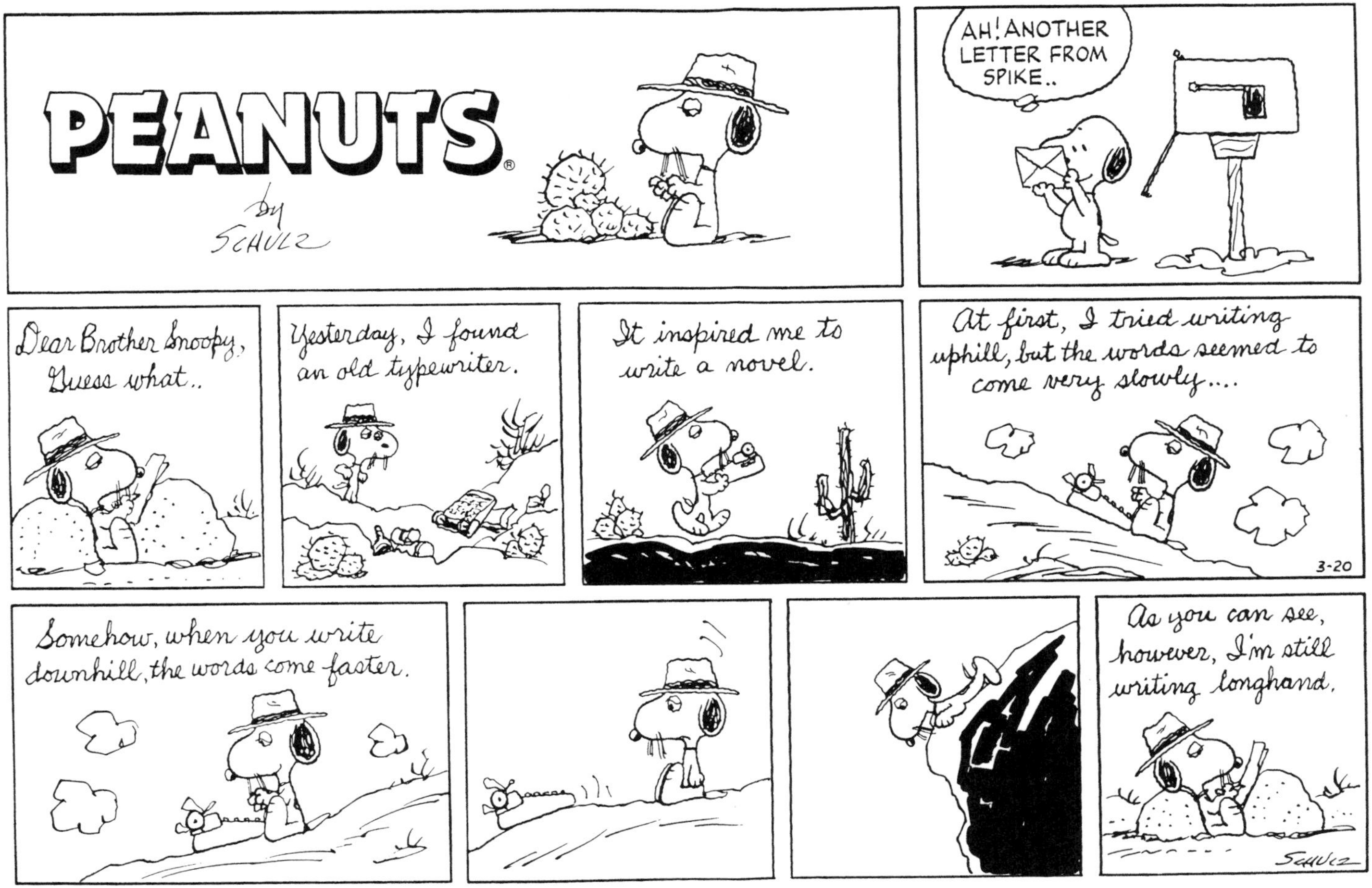
PEANUTS
by SCHULZ
AH! ANOTHER LETTER FROM SPIKE..
Dear Brother Snoopy, Guess what..
Yesterday, I found an old typewriter.
It inspired me to write a novel.
At first, I tried writing uphill, but the words seemed to come very slowly....
3-20
Somehow, when you write downhill, the words come faster.
As you can see, however, I'm still writing longhand.
SCHULZ

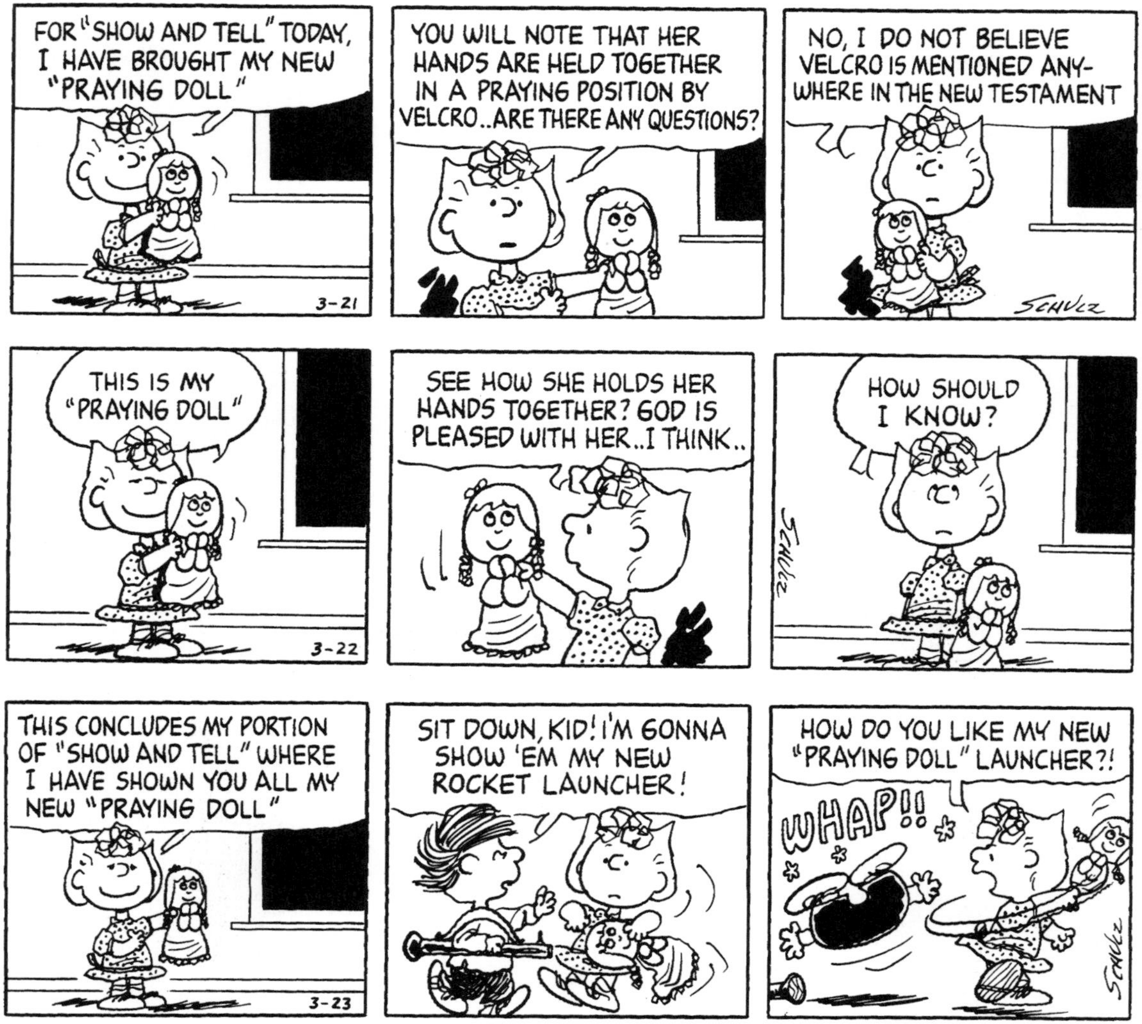
FOR "SHOW AND TELL" TODAY, I HAVE BROUGHT MY NEW "PRAYING DOLL"
3-21
YOU WILL NOTE THAT HER HANDS ARE HELD TOGETHER IN A PRAYING POSITION BY VELCRO..ARE THERE ANY QUESTIONS?
NO, I DO NOT BELIEVE VELCRO IS MENTIONED ANYWHERE IN THE NEW TESTAMENT
SCHULZ
THIS IS MY "PRAYING DOLL"
3-22
SEE HOW SHE HOLDS HER HANDS TOGETHER? GOD IS PLEASED WITH HER..I THINK..
SCHULZ
HOW SHOULD I KNOW?
THIS CONCLUDES MY PORTION OF "SHOW AND TELL" WHERE I HAVE SHOWN YOU ALL MY NEW "PRAYING DOLL"
3-23
SIT DOWN, KID! I'M GONNA SHOW 'EM MY NEW ROCKET LAUNCHER!
HOW DO YOU LIKE MY NEW "PRAYING DOLL" LAUNCHER?!
WHAP!!
SCHULZ

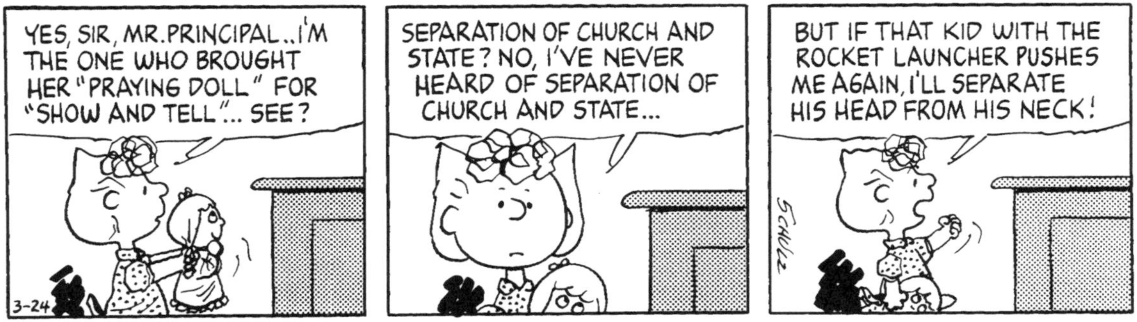
YES, SIR, MR. PRINCIPAL.. I'M THE ONE WHO BROUGHT HER "PRAYING DOLL" FOR "SHOW AND TELL"... SEE?
SEPARATION OF CHURCH AND STATE? NO, I'VE NEVER HEARD OF SEPARATION OF CHURCH AND STATE...
BUT IF THAT KID WITH THE ROCKET LAUNCHER PUSHES ME AGAIN, I'LL SEPARATE HIS HEAD FROM HIS NECK!
3-24

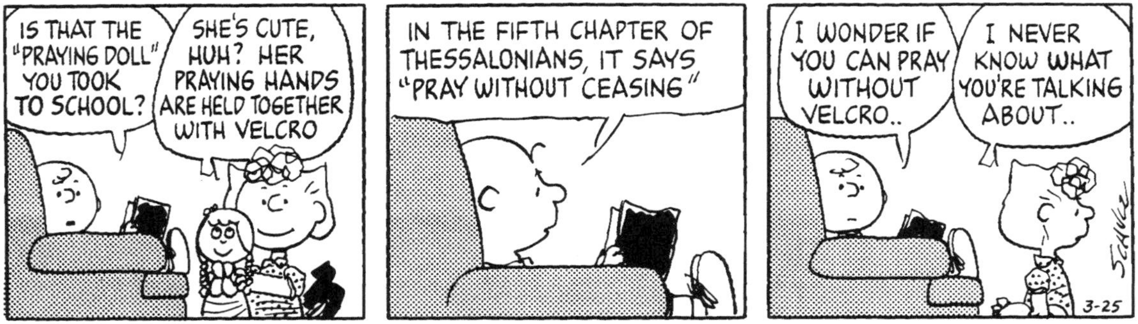
IS THAT THE "PRAYING DOLL" YOU TOOK TO SCHOOL?
SHE'S CUTE, HUH? HER PRAYING HANDS ARE HELD TOGETHER WITH VELCRO
IN THE FIFTH CHAPTER OF THESSALONIANS, IT SAYS "PRAY WITHOUT CEASING"
I WONDER IF YOU CAN PRAY WITHOUT VELCRO..
I NEVER KNOW WHAT YOU'RE TALKING ABOUT..
3-25

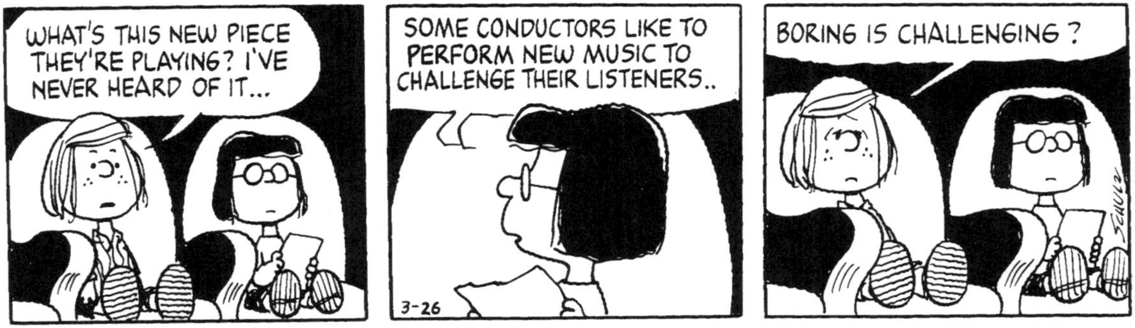
WHAT'S THIS NEW PIECE THEY'RE PLAYING? I'VE NEVER HEARD OF IT...
SOME CONDUCTORS LIKE TO PERFORM NEW MUSIC TO CHALLENGE THEIR LISTENERS..
BORING IS CHALLENGING?
3-26

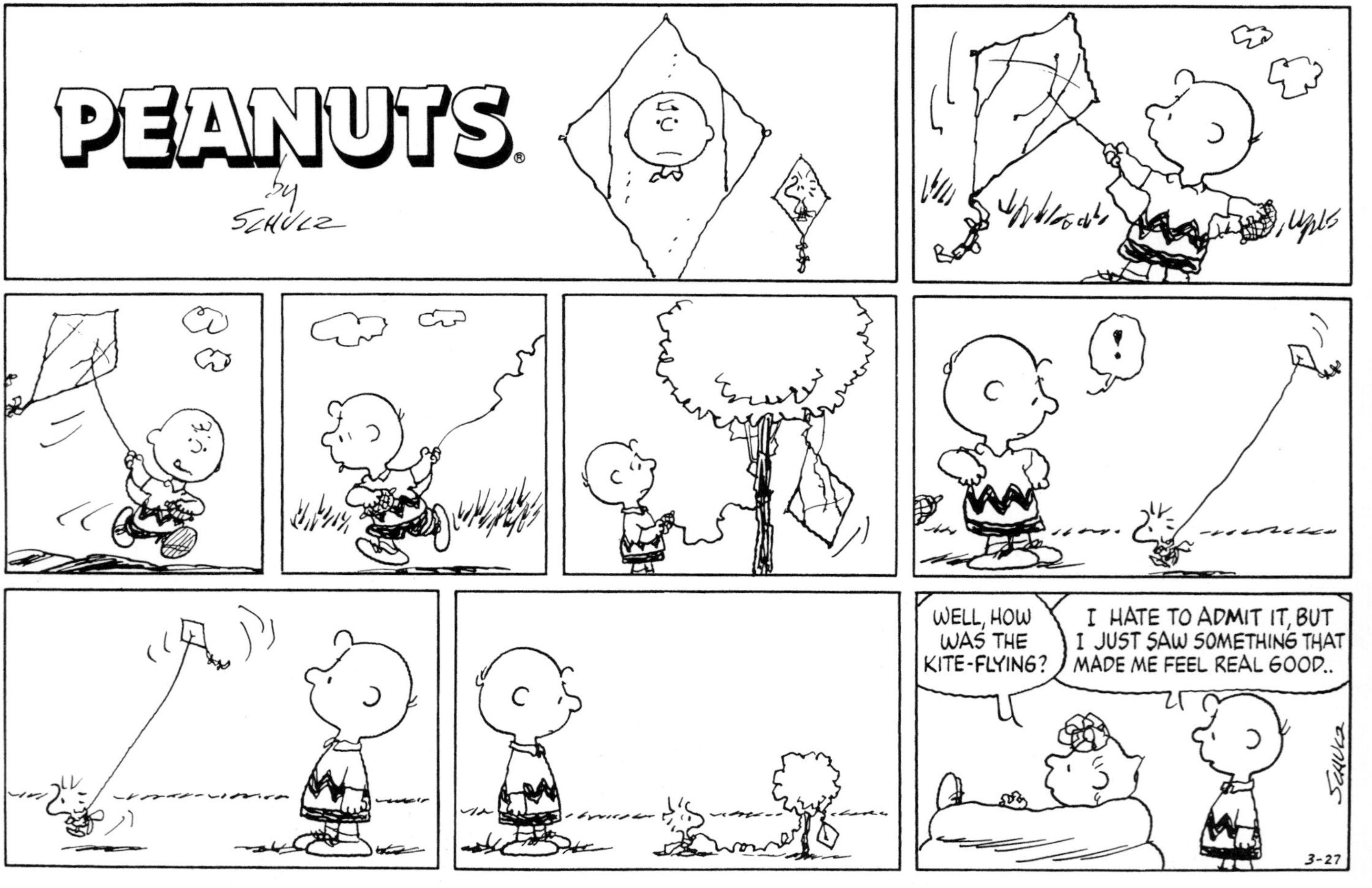
PEANUTS
by SCHULZ
!
WELL, HOW WAS THE KITE-FLYING?
I HATE TO ADMIT IT, BUT I JUST SAW SOMETHING THAT MADE ME FEEL REAL GOOD..
SCHULZ
3-27

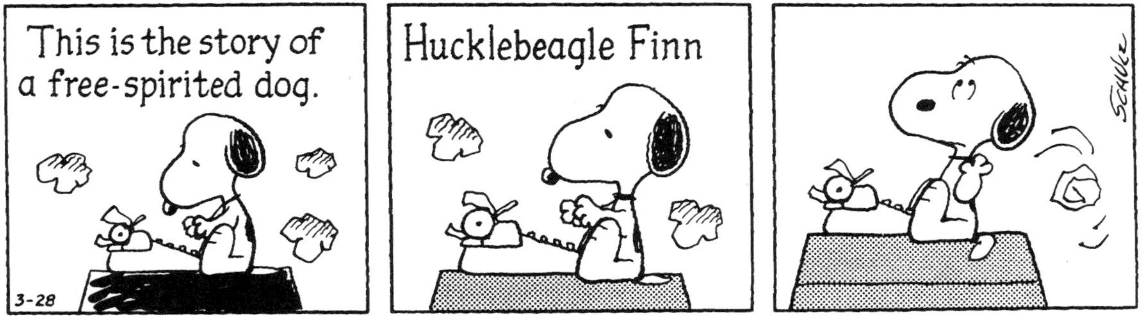
This is the story of a free-spirited dog.
Hucklebeagle Finn
3-28

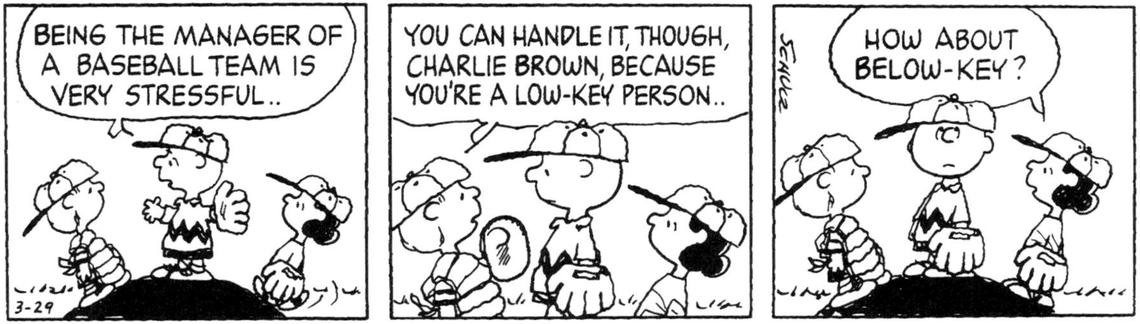
BEING THE MANAGER OF A BASEBALL TEAM IS VERY STRESSFUL..
YOU CAN HANDLE IT, THOUGH, CHARLIE BROWN, BECAUSE YOU'RE A LOW-KEY PERSON..
HOW ABOUT BELOW-KEY?
3-29

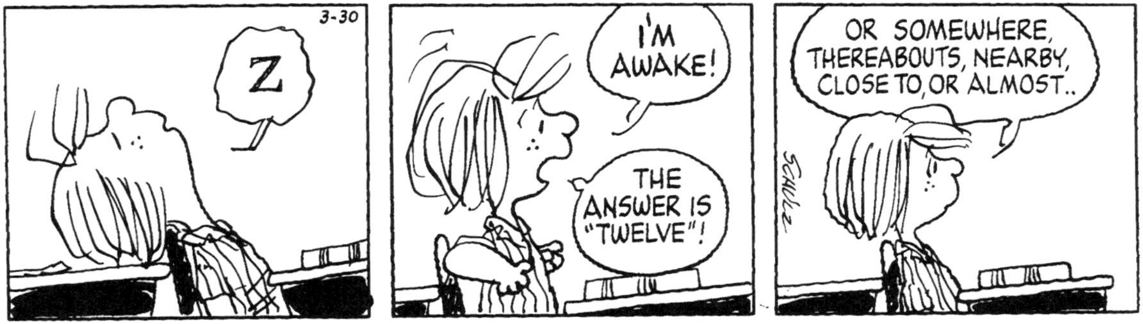
3-30
Z
I'M AWAKE!
THE ANSWER IS "TWELVE"!
OR SOMEWHERE, THEREABOUTS, NEARBY, CLOSE TO, OR ALMOST..

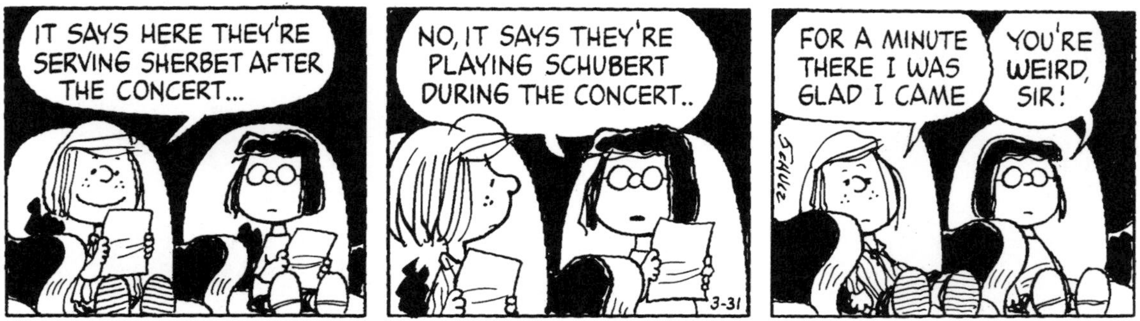
IT SAYS HERE THEY'RE SERVING SHERBET AFTER THE CONCERT...
NO, IT SAYS THEY'RE PLAYING SCHUBERT DURING THE CONCERT..
3-31
FOR A MINUTE THERE I WAS GLAD I CAME
YOU'RE WEIRD, SIR!

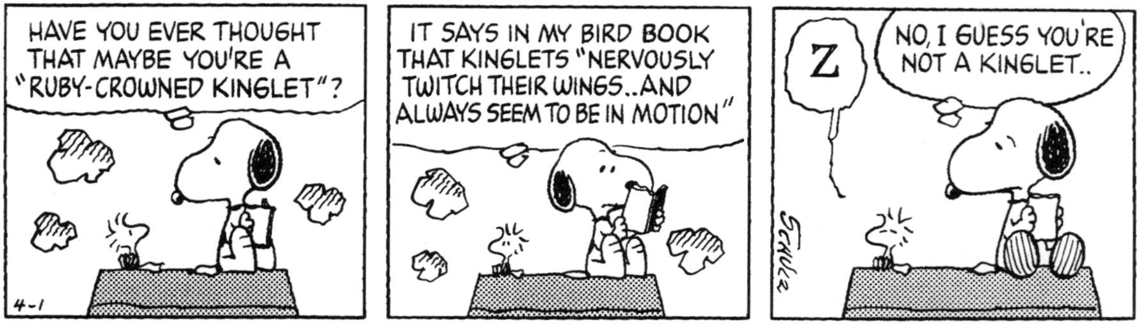
HAVE YOU EVER THOUGHT THAT MAYBE YOU'RE A "RUBY-CROWNED KINGLET"?
4-1
IT SAYS IN MY BIRD BOOK THAT KINGLETS "NERVOUSLY TWITCH THEIR WINGS..AND ALWAYS SEEM TO BE IN MOTION"
Z
NO, I GUESS YOU'RE NOT A KINGLET..

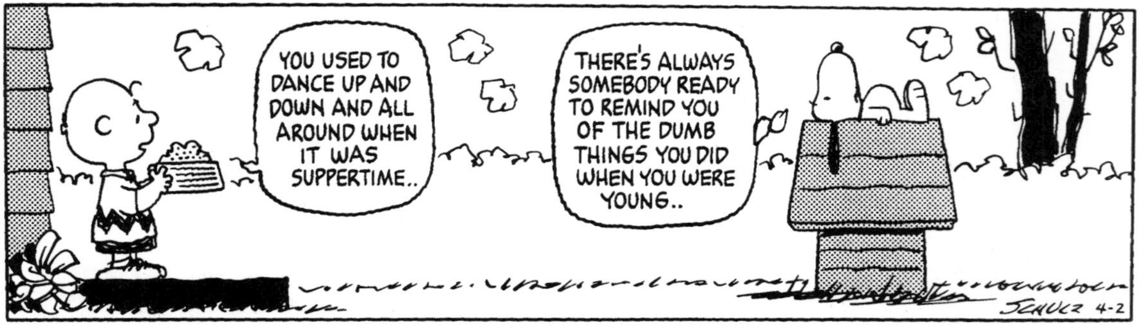
YOU USED TO DANCE UP AND DOWN AND ALL AROUND WHEN IT WAS SUPPERTIME..
THERE'S ALWAYS SOMEBODY READY TO REMIND YOU OF THE DUMB THINGS YOU DID WHEN YOU WERE YOUNG..
SCHULZ 4-2

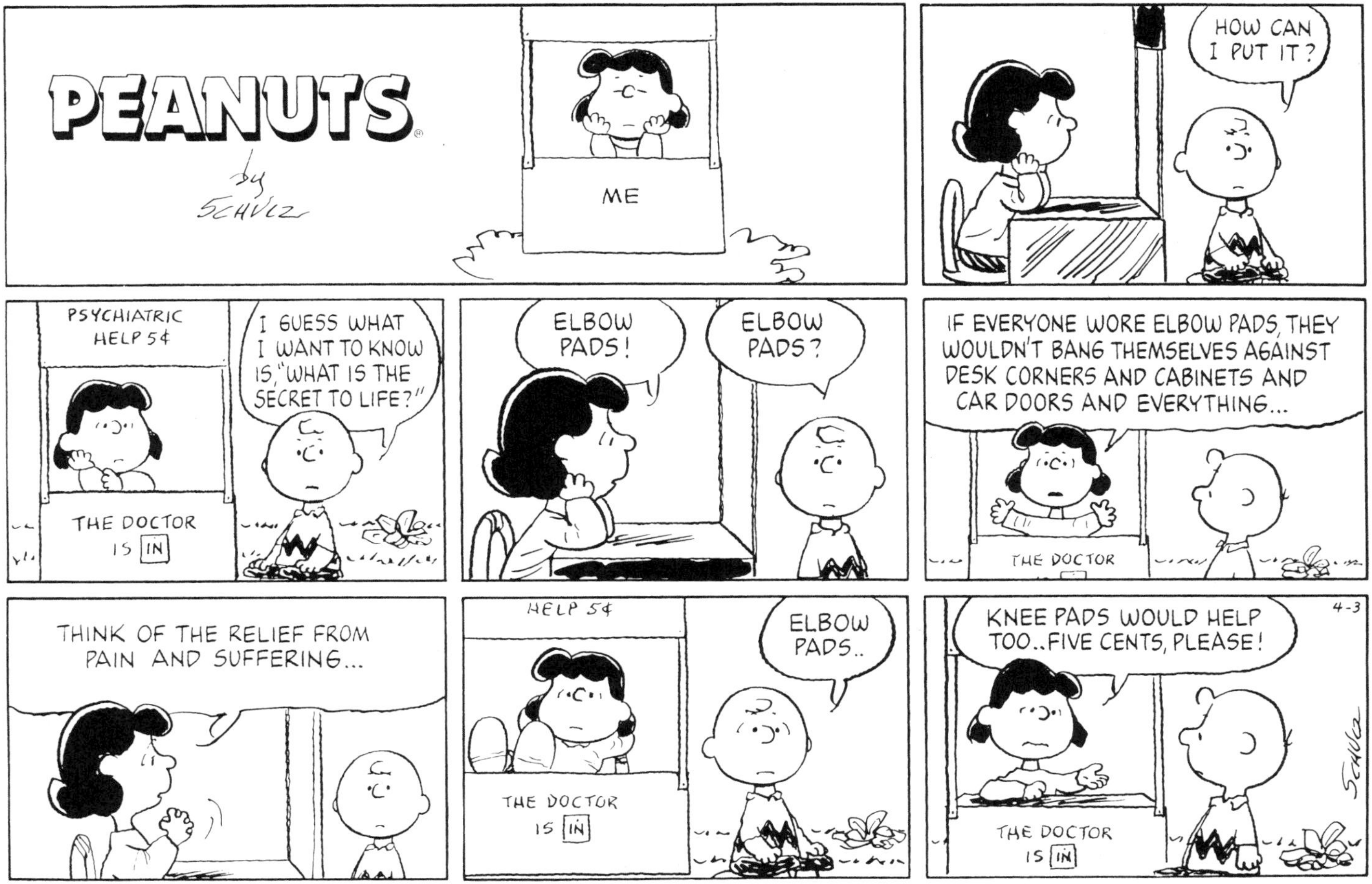
PEANUTS
by SCHULZ
ME
HOW CAN I PUT IT?
PSYCHIATRIC HELP 5¢
I GUESS WHAT I WANT TO KNOW IS, "WHAT IS THE SECRET TO LIFE?"
THE DOCTOR IS IN
ELBOW PADS!
ELBOW PADS?
IF EVERYONE WORE ELBOW PADS, THEY WOULDN'T BANG THEMSELVES AGAINST DESK CORNERS AND CABINETS AND CAR DOORS AND EVERYTHING...
THE DOCTOR
THINK OF THE RELIEF FROM PAIN AND SUFFERING...
HELP 5¢
ELBOW PADS..
THE DOCTOR IS IN
4-3
KNEE PADS WOULD HELP TOO..FIVE CENTS, PLEASE!
THE DOCTOR IS IN
SCHULZ

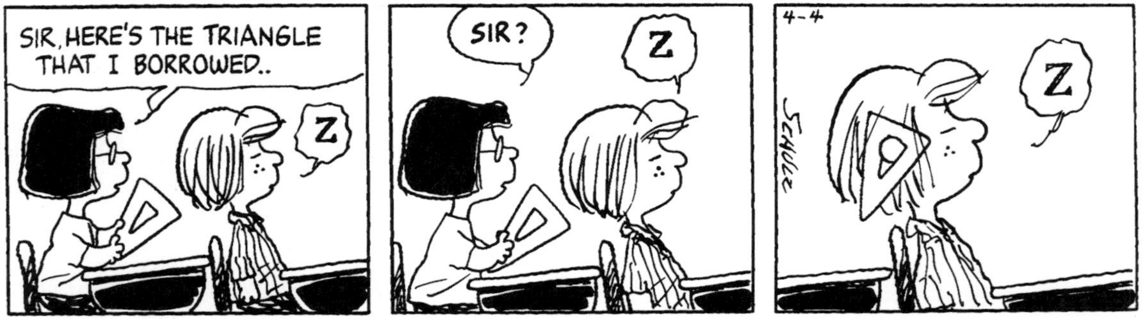
SIR, HERE'S THE TRIANGLE THAT I BORROWED..
Z
SIR?
Z
4-4
Z
SCHULZ

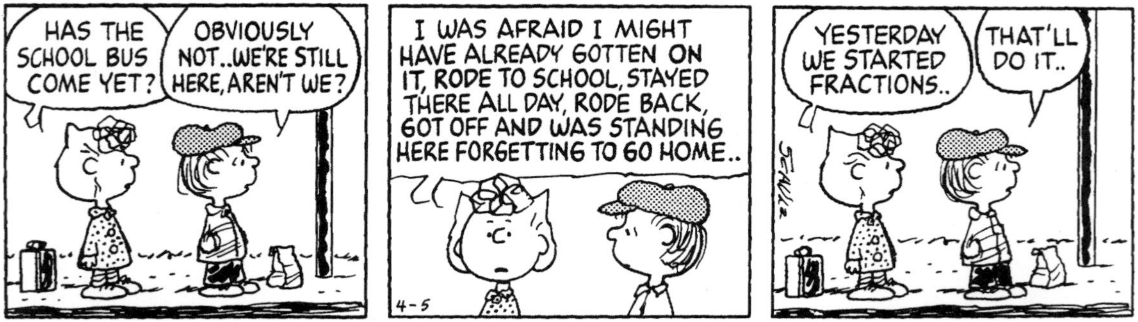
HAS THE SCHOOL BUS COME YET?
OBVIOUSLY NOT..WE'RE STILL HERE, AREN'T WE?
I WAS AFRAID I MIGHT HAVE ALREADY GOTTEN ON IT, RODE TO SCHOOL, STAYED THERE ALL DAY, RODE BACK, GOT OFF AND WAS STANDING HERE FORGETTING TO GO HOME..
4-5
YESTERDAY WE STARTED FRACTIONS..
THAT'LL DO IT..
SCHULZ

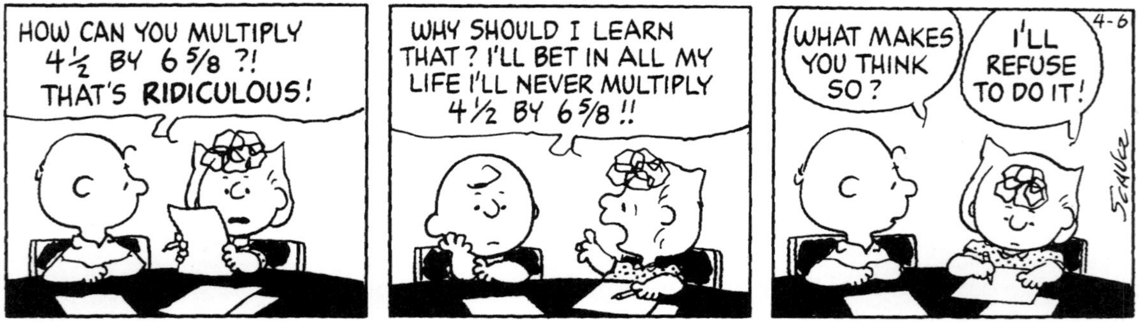
HOW CAN YOU MULTIPLY 4 1/2 BY 6 5/8 ?! THAT'S RIDICULOUS!
WHY SHOULD I LEARN THAT? I'LL BET IN ALL MY LIFE I'LL NEVER MULTIPLY 4 1/2 BY 6 5/8 !!
4-6
WHAT MAKES YOU THINK SO?
I'LL REFUSE TO DO IT!
SCHULZ

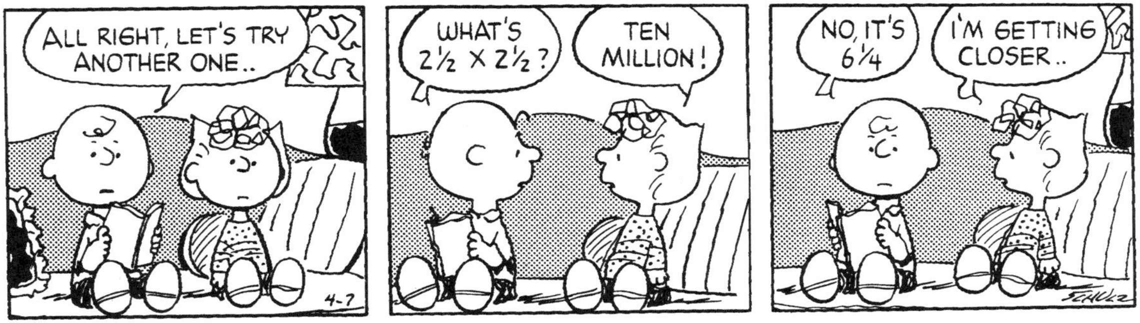
ALL RIGHT, LET'S TRY ANOTHER ONE..
4-7
WHAT'S 2½ X 2½?
TEN MILLION!
NO, IT'S 6¼
I'M GETTING CLOSER..
SCHULZ

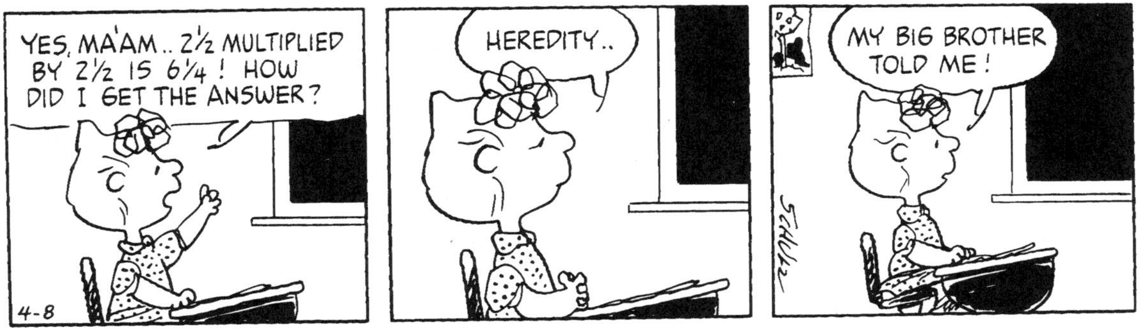
YES, MA'AM.. 2½ MULTIPLIED BY 2½ IS 6¼! HOW DID I GET THE ANSWER?
4-8
HEREDITY..
MY BIG BROTHER TOLD ME!
SCHULZ

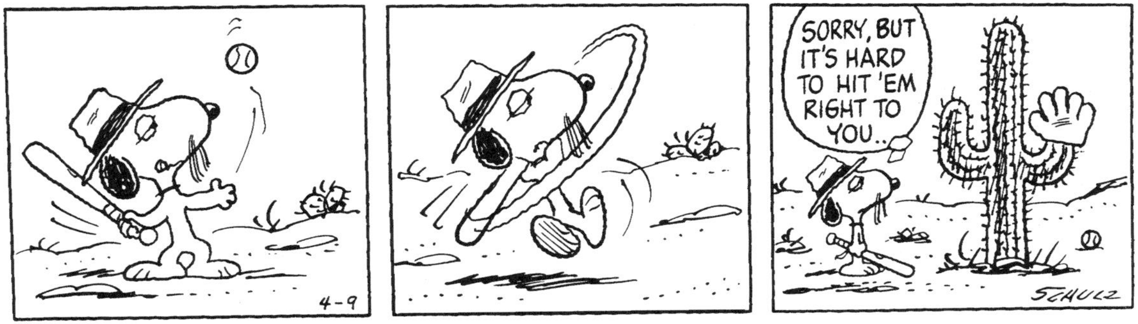
4-9
SORRY, BUT IT'S HARD TO HIT 'EM RIGHT TO YOU..
SCHULZ

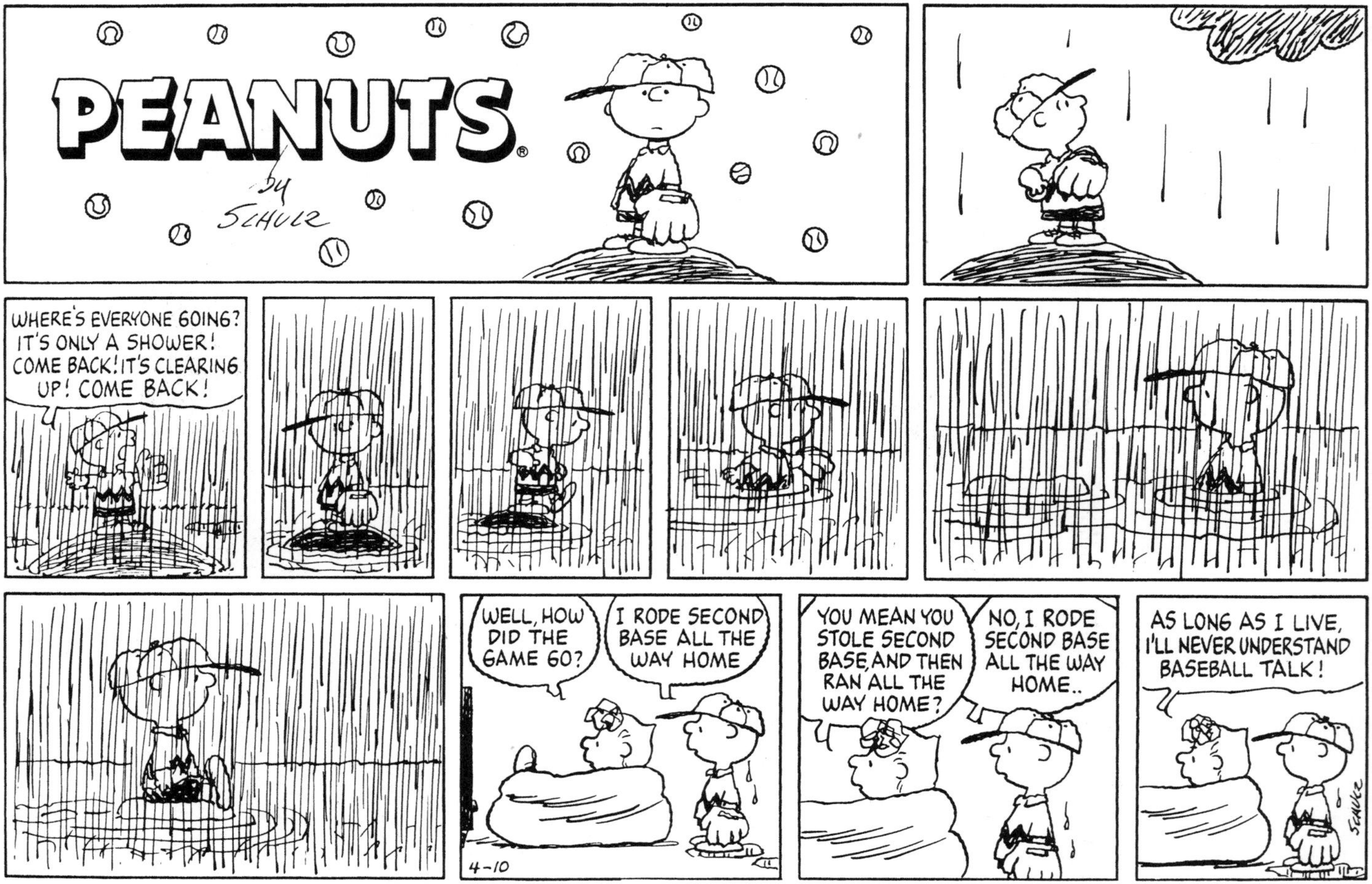
PEANUTS
by SCHULZ
WHERE'S EVERYONE GOING? IT'S ONLY A SHOWER! COME BACK! IT'S CLEARING UP! COME BACK!
WELL, HOW DID THE GAME GO?
I RODE SECOND BASE ALL THE WAY HOME
YOU MEAN YOU STOLE SECOND BASE, AND THEN RAN ALL THE WAY HOME?
NO, I RODE SECOND BASE ALL THE WAY HOME..
AS LONG AS I LIVE, I'LL NEVER UNDERSTAND BASEBALL TALK!
4-10
SCHULZ

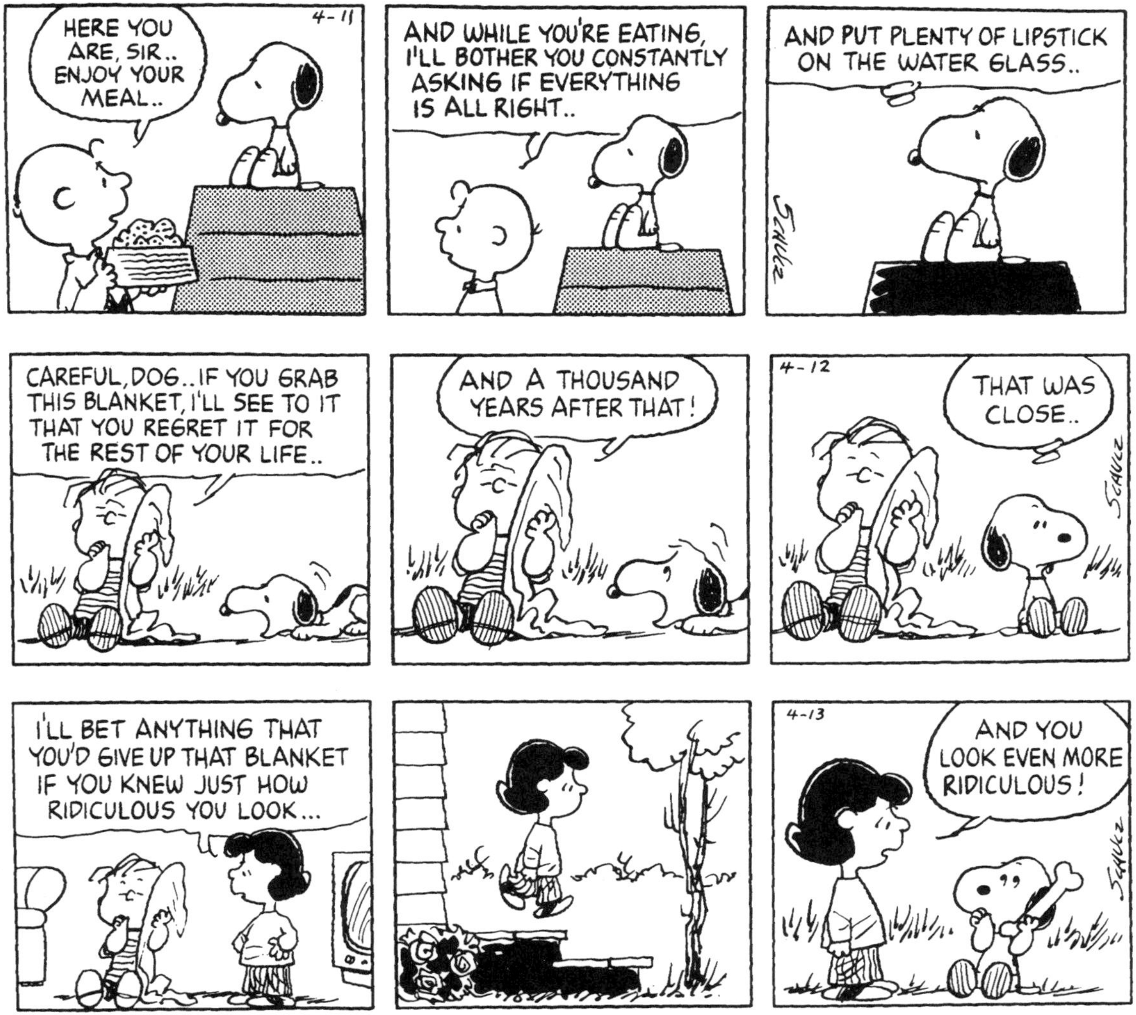
4-11
HERE YOU ARE, SIR.. ENJOY YOUR MEAL..
AND WHILE YOU'RE EATING, I'LL BOTHER YOU CONSTANTLY ASKING IF EVERYTHING IS ALL RIGHT..
AND PUT PLENTY OF LIPSTICK ON THE WATER GLASS..
SCHULZ
CAREFUL, DOG.. IF YOU GRAB THIS BLANKET, I'LL SEE TO IT THAT YOU REGRET IT FOR THE REST OF YOUR LIFE..
AND A THOUSAND YEARS AFTER THAT!
4-12
THAT WAS CLOSE..
SCHULZ
I'LL BET ANYTHING THAT YOU'D GIVE UP THAT BLANKET IF YOU KNEW JUST HOW RIDICULOUS YOU LOOK...
4-13
AND YOU LOOK EVEN MORE RIDICULOUS!
SCHULZ

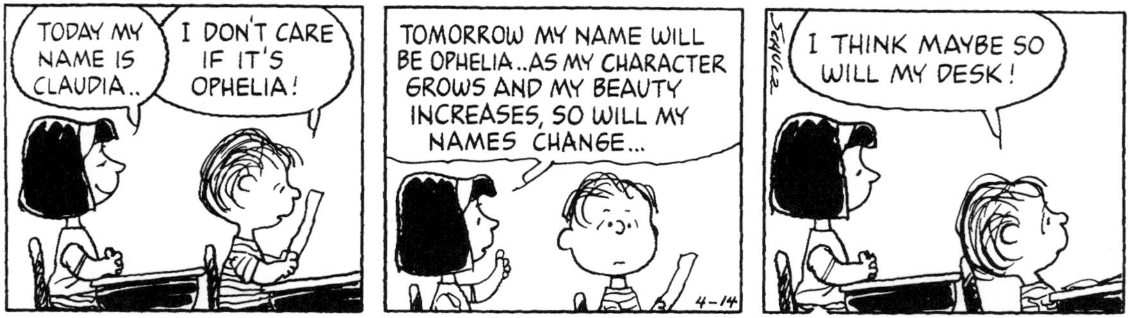
TODAY MY NAME IS CLAUDIA..
I DON'T CARE IF IT'S OPHELIA!
TOMORROW MY NAME WILL BE OPHELIA..AS MY CHARACTER GROWS AND MY BEAUTY INCREASES, SO WILL MY NAMES CHANGE...
I THINK MAYBE SO WILL MY DESK!
4-14

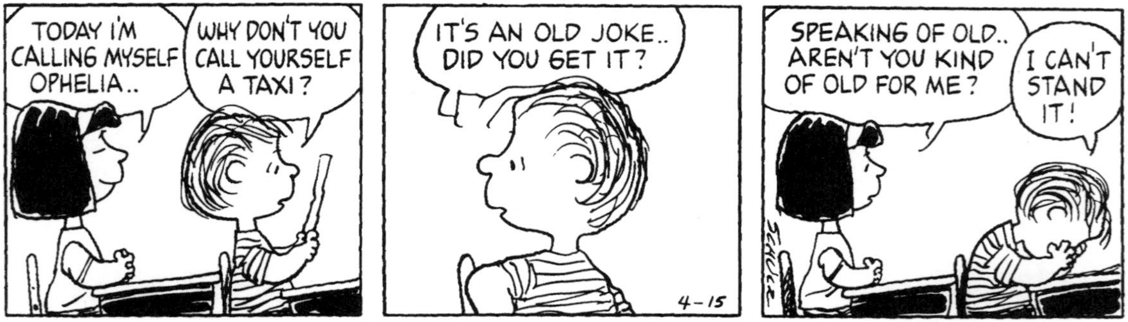
TODAY I'M CALLING MYSELF OPHELIA..
WHY DON'T YOU CALL YOURSELF A TAXI?
IT'S AN OLD JOKE.. DID YOU GET IT?
4-15
SPEAKING OF OLD.. AREN'T YOU KIND OF OLD FOR ME?
I CAN'T STAND IT!

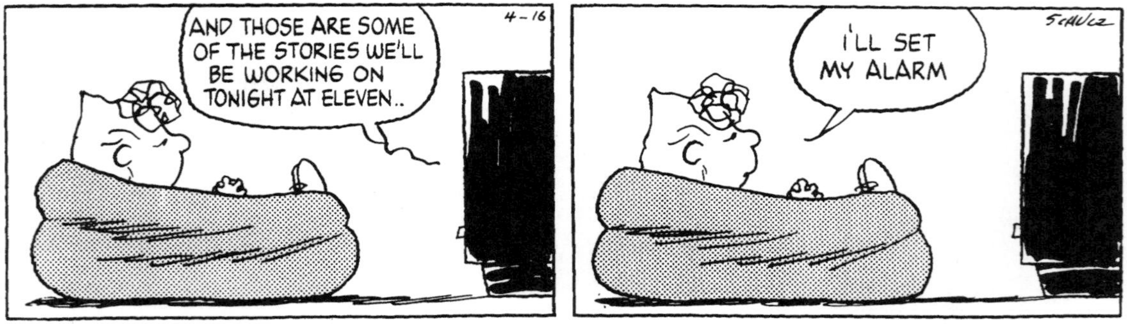
4-16
AND THOSE ARE SOME OF THE STORIES WE'LL BE WORKING ON TONIGHT AT ELEVEN..
I'LL SET MY ALARM

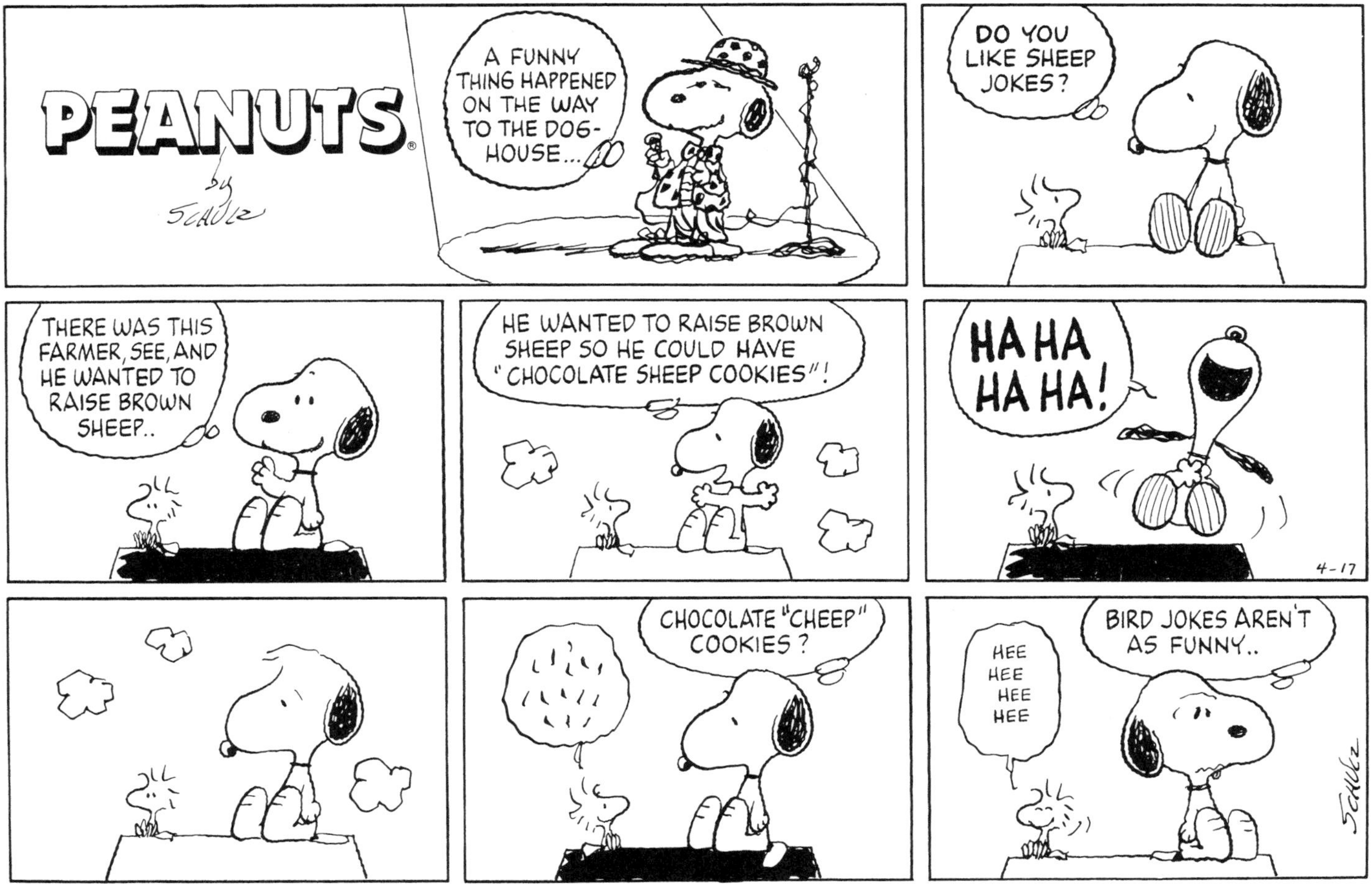
PEANUTS
by SCHULZ
A FUNNY THING HAPPENED ON THE WAY TO THE DOG-HOUSE...
DO YOU LIKE SHEEP JOKES?
THERE WAS THIS FARMER, SEE, AND HE WANTED TO RAISE BROWN SHEEP..
HE WANTED TO RAISE BROWN SHEEP SO HE COULD HAVE "CHOCOLATE SHEEP COOKIES"!
HA HA HA HA!
4-17
CHOCOLATE "CHEEP" COOKIES?
HEE HEE HEE HEE
BIRD JOKES AREN'T AS FUNNY..
SCHULZ

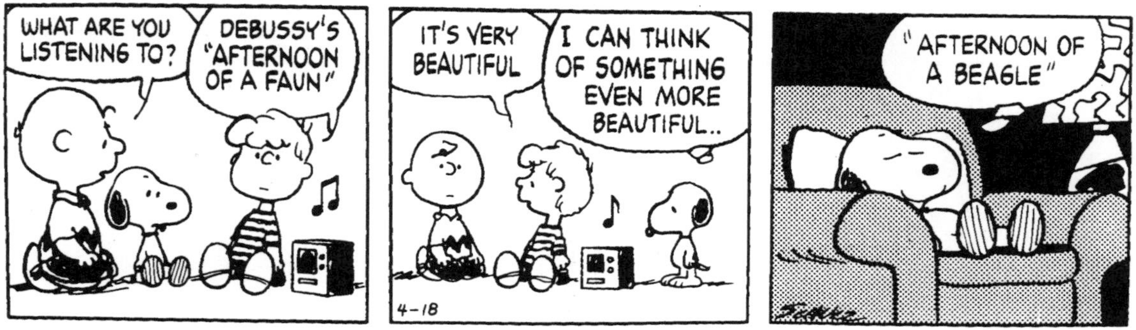
WHAT ARE YOU LISTENING TO?
DEBUSSY'S "AFTERNOON OF A FAUN"
IT'S VERY BEAUTIFUL
I CAN THINK OF SOMETHING EVEN MORE BEAUTIFUL..
4-18
"AFTERNOON OF A BEAGLE"

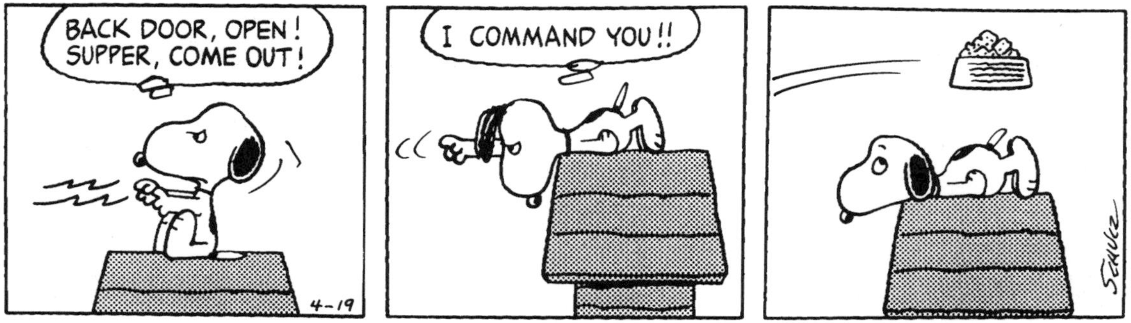
BACK DOOR, OPEN! SUPPER, COME OUT!
4-19
I COMMAND YOU!!

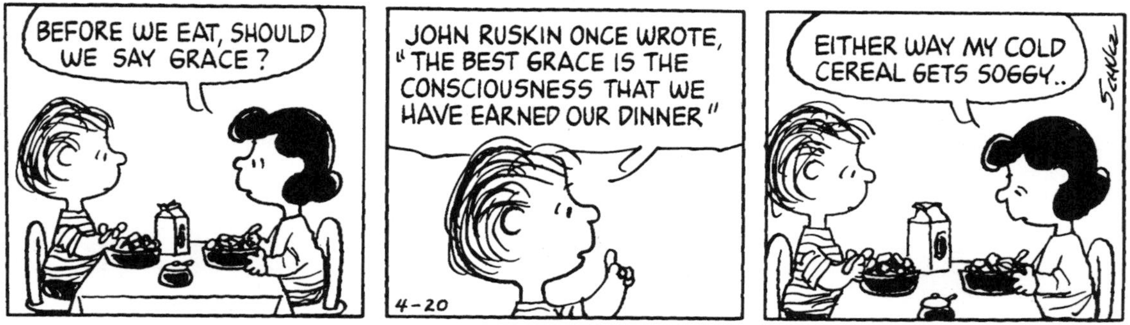
BEFORE WE EAT, SHOULD WE SAY GRACE?
JOHN RUSKIN ONCE WROTE, "THE BEST GRACE IS THE CONSCIOUSNESS THAT WE HAVE EARNED OUR DINNER"
4-20
EITHER WAY MY COLD CEREAL GETS SOGGY..

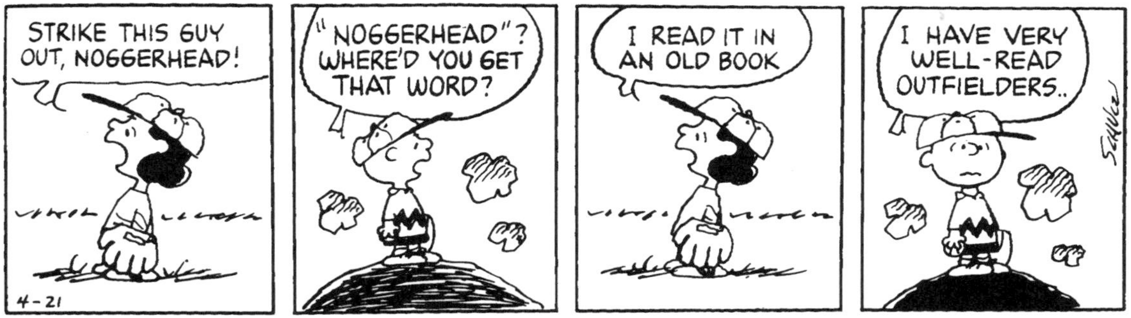
STRIKE THIS GUY OUT, NOGGERHEAD!
"NOGGERHEAD"? WHERE'D YOU GET THAT WORD?
I READ IT IN AN OLD BOOK
I HAVE VERY WELL-READ OUTFIELDERS..
4-21

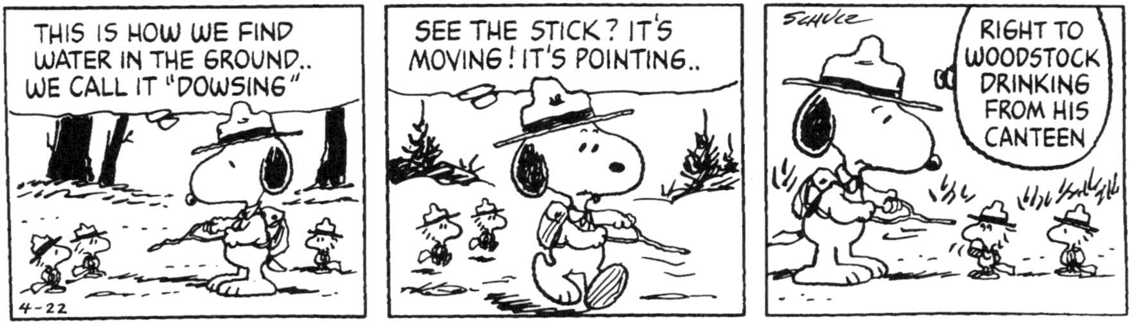
THIS IS HOW WE FIND WATER IN THE GROUND.. WE CALL IT "DOWSING"
SEE THE STICK? IT'S MOVING! IT'S POINTING..
RIGHT TO WOODSTOCK DRINKING FROM HIS CANTEEN
4-22

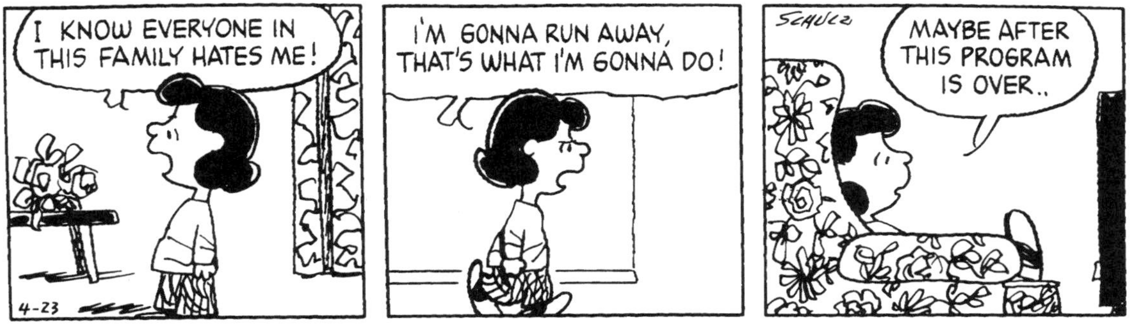
I KNOW EVERYONE IN THIS FAMILY HATES ME!
I'M GONNA RUN AWAY, THAT'S WHAT I'M GONNA DO!
MAYBE AFTER THIS PROGRAM IS OVER..
4-23

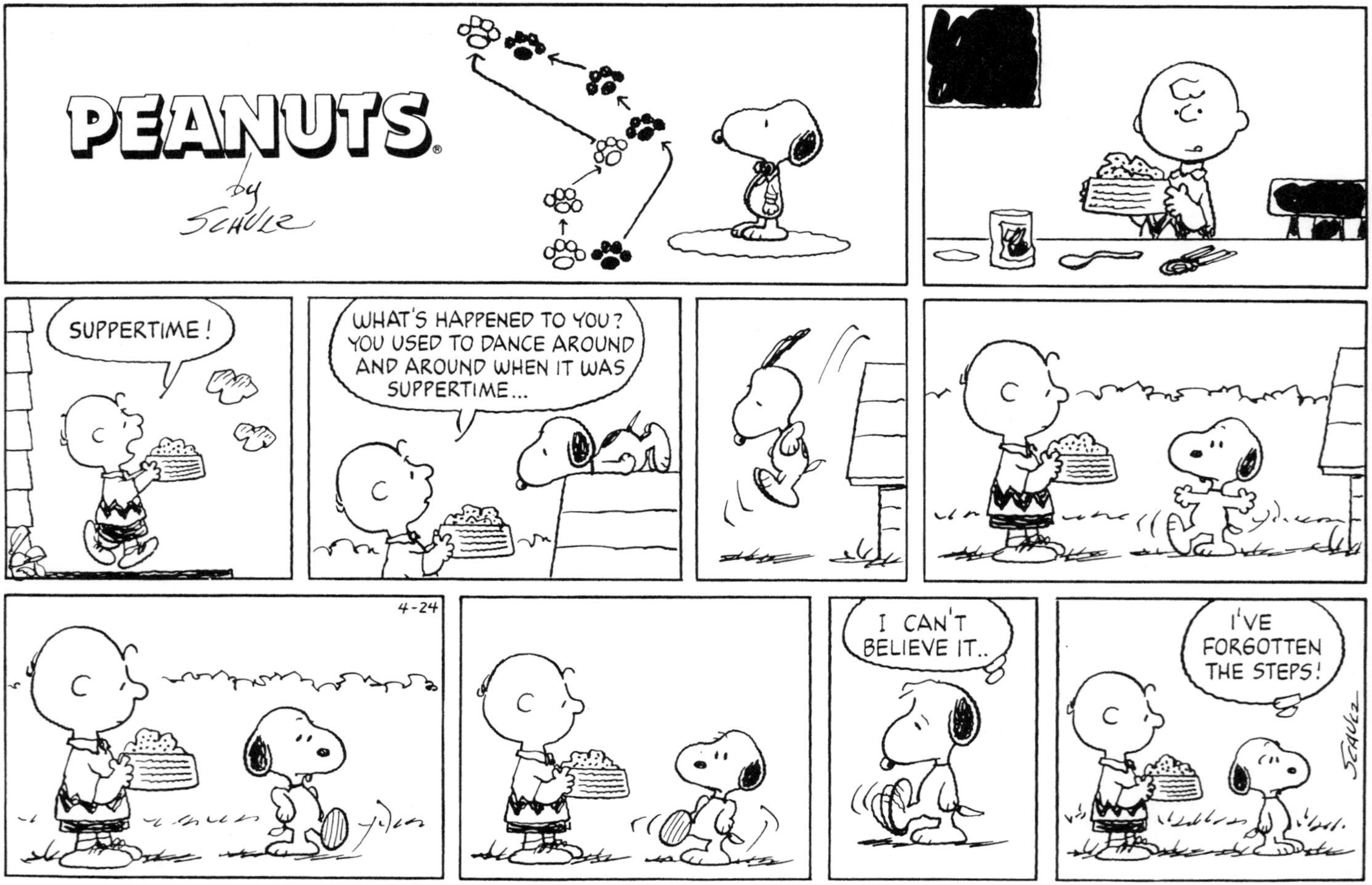
PEANUTS®
by SCHULZ
SUPPERTIME!
WHAT'S HAPPENED TO YOU? YOU USED TO DANCE AROUND AND AROUND WHEN IT WAS SUPPERTIME...
4-24
I CAN'T BELIEVE IT..
I'VE FORGOTTEN THE STEPS!
SCHULZ

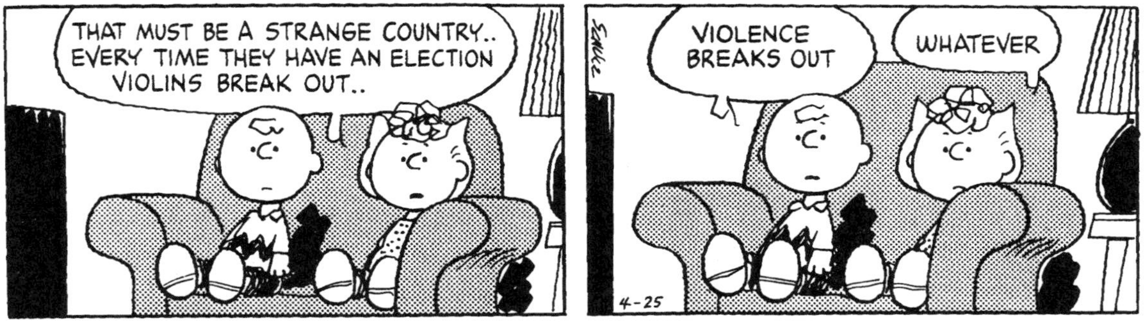
THAT MUST BE A STRANGE COUNTRY.. EVERY TIME THEY HAVE AN ELECTION VIOLINS BREAK OUT..
VIOLENCE BREAKS OUT
WHATEVER
4-25

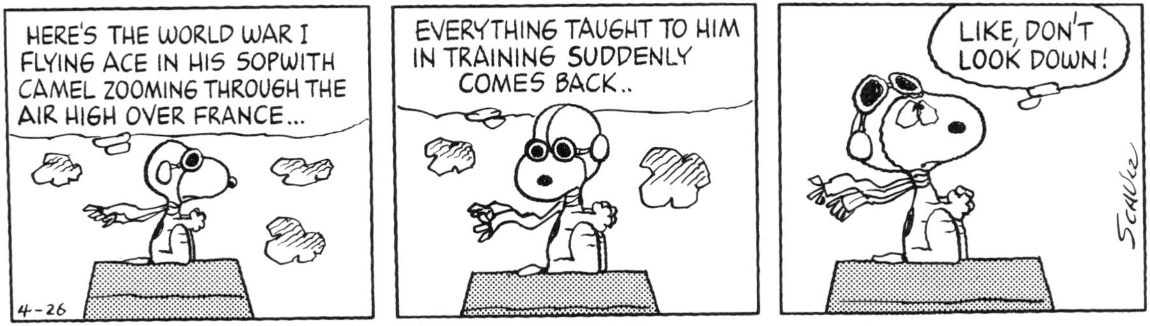
HERE'S THE WORLD WAR I FLYING ACE IN HIS SOPWITH CAMEL ZOOMING THROUGH THE AIR HIGH OVER FRANCE...
4-26
EVERYTHING TAUGHT TO HIM IN TRAINING SUDDENLY COMES BACK..
LIKE, DON'T LOOK DOWN!
SCHULZ

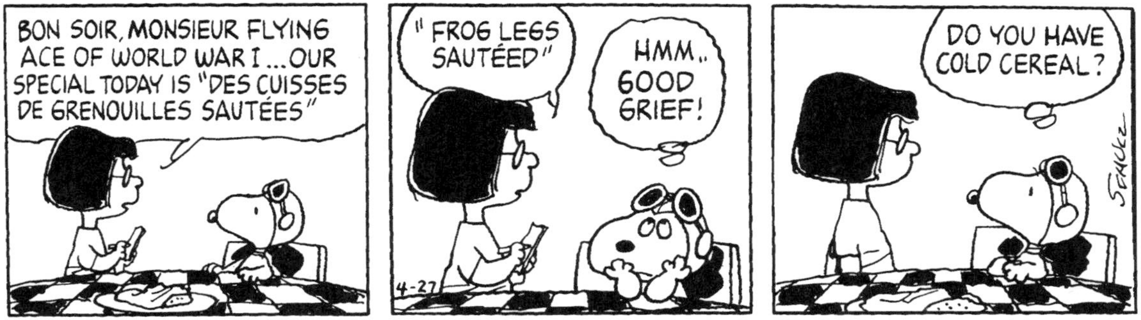
BON SOIR, MONSIEUR FLYING ACE OF WORLD WAR I ...OUR SPECIAL TODAY IS "DES CUISSES DE GRENOUILLES SAUTÉES"
" FROG LEGS SAUTÉED"
HMM.. GOOD GRIEF!
4-27
DO YOU HAVE COLD CEREAL?
SCHULZ

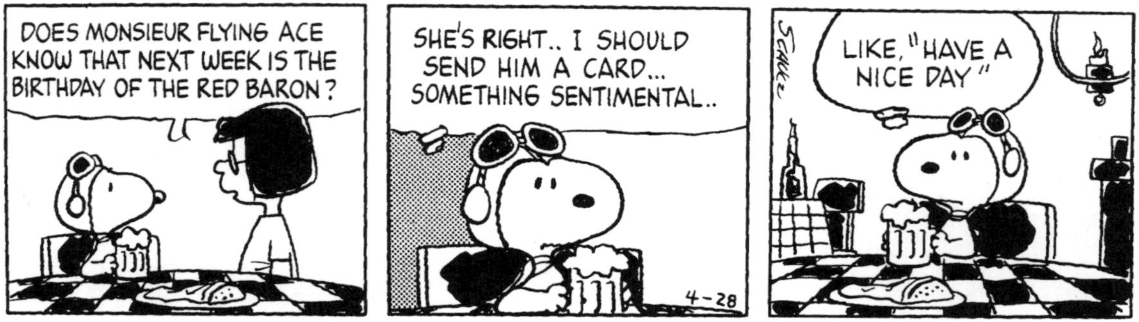
DOES MONSIEUR FLYING ACE KNOW THAT NEXT WEEK IS THE BIRTHDAY OF THE RED BARON ?
SHE'S RIGHT.. I SHOULD SEND HIM A CARD... SOMETHING SENTIMENTAL..
4-28
LIKE, "HAVE A NICE DAY"

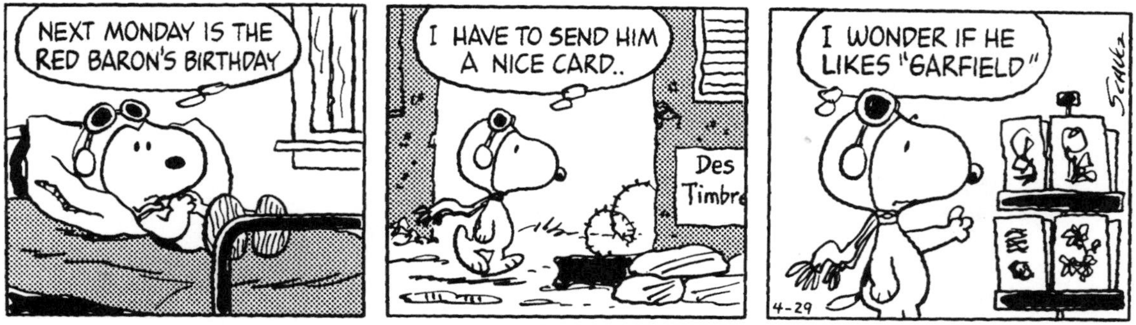
NEXT MONDAY IS THE RED BARON'S BIRTHDAY
I HAVE TO SEND HIM A NICE CARD..
Des
Timbre
I WONDER IF HE LIKES "GARFIELD"
4-29

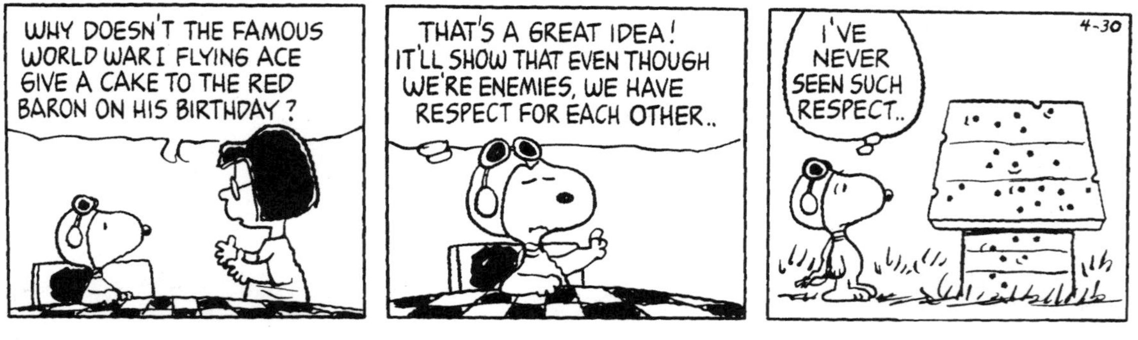
WHY DOESN'T THE FAMOUS WORLD WAR I FLYING ACE GIVE A CAKE TO THE RED BARON ON HIS BIRTHDAY ?
THAT'S A GREAT IDEA! IT'LL SHOW THAT EVEN THOUGH WE'RE ENEMIES, WE HAVE RESPECT FOR EACH OTHER..
4-30
I'VE NEVER SEEN SUCH RESPECT..

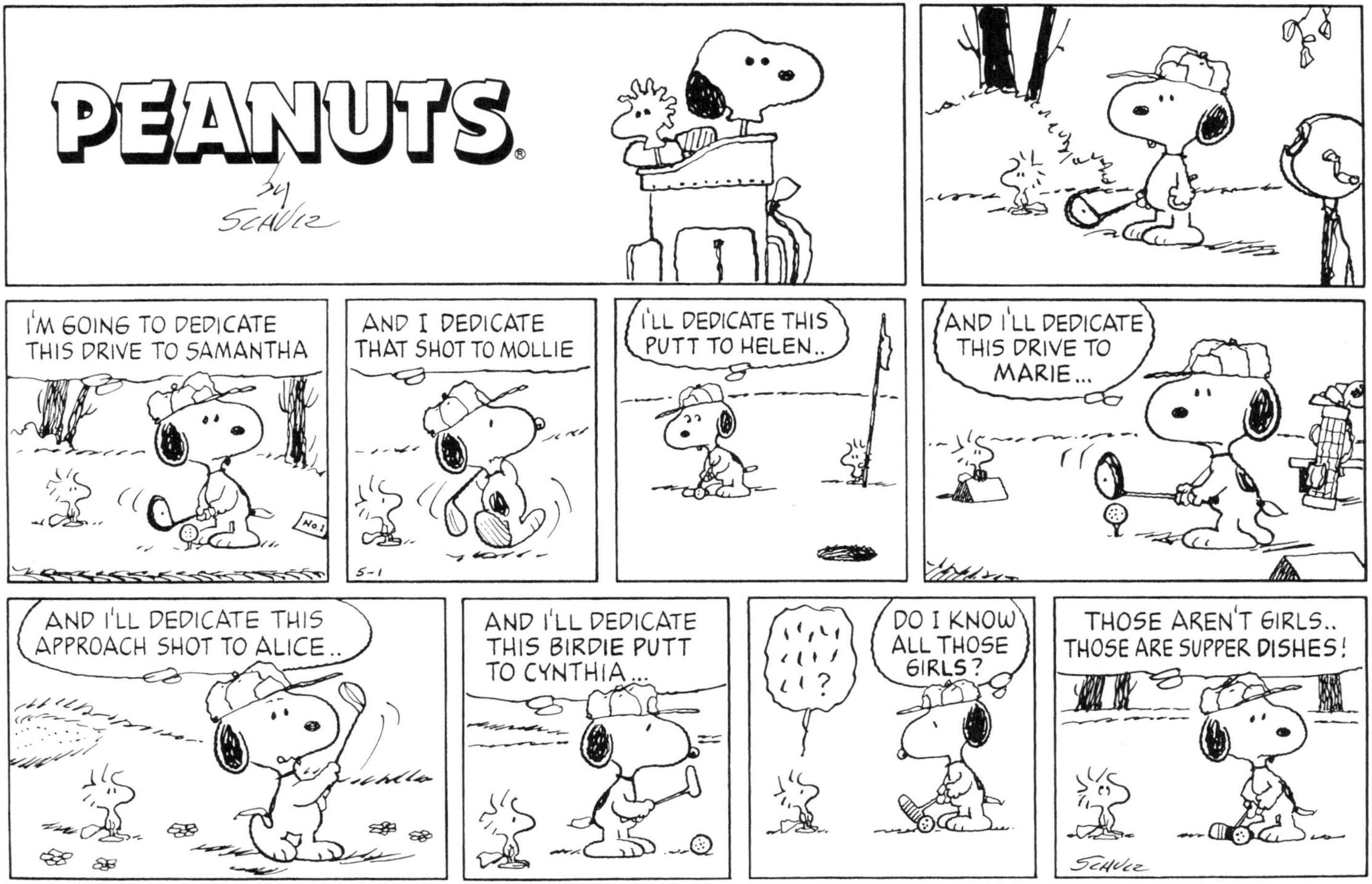
PEANUTS
by SCHULZ
I'M GOING TO DEDICATE THIS DRIVE TO SAMANTHA
NO. 1
AND I DEDICATE THAT SHOT TO MOLLIE
5-1
I'LL DEDICATE THIS PUTT TO HELEN..
AND I'LL DEDICATE THIS DRIVE TO MARIE...
AND I'LL DEDICATE THIS APPROACH SHOT TO ALICE..
AND I'LL DEDICATE THIS BIRDIE PUTT TO CYNTHIA...
?
DO I KNOW ALL THOSE GIRLS?
THOSE AREN'T GIRLS.. THOSE ARE SUPPER DISHES!
SCHULZ

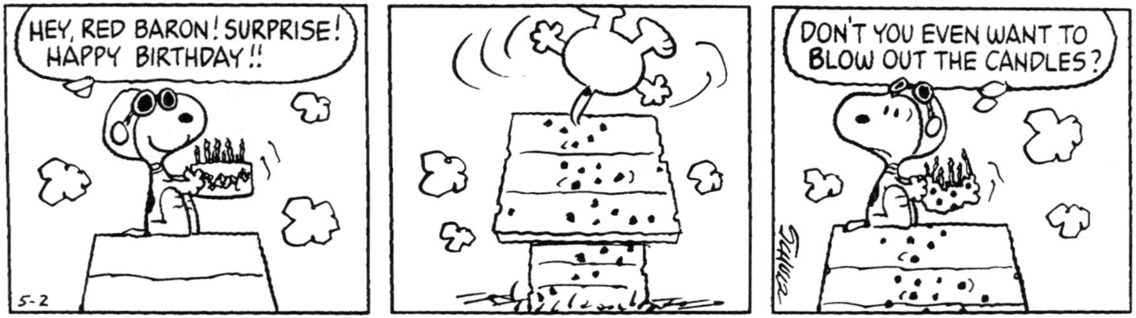
HEY, RED BARON! SURPRISE! HAPPY BIRTHDAY!!
5-2
DON'T YOU EVEN WANT TO BLOW OUT THE CANDLES?

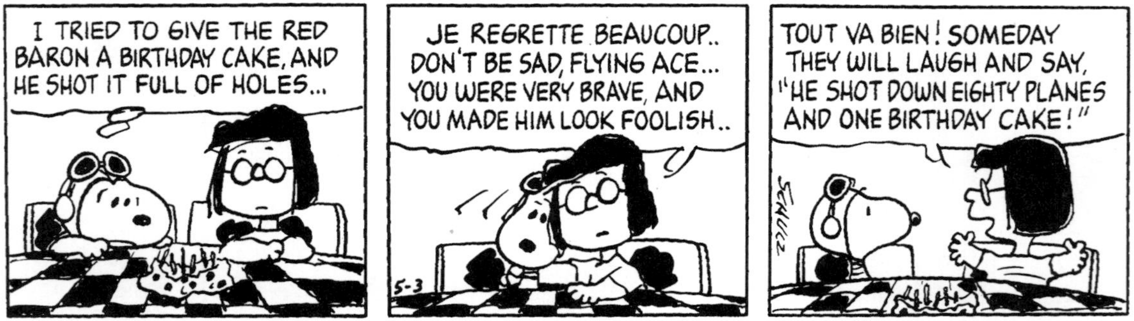
I TRIED TO GIVE THE RED BARON A BIRTHDAY CAKE, AND HE SHOT IT FULL OF HOLES...
JE REGRETTE BEAUCOUP.. DON'T BE SAD, FLYING ACE... YOU WERE VERY BRAVE, AND YOU MADE HIM LOOK FOOLISH..
5-3
TOUT VA BIEN! SOMEDAY THEY WILL LAUGH AND SAY, "HE SHOT DOWN EIGHTY PLANES AND ONE BIRTHDAY CAKE!"

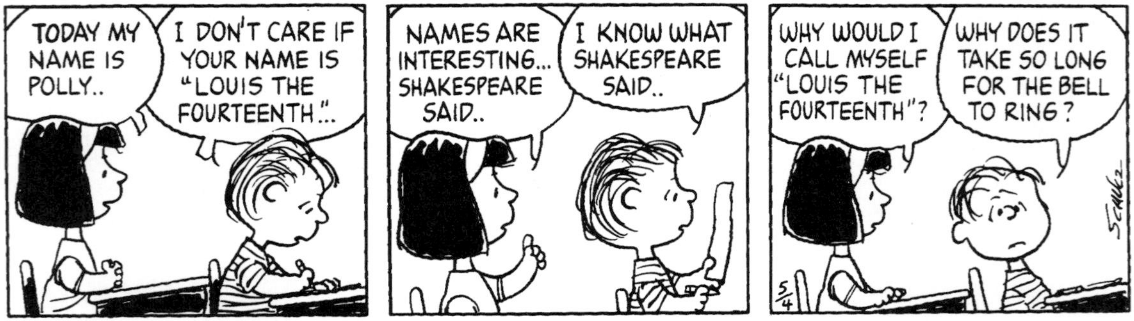
TODAY MY NAME IS POLLY..
I DON'T CARE IF YOUR NAME IS "LOUIS THE FOURTEENTH."..
NAMES ARE INTERESTING... SHAKESPEARE SAID..
I KNOW WHAT SHAKESPEARE SAID..
5/4
WHY WOULD I CALL MYSELF "LOUIS THE FOURTEENTH"?
WHY DOES IT TAKE SO LONG FOR THE BELL TO RING?

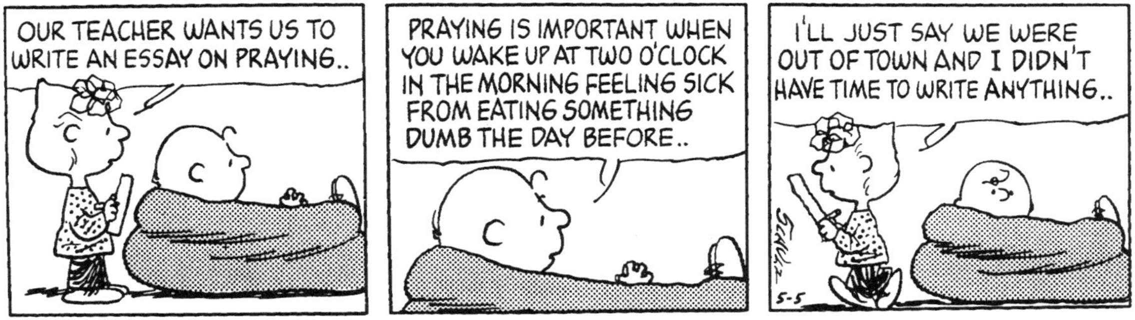
OUR TEACHER WANTS US TO WRITE AN ESSAY ON PRAYING..
PRAYING IS IMPORTANT WHEN YOU WAKE UP AT TWO O'CLOCK IN THE MORNING FEELING SICK FROM EATING SOMETHING DUMB THE DAY BEFORE..
I'LL JUST SAY WE WERE OUT OF TOWN AND I DIDN'T HAVE TIME TO WRITE ANYTHING..
SCHULZ
5-5

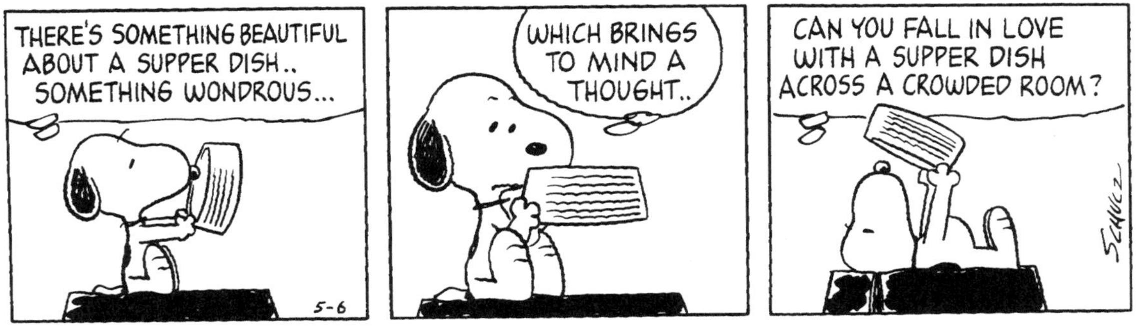
THERE'S SOMETHING BEAUTIFUL ABOUT A SUPPER DISH.. SOMETHING WONDROUS...
5-6
WHICH BRINGS TO MIND A THOUGHT..
CAN YOU FALL IN LOVE WITH A SUPPER DISH ACROSS A CROWDED ROOM?
SCHULZ

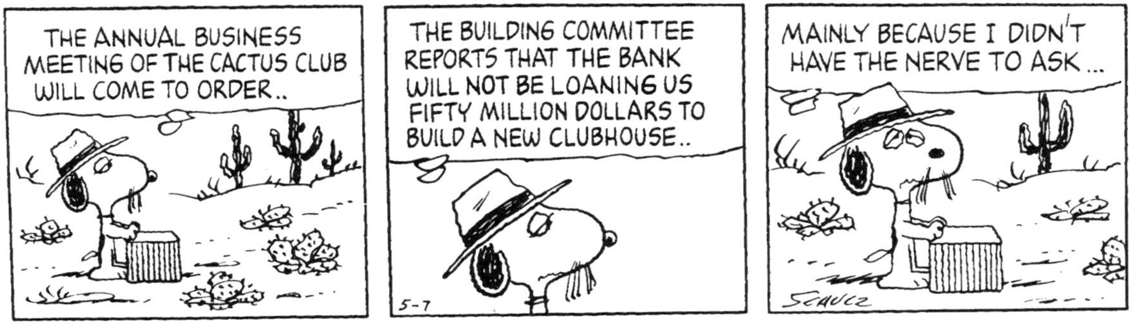
THE ANNUAL BUSINESS MEETING OF THE CACTUS CLUB WILL COME TO ORDER..
THE BUILDING COMMITTEE REPORTS THAT THE BANK WILL NOT BE LOANING US FIFTY MILLION DOLLARS TO BUILD A NEW CLUBHOUSE..
5-7
MAINLY BECAUSE I DIDN'T HAVE THE NERVE TO ASK...
SCHULZ

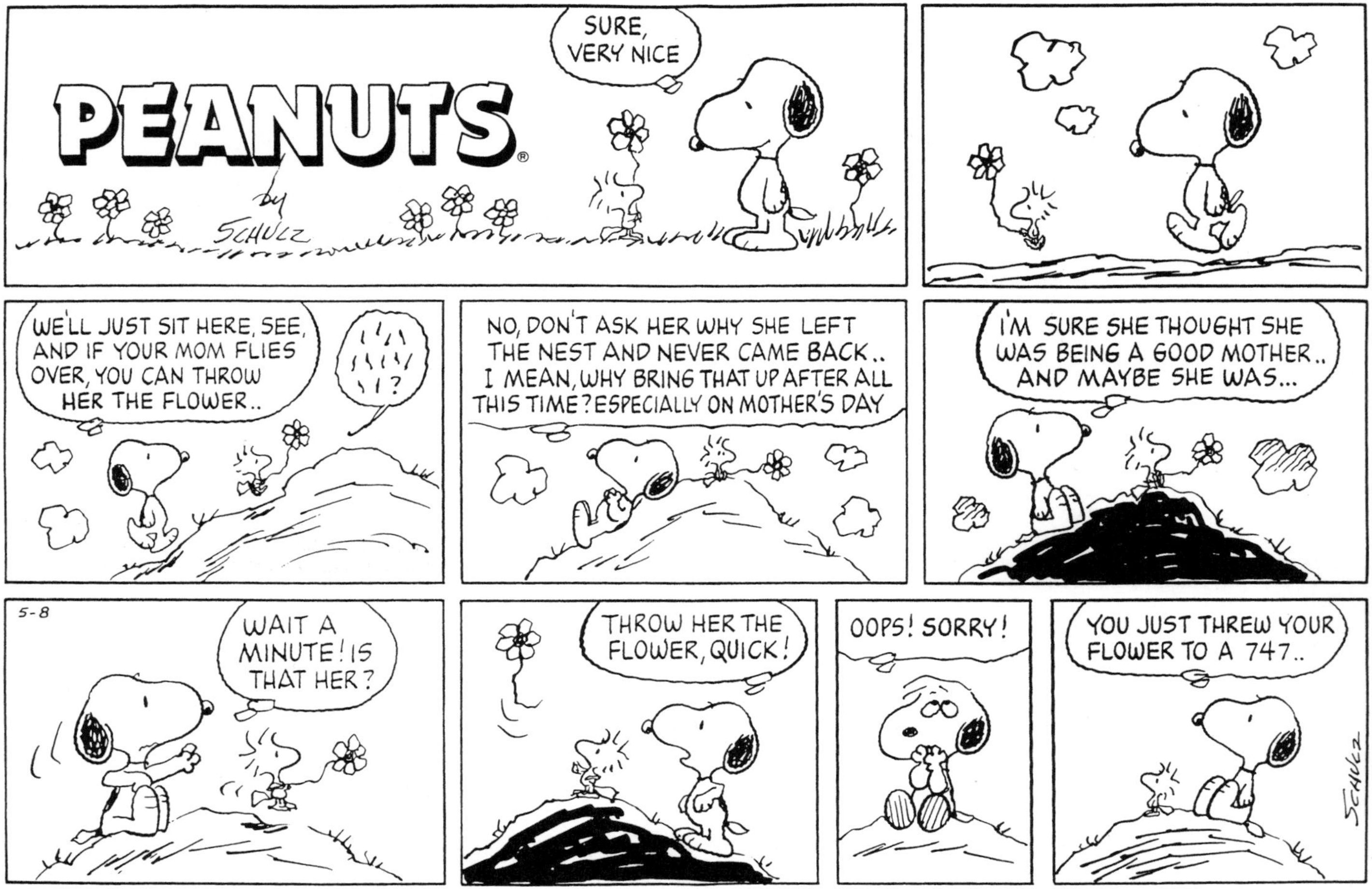
PEANUTS
by SCHULZ
SURE, VERY NICE
WE'LL JUST SIT HERE, SEE, AND IF YOUR MOM FLIES OVER, YOU CAN THROW HER THE FLOWER..
?
NO, DON'T ASK HER WHY SHE LEFT THE NEST AND NEVER CAME BACK.. I MEAN, WHY BRING THAT UP AFTER ALL THIS TIME? ESPECIALLY ON MOTHER'S DAY
I'M SURE SHE THOUGHT SHE WAS BEING A GOOD MOTHER.. AND MAYBE SHE WAS...
5-8
WAIT A MINUTE! IS THAT HER?
THROW HER THE FLOWER, QUICK!
OOPS! SORRY!
YOU JUST THREW YOUR FLOWER TO A 747..
SCHULZ

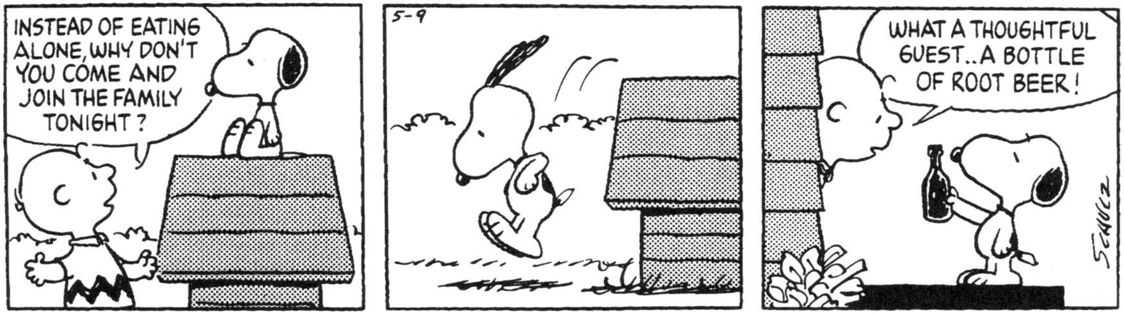
INSTEAD OF EATING ALONE, WHY DON'T YOU COME AND JOIN THE FAMILY TONIGHT?
5-9
WHAT A THOUGHTFUL GUEST.. A BOTTLE OF ROOT BEER!
SCHULZ

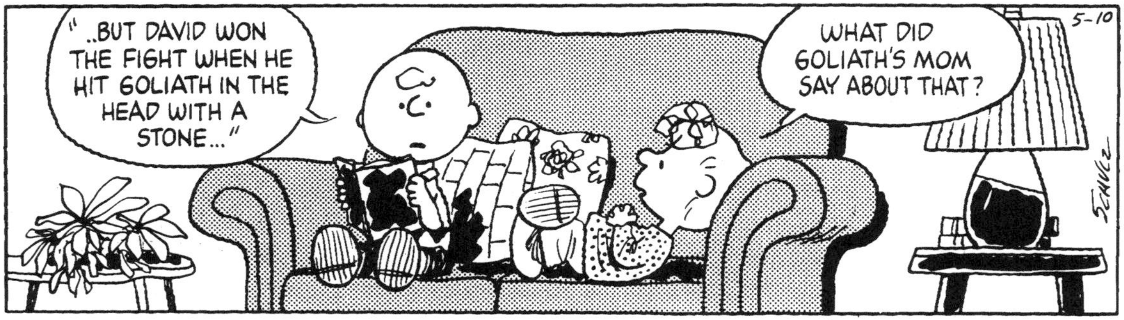
"..BUT DAVID WON THE FIGHT WHEN HE HIT GOLIATH IN THE HEAD WITH A STONE..."
WHAT DID GOLIATH'S MOM SAY ABOUT THAT?
5-10
SCHULZ

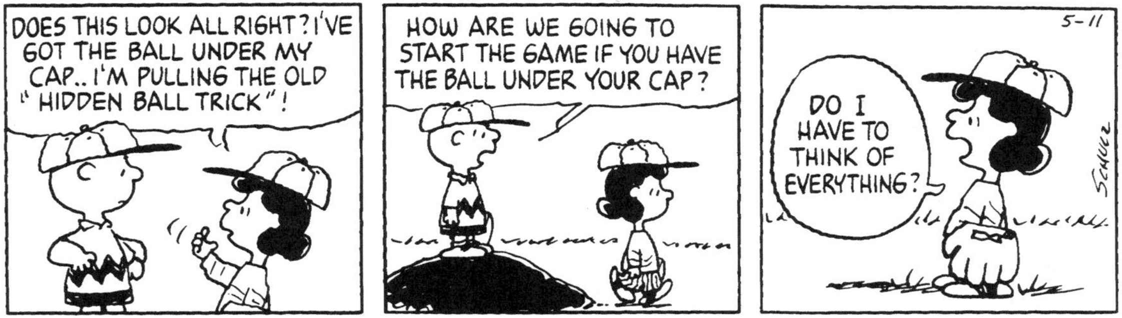
DOES THIS LOOK ALL RIGHT? I'VE GOT THE BALL UNDER MY CAP.. I'M PULLING THE OLD "HIDDEN BALL TRICK"!
HOW ARE WE GOING TO START THE GAME IF YOU HAVE THE BALL UNDER YOUR CAP?
5-11
DO I HAVE TO THINK OF EVERYTHING?
SCHULZ

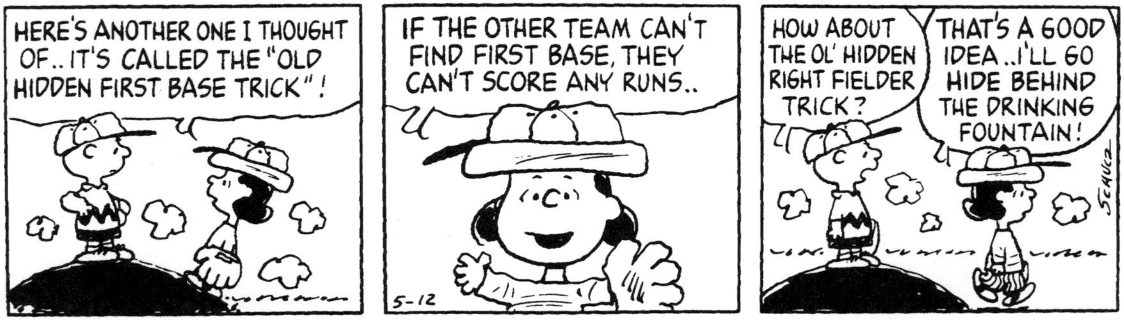
HERE'S ANOTHER ONE I THOUGHT OF.. IT'S CALLED THE "OLD HIDDEN FIRST BASE TRICK"!
IF THE OTHER TEAM CAN'T FIND FIRST BASE, THEY CAN'T SCORE ANY RUNS..
5-12
HOW ABOUT THE OL' HIDDEN RIGHT FIELDER TRICK?
THAT'S A GOOD IDEA..I'LL GO HIDE BEHIND THE DRINKING FOUNTAIN!
SCHULZ

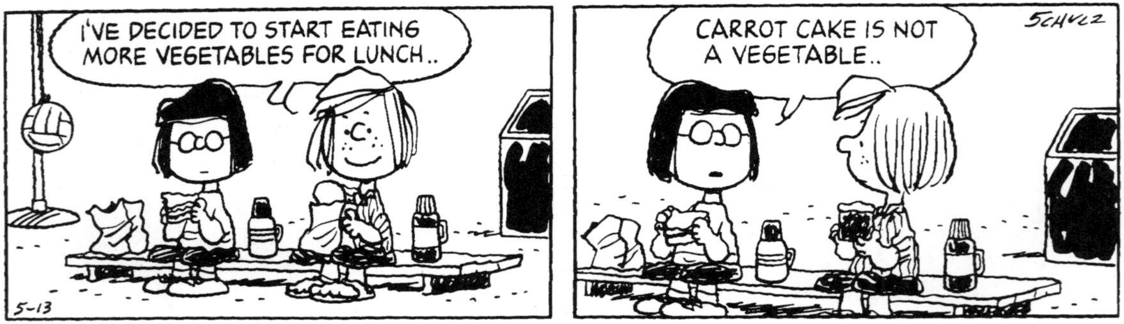
I'VE DECIDED TO START EATING MORE VEGETABLES FOR LUNCH..
5-13
CARROT CAKE IS NOT A VEGETABLE..
SCHULZ

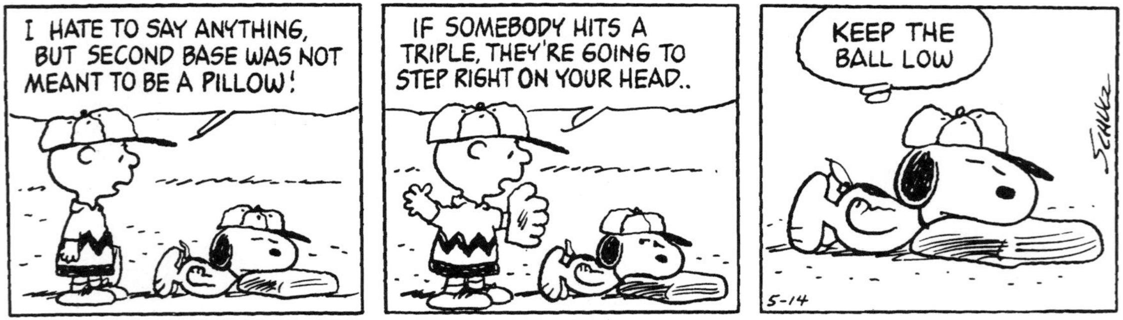
I HATE TO SAY ANYTHING, BUT SECOND BASE WAS NOT MEANT TO BE A PILLOW!
IF SOMEBODY HITS A TRIPLE, THEY'RE GOING TO STEP RIGHT ON YOUR HEAD..
KEEP THE BALL LOW
SCHULZ
5-14

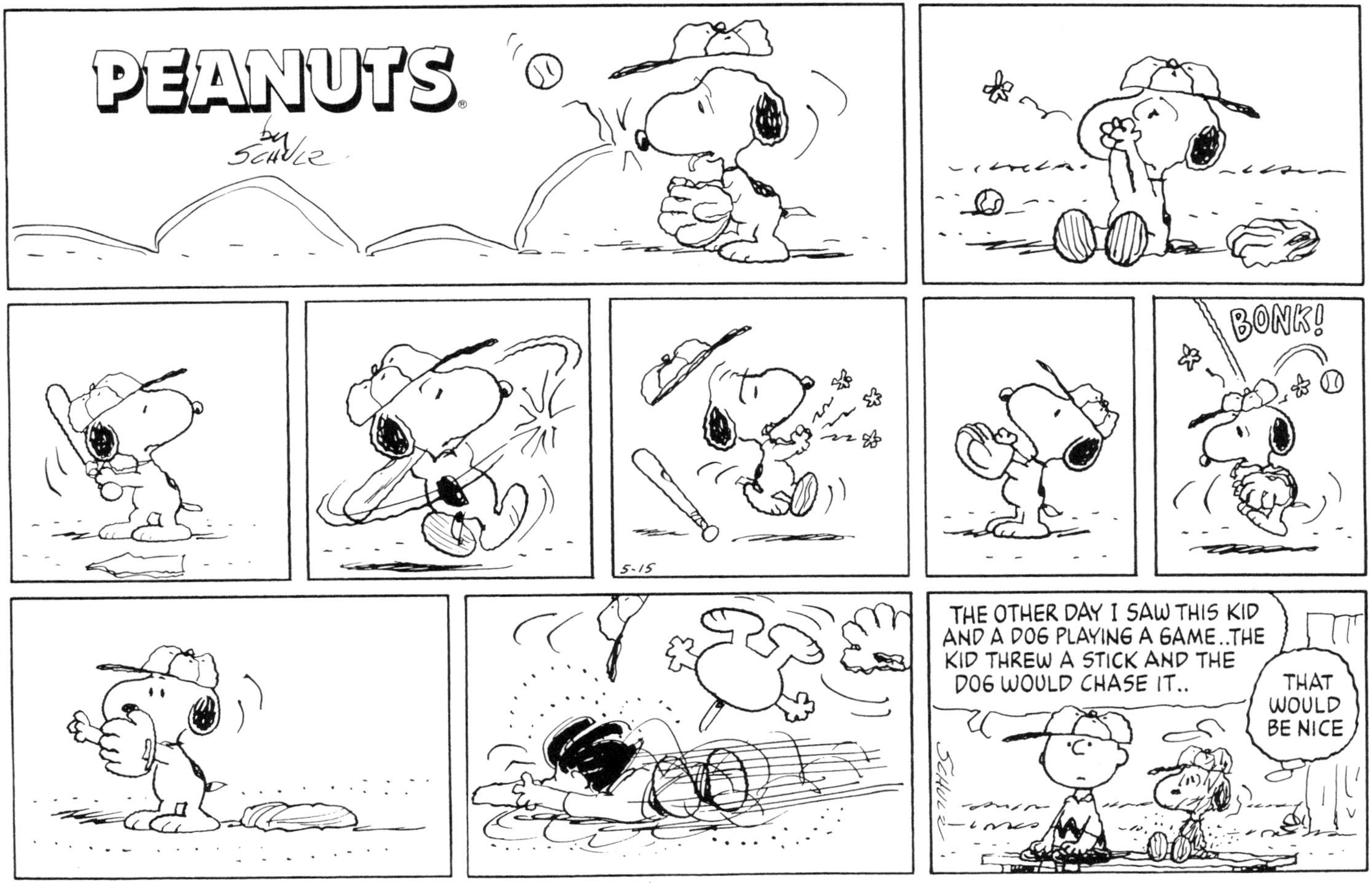
PEANUTS
by SCHULZ
BONK!
5-15
THE OTHER DAY I SAW THIS KID AND A DOG PLAYING A GAME..THE KID THREW A STICK AND THE DOG WOULD CHASE IT..
THAT WOULD BE NICE
SCHULZ

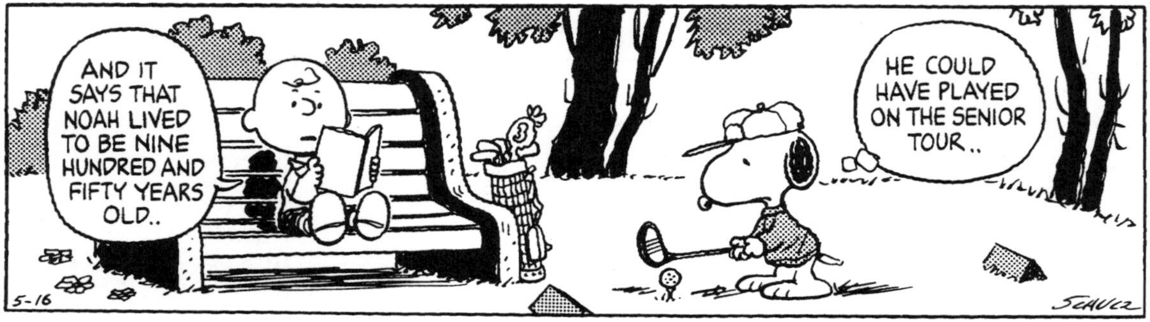
AND IT SAYS THAT NOAH LIVED TO BE NINE HUNDRED AND FIFTY YEARS OLD..
HE COULD HAVE PLAYED ON THE SENIOR TOUR..
5-16
SCHULZ

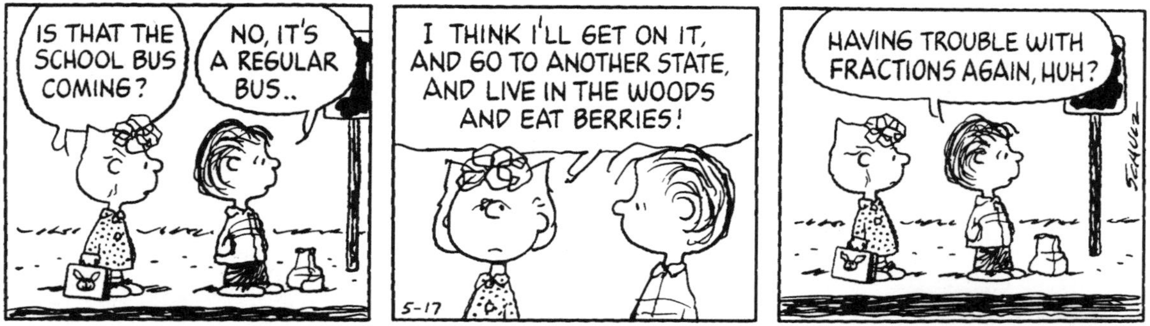
IS THAT THE SCHOOL BUS COMING?
NO, IT'S A REGULAR BUS..
I THINK I'LL GET ON IT, AND GO TO ANOTHER STATE, AND LIVE IN THE WOODS AND EAT BERRIES!
5-17
HAVING TROUBLE WITH FRACTIONS AGAIN, HUH?
SCHULZ

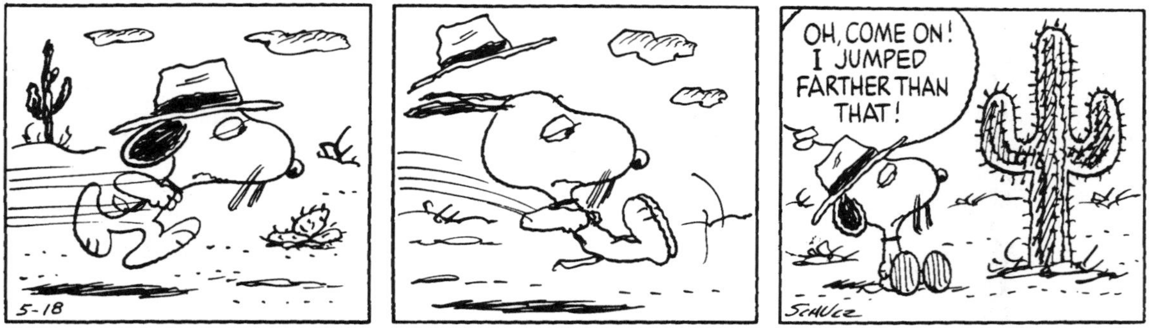
5-18
OH, COME ON! I JUMPED FARTHER THAN THAT!
SCHULZ

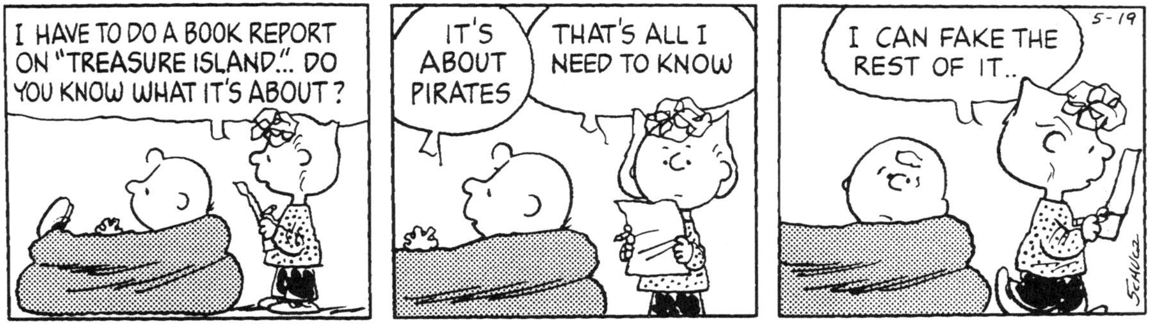
I HAVE TO DO A BOOK REPORT ON "TREASURE ISLAND"... DO YOU KNOW WHAT IT'S ABOUT?
IT'S ABOUT PIRATES
THAT'S ALL I NEED TO KNOW
I CAN FAKE THE REST OF IT..
5-19

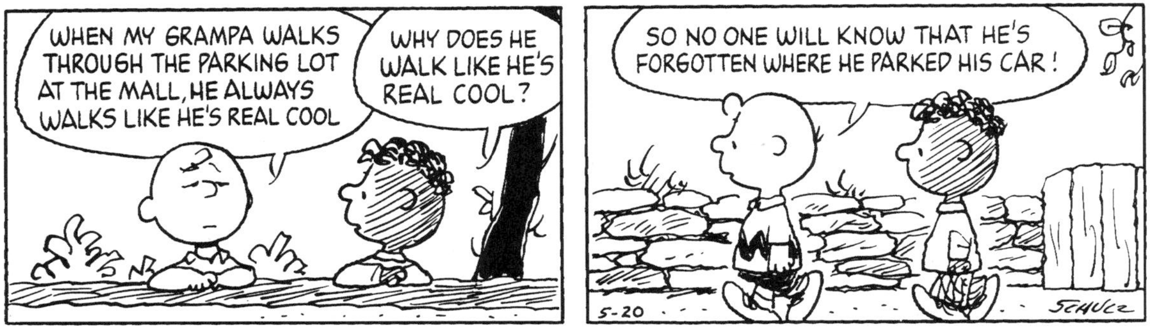
WHEN MY GRAMPA WALKS THROUGH THE PARKING LOT AT THE MALL, HE ALWAYS WALKS LIKE HE'S REAL COOL
WHY DOES HE WALK LIKE HE'S REAL COOL?
SO NO ONE WILL KNOW THAT HE'S FORGOTTEN WHERE HE PARKED HIS CAR!
5-20

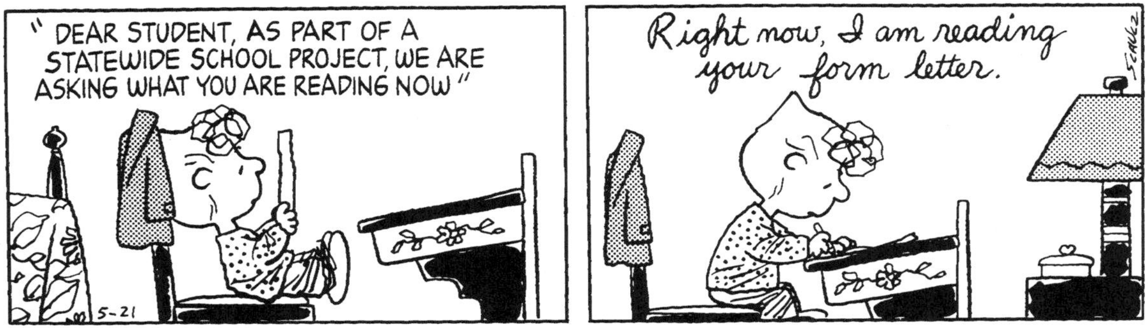
"DEAR STUDENT, AS PART OF A STATEWIDE SCHOOL PROJECT, WE ARE ASKING WHAT YOU ARE READING NOW"
5-21
Right now, I am reading your form letter.

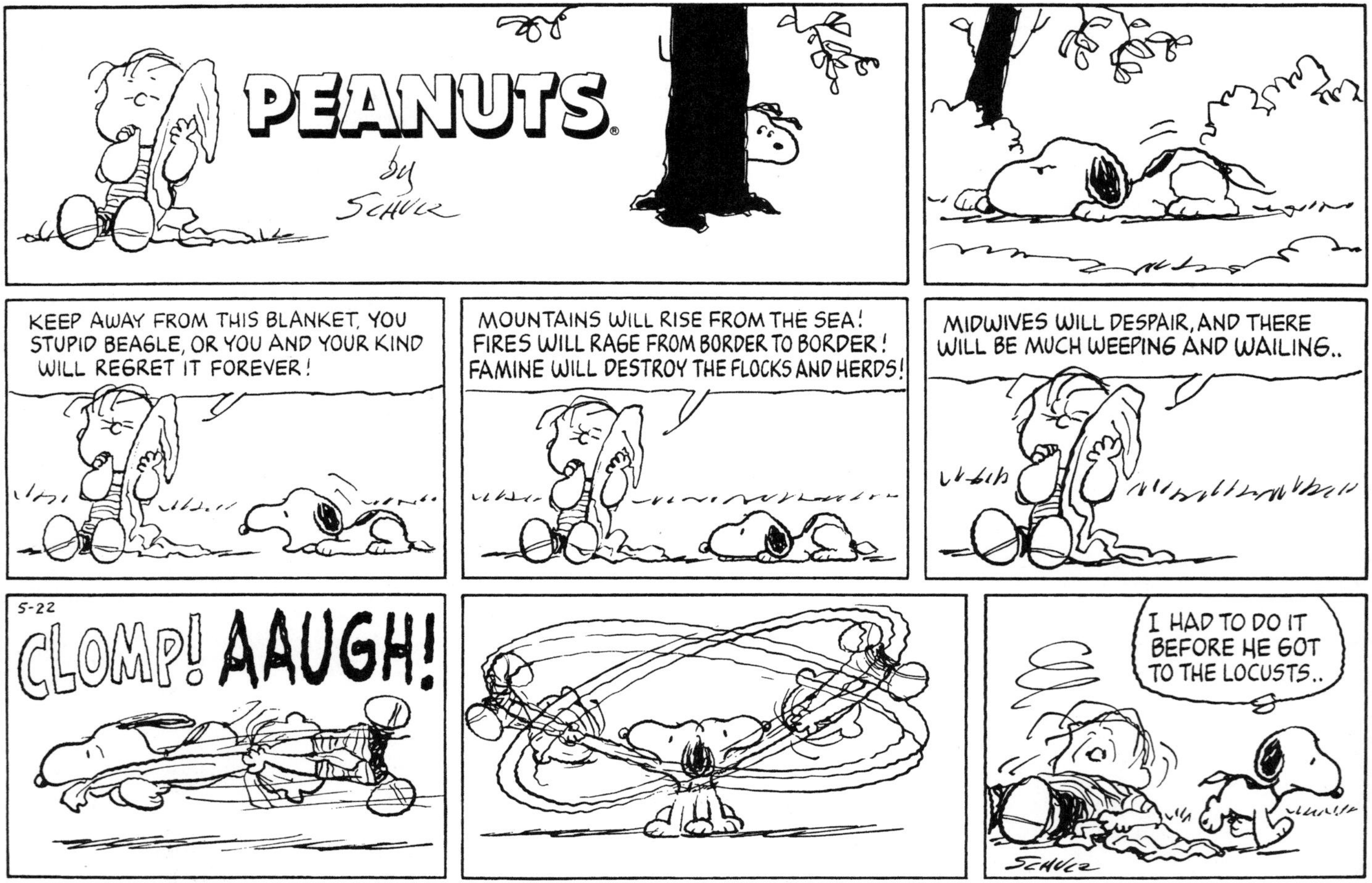
PEANUTS®
by SCHULZ
KEEP AWAY FROM THIS BLANKET, YOU STUPID BEAGLE, OR YOU AND YOUR KIND WILL REGRET IT FOREVER!
MOUNTAINS WILL RISE FROM THE SEA! FIRES WILL RAGE FROM BORDER TO BORDER! FAMINE WILL DESTROY THE FLOCKS AND HERDS!
MIDWIVES WILL DESPAIR, AND THERE WILL BE MUCH WEEPING AND WAILING..
5-22
CLOMP! AAUGH!
I HAD TO DO IT BEFORE HE GOT TO THE LOCUSTS..
SCHULZ

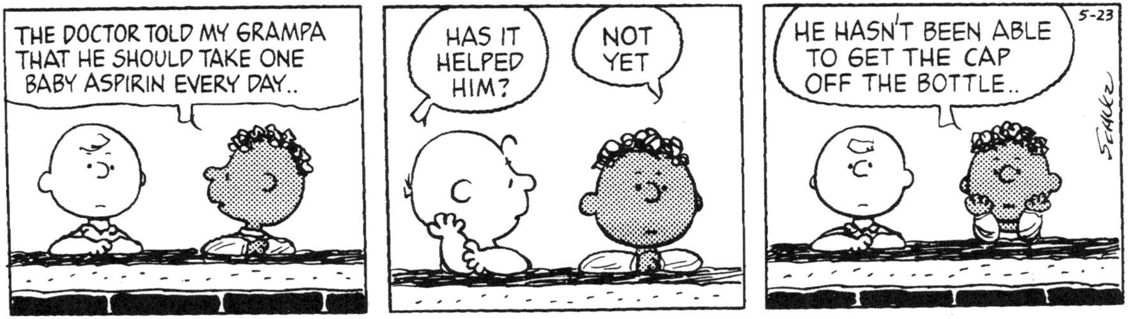
THE DOCTOR TOLD MY GRAMPA THAT HE SHOULD TAKE ONE BABY ASPIRIN EVERY DAY..
HAS IT HELPED HIM?
NOT YET
HE HASN'T BEEN ABLE TO GET THE CAP OFF THE BOTTLE..

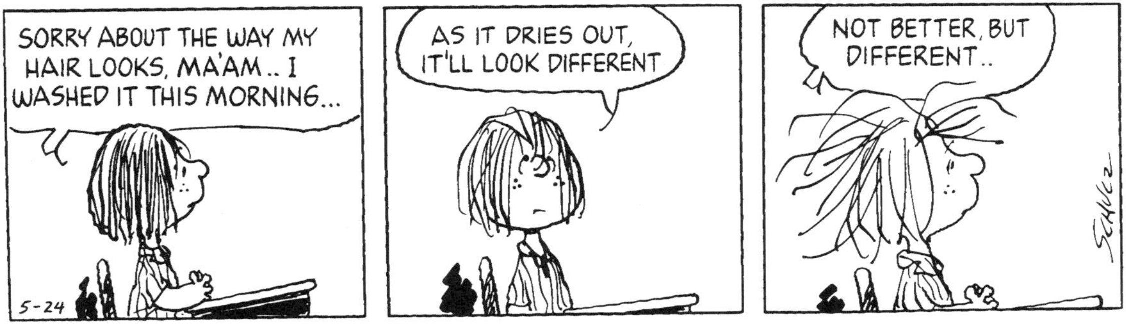
SORRY ABOUT THE WAY MY HAIR LOOKS, MA'AM.. I WASHED IT THIS MORNING...
AS IT DRIES OUT, IT'LL LOOK DIFFERENT
NOT BETTER, BUT DIFFERENT..

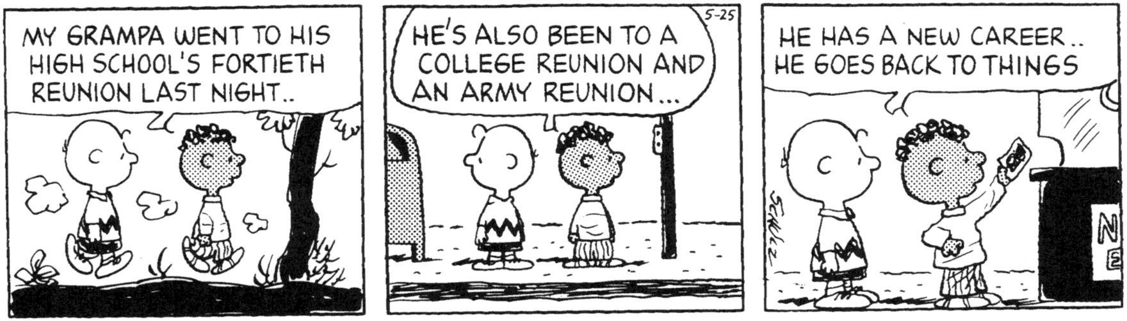
MY GRAMPA WENT TO HIS HIGH SCHOOL'S FORTIETH REUNION LAST NIGHT..
HE'S ALSO BEEN TO A COLLEGE REUNION AND AN ARMY REUNION...
HE HAS A NEW CAREER.. HE GOES BACK TO THINGS

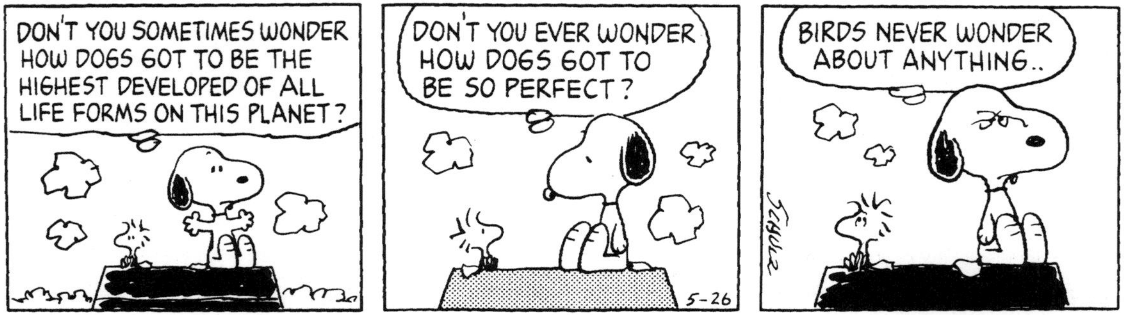
DON'T YOU SOMETIMES WONDER HOW DOGS GOT TO BE THE HIGHEST DEVELOPED OF ALL LIFE FORMS ON THIS PLANET?
DON'T YOU EVER WONDER HOW DOGS GOT TO BE SO PERFECT?
5-26
BIRDS NEVER WONDER ABOUT ANYTHING..

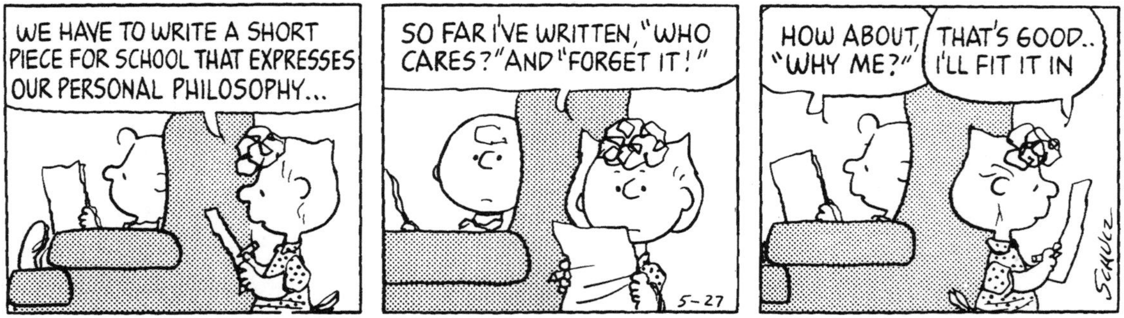
WE HAVE TO WRITE A SHORT PIECE FOR SCHOOL THAT EXPRESSES OUR PERSONAL PHILOSOPHY...
SO FAR I'VE WRITTEN, "WHO CARES?" AND "FORGET IT!"
5-27
HOW ABOUT, "WHY ME?"
THAT'S GOOD.. I'LL FIT IT IN

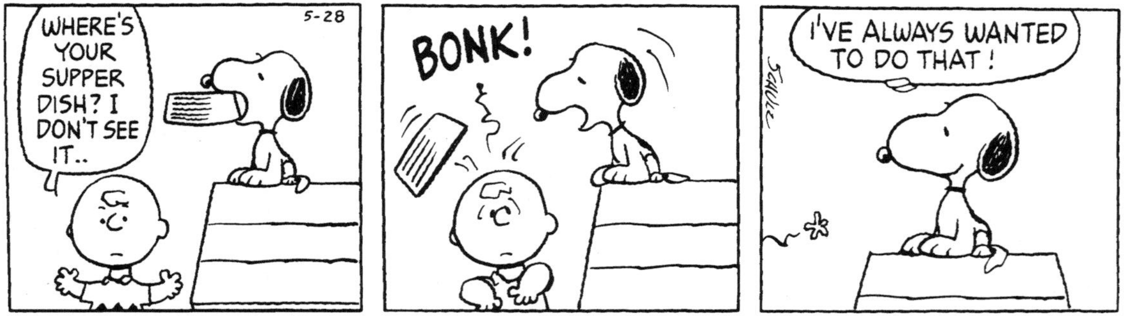
5-28
WHERE'S YOUR SUPPER DISH? I DON'T SEE IT..
BONK!
I'VE ALWAYS WANTED TO DO THAT!

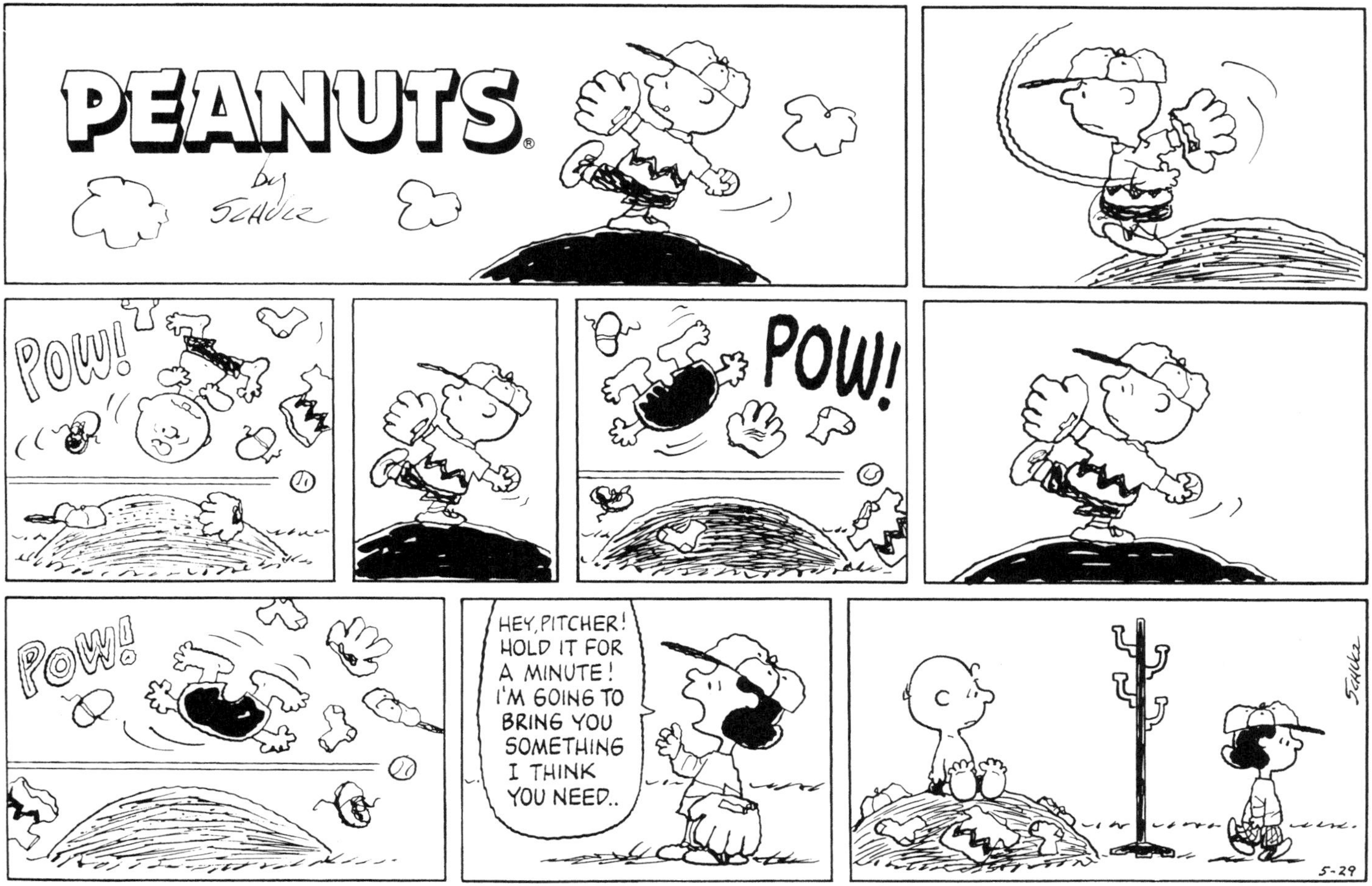
PEANUTS®
by SCHULZ
POW!
POW!
POW!
HEY, PITCHER! HOLD IT FOR A MINUTE! I'M GOING TO BRING YOU SOMETHING I THINK YOU NEED..
SCHULZ
5-29

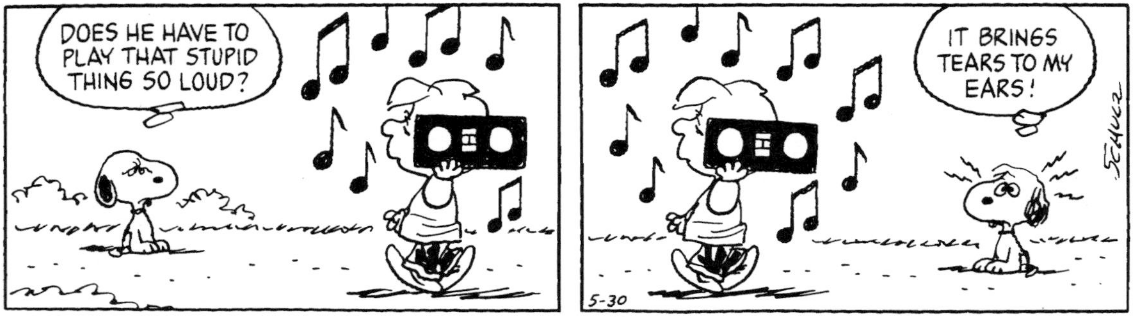
DOES HE HAVE TO PLAY THAT STUPID THING SO LOUD?
IT BRINGS TEARS TO MY EARS!
SCHULZ
5-30

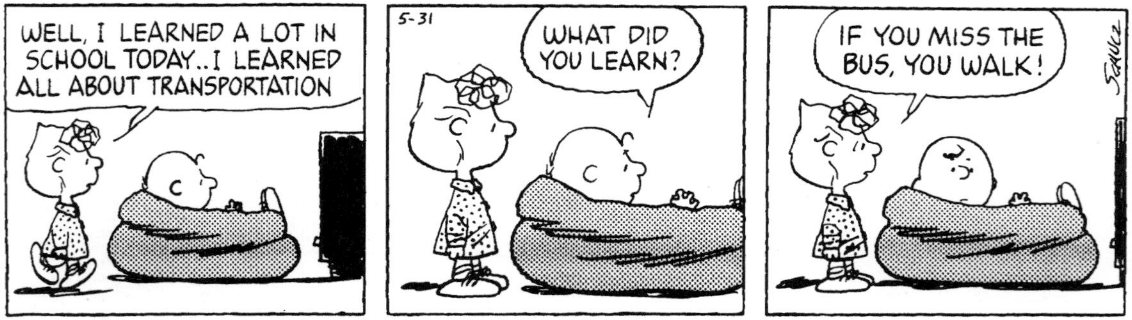
WELL, I LEARNED A LOT IN SCHOOL TODAY..I LEARNED ALL ABOUT TRANSPORTATION
5-31
WHAT DID YOU LEARN?
IF YOU MISS THE BUS, YOU WALK!
SCHULZ

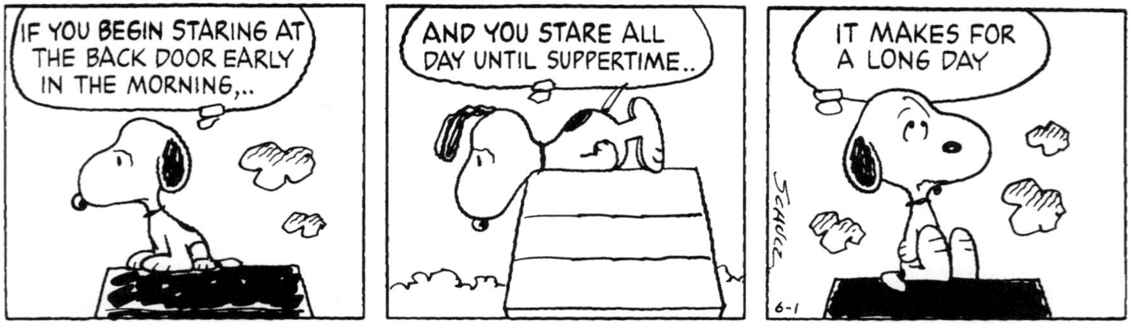
IF YOU BEGIN STARING AT THE BACK DOOR EARLY IN THE MORNING,..
AND YOU STARE ALL DAY UNTIL SUPPERTIME..
SCHULZ
IT MAKES FOR A LONG DAY
6-1

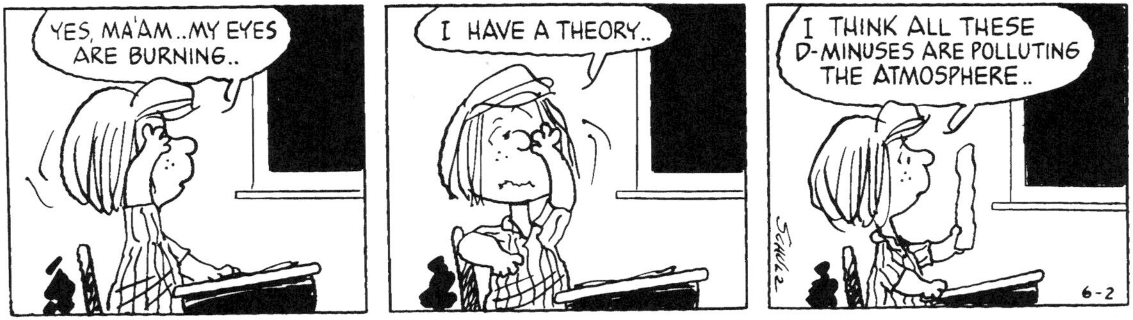
YES, MA'AM..MY EYES ARE BURNING..
I HAVE A THEORY..
I THINK ALL THESE D-MINUSES ARE POLLUTING THE ATMOSPHERE..
SCHULZ
6-2

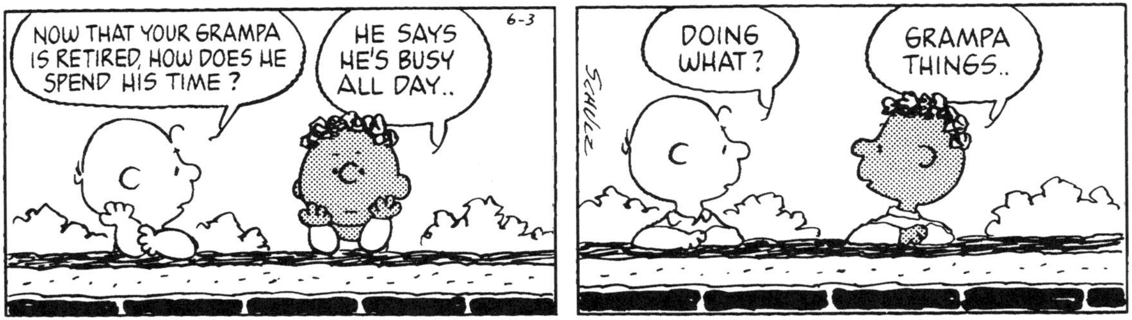
NOW THAT YOUR GRAMPA IS RETIRED, HOW DOES HE SPEND HIS TIME ?
HE SAYS HE'S BUSY ALL DAY..
6-3
SCHULZ
DOING WHAT ?
GRAMPA THINGS..

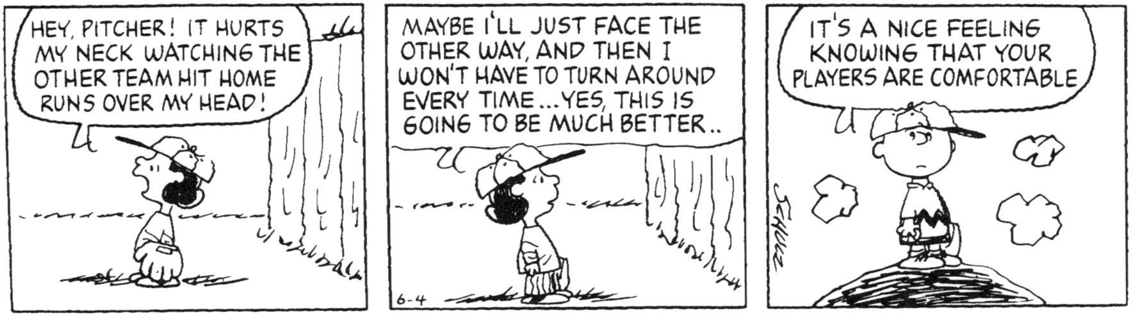
HEY, PITCHER! IT HURTS MY NECK WATCHING THE OTHER TEAM HIT HOME RUNS OVER MY HEAD!
MAYBE I'LL JUST FACE THE OTHER WAY, AND THEN I WON'T HAVE TO TURN AROUND EVERY TIME...YES, THIS IS GOING TO BE MUCH BETTER..
6-4
IT'S A NICE FEELING KNOWING THAT YOUR PLAYERS ARE COMFORTABLE
SCHULZ

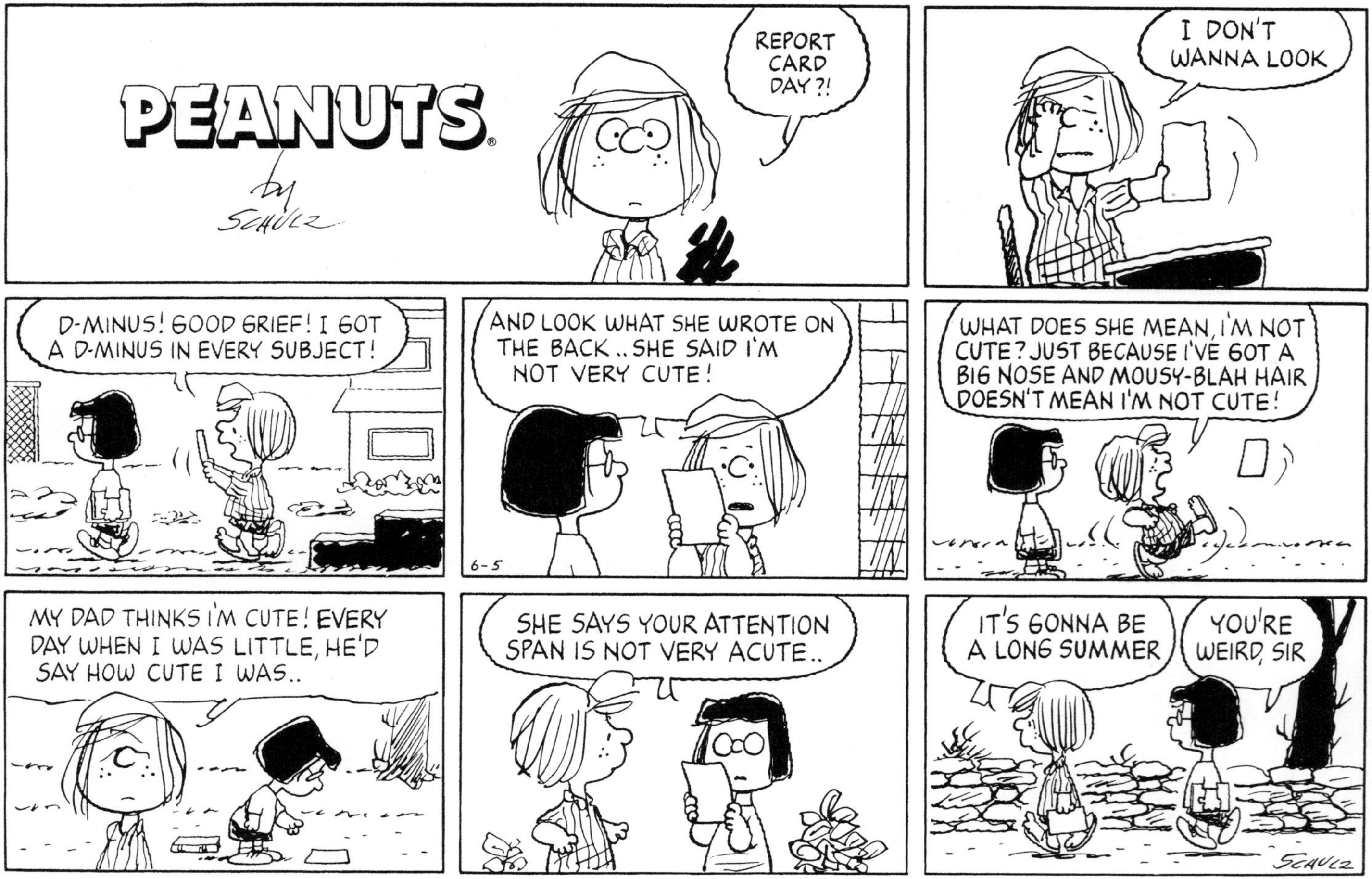
PEANUTS
by SCHULZ
REPORT CARD DAY?!
I DON'T WANNA LOOK
D-MINUS! GOOD GRIEF! I GOT A D-MINUS IN EVERY SUBJECT!
AND LOOK WHAT SHE WROTE ON THE BACK.. SHE SAID I'M NOT VERY CUTE!
6-5
WHAT DOES SHE MEAN, I'M NOT CUTE? JUST BECAUSE I'VE GOT A BIG NOSE AND MOUSY-BLAH HAIR DOESN'T MEAN I'M NOT CUTE!
MY DAD THINKS I'M CUTE! EVERY DAY WHEN I WAS LITTLE, HE'D SAY HOW CUTE I WAS..
SHE SAYS YOUR ATTENTION SPAN IS NOT VERY ACUTE..
IT'S GONNA BE A LONG SUMMER
YOU'RE WEIRD, SIR
SCHULZ

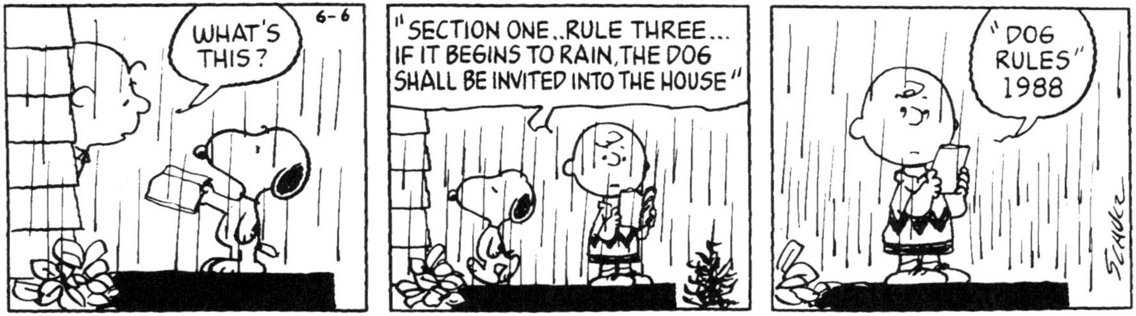
6-6
WHAT'S THIS?
"SECTION ONE..RULE THREE... IF IT BEGINS TO RAIN, THE DOG SHALL BE INVITED INTO THE HOUSE"
"DOG RULES" 1988
SCHULZ

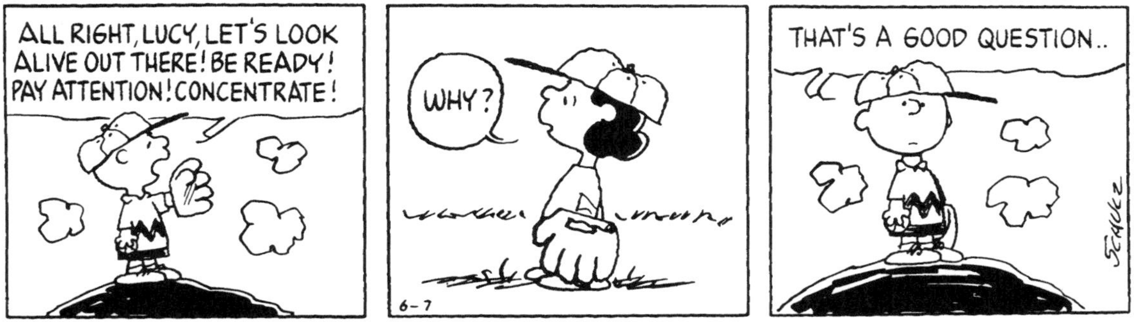
ALL RIGHT, LUCY, LET'S LOOK ALIVE OUT THERE! BE READY! PAY ATTENTION! CONCENTRATE!
WHY?
6-7
THAT'S A GOOD QUESTION..
SCHULZ

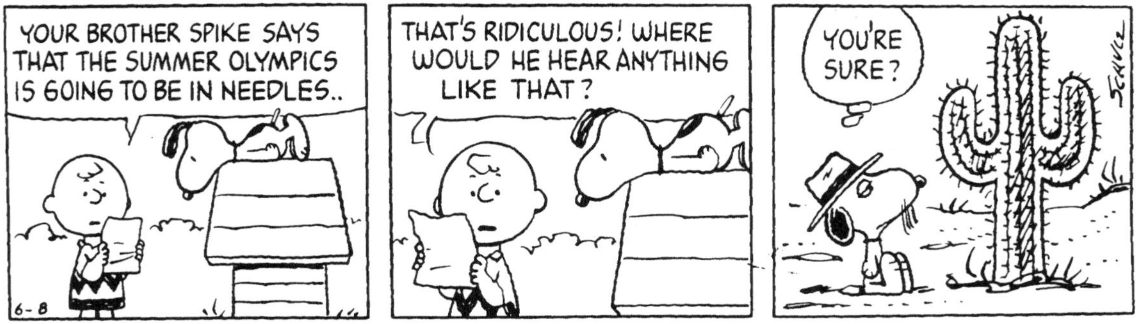
YOUR BROTHER SPIKE SAYS THAT THE SUMMER OLYMPICS IS GOING TO BE IN NEEDLES..
6-8
THAT'S RIDICULOUS! WHERE WOULD HE HEAR ANYTHING LIKE THAT?
YOU'RE SURE?
SCHULZ

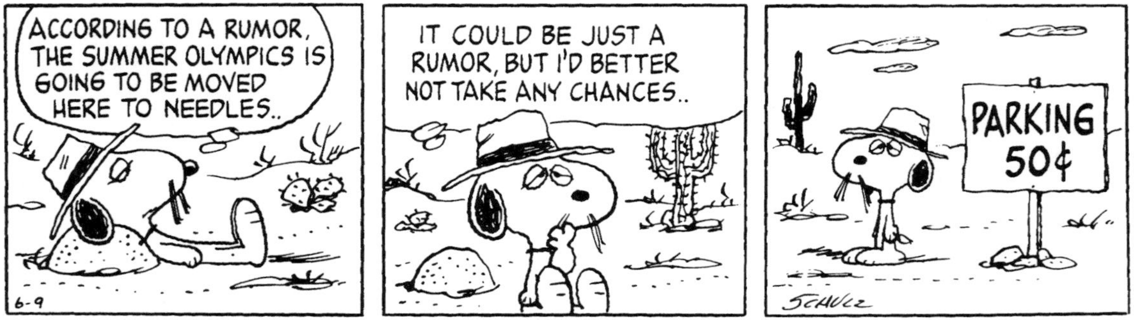
ACCORDING TO A RUMOR, THE SUMMER OLYMPICS IS GOING TO BE MOVED HERE TO NEEDLES..
IT COULD BE JUST A RUMOR, BUT I'D BETTER NOT TAKE ANY CHANCES..
PARKING 50¢

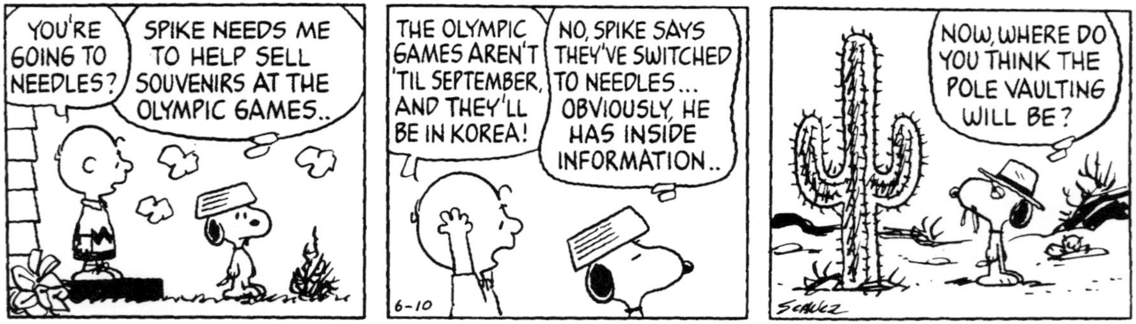
YOU'RE GOING TO NEEDLES?
SPIKE NEEDS ME TO HELP SELL SOUVENIRS AT THE OLYMPIC GAMES..
THE OLYMPIC GAMES AREN'T 'TIL SEPTEMBER, AND THEY'LL BE IN KOREA!
NO, SPIKE SAYS THEY'VE SWITCHED TO NEEDLES... OBVIOUSLY, HE HAS INSIDE INFORMATION..
NOW, WHERE DO YOU THINK THE POLE VAULTING WILL BE?

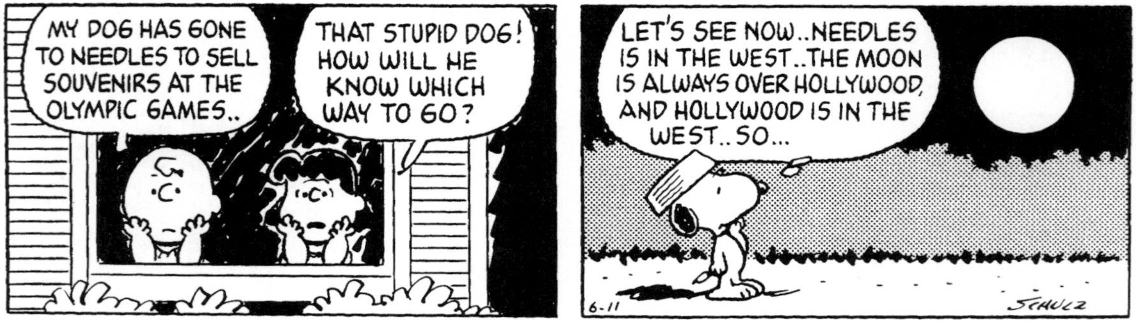
MY DOG HAS GONE TO NEEDLES TO SELL SOUVENIRS AT THE OLYMPIC GAMES..
THAT STUPID DOG! HOW WILL HE KNOW WHICH WAY TO GO?
LET'S SEE NOW..NEEDLES IS IN THE WEST..THE MOON IS ALWAYS OVER HOLLYWOOD, AND HOLLYWOOD IS IN THE WEST..SO...

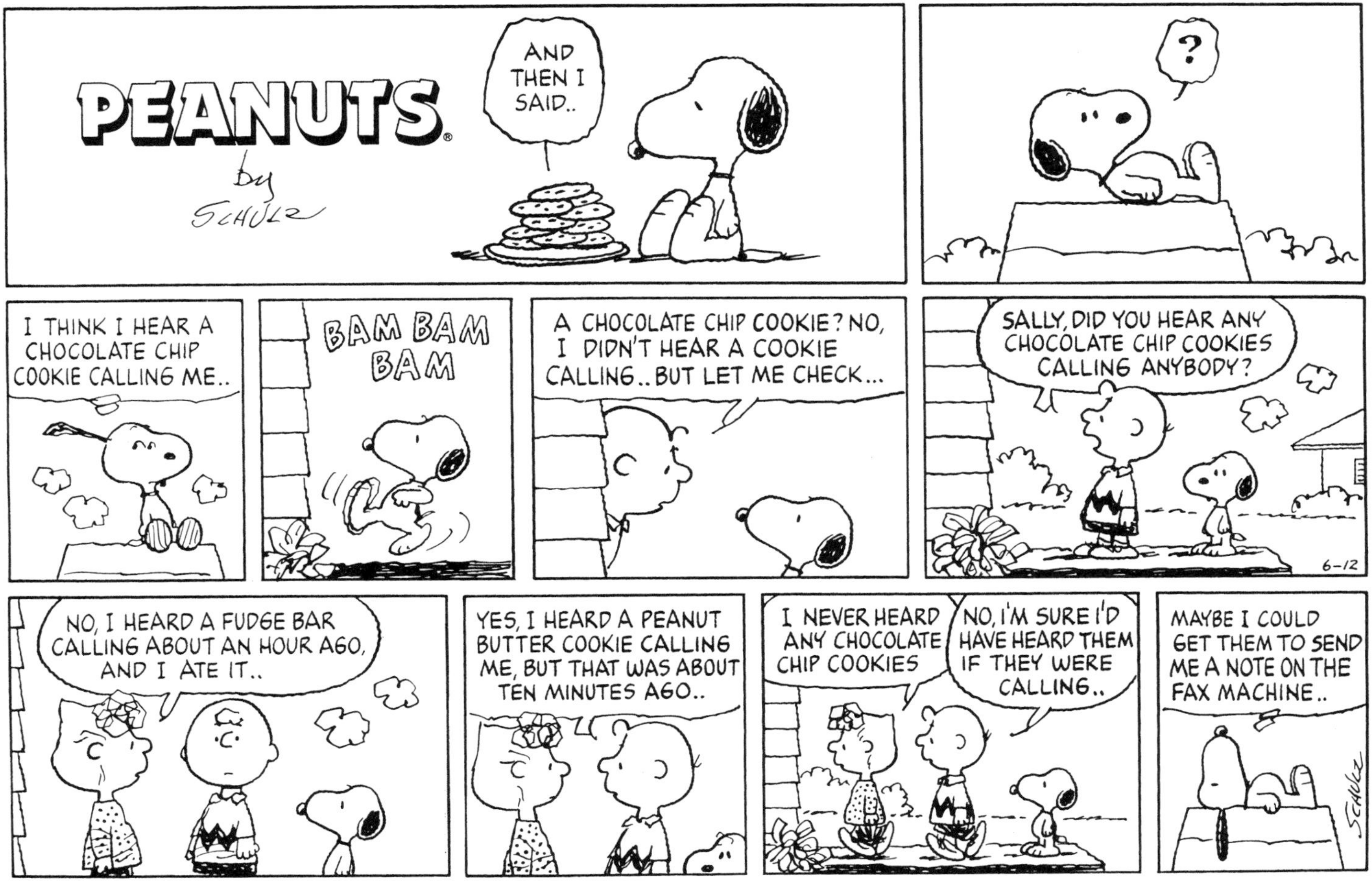
PEANUTS®
by SCHULZ
AND THEN I SAID..
?
I THINK I HEAR A CHOCOLATE CHIP COOKIE CALLING ME..
BAM BAM BAM
A CHOCOLATE CHIP COOKIE? NO, I DIDN'T HEAR A COOKIE CALLING.. BUT LET ME CHECK...
SALLY, DID YOU HEAR ANY CHOCOLATE CHIP COOKIES CALLING ANYBODY?
6-12
NO, I HEARD A FUDGE BAR CALLING ABOUT AN HOUR AGO, AND I ATE IT..
YES, I HEARD A PEANUT BUTTER COOKIE CALLING ME, BUT THAT WAS ABOUT TEN MINUTES AGO..
I NEVER HEARD ANY CHOCOLATE CHIP COOKIES
NO, I'M SURE I'D HAVE HEARD THEM IF THEY WERE CALLING..
MAYBE I COULD GET THEM TO SEND ME A NOTE ON THE FAX MACHINE..
SCHULZ

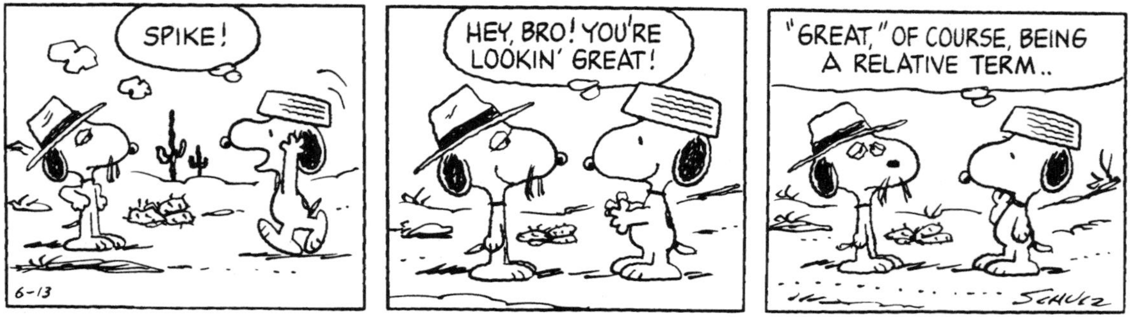
SPIKE!
6-13
HEY, BRO! YOU'RE LOOKIN' GREAT!
"GREAT," OF COURSE, BEING A RELATIVE TERM..

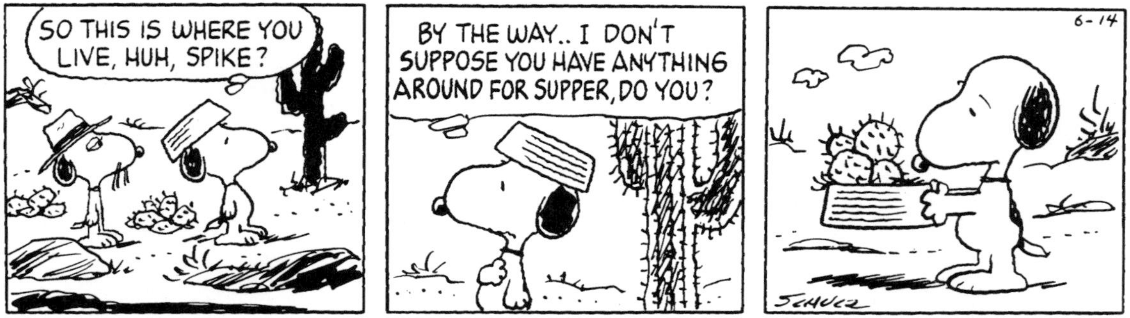
SO THIS IS WHERE YOU LIVE, HUH, SPIKE?
BY THE WAY.. I DON'T SUPPOSE YOU HAVE ANYTHING AROUND FOR SUPPER, DO YOU?
6-14

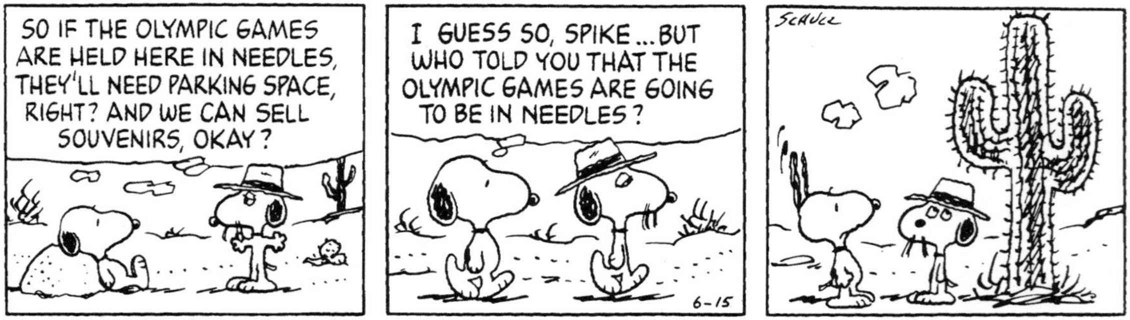
SO IF THE OLYMPIC GAMES ARE HELD HERE IN NEEDLES, THEY'LL NEED PARKING SPACE, RIGHT? AND WE CAN SELL SOUVENIRS, OKAY?
I GUESS SO, SPIKE...BUT WHO TOLD YOU THAT THE OLYMPIC GAMES ARE GOING TO BE IN NEEDLES?
6-15

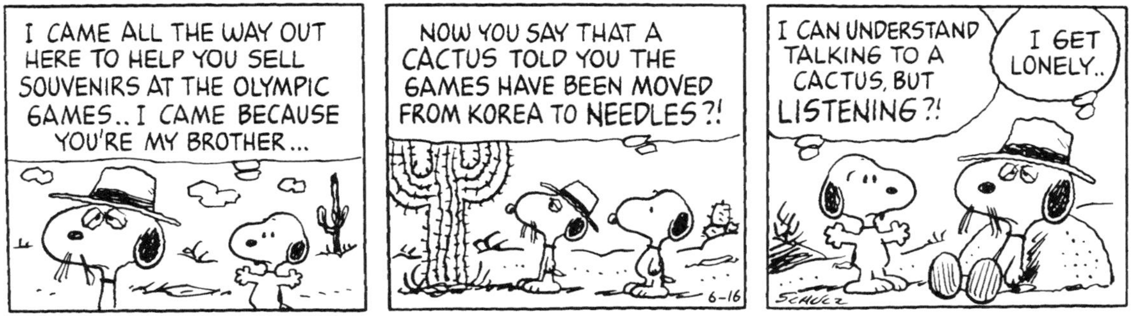
I CAME ALL THE WAY OUT HERE TO HELP YOU SELL SOUVENIRS AT THE OLYMPIC GAMES.. I CAME BECAUSE YOU'RE MY BROTHER...
NOW YOU SAY THAT A CACTUS TOLD YOU THE GAMES HAVE BEEN MOVED FROM KOREA TO NEEDLES?!
6-16
I CAN UNDERSTAND TALKING TO A CACTUS, BUT LISTENING?!
I GET LONELY..
SCHULZ

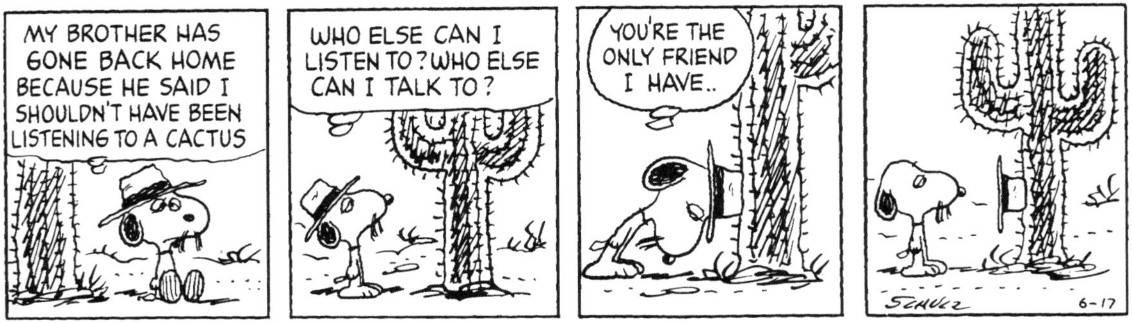
MY BROTHER HAS GONE BACK HOME BECAUSE HE SAID I SHOULDN'T HAVE BEEN LISTENING TO A CACTUS
WHO ELSE CAN I LISTEN TO? WHO ELSE CAN I TALK TO?
YOU'RE THE ONLY FRIEND I HAVE..
SCHULZ
6-17

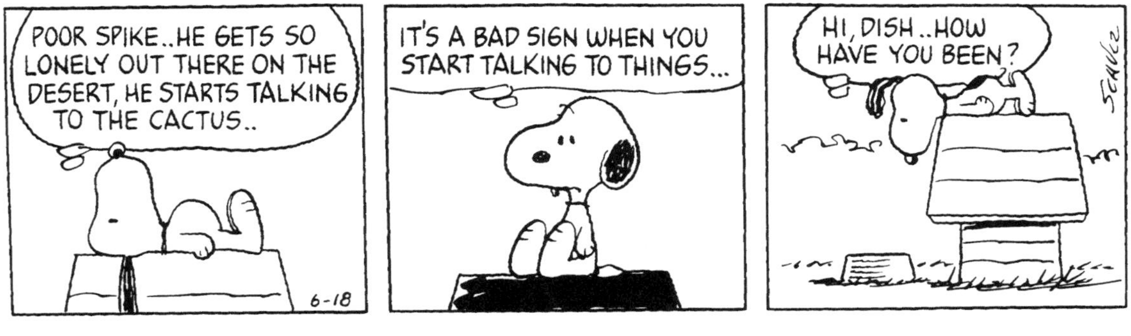
POOR SPIKE..HE GETS SO LONELY OUT THERE ON THE DESERT, HE STARTS TALKING TO THE CACTUS..
6-18
IT'S A BAD SIGN WHEN YOU START TALKING TO THINGS...
HI, DISH..HOW HAVE YOU BEEN?
SCHULZ

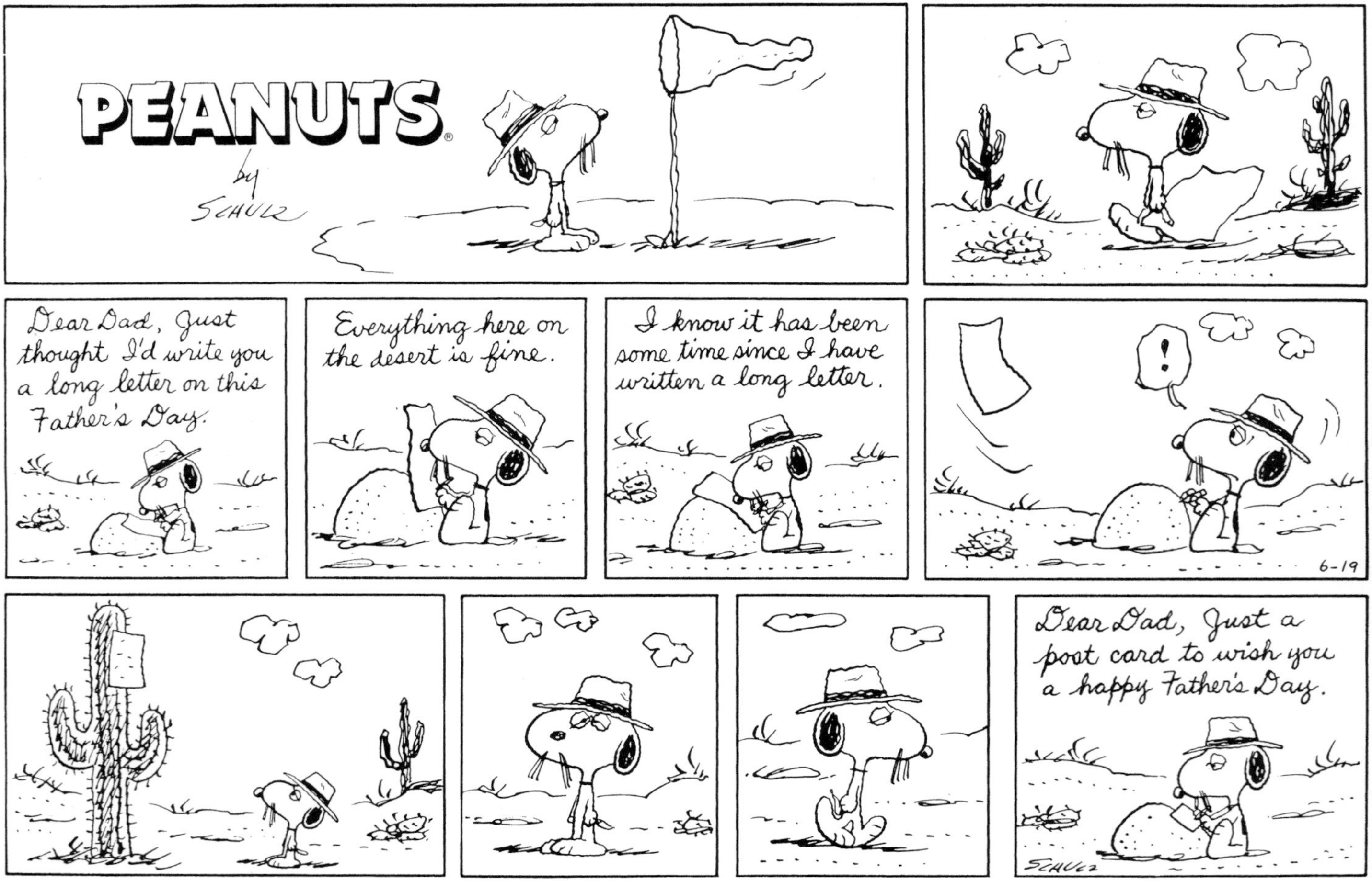
PEANUTS
by SCHULZ
Dear Dad, Just thought I'd write you a long letter on this Father's Day.
Everything here on the desert is fine.
I know it has been some time since I have written a long letter.
!
6-19
Dear Dad, Just a post card to wish you a happy Father's Day.
SCHULZ

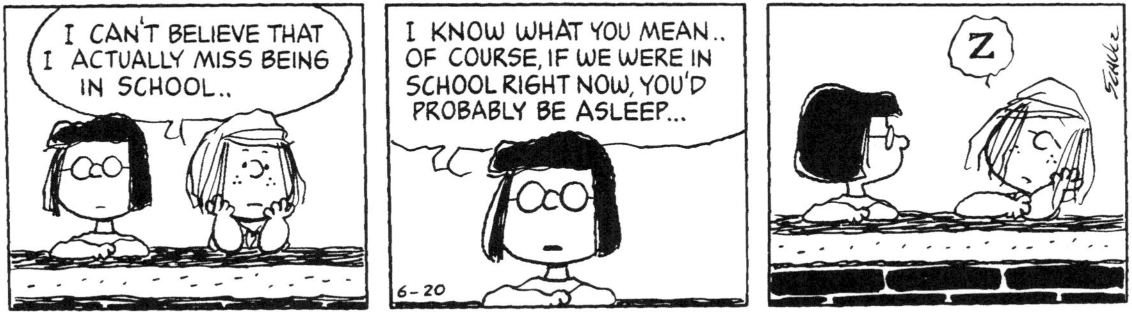
I CAN'T BELIEVE THAT I ACTUALLY MISS BEING IN SCHOOL..
I KNOW WHAT YOU MEAN.. OF COURSE, IF WE WERE IN SCHOOL RIGHT NOW, YOU'D PROBABLY BE ASLEEP...
6-20
Z

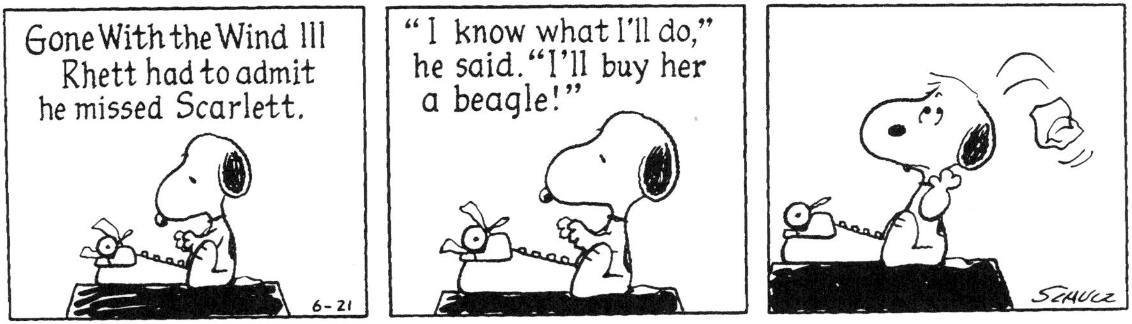
Gone With the Wind III
Rhett had to admit he missed Scarlett.
6-21
"I know what I'll do," he said. "I'll buy her a beagle!"

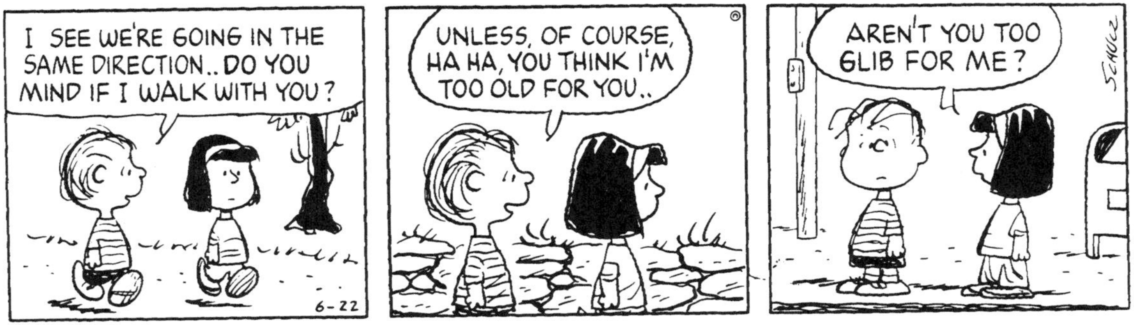
I SEE WE'RE GOING IN THE SAME DIRECTION.. DO YOU MIND IF I WALK WITH YOU?
6-22
UNLESS, OF COURSE, HA HA, YOU THINK I'M TOO OLD FOR YOU..
AREN'T YOU TOO GLIB FOR ME?

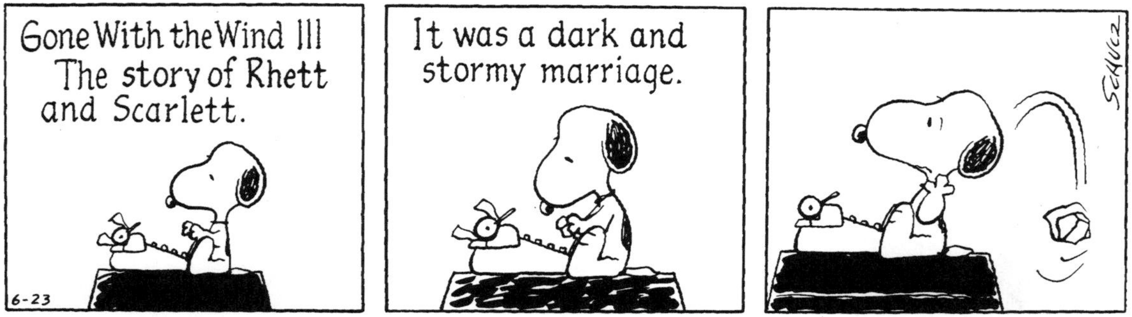
Gone With the Wind III
The story of Rhett and Scarlett.
It was a dark and stormy marriage.
6-23
SCHULZ

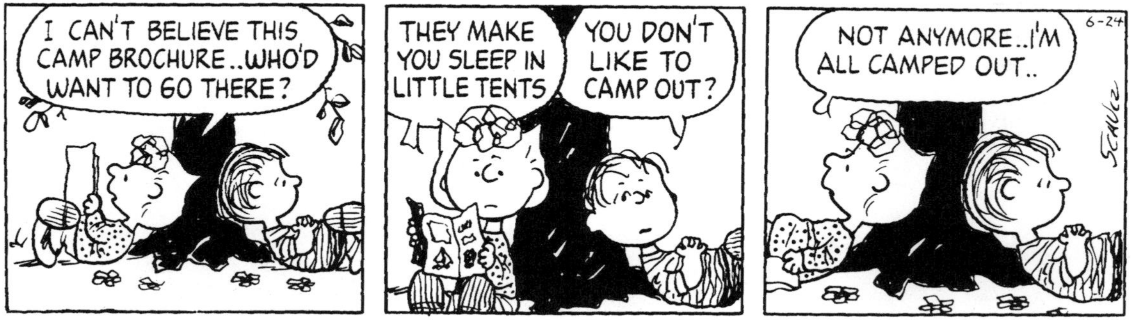
I CAN'T BELIEVE THIS CAMP BROCHURE..WHO'D WANT TO GO THERE?
THEY MAKE YOU SLEEP IN LITTLE TENTS
YOU DON'T LIKE TO CAMP OUT?
NOT ANYMORE..I'M ALL CAMPED OUT..
6-24
SCHULZ

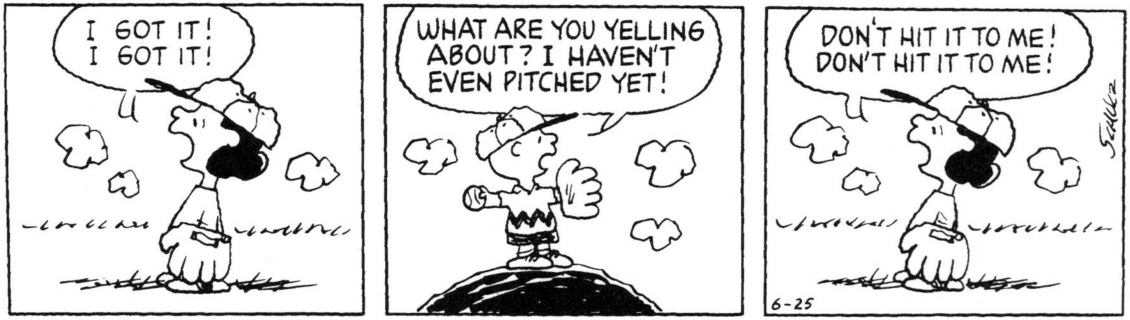
I GOT IT! I GOT IT!
WHAT ARE YOU YELLING ABOUT? I HAVEN'T EVEN PITCHED YET!
DON'T HIT IT TO ME! DON'T HIT IT TO ME!
6-25
SCHULZ

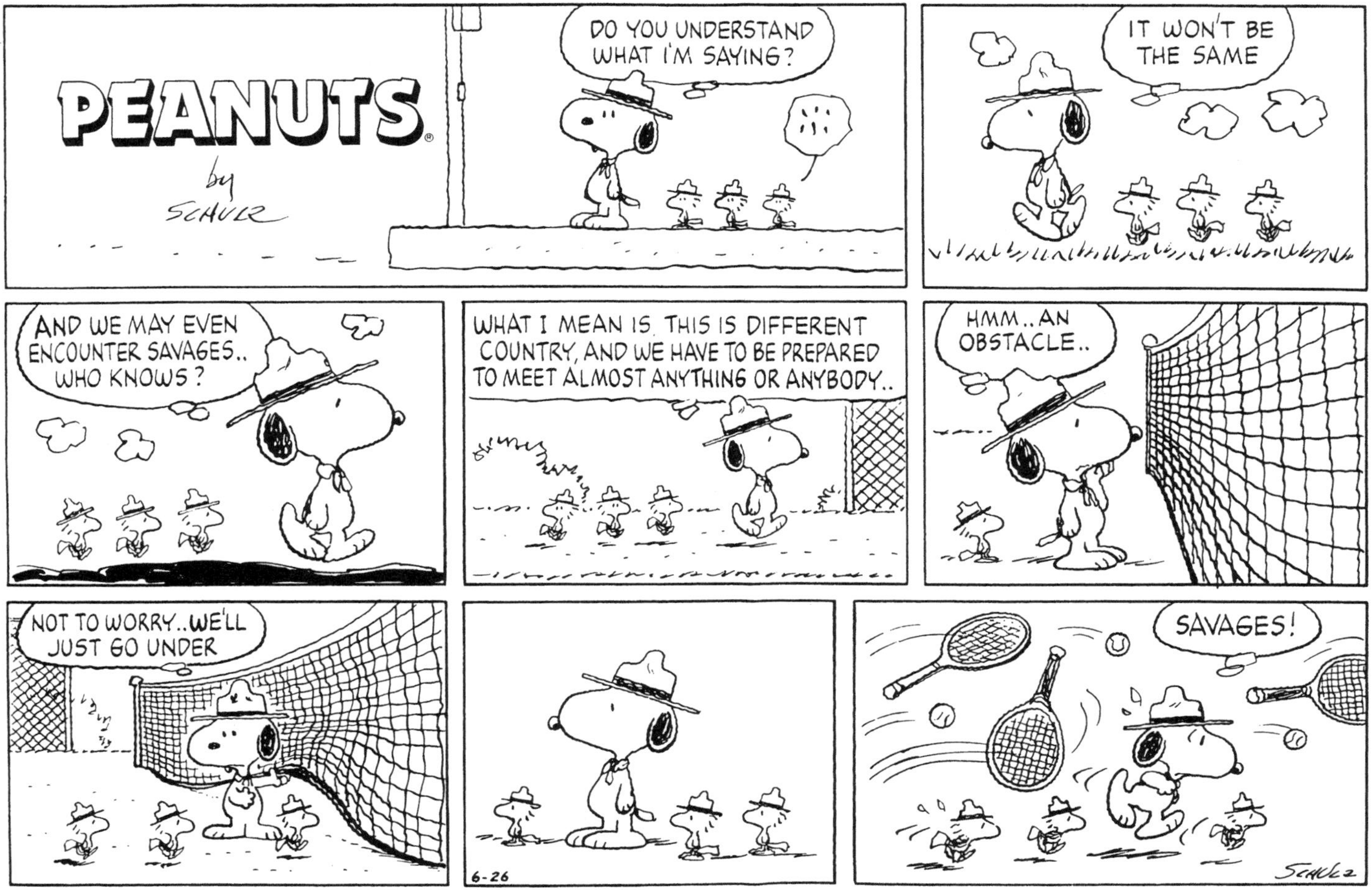
PEANUTS
by SCHULZ
DO YOU UNDERSTAND WHAT I'M SAYING?
IT WON'T BE THE SAME
AND WE MAY EVEN ENCOUNTER SAVAGES.. WHO KNOWS?
WHAT I MEAN IS, THIS IS DIFFERENT COUNTRY, AND WE HAVE TO BE PREPARED TO MEET ALMOST ANYTHING OR ANYBODY..
HMM..AN OBSTACLE..
NOT TO WORRY..WE'LL JUST GO UNDER
6-26
SAVAGES!
SCHULZ

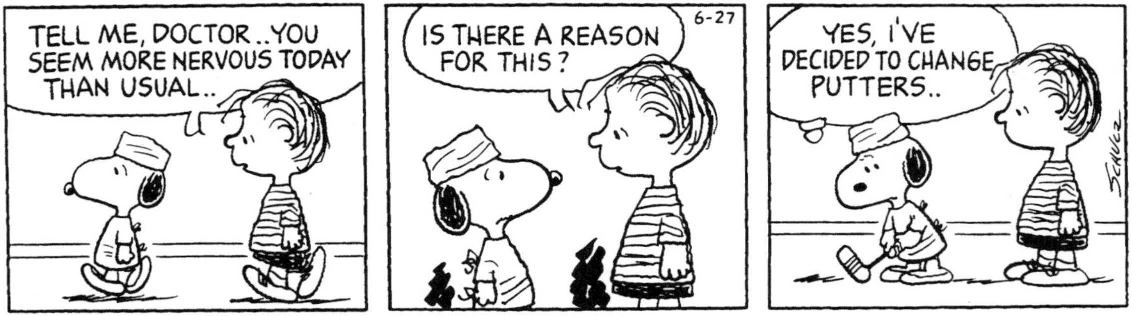
TELL ME, DOCTOR..YOU SEEM MORE NERVOUS TODAY THAN USUAL..
IS THERE A REASON FOR THIS?
6-27
YES, I'VE DECIDED TO CHANGE PUTTERS..

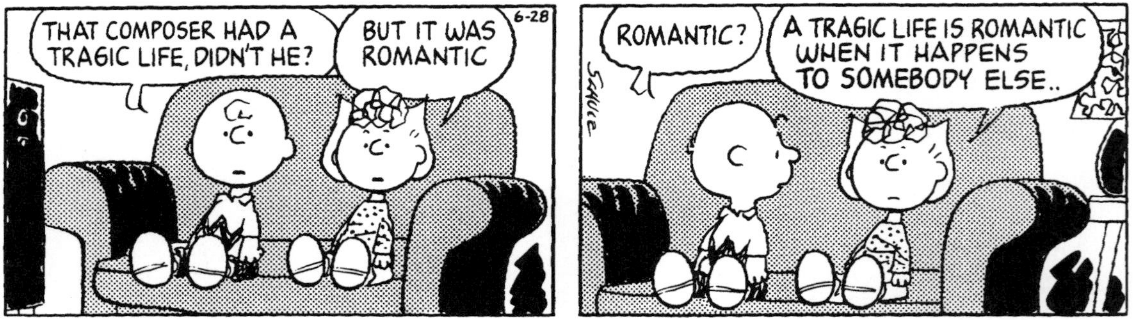
THAT COMPOSER HAD A TRAGIC LIFE, DIDN'T HE?
BUT IT WAS ROMANTIC
6-28
ROMANTIC?
A TRAGIC LIFE IS ROMANTIC WHEN IT HAPPENS TO SOMEBODY ELSE..

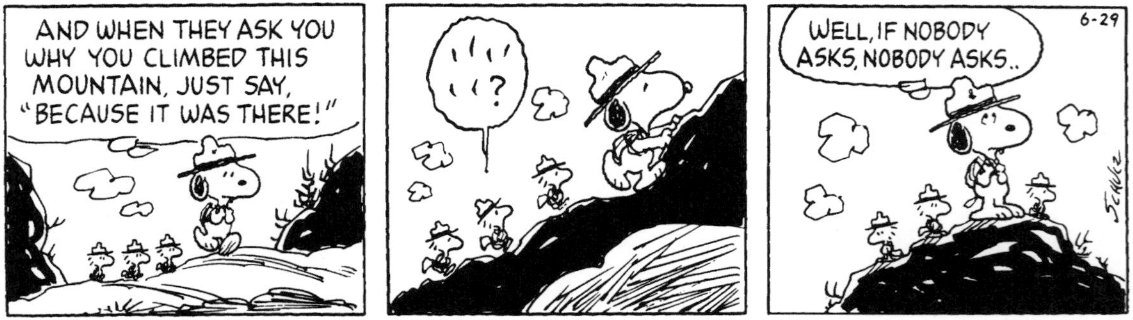
AND WHEN THEY ASK YOU WHY YOU CLIMBED THIS MOUNTAIN, JUST SAY, "BECAUSE IT WAS THERE!"
?
6-29
WELL, IF NOBODY ASKS, NOBODY ASKS..

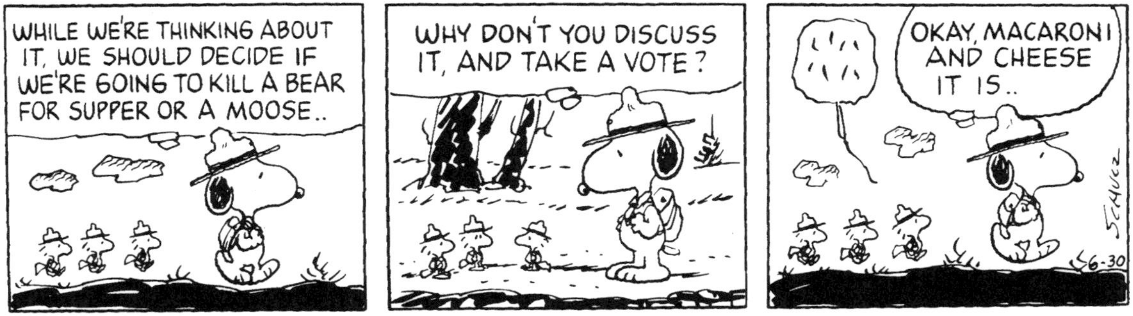
WHILE WE'RE THINKING ABOUT IT, WE SHOULD DECIDE IF WE'RE GOING TO KILL A BEAR FOR SUPPER OR A MOOSE..
WHY DON'T YOU DISCUSS IT, AND TAKE A VOTE?
OKAY, MACARONI AND CHEESE IT IS..

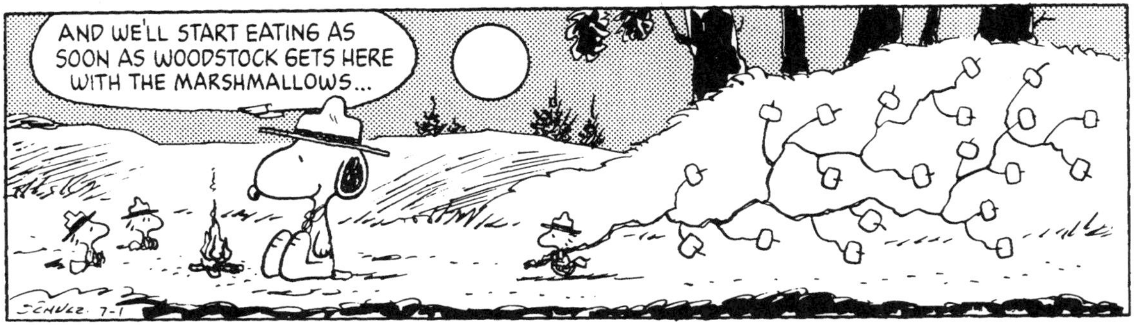
AND WE'LL START EATING AS SOON AS WOODSTOCK GETS HERE WITH THE MARSHMALLOWS...

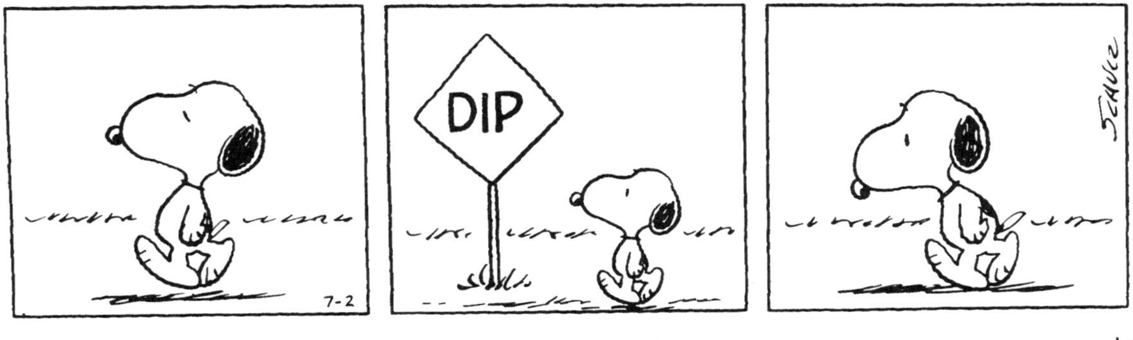
DIP

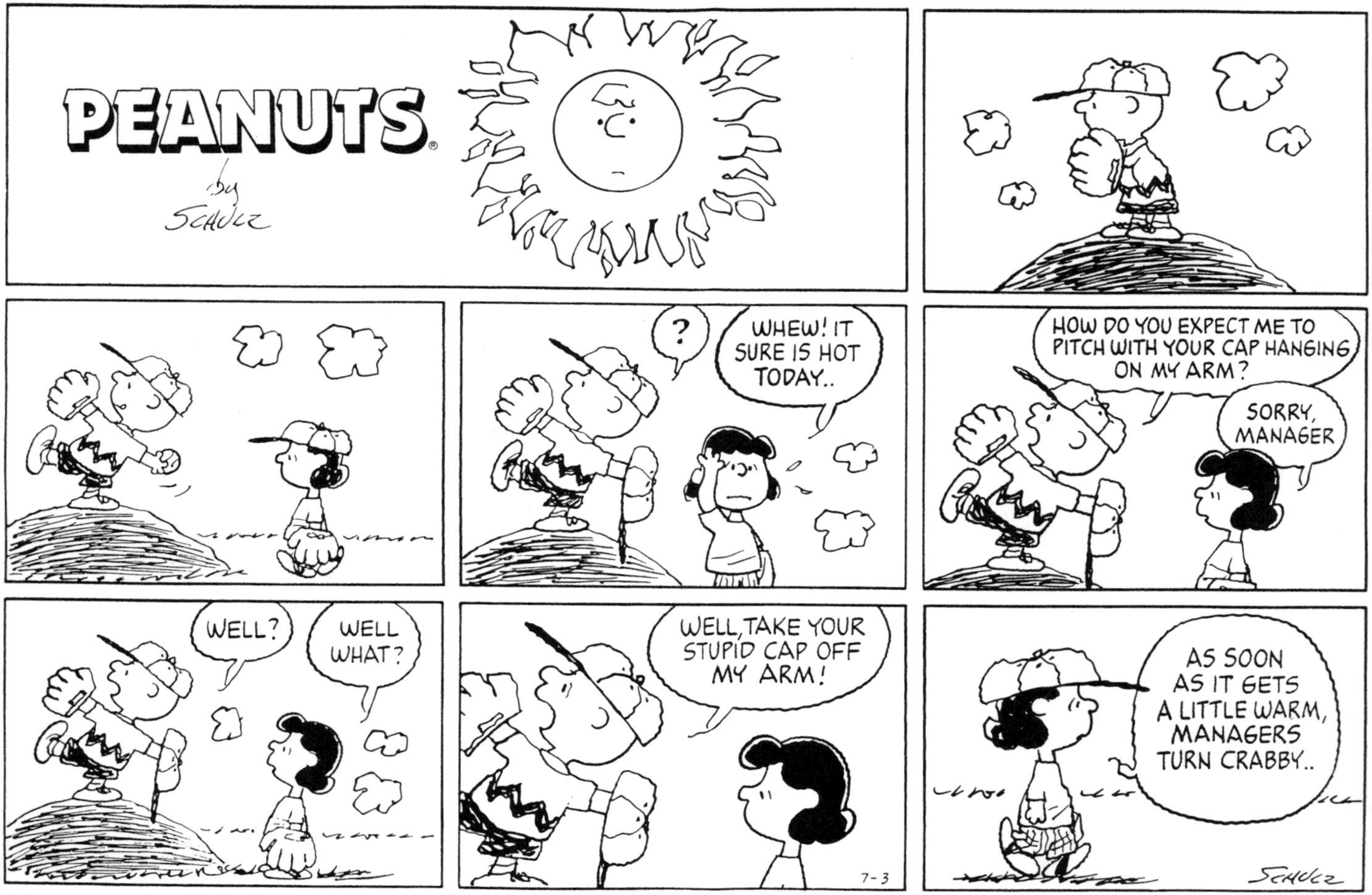
PEANUTS
by SCHULZ
?
WHEW! IT SURE IS HOT TODAY..
HOW DO YOU EXPECT ME TO PITCH WITH YOUR CAP HANGING ON MY ARM?
SORRY, MANAGER
WELL?
WELL WHAT?
WELL, TAKE YOUR STUPID CAP OFF MY ARM!
7-3
AS SOON AS IT GETS A LITTLE WARM, MANAGERS TURN CRABBY..
SCHULZ

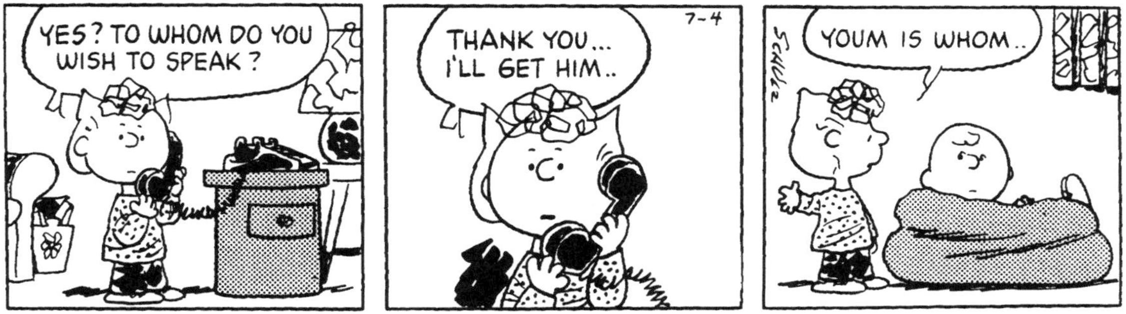
YES? TO WHOM DO YOU WISH TO SPEAK?
7-4
THANK YOU... I'LL GET HIM..
SCHULZ
YOUM IS WHOM..

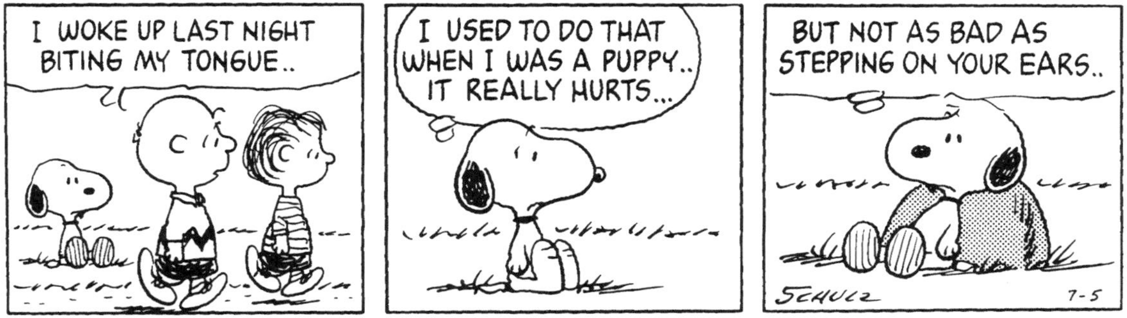
I WOKE UP LAST NIGHT BITING MY TONGUE..
I USED TO DO THAT WHEN I WAS A PUPPY.. IT REALLY HURTS...
BUT NOT AS BAD AS STEPPING ON YOUR EARS..
SCHULZ
7-5

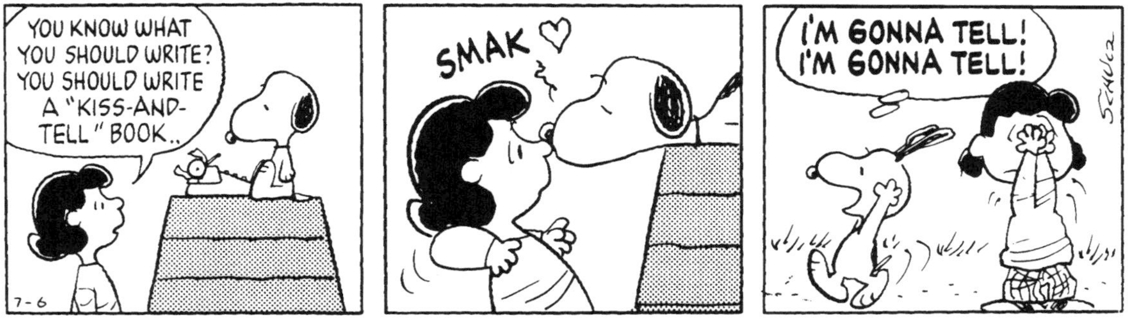
YOU KNOW WHAT YOU SHOULD WRITE? YOU SHOULD WRITE A "KISS-AND-TELL" BOOK..
7-6
SMAK
I'M GONNA TELL! I'M GONNA TELL!
SCHULZ

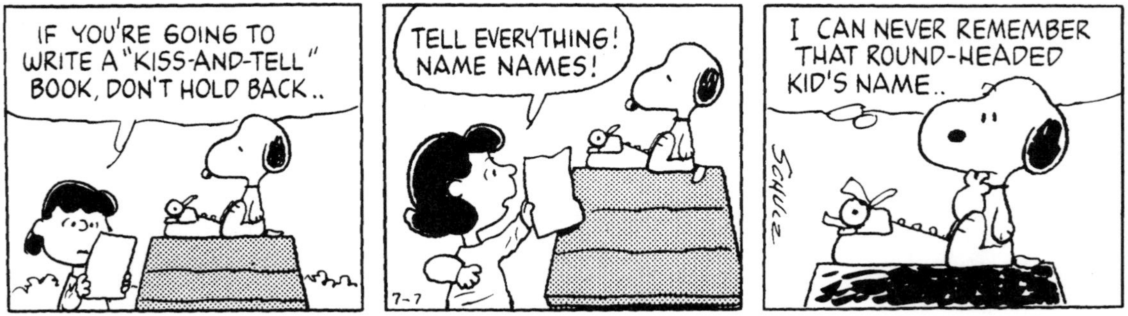
IF YOU'RE GOING TO WRITE A "KISS-AND-TELL" BOOK, DON'T HOLD BACK..
TELL EVERYTHING! NAME NAMES!
7-7
I CAN NEVER REMEMBER THAT ROUND-HEADED KID'S NAME..
SCHULZ

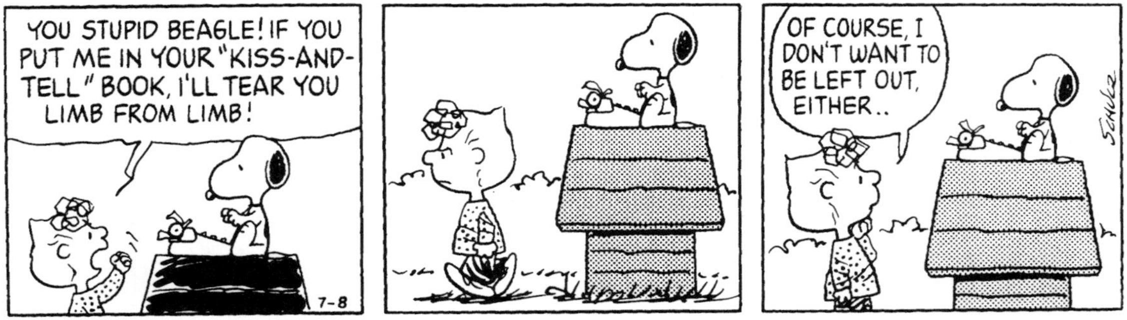
YOU STUPID BEAGLE! IF YOU PUT ME IN YOUR "KISS-AND-TELL" BOOK, I'LL TEAR YOU LIMB FROM LIMB!
7-8
OF COURSE, I DON'T WANT TO BE LEFT OUT, EITHER..
SCHULZ

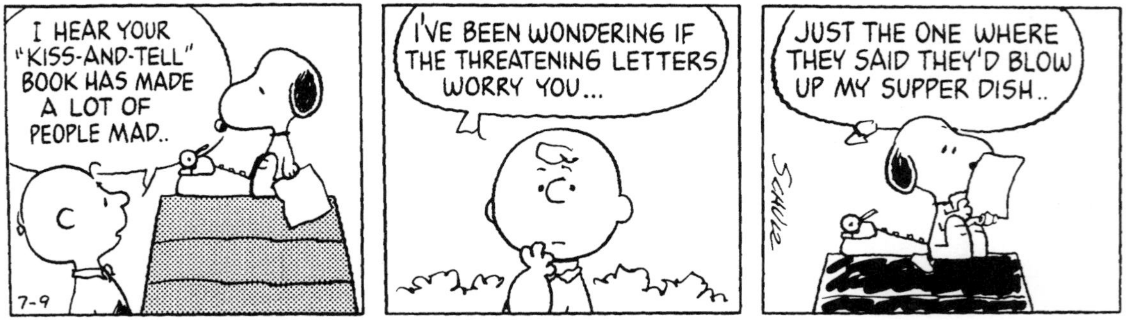
I HEAR YOUR "KISS-AND-TELL" BOOK HAS MADE A LOT OF PEOPLE MAD..
7-9
I'VE BEEN WONDERING IF THE THREATENING LETTERS WORRY YOU...
JUST THE ONE WHERE THEY SAID THEY'D BLOW UP MY SUPPER DISH..
SCHULZ

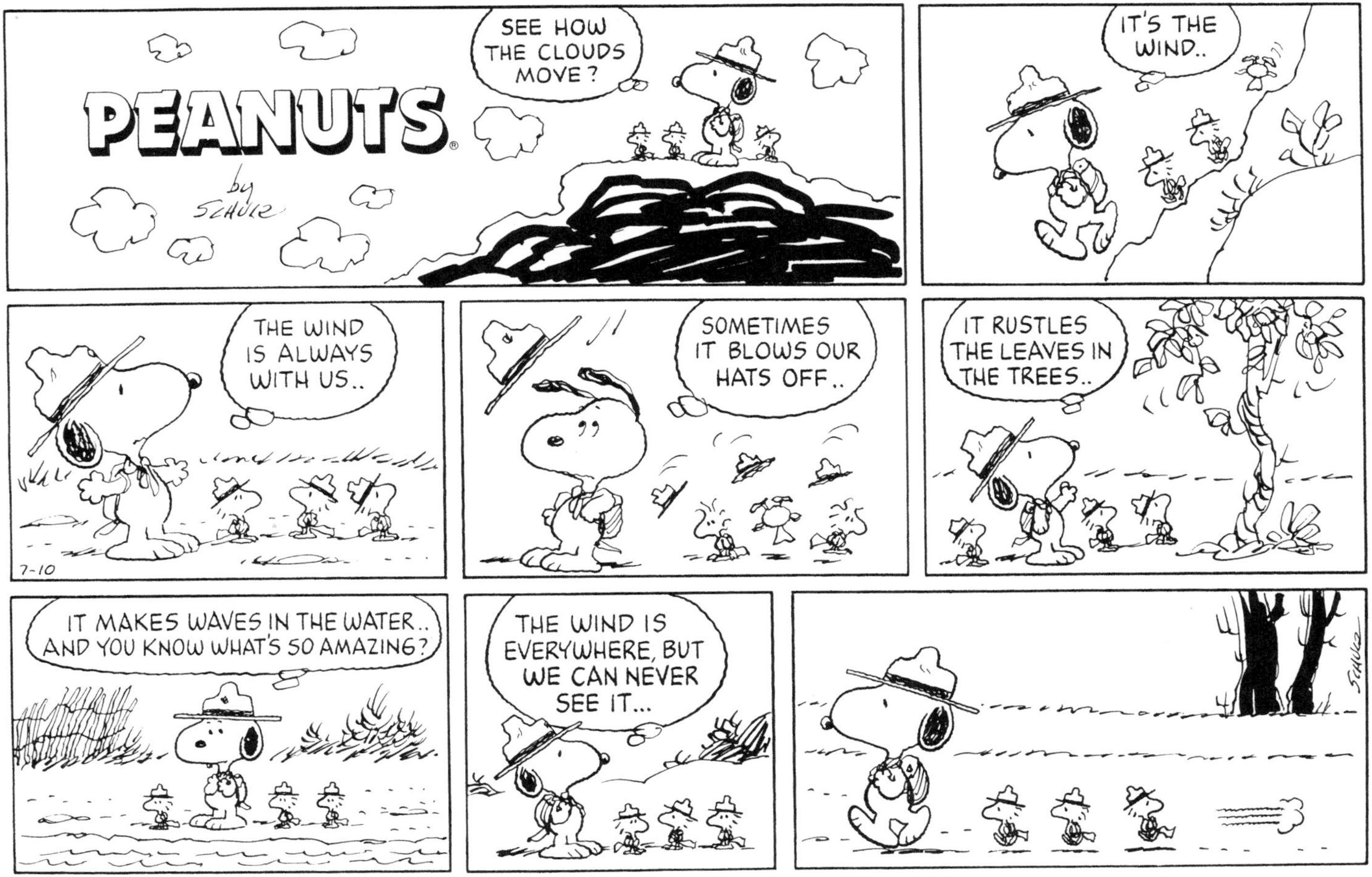
PEANUTS
by SCHULZ
SEE HOW THE CLOUDS MOVE?
IT'S THE WIND..
THE WIND IS ALWAYS WITH US..
7-10
SOMETIMES IT BLOWS OUR HATS OFF..
IT RUSTLES THE LEAVES IN THE TREES..
IT MAKES WAVES IN THE WATER.. AND YOU KNOW WHAT'S SO AMAZING?
THE WIND IS EVERYWHERE, BUT WE CAN NEVER SEE IT...
SCHULZ

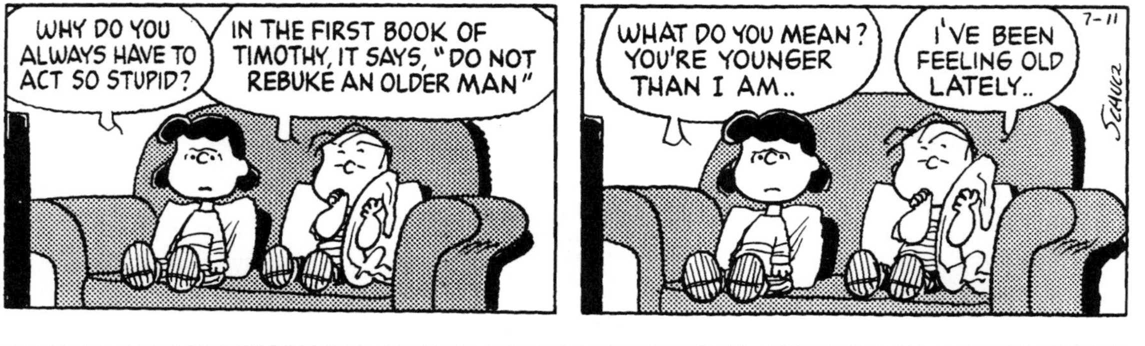
WHY DO YOU ALWAYS HAVE TO ACT SO STUPID?
IN THE FIRST BOOK OF TIMOTHY, IT SAYS, "DO NOT REBUKE AN OLDER MAN"
WHAT DO YOU MEAN? YOU'RE YOUNGER THAN I AM..
I'VE BEEN FEELING OLD LATELY..
7-11

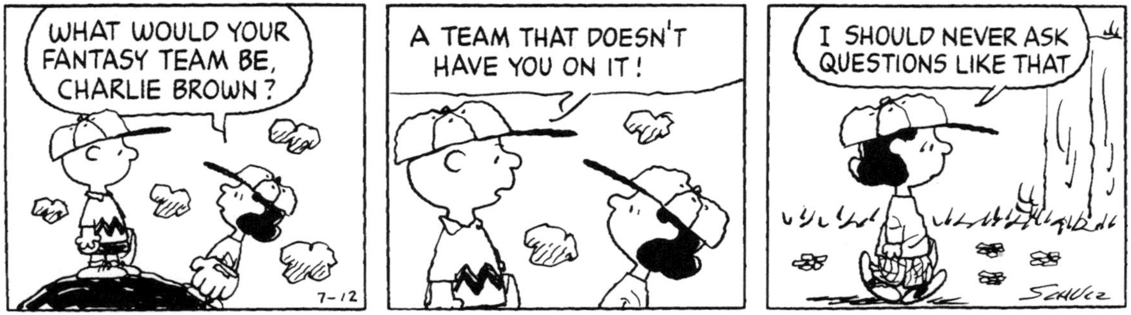
WHAT WOULD YOUR FANTASY TEAM BE, CHARLIE BROWN?
7-12
A TEAM THAT DOESN'T HAVE YOU ON IT!
I SHOULD NEVER ASK QUESTIONS LIKE THAT

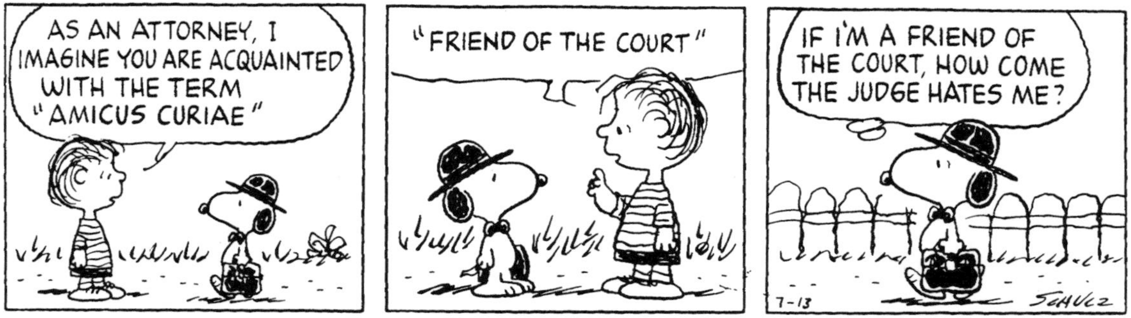
AS AN ATTORNEY, I IMAGINE YOU ARE ACQUAINTED WITH THE TERM "AMICUS CURIAE"
"FRIEND OF THE COURT"
IF I'M A FRIEND OF THE COURT, HOW COME THE JUDGE HATES ME?
7-13

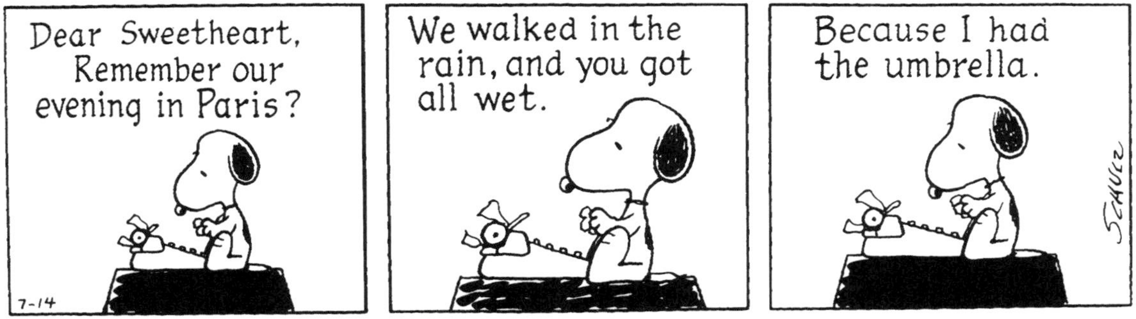
Dear Sweetheart,
Remember our evening in Paris?
7-14
We walked in the rain, and you got all wet.
Because I had the umbrella.
SCHULZ

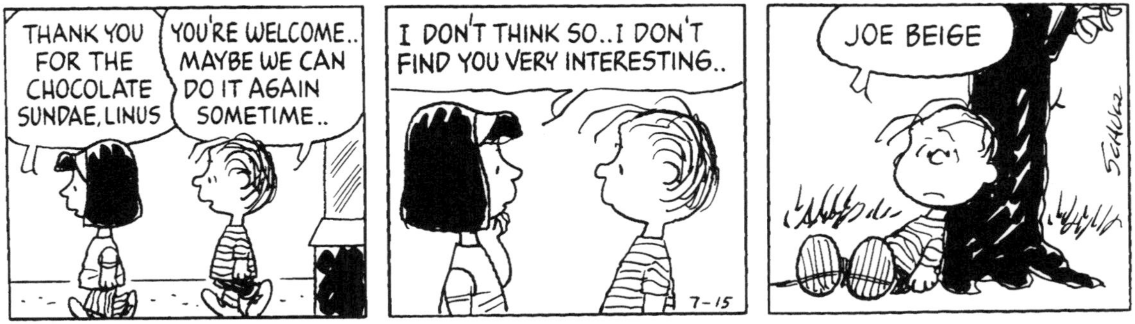
THANK YOU FOR THE CHOCOLATE SUNDAE, LINUS
YOU'RE WELCOME.. MAYBE WE CAN DO IT AGAIN SOMETIME..
I DON'T THINK SO..I DON'T FIND YOU VERY INTERESTING..
7-15
JOE BEIGE
SCHULZ

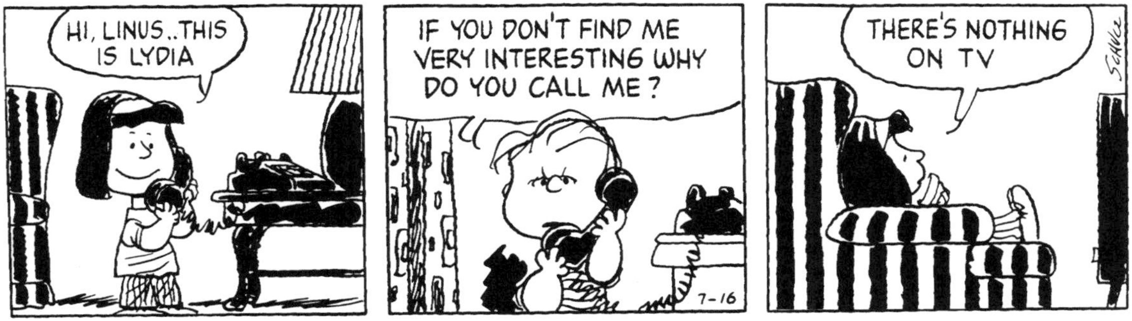
HI, LINUS..THIS IS LYDIA
IF YOU DON'T FIND ME VERY INTERESTING WHY DO YOU CALL ME?
7-16
THERE'S NOTHING ON TV
SCHULZ

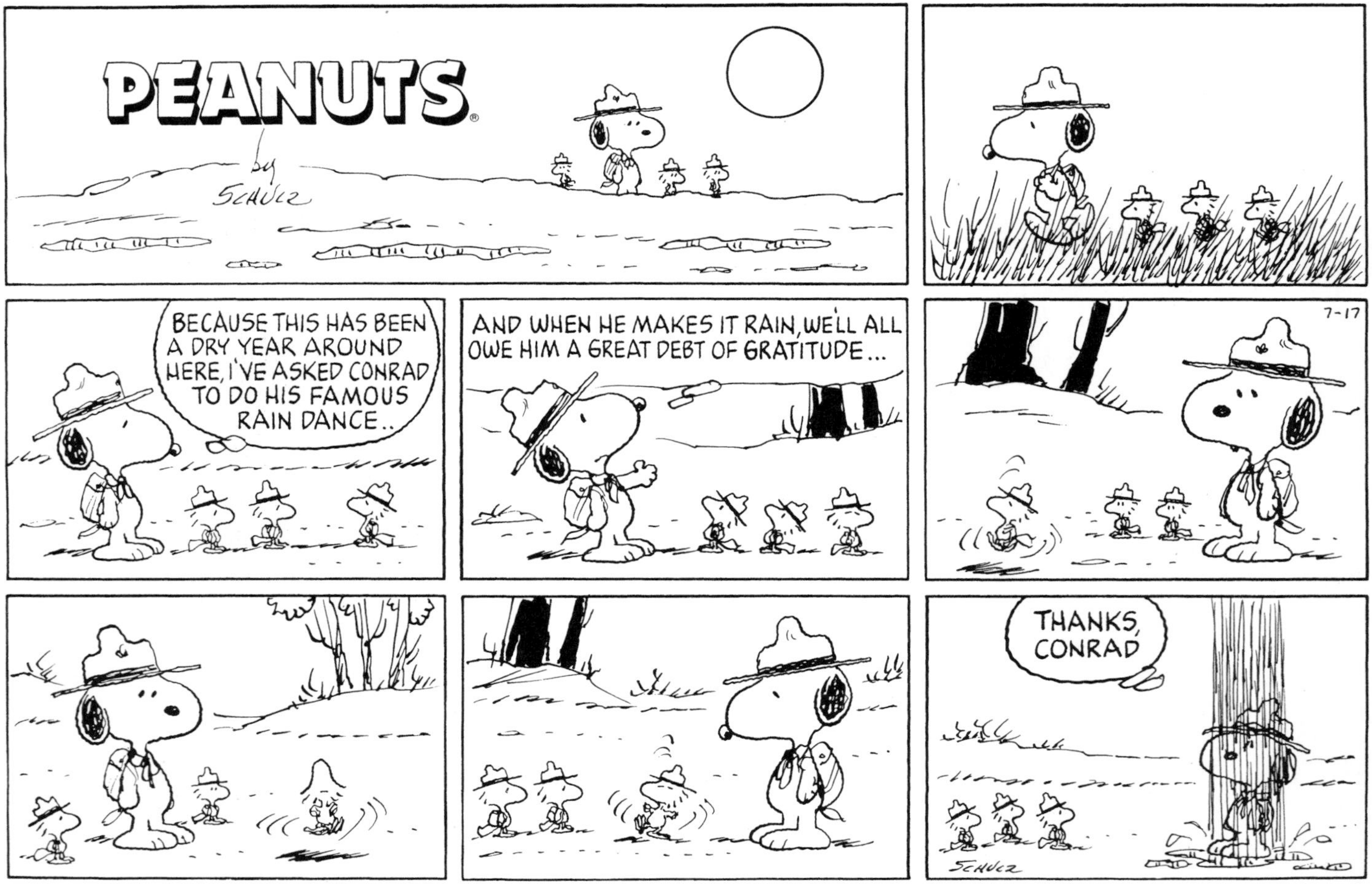
PEANUTS
by SCHULZ
BECAUSE THIS HAS BEEN A DRY YEAR AROUND HERE, I'VE ASKED CONRAD TO DO HIS FAMOUS RAIN DANCE..
AND WHEN HE MAKES IT RAIN, WE'LL ALL OWE HIM A GREAT DEBT OF GRATITUDE...
7-17
THANKS, CONRAD
SCHULZ

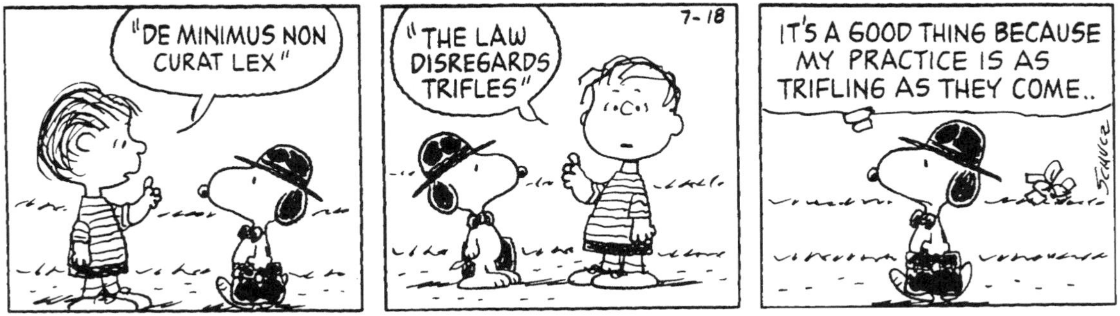
"DE MINIMUS NON CURAT LEX"
7-18
"THE LAW DISREGARDS TRIFLES"
IT'S A GOOD THING BECAUSE MY PRACTICE IS AS TRIFLING AS THEY COME..

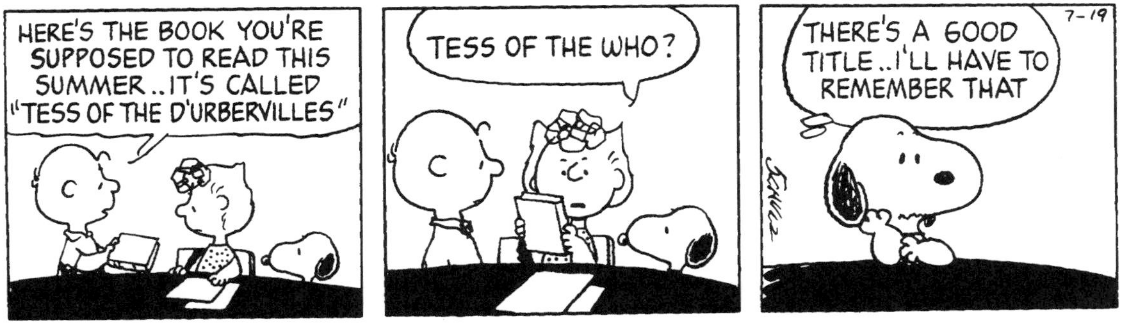
HERE'S THE BOOK YOU'RE SUPPOSED TO READ THIS SUMMER..IT'S CALLED "TESS OF THE D'URBERVILLES"
TESS OF THE WHO?
7-19
THERE'S A GOOD TITLE..I'LL HAVE TO REMEMBER THAT

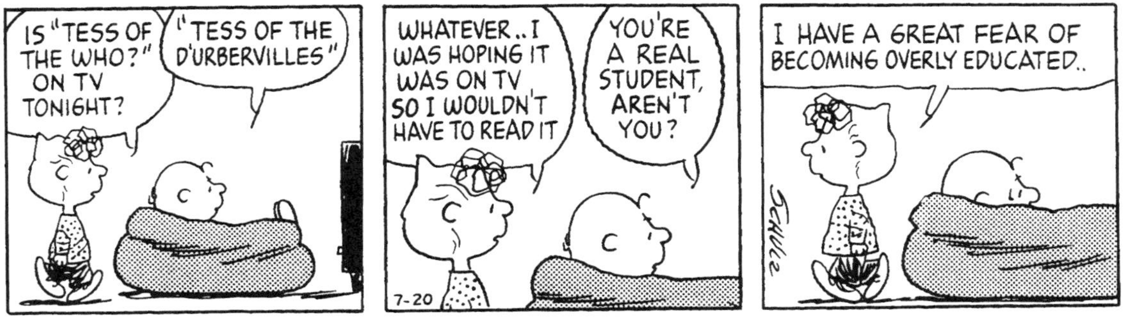
IS "TESS OF THE WHO?" ON TV TONIGHT?
"TESS OF THE D'URBERVILLES"
WHATEVER..I WAS HOPING IT WAS ON TV SO I WOULDN'T HAVE TO READ IT
YOU'RE A REAL STUDENT, AREN'T YOU?
7-20
I HAVE A GREAT FEAR OF BECOMING OVERLY EDUCATED..

HERE'S A LIST OF ALL THE BEST AND THE WORST JOBS

I HATE TO TELL YOU THIS...

ROCKS AREN'T EVEN ON THE LIST..

DO YOU FIND THAT BEING A ROCK IS BORING?

7-22

I MEAN, COMPARE YOUR LIFE WITH THE LIFE I LEAD...

SITTING ALONE IN THE DESERT TALKING TO A ROCK..

I'M FIXING YOUR DINNER RIGHT NOW..

WHILE YOU'RE WAITING, I THOUGHT YOU MIGHT LIKE SOME SOUP..AND WHILE YOU'RE WAITING FOR THE SOUP, I'LL BRING YOU SOME FRENCH BREAD..

7-23

AND WHILE YOU'RE WAITING FOR THE BREAD, I THOUGHT YOU MIGHT LIKE SOME CARROTS...

WHAT DO I EAT WHILE I'M WAITING FOR THE CARROTS?

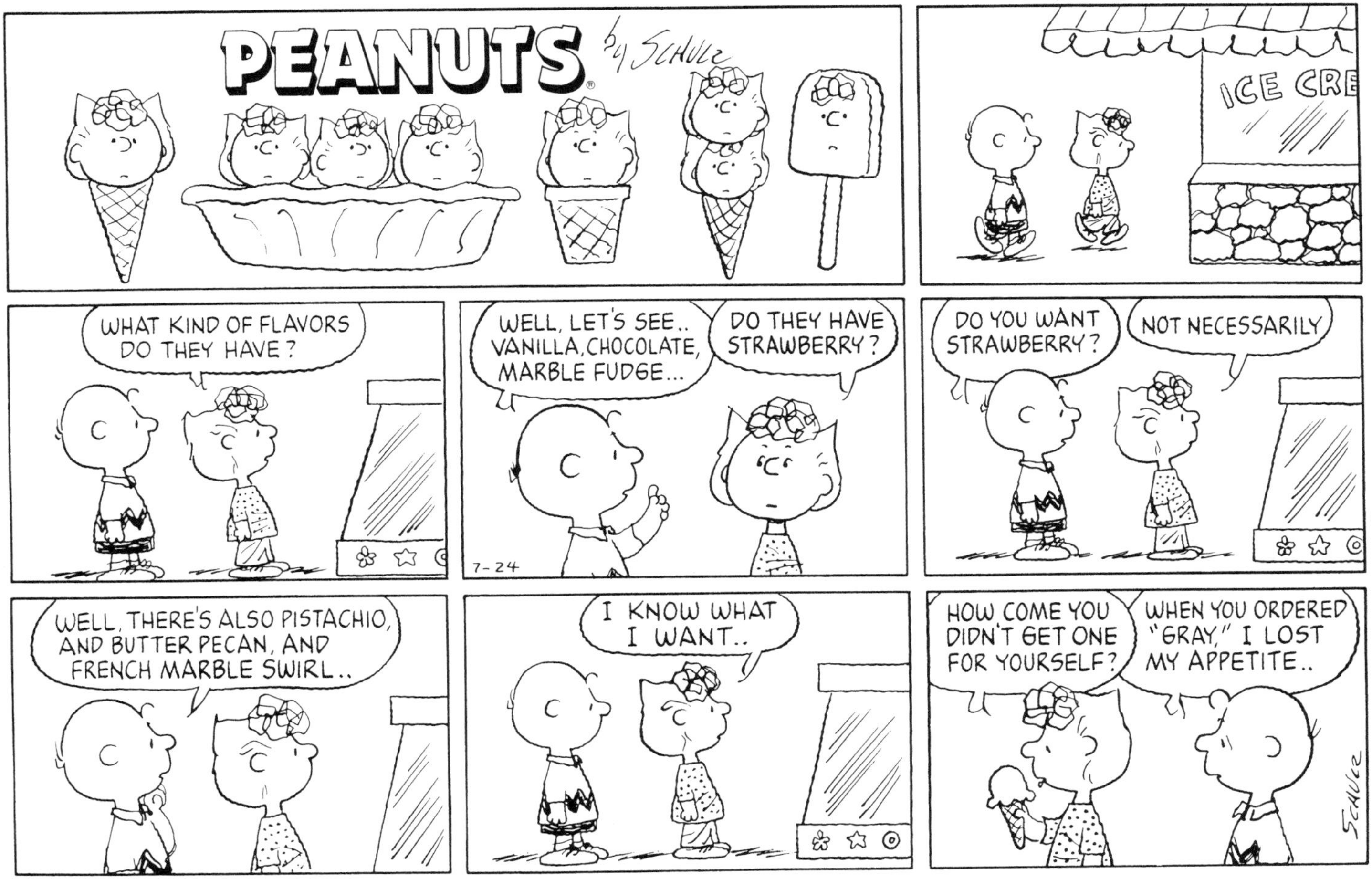
PEANUTS
by SCHULZ
ICE CRE
WHAT KIND OF FLAVORS DO THEY HAVE?
WELL, LET'S SEE.. VANILLA, CHOCOLATE, MARBLE FUDGE...
DO THEY HAVE STRAWBERRY?
7-24
DO YOU WANT STRAWBERRY?
NOT NECESSARILY
WELL, THERE'S ALSO PISTACHIO, AND BUTTER PECAN, AND FRENCH MARBLE SWIRL..
I KNOW WHAT I WANT..
HOW COME YOU DIDN'T GET ONE FOR YOURSELF?
WHEN YOU ORDERED "GRAY," I LOST MY APPETITE..
SCHULZ

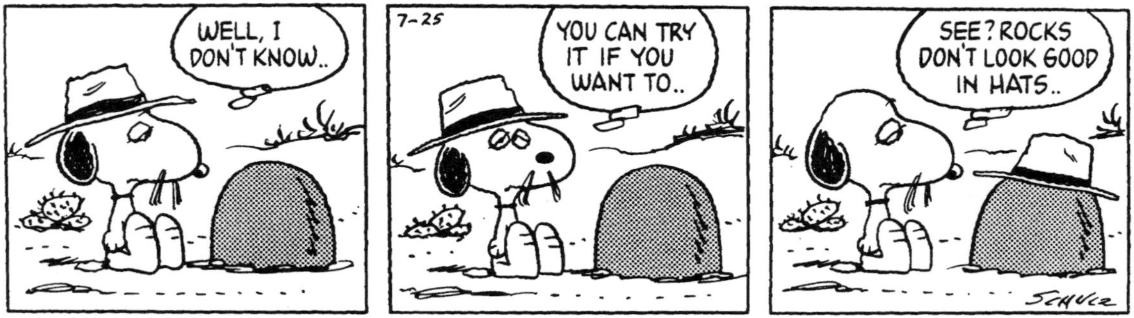
7-25
WELL, I DON'T KNOW..
YOU CAN TRY IT IF YOU WANT TO..
SEE? ROCKS DON'T LOOK GOOD IN HATS..

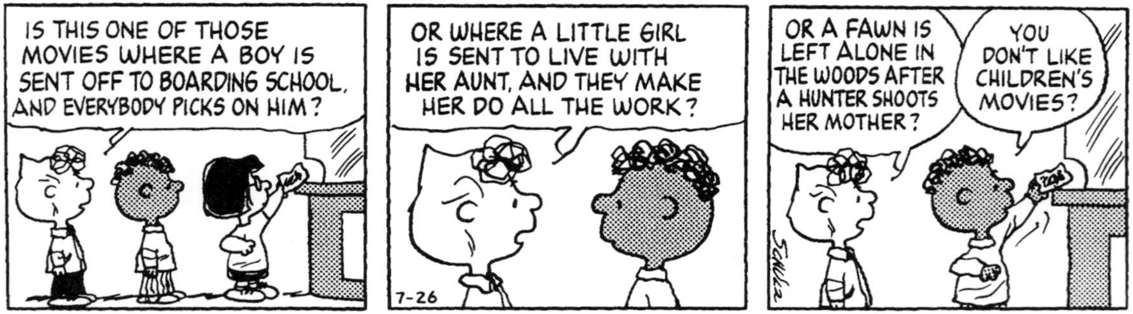
7-26
IS THIS ONE OF THOSE MOVIES WHERE A BOY IS SENT OFF TO BOARDING SCHOOL, AND EVERYBODY PICKS ON HIM?
OR WHERE A LITTLE GIRL IS SENT TO LIVE WITH HER AUNT, AND THEY MAKE HER DO ALL THE WORK?
OR A FAWN IS LEFT ALONE IN THE WOODS AFTER A HUNTER SHOOTS HER MOTHER?
YOU DON'T LIKE CHILDREN'S MOVIES?

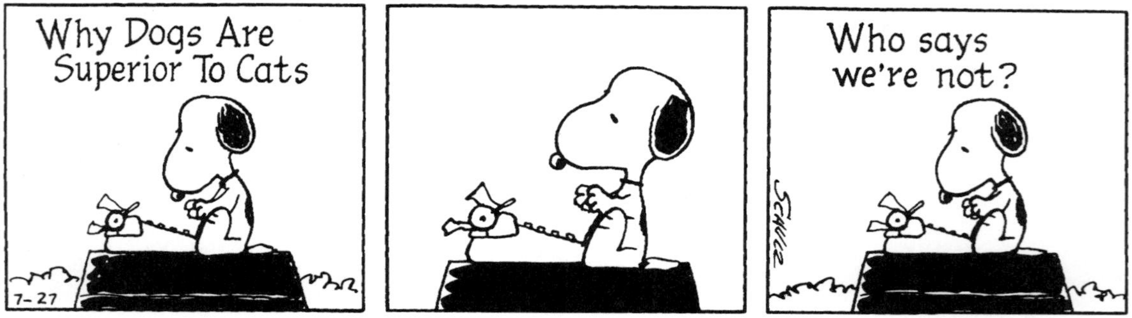
7-27
Why Dogs Are Superior To Cats
Who says we're not?

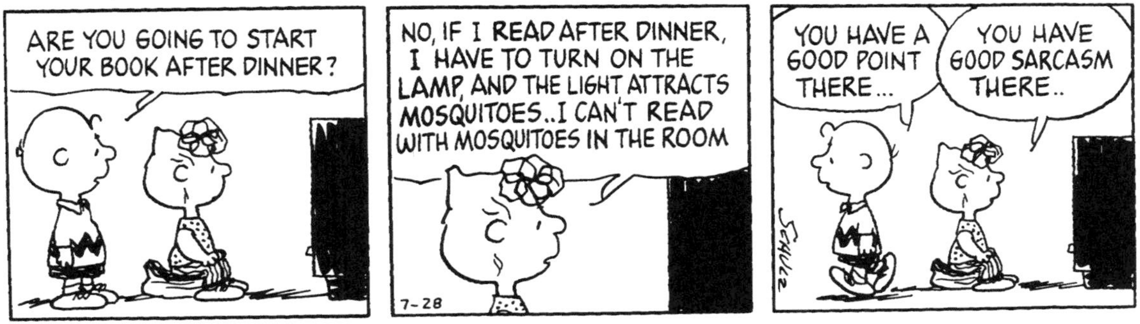
ARE YOU GOING TO START YOUR BOOK AFTER DINNER?
NO, IF I READ AFTER DINNER, I HAVE TO TURN ON THE LAMP, AND THE LIGHT ATTRACTS MOSQUITOES..I CAN'T READ WITH MOSQUITOES IN THE ROOM
7-28
YOU HAVE A GOOD POINT THERE...
YOU HAVE GOOD SARCASM THERE..
SCHULZ

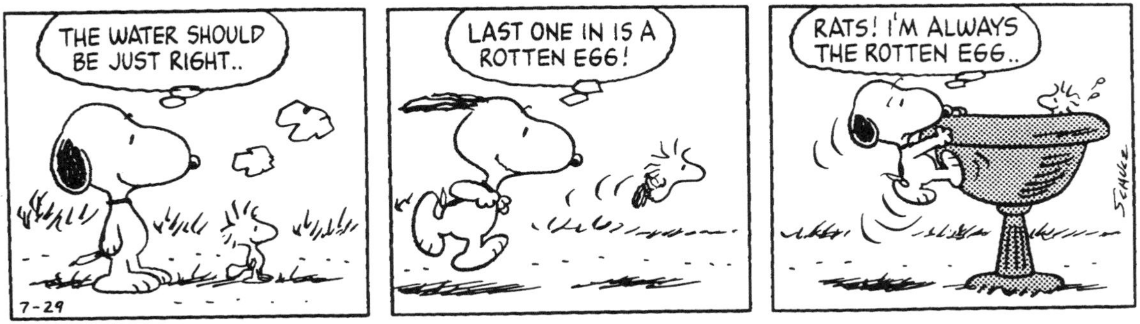
THE WATER SHOULD BE JUST RIGHT..
7-29
LAST ONE IN IS A ROTTEN EGG!
RATS! I'M ALWAYS THE ROTTEN EGG..
SCHULZ

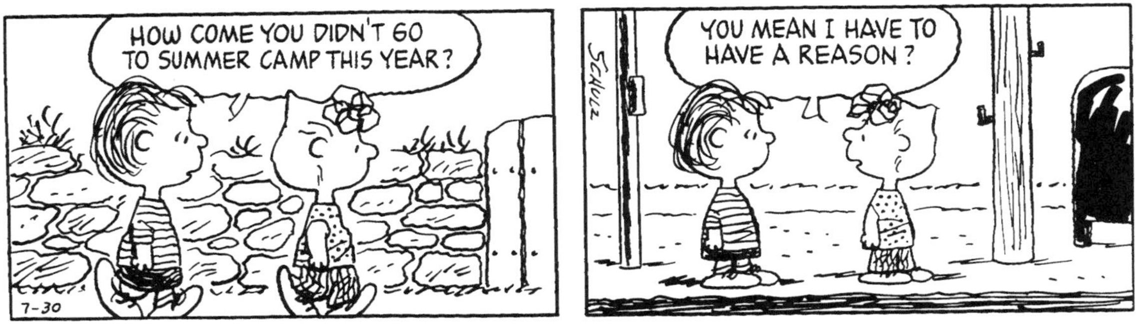
HOW COME YOU DIDN'T GO TO SUMMER CAMP THIS YEAR?
7-30
SCHULZ
YOU MEAN I HAVE TO HAVE A REASON?

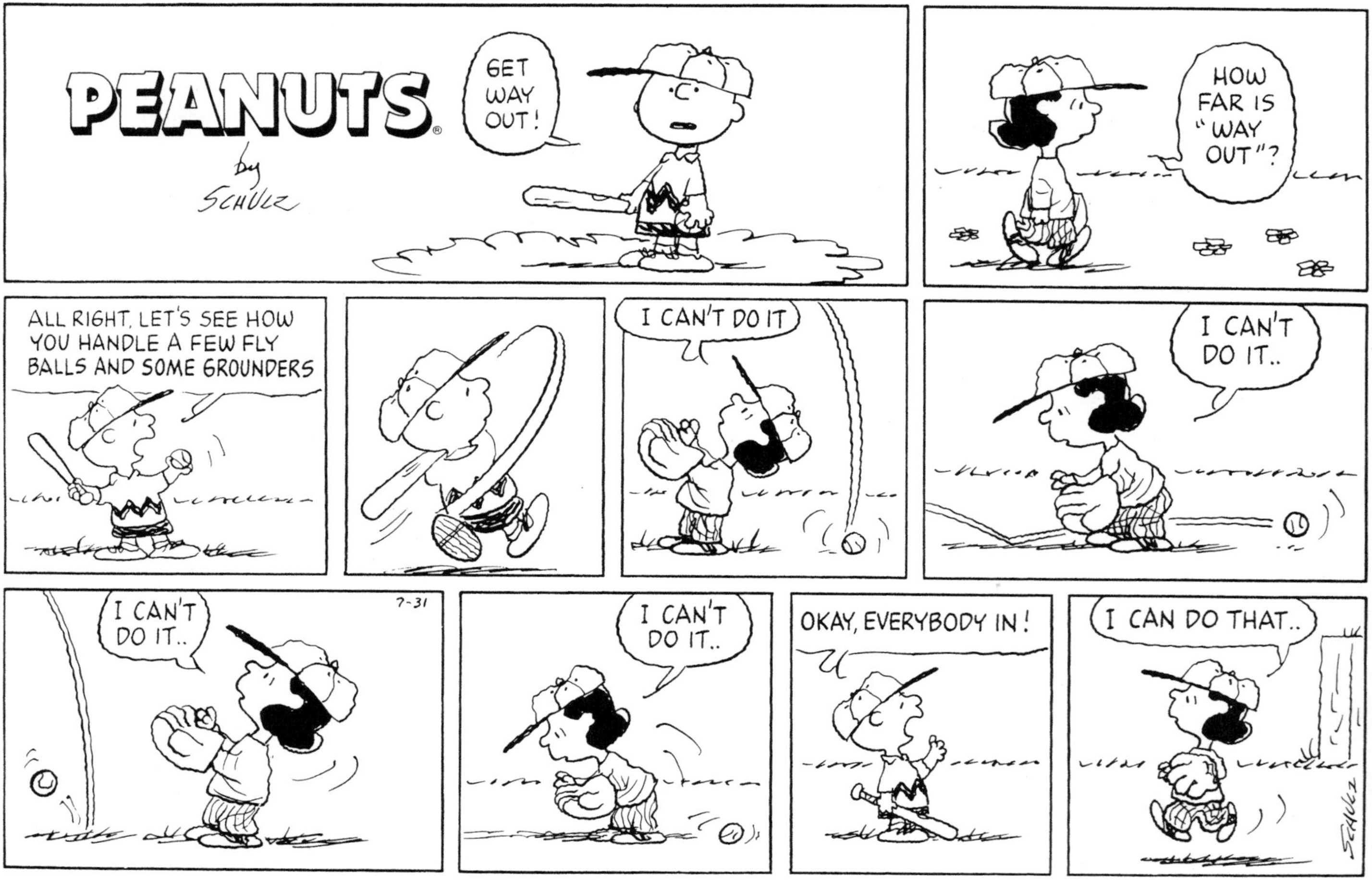
PEANUTS
by SCHULZ
GET WAY OUT!
HOW FAR IS "WAY OUT"?
ALL RIGHT, LET'S SEE HOW YOU HANDLE A FEW FLY BALLS AND SOME GROUNDERS
I CAN'T DO IT
I CAN'T DO IT..
7-31
I CAN'T DO IT..
I CAN'T DO IT..
OKAY, EVERYBODY IN!
I CAN DO THAT..
SCHULZ

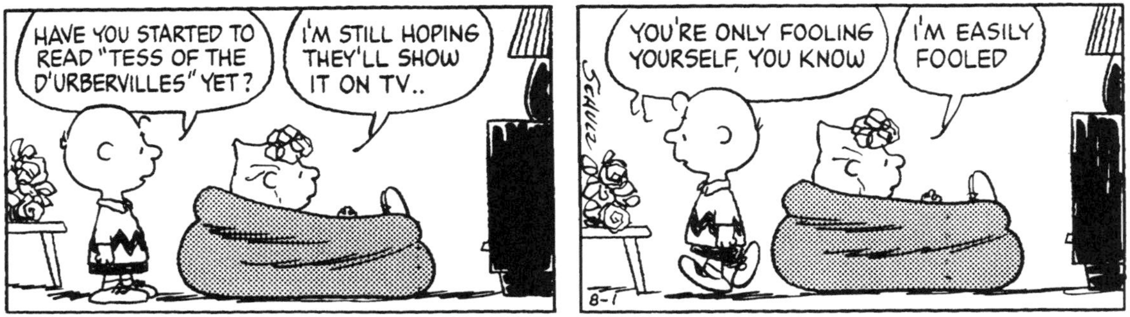
HAVE YOU STARTED TO READ "TESS OF THE D'URBERVILLES" YET?
I'M STILL HOPING THEY'LL SHOW IT ON TV..
YOU'RE ONLY FOOLING YOURSELF, YOU KNOW
I'M EASILY FOOLED
8-1

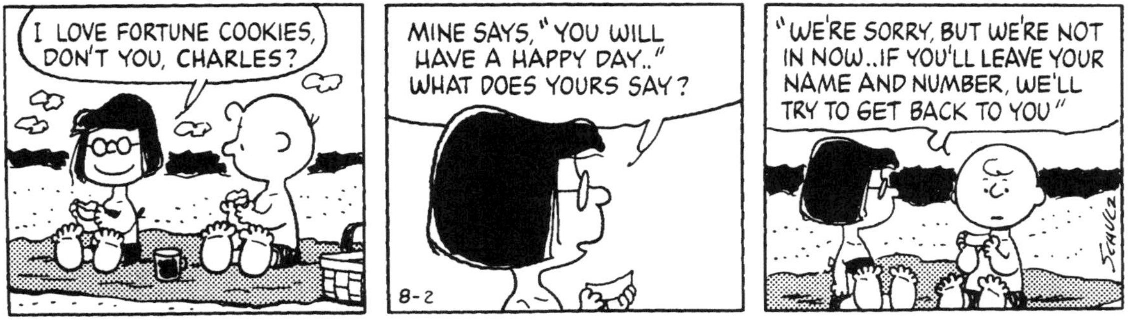
I LOVE FORTUNE COOKIES, DON'T YOU, CHARLES?
MINE SAYS, "YOU WILL HAVE A HAPPY DAY.." WHAT DOES YOURS SAY?
8-2
"WE'RE SORRY, BUT WE'RE NOT IN NOW..IF YOU'LL LEAVE YOUR NAME AND NUMBER, WE'LL TRY TO GET BACK TO YOU"

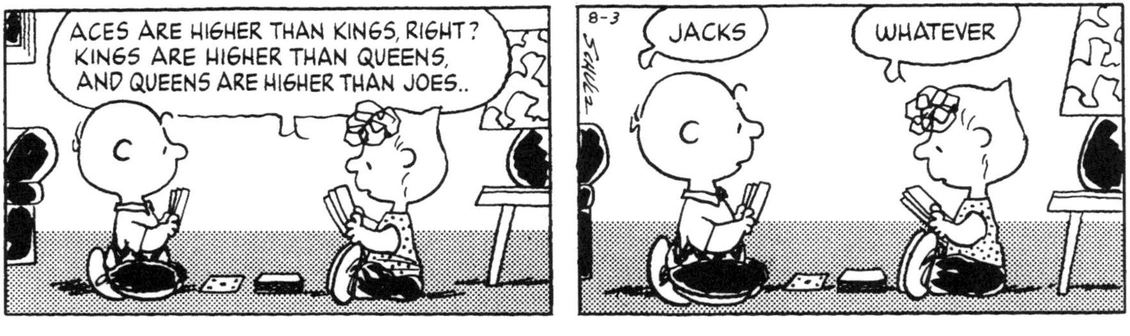
ACES ARE HIGHER THAN KINGS, RIGHT? KINGS ARE HIGHER THAN QUEENS, AND QUEENS ARE HIGHER THAN JOES..
8-3
JACKS
WHATEVER

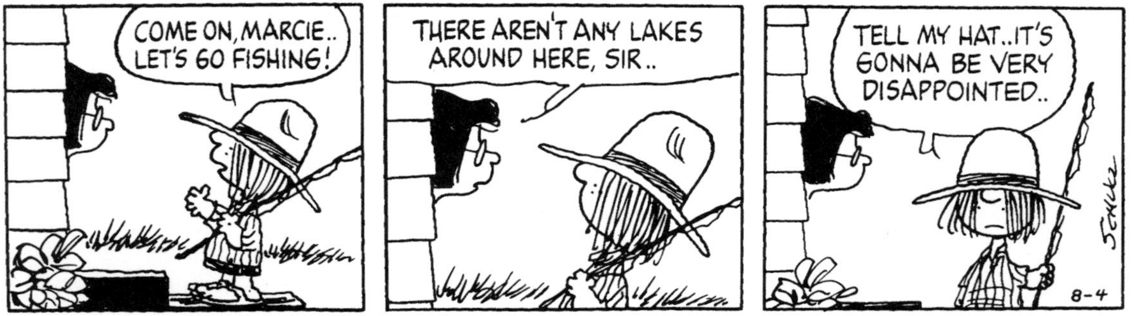
COME ON, MARCIE.. LET'S GO FISHING!
THERE AREN'T ANY LAKES AROUND HERE, SIR..
TELL MY HAT..IT'S GONNA BE VERY DISAPPOINTED..

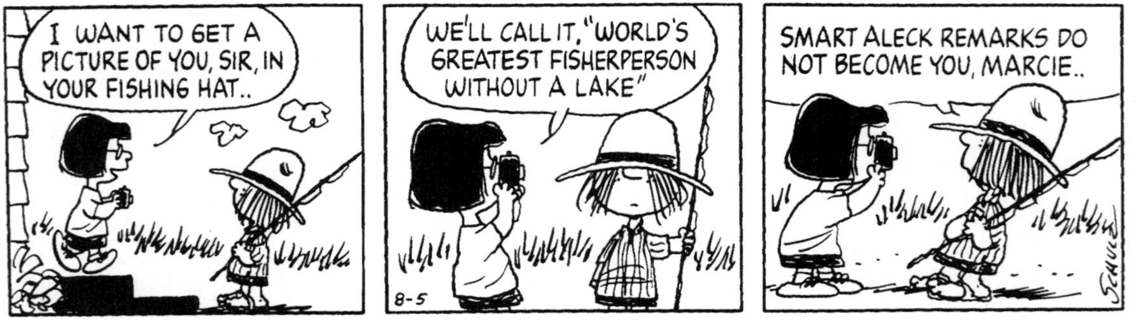
I WANT TO GET A PICTURE OF YOU, SIR, IN YOUR FISHING HAT..
WE'LL CALL IT, "WORLD'S GREATEST FISHERPERSON WITHOUT A LAKE"
SMART ALECK REMARKS DO NOT BECOME YOU, MARCIE..

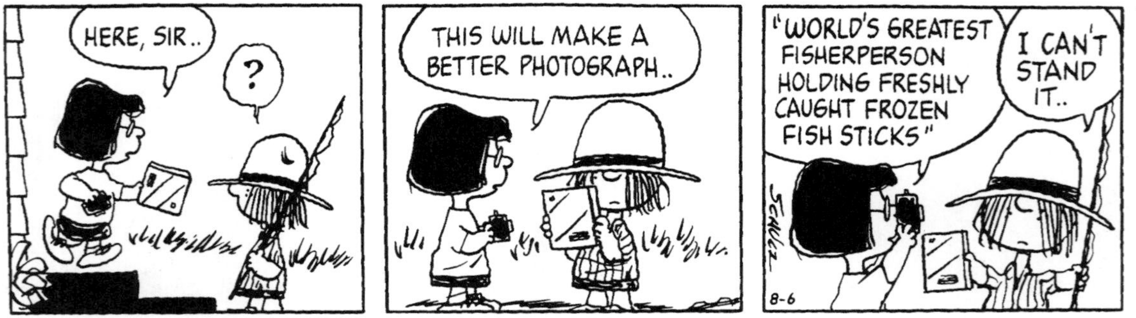
HERE, SIR..
?
THIS WILL MAKE A BETTER PHOTOGRAPH..
"WORLD'S GREATEST FISHERPERSON HOLDING FRESHLY CAUGHT FROZEN FISH STICKS"
I CAN'T STAND IT..

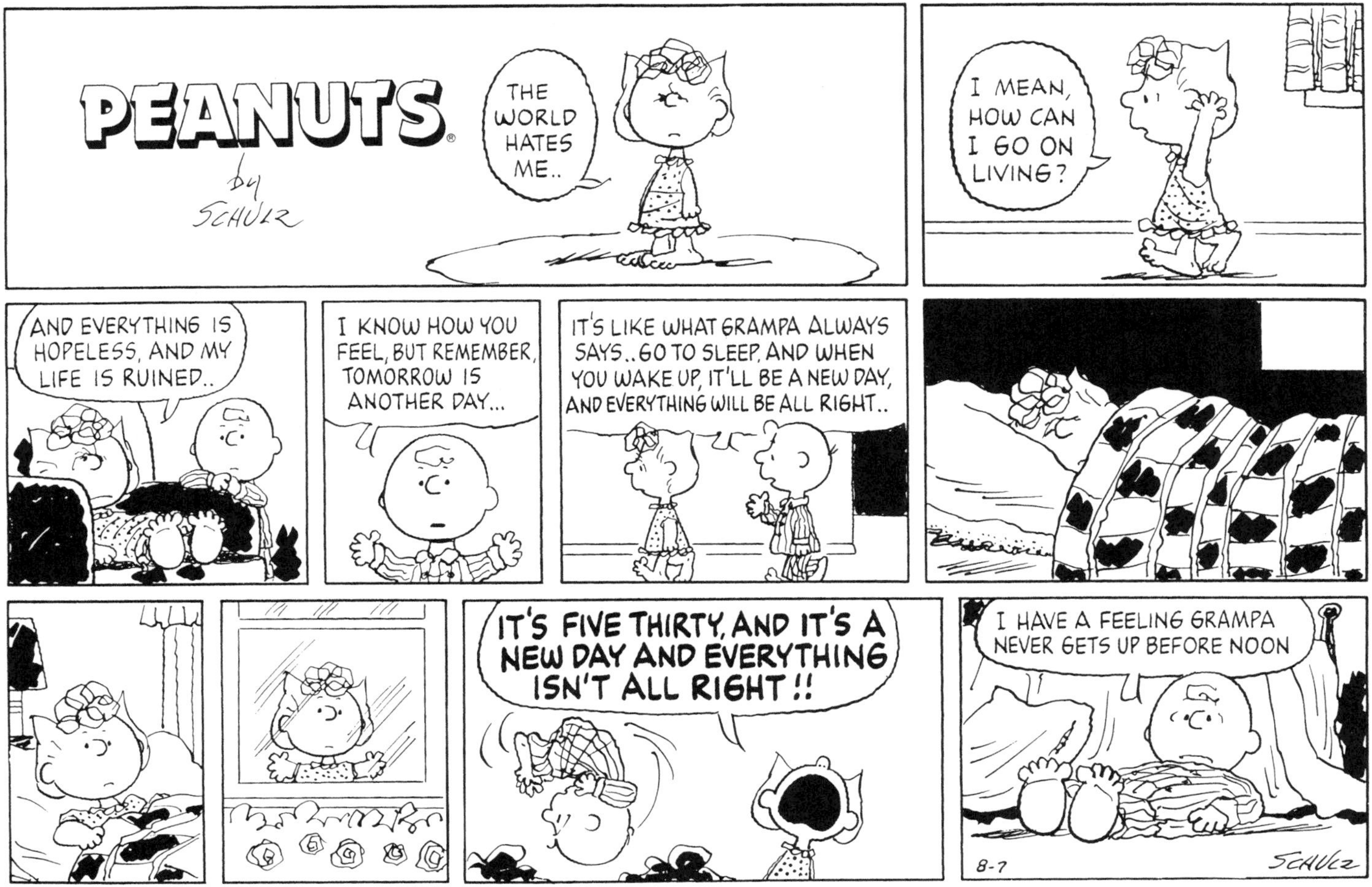
PEANUTS
by SCHULZ
THE WORLD HATES ME..
I MEAN, HOW CAN I GO ON LIVING?
AND EVERYTHING IS HOPELESS, AND MY LIFE IS RUINED..
I KNOW HOW YOU FEEL, BUT REMEMBER, TOMORROW IS ANOTHER DAY...
IT'S LIKE WHAT GRAMPA ALWAYS SAYS..GO TO SLEEP, AND WHEN YOU WAKE UP, IT'LL BE A NEW DAY, AND EVERYTHING WILL BE ALL RIGHT..
IT'S FIVE THIRTY, AND IT'S A NEW DAY AND EVERYTHING ISN'T ALL RIGHT!!
I HAVE A FEELING GRAMPA NEVER GETS UP BEFORE NOON
8-7
SCHULZ

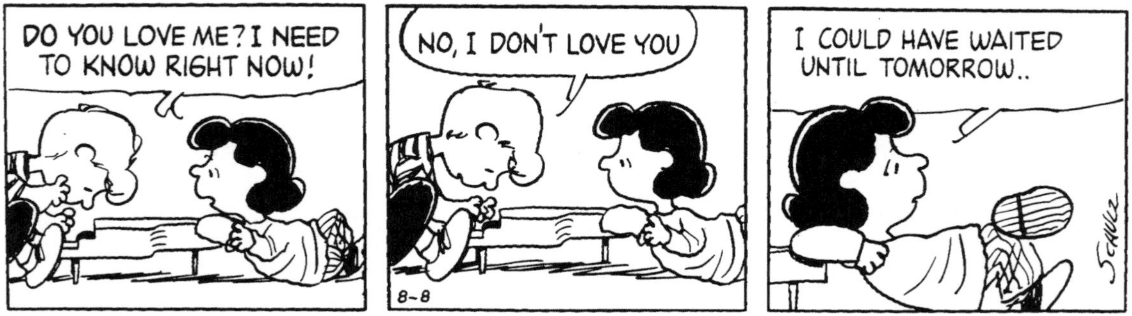
DO YOU LOVE ME? I NEED TO KNOW RIGHT NOW!
NO, I DON'T LOVE YOU
I COULD HAVE WAITED UNTIL TOMORROW..

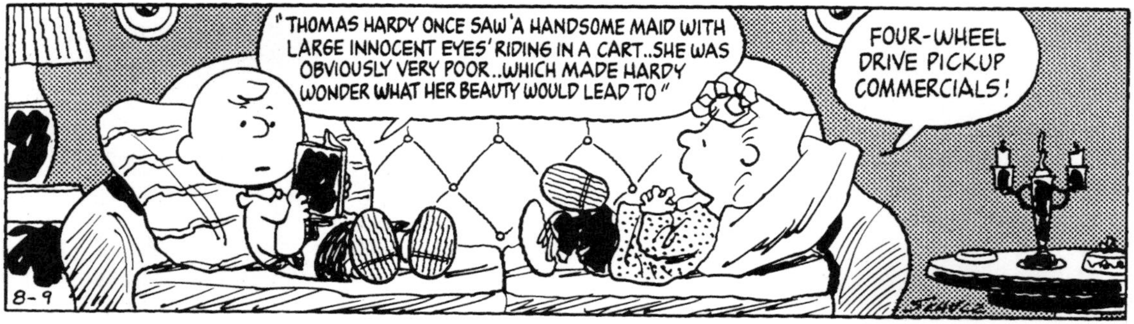
"THOMAS HARDY ONCE SAW 'A HANDSOME MAID WITH LARGE INNOCENT EYES' RIDING IN A CART..SHE WAS OBVIOUSLY VERY POOR..WHICH MADE HARDY WONDER WHAT HER BEAUTY WOULD LEAD TO"
FOUR-WHEEL DRIVE PICKUP COMMERCIALS!

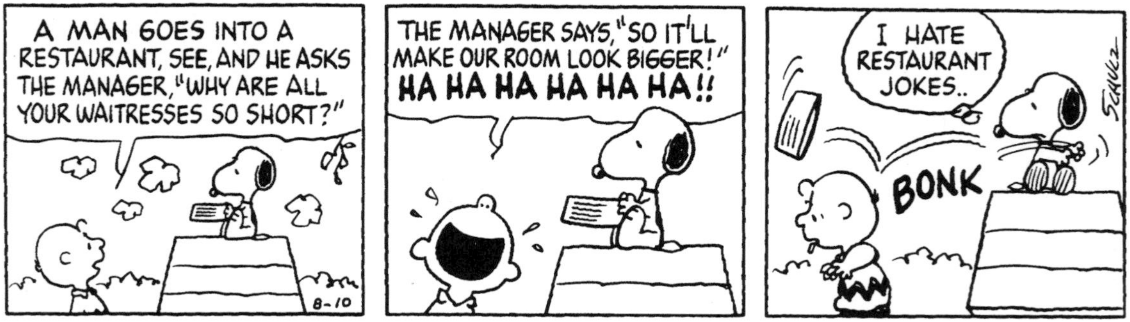
A MAN GOES INTO A RESTAURANT, SEE, AND HE ASKS THE MANAGER, "WHY ARE ALL YOUR WAITRESSES SO SHORT?"
THE MANAGER SAYS, "SO IT'LL MAKE OUR ROOM LOOK BIGGER!" HA HA HA HA HA HA!!
I HATE RESTAURANT JOKES..
BONK

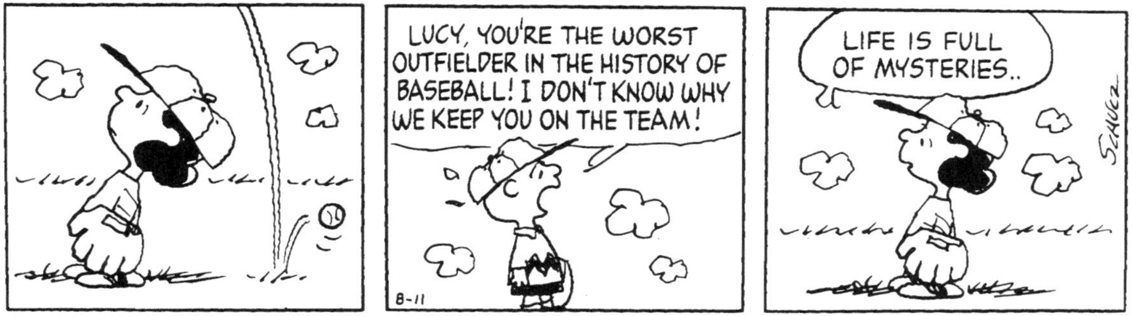
LUCY, YOU'RE THE WORST OUTFIELDER IN THE HISTORY OF BASEBALL! I DON'T KNOW WHY WE KEEP YOU ON THE TEAM!
8-11
LIFE IS FULL OF MYSTERIES..

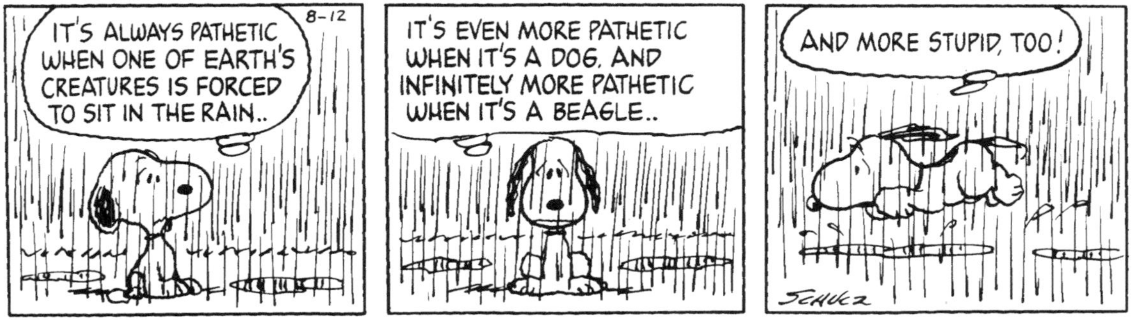
8-12
IT'S ALWAYS PATHETIC WHEN ONE OF EARTH'S CREATURES IS FORCED TO SIT IN THE RAIN..
IT'S EVEN MORE PATHETIC WHEN IT'S A DOG. AND INFINITELY MORE PATHETIC WHEN IT'S A BEAGLE..
AND MORE STUPID, TOO!

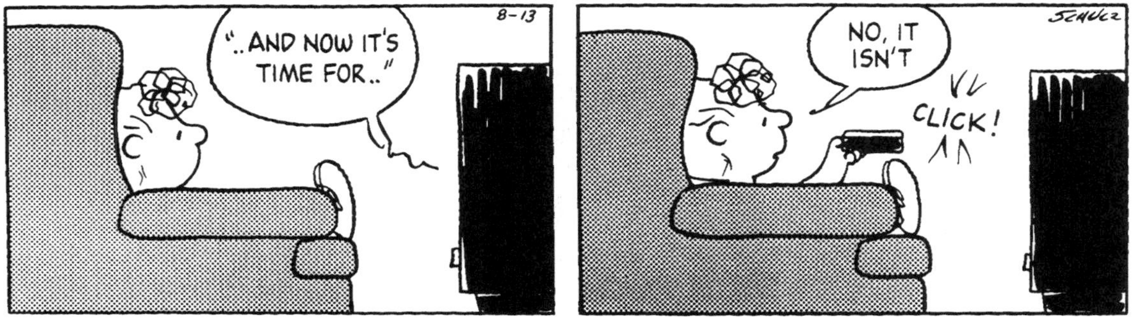
8-13
"..AND NOW IT'S TIME FOR.."
NO, IT ISN'T
CLICK!

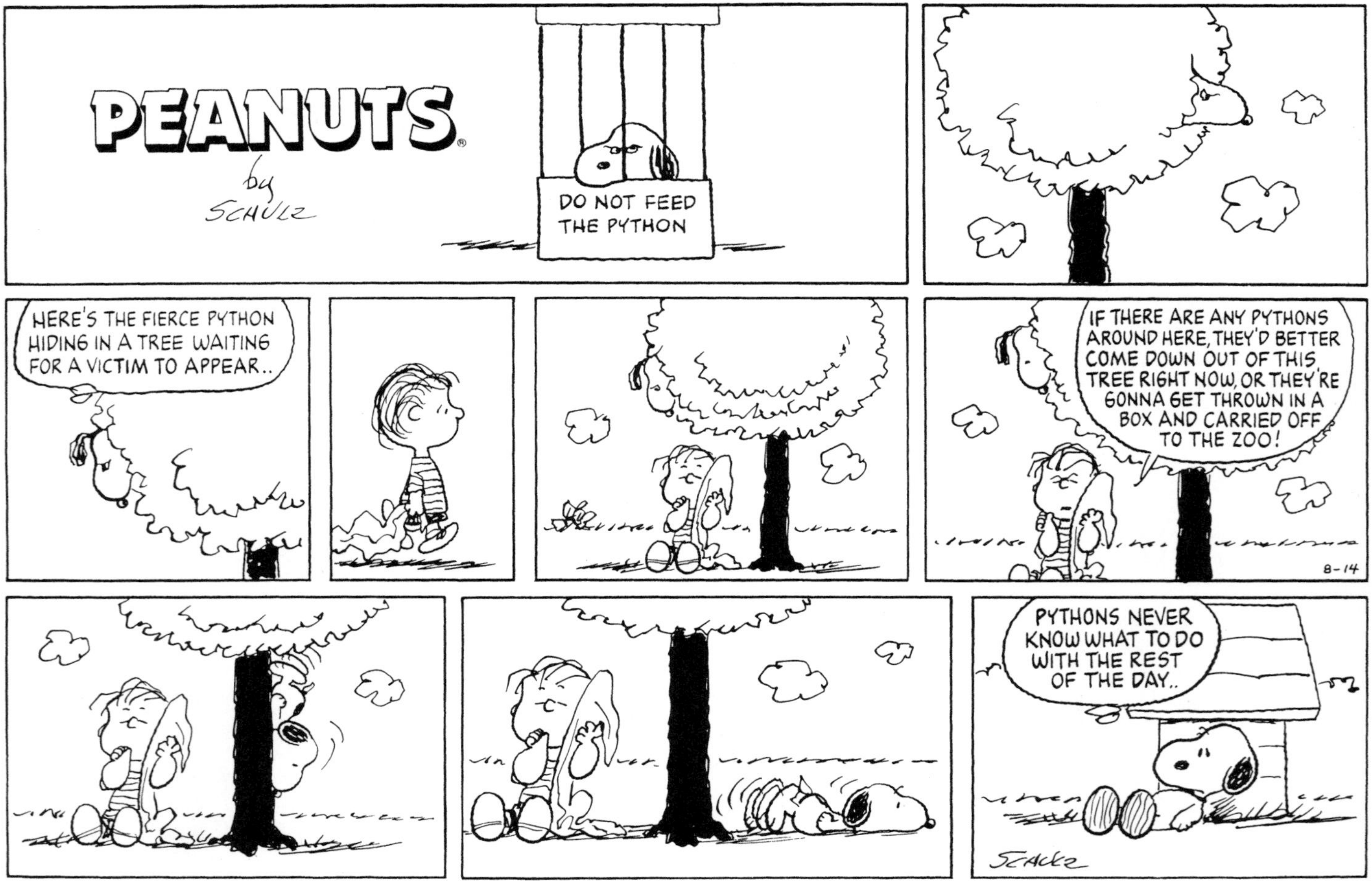
PEANUTS
by SCHULZ
DO NOT FEED THE PYTHON
HERE'S THE FIERCE PYTHON HIDING IN A TREE WAITING FOR A VICTIM TO APPEAR..
IF THERE ARE ANY PYTHONS AROUND HERE, THEY'D BETTER COME DOWN OUT OF THIS TREE RIGHT NOW, OR THEY'RE GONNA GET THROWN IN A BOX AND CARRIED OFF TO THE ZOO!
8-14
PYTHONS NEVER KNOW WHAT TO DO WITH THE REST OF THE DAY..
SCHULZ

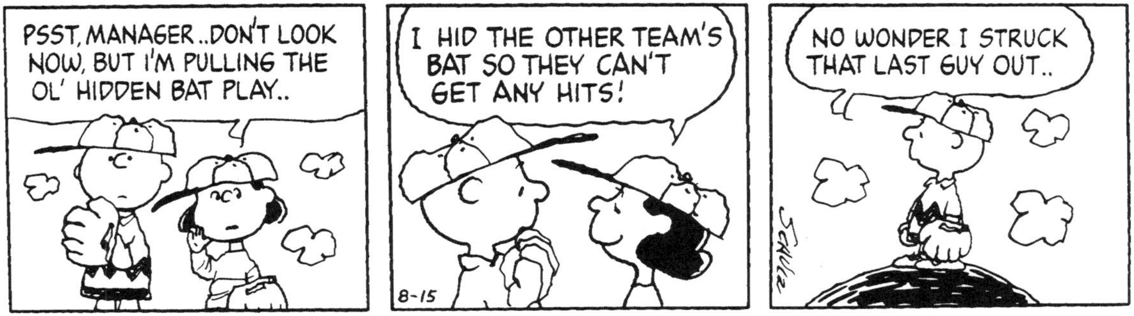
PSST, MANAGER..DON'T LOOK NOW, BUT I'M PULLING THE OL' HIDDEN BAT PLAY..
I HID THE OTHER TEAM'S BAT SO THEY CAN'T GET ANY HITS!
8-15
NO WONDER I STRUCK THAT LAST GUY OUT..
SCHULZ

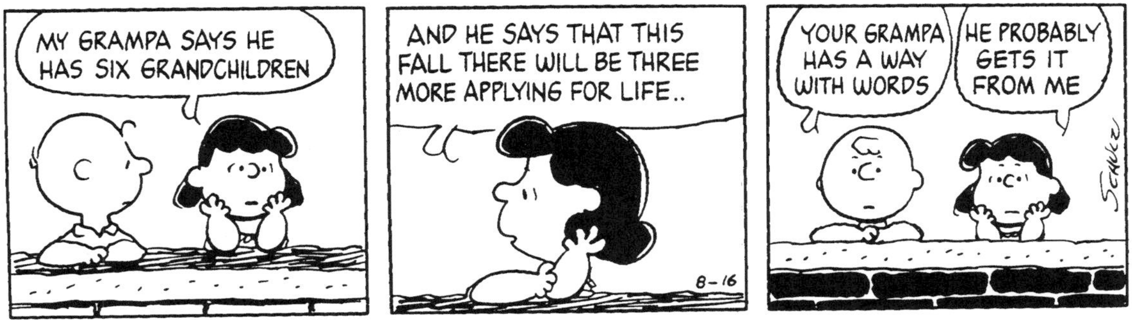
MY GRAMPA SAYS HE HAS SIX GRANDCHILDREN
AND HE SAYS THAT THIS FALL THERE WILL BE THREE MORE APPLYING FOR LIFE..
8-16
YOUR GRAMPA HAS A WAY WITH WORDS
HE PROBABLY GETS IT FROM ME
SCHULZ

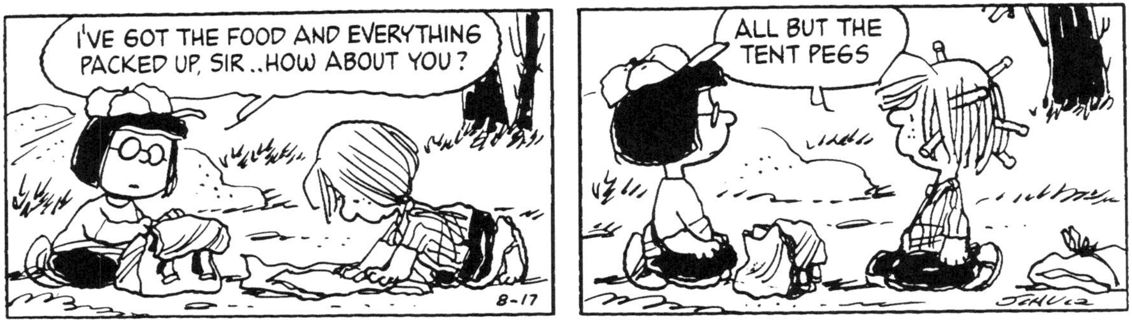
I'VE GOT THE FOOD AND EVERYTHING PACKED UP, SIR..HOW ABOUT YOU?
8-17
ALL BUT THE TENT PEGS
SCHULZ

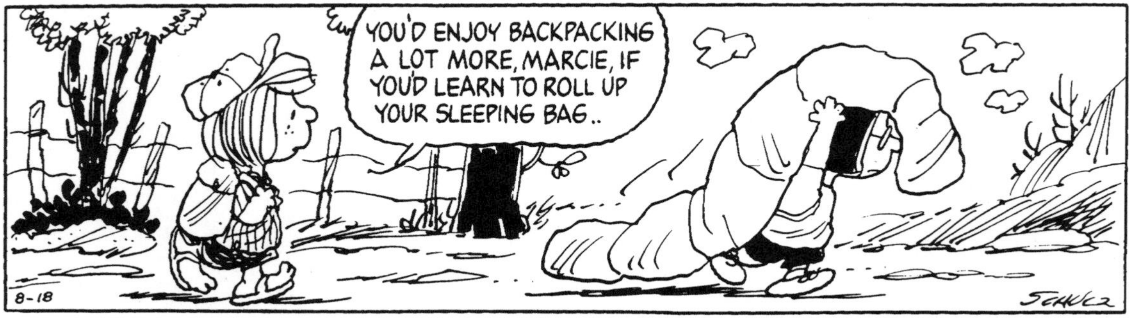
YOU'D ENJOY BACKPACKING A LOT MORE, MARCIE, IF YOU'D LEARN TO ROLL UP YOUR SLEEPING BAG..
8-18
SCHULZ

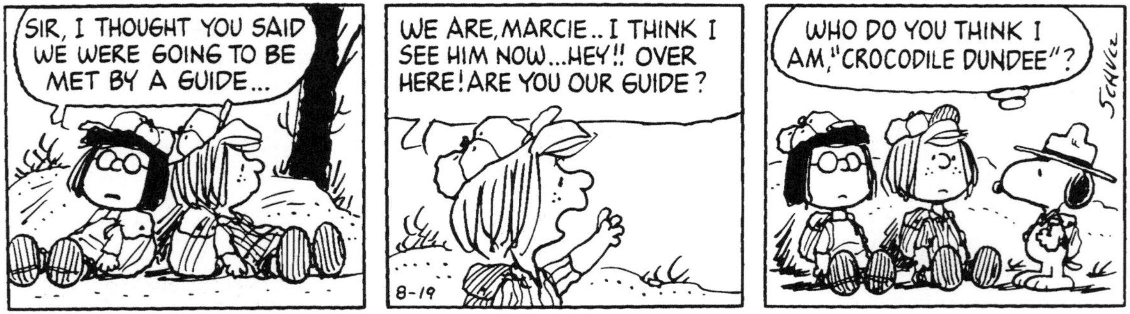
SIR, I THOUGHT YOU SAID WE WERE GOING TO BE MET BY A GUIDE...
WE ARE, MARCIE.. I THINK I SEE HIM NOW...HEY!! OVER HERE! ARE YOU OUR GUIDE?
8-19
WHO DO YOU THINK I AM, "CROCODILE DUNDEE"?
SCHULZ

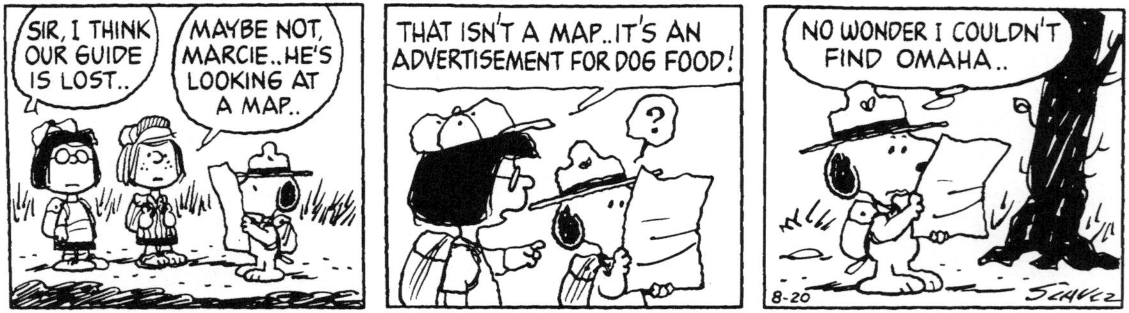
SIR, I THINK OUR GUIDE IS LOST..
MAYBE NOT, MARCIE..HE'S LOOKING AT A MAP..
THAT ISN'T A MAP..IT'S AN ADVERTISEMENT FOR DOG FOOD!
?
NO WONDER I COULDN'T FIND OMAHA..
8-20
SCHULZ

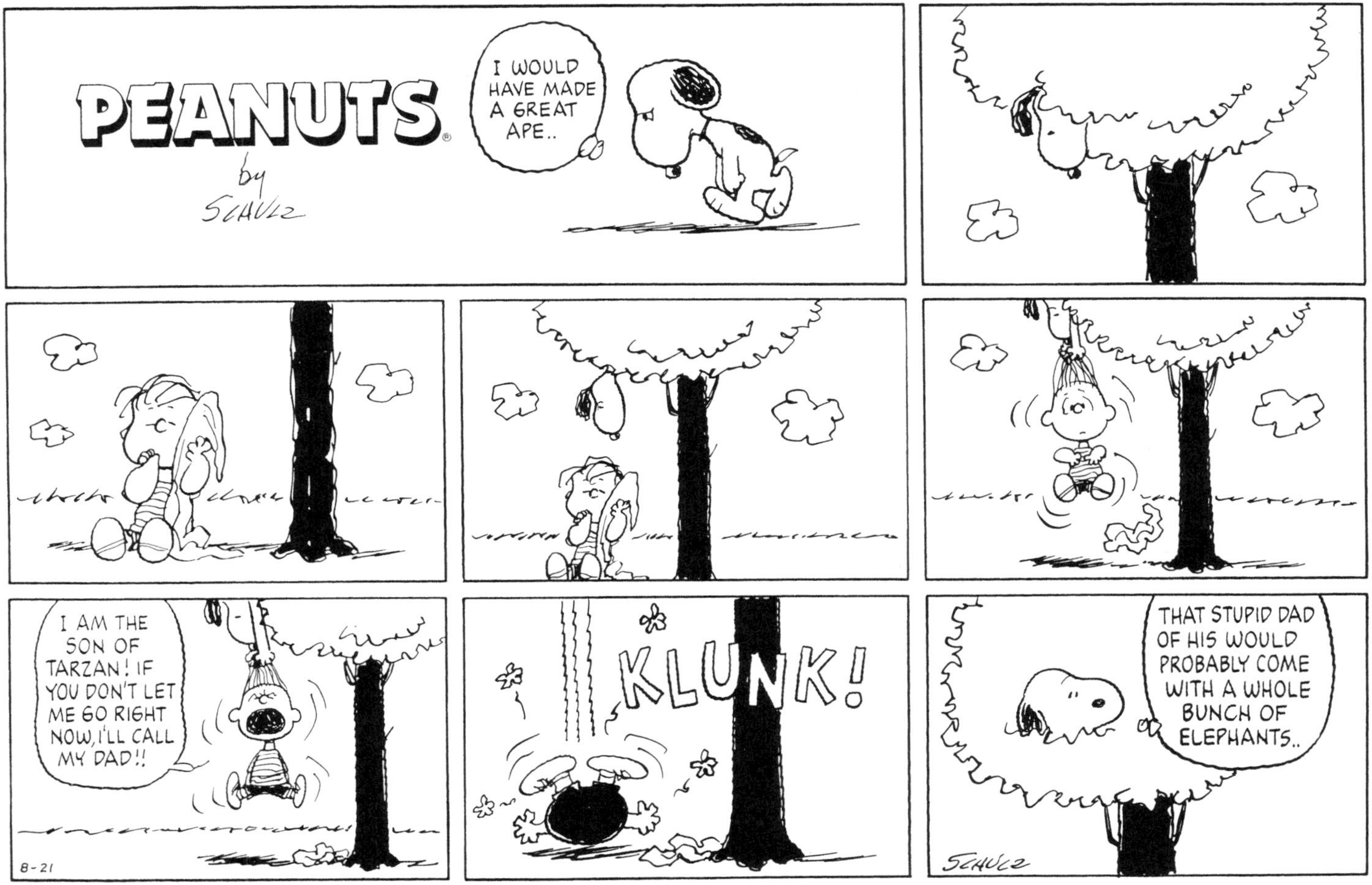
PEANUTS
by SCHULZ
I WOULD HAVE MADE A GREAT APE..
I AM THE SON OF TARZAN! IF YOU DON'T LET ME GO RIGHT NOW, I'LL CALL MY DAD!!
8-21
KLUNK!
THAT STUPID DAD OF HIS WOULD PROBABLY COME WITH A WHOLE BUNCH OF ELEPHANTS..
SCHULZ

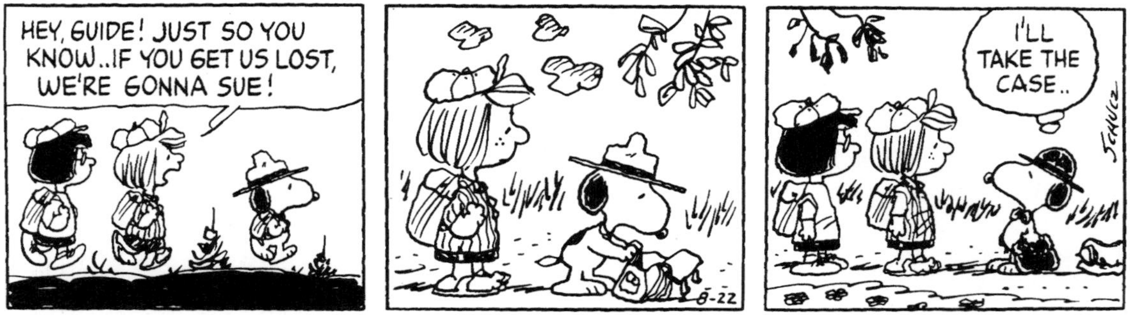
HEY, GUIDE! JUST SO YOU KNOW..IF YOU GET US LOST, WE'RE GONNA SUE!
8-22
I'LL TAKE THE CASE..
SCHULZ

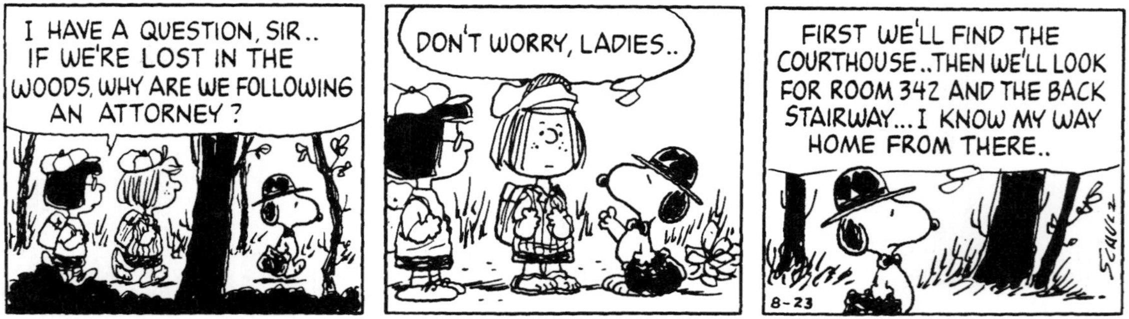
I HAVE A QUESTION, SIR.. IF WE'RE LOST IN THE WOODS, WHY ARE WE FOLLOWING AN ATTORNEY?
DON'T WORRY, LADIES..
FIRST WE'LL FIND THE COURTHOUSE..THEN WE'LL LOOK FOR ROOM 342 AND THE BACK STAIRWAY... I KNOW MY WAY HOME FROM THERE..
8-23
SCHULZ

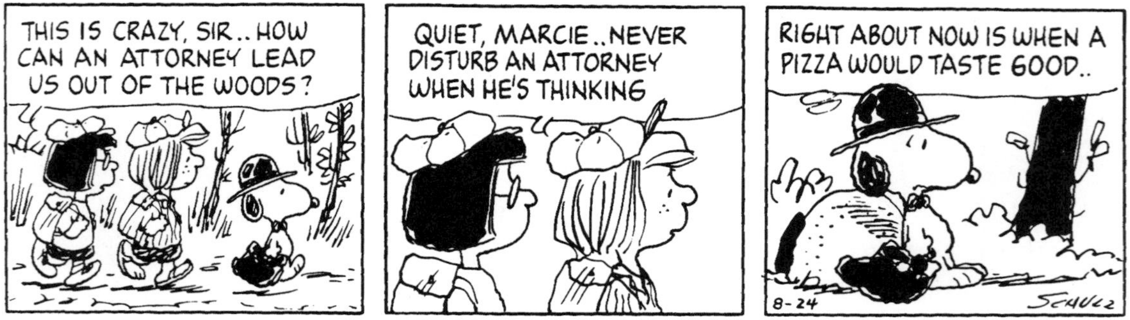
THIS IS CRAZY, SIR.. HOW CAN AN ATTORNEY LEAD US OUT OF THE WOODS?
QUIET, MARCIE..NEVER DISTURB AN ATTORNEY WHEN HE'S THINKING
RIGHT ABOUT NOW IS WHEN A PIZZA WOULD TASTE GOOD..
8-24
SCHULZ

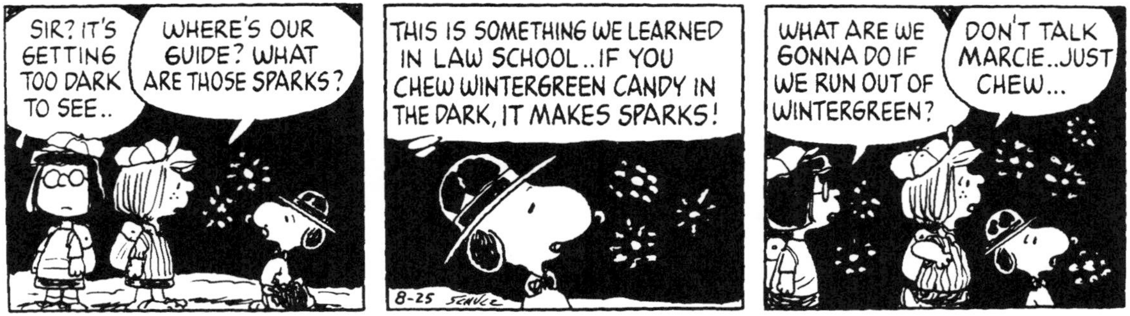
SIR? IT'S GETTING TOO DARK TO SEE..
WHERE'S OUR GUIDE? WHAT ARE THOSE SPARKS?
THIS IS SOMETHING WE LEARNED IN LAW SCHOOL..IF YOU CHEW WINTERGREEN CANDY IN THE DARK, IT MAKES SPARKS!
8-25 SCHULZ
WHAT ARE WE GONNA DO IF WE RUN OUT OF WINTERGREEN?
DON'T TALK MARCIE..JUST CHEW...

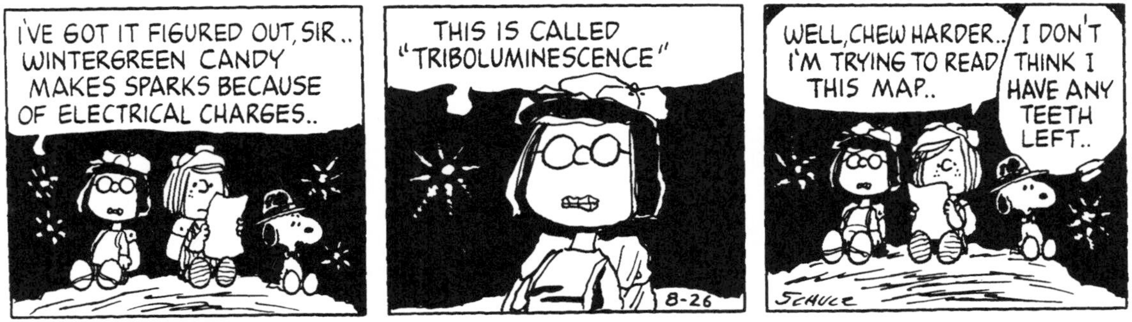
I'VE GOT IT FIGURED OUT, SIR.. WINTERGREEN CANDY MAKES SPARKS BECAUSE OF ELECTRICAL CHARGES..
THIS IS CALLED "TRIBOLUMINESCENCE"
8-26
WELL, CHEW HARDER.. I'M TRYING TO READ THIS MAP..
I DON'T THINK I HAVE ANY TEETH LEFT..
SCHULZ

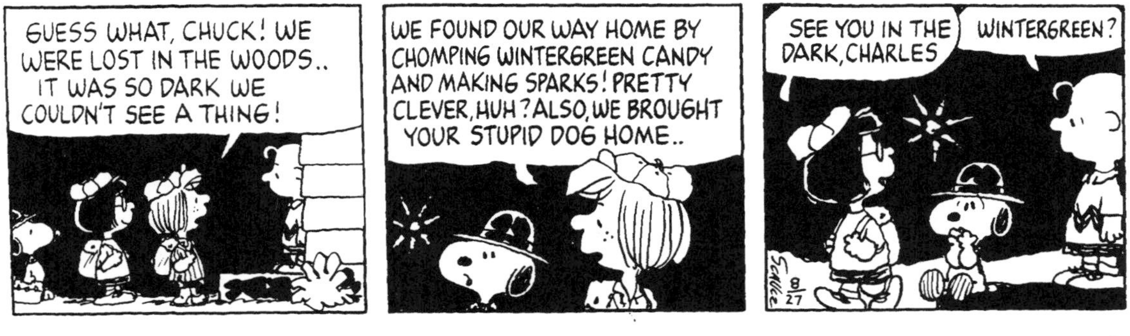
GUESS WHAT, CHUCK! WE WERE LOST IN THE WOODS.. IT WAS SO DARK WE COULDN'T SEE A THING!
WE FOUND OUR WAY HOME BY CHOMPING WINTERGREEN CANDY AND MAKING SPARKS! PRETTY CLEVER, HUH? ALSO, WE BROUGHT YOUR STUPID DOG HOME..
SEE YOU IN THE DARK, CHARLES
WINTERGREEN?
SCHULZ 8/27

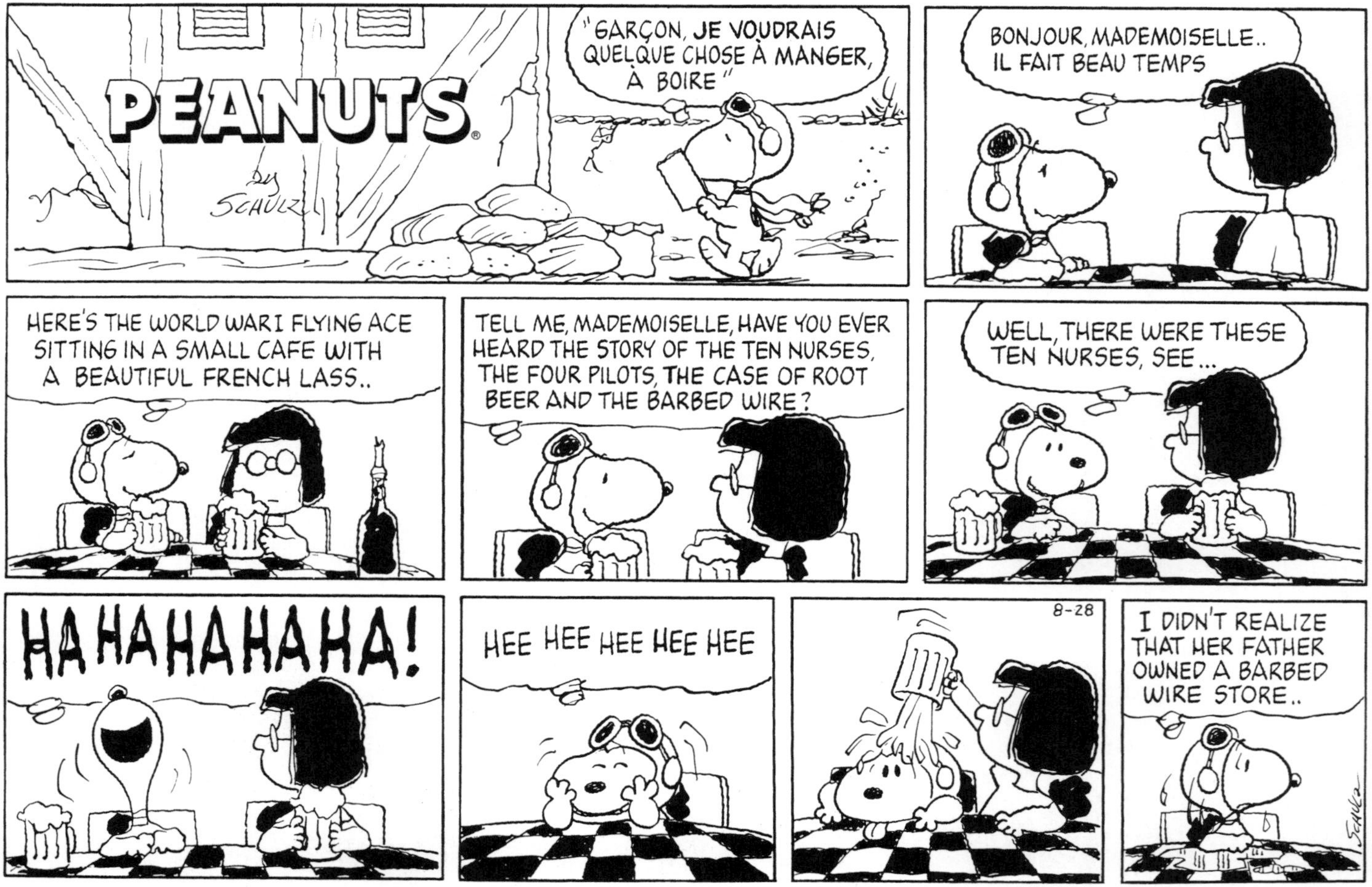
PEANUTS
by SCHULZ
"GARÇON, JE VOUDRAIS QUELQUE CHOSE À MANGER, À BOIRE"
BONJOUR, MADEMOISELLE.. IL FAIT BEAU TEMPS
HERE'S THE WORLD WAR I FLYING ACE SITTING IN A SMALL CAFE WITH A BEAUTIFUL FRENCH LASS..
TELL ME, MADEMOISELLE, HAVE YOU EVER HEARD THE STORY OF THE TEN NURSES, THE FOUR PILOTS, THE CASE OF ROOT BEER AND THE BARBED WIRE?
WELL, THERE WERE THESE TEN NURSES, SEE...
HAHAHAHAHA!
HEE HEE HEE HEE HEE
8-28
I DIDN'T REALIZE THAT HER FATHER OWNED A BARBED WIRE STORE..

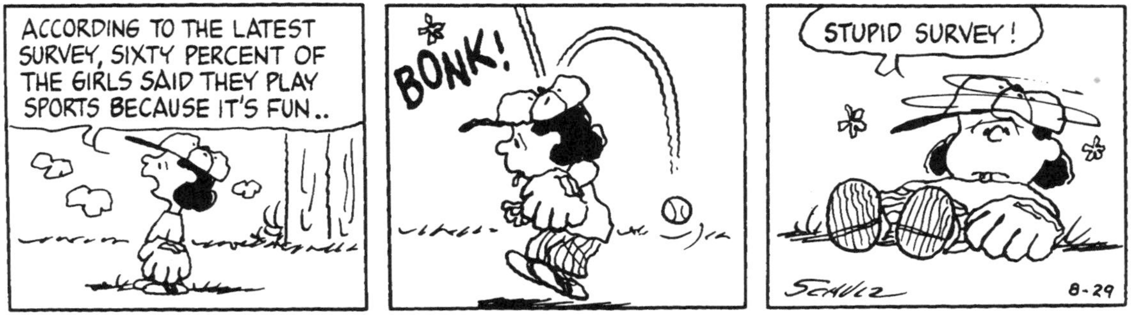
ACCORDING TO THE LATEST SURVEY, SIXTY PERCENT OF THE GIRLS SAID THEY PLAY SPORTS BECAUSE IT'S FUN..
BONK!
STUPID SURVEY!
SCHULZ
8-29

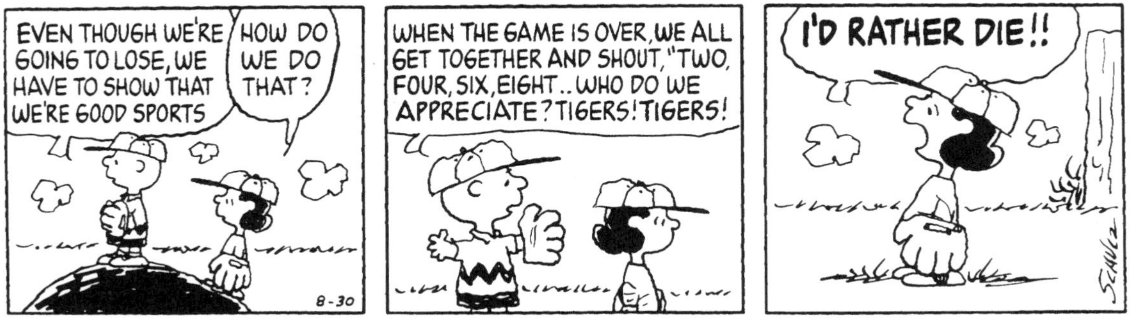
EVEN THOUGH WE'RE GOING TO LOSE, WE HAVE TO SHOW THAT WE'RE GOOD SPORTS
HOW DO WE DO THAT?
8-30
WHEN THE GAME IS OVER, WE ALL GET TOGETHER AND SHOUT, "TWO, FOUR, SIX, EIGHT.. WHO DO WE APPRECIATE? TIGERS! TIGERS!
I'D RATHER DIE!!
SCHULZ

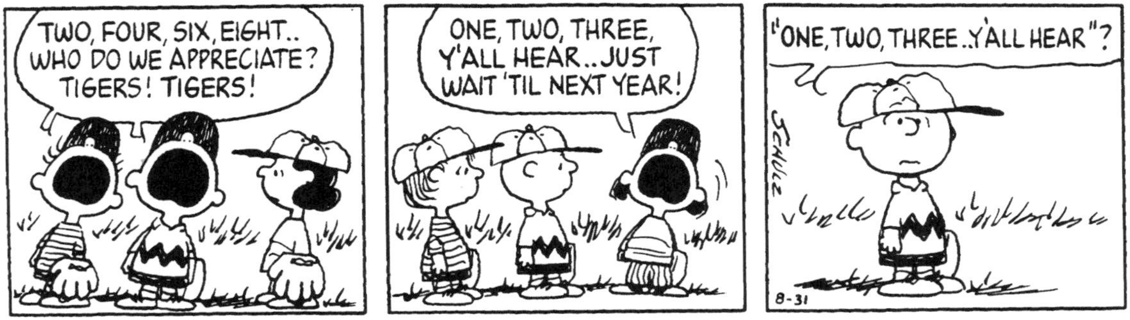
TWO, FOUR, SIX, EIGHT.. WHO DO WE APPRECIATE? TIGERS! TIGERS!
ONE, TWO, THREE, Y'ALL HEAR.. JUST WAIT 'TIL NEXT YEAR!
"ONE, TWO, THREE..Y'ALL HEAR"?
SCHULZ
8-31

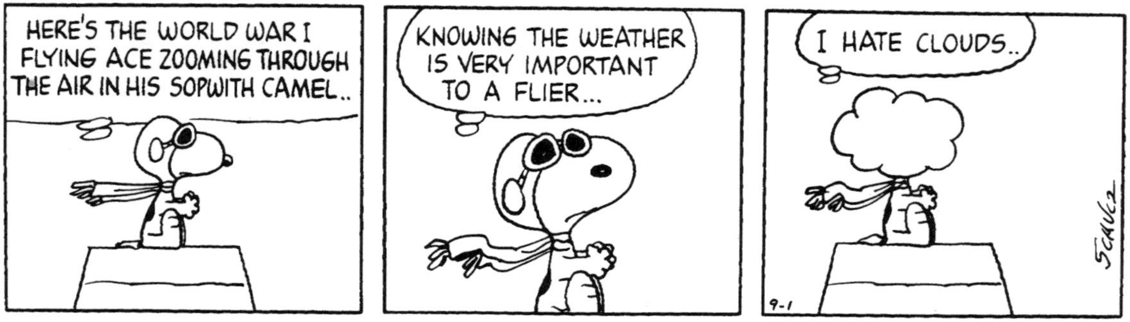
HERE'S THE WORLD WAR I FLYING ACE ZOOMING THROUGH THE AIR IN HIS SOPWITH CAMEL..
KNOWING THE WEATHER IS VERY IMPORTANT TO A FLIER...
I HATE CLOUDS..
9-1

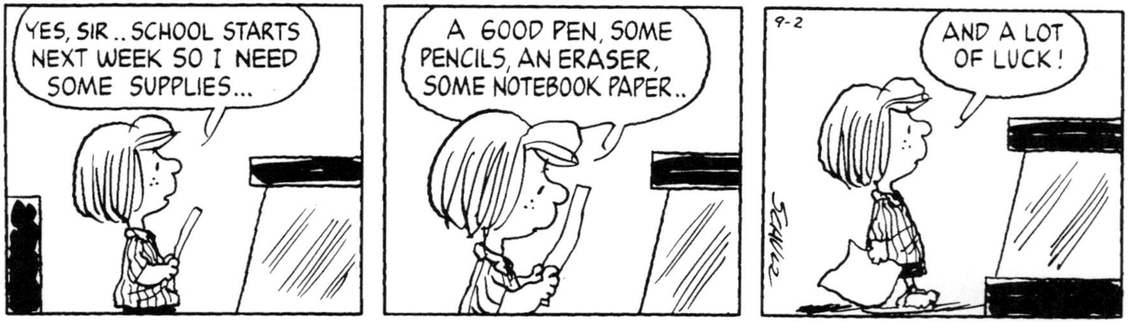
YES, SIR.. SCHOOL STARTS NEXT WEEK SO I NEED SOME SUPPLIES...
A GOOD PEN, SOME PENCILS, AN ERASER, SOME NOTEBOOK PAPER..
9-2
AND A LOT OF LUCK!

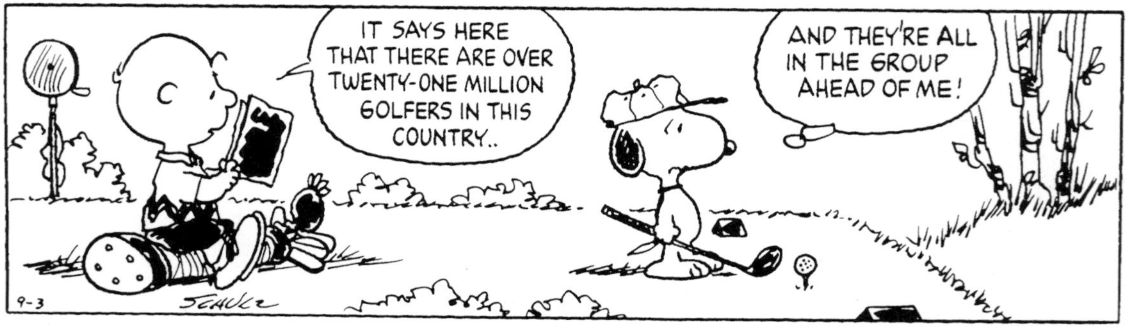
IT SAYS HERE THAT THERE ARE OVER TWENTY-ONE MILLION GOLFERS IN THIS COUNTRY..
AND THEY'RE ALL IN THE GROUP AHEAD OF ME!
9-3

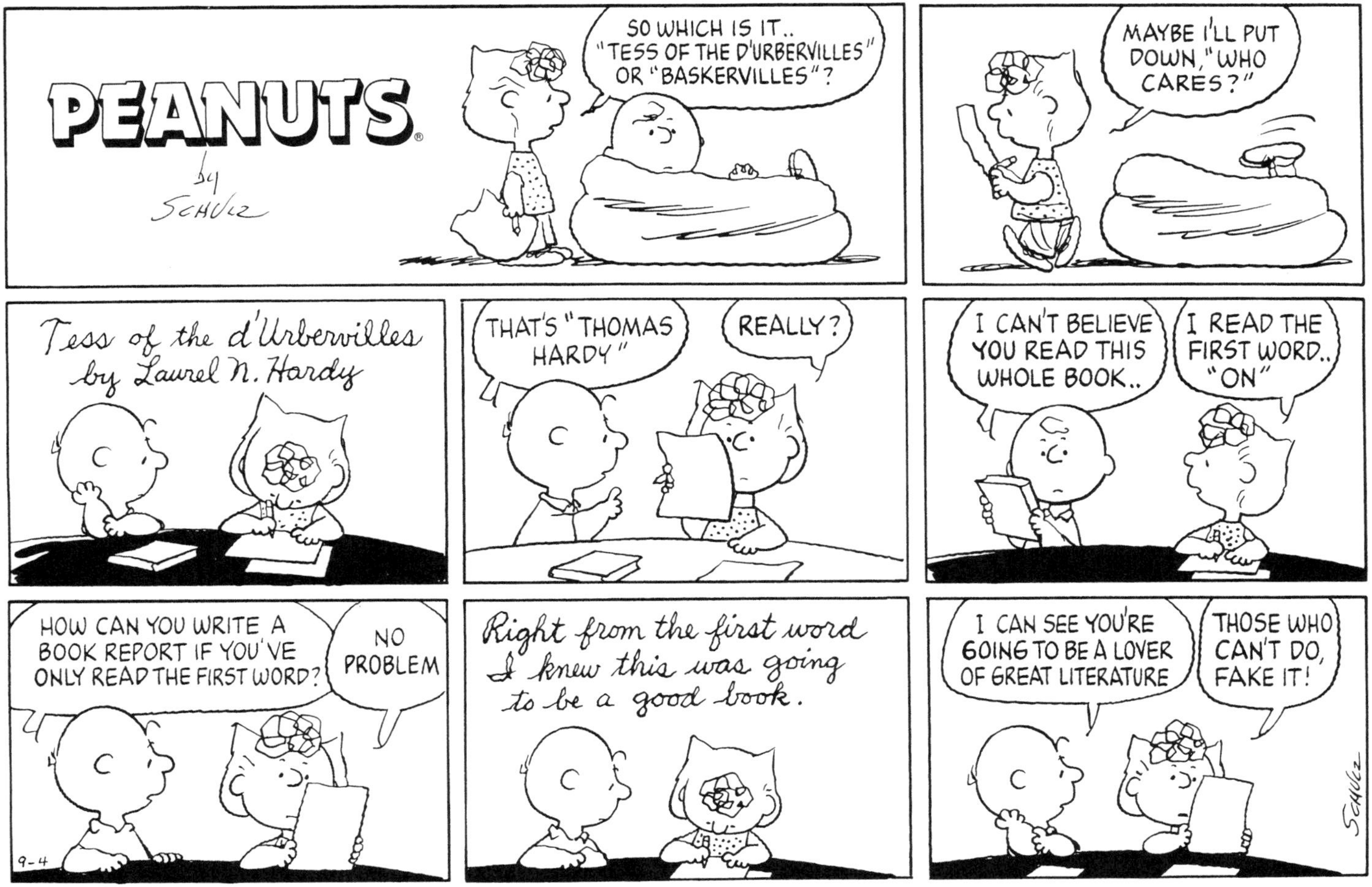
PEANUTS
by SCHULZ
SO WHICH IS IT.. "TESS OF THE D'URBERVILLES" OR "BASKERVILLES"?
MAYBE I'LL PUT DOWN, "WHO CARES?"
Tess of the d'Urbervilles by Laurel N. Hardy
THAT'S "THOMAS HARDY"
REALLY?
I CAN'T BELIEVE YOU READ THIS WHOLE BOOK..
I READ THE FIRST WORD.. "ON"
HOW CAN YOU WRITE A BOOK REPORT IF YOU'VE ONLY READ THE FIRST WORD?
NO PROBLEM
9-4
Right from the first word I knew this was going to be a good book.
I CAN SEE YOU'RE GOING TO BE A LOVER OF GREAT LITERATURE
THOSE WHO CAN'T DO, FAKE IT!
SCHULZ

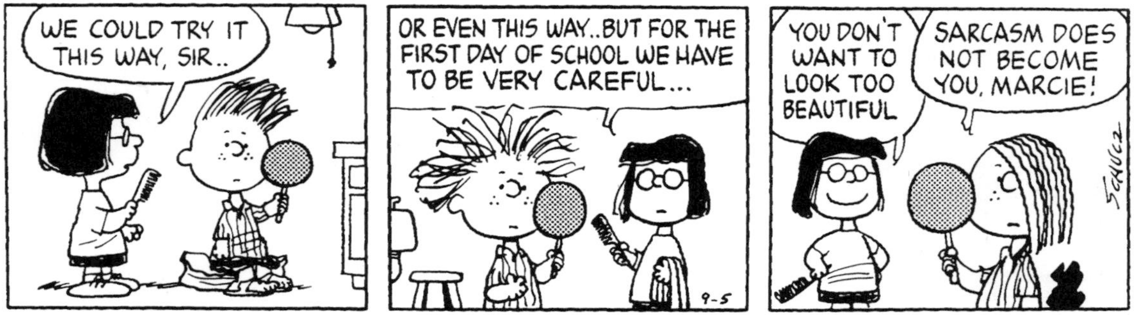
WE COULD TRY IT THIS WAY, SIR..
OR EVEN THIS WAY..BUT FOR THE FIRST DAY OF SCHOOL WE HAVE TO BE VERY CAREFUL...
9-5
YOU DON'T WANT TO LOOK TOO BEAUTIFUL
SARCASM DOES NOT BECOME YOU, MARCIE!

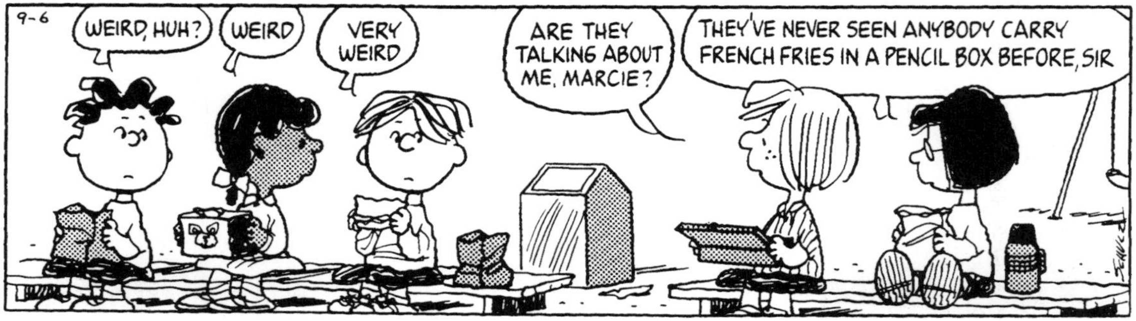
9-6
WEIRD, HUH?
WEIRD
VERY WEIRD
ARE THEY TALKING ABOUT ME, MARCIE?
THEY'VE NEVER SEEN ANYBODY CARRY FRENCH FRIES IN A PENCIL BOX BEFORE, SIR

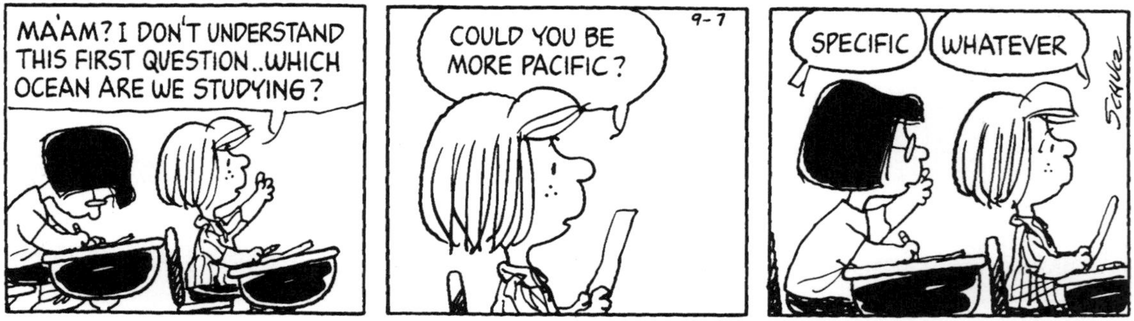
MA'AM? I DON'T UNDERSTAND THIS FIRST QUESTION..WHICH OCEAN ARE WE STUDYING?
9-7
COULD YOU BE MORE PACIFIC?
SPECIFIC
WHATEVER

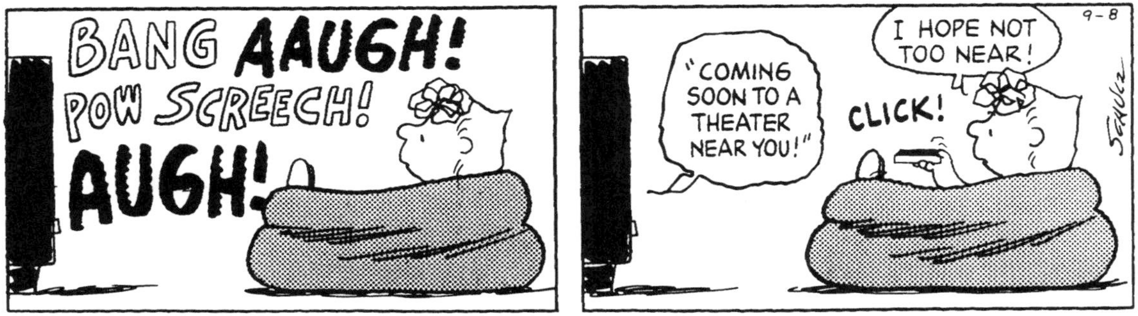
BANG AAUGH!
POW SCREECH!
AUGH!
"COMING SOON TO A THEATER NEAR YOU!"
CLICK!
I HOPE NOT TOO NEAR!
9-8

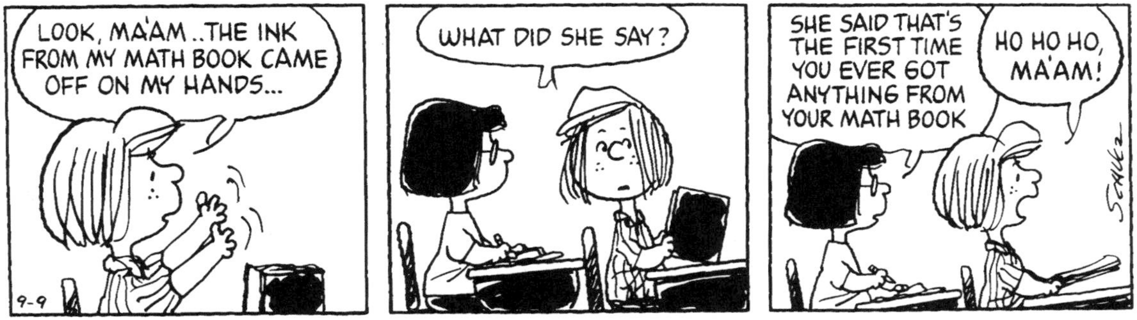
LOOK, MA'AM..THE INK FROM MY MATH BOOK CAME OFF ON MY HANDS...
9-9
WHAT DID SHE SAY?
SHE SAID THAT'S THE FIRST TIME YOU EVER GOT ANYTHING FROM YOUR MATH BOOK
HO HO HO, MA'AM!

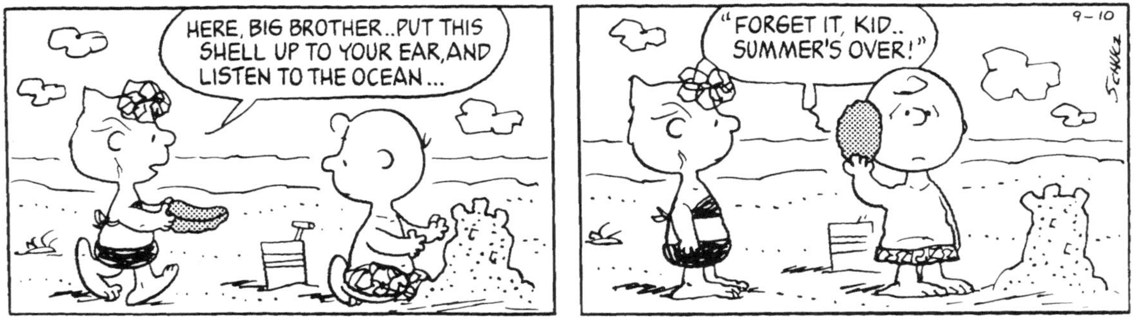
HERE, BIG BROTHER..PUT THIS SHELL UP TO YOUR EAR, AND LISTEN TO THE OCEAN...
9-10
"FORGET IT, KID.. SUMMER'S OVER!"

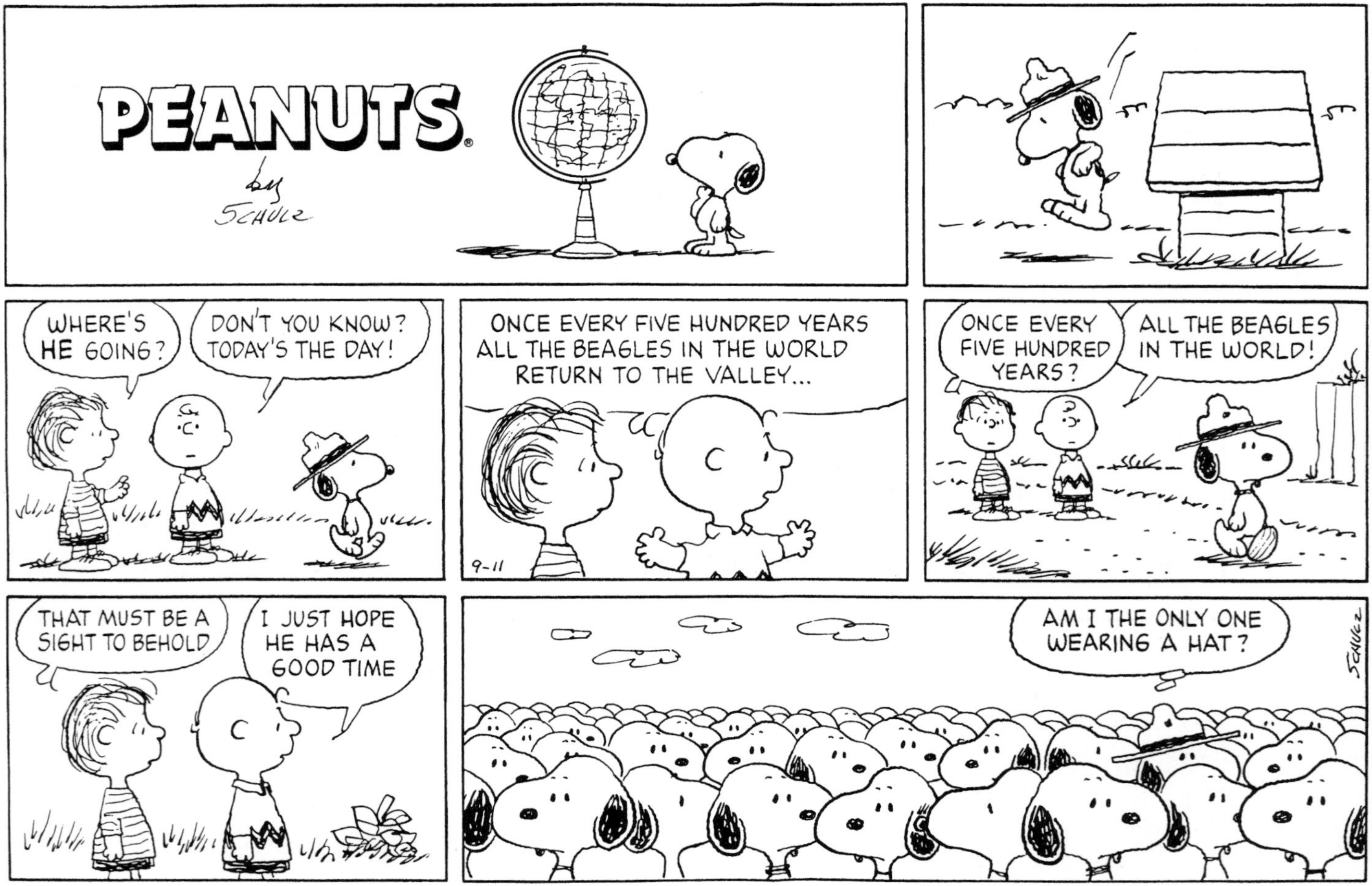
PEANUTS
by SCHULZ
WHERE'S HE GOING?
DON'T YOU KNOW? TODAY'S THE DAY!
ONCE EVERY FIVE HUNDRED YEARS ALL THE BEAGLES IN THE WORLD RETURN TO THE VALLEY...
9-11
ONCE EVERY FIVE HUNDRED YEARS?
ALL THE BEAGLES IN THE WORLD!
THAT MUST BE A SIGHT TO BEHOLD
I JUST HOPE HE HAS A GOOD TIME
AM I THE ONLY ONE WEARING A HAT?
SCHULZ

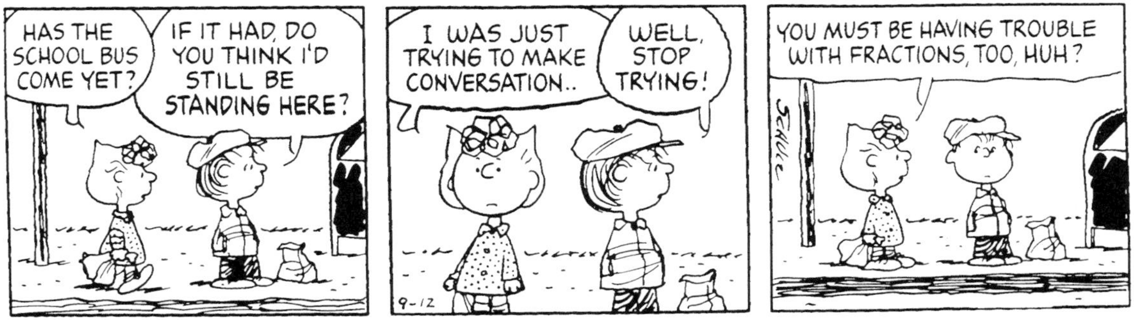
HAS THE SCHOOL BUS COME YET?
IF IT HAD, DO YOU THINK I'D STILL BE STANDING HERE?
I WAS JUST TRYING TO MAKE CONVERSATION..
WELL, STOP TRYING!
YOU MUST BE HAVING TROUBLE WITH FRACTIONS, TOO, HUH?
SCHULZ
9-12

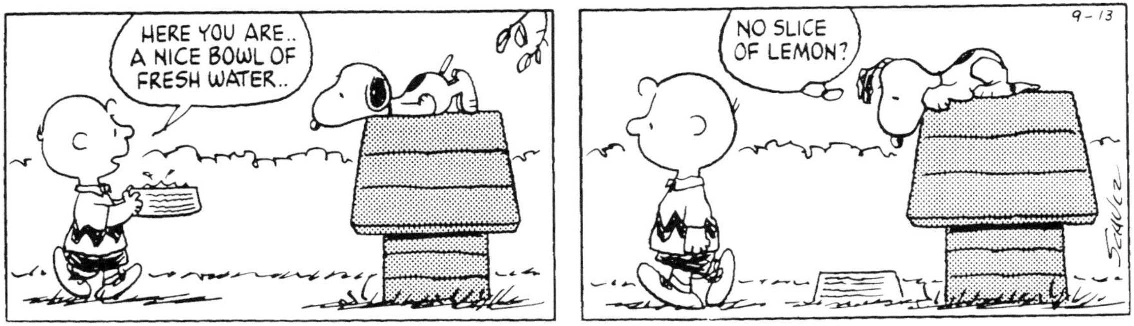
HERE YOU ARE.. A NICE BOWL OF FRESH WATER..
NO SLICE OF LEMON?
9-13
SCHULZ

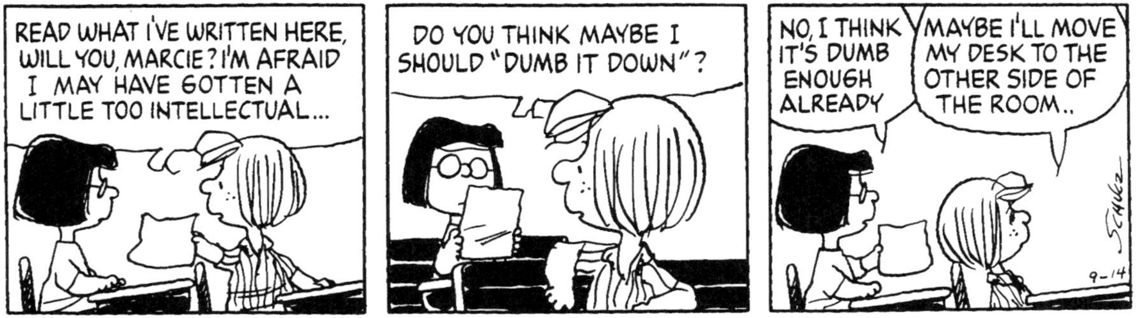
READ WHAT I'VE WRITTEN HERE, WILL YOU, MARCIE? I'M AFRAID I MAY HAVE GOTTEN A LITTLE TOO INTELLECTUAL...
DO YOU THINK MAYBE I SHOULD "DUMB IT DOWN"?
NO, I THINK IT'S DUMB ENOUGH ALREADY
MAYBE I'LL MOVE MY DESK TO THE OTHER SIDE OF THE ROOM..
SCHULZ
9-14

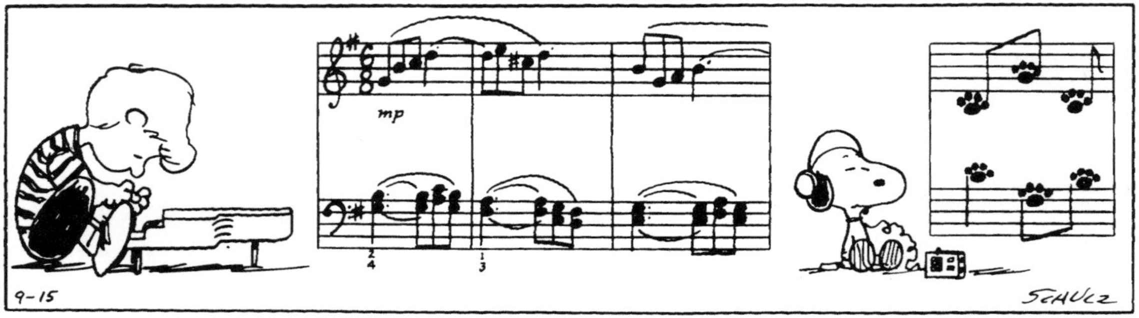
mp
9-15
SCHULZ

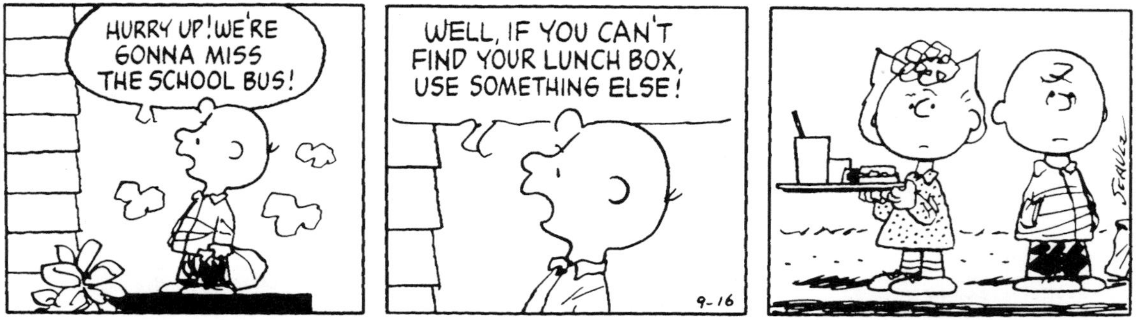
HURRY UP! WE'RE GONNA MISS THE SCHOOL BUS!
WELL, IF YOU CAN'T FIND YOUR LUNCH BOX, USE SOMETHING ELSE!
9-16
SCHULZ

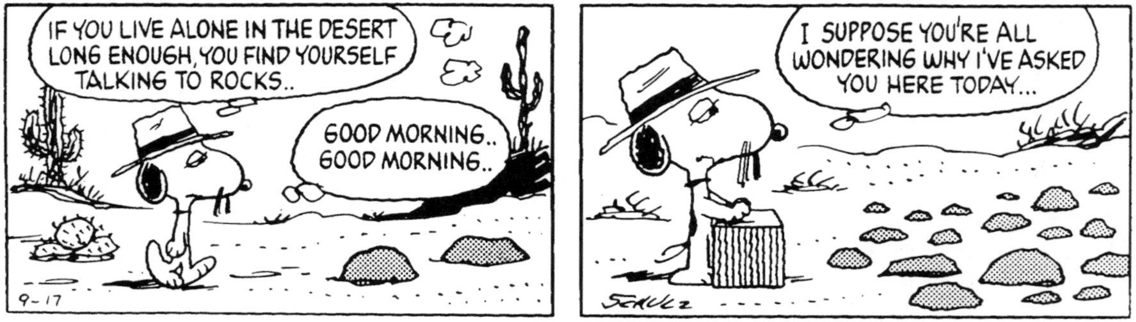
IF YOU LIVE ALONE IN THE DESERT LONG ENOUGH, YOU FIND YOURSELF TALKING TO ROCKS..
GOOD MORNING.. GOOD MORNING..
I SUPPOSE YOU'RE ALL WONDERING WHY I'VE ASKED YOU HERE TODAY...
9-17
SCHULZ

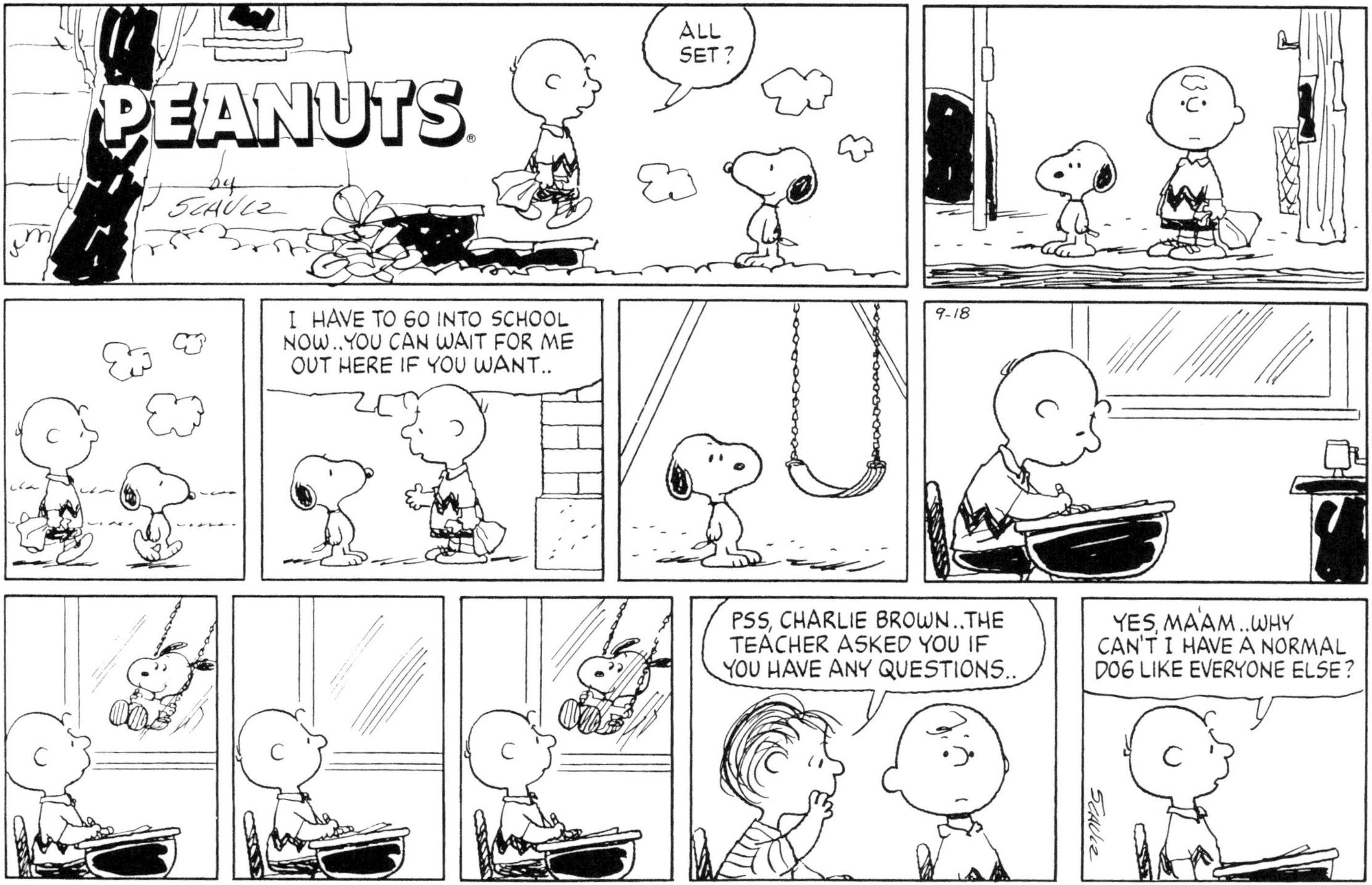
PEANUTS
by SCHULZ
ALL SET?
I HAVE TO GO INTO SCHOOL NOW..YOU CAN WAIT FOR ME OUT HERE IF YOU WANT..
9-18
PSS, CHARLIE BROWN..THE TEACHER ASKED YOU IF YOU HAVE ANY QUESTIONS..
YES, MA'AM..WHY CAN'T I HAVE A NORMAL DOG LIKE EVERYONE ELSE?
SCHULZ

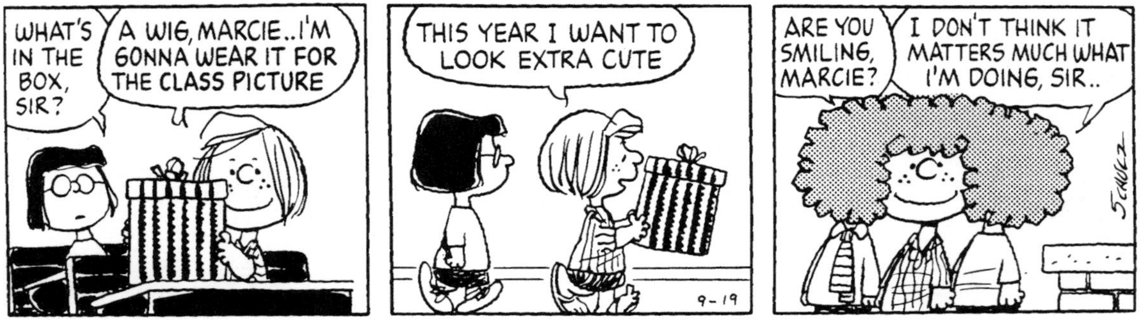
WHAT'S IN THE BOX, SIR?
A WIG, MARCIE..I'M GONNA WEAR IT FOR THE CLASS PICTURE
THIS YEAR I WANT TO LOOK EXTRA CUTE
9-19
ARE YOU SMILING, MARCIE?
I DON'T THINK IT MATTERS MUCH WHAT I'M DOING, SIR..
SCHULZ

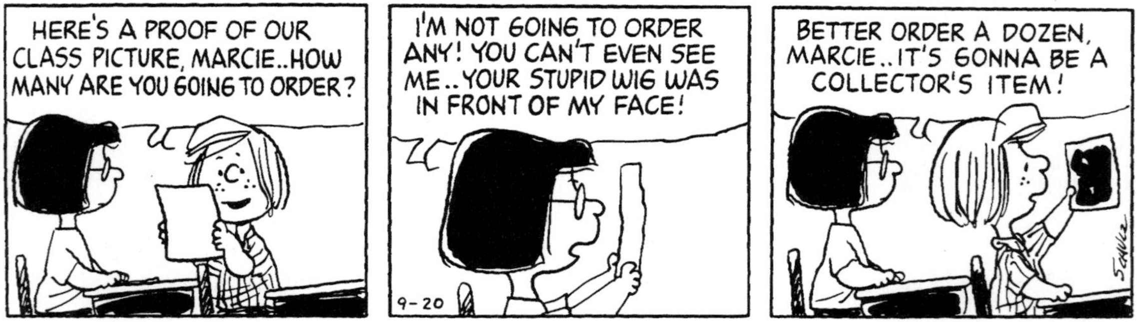
HERE'S A PROOF OF OUR CLASS PICTURE, MARCIE..HOW MANY ARE YOU GOING TO ORDER?
I'M NOT GOING TO ORDER ANY! YOU CAN'T EVEN SEE ME..YOUR STUPID WIG WAS IN FRONT OF MY FACE!
9-20
BETTER ORDER A DOZEN, MARCIE..IT'S GONNA BE A COLLECTOR'S ITEM!
SCHULZ

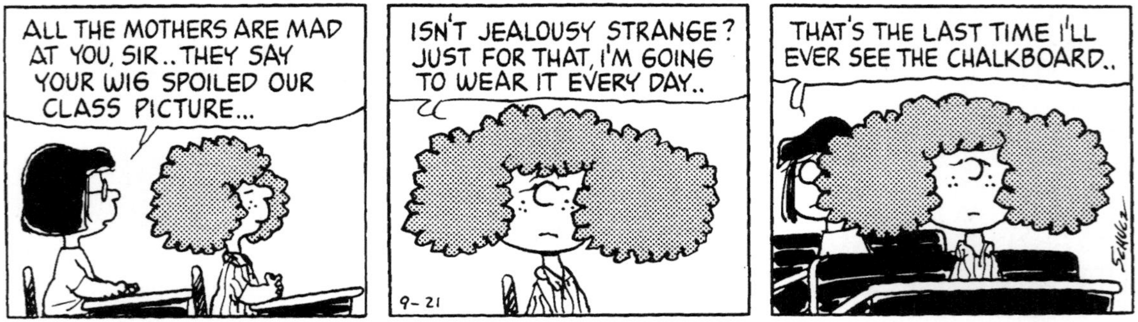
ALL THE MOTHERS ARE MAD AT YOU, SIR..THEY SAY YOUR WIG SPOILED OUR CLASS PICTURE...
ISN'T JEALOUSY STRANGE? JUST FOR THAT, I'M GOING TO WEAR IT EVERY DAY..
9-21
THAT'S THE LAST TIME I'LL EVER SEE THE CHALKBOARD..
SCHULZ

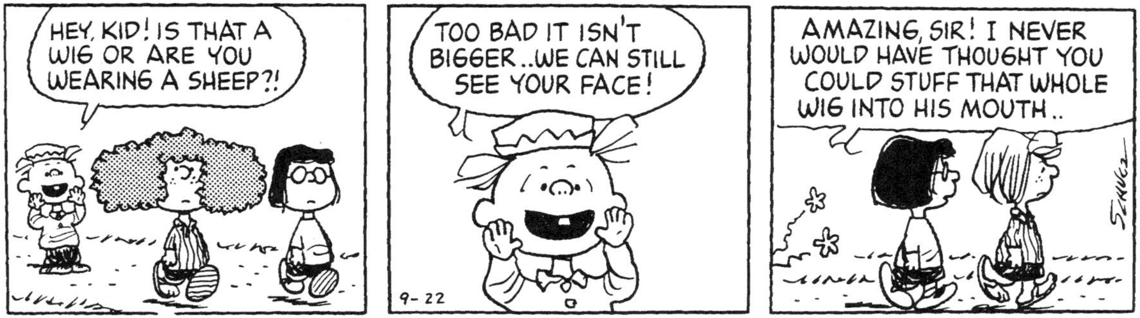
HEY, KID! IS THAT A WIG OR ARE YOU WEARING A SHEEP?!
TOO BAD IT ISN'T BIGGER..WE CAN STILL SEE YOUR FACE!
9-22
AMAZING, SIR! I NEVER WOULD HAVE THOUGHT YOU COULD STUFF THAT WHOLE WIG INTO HIS MOUTH..

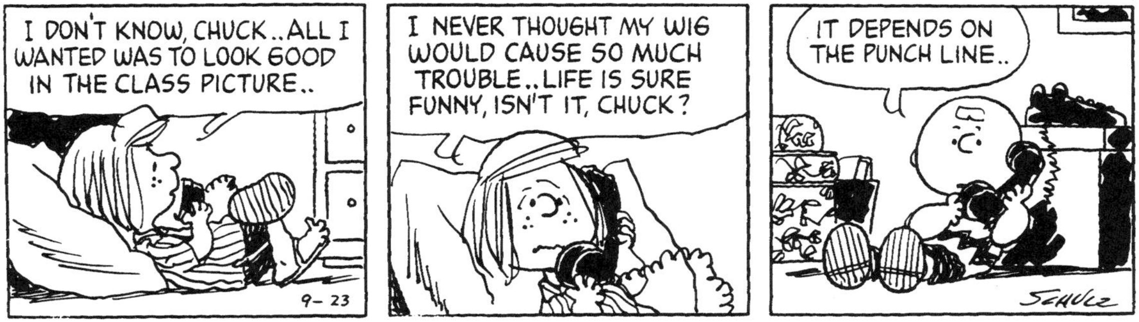
I DON'T KNOW, CHUCK..ALL I WANTED WAS TO LOOK GOOD IN THE CLASS PICTURE..
9-23
I NEVER THOUGHT MY WIG WOULD CAUSE SO MUCH TROUBLE..LIFE IS SURE FUNNY, ISN'T IT, CHUCK?
IT DEPENDS ON THE PUNCH LINE..

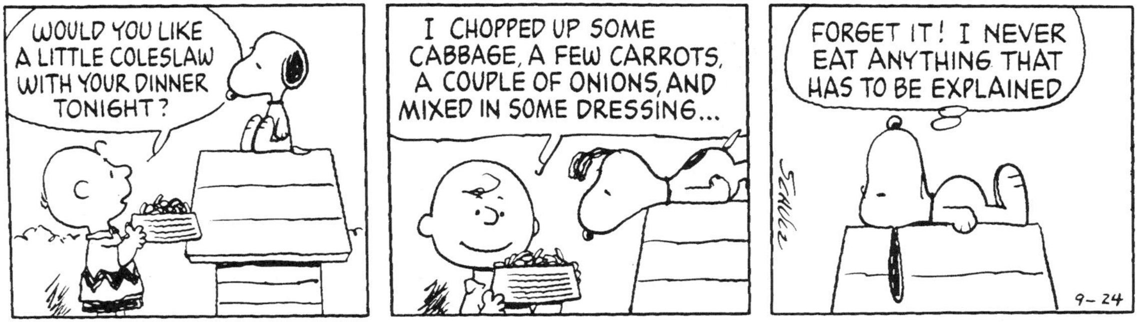
WOULD YOU LIKE A LITTLE COLESLAW WITH YOUR DINNER TONIGHT?
I CHOPPED UP SOME CABBAGE, A FEW CARROTS, A COUPLE OF ONIONS, AND MIXED IN SOME DRESSING...
FORGET IT! I NEVER EAT ANYTHING THAT HAS TO BE EXPLAINED
9-24

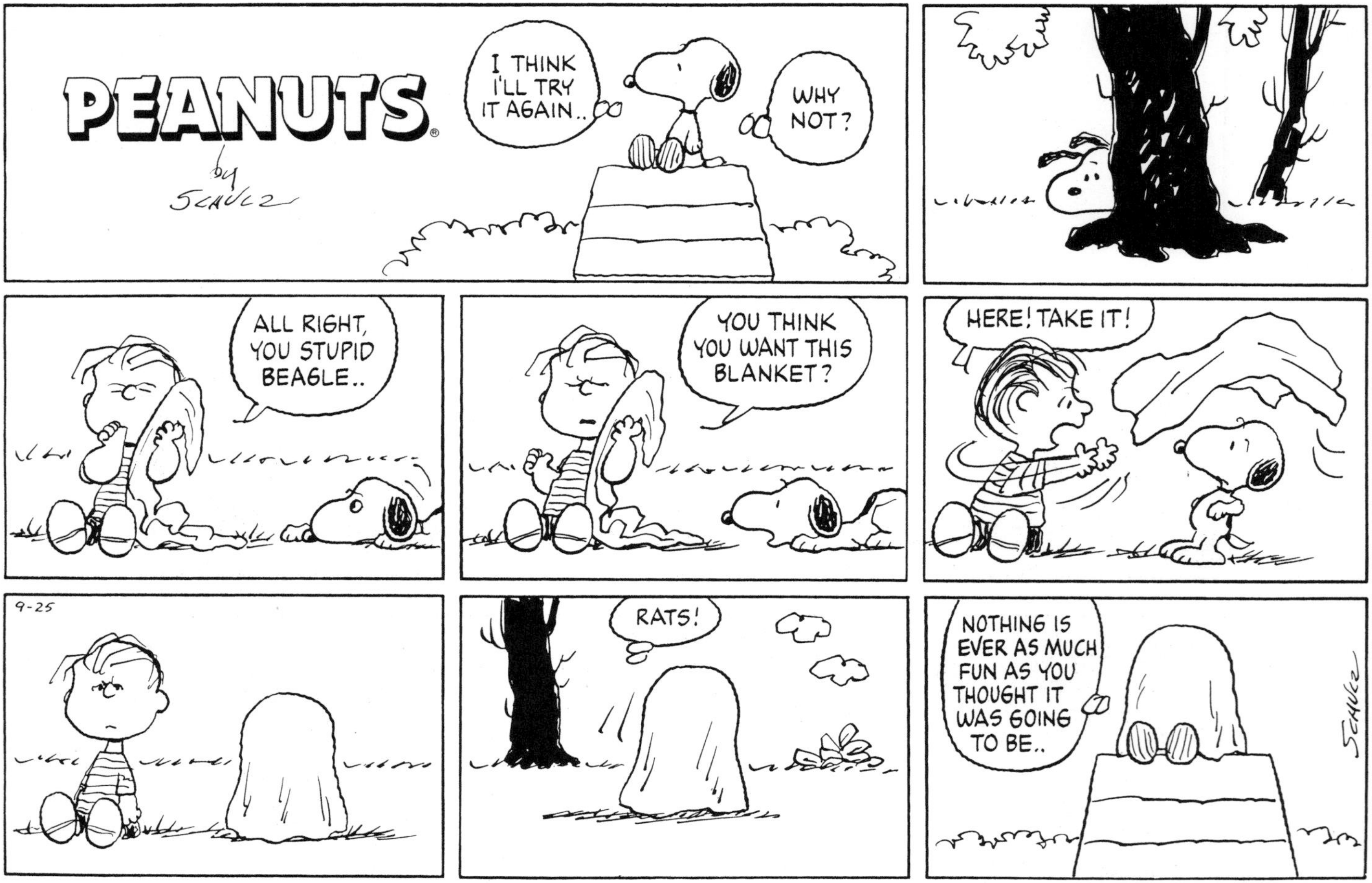
PEANUTS®
by SCHULZ
I THINK I'LL TRY IT AGAIN..
WHY NOT?
ALL RIGHT, YOU STUPID BEAGLE..
YOU THINK YOU WANT THIS BLANKET?
HERE! TAKE IT!
9-25
RATS!
NOTHING IS EVER AS MUCH FUN AS YOU THOUGHT IT WAS GOING TO BE..
SCHULZ

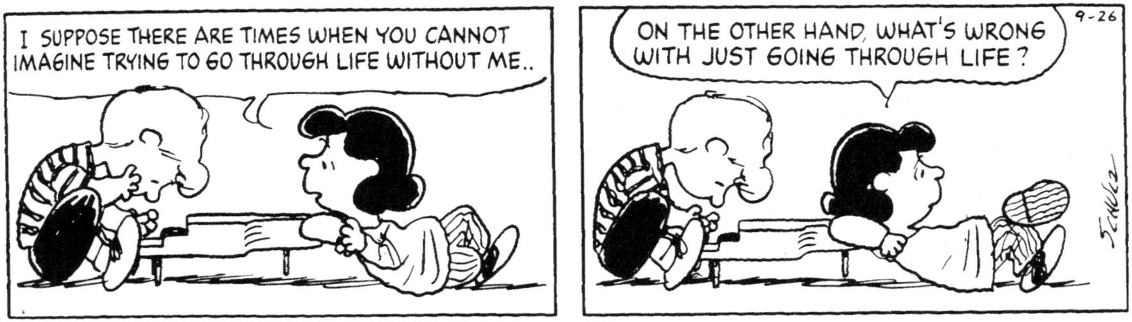
I SUPPOSE THERE ARE TIMES WHEN YOU CANNOT IMAGINE TRYING TO GO THROUGH LIFE WITHOUT ME..
ON THE OTHER HAND, WHAT'S WRONG WITH JUST GOING THROUGH LIFE?
9-26
SCHULZ

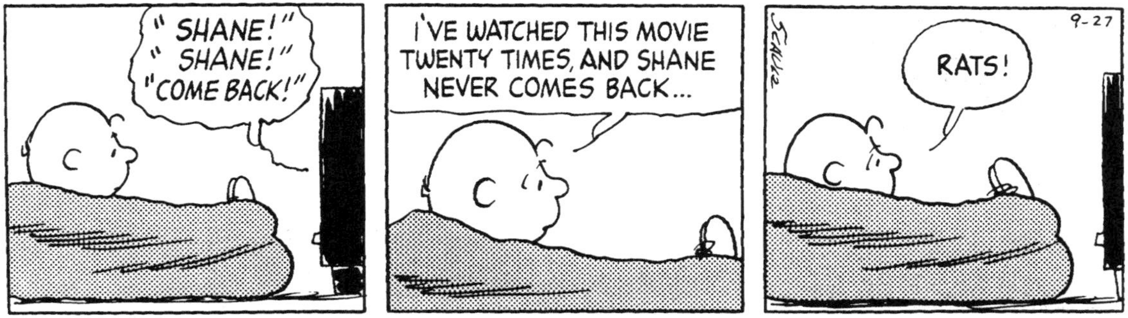
"SHANE!" "SHANE!" "COME BACK!"
I'VE WATCHED THIS MOVIE TWENTY TIMES, AND SHANE NEVER COMES BACK...
SCHULZ
9-27
RATS!

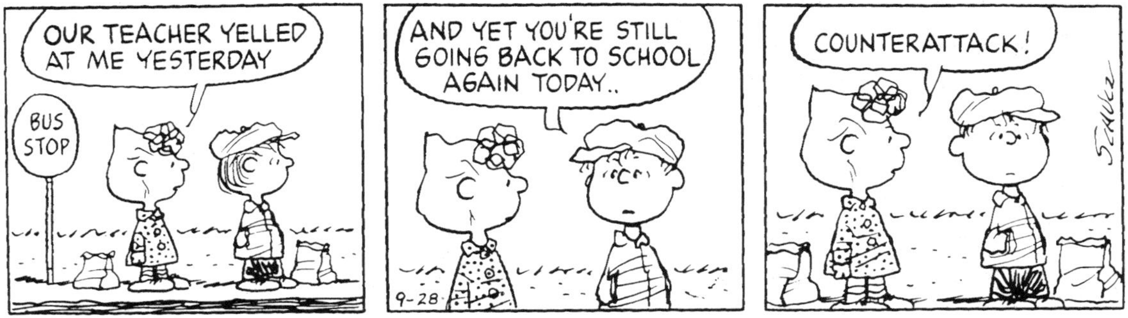
OUR TEACHER YELLED AT ME YESTERDAY
BUS STOP
AND YET YOU'RE STILL GOING BACK TO SCHOOL AGAIN TODAY..
9-28
COUNTERATTACK!
SCHULZ

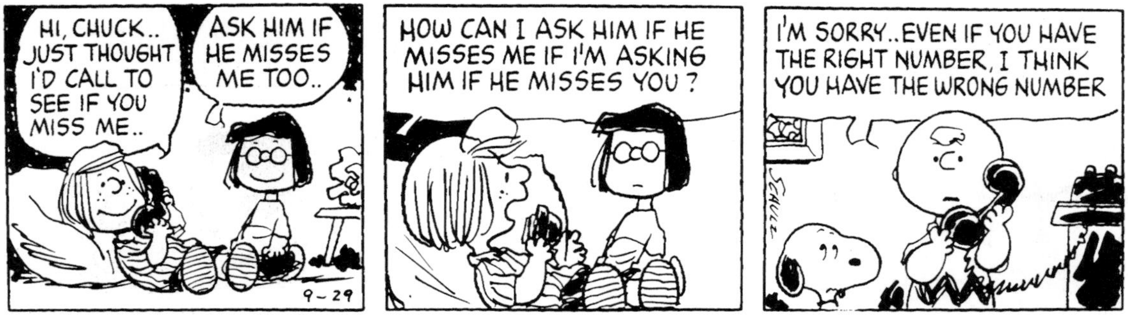
HI, CHUCK.. JUST THOUGHT I'D CALL TO SEE IF YOU MISS ME..
ASK HIM IF HE MISSES ME TOO..
9-29
HOW CAN I ASK HIM IF HE MISSES ME IF I'M ASKING HIM IF HE MISSES YOU?
SCHULZ
I'M SORRY..EVEN IF YOU HAVE THE RIGHT NUMBER, I THINK YOU HAVE THE WRONG NUMBER

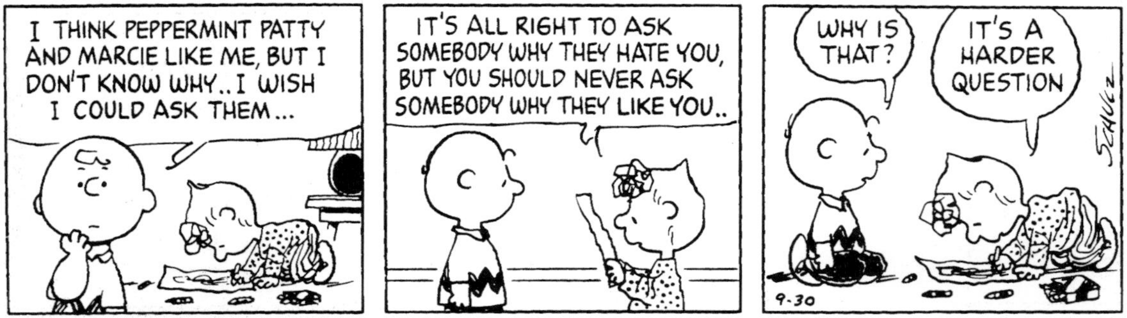
I THINK PEPPERMINT PATTY AND MARCIE LIKE ME, BUT I DON'T KNOW WHY.. I WISH I COULD ASK THEM...
IT'S ALL RIGHT TO ASK SOMEBODY WHY THEY HATE YOU, BUT YOU SHOULD NEVER ASK SOMEBODY WHY THEY LIKE YOU..
WHY IS THAT?
IT'S A HARDER QUESTION
SCHULZ
9-30

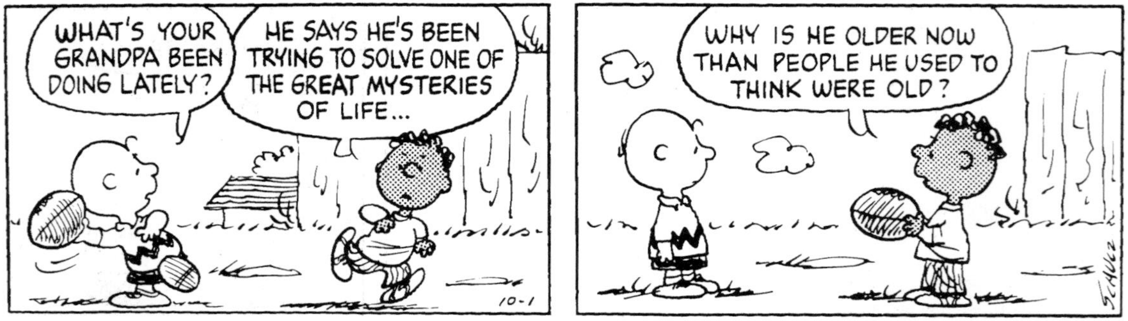
WHAT'S YOUR GRANDPA BEEN DOING LATELY?
HE SAYS HE'S BEEN TRYING TO SOLVE ONE OF THE GREAT MYSTERIES OF LIFE...
10-1
WHY IS HE OLDER NOW THAN PEOPLE HE USED TO THINK WERE OLD?
SCHULZ

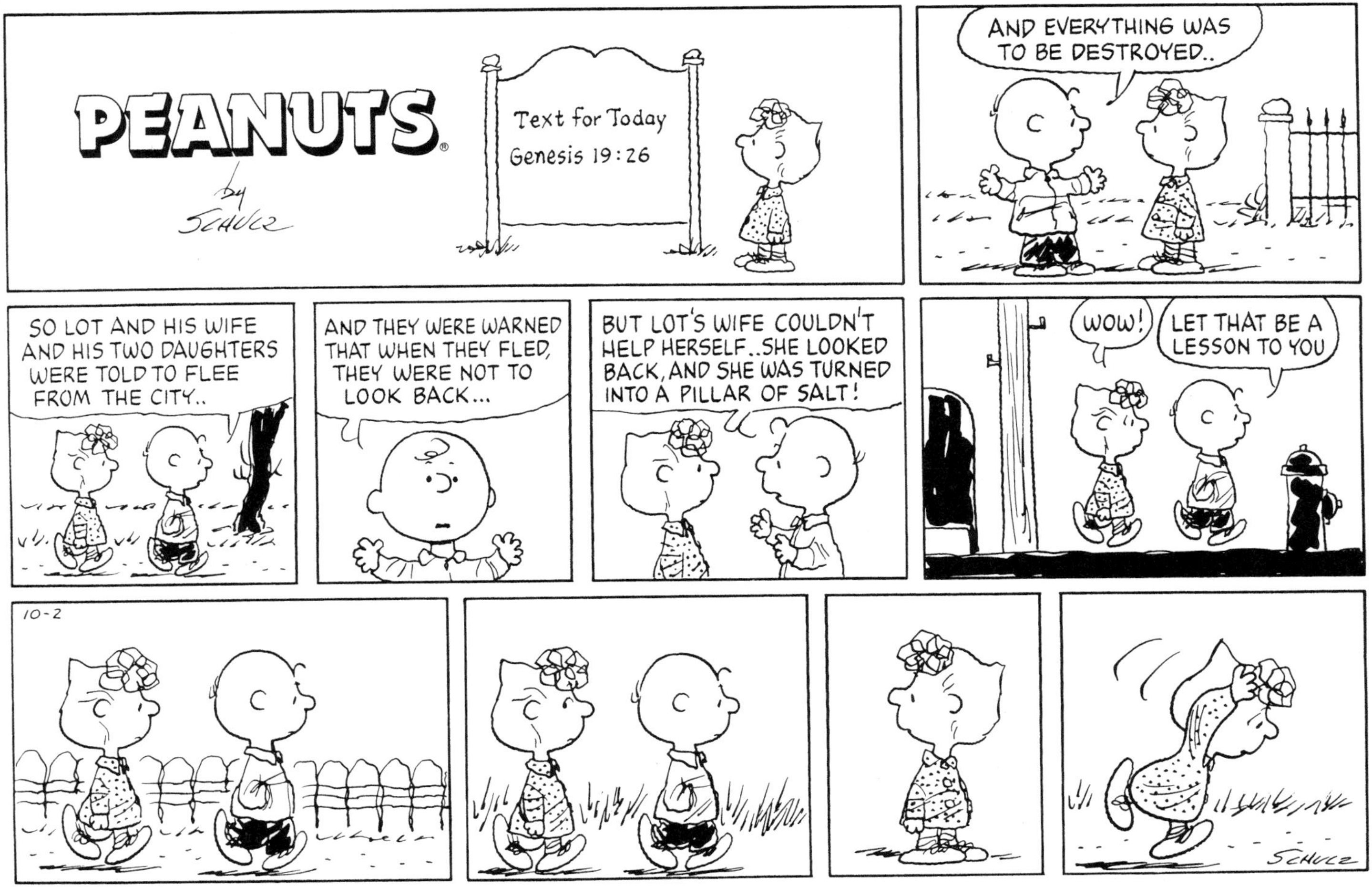
PEANUTS
by Schulz
Text for Today
Genesis 19:26
AND EVERYTHING WAS TO BE DESTROYED..
SO LOT AND HIS WIFE AND HIS TWO DAUGHTERS WERE TOLD TO FLEE FROM THE CITY..
AND THEY WERE WARNED THAT WHEN THEY FLED, THEY WERE NOT TO LOOK BACK...
BUT LOT'S WIFE COULDN'T HELP HERSELF..SHE LOOKED BACK, AND SHE WAS TURNED INTO A PILLAR OF SALT!
WOW!
LET THAT BE A LESSON TO YOU
10-2
SCHULZ

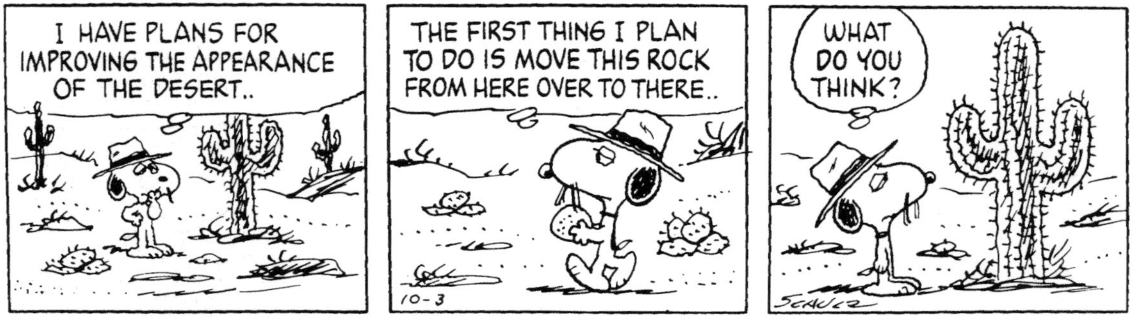
I HAVE PLANS FOR IMPROVING THE APPEARANCE OF THE DESERT..
THE FIRST THING I PLAN TO DO IS MOVE THIS ROCK FROM HERE OVER TO THERE..
10-3
WHAT DO YOU THINK?
SCHULZ

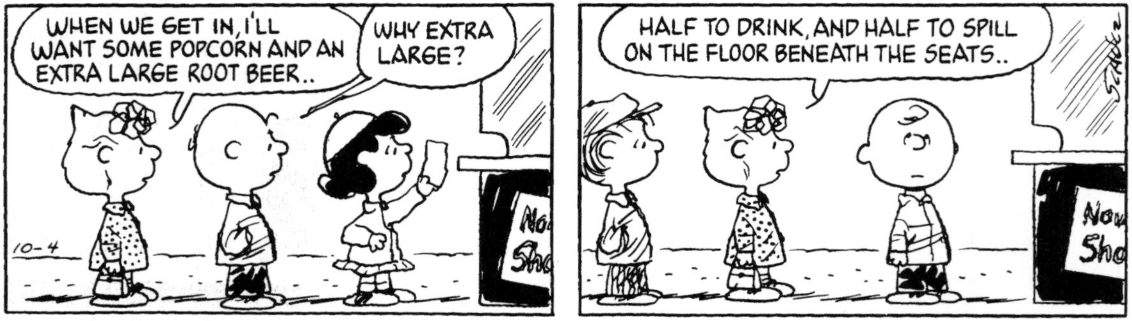
WHEN WE GET IN, I'LL WANT SOME POPCORN AND AN EXTRA LARGE ROOT BEER..
WHY EXTRA LARGE?
10-4
HALF TO DRINK, AND HALF TO SPILL ON THE FLOOR BENEATH THE SEATS..
SCHULZ

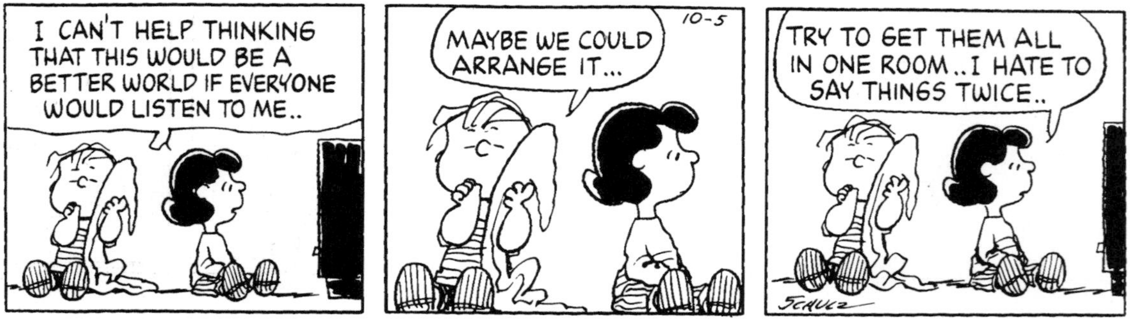
I CAN'T HELP THINKING THAT THIS WOULD BE A BETTER WORLD IF EVERYONE WOULD LISTEN TO ME..
10-5
MAYBE WE COULD ARRANGE IT...
TRY TO GET THEM ALL IN ONE ROOM..I HATE TO SAY THINGS TWICE..
SCHULZ

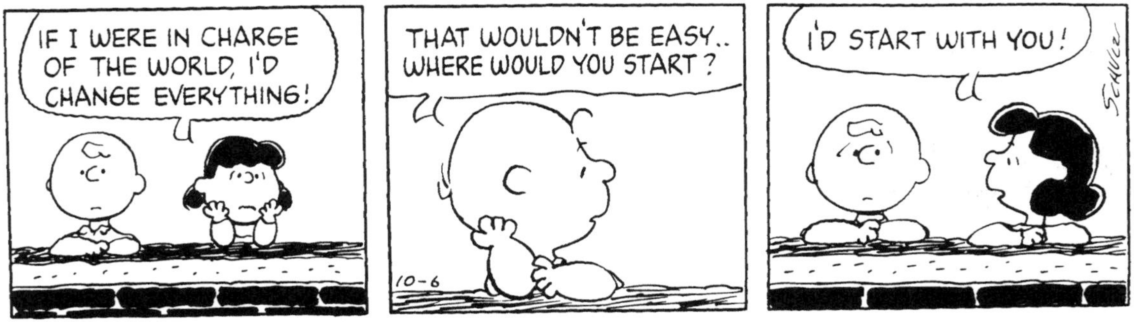
IF I WERE IN CHARGE OF THE WORLD, I'D CHANGE EVERYTHING!
THAT WOULDN'T BE EASY.. WHERE WOULD YOU START?
10-6
I'D START WITH YOU!

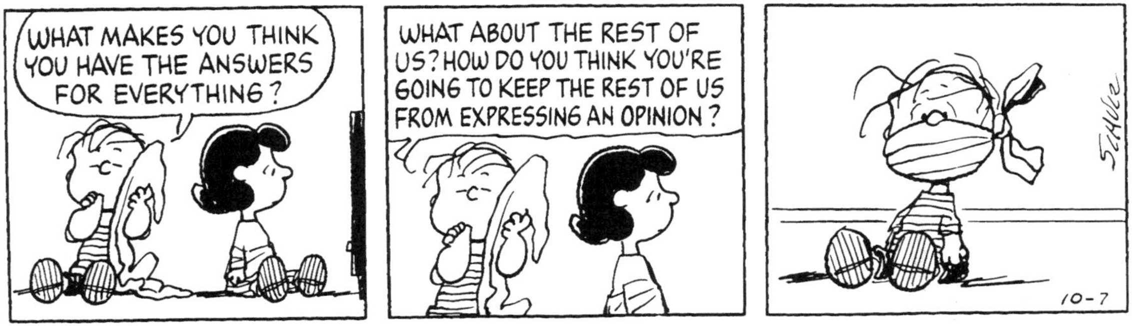
WHAT MAKES YOU THINK YOU HAVE THE ANSWERS FOR EVERYTHING?
WHAT ABOUT THE REST OF US? HOW DO YOU THINK YOU'RE GOING TO KEEP THE REST OF US FROM EXPRESSING AN OPINION?
10-7

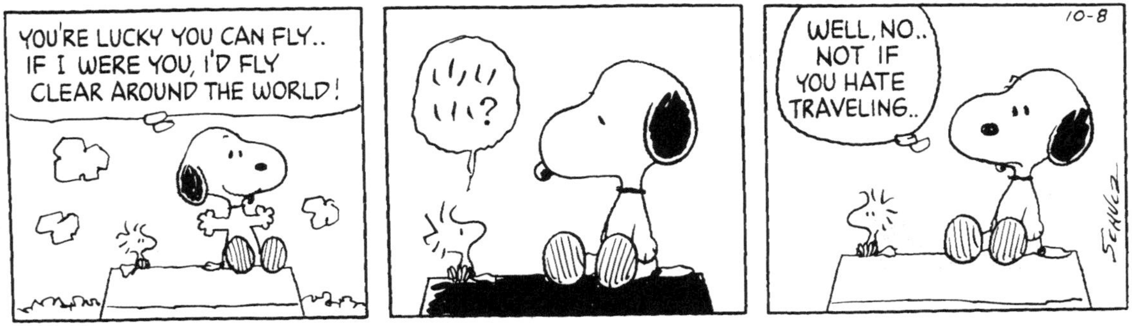
YOU'RE LUCKY YOU CAN FLY.. IF I WERE YOU, I'D FLY CLEAR AROUND THE WORLD!
?
10-8
WELL, NO.. NOT IF YOU HATE TRAVELING..

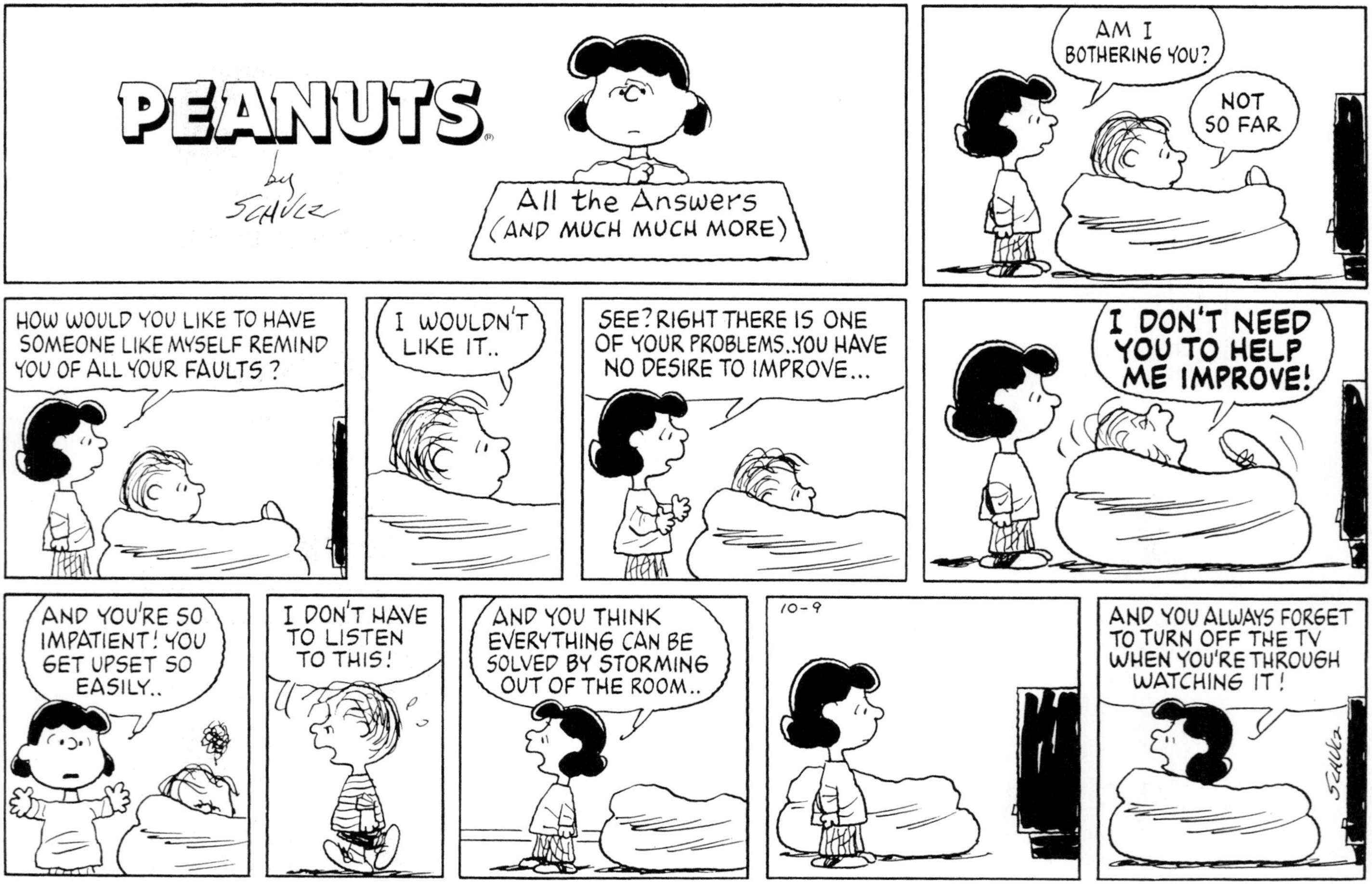
PEANUTS
by SCHULZ
All the Answers
(AND MUCH MUCH MORE)
AM I BOTHERING YOU?
NOT SO FAR
HOW WOULD YOU LIKE TO HAVE SOMEONE LIKE MYSELF REMIND YOU OF ALL YOUR FAULTS?
I WOULDN'T LIKE IT..
SEE? RIGHT THERE IS ONE OF YOUR PROBLEMS..YOU HAVE NO DESIRE TO IMPROVE...
I DON'T NEED YOU TO HELP ME IMPROVE!
AND YOU'RE SO IMPATIENT! YOU GET UPSET SO EASILY..
I DON'T HAVE TO LISTEN TO THIS!
AND YOU THINK EVERYTHING CAN BE SOLVED BY STORMING OUT OF THE ROOM..
10-9
AND YOU ALWAYS FORGET TO TURN OFF THE TV WHEN YOU'RE THROUGH WATCHING IT!
SCHULZ

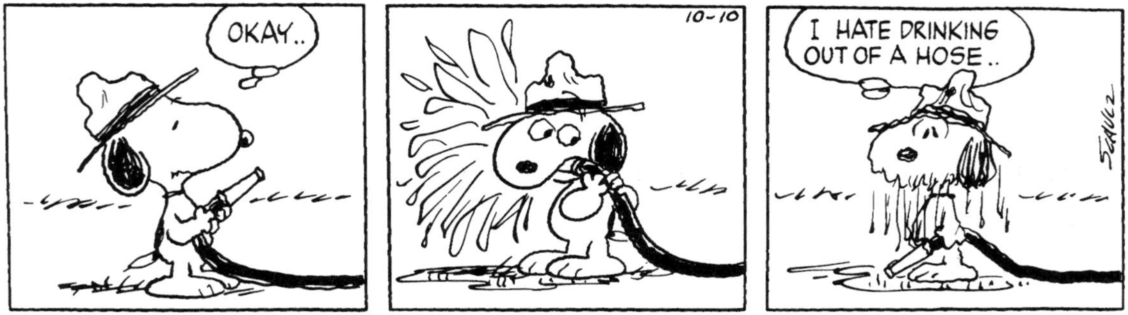
OKAY..
10-10
I HATE DRINKING OUT OF A HOSE..

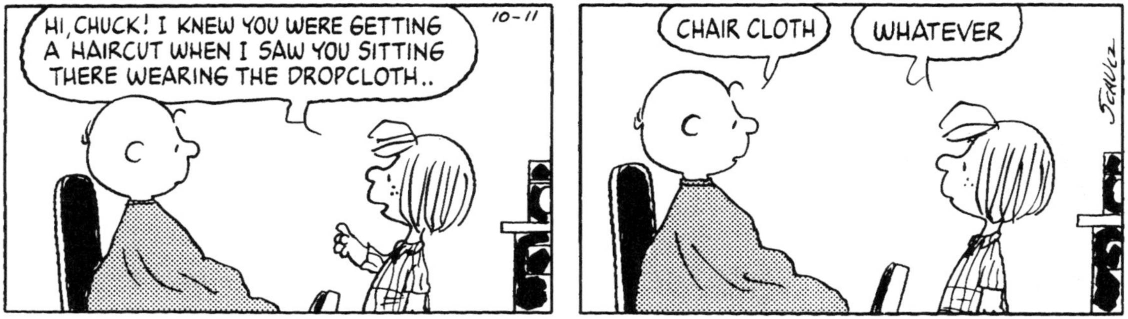
HI, CHUCK! I KNEW YOU WERE GETTING A HAIRCUT WHEN I SAW YOU SITTING THERE WEARING THE DROPCLOTH..
10-11
CHAIR CLOTH
WHATEVER

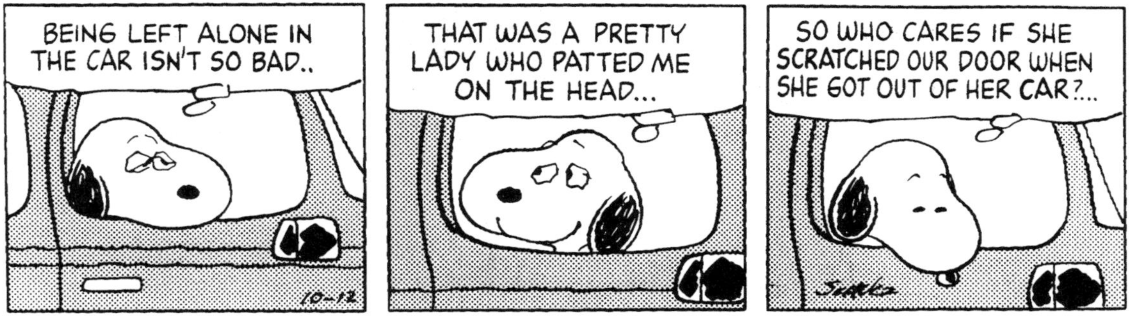
BEING LEFT ALONE IN THE CAR ISN'T SO BAD..
10-12
THAT WAS A PRETTY LADY WHO PATTED ME ON THE HEAD...
SO WHO CARES IF SHE SCRATCHED OUR DOOR WHEN SHE GOT OUT OF HER CAR?...

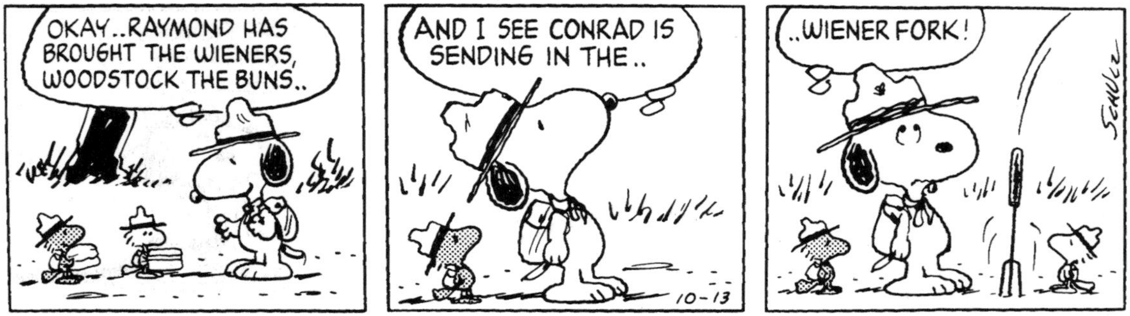
OKAY..RAYMOND HAS BROUGHT THE WIENERS, WOODSTOCK THE BUNS..
AND I SEE CONRAD IS SENDING IN THE..
10-13
..WIENER FORK!

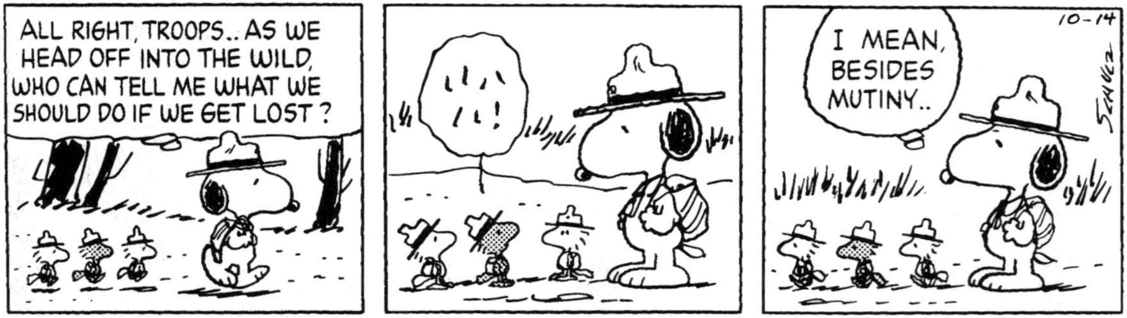
ALL RIGHT, TROOPS.. AS WE HEAD OFF INTO THE WILD, WHO CAN TELL ME WHAT WE SHOULD DO IF WE GET LOST?
10-14
I MEAN, BESIDES MUTINY..

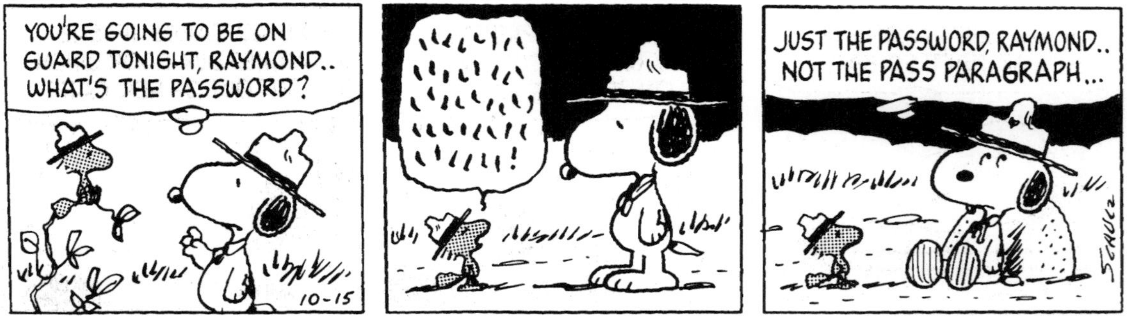
YOU'RE GOING TO BE ON GUARD TONIGHT, RAYMOND.. WHAT'S THE PASSWORD?
10-15
JUST THE PASSWORD, RAYMOND.. NOT THE PASS PARAGRAPH...

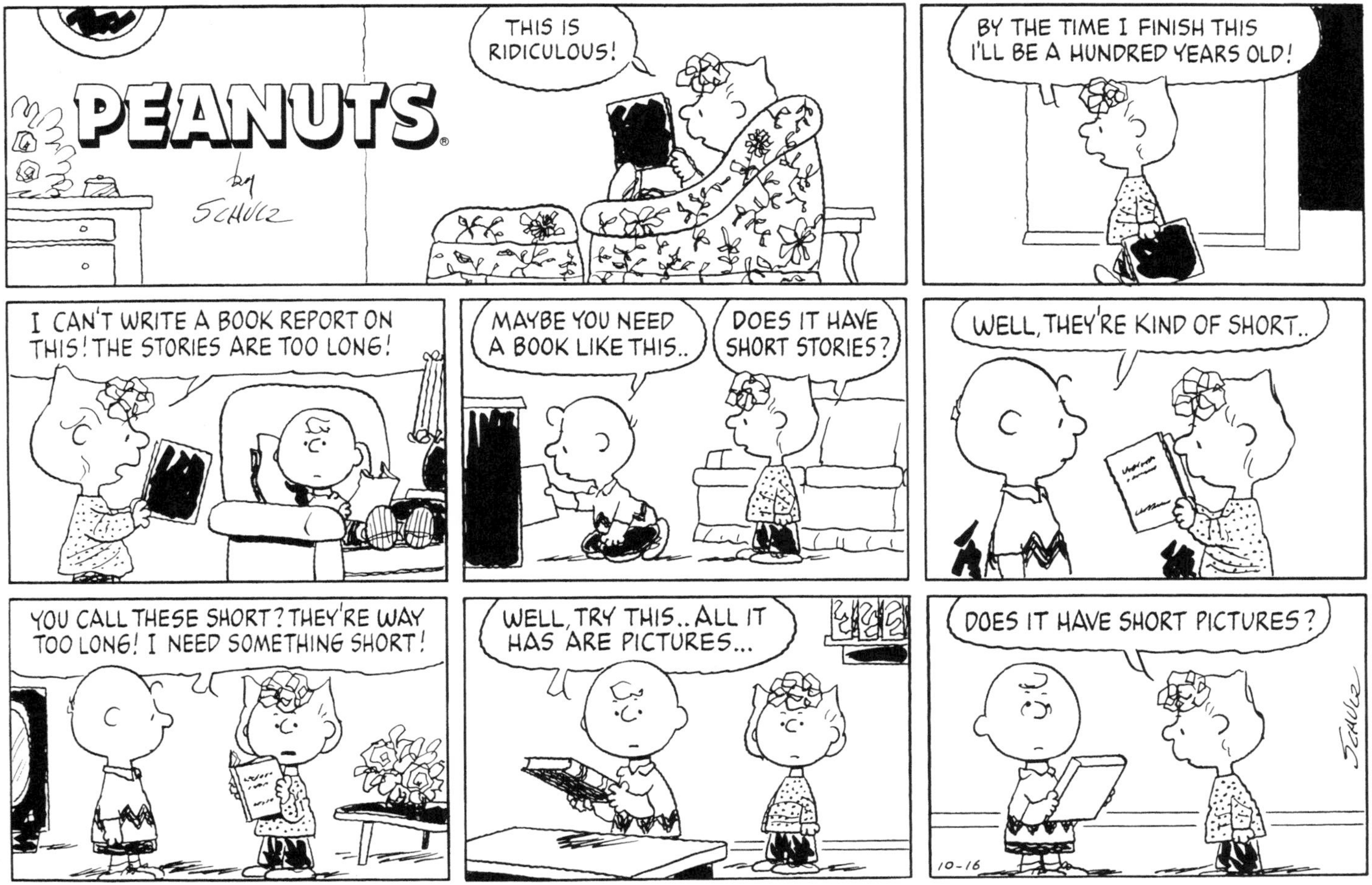
PEANUTS
by SCHULZ
THIS IS RIDICULOUS!
BY THE TIME I FINISH THIS I'LL BE A HUNDRED YEARS OLD!
I CAN'T WRITE A BOOK REPORT ON THIS! THE STORIES ARE TOO LONG!
MAYBE YOU NEED A BOOK LIKE THIS..
DOES IT HAVE SHORT STORIES?
WELL, THEY'RE KIND OF SHORT..
YOU CALL THESE SHORT? THEY'RE WAY TOO LONG! I NEED SOMETHING SHORT!
WELL, TRY THIS.. ALL IT HAS ARE PICTURES...
DOES IT HAVE SHORT PICTURES?
10-16
SCHULZ

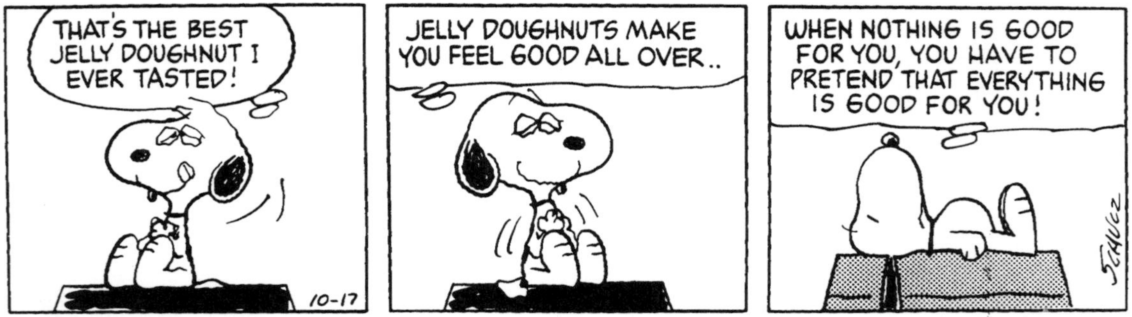
THAT'S THE BEST JELLY DOUGHNUT I EVER TASTED!
10-17
JELLY DOUGHNUTS MAKE YOU FEEL GOOD ALL OVER..
WHEN NOTHING IS GOOD FOR YOU, YOU HAVE TO PRETEND THAT EVERYTHING IS GOOD FOR YOU!
SCHULZ

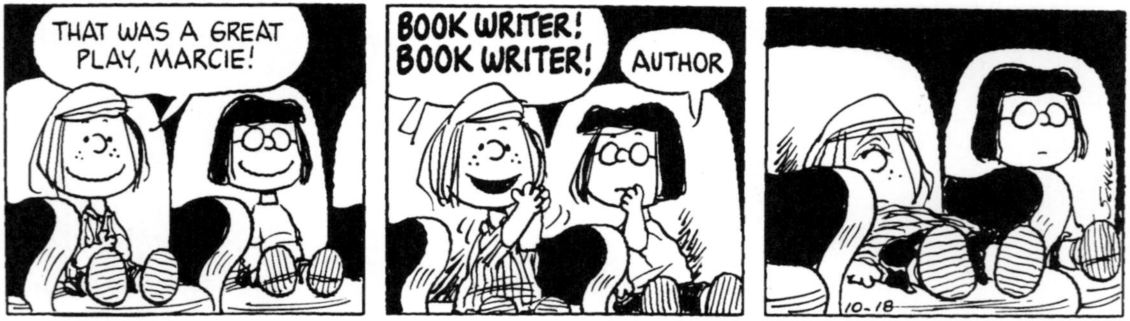
THAT WAS A GREAT PLAY, MARCIE!
BOOK WRITER! BOOK WRITER!
AUTHOR
SCHULZ
10-18

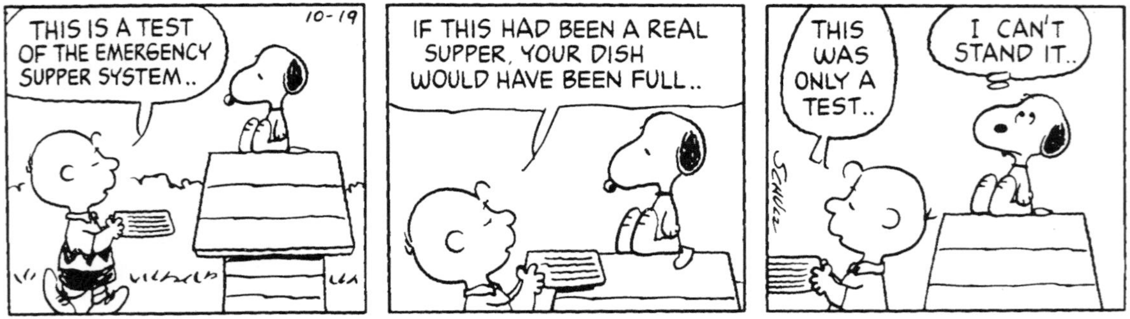
10-19
THIS IS A TEST OF THE EMERGENCY SUPPER SYSTEM..
IF THIS HAD BEEN A REAL SUPPER, YOUR DISH WOULD HAVE BEEN FULL..
THIS WAS ONLY A TEST..
I CAN'T STAND IT..
SCHULZ

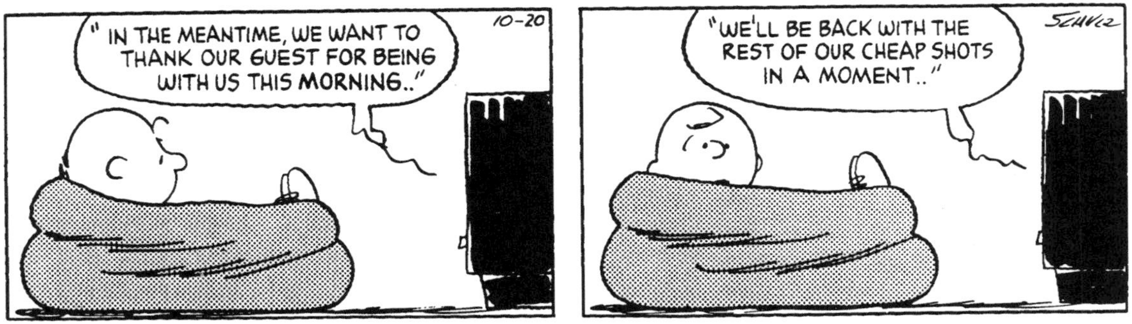
"IN THE MEANTIME, WE WANT TO THANK OUR GUEST FOR BEING WITH US THIS MORNING.."
10-20
"WE'LL BE BACK WITH THE REST OF OUR CHEAP SHOTS IN A MOMENT.."
SCHULZ

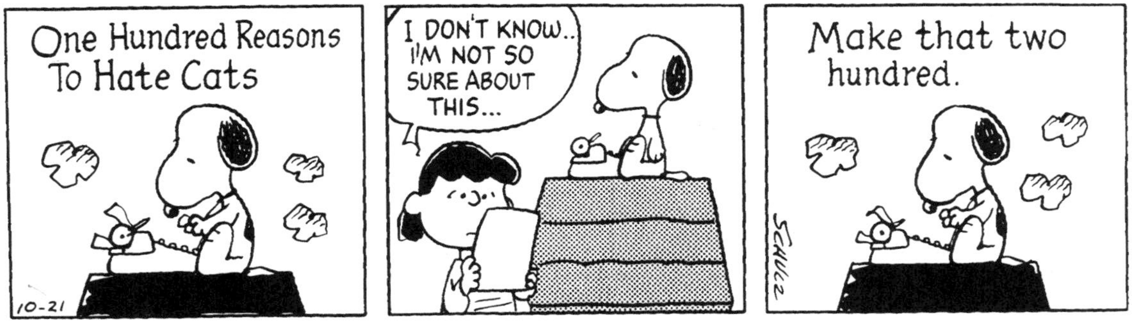
One Hundred Reasons To Hate Cats
10-21
I DON'T KNOW.. I'M NOT SO SURE ABOUT THIS...
Make that two hundred.
SCHULZ

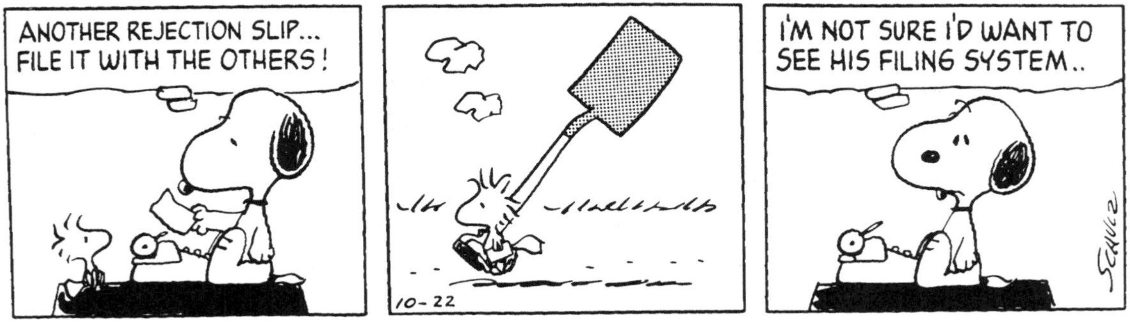
ANOTHER REJECTION SLIP... FILE IT WITH THE OTHERS!
10-22
I'M NOT SURE I'D WANT TO SEE HIS FILING SYSTEM..
SCHULZ

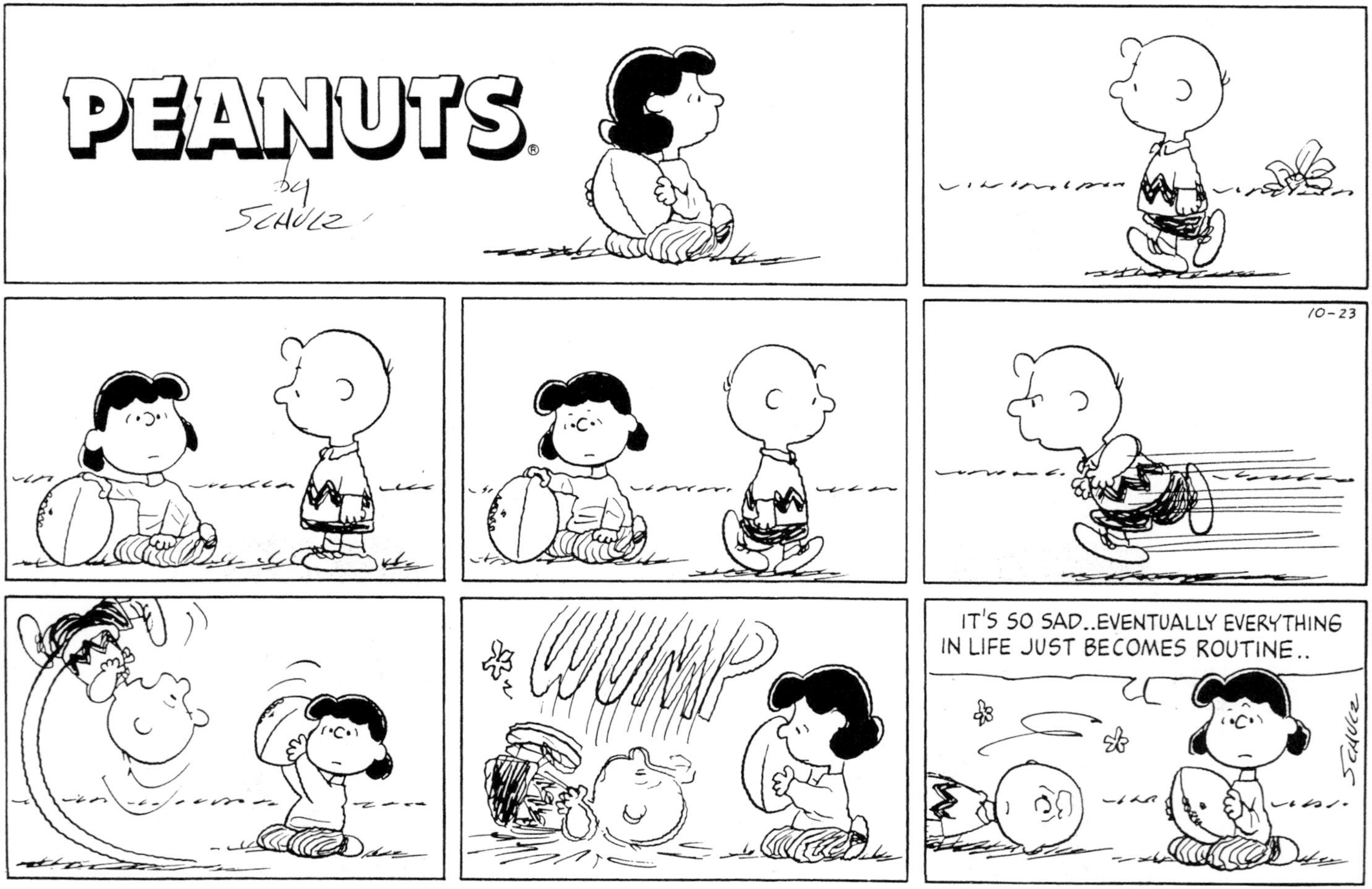
PEANUTS
by SCHULZ
10-23
WUMP
IT'S SO SAD..EVENTUALLY EVERYTHING IN LIFE JUST BECOMES ROUTINE..
SCHULZ

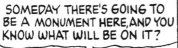

Panel 1: SOMEDAY THERE'S GOING TO BE A MONUMENT HERE, AND YOU KNOW WHAT WILL BE ON IT?

Panel 2: "THIS IS WHERE SALLY BROWN WASTED THE BEST YEARS OF HER LIFE WAITING FOR THE SCHOOL BUS..."

10/24

Panel 3: " SHE COULD HAVE SLEPT ANOTHER TEN MINUTES!"

Panel 4: I CAN'T BELIEVE ALL THE HOURS I'VE WASTED WAITING FOR THE SCHOOL BUS...

Z

Panel 5: GOOD GRIEF! WHAT TIME IS IT?

TEN O'CLOCK.. WE MISSED THE BUS.. I DIDN'T WANT TO WAKE YOU

10-25-

Panel 6: HAVE I DISCOVERED SOMETHING?

Panel 7: YES, MA'AM, I KNOW I'M LATE.. WELL, WE MISSED THE SCHOOL BUS.. MY SISTER FELL ASLEEP AGAINST A TELEPHONE POLE...

10-26

Panel 8: YES, MA'AM.. SITTING ON THE SIDEWALK.. WELL, I DIDN'T WANT TO WAKE HER UP, AND I FELT I COULDN'T LEAVE HER... SO I JUST SAT THERE, TOO...

Panel 9: ACTUALLY, I FELT A LITTLE BIT LIKE LASSIE..

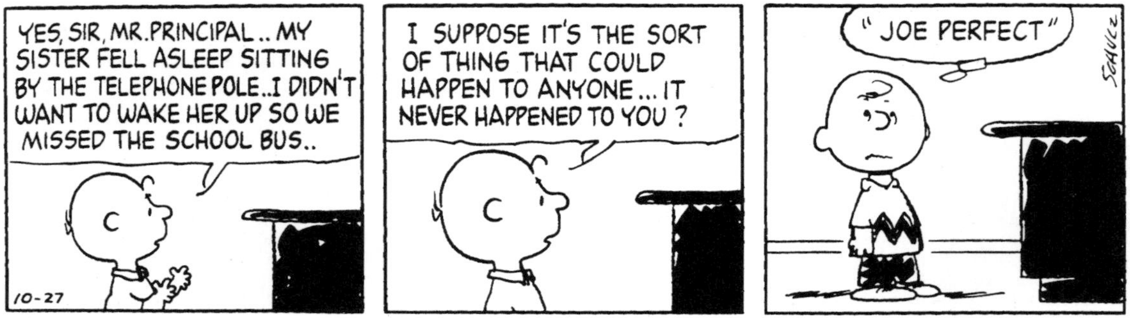
10-27
YES, SIR, MR.PRINCIPAL.. MY SISTER FELL ASLEEP SITTING BY THE TELEPHONE POLE..I DIDN'T WANT TO WAKE HER UP SO WE MISSED THE SCHOOL BUS..
I SUPPOSE IT'S THE SORT OF THING THAT COULD HAPPEN TO ANYONE... IT NEVER HAPPENED TO YOU ?
" JOE PERFECT "

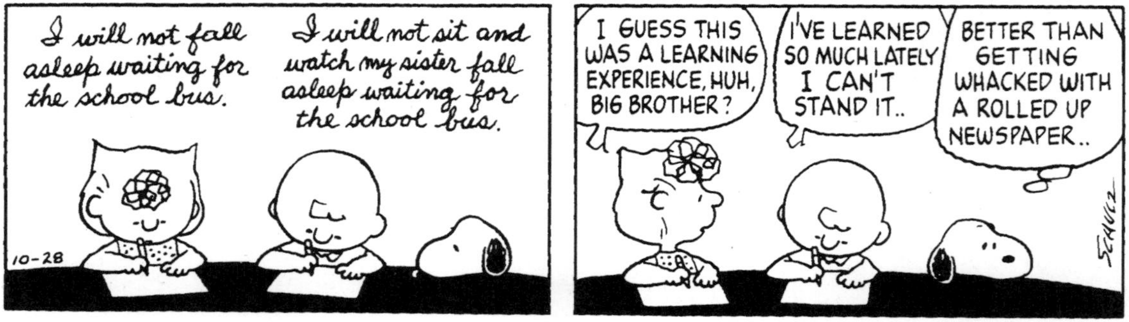
10-28
I will not fall asleep waiting for the school bus.
I will not sit and watch my sister fall asleep waiting for the school bus.
I GUESS THIS WAS A LEARNING EXPERIENCE, HUH, BIG BROTHER ?
I'VE LEARNED SO MUCH LATELY I CAN'T STAND IT..
BETTER THAN GETTING WHACKED WITH A ROLLED UP NEWSPAPER..

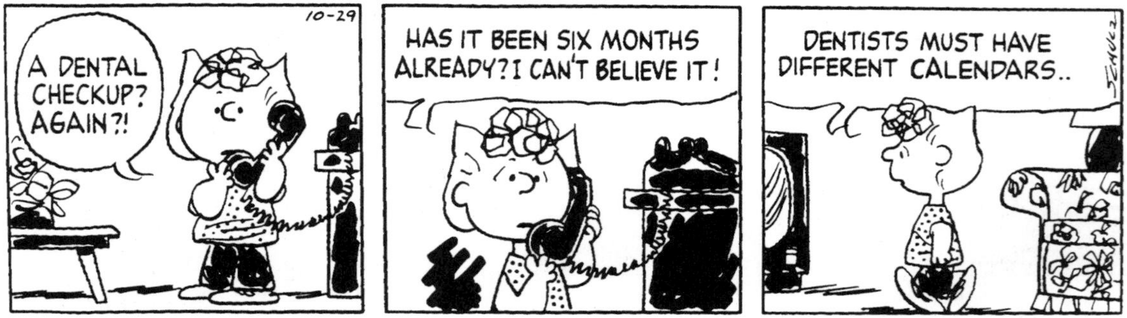
10-29
A DENTAL CHECKUP? AGAIN?!
HAS IT BEEN SIX MONTHS ALREADY? I CAN'T BELIEVE IT !
DENTISTS MUST HAVE DIFFERENT CALENDARS..

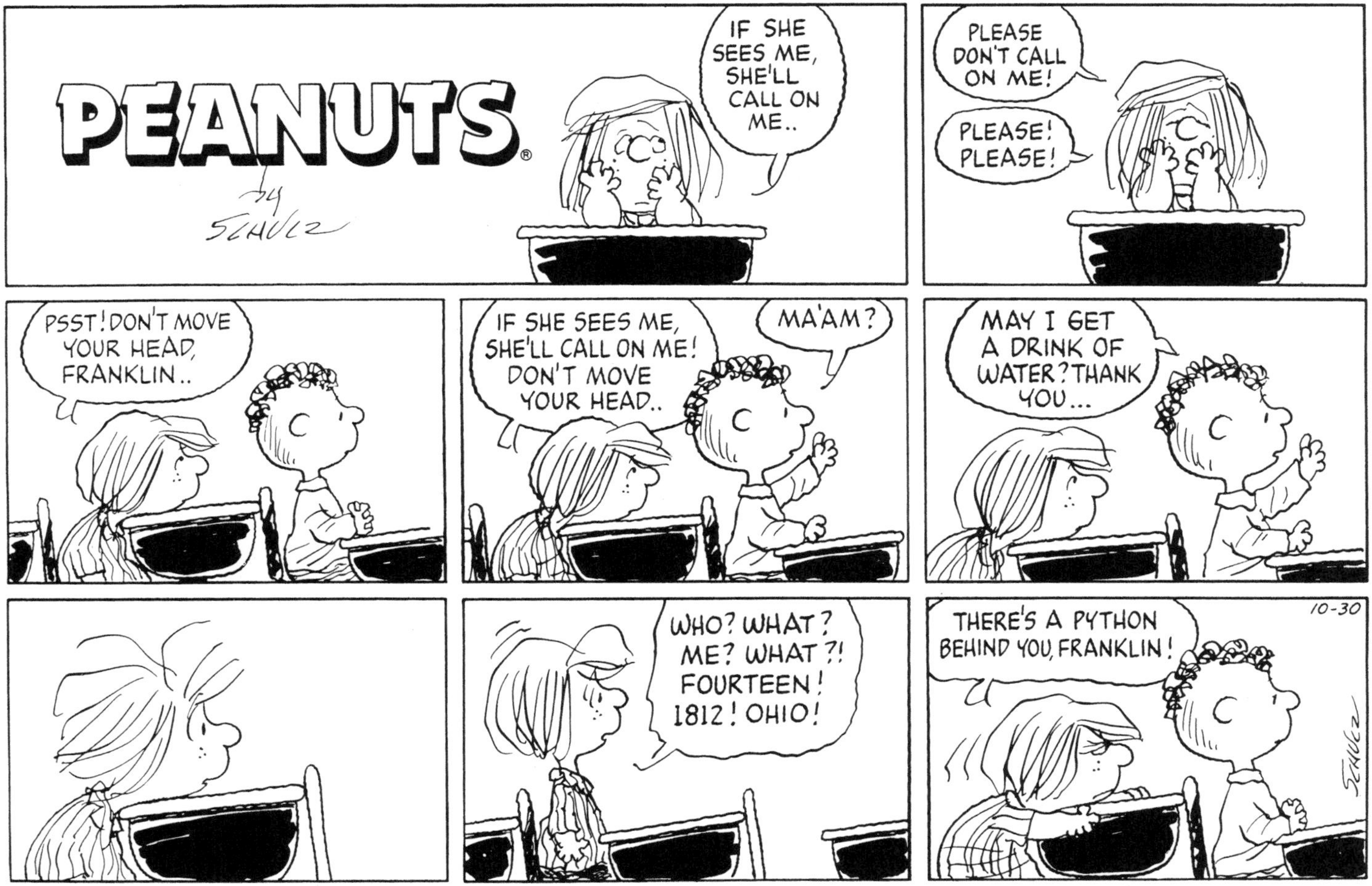
PEANUTS
by SCHULZ
IF SHE SEES ME, SHE'LL CALL ON ME..
PLEASE DON'T CALL ON ME!
PLEASE! PLEASE!
PSST! DON'T MOVE YOUR HEAD, FRANKLIN..
IF SHE SEES ME, SHE'LL CALL ON ME! DON'T MOVE YOUR HEAD..
MA'AM?
MAY I GET A DRINK OF WATER? THANK YOU...
WHO? WHAT? ME? WHAT?! FOURTEEN! 1812! OHIO!
10-30
THERE'S A PYTHON BEHIND YOU, FRANKLIN!
SCHULZ

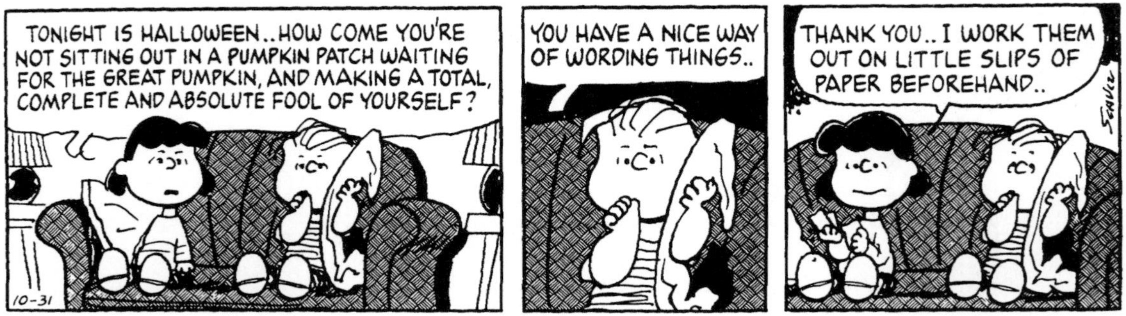
TONIGHT IS HALLOWEEN..HOW COME YOU'RE NOT SITTING OUT IN A PUMPKIN PATCH WAITING FOR THE GREAT PUMPKIN, AND MAKING A TOTAL, COMPLETE AND ABSOLUTE FOOL OF YOURSELF?
10-31
YOU HAVE A NICE WAY OF WORDING THINGS..
THANK YOU.. I WORK THEM OUT ON LITTLE SLIPS OF PAPER BEFOREHAND..
SCHULZ

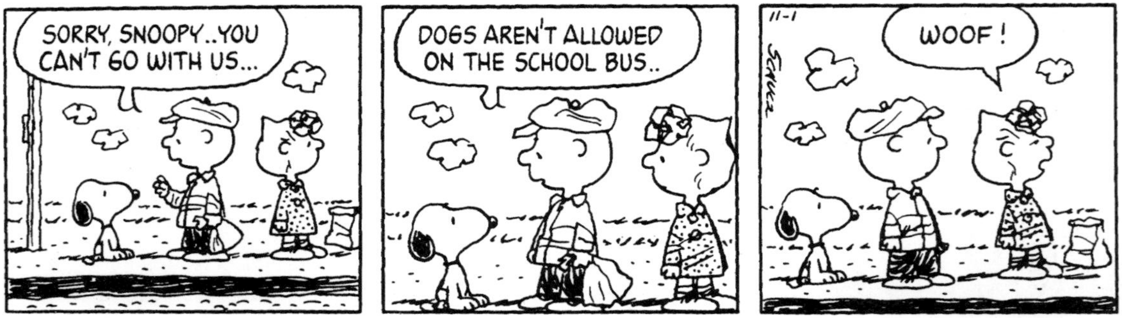
SORRY, SNOOPY..YOU CAN'T GO WITH US...
DOGS AREN'T ALLOWED ON THE SCHOOL BUS..
11-1
SCHULZ
WOOF!

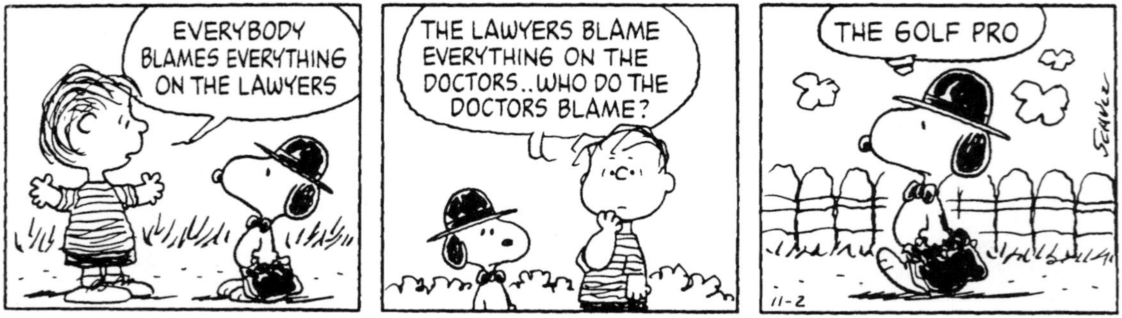
EVERYBODY BLAMES EVERYTHING ON THE LAWYERS
THE LAWYERS BLAME EVERYTHING ON THE DOCTORS..WHO DO THE DOCTORS BLAME?
THE GOLF PRO
SCHULZ
11-2

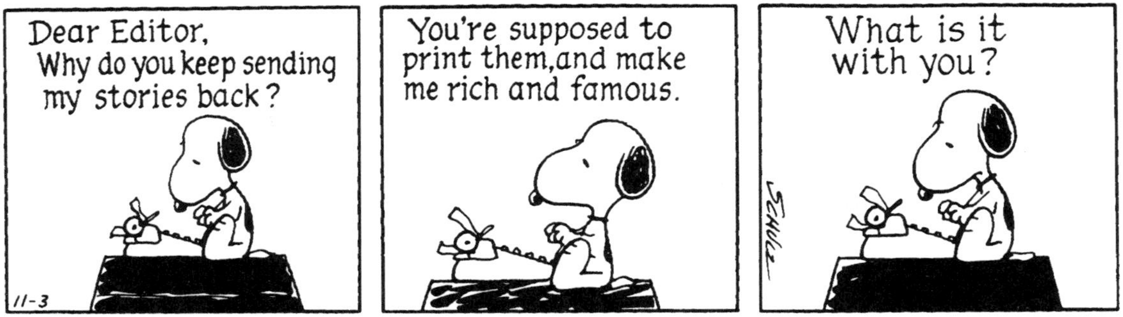
Dear Editor,
Why do you keep sending my stories back?
You're supposed to print them, and make me rich and famous.
What is it with you?

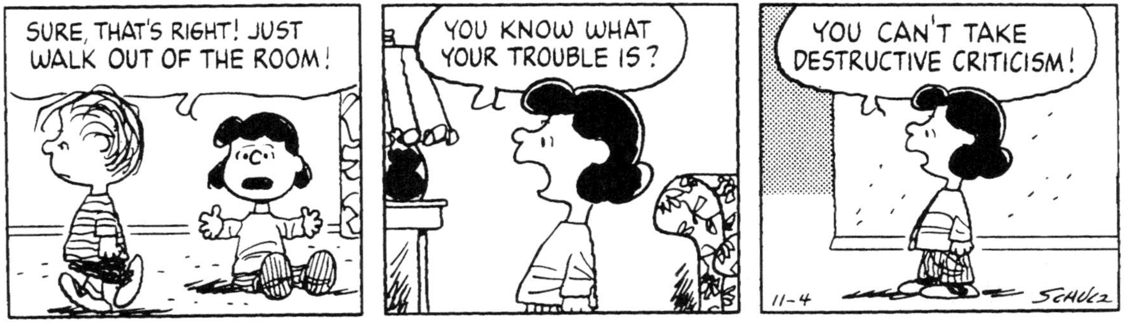
SURE, THAT'S RIGHT! JUST WALK OUT OF THE ROOM!
YOU KNOW WHAT YOUR TROUBLE IS?
YOU CAN'T TAKE DESTRUCTIVE CRITICISM!

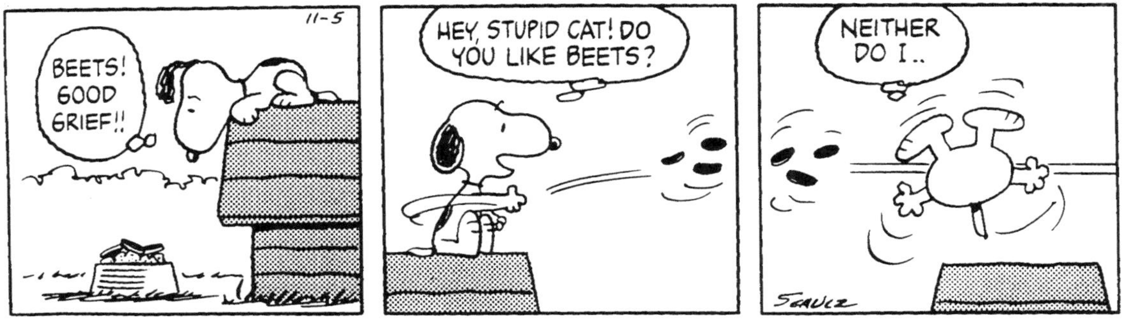
BEETS! GOOD GRIEF!!
HEY, STUPID CAT! DO YOU LIKE BEETS?
NEITHER DO I..

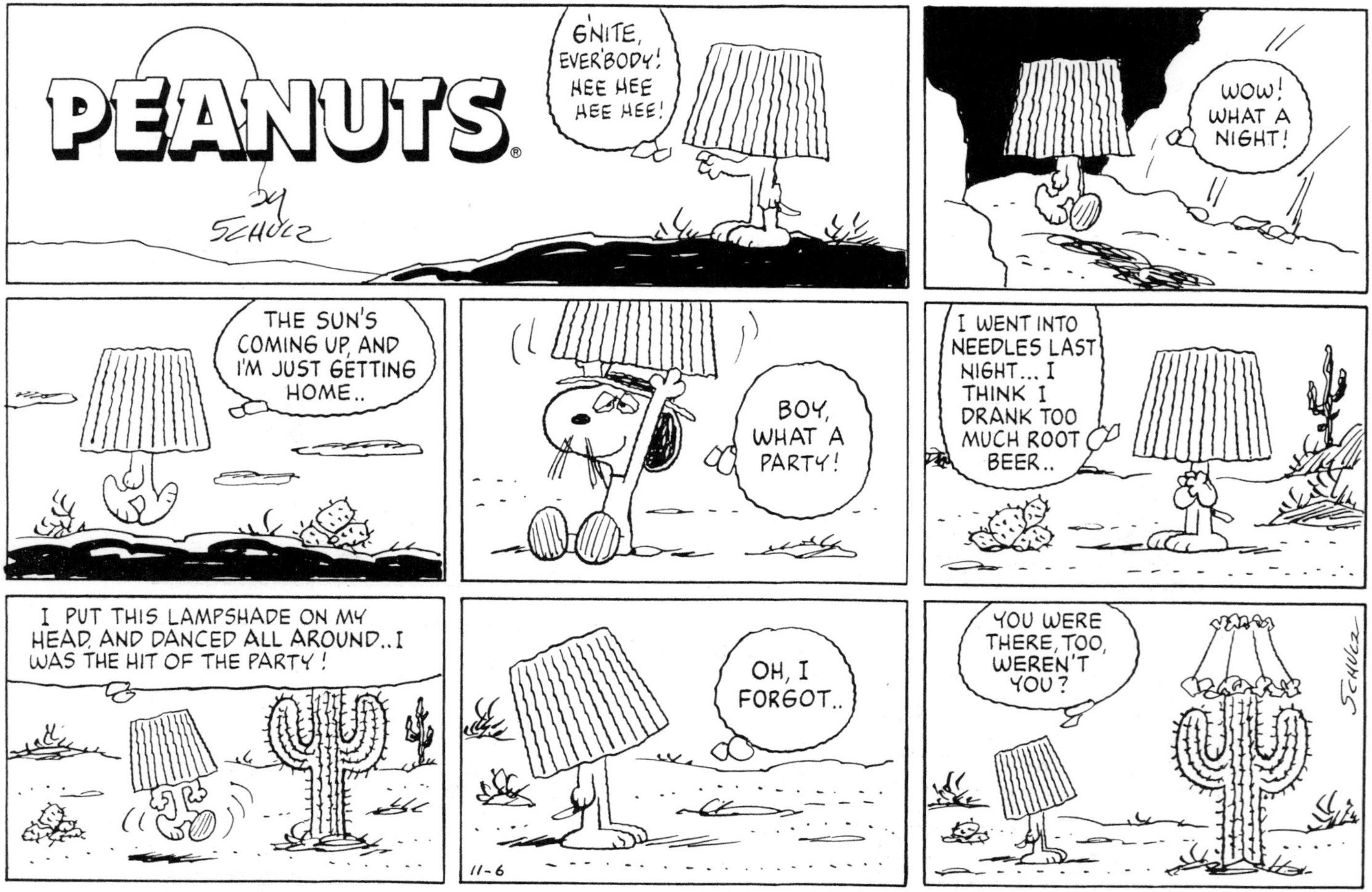
PEANUTS
SCHULZ
G'NITE, EVER'BODY! HEE HEE HEE HEE!
WOW! WHAT A NIGHT!
THE SUN'S COMING UP, AND I'M JUST GETTING HOME..
BOY, WHAT A PARTY!
I WENT INTO NEEDLES LAST NIGHT... I THINK I DRANK TOO MUCH ROOT BEER..
I PUT THIS LAMPSHADE ON MY HEAD AND DANCED ALL AROUND..I WAS THE HIT OF THE PARTY!
OH, I FORGOT..
11-6
YOU WERE THERE, TOO, WEREN'T YOU?
SCHULZ

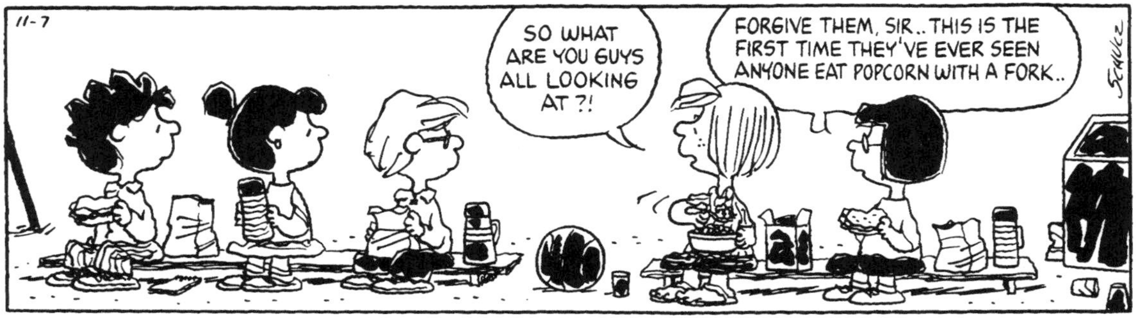
11-7
SO WHAT ARE YOU GUYS ALL LOOKING AT ?!
FORGIVE THEM, SIR.. THIS IS THE FIRST TIME THEY'VE EVER SEEN ANYONE EAT POPCORN WITH A FORK..
SCHULZ

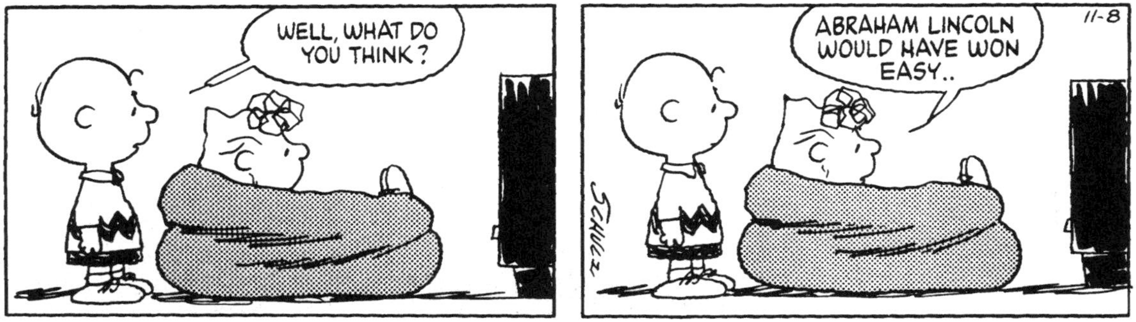
WELL, WHAT DO YOU THINK ?
11-8
ABRAHAM LINCOLN WOULD HAVE WON EASY..
SCHULZ

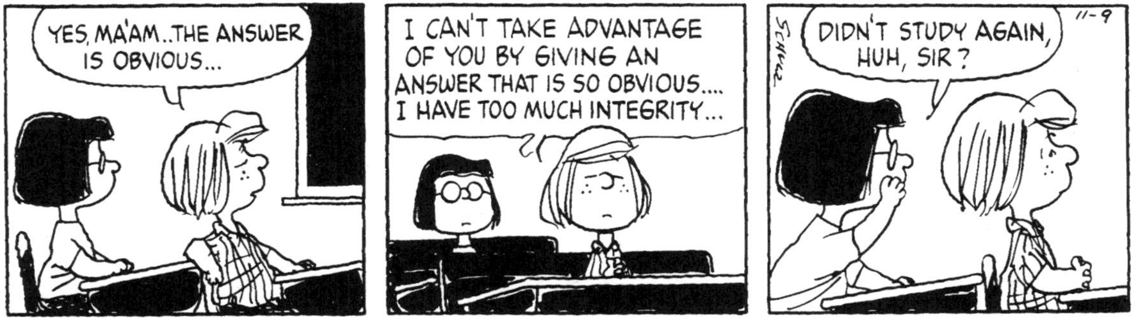
YES, MA'AM..THE ANSWER IS OBVIOUS...
I CAN'T TAKE ADVANTAGE OF YOU BY GIVING AN ANSWER THAT IS SO OBVIOUS.... I HAVE TOO MUCH INTEGRITY...
11-9
DIDN'T STUDY AGAIN, HUH, SIR ?
SCHULZ

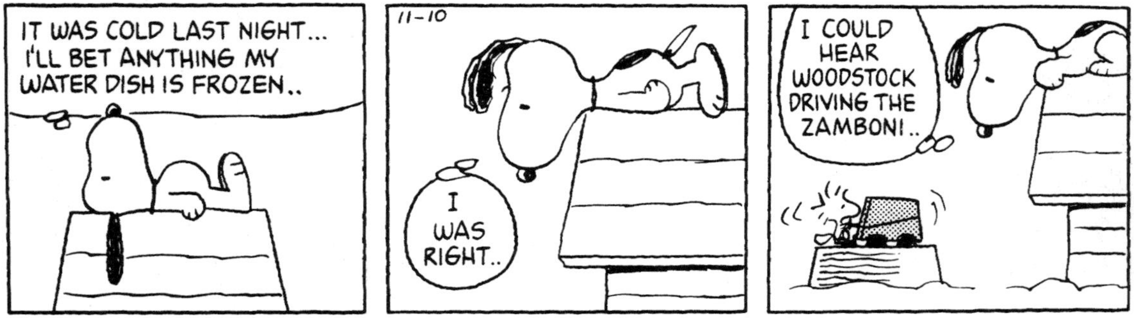
IT WAS COLD LAST NIGHT... I'LL BET ANYTHING MY WATER DISH IS FROZEN..
11-10
I WAS RIGHT..
I COULD HEAR WOODSTOCK DRIVING THE ZAMBONI..

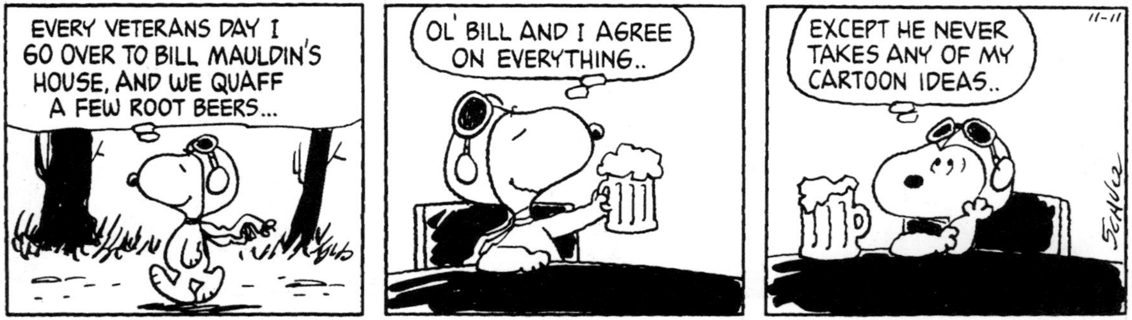
EVERY VETERANS DAY I GO OVER TO BILL MAULDIN'S HOUSE, AND WE QUAFF A FEW ROOT BEERS...
OL' BILL AND I AGREE ON EVERYTHING..
EXCEPT HE NEVER TAKES ANY OF MY CARTOON IDEAS..
11-11
SCHULZ

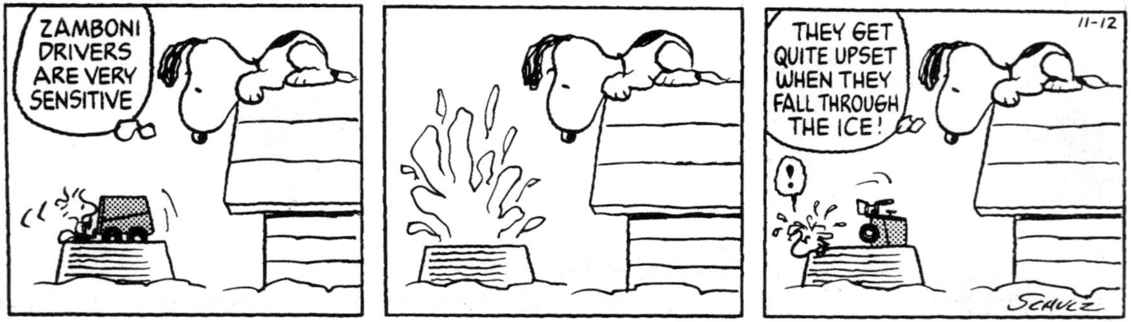
ZAMBONI DRIVERS ARE VERY SENSITIVE
THEY GET QUITE UPSET WHEN THEY FALL THROUGH THE ICE!
11-12
!
SCHULZ

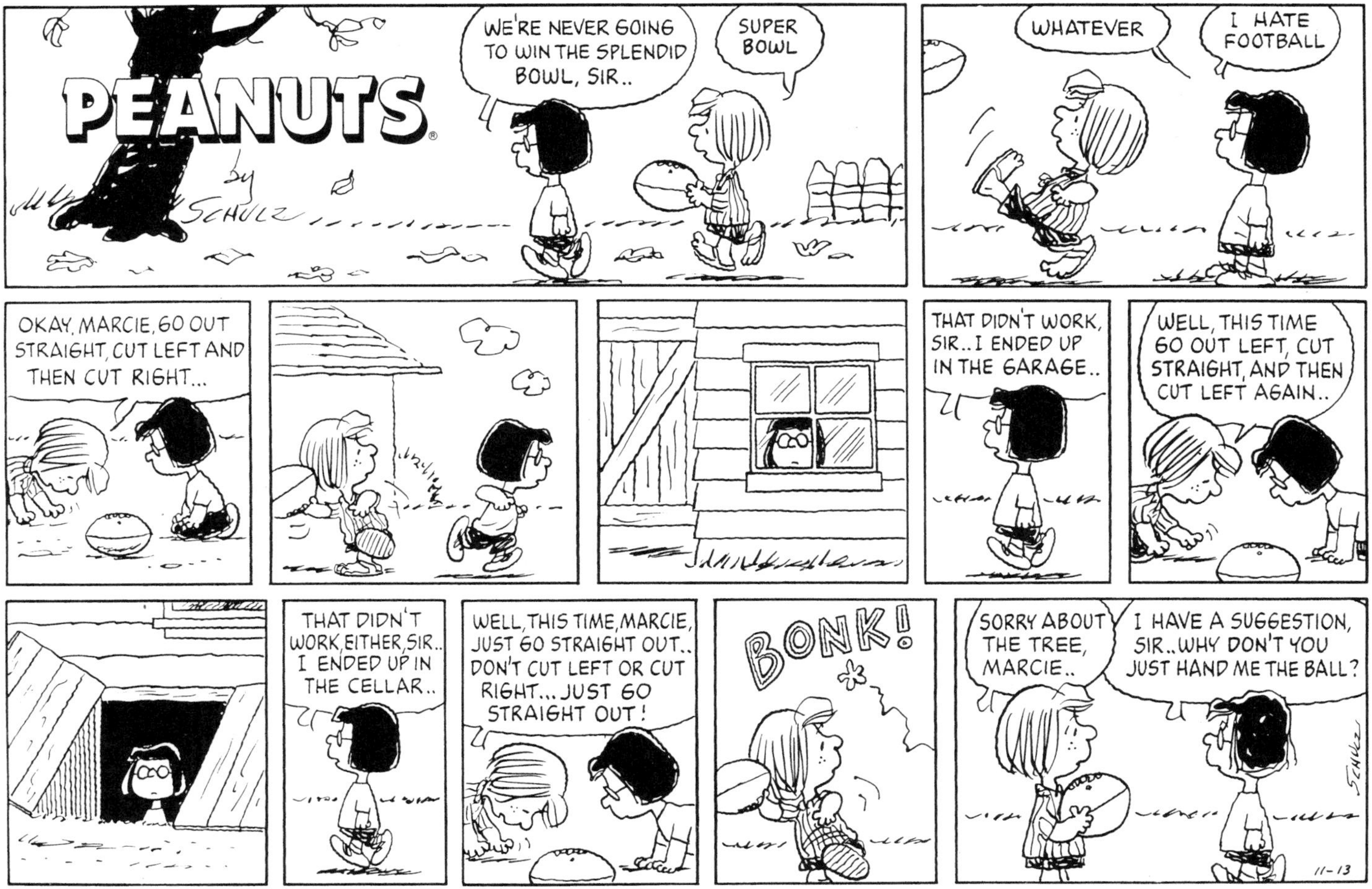
PEANUTS
by SCHULZ
WE'RE NEVER GOING TO WIN THE SPLENDID BOWL, SIR..
SUPER BOWL
WHATEVER
I HATE FOOTBALL
OKAY, MARCIE, GO OUT STRAIGHT, CUT LEFT AND THEN CUT RIGHT...
THAT DIDN'T WORK, SIR.. I ENDED UP IN THE GARAGE..
WELL, THIS TIME GO OUT LEFT, CUT STRAIGHT, AND THEN CUT LEFT AGAIN..
THAT DIDN'T WORK, EITHER, SIR.. I ENDED UP IN THE CELLAR..
WELL, THIS TIME, MARCIE, JUST GO STRAIGHT OUT.. DON'T CUT LEFT OR CUT RIGHT... JUST GO STRAIGHT OUT!
BONK!
SORRY ABOUT THE TREE, MARCIE..
I HAVE A SUGGESTION, SIR.. WHY DON'T YOU JUST HAND ME THE BALL?
SCHULZ
11-13

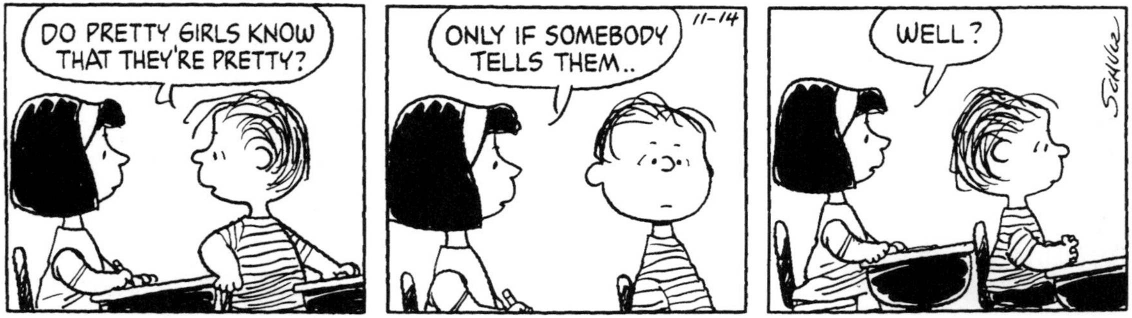
DO PRETTY GIRLS KNOW THAT THEY'RE PRETTY?
11-14
ONLY IF SOMEBODY TELLS THEM..
WELL?

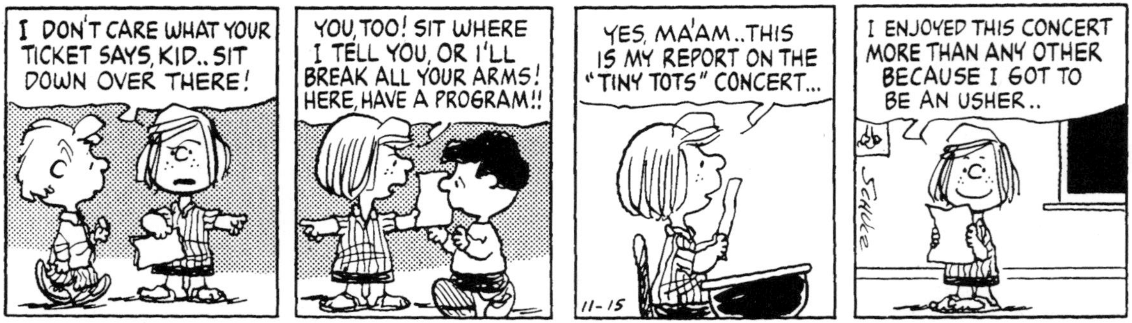
I DON'T CARE WHAT YOUR TICKET SAYS, KID.. SIT DOWN OVER THERE!
YOU, TOO! SIT WHERE I TELL YOU, OR I'LL BREAK ALL YOUR ARMS! HERE, HAVE A PROGRAM!!
YES, MA'AM..THIS IS MY REPORT ON THE "TINY TOTS" CONCERT...
11-15
I ENJOYED THIS CONCERT MORE THAN ANY OTHER BECAUSE I GOT TO BE AN USHER..

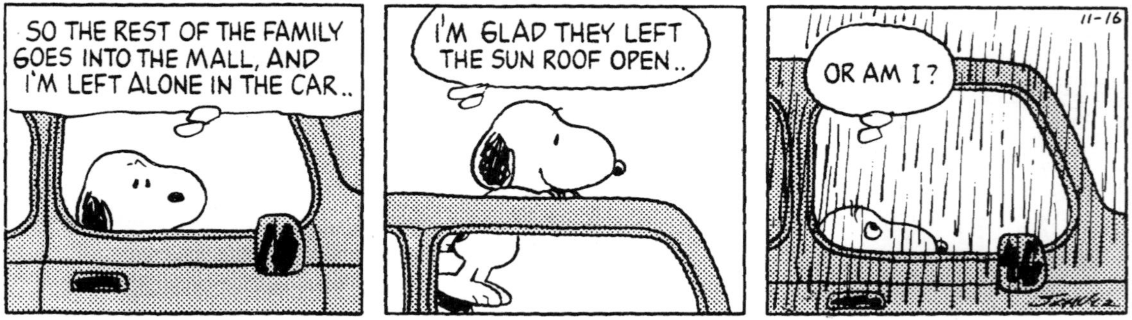
SO THE REST OF THE FAMILY GOES INTO THE MALL, AND I'M LEFT ALONE IN THE CAR..
I'M GLAD THEY LEFT THE SUN ROOF OPEN..
11-16
OR AM I?

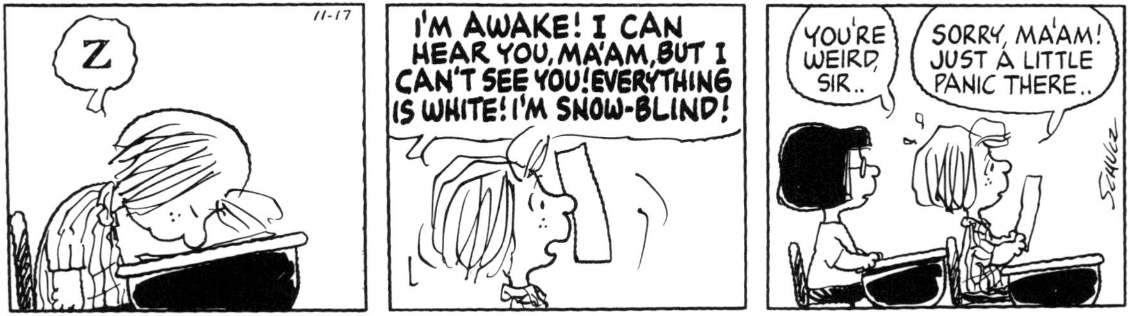
11-17
Z
I'M AWAKE! I CAN HEAR YOU, MA'AM, BUT I CAN'T SEE YOU! EVERYTHING IS WHITE! I'M SNOW-BLIND!
YOU'RE WEIRD, SIR..
SORRY, MA'AM! JUST A LITTLE PANIC THERE..
SCHULZ

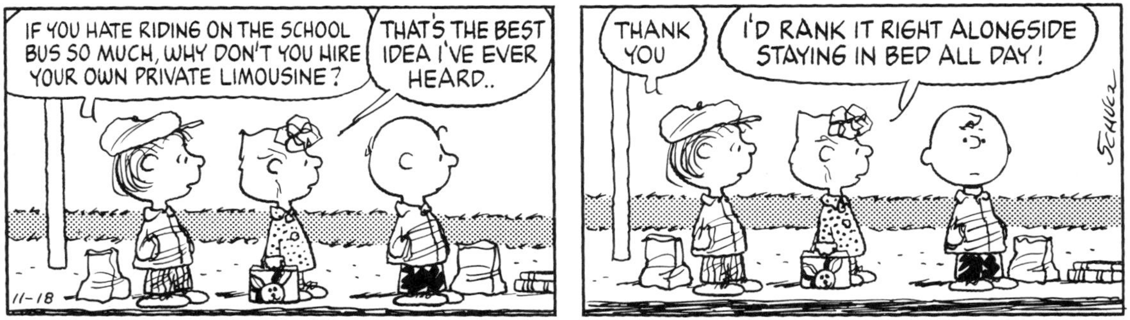
IF YOU HATE RIDING ON THE SCHOOL BUS SO MUCH, WHY DON'T YOU HIRE YOUR OWN PRIVATE LIMOUSINE?
THAT'S THE BEST IDEA I'VE EVER HEARD..
11-18
THANK YOU
I'D RANK IT RIGHT ALONGSIDE STAYING IN BED ALL DAY!
SCHULZ

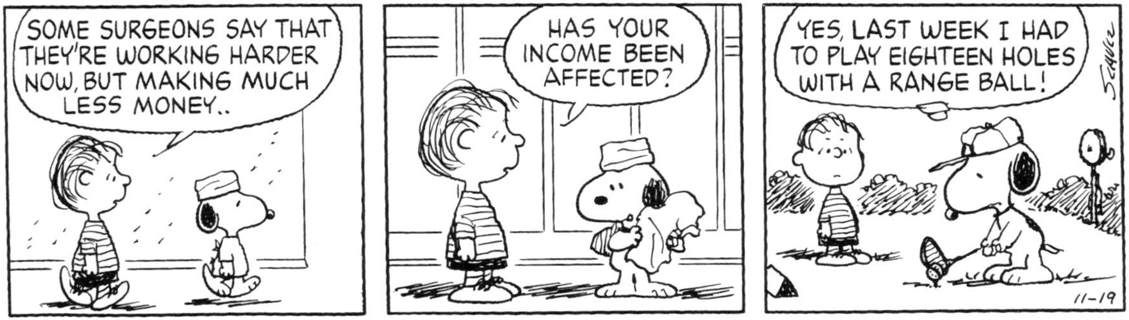
SOME SURGEONS SAY THAT THEY'RE WORKING HARDER NOW, BUT MAKING MUCH LESS MONEY..
HAS YOUR INCOME BEEN AFFECTED?
YES, LAST WEEK I HAD TO PLAY EIGHTEEN HOLES WITH A RANGE BALL!
SCHULZ
11-19

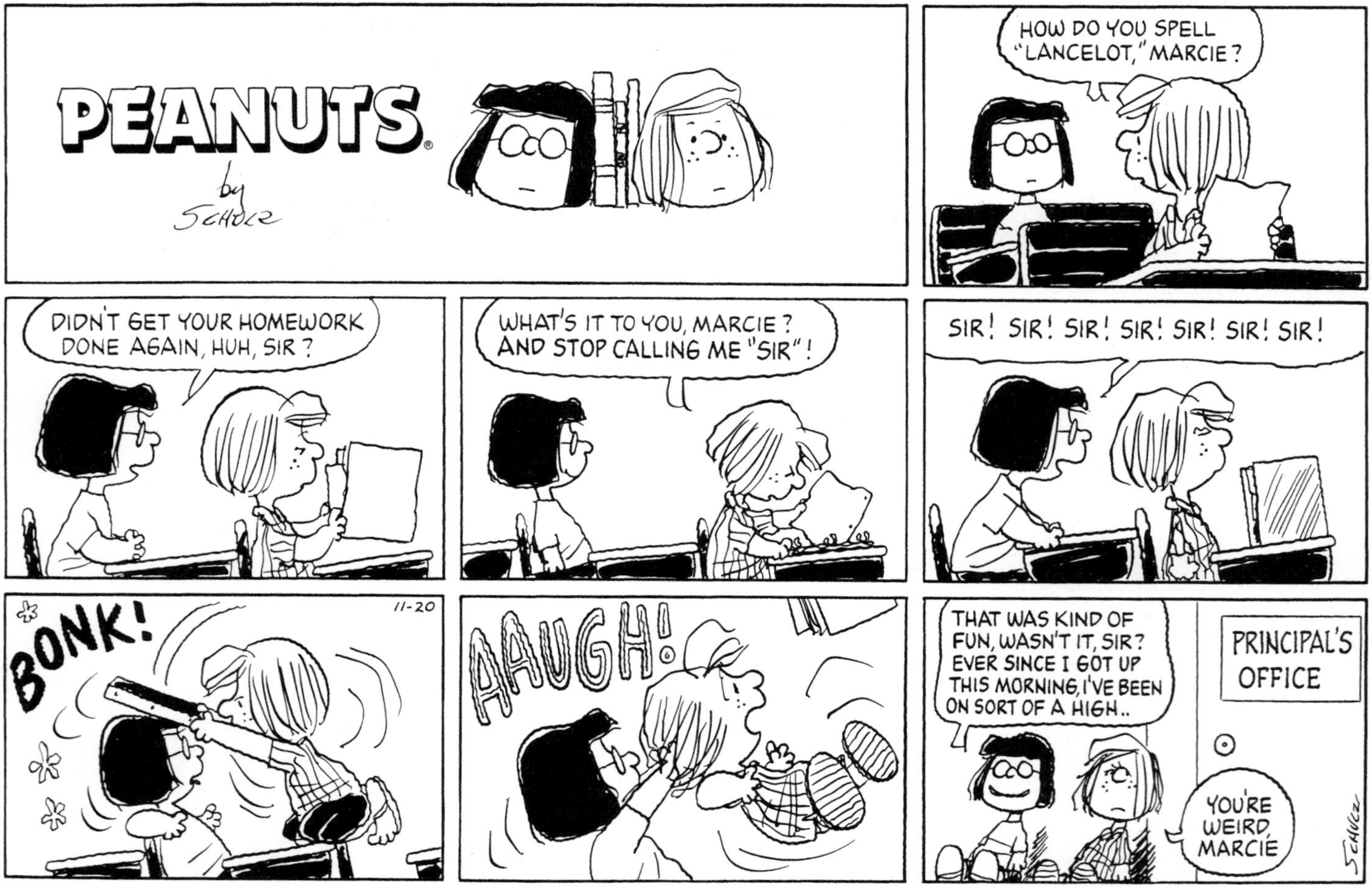
PEANUTS
by SCHULZ
HOW DO YOU SPELL "LANCELOT," MARCIE?
DIDN'T GET YOUR HOMEWORK DONE AGAIN, HUH, SIR?
WHAT'S IT TO YOU, MARCIE? AND STOP CALLING ME "SIR"!
SIR! SIR! SIR! SIR! SIR! SIR! SIR!
11-20
BONK!
AAUGH!
THAT WAS KIND OF FUN, WASN'T IT, SIR? EVER SINCE I GOT UP THIS MORNING, I'VE BEEN ON SORT OF A HIGH..
PRINCIPAL'S OFFICE
YOU'RE WEIRD, MARCIE
SCHULZ

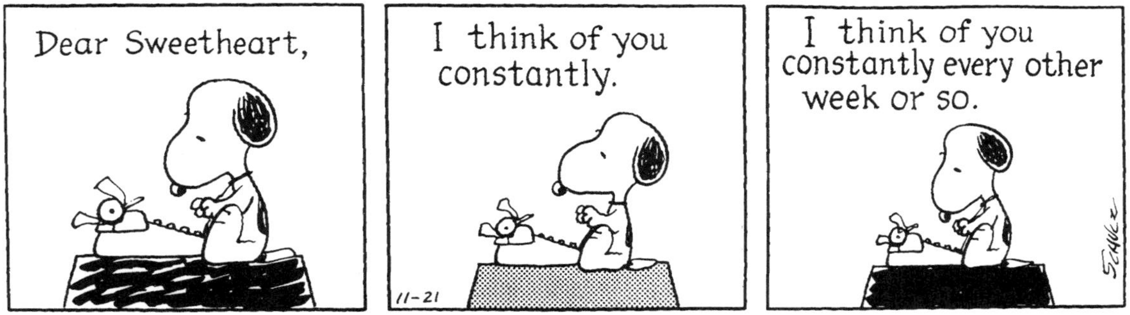
Dear Sweetheart,
I think of you constantly.
11-21
I think of you constantly every other week or so.
SCHULZ

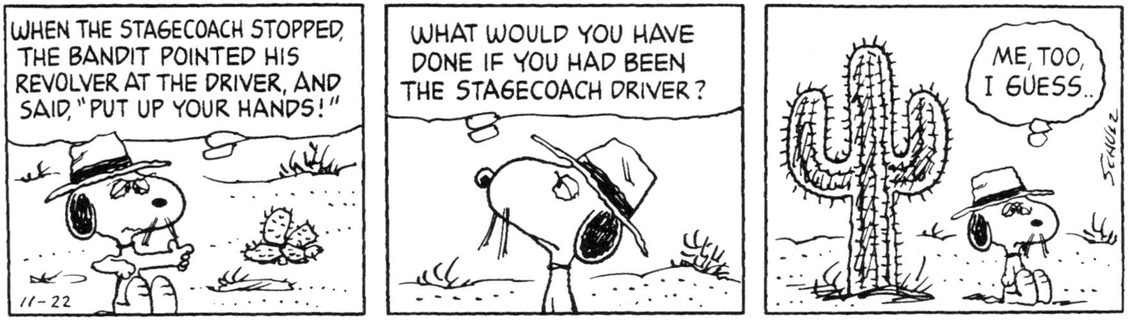
WHEN THE STAGECOACH STOPPED, THE BANDIT POINTED HIS REVOLVER AT THE DRIVER, AND SAID, "PUT UP YOUR HANDS!"
11-22
WHAT WOULD YOU HAVE DONE IF YOU HAD BEEN THE STAGECOACH DRIVER?
ME, TOO, I GUESS..
SCHULZ

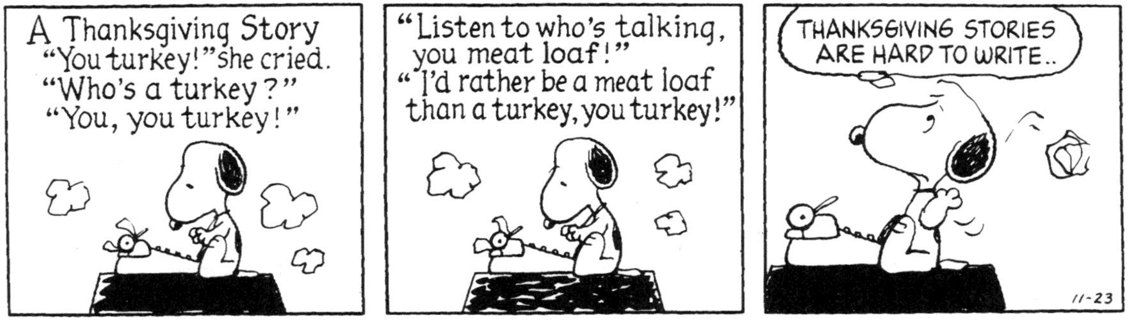
A Thanksgiving Story
"You turkey!" she cried.
"Who's a turkey?"
"You, you turkey!"
"Listen to who's talking, you meat loaf!"
"I'd rather be a meat loaf than a turkey, you turkey!"
THANKSGIVING STORIES ARE HARD TO WRITE..
11-23

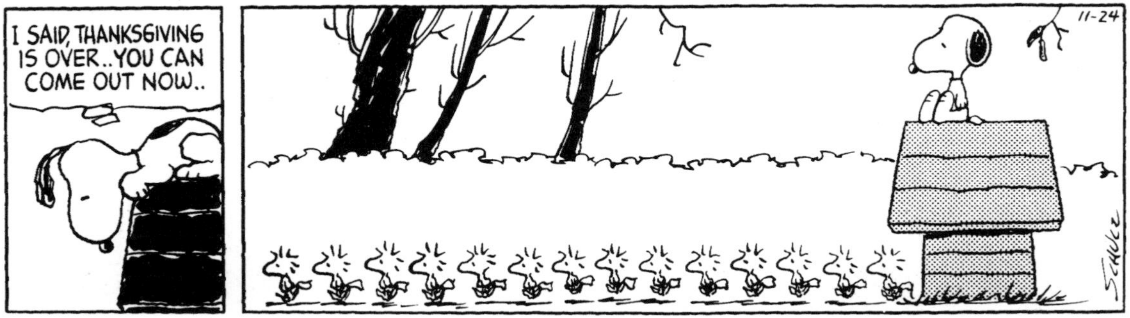
I SAID, THANKSGIVING IS OVER..YOU CAN COME OUT NOW..

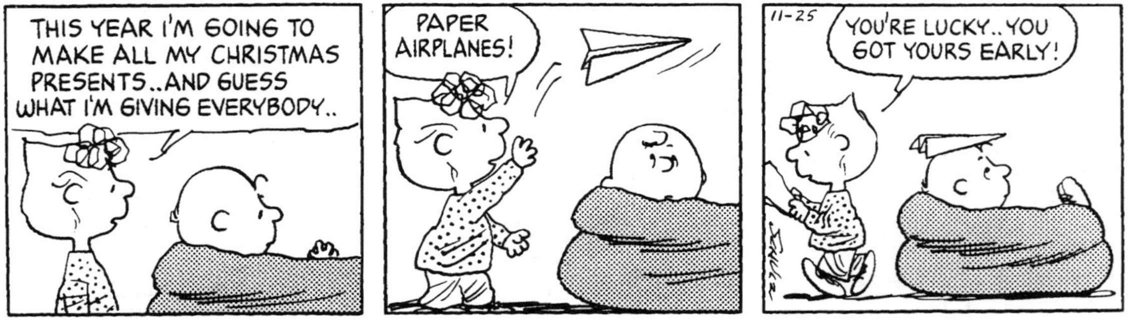
THIS YEAR I'M GOING TO MAKE ALL MY CHRISTMAS PRESENTS..AND GUESS WHAT I'M GIVING EVERYBODY..
PAPER AIRPLANES!
YOU'RE LUCKY..YOU GOT YOURS EARLY!

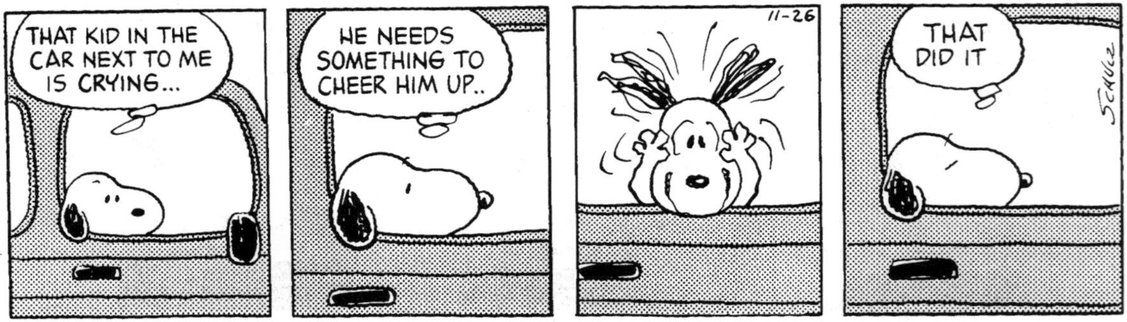
THAT KID IN THE CAR NEXT TO ME IS CRYING...
HE NEEDS SOMETHING TO CHEER HIM UP..
THAT DID IT

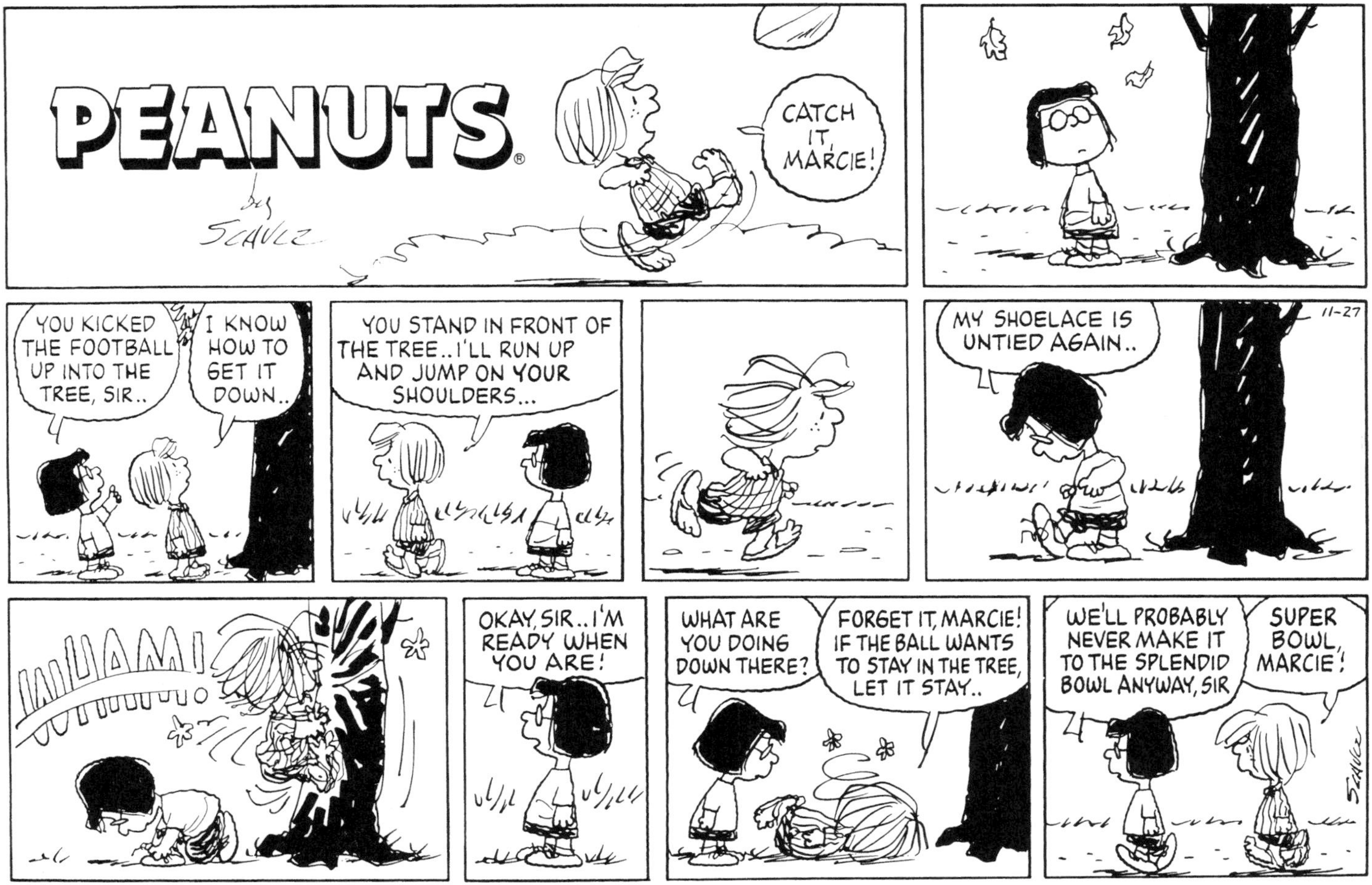
PEANUTS
by SCHULZ
CATCH IT, MARCIE!
YOU KICKED THE FOOTBALL UP INTO THE TREE, SIR..
I KNOW HOW TO GET IT DOWN..
YOU STAND IN FRONT OF THE TREE..I'LL RUN UP AND JUMP ON YOUR SHOULDERS...
11-27
MY SHOELACE IS UNTIED AGAIN..
WHAM!
OKAY, SIR..I'M READY WHEN YOU ARE!
WHAT ARE YOU DOING DOWN THERE?
FORGET IT, MARCIE! IF THE BALL WANTS TO STAY IN THE TREE, LET IT STAY..
WE'LL PROBABLY NEVER MAKE IT TO THE SPLENDID BOWL ANYWAY, SIR
SUPER BOWL, MARCIE!
SCHULZ

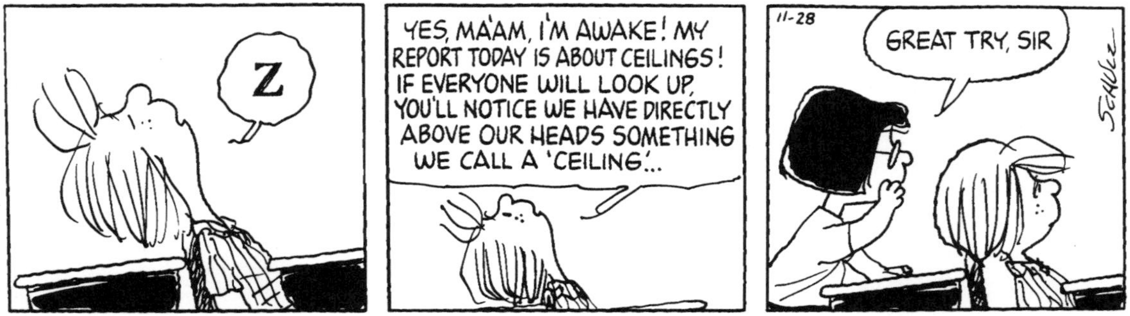
Z
YES, MA'AM, I'M AWAKE! MY REPORT TODAY IS ABOUT CEILINGS! IF EVERYONE WILL LOOK UP, YOU'LL NOTICE WE HAVE DIRECTLY ABOVE OUR HEADS SOMETHING WE CALL A 'CEILING'..
11-28
GREAT TRY, SIR
SCHULZ

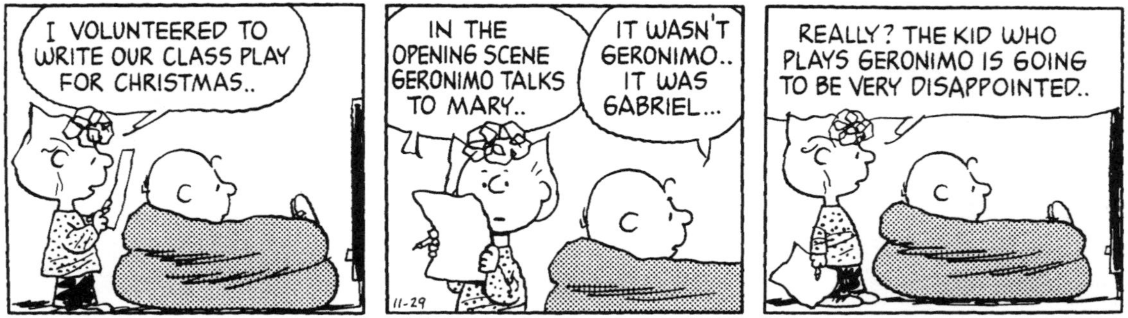
I VOLUNTEERED TO WRITE OUR CLASS PLAY FOR CHRISTMAS..
IN THE OPENING SCENE GERONIMO TALKS TO MARY..
IT WASN'T GERONIMO.. IT WAS GABRIEL...
11-29
REALLY? THE KID WHO PLAYS GERONIMO IS GOING TO BE VERY DISAPPOINTED..

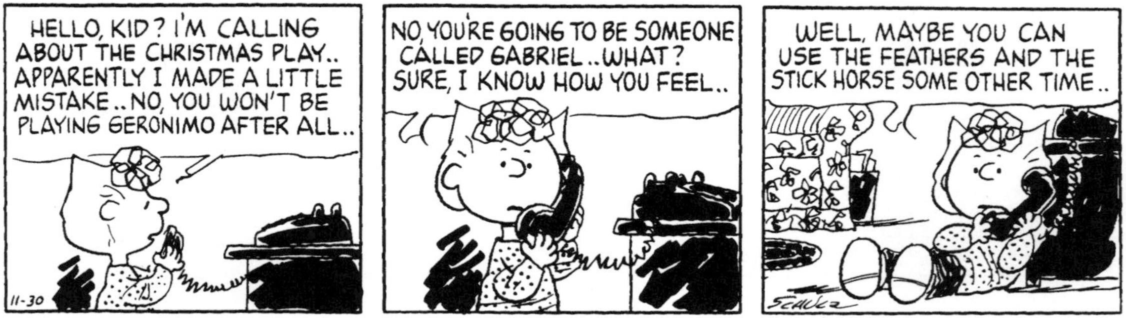
HELLO, KID? I'M CALLING ABOUT THE CHRISTMAS PLAY.. APPARENTLY I MADE A LITTLE MISTAKE..NO, YOU WON'T BE PLAYING GERONIMO AFTER ALL..
11-30
NO, YOU'RE GOING TO BE SOMEONE CALLED GABRIEL..WHAT? SURE, I KNOW HOW YOU FEEL..
WELL, MAYBE YOU CAN USE THE FEATHERS AND THE STICK HORSE SOME OTHER TIME..
SCHULZ

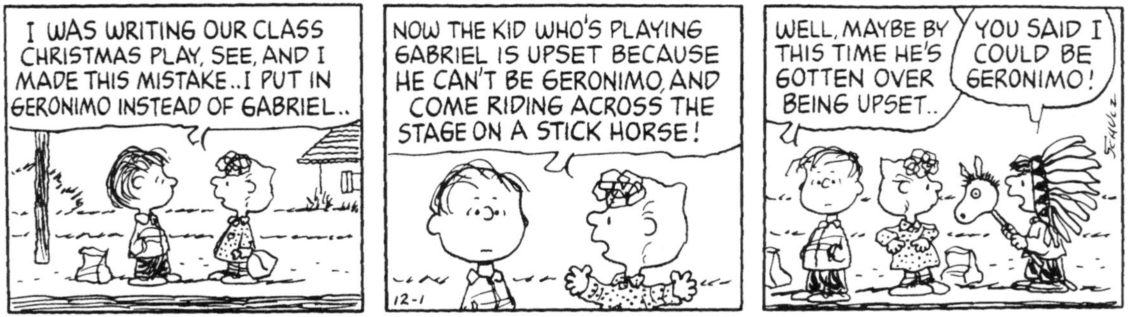
I WAS WRITING OUR CLASS CHRISTMAS PLAY, SEE, AND I MADE THIS MISTAKE..I PUT IN GERONIMO INSTEAD OF GABRIEL..
NOW THE KID WHO'S PLAYING GABRIEL IS UPSET BECAUSE HE CAN'T BE GERONIMO, AND COME RIDING ACROSS THE STAGE ON A STICK HORSE!
12-1
WELL, MAYBE BY THIS TIME HE'S GOTTEN OVER BEING UPSET..
YOU SAID I COULD BE GERONIMO!
SCHULZ

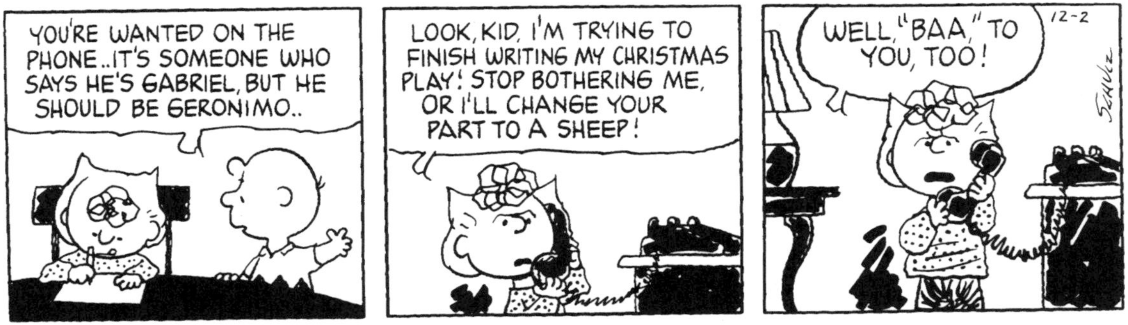
YOU'RE WANTED ON THE PHONE..IT'S SOMEONE WHO SAYS HE'S GABRIEL, BUT HE SHOULD BE GERONIMO..
LOOK, KID, I'M TRYING TO FINISH WRITING MY CHRISTMAS PLAY! STOP BOTHERING ME, OR I'LL CHANGE YOUR PART TO A SHEEP!
WELL, "BAA," TO YOU, TOO!
12-2
SCHULZ

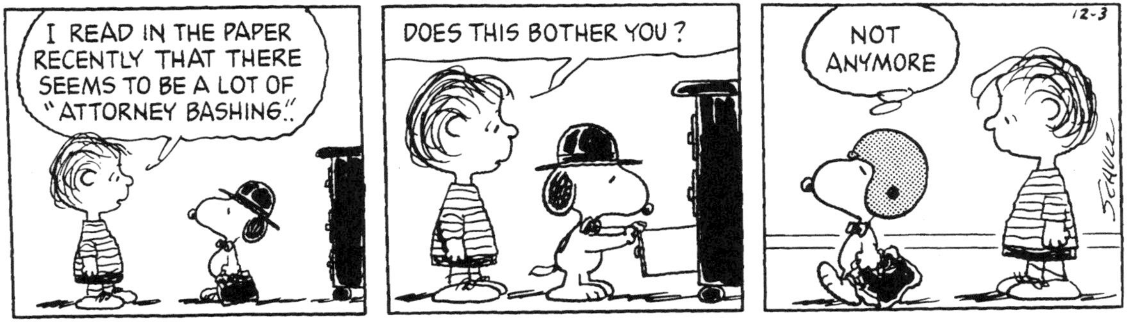
I READ IN THE PAPER RECENTLY THAT THERE SEEMS TO BE A LOT OF "ATTORNEY BASHING."
DOES THIS BOTHER YOU?
12-3
NOT ANYMORE
SCHULZ

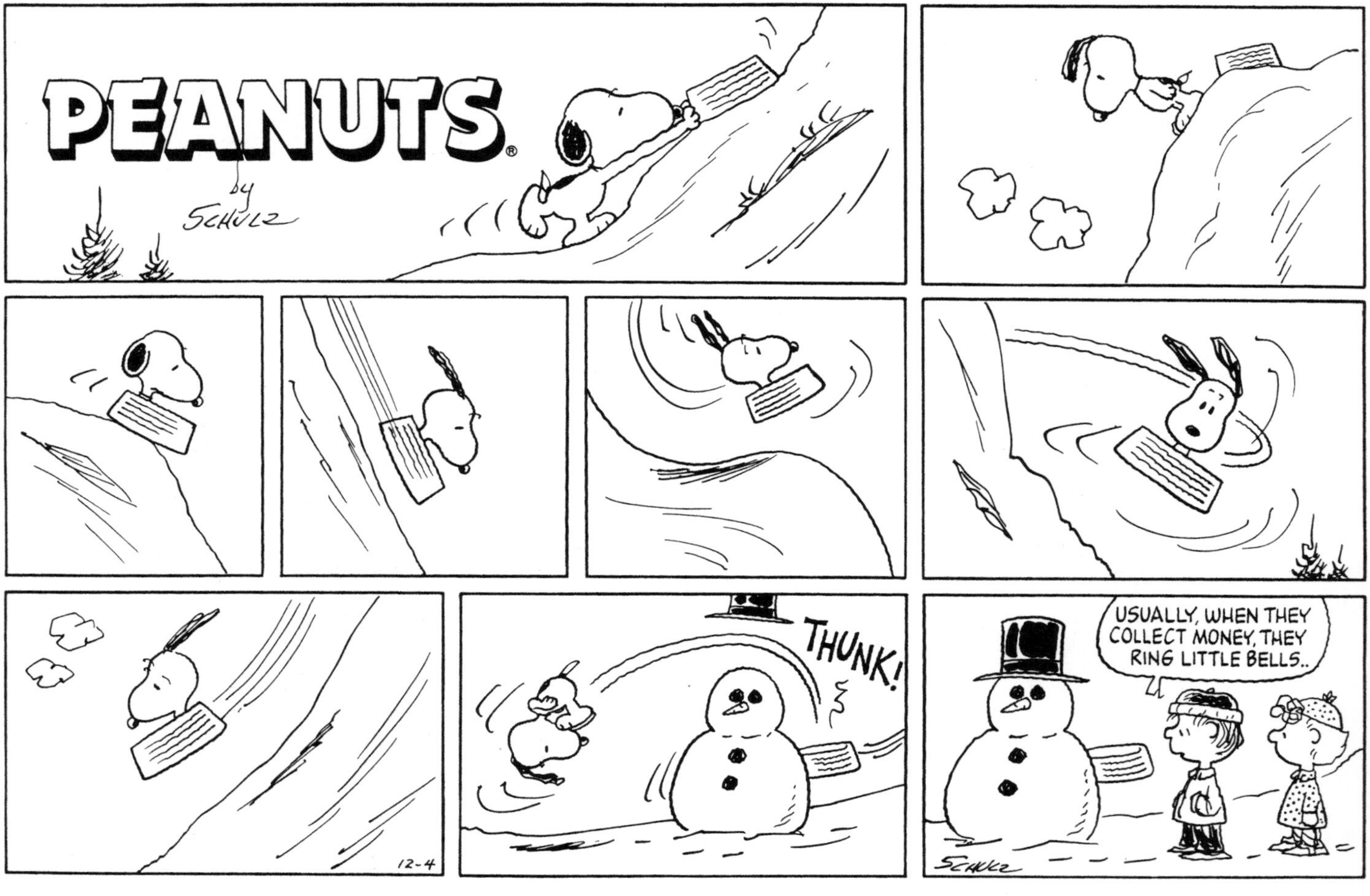
PEANUTS
by
SCHULZ
12-4
THUNK!
USUALLY, WHEN THEY COLLECT MONEY, THEY RING LITTLE BELLS..
SCHULZ

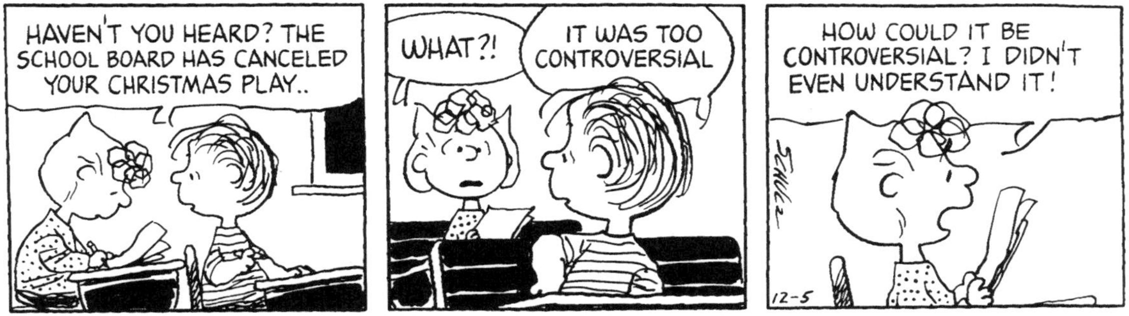
HAVEN'T YOU HEARD? THE SCHOOL BOARD HAS CANCELED YOUR CHRISTMAS PLAY..
WHAT?!
IT WAS TOO CONTROVERSIAL
HOW COULD IT BE CONTROVERSIAL? I DIDN'T EVEN UNDERSTAND IT!
12-5

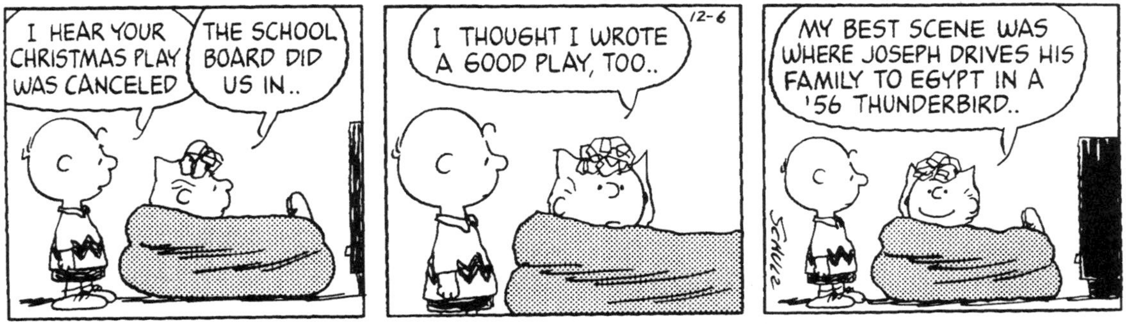
I HEAR YOUR CHRISTMAS PLAY WAS CANCELED
THE SCHOOL BOARD DID US IN..
12-6
I THOUGHT I WROTE A GOOD PLAY, TOO..
MY BEST SCENE WAS WHERE JOSEPH DRIVES HIS FAMILY TO EGYPT IN A '56 THUNDERBIRD..

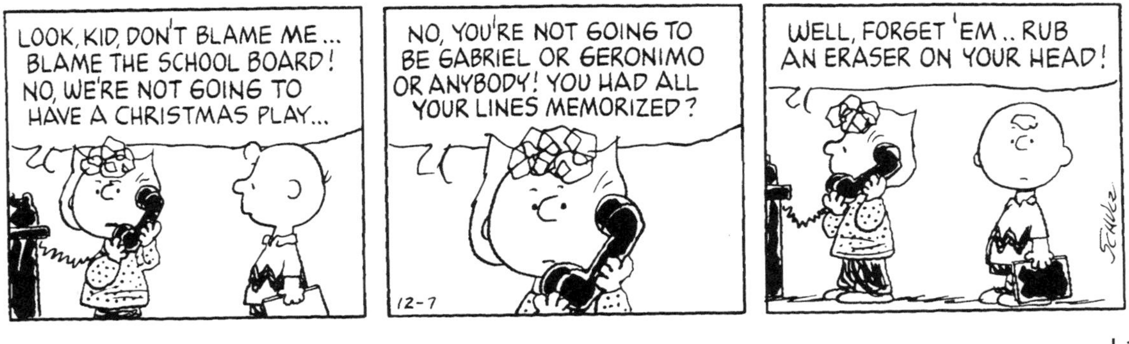
LOOK, KID, DON'T BLAME ME... BLAME THE SCHOOL BOARD! NO, WE'RE NOT GOING TO HAVE A CHRISTMAS PLAY...
NO, YOU'RE NOT GOING TO BE GABRIEL OR GERONIMO OR ANYBODY! YOU HAD ALL YOUR LINES MEMORIZED?
12-7
WELL, FORGET 'EM.. RUB AN ERASER ON YOUR HEAD!

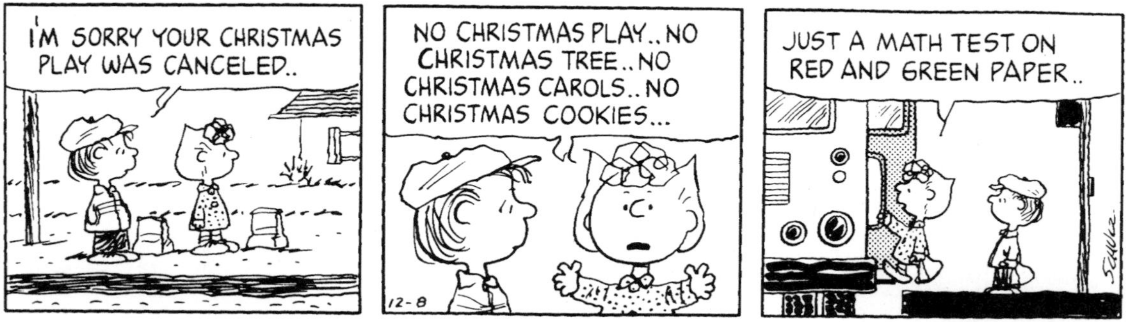
I'M SORRY YOUR CHRISTMAS PLAY WAS CANCELED..
NO CHRISTMAS PLAY.. NO CHRISTMAS TREE.. NO CHRISTMAS CAROLS.. NO CHRISTMAS COOKIES...
12-8
JUST A MATH TEST ON RED AND GREEN PAPER..
SCHULZ

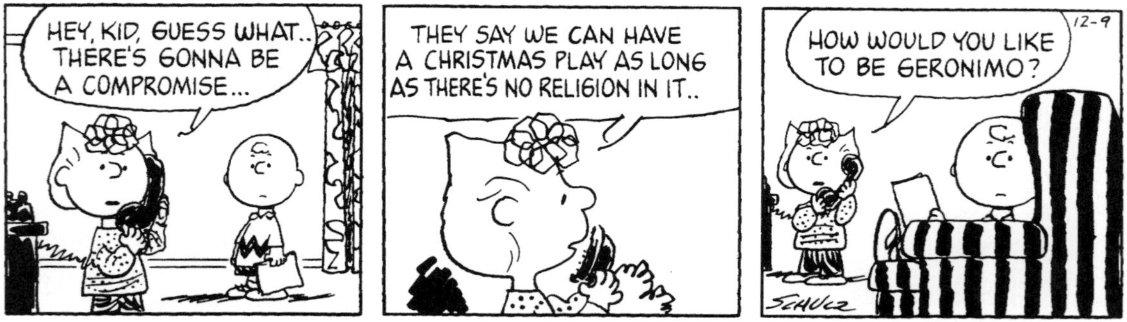
HEY, KID, GUESS WHAT.. THERE'S GONNA BE A COMPROMISE...
THEY SAY WE CAN HAVE A CHRISTMAS PLAY AS LONG AS THERE'S NO RELIGION IN IT..
12-9
HOW WOULD YOU LIKE TO BE GERONIMO?
SCHULZ

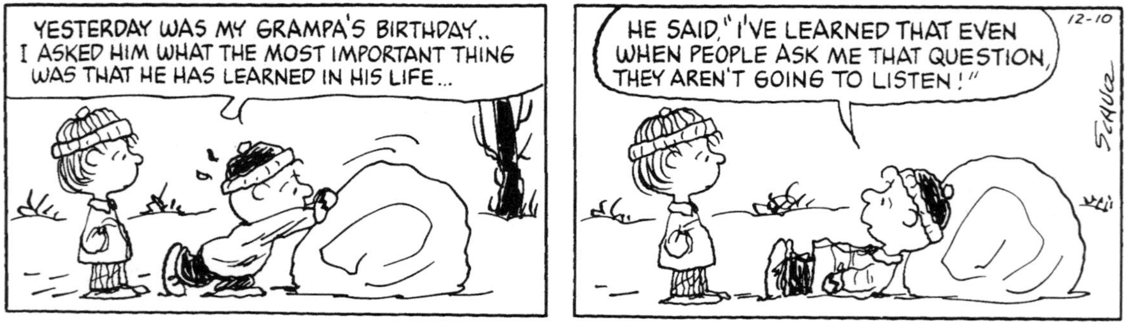
YESTERDAY WAS MY GRAMPA'S BIRTHDAY.. I ASKED HIM WHAT THE MOST IMPORTANT THING WAS THAT HE HAS LEARNED IN HIS LIFE...
12-10
HE SAID, "I'VE LEARNED THAT EVEN WHEN PEOPLE ASK ME THAT QUESTION, THEY AREN'T GOING TO LISTEN!"
SCHULZ

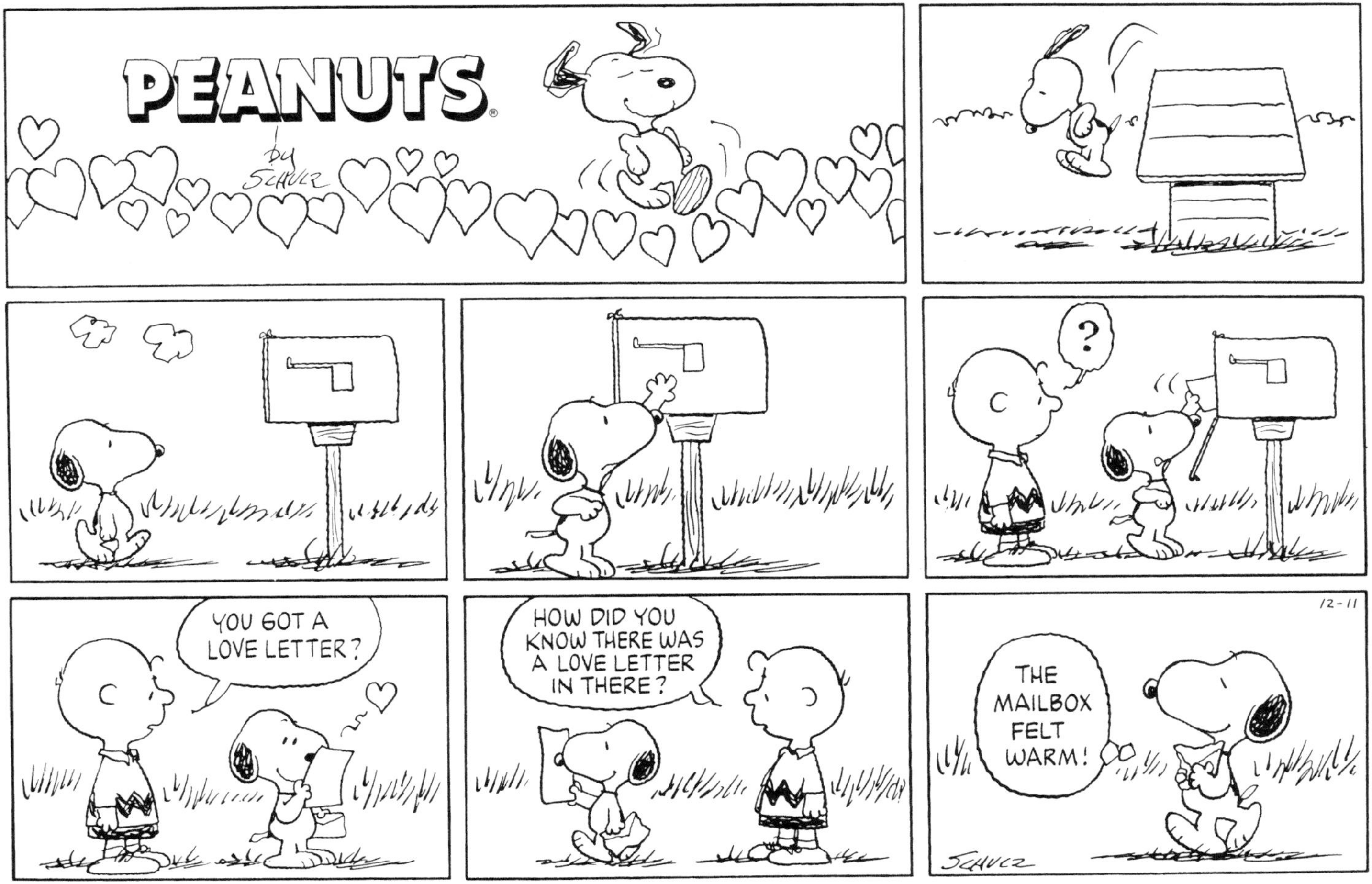
PEANUTS
by SCHULZ
?
YOU GOT A LOVE LETTER?
HOW DID YOU KNOW THERE WAS A LOVE LETTER IN THERE?
12-11
THE MAILBOX FELT WARM!
SCHULZ

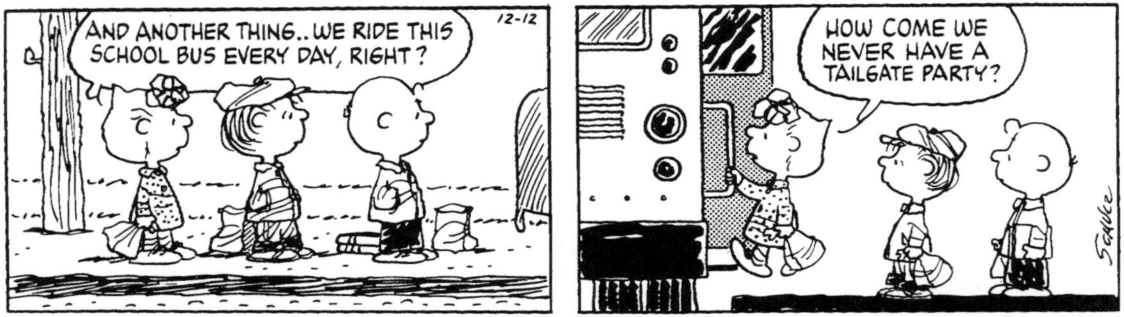
12-12
AND ANOTHER THING.. WE RIDE THIS SCHOOL BUS EVERY DAY, RIGHT?
HOW COME WE NEVER HAVE A TAILGATE PARTY?

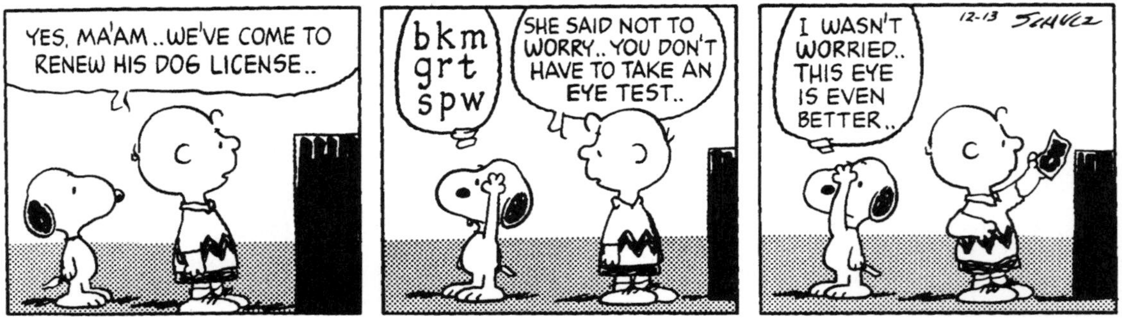
YES, MA'AM.. WE'VE COME TO RENEW HIS DOG LICENSE..
bkm grt spw
SHE SAID NOT TO WORRY.. YOU DON'T HAVE TO TAKE AN EYE TEST..
12-13
I WASN'T WORRIED.. THIS EYE IS EVEN BETTER..

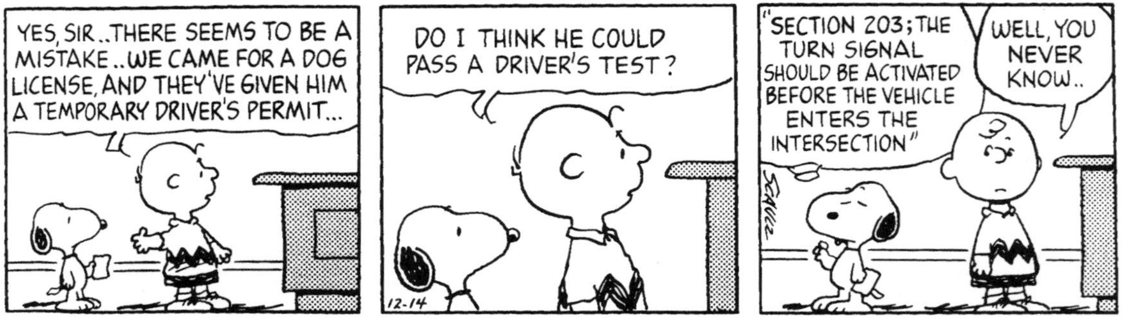
YES, SIR.. THERE SEEMS TO BE A MISTAKE.. WE CAME FOR A DOG LICENSE, AND THEY'VE GIVEN HIM A TEMPORARY DRIVER'S PERMIT...
DO I THINK HE COULD PASS A DRIVER'S TEST?
12-14
"SECTION 203; THE TURN SIGNAL SHOULD BE ACTIVATED BEFORE THE VEHICLE ENTERS THE INTERSECTION"
WELL, YOU NEVER KNOW..

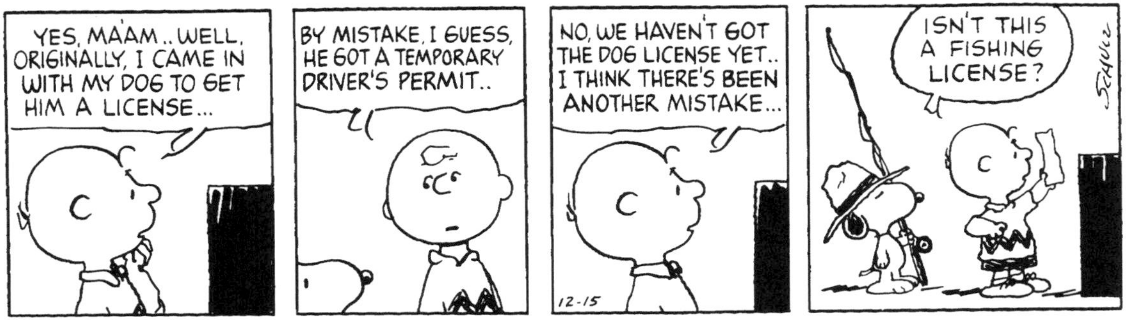
YES, MA'AM.. WELL, ORIGINALLY, I CAME IN WITH MY DOG TO GET HIM A LICENSE...
BY MISTAKE, I GUESS, HE GOT A TEMPORARY DRIVER'S PERMIT..
NO, WE HAVEN'T GOT THE DOG LICENSE YET.. I THINK THERE'S BEEN ANOTHER MISTAKE...
12-15
ISN'T THIS A FISHING LICENSE?
SCHULZ

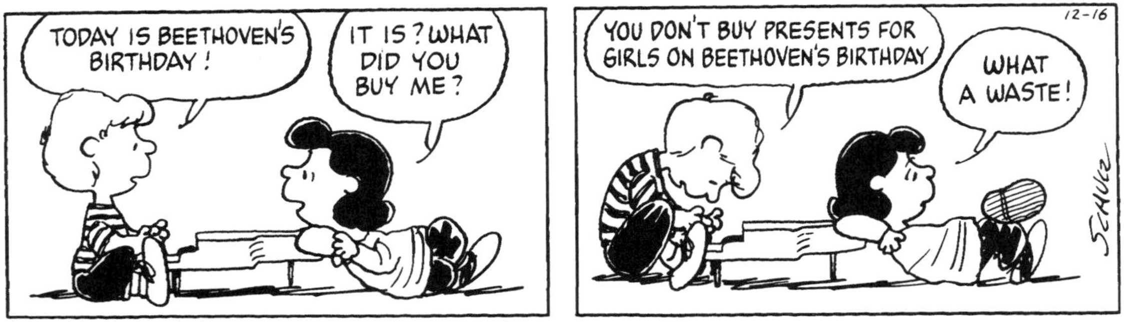
TODAY IS BEETHOVEN'S BIRTHDAY!
IT IS? WHAT DID YOU BUY ME?
12-16
YOU DON'T BUY PRESENTS FOR GIRLS ON BEETHOVEN'S BIRTHDAY
WHAT A WASTE!
SCHULZ

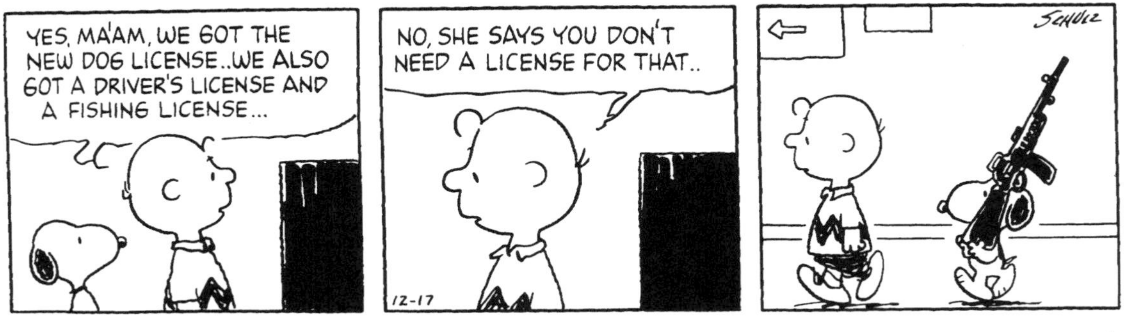
YES, MA'AM, WE GOT THE NEW DOG LICENSE..WE ALSO GOT A DRIVER'S LICENSE AND A FISHING LICENSE...
NO, SHE SAYS YOU DON'T NEED A LICENSE FOR THAT..
12-17
SCHULZ

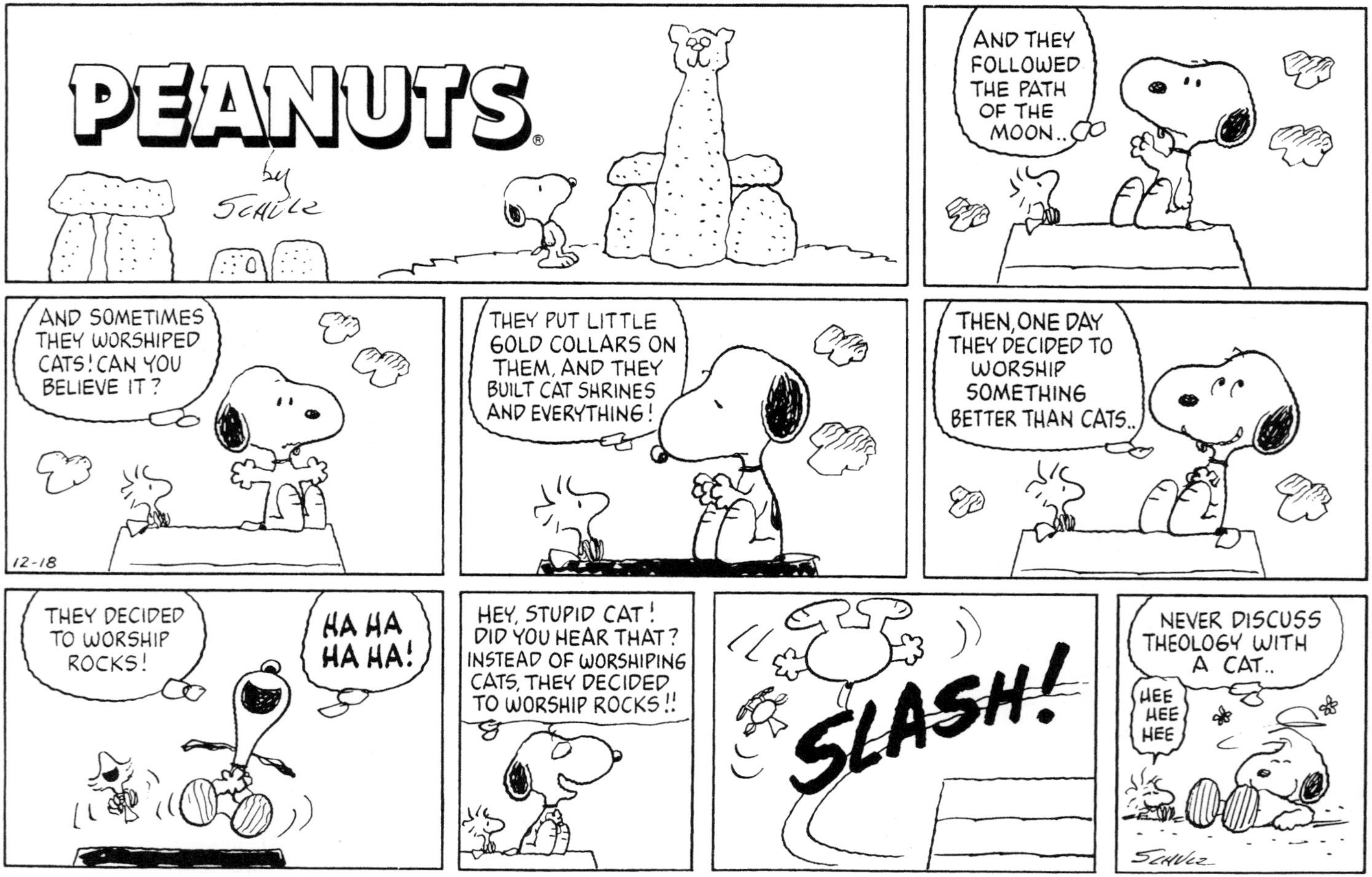
PEANUTS
by SCHULZ
AND THEY FOLLOWED THE PATH OF THE MOON..
AND SOMETIMES THEY WORSHIPED CATS! CAN YOU BELIEVE IT?
12-18
THEY PUT LITTLE GOLD COLLARS ON THEM, AND THEY BUILT CAT SHRINES AND EVERYTHING!
THEN, ONE DAY THEY DECIDED TO WORSHIP SOMETHING BETTER THAN CATS..
THEY DECIDED TO WORSHIP ROCKS!
HA HA HA HA!
HEY, STUPID CAT! DID YOU HEAR THAT? INSTEAD OF WORSHIPING CATS, THEY DECIDED TO WORSHIP ROCKS!!
SLASH!
NEVER DISCUSS THEOLOGY WITH A CAT..
HEE HEE HEE HEE
SCHULZ

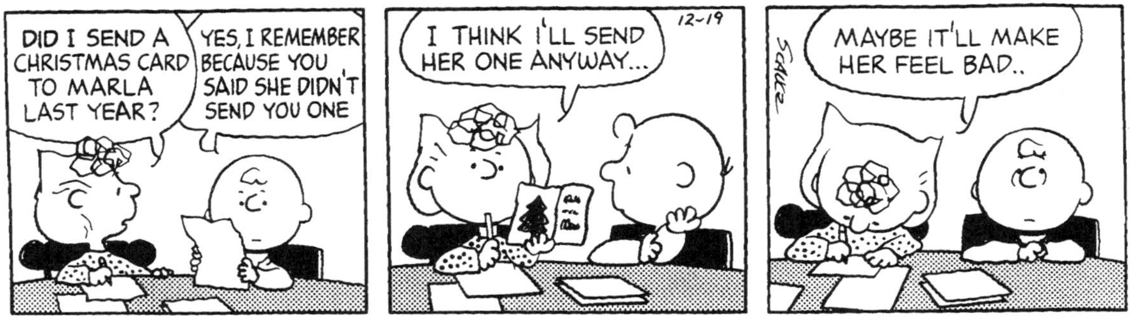
DID I SEND A CHRISTMAS CARD TO MARLA LAST YEAR?
YES, I REMEMBER BECAUSE YOU SAID SHE DIDN'T SEND YOU ONE
I THINK I'LL SEND HER ONE ANYWAY...
12-19
SCHULZ
MAYBE IT'LL MAKE HER FEEL BAD..

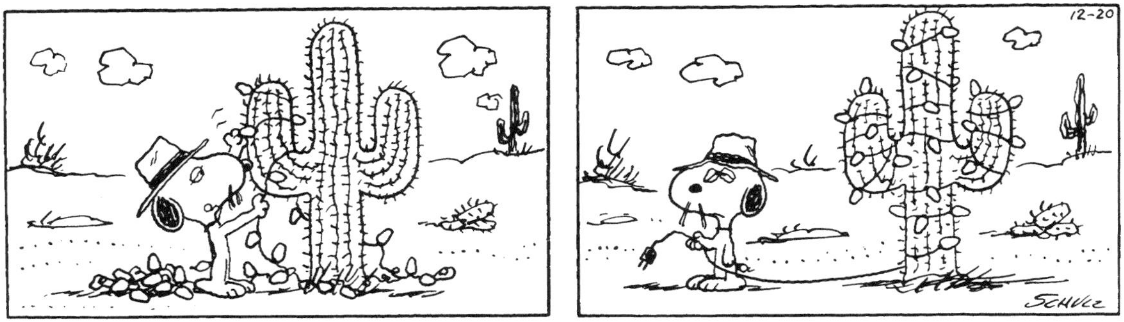
12-20
SCHULZ

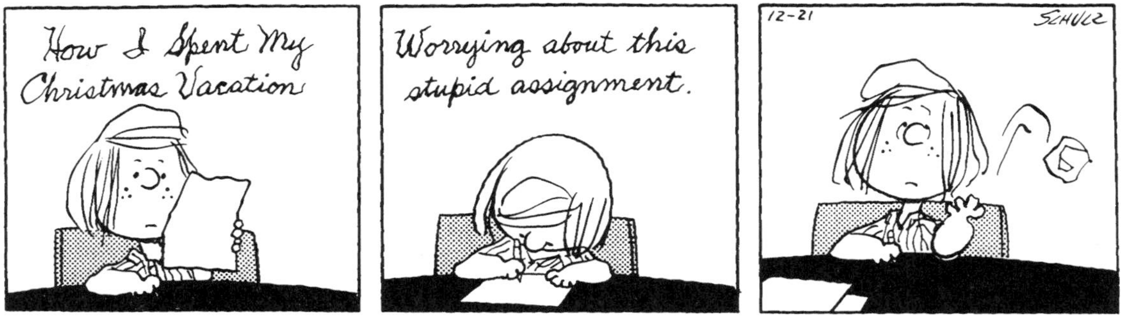
How I Spent My Christmas Vacation
Worrying about this stupid assignment.
12-21
SCHULZ

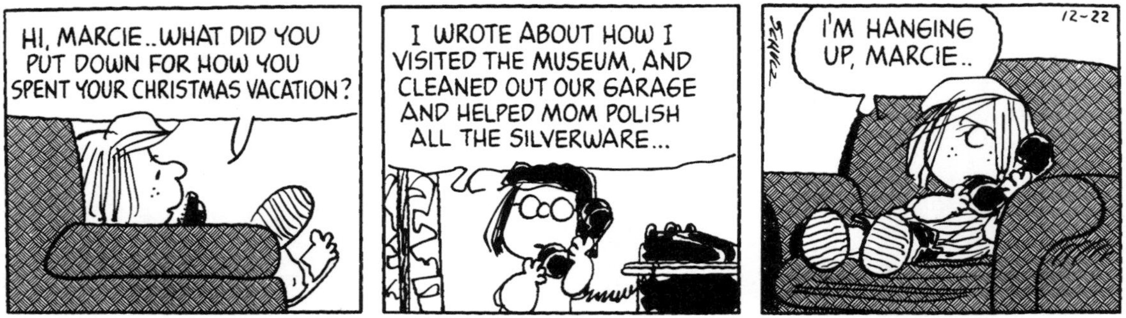
HI, MARCIE.. WHAT DID YOU PUT DOWN FOR HOW YOU SPENT YOUR CHRISTMAS VACATION?
I WROTE ABOUT HOW I VISITED THE MUSEUM, AND CLEANED OUT OUR GARAGE AND HELPED MOM POLISH ALL THE SILVERWARE...
I'M HANGING UP, MARCIE..
12-22

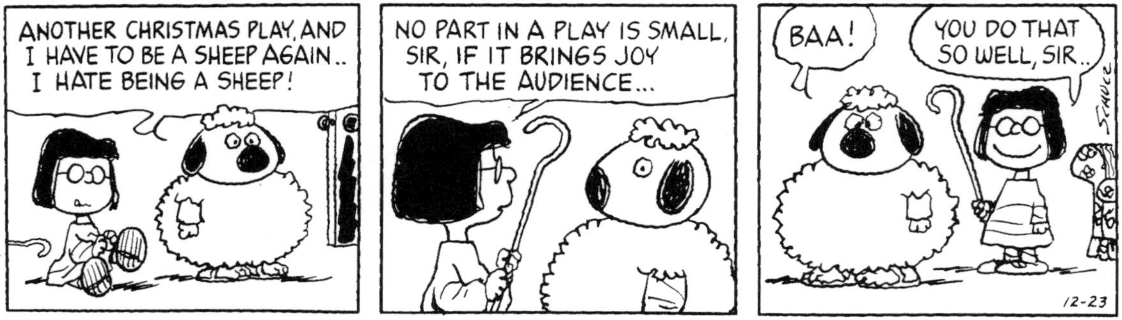
ANOTHER CHRISTMAS PLAY, AND I HAVE TO BE A SHEEP AGAIN.. I HATE BEING A SHEEP!
NO PART IN A PLAY IS SMALL, SIR, IF IT BRINGS JOY TO THE AUDIENCE...
BAA!
YOU DO THAT SO WELL, SIR..
12-23

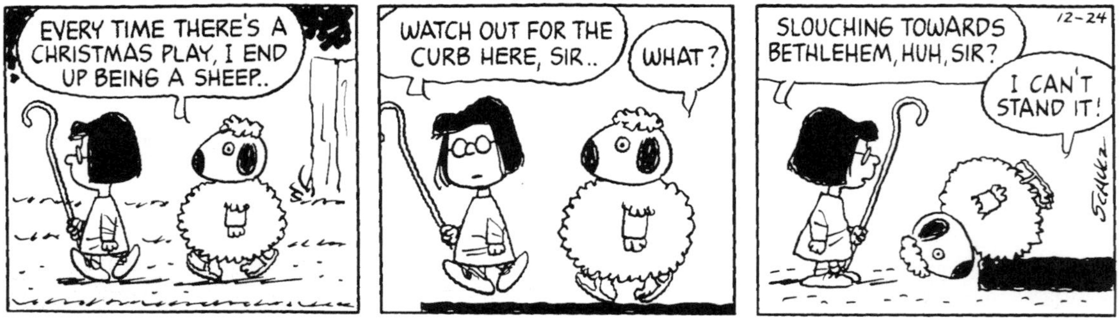
EVERY TIME THERE'S A CHRISTMAS PLAY, I END UP BEING A SHEEP..
WATCH OUT FOR THE CURB HERE, SIR..
WHAT?
SLOUCHING TOWARDS BETHLEHEM, HUH, SIR?
I CAN'T STAND IT!
12-24

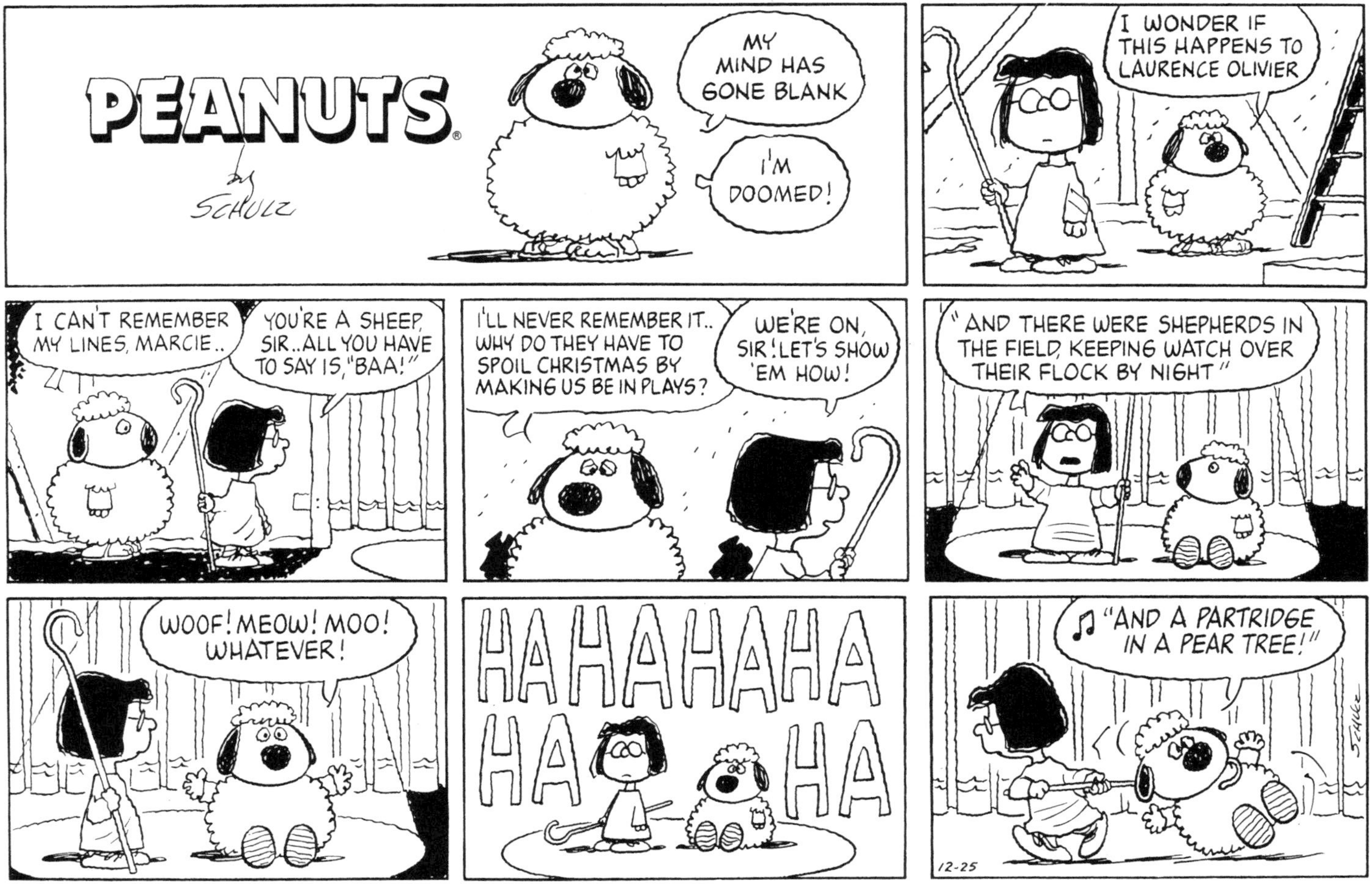
PEANUTS
by SCHULZ
MY MIND HAS GONE BLANK
I'M DOOMED!
I WONDER IF THIS HAPPENS TO LAURENCE OLIVIER
I CAN'T REMEMBER MY LINES, MARCIE..
YOU'RE A SHEEP, SIR..ALL YOU HAVE TO SAY IS, "BAA!"
I'LL NEVER REMEMBER IT.. WHY DO THEY HAVE TO SPOIL CHRISTMAS BY MAKING US BE IN PLAYS?
WE'RE ON, SIR! LET'S SHOW 'EM HOW!
"AND THERE WERE SHEPHERDS IN THE FIELD, KEEPING WATCH OVER THEIR FLOCK BY NIGHT"
WOOF! MEOW! MOO! WHATEVER!
HAHAHAHAHA
HA HA
"AND A PARTRIDGE IN A PEAR TREE!"
SCHULZ
12-25

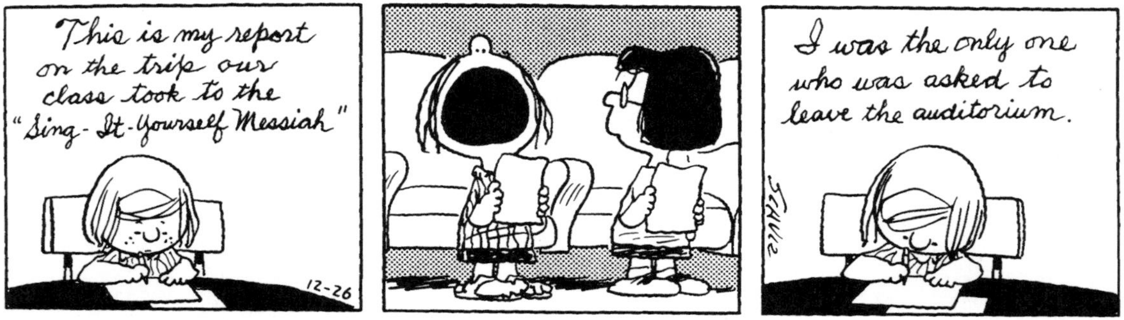
This is my report on the trip our class took to the "Sing-It-Yourself Messiah"
12-26
I was the only one who was asked to leave the auditorium.

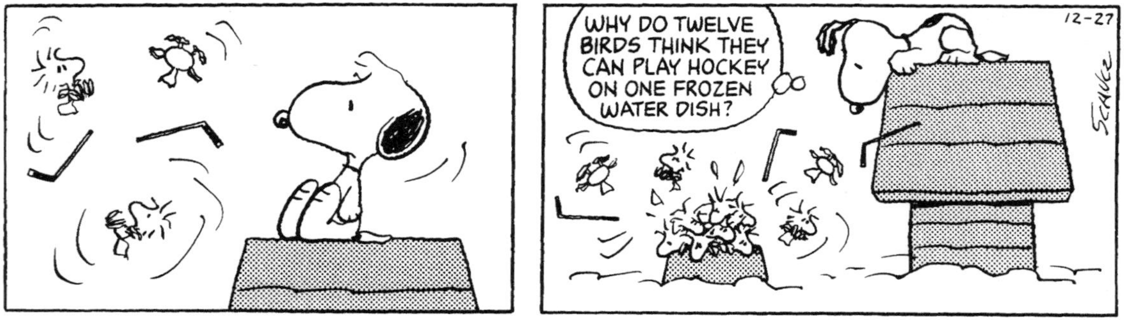
12-27
WHY DO TWELVE BIRDS THINK THEY CAN PLAY HOCKEY ON ONE FROZEN WATER DISH?

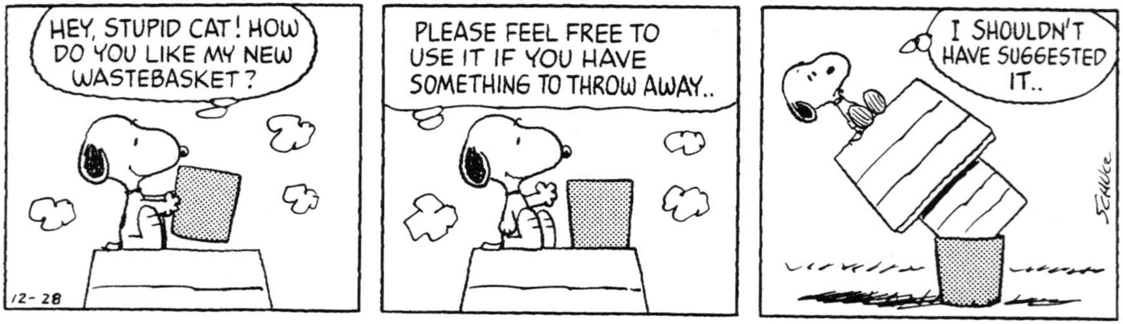
HEY, STUPID CAT! HOW DO YOU LIKE MY NEW WASTEBASKET?
12-28
PLEASE FEEL FREE TO USE IT IF YOU HAVE SOMETHING TO THROW AWAY..
I SHOULDN'T HAVE SUGGESTED IT..

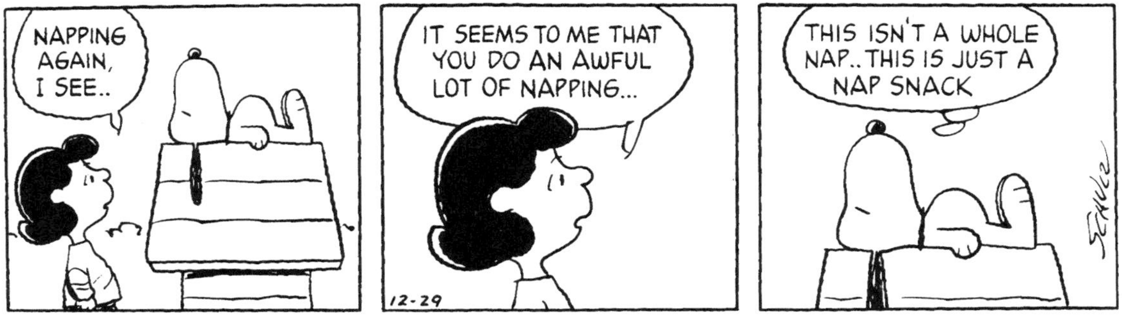
NAPPING AGAIN, I SEE..
IT SEEMS TO ME THAT YOU DO AN AWFUL LOT OF NAPPING...
12-29
THIS ISN'T A WHOLE NAP.. THIS IS JUST A NAP SNACK
SCHULZ

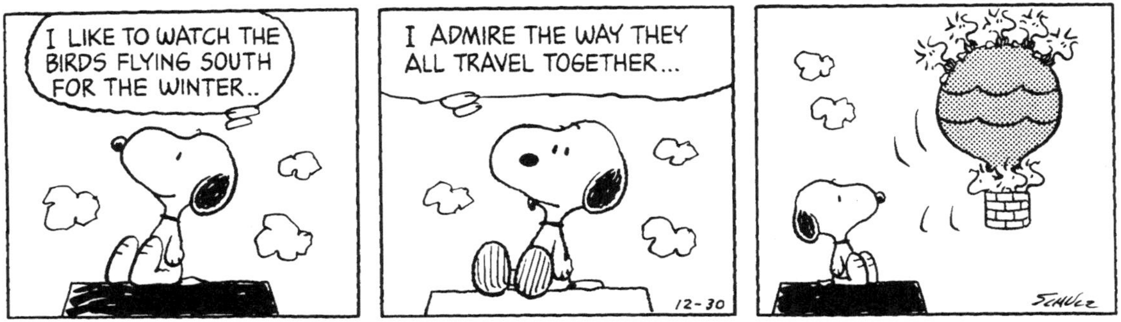
I LIKE TO WATCH THE BIRDS FLYING SOUTH FOR THE WINTER..
I ADMIRE THE WAY THEY ALL TRAVEL TOGETHER...
12-30
SCHULZ

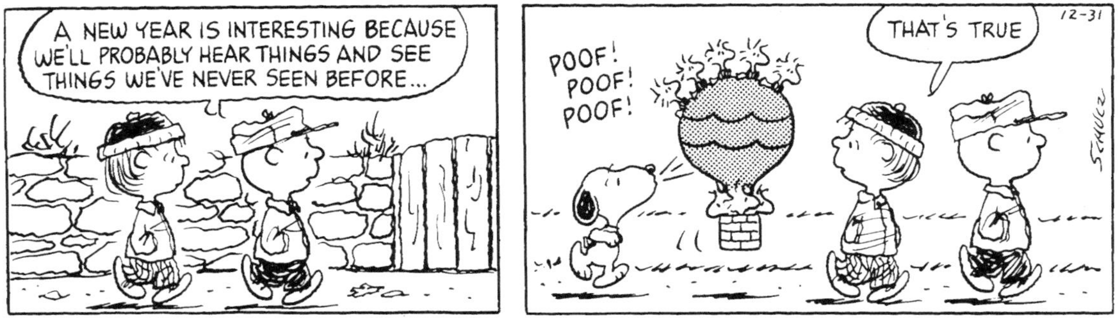
A NEW YEAR IS INTERESTING BECAUSE WE'LL PROBABLY HEAR THINGS AND SEE THINGS WE'VE NEVER SEEN BEFORE...
12-31
POOF! POOF! POOF!
THAT'S TRUE
SCHULZ

1922 CHARLES M. SCHULZ 2000

CHARLES M. SCHULZ WAS BORN NOVEMBER 26, 1922, in Minneapolis. His destiny was foreshadowed when an uncle gave him, at the age of two days, the nickname "Sparky" (after the racehorse Spark Plug in the newspaper strip *Barney Google*).

Schulz grew up in St. Paul. By all accounts, he led an unremarkable, albeit sheltered, childhood. He was an only child, close to both parents, his eventual career path nurtured by his father, who bought four Sunday papers every week — just for the comics.

An outstanding student, he skipped two grades early on, but began to flounder in high school — perhaps not so coincidentally at the same time kids are going through their cruelest, most status-conscious period of socialization. The pain, bitterness, insecurity, and failures chronicled in *Peanuts* appear to have originated from this period of Schulz's life.

Although Schulz enjoyed sports, he also found refuge in solitary activities: reading, drawing, and watching movies. He bought comic books and Big Little Books, pored over the newspaper strips, and copied his favorites — *Buck Rogers*, the Walt Disney characters, *Popeye*, *Tim Tyler's Luck*. He quickly became a connoisseur; his heroes were Milton Caniff, Roy Crane, Hal Foster, and Alex Raymond.

In his senior year in high school, his mother noticed an ad in a local newspaper for a correspondence school, Federal Schools (later called Art Instruction Schools). Schulz passed the talent test, completed the course, and began trying, unsuccessfully, to sell gag cartoons to magazines. (His first published drawing was of his dog, Spike, and appeared in a 1937 *Ripley's Believe It or Not!* installment.)

After World War II had ended and Schulz was discharged from the army, he started submitting gag cartoons to the various magazines of the time; his first breakthrough, however, came when an editor at *Timeless Topix* hired him to letter adventure comics. Soon after that, he was hired by his alma mater, Art Instruction, to correct student lessons returned by mail.

Between 1948 and 1950, he succeeded in selling seventeen cartoons to the *Saturday Evening Post* — as well

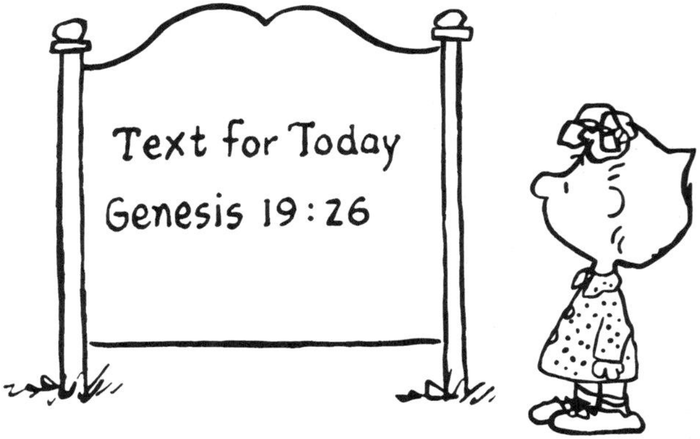
Text for Today
Genesis 19:26

as, to the local *St. Paul Pioneer Press*, a weekly comic feature called *Li'l Folks*. It was run in the women's section and paid ten dollars a week. After writing and drawing the feature for two years, Schulz asked for a better location in the paper or for daily exposure, as well as a raise. When he was turned down on all three counts, he quit.

He started submitting strips to the newspaper syndicates. In the spring of 1950, he received a letter from the United Feature Syndicate, announcing its interest in his submission, *Li'l Folks*. Schulz boarded a train in June for New York City; more interested in doing a strip than a panel, he also brought along the first installments of what would become *Peanuts* — and that was what sold. (The title, which Schulz loathed to his dying day, was imposed by the syndicate). The first *Peanuts* daily appeared October 2, 1950; the first Sunday, January 6, 1952.

Prior to *Peanuts*, the province of the comics page had been that of gags, social and political observation, domestic comedy, soap opera, and various adventure genres. Although *Peanuts* changed, or evolved, during the fifty years Schulz wrote and drew it, it remained, as it began, an anomaly on the comics page — a comic strip about the interior crises of the cartoonist himself. After a painful divorce in 1973 from which he had not yet recovered, Schulz told a reporter, "Strangely, I've drawn better cartoons in the last six months — or as good as I've ever drawn. I don't know how the human mind works." Surely, it was this kind of humility in the face of profoundly irreducible human question that makes *Peanuts* as universally moving as it is.

Diagnosed with cancer, Schulz retired from *Peanuts* at the end of 1999. He died on February 12, 2000, the day before his last strip was published (and two days before Valentine's Day) — having completed 17,897 daily and Sunday strips, each and every one fully written, drawn, and lettered entirely by his own hand — an unmatched achievement in comics.

— GARY GROTH

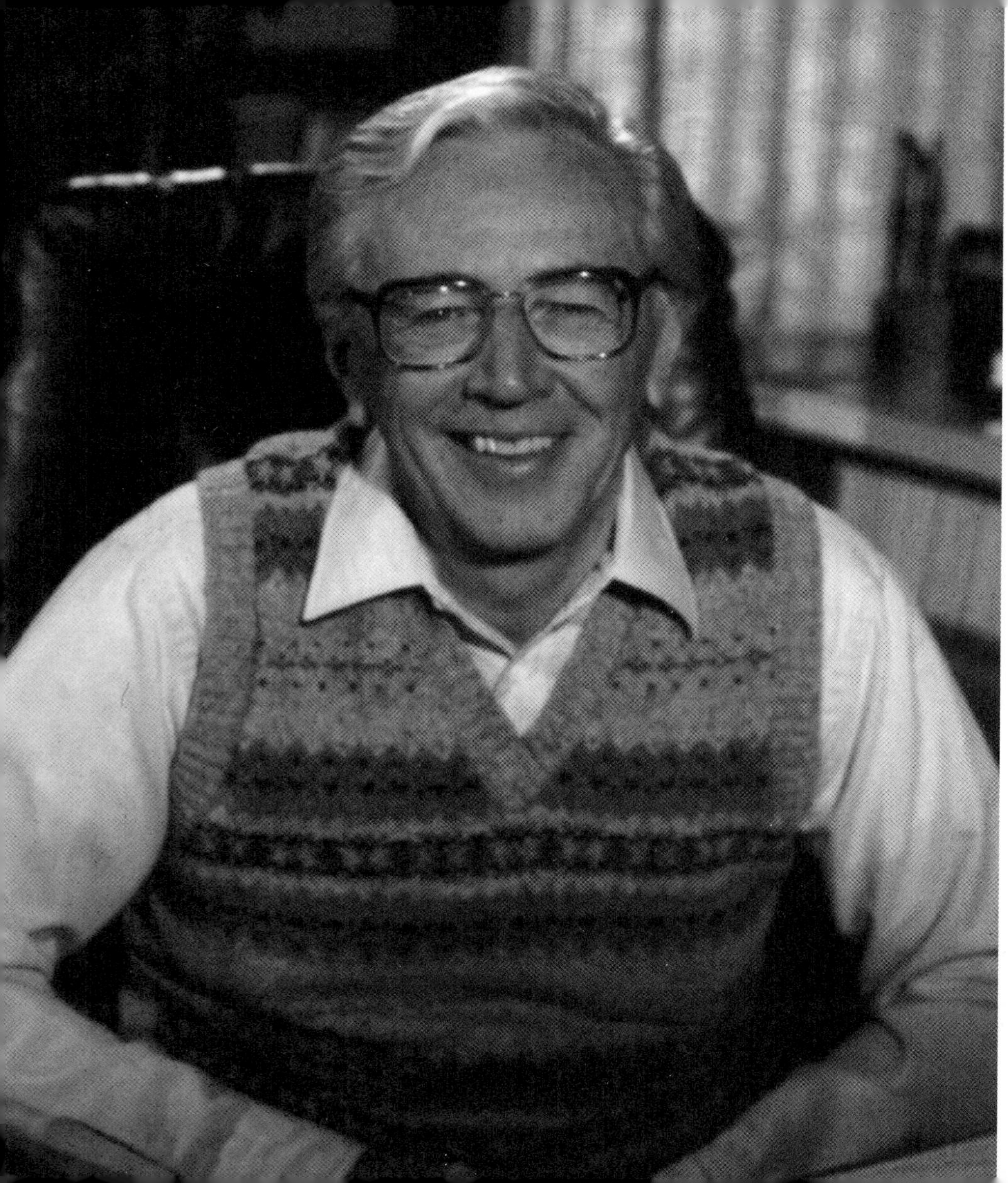

Charles M. Schulz in 1985 during the filming of *It's Your 20th Television Anniversary, Charlie Brown*. Courtesy of The Charles M. Schulz Museum and Research Center, Santa Rosa, California.